Society and Thought
in Modern America

Society and Thought in Modern America

A SOCIAL AND INTELLECTUAL HISTORY OF THE AMERICAN PEOPLE FROM 1865

by Harvey Wish

WESTERN RESERVE UNIVERSITY

LONGMANS, GREEN AND CO.

NEW YORK   LONDON   TORONTO

1952

LONGMANS, GREEN AND CO., INC.
55 FIFTH AVENUE, NEW YORK 3

LONGMANS, GREEN AND CO. LTD.
6 & 7 CLIFFORD STREET, LONDON W I

LONGMANS, GREEN AND CO.
215 VICTORIA STREET, TORONTO I

SOCIETY AND THOUGHT IN MODERN AMERICA

FIRST EDITION

Library of Congress Catalog Card Number 50-9981

Printed in the United States of America
AMERICAN BOOK—STRATFORD PRESS • NEW YORK

To

Anne and Dorothy

Preface

In the years since Lincoln's death, the pattern of American life has shown the deepening impress of the metropolis. Urban-industrial pressures born of the Industrial Revolution swept away the frontier, created the New South, secularized religion, "emancipated" women, commercialized recreation, and acted as an irresistible magnet in drawing countless rural folk and immigrants to the city. The captain of industry began awkwardly to fashion the tasteless world of the Gilded Age and then, with quickening perception, became a more worthy successor of the nobles and clerics who had once patronized the arts. Labor unions rose from a minor quantity to a giant social force in transforming laissez-faire individualism into something with a greater sense of social responsibility, thus making the state a guardian of economic security, educational opportunities, and public health. Western Europe stimulated and often initiated some of these welfare trends. With urban maturity, the United States ceased to be a mere cultural province of Europe and increasingly exported its institutions and ideas abroad until Americanization had affected much of the globe. The railroad, automobile, radio, and motion picture broke down regional differences by fostering centralization, but they contributed also to the debasement and standardization of the cultural inheritance.

Yet the city and the Industrial Revolution cannot stand alone as an explanation of recent social and intellectual history. The tremendous capacity of the human will and intelligence to transform the environment, responding perhaps to a distant challenge or a desired ideal, tends to vary the cultural pattern. Tradition has perpetuated ideals and motives borrowed from half-forgotten eras and prophets. Americans drew upon an inheritance of idealism, particularly a persistent faith in the worth and potentialities of man, to combat anti-democratic doctrines. Roger Williams and Emerson, Jefferson and Lincoln,

vii

all counted as contemporary influences for the mid-twentieth century. They armed the idealists against the age-old forces of intolerance and against those wedded to narrow concepts of material interest. The Great Depression, totalitarian threats, and the new lethal weapons, it is true, had shaken the nation's confident sense of direction inspired by the now-discarded doctrine of inevitable evolutionary progress and by the facts of material success; but a greater maturity was in the making to succeed the uncritical optimism of yesterday's pragmatists. Much of America's future depended upon such intangibles of morale and tradition as well as material successes. Urbanism, therefore, is only a limited explanation of the changes that have taken place since 1865. Man is too complex to be enclosed by a fatalistic philosophy of history.

The writer extends his gratitude to his co-workers in the social-intellectual field, particularly to those specialists who read chapters or discussed interpretations involved in this book. Among those scholars were: Jay Hubbell, editor, *American Literature*; E. Merton Coulter, University of Georgia; C. Vann Woodward, Johns Hopkins University; Roy M. Robbins, Butler University; James C. Malin, University of Kansas; Jessie Bernard (sociology), Pennsylvania State College; Thomas Cochran, University of Pennsylvania; Foster R. Dulles, Ohio State University; Philip D. Jordan, University of Minnesota; Carl F. Wittke, Richard A. Schermerhorn (sociology), and Lyon G. Richardson (American literature), all of Western Reserve University; Aaron I. Abell, University of Notre Dame; Bert J. Loewenberg, Sarah Lawrence College; Oliver W. Larkin, Smith College; and Julius W. Pratt, University of Buffalo.

Contents

Illustrations

1865-1885
between pages 36 and 37

Mark Twain
James B. Duke
"Making the Virginia Twist," by John Durkin
Booker T. Washington
Chain gang at Richmond
Buffalo Bill's Wild West Show
Helena, Montana, 1870
Geronimo, the Apache chief, at Fort Bowie
Two wood-burning locomotives at Merced, California, 1872
Carry Nation
The Great Chicago Fire of 1871
Frances E. Willard
Chicago's Prairie Avenue, 1880
"A Negro Baptism," Wake County, North Carolina
Billy Sunday
Mary Baker Eddy

1885-1905
between pages 180 and 181

"Not at Home," by Eastman Johnson
"Harlem" central telephone office, 1897
Potter Palmer mansion, Chicago
The Haymarket Riot, Chicago
The final assembly line at the Ford plant in Highland Park
Chinatown, San Francisco
"Cliff Dwellers," by George Bellows
"Steerage, 1907," by Alfred Stieglitz
Primrose & West's Big Minstrel Festival
Thomas A. Edison
The Wright brothers' airplane, 1903
"Stag at Sharkey's," by George Bellows
Lillian Russell

Reconstruction: The South of Wade Hampton

[1865-1876]

I

LEE HAD surrendered, but General Wade Hampton of South Carolina, "the giant in gray," was not quite through with the Yankees. He was ready to carry on the war from Texas and the Mexican border at the head of guerrilla cavalry troops. A small band of diehards wanted to follow him, but they were dissuaded by Confederate leaders. The belligerent South Carolinian had once been the richest planter in the South, ruling paternalistically over a kingdom of 3000 slaves. Now he bitterly contemplated the ruins of his elegant plantation, "Millwood," burnt and sacked by Union soldiers. In Mississippi, the regal Hampton estate of "Wild Woods" was deserted and over a million dollars in cotton had been destroyed by retreating troops. Land-poor, the general declared himself bankrupt in 1868, overwhelmed by personal debts exceeding a million dollars. But meanwhile, Hampton owned enough property to be disfranchised on that account (and also because of his military rank) by the federal government, and the Radicals were clamoring for his head as a war criminal. As a planter and former politician, he represented a ruling class that the Radicals were determined to liquidate.

Hampton viewed the wreckage of war and was profoundly moved. His favorite city of Columbia, South Carolina, was but a

shell and Northern leaders insisted that he himself—not Sherman—
had burnt that state capital. Richmond, the "beleaguered fortress of
the Confederacy," was partly destroyed. Georgians gazed hopelessly
at the wreck of Atlanta and of entire counties stripped bare by
Sherman's innovation of "total war." The fresh graves of 134,000
Confederates were deeply impressed in the consciousness of the
living. Northerners, too, wept, not for their cities, for they had
escaped unscathed, but for the 359,000 men in blue who had given
their lives to keep America one and inseparable. There was bitterness
in the air. Returning Southern soldiers sang these defiant words to
ease their frustration:

> Three hundred thousand Yankees
> Lie mouldering in the dust—
> We got three hundred thousand
> Before you conquered us.
> They died of Southern fevers
> And Southern steel and shot,
> And I wish it was three million
> Instead of what we got.

Hampton and many other wealthy planters did not feel like war
criminals. They had resented the Southern fire-eaters of 1861 who
had pushed the South into secession. Possibly these solid men of
property had foreseen the ultimate cost of a crusade for Southern
nationalism. The cultivated planters, Hampton included, had tended
to deprecate slavery as a necessary evil even after the defiant
Calhoun had praised it as a positive good. Once war began, Hampton
had thrown his huge muscular body and long-acquired skill as a
horseman into the severest battles for the Southland and had developed an uncompromising will to fight until victory. Now that
the war was over, the proud Hamptons, for several generations the
political Warwicks among cotton planters, were reluctant to abdicate their power. The forty-seven-year-old veteran licked his wounds,
watched the Radicals enfranchise the Negroes and weaken the
planter class, and planned the day of reckoning.

The planters had suffered some serious defections. Hampton attacked the "deserters" who fled the South in despair after Appomat-

tox. About ten thousand left for slaveholding Brazil, which then offered the immigrant cheap lands on generous credit terms. Others went to Mexico. Scores of prominent lawyers and planters, like Judah P. Benjamin, departed for England or France. But most Southerners were too short on capital to begin a new life in a strange land. George Fitzhugh, the proslavery propagandist, lost his already dilapidated mansion at Port Royal, Virginia, when a Union shell crushed the roof. He professed himself entirely reconciled to defeat and even accepted a minor post as a Freedmen's Bureau judge to supervise Negro labor contracts with the planters. Still, he persistently attacked the Radicals as latter-day Puritan fanatics who were plotting to exploit the South as a colony of Northern capitalism. In 1878 he moved to Kentucky and two years later, like so many postbellum Southerners, he left for Texas. That cotton and cattle empire, which in 1860 had ranked ninth among Southern states in population, rose to first place by 1880.

In the meager literature of the planter class during Reconstruction, Alexander H. Stephens' book, *A Constitutional View of the Late War between the States* (1868-70), revealed how little the late ruling class had learned from the Civil War. The former vice-president of the Confederacy, like Hampton and others of this group, admitted that slavery was dead and that there were none to seek its revival. But slavery, he argued, was not the true cause of the war "but [was] a drop in the ocean compared with those other considerations involved in the issue." The South had fought for the revolutionary right of secession affirmed in 1776. "It was the cause of the Federative principle of Government against the principle of Empire," he insisted, "the cause of the Grecian type of civilization against the Asiatic!" His "federative principle" was a watered-down variety of antebellum states' rights but it was a useful defense for an agrarian society against the pressures of urban-industrial interests. The historic principle of states' rights would be found helpful by planters and farmers in maintaining white supremacy and a dual racial society. It constituted a rock against which the most basic civil rights bills from Washington would not prevail. Stephens and other Southerners came to believe that the South was the true custodian of American values and that Calhoun and Jefferson Davis were but the contemporary prophets of the agrarian ideals of Jefferson, Washington, and George Mason. From this point of view, Lincoln's armies had overthrown historic American agrarianism to set up the centralized capitalist structure once advocated by Alexander Hamilton.

While Alexander Stephens looked backward to an outmoded agrarian ideal, George Fitzhugh was one of the earliest prophets of an industrialized New South, for he had propagandized for large-scale industry back in antebellum times. In his articles of 1869-70 for *Lippincott's Magazine,* he grafted a new philosophy of industrial monopoly upon his older aristocratic agrarian ideas. He had always denounced laissez-faire liberalism because the idea of freedom of contract for the laborer ran counter to the system of slavery; now he attacked free competitive enterprise as inefficient compared to big business and monopolistic methods. Thus he offered an intellectual rapprochement between the planter and the industrialist, the South and the North.

Fitzhugh's article on "Land Monopoly" repeated his antebellum views that land monopoly by a few was essential to civilization because it provided the strongest incentives for efficient large-scale production. Looking benevolently at the contemporary growth of railroad monopoly, he asserted in his usual sweeping language, "... the monopoly of property, or capital, by the few, and the consequent subjection of the many to the dominion, taxation, and exploitation of these few, is not an evil, as generally esteemed, but the greatest of human blessings, because it is the only means of begetting, sustaining and advancing civilization." He restated this idea most emphatically: "Millionaires, without intending it, are the benefactors of mankind ... and one of them with a hundred clerks in his employ, will do more business, and do it better and more cheaply, than a thousand independent petty, vulgar shopkeepers." He argued that "slavery to capital" like the chattel slavery of Negroes and serfdom in medieval times was right, necessary, and the greatest of blessings. Still, Fitzhugh was now ready to accept trade unions as a check upon the power of employers and he even endorsed the idea of class war within limits: "The war between Capital and Labor is evidence of a healthy state of society. When it ceases, despotism, ignorance, and pauperism will supervene." Only the Negro, he said, was unfitted by his improvident nature from entering the portals of a capitalist society except under the control of the white. However, Fitzhugh's new enthusiasm for big business was far in advance of Southern thought, which continued to cling to historic agrarian ideals during these years of Reconstruction.

2

The chief ally of the planter continued to be, as in antebellum times, the yeoman white farmer who constituted the majority of the Southern people. Whatever differences existed between them—and these became patent in the Populist Revolt of the nineties—were submerged by the necessities of white man supremacy and the traditional clannish attachment between the two groups. Besides, class lines were very fluid in antebellum times and many small farmers could reasonably hope to become substantial planters. The Jacksonian revolution of the twenties and thirties had carried innumerable non-slaveholders into the governorships, legislative seats, and other positions of honor, but these men were as zealous spokesmen of the Old Order as the planters themselves. Rebels like Ben Tillman of South Carolina might feel restive in asserting the traditional program of the planters, but the issue of "Africanization" kept them cooperative until the passing of Reconstruction.

Scarcely higher than the Negro economically, though asserting a much higher social status, was the poor white. He had proudly worn the dignified Confederate gray uniform and enjoyed the plaudits of the crowd until military discipline began to irk him. Rumors spread that rich men did not have to fight in this "poor man's war" and that the planters were not keeping their promises of taking care of poor white families. Mass desertions followed and thousands took the Union oath in return for "vittles." After the war, those who turned sharecropper found themselves in a new bondage, this time in direct competition with the Negro, a situation that endangered even the modest rank that the poor white enjoyed in the Southern caste system. As a result the hatreds of prewar times stiffened considerably between the "po' buckra" and the Negro. Some returned to become squatters as of old, others to operate grogshops in the piney woods or to deal in stolen goods. Their womenfolk begged ever more assiduously from other classes or resorted to prostitution. So many Southern women were widowed by the war that travelers noted quite a few instances of such poor white females taking husbands from among the self-supporting Negroes. Union soldiers of occupation, like the sailor with a proverbial wife in every port, fathered many an illegitimate child among this class.

A substantial part of the highlanders had fought for the Union and in many cases had been evicted from their homes by the Confederates. These dispossessed people flocked to the Freedmen's Bureau or to the missionaries for handouts of rations and carried tales of Southern persecution. Reconstruction offered them only temporary relief and emergency remedies. Their future was bound up with the industrialization of the South.

One of those who considered himself a spokesman for the small farmers and laborers was the belligerent Hinton Rowan Helper of Davie County, western North Carolina, who returned to his native state in 1866. Not so long before, his bitter book upon the "slavocracy," *The Impending Crisis of the South* (1857), had gratified antislavery men while angering Southern nationalists, for it had sold 142,000 copies by the election of 1860 and had won for its author a consulship in Buenos Aires. Previously he had argued that slavery retarded the progress of the white race; now he insisted that the very presence of the Negro was an obstacle to the whites. In 1867, he published *Nojoque: A Question for a Continent* with the avowed object "to write the negro out of America." He would expel all colored peoples, Chinese and Indians as well as Negroes. Using the most offensive characterizations of the Negro as an inferior being, he called for a world society that would be "peopled exclusively by those naturally and superlatively superior races—the pure white races—to whom we are indebted for all human achievements." He outdid the unreconstructed Southerner in attacking the Radicals, the Black Republicans, who were "shortwitted and hypocritical blatherskites, who howled and whined in the interest of the accursed negro." This tirade was continued in *The Negroes in Negroland* (1868), which stressed the superstition and backwardness of Africa.

Yet Helper envisaged a new labor party of all white workers to replace the existing parties and offered a number of liberal ideas (of course within a Caucasian framework), such as the equality of women and freer immigration to the South. On the international scene, he was an avowed imperialist who believed that the smaller nations should be absorbed by the larger and that the United States should take over all of North America. Helper's fear of Africanization and racial equality was commonly shared during Reconstruction times, though his influence was undoubtedly less than in 1857-60 when his *Impending Crisis* shook the nation.

3

For the Negro, Reconstruction was obviously a period of bewildering change, not all of it to his benefit. He was no longer a chattel slave but a free wage worker who hoped that the federal government would follow the example of Russia and other states in combining emancipation with an opportunity to own farms. Sometimes, as in Louisiana, bands of Negroes tried to seize large estates for distribution among themselves. "Forty acres and a mule" seemed a reasonable slogan that the speeches of the Radicals encouraged. Instead, Congress, while steadily increasing its bounty to the Indian to perpetuate his status as a helpless ward of the nation, chose to ignore the basic land problem of the self-supporting Negro who wanted a farm. This question was left to private philanthropy and the state legislatures. Northern Republicans refused to follow Thaddeus Stevens' advice to confiscate the plantations of Confederates in behalf of the Negroes. Fortunately for some, the price of many good Southern farms was unusually low in Reconstruction times and those ambitious Negroes with some savings were able to acquire land. By 1880, Georgia Negroes owned almost 600,000 acres of farm land. But for most Negroes of the Black Belt (originally named for the rich black soil of the Deep South) there was only the sharecropper's lot as a permanent status—and even that had to be held against increasing competition with whites who now entered the cotton fields in very large numbers.

The Negro continued as in slavery times to furnish the vast reserve of unskilled labor. European immigrants were almost as indifferent as before to settling south of the Mason and Dixon line. Competition with cheap Negro labor and the race conflicts discouraged many. In freedom, the Negro had to acquire the economic drives that the West European ancestors of white Americans had slowly learned after the Middle Ages; and the inheritance of mass illiteracy and racial antagonisms had to be drastically reduced. Freedom proved a strong intoxicant to many Negroes who tended at first to work no longer than was necessary to meet immediate needs. During this era of painful adjustment considerable aid came from the Freedmen's Bureau in arranging labor contracts with the planters and in securing relief.

The stability of Negro life suffered from the slave inheritance of family disorganization. Under slavery the Negro husband did not have to support his wife and children and a matriarchal system had existed. Among the freedmen, family duties remained indistinct, and economic disorganization led to an alarming increase in their mortality. However, freedom did add to the Negro's feeling of self-respect and his sense of having risen in status. He felt that his personality was enhanced by the luxury of having two or three names, a privilege that had to be deferred until freedom. Thus, Booker Taliaferro Washington, so famous in the history of his race, had to improvise much of his name. He knew little of his father, who, he believed, may have been a white man. Leadership for the race, once monopolized by the planters, was taken over during Reconstruction by Negro ministers, businessmen, and artisans whose freedom antedated the Civil War, or by cultured mulattoes of the cities. One step forward in adopting the white man's social standards was the frequent refusal of Negroes to permit their women to do heavy work in the fields.

Negro illiteracy fell rapidly. After two centuries of slavery, less than 10 per cent could read or write in 1861. Conscientious masters, anxious that their slaves should be able to read the Bible, had sometimes evaded state laws and local opinion to teach them to read and even to write. But the necessities of white-man supremacy prevented slavery from achieving very much as an educational institution. During Reconstruction, when thousands of Northern schoolteachers opened schools in the South with the protection and financial support of the Freedmen's Bureau, Negroes rushed to school *en masse*. "It was a whole race trying to go to school," wrote Booker T. Washington, who was one of this eager group. "Few were too young; and none too old, to make the attempt to learn." Day schools, night schools, and Sunday schools were crowded with Negroes from six to seventy, who regarded reading and writing as the evidence of free status. Literate Negroes were promptly drafted as teachers in colored communities. Idealistic Northern women, some of them from old Massachusetts families, conducted numerous schools for freedmen, since Southern whites would lose caste by teaching Negroes. Besides, many Southern farmers believed that education unfitted a Negro for the only work he could do. "Whenever it is written," declared Washington, "... the part that the Yankee teachers played in the education of the Negroes immediately after the war will make one of the most thrilling parts of the history of this country."

4

Historians often explain Reconstruction as the efforts of industry-minded Republicans to monopolize national power at the expense of agrarian Democrats. Too often they have minimized the unique experiment in race relations and social indoctrination. Cynics who believe that the Fourteenth Amendment was written primarily to serve corporate privilege rather than the civil rights of the freedmen overlook the sincerity and depth of the antislavery crusade and the humanitarian faith of antebellum times.

Thaddeus Stevens of Pennsylvania is often presented as a pathological politician who desired only to torture the South, to exalt his party, and to reap tariff benefits for the industries he owned. Yet he had spent much of his threescore and ten years in fighting social inequality. A lame, sickly person, the son of a Vermont shoemaker, he had lived on a frontier farm, attended Dartmouth and the University of Vermont and had once written a play, "The Fall of Helvetic Liberty." As a lawyer he had frequently defended fugitive slaves without a fee, and in antebellum politics he fought slavery, segregation, and Negro suffrage restrictions, and did a great deal to secure a free school law for Pennsylvania. When Russia emancipated its serfs during the 1860's he followed the reform with keen sympathy. Vitriolic in language and intolerant of those who disagreed with him, he proved a painful gadfly to Lincoln and even led the movement to impeach and convict President Andrew Johnson. He disregarded the fact that so few Northern states were ready to grant Negroes social equality and he looked upon Reconstruction as a great opportunity to solve the race question in the South. Just before his death in 1868, he composed this epitaph for himself:

I repose in this quiet and secluded spot, not from any natural preference for solitude, but, finding other cemeteries limited by charter rules as to race, I have chosen this, that I might illustrate in my death the principles which I advocated through a long life—Equality of Man before his Creator.

Charles Sumner of Massachusetts, who led the fight for Radical Reconstruction in the Senate while Stevens did so in the House, showed a similar lifetime devotion to social equality and the same readiness to hurl bitter words at adversaries in the righteous spirit of the ancient Hebrew prophets. He had been a leader in the prewar movement to end all wars, an opponent of the War with Mexico because of its slavery aspects, an active counsel for Negroes seeking relief from racial segregation, and an enthusiastic supporter of Negro suffrage. Other Radicals, too, such as crude Ben Wade of Ohio, had come by their moral fervor honestly in decades of battle in the antislavery cause.

But once the war emotions had begun to decline, the North turned readily to the Southern view that the experiment of Reconstruction was fanatical and inherently corrupt. Besides, Northern attitudes toward the Negro may be inferred from the fact that in 1865 Negro

suffrage had been voted down by Connecticut, Wisconsin, and
Minnesota and that few states had granted this right before 1861.
There were propertied Northerners who feared the socialistic implications of the wholesale confiscation of Southern property suggested by Stevens. As it was, the confiscation of several billion
dollars' worth of slaves and millions of dollars in cotton set an uncomfortable precedent for property rights. The antislavery crusade
was definitely over and the spearhead of equal rights failed to
advance beyond the issues of emancipation and the indissoluble
Union.

Northern Radicals considered the passage of the Black Codes of
1865-66 by various Southern states as a defiant effort to revive the
slave regime. Most heinous to them, and to the Negroes themselves,
was the provision forbidding Negroes to testify against whites and
to act as jurors. The subsequent story has often been told: of the
setting aside of moderate policies by military reconstruction; of the
race clashes in Memphis, New Orleans, and elsewhere; of the temporary disfranchisement of Confederate leaders and wealthy
planters like Wade Hampton; of the new constitutions and the Radical biracial legislatures set up in 1867 and afterwards; and of the
rise of the Ku Klux Klan and other underground movements.

Many impecunious Northerners whose possessions were so few
as to fill no more than a "carpetbag" hurried South to befriend the
Negro. Some apparently acted for the sake of quick wealth, others
from moral conviction. Conservative Southerners stigmatized the
native allies of the Radicals as traitors and "scalawags"—though the
South had never been completely of one mind in its attitude toward
the Negro. The corruption of some of the carpetbag regimes, which
was widely publicized by the Conservatives, must be weighed
against the facts of that day: the postwar decline in public morals
as witnessed by the Tweed Ring swindles in New York city, estimated up to $200,000,000 for the six years following the war; the
notorious scandals of the Grant era; and the corrupt political machine of postbellum Philadelphia and other cities and states.

Much more significant is the fact that the carpetbag regime made
the most far-reaching effort in Southern history to establish a system

of free public schools for both races. Southerners had clung to the old English tradition of private schools and taxpayers had usually been reluctant to vote for large educational appropriations in behalf of the public school movement that had been developing before the Civil War. Education has always been one of the most expensive enterprises in American government and this cause meant a new heavy tax load for Southern states. In addition, more state support than ever went for orphan homes (including those for colored children), modern penitentiaries, and asylums for the mentally ill.

Northern Republican leaders tried to make the Negro vote count in the balance against Southern Conservatives through biracial political clubs and the protection given by federal troops. The Yankee "schoolmarms" taught a distinctly non-Confederate interpretation of the war and were usually ostracized by patriotic Southerners. Conservative forces rallied behind a secret lodge, the Ku Klux Klan, which had begun in 1865 at Pulaski, Tennessee, in the spirit of rural horseplay, and converted it in 1868 into an underground movement embellished with organizational lodge mummery, ranging from the Grand Wizard down to the rank and file member "ghouls" in the various Dens. Wade Hampton himself was too dignified to take an active part in this movement, but he defended the motives of its members, and tried to get Northern lawyers to take the cases of Klansmen who ran afoul of the law. The Klan was justified in his mind as a liberating army to save the South from "Africanization." Its tactics became increasingly brutal and inspired many imitators to act as free-lance Klansmen: nightriding, beatings, lynchings, the burning of Negro schools, and other kinds of sadism intended to intimidate the Negroes and their Northern friends.

This romantic pose of the Klan as a champion of the oppressed whites against Negro attacks attracted the unthinking who rushed out to buy "Klan hats," sang Klan songs, danced to Klan tunes, and bought Klan knives. Though the violence was suppressed by federal troops, similar resistance continued through the 1870's until the Conservatives swept into power. Louisiana's White League, South Carolina's Rifle Clubs, Sabre Clubs, and artillery clubs, and similar extra-legal organizations arose to harass the Radical governments.

Even as they were outlawed successively, their leaders used the weapon of ridicule by taking such incongruous names as the Mounted Baseball Club, with a team of 150 members, and later, "Mother's Little Helpers." In South Carolina, the Red Shirts, who had adopted the banner of Garibaldi's army, intimidated Negro voters and swept Wade Hampton into the governor's seat in 1876. This spirit of lawlessness was revived after 1915 when a new Ku Klux Klan was organized, this time adding Catholics, Jews, and others to the proscribed list.

5

The war had stunted the intellectual life of the South and diverted its esthetic energies into destructive channels. It maimed the lyric poets of the Confederacy—Henry Timrod, Paul Hamilton Hayne, and Sidney Lanier—and wasted away their health in filthy, ill-supplied army camps. After the war, they faced broken sickly lives. "You ask me to tell my story for the last year," wrote Timrod to Hayne, just before his death in 1867. "I can embody it all in a few words, *Beggary, starvation, death, bitter grief, utter want of hope.*" He wrote his faith in the Lost Cause in an ode that was sung at the occasion of decorating the graves of the Confederate dead at Charleston in 1866:

> Sleep sweetly in your humble graves,
> Sleep, martyrs of a fallen cause;
> Though yet no marble column craves
> The pilgrim here to pause.

Timrod, Hayne, and William Gilmore Simms, the most gifted members of the Charleston literary circle, lost their homes and most of their libraries in the path of the destruction wreaked by Sherman's men. Simms died in 1870. Hayne lived on to 1886, an invalid residing in the pine barrens near Augusta, Georgia, and getting food as best he could from his garden. Those who liked to relive the excitement of the war read his *War Poetry of the South.* Later works such as *Legends and Lyrics* (1872) and *Mountains and Lovers* (1875) gave him a reputation in the South as "the last literary cavalier." He expressed a mood of sadness and melancholy retrospection in one of his last poems, "A Little While I Fain Would Linger Yet."

Perhaps the brightest star that shone in the postwar South was Sidney Lanier of Georgia. Like Timrod, Hayne, and Simms, he had written war poetry and the war had ruined his health. As a soldier he had contracted tuberculosis and this disease devitalized him during his remaining years. Educated at Oglethorpe College in Georgia, he turned for a time to the academic life, lecturing in English literature at the new Johns Hopkins University. Out of this emerged several critical writings, *The Science of English Verse* (1880) and *The English Novel* (1883). He added to his slender income by writing numerous boys' books dealing with the King Arthur tales.

Lanier combined exceptional talents as a musician, which won the praise of Theodore Thomas and Leopold Damrosch, with his art as a lyric poet. In social consciousness he was considerably ahead of most Southern writers in Reconstruction times, particularly in his sincere interest in the poor white, apart from the sentimental idealization attempted by the local colorists. He attacked the rising commercial spirit, although this was before industrial Bourbonism came into full flower. In *The Symphony* (1875) he showed the traditionalist's distrust of the new age of business and expressed a sensitive social conscience. Hamlin Garland, midwestern realist in both prose and verse, even compared him with Walt Whitman in cosmic sympathies. He liked to quote these verses from Lanier's *The Symphony:*

> Look up the land, look down the land,
> The poor, the poor, the poor, they stand
> Wedged by the pressing of Trade's hand
> Against an inward-opening door
> That pressure tightens evermore: . . . .
> But who said once, in the lordly tone,
> *Man shall not live by bread alone*
> *But all that cometh from the Throne?*
>   Hath God said so?
>   But Trade saith *No:*
> And the kilns and the curt-tongued mills say *Go!*
> *There's plenty that can, if you can't: we know.*

Move out, if you think you're underpaid.
The poor are prolific; we're not afraid;
Trade is trade.

Garland liked the nostalgic note of sweet melancholy and the love
of justice expressed in this verse:

> Shall Trade aye salve his conscience-aches
> With jibes at Chivalry's old mistakes—
> The wars that o'erhot knighthood makes,
> For Christ's and ladies' sakes,
> Fair Lady?

Southern litterateurs and occasionally Northern writers as well continued even in the twentieth century to echo the idea of an antithesis between the exploitative "little foxes" of the new industry
and business, and the paternalistic, chivalric life of the antebellum
planter's world of tradition. Less moralistic, but more revelatory of
Lanier's lyric qualities were his descriptions of Georgia's primitive
beauty in *The Marshes of Glynn* (1880), which spoke of

> Beautiful glooms, soft dusks in the noon-day fire,—
> Wildwood privacies, closets of lone desire,

He reveled in his inner mind over the mystery of the dimly lit
marshes and the wide overflowing sea that swept in with the tide,
symbolizing his search for infinity:

> . . . I stand
> On the firm-packed sand,
> Free
> By a world of marsh that borders a world of sea.

Culturally, Latin New Orleans seemed to be in decline. The war
had bankrupted too many old Creole planter families and the end
had come to the native Creole literature that had been written
largely in French by a Paris-educated elite. Inevitably assimilation
as well as war took its toll of this unique Latin civilization. Its leading representative, Charles Étienne Gayarré, was still alive and
active as a statesman, historian, and literary leader. He wrote the

monumental four-volume *History of Louisiana* (1851-66) as well as several novels and an interesting biography, *Philip II of Spain* (1866). As for the Anglo-American residents of the city, their cultural life suffered with the death in 1867 of James D. B. De Bow, editor of *De Bow's Review* and a former professor of political economy at the University of Louisiana who had introduced modern methods of teaching accounting.

With the coming of the carpetbag regimes, however, which stimulated popular education and the growth of public institutions, a fruitful influence began to permeate Southern literature. Northern readers had been deeply interested in Southern life since the days of *Uncle Tom's Cabin* and Frederick Law Olmstead's *Cotton Kingdom,* but Reconstruction whetted their curiosity regarding the South even more. Publishers' agents roamed the South to discover native writers capable of satisfying this demand. Edward King, a Massachusetts-born journalist who visited New Orleans in 1872 to gather material for his Southern sketches, persuaded Scribner's to issue George Washington Cable's short story, " 'Sieur George." Thus Cable was "discovered" and his popularity quickly spread throughout this country and even abroad. Many Southern writers, like old George Fitzhugh, found a literary outlet in the Philadelphia journal, *Lippincott's Magazine,* after the demise of *De Bow's Review.* The obvious parochial limitations of the newer Southern magazines offered little inspiration or fiscal reward for the gifted Southern writer.

The groundwork for the Southern Cultural Revival of the 1880's was laid in Reconstruction times. Edward King, friend of Cable, published in 1875 a sympathetic volume on Southern conditions in *The Great South.* He gratified Southerners by his generosity to that defeated section and by his understanding of the problems of race and labor. More in the abolitionist mode, however, were the novels of an Ohio lawyer, schoolmaster, and Union veteran, Albion W. Tourgée, who was a judge and a carpetbag leader in North Carolina. In *A Fool's Errand* (1879), he told about the brutality of Klansmen and the experiences of a Northern lawyer who bought a run-down plantation just after the war. Tourgée dwelt upon the reign of terror against Negroes and their sympathizers and the failure of Southern jurors to grant justice to the freedmen. Writing in the sentimental style popularized by Harriet Beecher Stowe, he denounced the methods of Southern conservatives in buttressing white-man domination. His incidental use of Negro dialect forecast something of the local color school.

A keener observer than Tourgée, and one who tempered romantic descriptions of proud Southern belles with realistic portraits of the drunken, foul-smelling poor white was Major John W. De Forest, an administrator of the Freedmen's Bureau. De Forest later won the enthusiastic praise of William Dean Howells, father of the American realistic novel, for his convincing tale, *Miss Ravenel's Conversion from Secession to Loyalty* (1867). Knowing at first hand the genuine "low-down people" whom he met at his office begging for federal relief, he gave Northerners a nauseating introduction to the filthy, lecherous, half-civilized, and diseased "trashy crackers." Here was a pioneer effort in the direction of the "naturalistic" novel with its frankness and freedom from moralizing. Here was a definite anticipation of the decadent poor white types later described in *Tobacco Road*.

6

Economically, the Reconstruction era witnessed revolutionary changes in the lives of Southerners of both races. Planters were injured by the blows of war, vandalism, cotton confiscations by federal agents, and the breakup of so many plantations by forced sale. Disruption of labor and markets, the lack of fluid capital, and mounting taxes led to a drastic fall in land values. The sudden advance of tenantry, both white and black, meant that many planters became absentee landlords dwelling in the city, indifferent to the efficiency and welfare of their tenants. One of the chief reasons for the adoption of the sharecropper system was the inability of the planter to pay cash to his workers. Instead, he could furnish the cropper with a cabin, an acre or two for a truck patch, mules, implements, seeds, and part of the fertilizer and ginning costs. In return he received a stipulated share of the crop.

Some planters joined the new class of merchant-storekeepers who dominated the credit and marketing system of the postbellum South. These rural merchants established the crop-lien system that extended credit to the tenant or farm owners through a chattel mortgage upon the crop. This meant that the debtor-tenant paid high arbitrary prices for the store goods sold on credit by the merchant, and had to abide by the latter's decision on what crops he might raise—usually cotton. Thus the one-crop system was fastened more tenaciously than ever on the South. Unscrupulous merchants could resort to trick bookkeeping and keep the illiterate tenant in a perpetual state of debt peonage. On the other hand, defenders of the merchants point out that these men also had to borrow their money at usurious rates because of the tight credit situation in the South. But the social effect of the merchant-landlord system was to put white and Negro "croppers" in sharp competition with each other and to deepen race hatreds.

Recovery from the physical effects of war and Reconstruction was not too difficult in a rich farm country, and by 1878 the cotton crop matched the large antebellum harvest of 1860. In 1880 the census reported the surprising information that there were more than twice as many Southern farms as in 1860. This was due not only to the subdivision of large plantations into small farms, but even more to the remarkable revival of homesteading resulting from the sale of new lands at very low rates. Once more, the sun shone pleasantly upon the Southland.

7

The Southern churches were directly affected by Reconstruction and the race issue. Many Northern clergymen in antebellum days had denounced the Southern churches for defending slavery and after the war insisted on a sweeping policy of "reconstructing" them in order to insure loyalty. Aggressive Northern missionaries in the South had done much for Negro education and thereby had offended Southern mores. The antebellum split between Northern and Southern wings of the Methodists, Baptists, and Presbyterians remained throughout this era and helped to foster the "Solid South."

During these years, Negroes seceded on a large scale from the

Southern white denominations. This was due primarily to the desire
of the freedmen to express their own varieties of religious experience, or to unite with Northern churches, either white or Negro,
rather than to any new policy of discrimination in the South. As a
result, ministers made up much of the Negro racial leadership. So
numerous were the exhorters "called to preach" that Booker T.
Washington recalled one colored congregation of 200 with 18 such
ministers. He described what happened when such exhorters
suddenly felt the "call": "Without warning the one called would
fall upon the floor as if struck by a bullet, and would lie there
for hours, speechless and motionless." For the illiterate Negroes,
living in windowless shacks with dirt floors and under a roof lacking
a chimney but full of generous-sized holes, there was a genuine
emotional outlet in listening to eloquent exhorters and taking part
in the stirring revivalist hymns, dances, and hand clappings.

Whites of the same class had a similar fondness for the exciting
revivalist ways of the old-time religion. Ever since Jefferson's death,
most Southern sects had been moving toward increased orthodoxy
at the expense of the eighteenth-century rationalist cults. In the
rural South, isolated by poor transportation and communication,
orthodoxy was secure from the secular spirit of the great cities. The
camp meeting had its devotees in the North, but its richest expression was found largely in the South. Semi-literate preachers and
their ranting styles left their influence on the tone of the rural community and retarded the free growth of Southern mass education.
One of their persistent crusades was directed against alcohol. By
1882, a conference of the Methodist Episcopal Church South finally
succeeded in adding temperance as a special chapter of church
discipline: " . . . in cases of drunkenness let the discipline be administered as in the case of immorality." Prohibition also had the
value of keeping liquor from inflaming race conflicts. Despite the
persistence of heavy drinking, especially among the poor whites
and highlanders, and despite the existence of widespread poverty,
the Southern churches among the masses tended to stick to fundamentalist doctrine, prohibition, and revivalism as the chief panaceas. To a large extent religious orthodoxy had its counterpart in

economic orthodoxy and discouraged the "isms," as Fitzhugh once observed, from penetrating the South.

8

Even Reconstruction could not extinguish the Southerner's love for gaiety and frontier excitement. Local Granges brought many isolated Southern farmers together for social gatherings as well as for cooperative marketing and mutual protection, just as they did in the North. Excursion trains, picnics, lavish funerals, minstrel shows, carnivals, and circuses attracted thousands of both races. Baseball, which went back to the old English child's game of "rounders," had already been professionalized in the Northern cities shortly before the Civil War. Now, during Reconstruction, Southerners of all classes (and both races—separately) showed a real enthusiasm for the sport. In 1868 five Southern cities organized the Alabama Association of Base Ball Players at Montgomery. Tom Watson, later Georgia's vitriolic Populist journalist and political "demagogue," was, in the 1870's, captain and pitcher of the "Up and At 'Em" Club.

Southerners enjoyed their customary front porch and rocking chair, their seasoned fried chicken rolled in flour, their hot biscuits, and their succulent varieties of pork dishes. During the lean years after the war even the middle class shared the crude delicacies of the poor whites, such as chitterlings (a kind of fried or boiled variety of the smaller intestines of swine), cowpeas, and cracklings (the crisp end of roasted pork). For the lowly sharecropper, diet was apt to consist of "fat back," salt pork, sowbelly, bacon, sweet potatoes, and occasionally corn whiskey or "rot gut." Despite the preachers and local laws, prohibition met serious setbacks and evasion.

The Southern love of horse racing took on a medieval twist in the revival of tournaments, featuring local knights on horseback who competed for prizes in a gaily bedecked setting. Whatever the real origins of these tournaments, popular opinion attributed them to Walter Scott's romantic influence. After 1875 a Kentucky Derby was held each May at Churchill Downs, Louisville, but this event did not become the famous national festival until after 1902.

New Orleans quickly recovered its fame as a city of laughter and sin with a Mardi Gras carnival season which took on more and more frills for all classes, beginning with upper-class balls. "It is a thing which could hardly exist in the practical North," asserted Mark Twain, "for the soul of it is the romantic, not the funny and the grotesque." There were flashy gambling houses, huge lotteries, exciting prize fights, openly advertised prostitutes, and cheap "honky-tonks." In these dives jazz music is said to have spent its period of incubation, developing from constant improvisations by Negroes who knew music by ear rather than by note.

· 2 ·

The New South: Hampton
and the Bourbon Era

[1876-1890]

I

THE overthrow of Reconstruction by 1876 marked the accession of the "Bourbons" under such leaders as Governor Wade Hampton of South Carolina. Populist-minded critics coined the terms "Bourbon" and "Confederate brigadier" for the conservative planters and industrialists who were now in power. They knew them by their broad-brimmed hats, their long coats, their flair for spread-eagle oratory, and their penchant for Latin phrases. Clever politicians among them could doff this dignified garb and manner in back-country campaigns for the crude trousers and shirt and the picturesque epithets of the small farmer, hillbilly, or "cracker." They gloried in the good old days "befo' the wah," but they did not permit the pleasant cult of Confederate patriotism with its monuments, memorial days, and historical societies to block the road to Southern industrialization. Northern capital was invited amid sentimental appeals for sectional reconciliation. Wade Hampton preached "Reconciliation, Retrenchment, and Reform" and joined his friends General John B. Gordon and Benjamin H. Hill in organizing the Southern Life Insurance Company of Atlanta. They offered the presidency to Lee himself, but received a courteous refusal. Planters joined with merchants and bankers to finance the mills, factories, and furnaces of the New South and they led the movement to undo the results of Reconstruction by partially disfranchising the Negro.

A striking example of Bourbonism is the case of Colonel Henry Watterson, editor of the *Louisville Courier-Journal*. He had served in the Confederate army and now advocated sectional conciliation, free trade, and an end to the violence of the Ku Klux Klan. In 1883 he made his siren appeal to attract Northern capital for Southern industry in a speech before the American Bankers Association. "No Southerner," declares Shields McIlwaine, "ever wooed Northern cash with such rare humor in the grand old manner." His *Louisville Courier-Journal* together with Henry Grady's *Atlanta Constitution* led the procession of the New South.

Planting, writes Daniel M. Robison, now became secondary to merchandising, moneylending, railroad promotion, factory building, and the development of resources. The Bourbons reversed the welfare trend of the Reconstruction legislatures and called for lighter taxes, economy, low official salaries (this would also discourage poor men from seeking office), and laissez faire. In Congress, their representatives demanded lower tariffs, continued to talk abstract states' rights, and turned down the Blair bill, which provided federal subsidies to eradicate illiteracy in the backward states.

The Bourbons disfranchised the Negro except where they could count on his vote but control, rather than disfranchisement, was the aim of Hampton and other Bourbons. Although the election of large numbers of Negro legislators was no longer tolerated, occasionally a Negro was permitted to hold office. Thus a Negro sat in the Mississippi legislature in 1882 and four Negroes of the Lower South even went to Congress during this era. Where disfranchisement was desired, the Bourbons and their allies among the other classes resorted to literacy tests and an Eight-Box law (as in South Carolina) requiring separate boxes and ballots for each office in order to baffle illiterate Negroes—and incidentally illiterate poor whites as well. Young Negro voters were frequently challenged for documentary proof of age while white youths had no such difficulty.

With disfranchisement went a decline in the social status of the Negroes. "Jim Crow" laws segregated them in public conveyances, depots, and wharves as well as in schools and hotels. Private citizens, encouraged by state law, refused to admit Negroes into theaters, restaurants, and other semi-public places. By 1883, the federal Supreme Court itself declared that segregation was legal. In five significant civil rights cases, the Court overthrew the substance of the Civil Rights Act of 1875, which guaranteed all persons "the full and equal enjoyment of the accommodations, advantages, facilities, and privileges of inns, public conveyances on land or water, theaters, and other places of public amusement." These were *social* rights, not civil rights, argued the Court, and therefore the federal government had no control over such matters. The civil rights section of the Fourteenth Amendment, forbidding states to deny to any person the equal protection of the laws, was therefore irrelevant in these cases. As for the application of the Thirteenth Amendment abolishing slavery, Justice Bradley said that free Negroes, even before this amendment, had never enjoyed all the privileges held by white citizens. "Mere discrimination on account of race or color were not regarded as badges of slavery." The principle was laid down that the Reconstruction amendments did not prevent private individuals, even the owners of theaters, inns, and other semi-public places, from denying service to anyone on the ground of race. In fact, as will be seen, the Southern states later used their police power in the alleged interest of racial peace to require segregation in railways, hotels, and restaurants.

The Bourbon bid for reunion with the North had to surmount Northern indignation against the disfranchisement of the Negro. Undoubtedly the best apologist of this industrial "New South"—and the popularizer of the term that had originated with Grant's military secretary, General Adam Badeau—was Henry Woodfin Grady, editor of the *Atlanta Constitution*. He was the son of a Georgia major who had died for the Confederacy; and he had been educated at the University of Georgia and the University of Virginia Law School. A Northern financier, Cyrus W. Field, promoter of the first Atlantic cable, had lent him $20,000 to buy an interest in the *Atlanta Constitution*. With a keen sense for news, he and his talented associate, Joel Chandler Harris, gained for the paper a wide circulation.

Readers liked Grady's wit and sentimentality, his Methodist piety
and prohibitionist leanings, as well as the literary articles of Harris.
Grady campaigned for an industrialized South, a diversified Southern agriculture with special attention to forest products, and the
local manufacture of all necessities.

In December, 1886, he attracted national attention by a skillful
appeal before the New England Society of New York. He praised
Lincoln as a genuine American, a fusion of Puritan and Cavalier;
and he drew a roseate picture of race relations and the progress of
the New South:

We have found out that in the summing up the free Negro counts for
more than he did as a slave. We have planted the schoolhouse on the
hill top, and made it free to white and black. We have sowed towns and
cities in the place of theories and put business above politics. We have
challenged your spinners in Massachusetts and your ironmakers in
Pennsylvania.

He reminded his listeners, "Your fathers sold their slaves to our
fathers" and declared that the Southerner, not the outside meddler,
was the best friend of the Negro, hence the race problem must
be left to the South. Socially and economically everything pointed
toward the victory of white democracy:

The new South presents a perfect democracy, the oligarchs leading in
the popular movement—a social system, compact and closely knitted,
less splendid on the surface, but stronger at the core—a hundred farms
for every plantation, fifty homes for every palace—and a diversified
industry that meets the complex needs of this complex age.

The speech ended with a plea that New England emulate the conciliatory spirit of Grant at Appomattox, though he quickly added,
aware of how his words would look in print to Atlanta readers:

The South has nothing for which to apologize. She believes that the late
struggle between the States was war and not rebellion, revolution and
not conspiracy, and that her convictions were as honest as yours. . . .
The South has nothing to take back.

When he finished, many of his listeners were in tears and some
were on their feet shouting enthusiastically. Grady had won his

case. In December, 1889, he gave another influential speech—his last —before the Boston Merchants' Association, stressing the idea that Northerners must not allow the issue of Negro rights to estrange them from the South. "Never before in this Republic has the white race divided on the rights of an alien race," he asserted. "The red man was cut down as a weed, because he hindered the way of the American citizen." He mentioned casually that he had recently read that a G.A.R. post in Connecticut had closed its doors to a Negro veteran. Like many defenders of white-man supremacy, Grady found it easy to relapse into a purely racialist argument directed against Negroes, Indians, Chinese, and other "aliens." Once more he scored his point with an important audience, but the Boston climate itself struck him down, for he contracted pneumonia and died within a few days, at the early age of thirty-nine.

The concerted effort of the Bourbons to relegate the Negro to a permanently inferior status aroused the criticism of liberal Southerners. The most outspoken critic was a former Confederate soldier, George Washington Cable of New Orleans. His sympathetic and successful literary interpretation of the French Creole and the racial types of Louisiana had fascinated readers all over the world. In 1885 he published *The Silent South* to express the feelings of those thousands of dissidents who had listened with approval to his lectures on the plight of the freedman:

There are those among us who see that America has no room for a state of society which makes its lower classes harmless by abridging their liberties, or, as one of the favored class lately said to me, has "got 'em so they don't give no trouble." There is a growing number who see that one thing we cannot afford to tolerate at large is a class of people less than citizens; and that every interest in the land demands that the freedman be free to become in all things, so far as his own personal gifts will lift and sustain him, the same sort of American citizen he would be if, with the same intellectual and moral calibre, he were white.

Cable condemned the ingrained tendency of Southerners to regard the Negro as a perpetual alien in their midst and attacked the current insistence on "the hot branding-iron of ignominious distinctions" such as segregation on steamboat landings, railway platforms, theaters, concert halls, art displays, public libraries, public schools, courthouses, and churches. The Negro became tolerable in the favored sections of public conveyances only when he accompanied a white person as a servant. Cable pleaded for a torrent of Southern protests to raise the freedman to the status of genuine freedom. But his followers were too inarticulate, and angry men denounced him as a traitor. It was this situation, in all likelihood, as well as his desire to be near his literary outlets, that induced him to find a home in Northampton, Massachusetts.

2

In their drive for economy, the Bourbons gave the Southern penal system its reputation as an "American Siberia." Governor Wade Hampton tried to carry out the pledge for strict economy by leasing prisoners to private contractors. When a conscientious prison official protested against the cruelty of the lease system, he soon found himself without a post. The more corrupt carpetbaggers had already discovered a handsome source of revenue in hiring out convicts as laborers for railroads, road companies, and mines, but the Bourbon governors of the Deep South like Hampton became deeply attached to this budget-balancing device. The result was a brutal chain gang and prison system which drew national condemnation.

Northern states also used the convict leasing system for a time until organized labor and public opinion compelled its abolition. But in the South, union pressure was too weak. The powerful Tennessee Coal and Iron Company was the lessee of most of Tennessee's state prisoners and found them indispensable in breaking strikes and discouraging unionization among their free mine workers. Besides, the inevitable race issue divided Southern opinion on the evils of chain gangs and the convict lease system. As a result, most of those sentenced, especially those given the longest terms, were Negroes. Vagrancy laws and petty theft statutes were effective in trapping foot-loose Negroes while the trial procedures were likely to penalize the innocent as well as the guilty.

Cable wrote a savage arraignment of the convict lease system and dwelt upon the racial aspects of it. Negro prisoners were convicted in large numbers, often for fanciful crimes, by exclusively white juries. Ray Stannard Baker, biographer of Woodrow Wilson, observed the operations of Southern courts and reported, "The white man sometimes escaped with a reprimand, he was sometimes fined three dollars and costs, but the Negro, especially if he had no white man to intercede for him, was usually punished with a ten or fifteen dollar fine, which often meant that he must go to the chain-gang." As for cases involving Negroes against whites, the biased atmosphere of rural communities may be inferred from the eloquent summing up of a zealous lawyer in defending a white client accused of killing a rebellious Negro: "God forbid that a jury should ever convict a white man for killing a nigger who knocked his teeth down his throat!"

It should be noted that while Southern governors and county sheriffs turned the clock back in the field of scientific penology and court procedures, the North was making unusual progress. Zebulon Brockway of New York and the various prison leagues were making the prewar ideal of reformation rather than retaliation the chief goal of penology. Brockway's idea of the indeterminate sentence as an incentive to self-improvement was adopted at his new Elmira Reformatory opened in 1877. State after state imitated the Elmira plan of incentives and education. Northern prisons also borrowed the advanced European theories of probation and parole. But the reformatory ideal and the modern penitentiary system affected few Southern states before the twentieth century.

Blake McKelvey, historian of American prisons, has left a dark picture of the leasing system and the chain gang in which the paternalism of plantation slavery was wholly lacking. A convict had no cash value as the slave had had and if disease or the lash took his life, he would scarcely be missed under this scheme of things. A hundred chained men might be squeezed into a loathsome, foul-smelling shack at night and the doors or windows kept tightly shut as a precaution against escape. Convicts in striped suits toiled on rockpiles, in dust-choked mines, and up to their knees in malarial swamps, guarded by armed men who did not hesitate to shoot fugitives or set huge dogs upon them. In Florida, guards sometimes broke the spirit of rebels with the "water-cure"—pouring large quantities of water down the throat of a prisoner while he was held down on the ground. There was every incentive for these wretches to take the most desperate chances to escape and far more convicts ran away in the South than in the North. State legislators left only the most perfunctory arrangements for inspection. Things were even worse in the counties, for the local taxpayer asked no questions regarding what the sheriff did with his chain gang in building roads.

With the overthrow of the Bourbon statesmen in the 1890's by Populist-minded champions of the white yeoman farmer, some improvement took place, especially for white prisoners. The convict lease system was dropped in state after state, partly because it was proving to be less profitable than expected, although the chain gang seemed too well adapted to the warm climate of the South for it to be abolished altogether. However, new industrial prisons were built and more humane experiments were made with convict labor in plantations and road camps. Gradually, the influence of Northern and European penal systems infiltrated the more enlightened Southern communities.

3

The crowning glory of the Bourbon era was the sensational success of the campaign "to bring the cotton mills to the cotton." While New Englanders felt unhappy at this industrial competition, enthusiastic Southern journalists, businessmen, lawyers, and even ministers organized a drive for small native capital to build mills. A handful of Southerners like James D. B. De Bow and George Fitzhugh had long preached the blessings of industrialization and a diversified economy as the solution to the colonial status of the South. Some results had been achieved by 1861 when the South had about 25,000 factories worth $175,000,000, although most of these plants were very small.

The Civil War proved—if one needed proof—how far the South really was from economic self-sufficiency. Even professional patriots paid their reluctant tribute to the wealth and power of Northern industry. After the war, the Northern example of rapid industrial expansion inspired ambitious Southerners with a little capital to build many small factories. But the real growth of Southern mills on a large scale began with the Bourbon era.

During the 1880's energetic citizens of all classes joined the campaign to raise capital for the mills. Hundreds of people bought small shares in a single enterprise. Speakers argued that the cotton mills would furnish work for the poorer classes and raise the general standard of living. In North Carolina, the camp meeting revivals were often concluded with a fund-raising appeal for the factories. The rapidly growing evangelical cults could point out that by encouraging temperance and steady habits they had made available many thousands of reliable workers. Wealthy philanthropists joined the drive. "Every little town wanted a mill," wrote an observer, "if it couldn't get a big one, it would take a small one; if not a sheeting, then a spinning mill."

It was impossible to exaggerate the local advantages of the South for industrialization. All along the Piedmont, stretching from southwestern Virginia to Georgia and Alabama, the "fall line" offered the attraction of unlimited water power. Besides, there was a vast market for the Southern textile mills in the enormous local demand for cheap, coarse, cotton manufactures. The results were immediate. Between 1880 and 1890, the number of textile factories rose from 161 to 239 and from a modest capitalization of less than $18,000,000 to nearly $54,000,000, while the number of operatives more than doubled, totalling over 36,000 at the end of the decade. The great Atlanta Expositions and lesser fairs in other cities proudly exhibited the wares of the New South and took millions of dollars worth of orders.

One of the leading Southern advantages over New England was the low wages paid. To Southern rural folk, accustomed to a subsistence standard of living, factory pay seemed very high in these years. Mill jobs were hoarded for whites despite the admitted qualifications of many Negroes for such semi-skilled work. One manufacturer, according to Broadus Mitchell, declared that factory owners "have recognized the fact that the mill life is the only avenue open today to our poor whites, and we have with earnestness and practically without exception kept that avenue open to the white man alone." This, he believed, meant escape from competition with the Negro.

Into the small mill towns, virtually owned by the cotton manufacturers, poured wagon loads of poor highlander families, poor whites from the lowlands, and even village ne'er do wells. As in the early industrial history of England and New England, the rule was long hours, low hourly rates, and the employment of women and children as well as adult males. Youngsters had little opportunity for schooling, though some mill owners showed a paternalistic regard for the welfare of the textile workers and built schools, hospitals, and churches.

Even more impressive and significant was the rise of the tobacco kingdom of James Buchanan Duke and his rivals. During the war and afterwards, Union soldiers stationed at Durham, North Carolina, had carried away a pleasant recollection of "bright tobacco" developed in that area through a charcoal process that produced a mild smoke or "chaw" that would not bite the tongue. Washington Duke, James's father, an antislavery farmer who is said to have voted for Lincoln in 1860 but who, nevertheless, had served in Lee's army, had returned from the war to find his farm stripped by marauders, except for a barn of bright tobacco. Thereafter, he went peddling with James and eventually developed his own bright leaf variety of smoking tobacco known widely as "Duke's Mixture."

James Duke was no soft Southern Bourbon, though he shared their industrial enthusiasm. He took John D. Rockefeller as his model and displayed a commercial ruthlessness and promotional ingenuity that had been almost forgotten in the South during the days when cotton was king. When his father offered him a chance to get a liberal arts education befitting the station of a traditional Southern gentleman, James decided instead to go off to a business college in the North and returned to Durham with aggressive commercial ideas. His neighbors had already begun to popularize "Bull Durham" with a bovine symbol borrowed from an English mustard label, and makers of the plug and pipe tobacco were beginning to look into the possibilities of the cigarette. James Duke outdid his rivals in gaining patent control of the best cigarette-rolling machines, and revolutionized production.

Since Southerners tended to regard cigarettes as an effeminate importation from Russia and Turkey, Duke reached out for a wider market in the North, hired expert Russian Jews to teach his Negro workers the best techniques, and originated a nation-wide sales campaign. He cut prices, gave away premiums, and introduced billboard advertising with alluring actresses smoking away in queenly style. (Personally, James Duke, who came of strict Methodist ancestry, did not like to see ladies smoke.) Adopting the latest techniques of the Yankee monopolists in oil, steel, railroads, and other swiftly expanding fields, he launched bitter price wars to force competitors to sell out to him, used spies and rebates against competitors, gained control of retail outlets through the United Cigar stores, learned the intricacies of trust and holding company evasions, and forced tobacco farmers to sell to him at ever-lower prices. After a severe cigarette war, Duke brought his rivals under his hegemony in 1890 when the American Tobacco Company was organized with himself as president and leading stockholder.

The great railroad revival took place in the 1880's when the South completed her recovery from the damage of war and neglect. In 1883 occurred the long-discussed union of New Orleans and San Francisco through the efforts of the Southern Pacific Railway. That same year new lines reached out from St. Louis to Houston, Galveston, and other Southern towns. By the nineties, Northern financiers, J. P. Morgan particularly, were untangling the finances of the Virginia railroads and those elsewhere, thus making possible the extensive Southern Railway network. Railroads actively stimulated the growth of Southern cities and towns and broke down rural isolation in many areas.

In 1871, during the opening phase of the New South, Birmingham, "the Pittsburgh of the South," was founded at the junction of two railway lines. Surrounded by cotton fields, it was in 1880 a town of only 3000, but a decade later, as its coal and iron activities developed, its population increased to over 26,000. Capital from the

North—especially from Pennsylvania—stimulated its growth. Before the eighties had ended, Andrew Carnegie and other Eastern promoters had investigated this area and had returned home with an enthusiasm for investing in the Birmingham coal and iron industries. Thus the Birmingham-Chattanooga area eventually became a province of the United States Steel Corporation and the city claimed in 1890 to be the third largest iron-shipping point in the world.

Atlanta, later called the New York of the South because of its distributing facilities, was almost as new in appearance as Birmingham, for Sherman had done his work methodically on that munitions center of the Confederacy. During the eighties its citizenry expanded from 37,000 to 65,000. Flour mills, meat-packing plants, lumber companies, and machine shops thrived.

Meanwhile, Richmond dug itself out of the ruins and advanced as the chief entrepôt for cigars, cheroots, and other tobacco products, as well as flour, iron, and steel. Her historic Tredegar Iron Works manufactured thousands of freight cars. Charleston recovered only slowly, her rice planters injured by the wartime destruction of canals and floodgates and by the competition of Louisiana.

New Orleans, on the contrary, recovered swiftly from the war, her cotton, sugar, and rice hinterland richer than ever; her population, which had been less than 169,000 before the war, expanded to 216,000 by 1880. Thereafter, as the railroad gained dominance over the Mississippi steamboat, the city lost out increasingly to the upriver cities of St. Louis, Louisville, and Chicago, and not until after 1875 did the city improve its water channels to admit modern ocean steamers. Still, she had numerous factories to process cotton, rice, and sugar products, many machine shops, and several men's clothing factories. In 1890 New Orleans modernized her sewage disposal plant and ended the unsanitary practice of relying upon the gutters for this purpose. At the same time she replaced her cobblestone walks with modern pavements.

4

The Bourbons were too concerned with bringing back the good old days of light taxation and private schools to conduct a public school crusade, but even they made some mild advances toward the goal of general literacy. Although the carpetbaggers had sometimes dissipated Southern school funds, they left behind them the principle that the child's education was the responsibility of the state. However, universal education in the South was severely handicapped not only by poverty but by the insistence on a dual system of schools as the bulwark of the segregated racial structure of Southern society. Even the carpetbaggers had not dared to violate the taboo on mixed schools. From the primary grades through the universities, whites and Negroes were kept strictly apart regardless of the costly duplication of school facilities and teachers in thinly settled communities. Burton J. Hendrick, biographer of the liberal Southern writer and statesman, Walter Hines Page, drew this dark picture of Southern education in Bourbon times:

A few wretched hovels, scattered through a sparsely settled country, served as schoolhouses; a few uninspiring and neglected women, earning perhaps $50 or $75 a year, did weary duty as teachers; a few groups of anemic and listless children, attending school for only forty days a year —such was the preparation for life which most Southern states gave the less fortunate of their citizens. The glaring fact that emphasized the outcome of this official carelessness was an illiteracy among white men and women, of 26 per cent. Among the negroes it was vastly larger.

Although the school term and salary figures were exaggerated, the general picture was quite true. In 1880 the illiterate part of the population in North Carolina included 32 per cent of the whites and 77 per cent of the Negroes. Alabama, that year, reported that 25 per cent of the whites and 81 per cent of the Negroes were unable to read or write. Texas had only 14 per cent of white illiterates, but counted 75 per cent of the Negroes in this class. The rural schoolteacher was paid poorly everywhere, but North Carolina paid less than any other state, offering, as late as 1900, an average monthly wage of $26.18 to schoolmasters and $23.14 to schoolmistresses. In

1900, after the Bourbons and Populists had been in control several
decades, Georgia's Superintendent of Education reported gloomily:

All the States in the Union except a small group of Southern States now
have a nine months absolutely free term for all the children of school
age. Georgia has only a five months term. Massachusetts spends $39.10
every year for each child enrolled . . . while Georgia spends $6.31. As a
matter of fact, Georgia spends on her country children each year less
than $4 for each child enrolled.

He pointed out that the Middle and Western states spent ten times
as much as Georgia did for each child of school age. In 1882 the
school term in Alabama averaged eighty-four days for whites and
seventy-six days for colored, and teachers' salaries were about $23
a month. Other Southern states were not much better off. In the
same year Florida reported only fifty-five days of schooling for
whites and forty-one for Negroes though white schoolmasters
received $44.49 monthly while colored teachers got $29.89. Not
only did Negro teachers receive less compensation than white
but Negro schools ran shorter terms. Exceptions to this discouraging picture of course existed. New Orleans, which had an excellent
school system in antebellum times, retained a stable nine-month
school year in 1882 and afterward.

In contrast, Bourbon preparatory schools and colleges did very
well, although they were not as prosperous as in antebellum times.
Excellent sectarian and private schools, academies, and colleges
could be found all over the South. The number of colleges was
astonishing. While six New England states were provided with
seventeen colleges, six Southern states had sixty-six! However, most
of the latter were no better than preparatory schools and were
weighted down with poor students who were able to enroll because
of low entrance standards. But there were first-rate schools like the
University of Virginia where George Frederick Holmes was offering
one of the earliest sociology courses to be taught in the nation. Basil
Gildersleeve, who had left this institution for the new Johns Hopkins
in 1876, had established a distinguished tradition in philology. At
the Johns Hopkins University, he founded in 1880 the *American*

Journal of Philology. Southern colleges were particularly strong
not only in the classics but in the relatively new professional field of
the English language. Tulane University, opened in 1884, had an
excellent record under William P. Johnston who stressed the Jeffersonian ideal of religious freedom and academic liberty.

The fundamentalist spirit of the Southern churches, especially
among the Baptists, Methodists, and a wing of the Presbyterians,
played havoc with the ideal of academic freedom, particularly on
the issue of evolution. Vanderbilt College, endowed in 1873 by the
fortune of Cornelius Vanderbilt, the railroad magnate, dismissed
a professor of geology for upholding evolutionary doctrines. Its
decision had the backing of the Tennessee Conference of the Southern Methodist Church. Baptist colleges had their own heretics to
expel. A *cause célèbre* arose among Presbyterians in 1884 when a
fundamentalist wing under Robert L. Dabney demanded the dismissal of Professor James Woodrow of the Presbyterian Theological
Seminary at Columbia, South Carolina, for publicly defending
evolution. Dabney was himself an unreconstructed Southerner who
opposed public schools as Yankee inventions and fought the reunion of the Northern and Southern wings of the Presbyterian
Church. During the war, he had served as Stonewall Jackson's chaplain. Although the General Assembly of the Southern Presbyterian
Church supported Dabney and decided against Professor Woodrow's heresies, the evolutionist found a refuge in the Bourbon
institution of South Carolina College where many of his former
students joined him. Thoughout this era and in the succeeding
decades the fundamentalists continued their attack upon the teaching of the new biology in the colleges. Thousands of impressionable
hearers listened to the semi literate, itinerant preachers, like Sam
Jones of Alabama, who shouted down sinners and attacked Darwin's
evolution and the new geology of Lyell, which extended the age
of the earth considerably beyond the year 4004 B.C., as estimated
by some churchmen.

That the Bourbons had learned nothing and forgotten nothing is
evident in their rejection of the federal Blair bill, which sought to
subsidize elementary education in backward states. Even Woodrow

1865-1885

Mark Twain (1835-1910), humorist and author.
(*Cleveland Plain Dealer*)

James B. Duke
as a young man.
(Underwood-Stratton)

"Making the Virginia Twist," by John Durkin. (Bettmann Archive)

A Virginia Mammy

J. Durkin

MAKING THE VIRGINIA TWIST

Booker T. Washington,
Negro educator.
(Bettmann Archive)

"Chain gang at Richmond," by W. S. Sheppard. (Bettmann Archive)

Buffalo Bill's Wild West and Congress of Rough Riders of the World. *At right:* Col. W. F. Cody, "Buffalo Bill." (Lithographic poster, 1899, by Courier Litho. Co.; Bettmann Archive)

Main Street, Helena, Montana, 1870. (Collection of L. H. Jorud, Helena, Montana)

Geronimo, famed Apache chief (wearing a black alpaca coat) at Fort Bowie, Arizona Territory, September 7, 1886. Fourth Cavalry soldiers are in the background. (National Archives)

El Capitan Hotel, Merced, California, in 1872 with two Central Pacific wood-burning locomotives in the foreground. (Southern Pacific Railroad)

Carry Nation, prohibitionist, on a visit to Cleveland in 1907. (*Cleveland Plain Dealer*)

The Great Chicago Fire of 1871, Michigan Avenue. (Chicago Historical Society)

Frances E. Willard, educator and reformer. (Engraving from a photograph; Bettmann Archive)

Chicago's Prairie Avenue, street of the elite, 1880. (Chicago Historical Society)

Above: "A Negro Baptism," Wake County, 1903. (State Department of Archives and History, Raleigh, N. C.)

Below, left: Billy Sunday, evangelist, in Cleveland. *(Cleveland Plain Dealer)*

Below, right: Mary Baker Eddy, founder of the Christian Science Church, speaking in June, 1903, from the balcony of her retreat at Pleasant View, N. H. (Copyright, 1904, 1932, by the Christian Science Publishing Society. Used by permission.)

Wilson sympathized with their refusal to compromise with their belief in states' rights and their suspicion of federal control. The bill required the states and localities to match the federal contribution and to tolerate a certain degree of federal supervision over such expenditures. It would have apportioned federal funds to the states according to the amount of illiteracy. The bill was defeated by the Bourbons and by certain Northern industrialists, and by Catholic sentiment against the exclusion of parochial schools from public school benefits. On the other hand, the conservatives showed an increasing interest in vocational education. Grant's victory, in part attributed to superior Northern technology, together with the new technical needs of the South, led to a greater enthusiasm for the applied subjects. These came to supplement the traditional, classical upper-class curriculum. The Morrill Act of 1862, intended to encourage scientific and technical education by subsidizing colleges for this purpose, did much to strengthen or initiate Southern as well as Northern colleges. General Robert E. Lee at Washington College proved not only an efficient and beloved administrator, but a vigorous innovator in encouraging the applied sciences, modern languages, and journalism. The New South recognized the importance of a technical education.

Northern philanthropy tried to fill the gap left by Southern poverty and by Bourbon indifference to elementary education. No kindness had touched the hearts of Southerners quite as much as the huge educational bequest of the Massachusetts-born financier, George Peabody of England. In 1867, Peabody decided to make an effort to raise the educational level of the South. He had already given museums of science to both Yale and Harvard and he left a $2,500,000 gift to construct homes for London's poor. The Peabody Education Fund totalled $3,500,000 and aimed at the improvement of existing public schools rather than at the building of new ones or at aid to private and sectarian schools. From this fund also grew the George Peabody College for Teachers in Nashville. Under the administration of the devoted educator, Jabez L. M. Curry of Alabama, this legacy stimulated state taxation for the building and maintenance of public schools for both races.

Curry, the official agent for both the Peabody and Slater Funds (the latter a million-dollar fund for the education of freedmen) and later the director of the Southern Education Board, was the South's best-known educator. The son of an Alabama slaveholder, he had once taken an ardent proslavery and secessionist position and had fought for the Confederacy. But he had also been educated in Massachusetts and had been deeply impressed by Horace Mann's crusade for public schools. Despite his states' rights ideas and his Bourbon economic conservatism, he agitated during the eighties for the passage of the Blair bill. He had accepted the administration of the Slater Fund for the education of the Negro despite strong Southern prejudices against this type of racial contact.

Curry used his control over the Peabody Fund to block the efforts of certain Southern states to restrict Negro school expenditures to the amount of taxes paid directly by the colored race. This was done simply by withholding Peabody Fund money from any state practicing this type of discrimination. He did much for vocational education because he shared the Bourbon enthusiasm for the industrialization of the South. His goal of general literacy was to make the school the conservator of the existing social order, rather than an instrument for major economic changes. But he had a far more enlightened view of racial justice and the value of mass literacy than most Bourbons.

5

Just as the Bourbons of the 1880's invoked the Northern capitalist to stand as godfather to the New South of commerce and industry, so the Southern writers of that era found their best patron in the Northern publisher of books and magazines. Southern patronage had never been adequate in antebellum times. Simms, De Bow, G. F. Holmes, Fitzhugh, and others had lamented this fact many a time. Reconstruction, as already noted, brought with it a keen interest among Northern readers in the life of the South. "Between 1882 and 1887," writes Shields McIlwaine, "the annual average of articles published on the South was about ten times that during the preceding period of eighty years." The plantation tradition, as in

antebellum years, had its devotees in New York city and the prairies
of the Middle West. Poor whites, long the concern of abolitionists
who attributed their debasement to the planter's monopoly of the
best land, were introduced in a much more sympathetic guise by
Southern novelists and short story writers. The entire local color
genre was stimulated by the successful example of Bret Harte of
California and his western mining camp stories.

George Washington Cable was not the only Southern writer
"discovered" by Northern publishers. Walter Hines Page, too, found
a literary career on the staff of the *Forum* of New York, as editor
of the *Atlantic Monthly* and *The World's Work,* and later as a
publishing partner in Doubleday, Page and Company. The real
start for Thomas Nelson Page came in 1884 when *Century Magazine*
published his story, "Marse Chan." Joel Chandler Harris wrote
innumerable sketches and editorials for the *Atlanta Constitution,* but
it was not until a manuscript scout for Appleton's persuaded him
to collect some of his sketches for a book that Harris became a
national idol as the father of Uncle Remus. Recognition came to
Mary N. Murfree of Tennessee (Charles Egbert Craddock) after
Thomas Bailey Aldrich of the *Atlantic Monthly* decided to go
ahead with her story, "The 'Harnt' that Walks Chilhowee." *Lippincott's Magazine* helped introduce Sidney Lanier's poetry to the
world and maintained a policy of encouraging Southern writers.
This sponsorship by the North made possible the Southern cultural
revival of the 1880's.

While Tourgée and De Forest had incidentally tapped the rich
local color sources of Negro dialect and poor white characteristics,
it remained for the Southern revival writers to refurbish the con-
tented Negro of the plantation tradition and other ethnic types with
a greater degree of realism through the use of accurate dialect.
They enhanced the poor white's appeal through pathos, tragi-
comedy, and uninhibited sentimentality. Unlike Longstreet, forerunner of the local colorists who described the world of the illiterate
Georgia "crackers," they did not poke fun at them, but instead drew
a sympathetic (properly censored) portrait of the Jeeter Lesters of
that day.

Joel Chandler Harris was too democratic in his sympathies to fit easily into the Bourbon category. Yet, as associate editor of the *Atlanta Constitution* under Henry Grady, he agreed completely with the policies of that prophet of the New South. However, he showed a more generous faith in the future social emancipation of the Negro. Booker T. Washington and even less conservative Negro leaders wrote him their appreciation of his enlightened attitude toward their race. By nature he was about as benevolent as his own Uncle Remus and by rearing he was a product of the unique equalitarian spirit of Middle Georgia where planters and farmers did not lose caste by working alongside Negroes or the poorest of the white farmers. His father had been a laborer who deserted Joel's mother shortly after his birth and the boy had worked his way upward and educated himself in the country printing shops. He felt little rancor toward the Yankees and taught his children that Lincoln's death was the greatest tragedy of the South.

The Negro myths and legends that young Joel heard might have remained but a pleasant memory as they did with so many Southerners raised by Negro servants or slaves. For a time Uncle Remus was known only locally through the sketches in the *Atlanta Constitution*. Not until the 1870's, when *Lippincott's Magazine* published articles on Negro folklore did Harris realize the full literary value of such materials. In 1880 there finally emerged from the presses of D. Appleton and Company the first volume, *Uncle Remus: His Songs and His Sayings*. Although Harris modestly assigned credit for the literary introduction of genuine Negro dialect to Irwin Russell of Mississippi, he succeeded in making the most skillful blend of such dialect with Negro legends. Few Southerners received as great a literary ovation as did this shy, kindly journalist of Atlanta. Not only did the discriminating *Springfield Republican* and *New York Evening Post* sing his praises, but he was sought after by Mark Twain, James Whitcomb Riley, and Theodore Roosevelt. The entire Roosevelt family adored Harris, whom they had to cajole to dine with them, and the President afterwards recalled that he had first heard "Brer Rabbit" stories from his own mother and aunt who had been raised in Georgia. An insatiable public of all ages demanded more Uncle Remus books until ten had been published by 1917.

To put the various Negro folk tales together Harris had created Uncle Remus as a devoted eighty-year-old plantation Negro who amused a small boy nightly with some new tale of Brer Rabbit's adventures with Brer Fox and other loquacious animals. When Harris insisted that he was a mere compiler of such stories, Mark Twain snorted, adding in effect that the character of Uncle Remus was itself a literary achievement of the first order. Most striking was the Tar Baby story. In this, Brer Fox mixed tar and turpentine in the shape of a "tar baby" and put this in the road to trap Brer Rabbit who finally came along "des ez sassy ez a jay-bird." The rabbit became tangled with the Tar Baby to the delight of Brer Fox. " 'Well, I speck I got you dis time, Brer Rabbit,' sezee; 'maybe I ain't, but I speck I is.' " Upon this, the quick-thinking rabbit replied, "I don't keer w'at you do wid me, Brer Fox, . . . so you don't fling me in dat brier patch." Brer Fox was so anxious to even up scores with his old enemy that he gleefully threw Brer Rabbit into the briar patch. Upon this, of course, the rabbit escaped with the taunt, "Bred en bawn in a brier patch, Brer Fox—bred en bawn in a brier patch!" And with that he skipped out "des ez lively ez a cricket in de embers."

This tale, among others, attracted the attention of readers in far away India and the Philippines as well as at home. Letters from folklorists and others astonished Harris with the news that variants of the Tar Baby story were known among American Indians, Caribbean natives, Indians of Brazil, African bushmen, Moros of the Philippine Islands, and treasured even among Hindus in their tradition of Buddha's "Birth Stories." Harris, who had attempted to explain the stories by reference to Negro psychology, turned amateur folklorist and discovered the wide distribution of these Georgia tales. Modern anthropologists have pointed out that many American Indians west of the Mississippi from Alaska to New Mexico know the Tar Baby story and are familiar with the white rabbit as a combination of demigod and trickster. Quite possibly Uncle Remus had learned most of his stories from slaves belonging to the Cherokee Indians who had once owned plantations in North-western Georgia.

While Joel Chandler Harris could make his Negroes talk in every-day dialect, he did not venture to go beyond the happy "darky" stereotype of the plantation tradition. But he could be much more realistic—though still restrained by the Victorian conventions of that day regarding sex and "hard-boiled" realism—in dealing with the poor whites of Georgia. Other Georgians, not only Longstreet but Richard Malcolm Johnston, author of *Georgia Sketches* (1864), had explored with some nostalgia the "cracker" background of horseplay, frontier fighting, and native humor. Harris' story "Mingo" (1882) depicts a tragic half-witted Georgia "Tacky," Bud Stucky, in red jeans and striped shirt, and touches briefly on the hatred of this poor class for the gentry. But Harris, sympathetic as he was to the underprivileged whites, was no literary propagandist, for he colored his stories by sentimental situations in which pity and sympathy dominate. He always remained well within the bounds of respectability for middle class America.

The local color school thrived particularly well in Gallic Louis-iana, land of the aristocratic Creole and the illiterate "Cajun"— the Acadian of Longfellow's *Evangeline*. Most important of the Louisiana regionalists was George Washington Cable, descended from an old Virginia slaveholding family on his father's side and from New England Puritan stock on his mother's. His Confederate cavalry service and his sympathetic writings on behalf of the freed-man have already been noted. He could depict the haughty Creole aristocrat of New Orleans and the down-at-the-heels Creole gambler of the River. His "Posson Jones" tells the story of a semi-literate "American" minister of the West Florida frontier who meets "Jools," a Creole gambler who hopes to pick his pocket. "Jools" ingratiates himself with the naïve parson, " 'I am a *Catholique, mais,*'—bright-ening as he hoped to recommend himself anew—'not a very good one.' " Then, with a tenderhearted treatment suggestive of Bret Harte and O. Henry, the author allows the cynical "Jools" to be completely converted to a better life by his contact with "Posson Jones" whose goodness is irresistible.

The beautiful secretive quadroons of Cable's novels lured many Europeans as well as Northern visitors to New Orleans and lent color to such books as *Old Creole Days* (1879), *The Grandissimes* (1880), and *The Creoles of Louisiana* (1884). His readers loved *Bonaventure* (1888) for the pastoral beauty of the Cajun country in southern Louisiana. Amid the bayous and western prairies lived the descendants of Evangeline's French-speaking people—now barefoot, illiterate squatters, still peasant in outlook, and isolated by language, religion, and geography from their Anglo-Saxon fellow countrymen. Their Latin temperament, ancient folkways, distinctive beards and broad-brimmed hats, their "pirogues" (scooped-out shallow boats) and little patches of land set them apart from the advancing pioneers. The Civil War did much to break up this unique pastoral culture in which the priests played a large role in resisting the "progress" and materialistic aims of the Anglo-Saxon. Intermarriage, as McIlwaine points out, had strengthened the clannish feeling of the Cajuns, though a large Indian admixture was obvious. Cable, ever a moralist, combined his love tale in *Bonaventure* with an "uplift" story of a Creole schoolmaster who sought to raise the lot of the Cajuns.

This rich vein of human material was skillfully exploited by the unconventional Kate Chopin, née Katherine O'Flaherty, who was born in St. Louis and had become the mistress of a Red River plantation. She knew the Cajuns of the mid-Louisiana parishes and could tell their story with humor and suspense, with a suggestion of Maupassant's realism, and the pathos of that Victorian era. Readers knew her best for *Bayou Folk* (1894) and other short stories.

The most exotic of the literary men who loved Creole Louisiana was Lafcadio Hearn, born in Greece of Greek and Irish parents, and fated to be a perennial rolling stone. Observing the quaint homes of old New Orleans and the diverse wanderers from all over the globe, he described the "fairest city of the South" in *The Glamour of New Orleans* (1878) and in various Creole sketches—always sensing some exotic mystery beneath the surface of things. Far more Victorian as an interpreter of the Creole was Grace King, eager to correct the blemishes that Cable and others had cast upon the middle class population of New Orleans. In 1903, she showed her regard for the respectable Creole tradition by editing the works of Charles Étienne Gayarré.

The literary discovery of the white mountaineers in the Cumberlands and Great Smokies of Tennessee belongs to a native-born, retiring, crippled woman, Mary N. Murfree, who adopted the device of George Eliot and George Sand in gaining entree into a male world of arts and letters by using a male nom de plume, Charles Egbert Craddock. Her first collected stories, *In the Tennessee Mountains* (1884), showed a mastery of local dialect and characterization. In one of the stories published in the *Atlantic Monthly,* "The 'Harnt' That Walks Chilhowee," she depicted the forthright attitude of an illiterate highlander, Simon Burney, who supported an ungrateful outcast for the rest of the latter's life. To him, he had said in dialect reminiscent of the seventeenth century, "I ain't a-goin' ter holp no man ter break the law an' hender jestice; but ef ye will go an' stand yer trial, I'll take keer of ye agin' them Grims ez long ez I kin fire a rifle. . . . " In Kentucky the Blue Grass region was preempted by James Lane Allen, a schoolteacher whose novels were highly praised by the critics of his day. His novels were usually romantic, though in a later work, *The Choir Invisible* (1897), he tempered his sentimental tendencies with considerable realism of character.

While most local color writers respected the proprieties and disdained to pry into such questions as actual race relations, sex mores, and disease, a transplanted Yankee lady, Octave Thanet, who wrote under the pseudonym of Alice French, showed considerable willingness to discuss these forbidden themes. Her discovery of the Arkansas "rednecks" of the 1880's and 1890's added more subject matter for the local colorists. Residing in a decayed plantation house, she told of the hard-headed, backward trash who were by Southern standards so degraded as to be jailed together with Negroes in a chain gang. In numerous stories she described promiscuous poor white women, anemic tenants, drunken croppers, sadists, and tragic families whose women died early from overwork and child-bearing. Much of her work, however, appeared later than the 1880's and showed the effect of the new realism that was captivating Northern as well as Southern writers.

Leading Virginians of the local color school had not given up the older forms of the plantation tradition of John Pendleton Kennedy and John Esten Cooke (who continued to write his tales of chivalry). One of the direct heirs of this genteel tradition who devoted his attention to poor whites as well as to romantic ladies and gentlemen was Thomas Nelson Page. He showed a successful handling of Negro dialect in his collection of short stories, *In Ole Virginia* (1887), which followed his highly popular dialect story, "Marse Chan," published in *Century Magazine* in 1884. But he could not easily avoid a mannered style and the prevailing tendency to deal lavishly in sentiment and pathos. Dickens and Walter Scott were still literary models.

Although Mark Twain is usually considered a humorist and storyteller of the frontier West, he often spoke of himself as a Southern writer and expressed that type of liberal dissent that George Washington Cable and later, Walter Hines Page, stood for. In 1901, he introduced the Louisville editor, Henry Watterson with these words, "I was born and reared in a slave state, my father was a slaveowner; and in the Civil War I was a second lieutenant in the Confederacy." This was rather misleading, for his military record had been less than perfunctory. He had been inducted into a Hannibal, Missouri, regiment and after it had been absorbed into the Confederate service, he had decided against army life and left. Some of his best books, however, dealt with life in the South, or at least along the lower Mississippi; these appeared in the seventies and eighties when Southern stories were most popular.

During this era, he wrote *Life on the Mississippi* (1883), which dealt with his stirring youth as a pilot on a Mississippi steamboat. Of special interest are his comments on the postwar South. He blamed the Civil War on the "Walter Scott disease" that infected the South, and he wrote a scathing comment on the nostalgic tendency to romanticize the war. "Mention of the war will wake up a dull company and set their tongues going when nearly any other topic will fail. In the South, the war is what A.D. is elsewhere; they date from it."

Southern journalism amused him for its chivalric flourishes and hyperbole—though he could hardly have included Henry Grady's *Atlanta Constitution* as illustrative of this. He marked this sentence in the *New Orleans Times-Democrat,* "On Saturday, early in the morning, the beauty of the place graced our cabin, and proud of her fair freight the gallant little boat glided up the bayou." The trouble with Southern reporters, he explained, was women. Take another example, this time a description of the ladies at a New Orleans mule race:

The New Orleans women are always charming, but never so much so as at this time of the year, when in their dainty spring costumes they bring with them a breath of balmy freshness and an odor of sanctity unspeakable.

· 3 ·

Southern Demagogues and Liberals:
From Tillman to Wilson

[1890-1917]

I

In 1890, Senator Wade Hampton—he was a United States senator by then—and other Bourbon leaders were overthrown by an upsurge of rural radicals like Ben Tillman of South Carolina. Southern farmers as well as their Northern brethren were suffering from declining prices and fixed debts. The Bourbons and their middle-class allies staved off defeat for a time by a strategic use of the Negro vote. In the Alabama elections of 1892, for example, they defeated the Populists, who were victorious everywhere else in the state, by carrying twelve counties in the Black Belt where the Negro made up two-thirds of the vote. To meet this strategy Tom Watson of Georgia even urged solidarity between white and black farmers, but he soon reversed his position. He joined the radical farmers in destroying the Negro as a political factor by a ruthless program of disfranchisement, sharper social discriminations, and even willingness, on occasion, to abet lynching. Thus Populism and other radical programs were not permitted to destroy the monolithic Democratic one-party system, regarded as the shield of white supremacy.

In his Manifesto of 1890, Benjamin F. Tillman, an ex-farmer with

47

a middle-class background, attacked the Bourbon strategy of antebellum days that made the need for white unity an effective bar to
the economic and social changes desired by small farmers:

South Carolina has never had a real Republican Government. Since the
days of the "Lords Proprietors" it has been an aristocracy under the forms
of Democracy. . . .
Fear of a division among us and consequent return of a negro rule has
kept the people quiet, and they have submitted to many grievances
imposed by the ruling faction because they dreaded to risk such a
division. . . .
Can we afford to leave [power] in the hands of those who, wedded
to ante-bellum ideas, but possessing little of ante-bellum patriotism and
honor, are running it in the interest of a few families and for the benefit
of a selfish ring of politicians?

Most of the so-called demagogues (though not Tillman) had some
college training, as Robison points out, but they found it expedient
to speak the dialect and echo the prejudices of the semi-literate
white masses. "If I didn't," explained Tillman privately, "the damn
fools wouldn't vote for me." His rasping voice, violent language, and
affected carelessness of attire and manners were prime assets for a
successful demagogue. This type of leader from Tillman to Long
usually denounced corporate wealth, speculators, and railroad
lobbies, introduced numerous public schools, hospitals, welfare institutions, vocational colleges, and agricultural aid bureaus. Although
Tillman was a Democrat, he fought the conservatism of another
Democrat, President Cleveland, and took an important part in the
progressive program of a Republican president, Theodore Roosevelt. Another such type, Governor Jeff Davis of Arkansas, sponsored
major social legislation during his term of 1901-5, including laws
prohibiting child labor and protecting miners and other laborers.
Generally, however, the demagogues were far more interested in
rural aid than in urban reform.

The forgotten man, more than ever, was the Negro who lost the
limited franchise that the Bourbons had left him since Reconstruction. The devices of disfranchisement became more ingenious than
ever. To Mississippi's old residence requirement for voting, aimed

at the itinerant Negro, was added a poll tax and a provision that voters be able either to read or to understand any section of the state constitution. White officials, of course, decided whether the Negro had passed the test. If a voter, particularly a Negro, gave even slightly inaccurate facts about himself, he could he held guilty of perjury and disfranchised. Finally, Tillman and his imitators perverted a progressive device, the primary system, by using it to eliminate Negro voters. The primary was defined as a private activity of the Democratic party and hence it could be restricted to white voters. Since the Republican party in the South was scarcely more than a patronage cult, the Democratic primaries determined the outcome of elections. One illustration of the effect of these devices of Negro disfranchisement can be seen in Alabama where the number of registered Negro voters fell in 1900 to 3000 out of 181,000 of voting age.

The federal Supreme Court itself gave its imprimatur to these fundamental constitutional changes in the legal status of the Negro in the case of *Plessy* v. *Ferguson* (1896). Plessy, a Louisiana Negro, vainly challenged a state statute requiring railroads to provide "equal but separate accommodations" for both races. Federal judges, acting on the precedent of an early Massachusetts case, agreed that this was a "reasonable classification." Thereafter the dual racial system was sanctioned for public conveyances, parks, beaches, playgrounds, and public waiting rooms. By 1910 many Southern cities had introduced residential segregation laws. Northern cities with large Negro populations secured the same result through private covenants. However, in 1917 the Supreme Court nullified Louisville's segregation law and compelled restrictionists to resort to more ingenious methods of keeping the races apart.

Still worse was the startling increase of all kinds of violence against Negroes, especially in those counties where white tenants and croppers were in sharp competition with them. Tillman had taken part in the provocative race riots of 1876 and privately justified the lynching of Negroes in cases of rape. Still, he made the gesture in 1895 of putting through an anti-lynching law which died a natural death through disuse. The greatest record for lynching in

the South was reached in 1892 when 235 were reported as victims.
In 1900 (according to the figures of Tuskegee Institute), 115
Negroes were lynched, in 1901, 105; and subsequently up to 1918,
the numbers declined but never fell below 50 a year. The lynchers
were usually young men from poor, uneducated rural families.
Frequently they hanged their victims with the approval or tolerance
of substantial citizens, and cut the law's delays by hanging alleged
killers, rapists, and arsonists. Even if the Negro was innocent, this
did not matter if the desired result of racial intimidation was obtained. "Uppity niggers," who did not "know their place," and successful competitors of the whites were likely to be the lynching
victims instead of the real criminals. Poverty, ignorance, as well as
pure sadism motivated the lynchers and there were too few sheriffs
ready to endanger their lives to save a prisoner from a mob—
although there were some courageous exceptions. Theodore Roosevelt underestimated the strength of racial feeling in the South in
1901, for he was surprised when his luncheon engagement with
Booker T. Washington aroused an indignant outcry in the Southern
press.

2

In this critical era of the Tillman-style demagogues, President
Booker T. Washington of Tuskegee Institute held out the hand of
Christian conciliation and frankly accepted the system of segregation. He had risen from slavery and poverty to the leadership of
his race and was convinced that the times called for a conservative
strategy. The solution to the problem, he felt, lay in the South where
most Negroes lived; emigration to the North would not help very
many. Negroes should avoid a direct battle with the whites for civil
rights and instead should concentrate on winning a secure place in
the national economy as skilled workmen and businessmen. Thus,
he reasoned, the Negro would make himself economically indispensable to the whites and his civil rights would then come as an
inevitable consequence.

At Tuskegee, founded in 1881, Washington had built a promising
vocational institution. He opposed the tendency of literate Negroes

to acquire "the craze for Greek and Latin learning," the symbol of a free leisure class tradition. These intellectuals wished to form an elite of their own, as in Haiti, rather than descend to manual work and learn modern farming and skilled trades. Washington later wrote that he began his work at Tuskegee with "the gospel of the tooth brush," teaching cleanliness and self-reliance, and emphasizing vocational subjects. His conciliatory attitude toward the whites brought him generous gifts from the South as well as from Northern philanthropists. At a time when Northern unions were excluding Negroes it seemed natural for him to seek an alliance with the "best people"—the employer class. Under existing circumstances, when Negroes must first solve the problem of livelihood, even strike-breaking did not seem out of place for Negro strategy. So it seemed to Negro conservative leaders.

It was not surprising, therefore, that Southerners paid Washington the compliment of inviting him in September, 1895, to be one of the chief speakers at the Atlanta Exposition. This was the first time that anyone could recall that a Negro had shared such a speaker's platform with a white. On the appointed day, Washington expounded his ideas on race relations and dwelt upon the futile attempts to replace Southern Negro workers with immigrants:

To those of the white race who look to the incoming of those of foreign birth and strange tongue and habits for the prosperity of the South, were I permitted I would repeat what I say to my own race, "Cast down your bucket where you are."

He praised the loyalty of Negro workmen with whom strikes and labor wars were almost unknown. Most important to Southern listeners who awaited his formula on race contacts was the statement, "In all things that are purely social we can be as separate as the fingers, yet one as the hand in all things essential to mutual progress." Appealing to the enlightened self-interest of the whites, he asked whether Southerners wished Negroes to "constitute one-third and more of the ignorance and crime of the South, or one-third of its intelligence and progress." He went on to explain his position on social equality:

The wisest among my race understand that the agitation of questions of social equality is the extremest folly, and that progress in the enjoyment of all the privileges that will come to us must be the result of severe and constant struggle rather than of artificial forcing. No race that has anything to contribute to the markets of the world is long in any degree ostracized. . . . The opportunity to earn a dollar in a factory just now is worth infinitely more than the opportunity to spend a dollar in an opera-house.

This speech received an ovation from the huge audience which had been tense with expectation about what the Negro spokesman might say. Hearty congratulations and handshakes came from all sides, including the warm praise of former governor Bullock of Georgia. Newspapers in Boston as well as in Atlanta agreed that Washington had created a sensation.

In the ensuing years more millions for Negro institutions poured in from wealthy philanthropists. By 1915, the year of his death, Washington could point out not only the educational progress of his race but its material advancement on other frontiers as well. He had organized in 1900 the National Negro Business League in Boston; now Negroes owned 30,000 businesses in the South, operated 900,000 farms, owned 1000 millinery stores, 7000 grocery stores, 100 drugstores, 200 sawmills, 50 banks, and 120 insurance companies. Some 34,000 Negroes taught in thousands of schools and colleges for Negro youth. A small elite of lawyers, businessmen, and architects were contesting racial leadership with the traditional ministers and exhorters whom Washington despised. One factor that Washington overlooked is that the new class of Negro businessmen held to some extent a stake in the perpetuation of segregation, at least in their desire to control the Negro's trade.

Not all Negroes agreed with the philosophy of Tuskegee's president. Among the brilliant younger men was a Massachusetts intellectual, Dr. William Edward Burghardt Du Bois, who had taken a Ph.D. at Harvard and studied at the University of Berlin. In 1896 he became a professor of economics and history (later of sociology) at Atlanta University. Intellectually Du Bois belonged to the tradition of Frederick Douglass who had fought uncompromisingly for Negro civil rights. In 1903 he published an influential interpretation of race relations, which was also an attack on the Washington strategy, *The Souls of Black Folk*. He charged that industrial education had been overemphasized at the expense of liberal collegiate training for Negroes and asserted that political activity offered salvation for the race. Without the ballot, he argued, the Negro laboring class was helpless, ignorant, and the "plaything of mobs." In 1909 he helped to found the National Association for the Advancement of Colored People. This organization took as its purpose the recovery of all the Negro's social and civil rights under the Constitution. As editor of *The Crisis*, Du Bois pressed home his assault on the Washington tactics and demanded full civil liberties for his race.

Negro protest partly took the form of migration, though obvious economic motives were inseparable from other motives for escape. Even before the Civil War tens of thousands of Negroes had left for Liberia and Haiti. The largest single migration, including over 43,000 "exodusters," went to Kansas during the seventies, a move that aroused investigations by Congressmen. However, many of these homeseeking Negroes who had yielded to "Kansas fever" received only a chilly welcome from white residents there and some began to return to Mississippi, the chief source of this movement. Less than 136,000 Negroes were living in the West by 1910, and they preferred Texas and Oklahoma despite Jim Crow. Industrial expansion in the Northern cities, growing white competition for Southern jobs, and the crop destruction wrought by the boll weevil set in motion the Great Migration after 1915. This movement swelled with the economic opportunities of World War I. By that time over a million Negroes were residing in the Northern and Western states.

Despite setbacks, Negroes gained in material goods as well as in educational opportunities. Between 1890 and 1910, Negro farm owners almost doubled, totaling nearly 219,000, almost all of them in the South. Their lands comprised nearly 13,000,000 acres valued at over $620,000,000. Negro farm tenants increased from approximately 470,000 to 670,000 in the same period. In the North thousands of Negro migrants, although denied skilled employment by the trade unions, were finding fresh opportunities in an expanding industrial economy. The nearly static world of slavery was gone.

One of the brightest hopes for the Negro's future lay in the multiplication of educational opportunities. Tuskegee grew so rapidly that in 1902 there were nearly 1400 Negro men and women taking vocational courses there and specializing in one of the thirty-four different industries, especially in brickmaking, which Washington felt was vital to the South. The college also offered afternoon cooking classes, town night schools, and a Children's House, which served as an experimental elementary school for prospective teachers. While Tuskegee stressed vocational training, new Negro institutions, like Fisk University in Nashville and Atlanta University, rose from preparatory schools to train teachers and eventually came to offer the race a liberal education. Fisk attained international fame for its magnificent Jubilee Singers who sang the Negro's rich songs North as well as South and even in England.

Elementary schools for Negroes remained poor in quality of teaching and equipment throughout this period, but important advances were being made. State grants and philanthropic agencies such as the General Education Board, the Slater Fund, the Jeanes Fund, the Julius Rosenwald Fund, and various church societies helped the public schools reduce Southern Negro illiteracy to 44 per cent by 1904, a proportion that Washington compared favorably with the 68 per cent illiteracy in Spain and 80 per cent in Latin America. In 1908 a kindly Philadelphia Quaker, Miss Anna T. Jeanes, left a large bequest to improve rural Negro schools in the South. "Jeanes Teachers" were sent from school to school in the county to act as rural industrial arts supervisors and to help teachers organize courses in domestic science, gardening, home carpentering, and other useful skills. Eventually this idea caught enough general interest for the county school boards to take over and to administer the Jeanes Fund.

On a far larger scale were the frequent contributions to Negro education by Julius Rosenwald, president of the Chicago mail order house, Sears, Roebuck and Company. In 1911 he offered to pay one-third of the costs of new rural school buildings for Negroes, provided that local authorities and private sources made up the remainder. The Rosenwald Fund of $40,000,000, created in 1917 "for the well-being of mankind," eventually helped build 5000 Negro schools in fifteen Southern states. Rosenwald served as a trustee for Tuskegee Institute and gave $200,000 to that school.

Other merchants and industrialists also aided Negro education—Rockefeller, Carnegie, Du Pont, Duke, the Guggenheims, and many Negro philanthropists as well. Stimulated by this encouragement, Southern states and counties stepped up their annual grants for Negro schools. In 1910 47.7 per cent of the Negro school age population were attending school, compared with 9.2 in 1870; in 1910, it should be noted, 61.3 per cent of the white children were in school. Here was a remarkable achievement.

3

The Populist record for education outstripped the work done in this field by the Bourbons. In the public school crusade at the turn of the century, Governor Charles B. Aycock of North Carolina, and Walter Hines Page played a major role. This state had once been in the forefront of the free school movement just before the Civil War; thereafter, its decay was manifest. In 1883, Walter Hines Page began his editorship of the *Raleigh State Chronicle* with an incessant demand for a revival of the public school movement. He was often brutally frank in his criticism of the South and he displeased many before he decided to give up Carolina journalism and move North for a literary career.

In 1897, when Page was on the staff of the *Atlantic Monthly*, he returned to his native state to deliver at the normal school in Greensboro a widely-quoted address, "The Forgotten Man"— a phrase re-echoed by another Wilsonian a generation later, Franklin D. Roosevelt. The extremely individualistic sociologist, William Graham Sumner, used this title years after Page did, but to depict the suffering taxpayer compelled to pay the cost of expensive social services. However, Page had in mind the poverty-stricken Southerner deprived of an education by a small unprogressive aristocracy. Sectarian schools, he thought, had failed to meet the challenge of mass education. The forgotten man had been lulled into apathy by the politician on the stump who dwelt tenderly on each detail of the battles of the late war. Page declared that three "ghosts" were the chief barriers to Southern progress: "The Ghost of the Confederate dead, the Ghost of religious orthodoxy, the Ghost of Negro domination." Failure to propitiate all of these ghosts meant exclusion from material rewards in the South. "Our civilization has been a failure," he concluded boldly. "I believe in the free public training of both the hands and the mind of every child born of woman. . . . I believe in the perpetual regeneration of society and in the immortality of democracy and in growth everlasting."

Though abusive letters were showered on Page, he left a strong impression on many minds, especially in North Carolina. Within a few years of his speech, Governor Charles Aycock, one of Page's well-wishers, went far in building public elementary schools, high schools, normal schools, and trade schools. The state was on its way back to leadership in Southern education. Other states in the South followed this progressive example to some extent. Page's campaign in the press and on the platform induced John D. Rockefeller to charter in 1903 the General Education Board, which he endowed with $53,000,000 by 1909, one of the largest philanthropies of this type in history. Page devoted much of his time to work on the executive committee of the Board and during these early years did much to strengthen the South's public high school system, agricultural training, and Negro education. Later, the Board added emphasis on college to its program for improving secondary and elementary education.

Page's role in promoting public health in the South is worthy of considerable attention. Shortly before World War I, the Southern masses became the beneficiary of the discoveries made by the public health movement in eradicating hookworm. Tropical medicine, reflecting the nation's advance in the Caribbean, had gone far under American and native doctors in Cuba, Puerto Rico, and the Canal Zone. In Puerto Rico, Colonel Bailey K. Ashford, an army surgeon in the Spanish-American War, found that the anemia affecting thousands of poor islanders was due to hookworm. A native of North Carolina, Dr. Charles W. Stiles, who taught medical zoology at the Johns Hopkins University, identified in 1902 the parasite *Necator Americanus* (American murderer) as the hookworm of the Southern poor white. He pointed out to Walter Hines Page in 1909 that the anemic "dirt-eater" whom they saw near a Greensboro train platform was a typical hookworm case. Stiles asserted that this man could be cured with "about fifty cents worth of drugs" and that at least 2,000,000 Southerners, especially poor whites, suffered from the parasite.

While local newspapers resented a fancied slur upon the South, and Northern journalists joked about the discovery of the "germ of laziness," Page used his intimate contacts with Rockefeller to initiate the Rockefeller Commission for the Eradication of Hookworm Disease. The ensuing drive to cure the pale, enervated parasite victims, conspicuous for their listlessness and distended bellies, revealed in 1911-14 that almost 60 per cent of all Southern school children had some hookworm infestation. Yet, by 1918 about one-third of those infected were cured and the proportions of those affected dropped steadily thereafter. Elsewhere in backward areas of the world, from the West Indies and Egypt to India and China, the Rockefeller Commission applied these lessons to save millions from a lifetime of futility and hopelessness.

4

The careers of Walter Page, George W. Cable, and Joel Chandler Harris illustrate that Southern liberalism of the Jeffersonian variety was not dead, though it was usually confined to a dissenting role in this era. Most Southern liberals agreed on the necessity of more Negro education and a stronger policy on civil rights in the South, but they quarreled on other parts of their program. Governor Aycock demanded more schools for Negroes, but he also urged their disfranchisement and upheld segregation. Josephus Daniels, fighting liberal editor of the *Raleigh News and Observer*, assailed the Duke interests and other monopolies, but he showed a fundamentalist regard for prohibition and anti-smoking causes; even his stand on race showed some surprising inconsistencies. Walter Page, too, who was a liberal in most respects, could show Bourbon attitudes at times in his opposition to government regulation of business. Woodrow Wilson, as will be noted, evolved from a conservative, almost of the Bourbon stripe, to one of the greatest liberals in American history, emancipating himself, one by one, from the prejudices of his earlier years. Under these circumstances, it is impossible to offer a sound definition of Southern liberalism, although one may be guided by the persistence of Jeffersonian ideals among these men. All agreed upon that dignity of the individual which is so fundamental to democracy, and they shared cultural values of their Northern counterparts.

Too many of the Southern liberals, like Cable and Page, were actually expatriates. Among this group was the exceptionally talented and prolific William P. Trent, formerly professor of English and dean of the University of the South at Sewanee. In 1892, he aroused the most bitter resentment by his critical—it was not unflattering—biography of the Southern novelist, William Gilmore Simms. Trent was among the first to see the literary and intellectual shortcomings of Simms and to write honestly about them. He made it evident that he thought secession was wrong and that the South had fought merely to preserve slavery. Although his university resisted the popular demand that he be dismissed, he found himself ostracized and pointed out on the street as a traitor. His letters to his friend, Herbert Baxter Adams of the Johns Hopkins University, reveal the deep anguish he suffered daily until he left for a new distinguished career as professor of English at Columbia University. Meanwhile, he had left behind a remarkable literary tradition in the *Sewanee Review*, which he had edited since 1892 when it was founded. The *Review* had a strong creative influence upon the new critical tendencies in Southern literature, particularly among the magazines.

Another able liberal expatriate was the historian, John Spencer Bassett of Trinity College, who edited the *South Atlantic Quarterly* at its inception in 1902. He had never concealed his dissatisfaction with the backward state of things in the South. "The people of the South," he once wrote, "are not a poor people. They have too long hidden some other failures behind this idea." His letters to Herbert B. Adams reveal his deep concern over the mistreatment of Negroes in his state. In one outspoken article, "Stirring Up the Fires of Race Antipathy," he took occasion to praise Booker T. Washington as the greatest man, next to Lee, who had been born in the South for the past century. In the ensuing outcry for Bassett's dismissal, Josephus Daniels led the pack by editorializing in his *Raleigh News and Observer* about the *treason* of "bASSett" as he spelled the name. The faculty quickly came to Bassett's rescue and cited the Jeffersonian ideal of academic freedom as justification for their stand in his behalf. His colleagues, according to Virginius Dabney, threatened to resign in a body if the Board of Trustees dismissed him. However, Bassett left for Smith College in 1906 and there began the most productive years of his life.

The evolution of Woodrow Wilson into a liberal leader of world stature involves a good deal of Southern history. He was born in Staunton, Virginia, of Scotch-Irish ancestry, and was raised in Georgia and South Carolina during the Civil War and Reconstruction. He had briefly attended an orthodox Presbyterian college, Davidson College, in the piedmont section of North Carolina and then, in 1875, went on to Princeton where he widened his intellectual horizon greatly. Resolving upon a legal career, he entered the University of Virginia Law School. By this time the stern Calvinist morality of his minister-father and a good deal of Jeffersonian idealism had saturated his outlook, but he retained a sense of humor— though outsiders doubted this. He developed a critical attitude toward Southern history as he grew older, "I yield to no one precedence in love for the South but *because* I love the South, I rejoice in the failure of the Confederacy.... We cannot conceal from ourselves the fact that slavery was enervating our Southern society and exhausting to Southern energies."

As a lawyer in Atlanta during 1882 he showed a marked conservative bias, which led him to join the Bourbons in denouncing the

federal Blair education bill as mere begging by the South and as a
violation of Southern self-respect. The Greenback inflationist movement, whatever it might mean to farmers hard-pressed for credit,
was sheer dishonesty to him and Southern free trade doctrines
seemed to offer an ample program for the nation's ills. He affected
an aristocratic disdain for the money-making spirit of the New
South, observing that in Atlanta "money cannot be made except by
the most vulgar methods." There were too few Southerners like his
literary friend, Walter Hines Page, whom he first met in Atlanta;
he felt starved intellectually. "I can never be happy unless I am
enabled to lead an intellectual life," he wrote privately at this time,
"and who can lead an intellectual life in ignorant Georgia?" There-
upon, Wilson turned to a professional career in political science and
history.

At the new Johns Hopkins University, founded by a wealthy
Baltimore financier, he wrote a doctoral dissertation, *Congressional
Government* (1885), which reflected the political experiences of
Reconstruction as well as the British parliamentary ideas of so many
intellectuals of the Anglo-Saxon South. His admiration for English
institutions was encouraged in the Johns Hopkins seminar of
Professor Herbert B. Adams and by his enthusiastic reading of
Walter Bagehot's treatise on English cabinet government with its
centralized responsibility and its sensitivity to the mandates of the
electorate. In contrast, the American system of congressional government lacked effective direction and democratic leadership, even
allowing the Speaker of the House to be an autocrat and a crude
partisan. The depths to which this system could sink were revealed,
he thought, during Reconstruction when Congressman Thaddeus
Stevens at one time almost dominated the entire government.

In 1889, Wilson wrote a textbook, *The State*, which reflected the
evolutionary theories taught at Johns Hopkins regarding the progressive adaptation of political institutions from popular Anglo-
Saxon and Germanic origins to modern English forms of democracy.
Although he stressed the Hegelian notion of continuity in history,
which minimized economic factors, he moved away from the old-
fashioned liberal's distrust of the state to insist upon the popular

Germanic idea that the state was a beneficent organ of society capable of harmonizing individual rights with public duties and social development. The Constitution itself, as he remarked elsewhere, was not a mere lawyer's document intended "to hold the government back to the time of horses and wagons" but an ever-evolving organism reflecting a changing society. His five-volume *History of the American People* (1902), however, showed the conservative philosophic influence of the English traditionalist, Edmund Burke, and the champion of pure laissez faire, Herbert Spencer. Wilson had the opportunity to think through some of the inconsistencies in his political philosophy while he was professor of history at Bryn Mawr and of jurisprudence and political economy at his alma mater, Princeton.

His open conversion to a concrete social welfare program based on active state intervention came just before his election as governor of New Jersey, where conservative machine Democrats had intended that he serve merely as a respectable front for the entrenched interests. Instead he turned the tables on the political bosses and brought New Jersey, previously the "mother of trusts," into the forefront of the progressive states. He put through legislation for direct primaries, a corrupt practices act, public utility regulation, and workmen's compensation. In 1912 he campaigned for president on the slogan of *The New Freedom.* "Human freedom," he said, "consists in perfect adjustments of human interests and human activities and human energies." As for Jefferson's doctrine spoken "in those early days of simplicity," of the best government being that which governs least, he observed,

It is still intolerable for the government to interfere with our individual activities except where it is necessary to interfere with them in order to free them. . . . Without the watchful interference, the resolute interference, of the government, there can be no fair play between individuals and such powerful institutions as the trusts. Freedom today is something more than being let alone. The program of a government of freedom must in these days be positive not negative merely.

The election of President Wilson was also a victory for Southern liberalism. He brought with him as Secretary of the Navy Josephus

Daniels, the militant editor of the *Raleigh State Chronicle* and the *Raleigh News and Observer*. From the same state came Walter Hines Page, an "original" Wilson man, who became ambassador to Great Britain. Page, as already seen, had been a leader in mass education and public health movements for both races. More influential than either of these was Wilson's "alter ego," Edward Mandell House of Houston, a planter and literary dilettante who was known during the Bryan era as one of the most influential progressive leaders in Texas politics. Working behind the scenes in Washington, just as he had liked to do in Texas, he played a major role in planning and carrying out several of Wilson's chief domestic and foreign programs. These liberals had broken with Southern Bourbonism and had continued a Southern agrarian distrust of big business and speculative finance. The South, out of the saddle for so many decades, sponsored important farm legislation such as the Smith-Lever Act, which was a federal grant-in-aid system to subsidize agricultural education and community services, thus making farm life far more attractive than before. Other Southern victories were the Clayton Act to revive competition in business and the Underwood Act to revise the tariff downward.

5

In literature genuine modern realism came to the South with the Richmond-born novelist, Ellen Glasgow, a rebel against the inhibited "genteel tradition" of the North as well as the "sentimental fallacy" of the Southern plantation tradition. Unlike most writers of the New South, who dwelt upon the Old South with nostalgia but had no intention whatever of giving up the social order of the Industrial Revolution, Miss Glasgow sought fidelity to experience through the example of Balzac, Flaubert, Maupassant, and the English realists—she read the Russians much later. "What the South needs is blood and irony," she declared.

Her first novel, *The Descendant* (1897), was begun when she was eighteen and had already determined to seek realism. She took as her central figure "one of the despised and rejected of society, an illegitimate offspring of the peasant or 'poor white' class." Critics were not only shocked to find a well-brought-up Southern girl writing about illegitimacy but they also disliked the frank naturalistic philosophy expressed on her title page—a quotation from Haeckel, the evolutionist.

In 1902, she published *The Battleground*, first of a long series of novels dealing with the social history of Virginia since 1850. Although she did not wholly escape the temptation to romanticise, she kept her story remarkably close to actuality in delineating character, costume, and the tobacco fields she had known at first hand from childhood days. She could be as unconventional as Octave Thanet, at least in portraying classes, the irregular sex life among the farmers, and the degraded sharecroppers who lacked real incentives in a planter's society. Her women were not pretty, empty-headed Southern belles, but substantial human beings, capable of struggling against the dicta of a man-made society. Occasionally, she pictured a Negro with real authenticity, but generally confined herself to the Southern white. Her best work was yet to come in the 1920's and afterwards, but she was never to permit her realism to take the form of "hard-boiled fiction" and a mechanistic "stream of consciousness."

Despite the growing vogue of literary realism, multitudes of both Northern and Southern readers never lost their love for the romantic magnolia tradition of the antebellum South. Harriet Beecher Stowe had not permitted the woes of Uncle Tom to obscure her perception of the literary values inherent in Southern life and its fanciful myths; she had pointed this out in a preface to *Dred*. Only for a brief painful decade or so after the Civil War did Northern publishers reject the Southern interpretation of slavery, secession, the War, and Reconstruction. The highly remunerative literary road that was to lead to Margaret Mitchell's *Gone with the Wind*, idealizing the planter's society and the pathos of the Lost Cause, had been discovered before the turn of the century by Southern fiction writers. While some Dixie writers sought a literary "road to reunion" by avoiding any references to the "late unpleasantness between the states" or in stressing Americanism, others like Thomas Dixon learned that Northerners too were ready to weep in nostalgia for the chivalrous Old South they had crushed. Only a minority felt Mark Twain's skepticism for the cult of chivalry.

The extraordinary popularity of Dixon's novel, *The Clansman* (1905), illustrates this romantic tendency. Dixon was a North Carolina Baptist clergyman who had moved to a pastorate in New York city where he wrote several pro-Southern novels, but none with such success as *The Clansman*. This pictured violent race wars during Reconstruction in which the Negro appeared as a lustful, degraded creature and the Ku Klux Klan emerged as the shield of white womanhood and Anglo-Saxon civilization. Millions were to read this exciting tale. One Kentucky-born motion picture producer, David W. Griffith, who popularized the innocent Southern belle on the screen, adapted it for his noteworthy *Birth of a Nation* (1915). Although this motion picture was a pioneer triumph in realistic cinema craft, it perpetuated the romantic stereotypes and the conservative Southern interpretation of history. White liberals as well as Negroes felt outraged by the cinema treatment of the Negro and many feared new race conflicts; Griffith himself later regretted the theme he had chosen. Interestingly, Woodrow Wilson, a professional historian as well as President of the United States, was sufficiently an unreconstructed Southerner to see in the Dixon motion picture only an excellent way to teach history.

6

The revolt of the farmers in the nineties did not arrest the accelerated pace of Southern industrialization. New England competition was overwhelmed by the powerful movement of the mills to the cotton. In 1900, there were over four hundred textile factories in the South with a total capital of nearly $125,000,000 and a working force of over 97,000 men, women, and children. Most of the spindles were concentrated within a one-hundred-mile radius of Charlotte, North Carolina. By 1915, the Southern cotton mill owners could boast that the South had definitely surpassed New England. Not all of this result had come from cheap labor. Transportation advantages, raw materials, ample power sources, and other factors favored the South.

At the same time other major industries were coming into existence and transforming the Southern rural way of life. By the nineties, furniture-making, which thrived upon the vast forests of the South, made High Point, North Carolina, the Grand Rapids of the South. The iron and coal industry of the Birmingham area was reflected in the rapid growth of population during 1890-1910 from 26,000 to 132,000. In 1907, the union of Northern and Southern steel was blessed by President Theodore Roosevelt when he granted immunity from antitrust prosecution to the United States Steel Corporation in its successful efforts to acquire the powerful Tennessee Coal and Iron Company.

The amazing rise of James B. Duke and his tobacco empire continued after his organization of the monopolistic American Tobacco Company in 1890. By the end of the century he had practically divided the tobacco business of the entire globe with a British syndicate and the assets of the reorganized A.T.C. were over a half billion dollars. Even the dissolution of the A.T.C. ordered by the federal court in 1911 did not cripple the ambitions of the indefatigable Duke, though vigorous competition was revived in the cigarette field. His neighbor, R. J. Reynolds, went on independently of the old trust to develop and advertise an improved variety of bright leaf tobacco, making Camels and Lucky Strike cigarettes among the most popular in the nation. Liggett and Myers pushed Chesterfield with sensational results. As for Duke himself, he not only remained a leader in the tobacco field, but also entered the hydroelectric power business on a large scale. In the Southern piedmont area (and elsewhere), his Duke Power Company was supplying electricity to one-third of all the spindles in the South by the 1920's. His crowning monument appeared in 1924 as Duke University, formerly the small Methodist school, Trinity College, enriched by a forty-million-dollar endowment to which a similar sum was added in his will. This did not prevent him, in that day of low income taxes, from leaving a quarter of a billion dollars to his daughter, Doris.

Duke had disturbed Southerners too much to escape severe criticism. Josephus Daniels directed an incessant attack in his newspaper upon Duke's control over the state and the spread of the smoking habit attributed to his advertising. Tobacco farmers in Kentucky and North Carolina carried on their own war with Duke's tobacco enterprises. In 1906, an angry Kentucky mob even burnt a valuable warehouse belonging to the American Tobacco Company. However, public relations eventually improved as his organizations stopped the aggressive methods of the turn of the century. One of his chief beneficiaries, President John C. Kilgo of the old Trinity College, stated publicly, according to Duke's biographer, John K. Winkler, that trusts and monopolies were not "the awful curse to society that we are led to believe by demagogues."

7

The coming of industry broke down part of the isolation of the highlander, particularly in the Southern Appalachians where over 5,000,000 of this class lived in eight different states in 1910. Two years later, coal mining and railroading invaded the isolated counties of the Kentucky mountains and brought thousands of men from the hills to live in company-owned towns and shacks. Numerous communities of highlanders also dwelt in the Ozark-Ouachita mountains, but these too were partly absorbed in the new industrial world by the expansion of lead and zinc mines in that area. It was difficult for the more backward of these people, whose dialect was reminiscent of Elizabethan England and whose outlook was still colonial, to acquire the competitive drives of the Industrial Revolution. Traditionally one worked when food was lacking and rested when it was supplied.

They were set apart by the habit of feuding, religious fundamentalism, illiteracy, peculiarities of dialect ("you uns" and "tote"), and frontier simplicity. Their strong sense of kinship—intermarriage made a single clan of entire settlements—their ancient games and songs, their ubiquitous hunting dogs, and their unique rifle marksmanship also set them apart as a distinct people. Many supplemented their living with "moonshining," and carried jugs of corn liquor to market as their Revolutionary ancestors had done. Transportation difficulties in the hills made it advantageous to convert the corn into liquid form. They were often as poor as Job, but never as poor in spirit as the lowland Red Necks, Crackers, and Sandhillers of antebellum days. Despite cultural handicaps, many thousands made the adjustment to life in the mill town and the mining communities.

A careful student of the highlanders, J. Wesley Hatcher, has pointed out that the culture and outlook of this group was far from homogeneous, but varied according to the relative fertility of the soil and the degree of accessibility to markets. Thus, visitors to the communities along the creeks and rivers where the soil was not so thin might find substantial, picturesque farms with two-story colonial white frame houses, comfortable beds with goose or duck feather mattresses and pillows covered by skillfully woven wool blankets or daintily stitched quilts, and abundant foods of the usual Southern varieties, including fried apple pie and candied sweet potatoes. Here cleanliness was the rule and the abundance reflected the ownership of orchards, a small corn patch, turkeys and chickens, cows and sheep, and a vegetable garden. Between this relatively affluent group and the poor mountaineer were other classes, lower on the economic scale but still above the subsistence level.

The highlanders that attracted most attention were those from the steepest lands and thinnest soils, and the most inaccessible communities. Life remained a hard primitive struggle to achieve a bare subsistence. One saw crude single-room log houses lacking stoves and even fireplaces, where the few furnishings were set about on an unadorned clay floor and the kitchen equipment was of the most elementary character. Repeated division of lands among descendants had left only small farms of corn, onion, and turnip patches to support the huge families of the mountaineer. Poverty, disease, ignorance, and degeneracy often went hand in hand and furnished a tragic picture that became the literary staple of Southern novelists and other writers. It was not difficult to find illegitimacy, gross sensualism, and even incest among them. The lack of milk, butter, and vegetables left a diet that insured a high mortality. Women were but beasts of burden and children were much too occupied to attend school.

A great deal has been said without exaggeration of their feuding habits. For generations, they had distrusted courts and sheriffs and stubbornly upheld the "code of the hills" in their own way. There was no place for chivalry, except to spare women and children, in these relentless feuds that went on between families and clans for many decades. Kentucky mountaineers, for example, were obviously good shots, but this did not prevent them from firing from ambush or from shooting their enemies in the back. As for the causes of feuds, they varied from resentment at a slightly offensive remark to revenge for murder or violation of their women.

Highlanders of this class came from pure Anglo-Saxon stock—or at least the nearest thing to it. Their ancestors had been British or German pioneers probably of a much higher cultural level. Calvinist Presbyterianism had been predominant among the Appalachian pioneers, but the Methodists and Baptists who offered universal salvation instead of the doctrine of the elect won over most of them, though there were a good number of Calvinist Baptists. The Baptist rite of total immersion was especially popular. They disliked church ritual and admired vigorous preaching; they believed that the Bible was infallible and the sole guide to conduct. Among illiterate, backward people, the belief that every man was his own priest could produce some religious anomalies in which superstition played a larger role than traditional church doctrine. When a mountaineer noted that his cow had gone dry, he knew that a witch had been at work. The only thing to do was to shoot a silver bullet through an effigy of the witch. However, these traits were not limited to highlanders, but were found in varying degree among poor illiterate Southerners of other areas.

Although the mountaineer has been credited with a near-monopoly of old English folklore and song, most Southerners knew the ballads and dances of the British tradition. Perhaps the highlander sang more than any other group, for he impressed English folklorists with his large store of Elizabethan and more recent stories, ballads, and other folk expressions. One heard song themes that Chaucer had dealt with in his Canterbury tales, long-forgotten nursery rhymes, and ancient game songs like "A Frog Went a-Courting." Highlanders and other Southerners too sang songs of the Revolution like "We're Marching to Old Quebec" or old English ballads like "Fair Margaret and Sweet William." Dancing was popular with all. Arthur P. Hudson, commenting upon the general vogue of the square dance in the South, notes these homely lines of the caller:

> Men ketch hands an' women to the center
> Watch yo' step an' don't ketch a splinter

The postwar history of the poor white is difficult to follow. Southern industry and the taking-up of most of the remaining farm lands drove the poor white squatter out of his usual haunts. Once the public health movement began to eliminate the dreaded hookworm that had given so many of the barefooted poor whites their characteristic listlessness and distended bellies, these people found new energies and a more secure niche in society. The term, "poor white" was then generally applied to the most backward of the cotton and tobacco croppers. But the extensive isolation of antebellum times that had made possible the poor white squatter was gone.

The final advent of a Southerner to the White House in 1913 (if one excludes Andrew Johnson) symbolized the reunion of the North and the South. To some extent, this process had been promoted by the common experience in the Spanish-American War in which Southerners and Northerners marched shoulder to shoulder against a foreign foe—the first since 1846. Northern investors, Northern philanthropists, and Northern patrons of Southern literature helped to soften the scars of war and military Reconstruction. In the same conciliatory direction, Bourbon efforts to industrialize the South and thus to assimilate it to the commercial-industrial culture of the North also drew the two sections together. Southern novelists, poets, and journalists wrote more than ever for Northern readers and succeeded in striking a sympathetic chord of mutual understanding.

In this integrative process, the Negro played only a passive role.

The New South of Wade Hampton and Ben Tillman disfranchised him and barred him from employment in the cotton mills, though not from the Birmingham blast furnaces. His gains of Reconstruction days were among the major casualties of the course of sectional reunion. There still remained, it is true, important precedents in civil rights and solid achievements in Negro education. But the reunion of North and South was consummated largely by the surrender of the antebellum crusade for social equality.

· 4 ·

The Last Frontier
and Frederick Jackson Turner

I

During Chicago's World's Fair of 1893, when Americans looked back with self-conscious pride over the history of four centuries, two remarkable men observed, each in his own way, that one phase of American life had ended—the frontier. One of these visitors, William F. Cody, whose mother had predicted that he would be president, was quite willing to settle for what he was then—Buffalo Bill, the hero of the Wild West Show. At forty-seven years of age he could easily recall (but unfortunately, only with embellishments) his exciting youth on the primitive Kansas and Nebraska frontier, his days as a swift pony express rider, a Civil War soldier, and a magnificent buffalo hunter. He had initiated the Grand Duke Alexis of Russia into the mysteries of the buffalo hunt at a time when all America craved to honor the heir of the Romanovs. Cody knew Jim Bridger, Kit Carson, and Wild Bill Hickok as flesh-and-blood heroes. He had served the army well as a chief scout during the Sioux War of the seventies and had thrilled the nation with his story, properly touched up, of how he had killed Yellow Hand, son of a Cheyenne chief, and carried off his enemy's scalp. At various times, he tried ranching and farming, but his most lasting career began in the seventies when he went on the stage in "Scouts of the Prairies." He was apparently quite content to have become one of America's leading exhibits and to enjoy the plaudits of the thousands at the Fair who watched his cowboys and scouts defeat the redskins with unfailing regularity.

The lesser luminary was a quiet college professor of history from the University of Wisconsin, Frederick Jackson Turner who had been born and reared along the historic Wisconsin route taken by the French explorers of the St. Lawrence Valley. Now he read a momentous paper before the scholars of the American Historical Association, "The Significance of the Frontier in American History." Although he had not written a text for pessimists during that year of the great depression, his address came to be looked upon by some as a dirge for the American dream. In his paper was this striking passage:

What the Mediterranean Sea was to the Greeks, breaking the bond of custom, offering new experiences, calling out new institutions and activities, that, and more, the ever retreating frontier has been to the United States directly, and to the nations of Europe more remotely. And now, four centuries from the discovery of America, at the end of a hundred years of life under the Constitution, the frontier has gone, and with its going has closed the first period of American history.

The last frontier—if one excepts Alaska and the newer island possessions—was extinguished with the conquest of the Great Plains beyond the ninety-eighth meridian where the cattle and mining frontiers had had their day. The insatiable demands of the booming cities and the new technology had speeded up the winning of the West. Unlike the slow retreat of the Indians east of the Mississippi, a process taking two centuries, tribal resistance in the West had collapsed within a few decades. Homesteaders were spurred on by the lure of profitable eastern markets to defy nature itself by attempting to wrest a living from semi-arid lands where recurrent droughts mocked their efforts. The irresistible pressure came from a people whose political unity had been assured by the Civil War and whose standard of living was rising. Isolated self-sufficient farms were gradually disappearing with the advance of better roads, railways, ocean steamships, telegraphs, and other new technological gains.

2

The cattle era, with its romantic cowboy and the "thundering herd" on the way to a cow town, gave the passing frontier its final brilliance. In American history the famous "long drive" dated back to colonial days when animals were driven from the Southern cowpens to markets in Charleston, Philadelphia, and New York. "Travellers at the close of the War of 1812," wrote Turner, "met droves of more than a thousand cattle and swine from the interior of Ohio going to Pennsylvania to fatten for the Philadelphia market." Such experiences, Turner felt, guided the ranchers of Texas. Toward the end of the Civil War, with Eastern meat supplies being consumed by regiments of the Blue and the Gray as well as by civilians, New York merchants were ready to pay ten times more than local Texan quotations for cattle. The Lone Star state was cut off by Union armies from Confederate markets during the war and had allowed its cattle to multiply, often in wild herds on the Southern range. Once the war blockade ended, cattlemen drove their herds to railway points such as Sedalia, Missouri, where the Missouri Pacific Railroad completed connections with St. Louis and the East in 1866. Cattle rustlers waylaid the herds, beat up the drovers, and themselves sold the animals. Life was cheap on the cattle trails. To escape the savage Missourians and establish a safe cattle trail, J. G. McCoy, a Texan drover, bargained in 1867 with the Kansas Pacific to build a "cow town" in Abilene, Kansas, connecting with the new meat-packing center, Chicago. Thus, in 1867, 35,000 cattle were driven to Abilene and in 1871, 700,000—altogether a total of almost 1,500,000 animals between those two years. Over a million head were driven across the plains in the next three years. Abilene, furnishing so much of the meat supply of the nation, flourished overnight as a bold, wicked, cow town, so often portrayed by Hollywood westerns, with swinging-door saloons and gambling houses, gaudy dance halls, painted ladies, and feuding bad men. It was here that Wild Bill Hickok won his awesome reputation as a swift, straight-shooting federal marshal who subdued his foes and carried on a feud or two on the side. As the railroads moved westward, Wichita and Dodge City shared the cattle traffic.

To fatten cattle as well as to hold them off the market for more favorable prices, cowboys herded the animals on the ranges of the Southwest; and as the practicality of wintering on the Northern plains became clear, they drove them along the Missouri and the Bozeman Trail to supply ranches as far away as Montana, the Dakotas, and even Canada. The southern drawl of the Texan spread to the entire Great Plains as the cattle industry expanded over the grasslands. Ranch owners, many of them Easterners, Englishmen, Scotchmen, Australians, and a few Continental noblemen, fenced in the precious water holes and streams on which survival depended. In Dakota Territory a "four-eyed dude from New York," Theodore Roosevelt, turned ranchman in 1883, risking his small fortune of $50,000. Although unsuccessful financially at a time when the range was being overstocked and the grasslands depleted, he developed robust health and a love of the West and its traditions which was to benefit the conservation cause and enable him to write a highly readable if unreliable history in his four-volume *The Winning of the West* (1889-96). Some of the ranches attained astonishing size. Witness the XIT ranch, one of the largest, which covered 3,000,000 acres and was stocked with 160,000 cattle and fenced in by hundreds of miles of barbed wire.

Sharing the sparse grass and uncertain water supplies of the open range were millions of sheep, originating to a large extent from Spanish silky-fleeced ancestors. They filled Colorado, Wyoming, Montana, and other Rocky Mountain states in the 1880's, then overflowed into the Dakotas, Kansas, and Nebraska. Wealthy sheep ranchers contested the range with the cattle barons. The sheep stripped bare wide grazing areas in a few weeks, provoking charges from the cattlemen that the sheep killed the grass and young trees and tainted the water. In the middle 1890's cattlemen were openly raiding the sheep camps, poisoning, burning, and clubbing the sheep.

The pageantry and excitement of cowboy life caught the imagination of the East. Originating as a Great Plains version of the Mexican *vaquero*, the cowboy borrowed much from his neighbor south of the border. He worked on a Mexican type of ranch (Spanish *rancho*), caught his animals with a lariat (*la reata*), subdued unruly *bronchos, corralled* cattle in a roundup or *rodeo*, went to a "hoosegow" (*juzgado*) for his misdeeds, and sprinkled numerous other Spanish terms into his everyday speech. His distinctive garb was basically utilitarian as well as ornamental. The high heels of his boots gave him a better grip on his stirrup; the fringed "chaps" (*chaparejos*) served as a protective covering for his trousers and legs. The large handkerchief around his neck had obvious uses on the hot plains, his vest had useful pockets, while his broad-brimmed hat not only protected him from the sun but served to hold water or as a weapon to subdue a rearing horse. His saddle was also his pillow at night, while he rolled himself up in a blanket under the stars around a campfire. He kept busy on the ranch and the plains branding and tending the cattle, feeding and doctoring the animals, and following the cattle trail; yet he led a lonely life. The sentimental words he sang to soothe the restless cattle cheered him too and whiled away the long days on the Chisholm Trail. "O Bury Me Not on the Lone Prairie," ran his best-remembered ballad with its numerous stanzas of tears and self pity:

> O bury me not on the lone prairie
> Where the wild coyotes will howl oe'r me,
> Where the rattlesnakes hiss and the crow flies free,
> O bury me not on the lone prairie.

When he reached a cow town he often went off on a spree, shot out the lights in a saloon, gambled recklessly, drank himself into a stupor, or ran off to see the excitement of a vigilante hanging. The scarcity of women on the range encouraged an exaggerated chivalry toward them and made courting a strenuous and highly competitive adventure. Stag dancing was too frequently a painful necessity. It is noteworthy that the cowboy territory of Wyoming, where women were few, was first to sanction woman suffrage. In the cattle "roundup" of spring and fall the cowhand branded the "mavericks" (unbranded animals, usually motherless calves) and made the occasion a festive community celebration. The cowboy came to be regarded in the Western tradition as both brave and chivalrous, taciturn, yet capable of gargantuan horseplay, and phenomenal as rider and marksman.

The idyllic era of the long drive and the open range ended with the opening of the transcontinental railroad, overspeculation, and the general adoption of barbed wire fencing after 1874. This economical and highly practical kind of fencing turned out to be indispensable on the treeless plains, but provoked wire-cutting wars as rival cattlemen or farmers fought to inclose water holes. During the unusual winter of 1886-87, when temperatures fell to fifty or sixty degrees below zero on the plains, and giant snowdrifts buried settlements and livestock, the barbed wire fences prevented cattle from escaping and their heaped-up bodies fed the ravenous wolves and coyotes.

So destructive was that unusual winter, when millions of cattle and sheep were wiped out, that innumerable ranch owners gave up and turned to more predictable occupations. Besides, it was clear that the limits of cattle grazing on the semi-arid plains had been reached. Huge herds and large wasteful ranches gave way to smaller units and more scientific methods. The West had never furnished more than one-third of the nation's cattle and this proportion fell with the increased livestock activities of the average farm. Nevertheless, the Great Plains did much to encourage the rise of large-scale packing plants at St. Louis, Kansas City, and Chicago. Improvements and inventions in meat-cutting, canning, curing, refrigeration, and industrial by-products gave the meat industry increasing national importance and prosperity.

3

In the mountain territories and states mining continued, as in California gold rush days, to produce its peculiar form of frontier life and to build cities and towns where cattlemen and homesteaders seemed indifferent to venture. In 1885, Idaho miners not only began panning for gold on a large scale in the rich Coeur d'Alene

forests but discovered one of the largest silver and lead mines at
Bunker Hill and Sullivan. Especially significant in the history of
Montana was the success story of Marcus Daly, an Irish immigrant
who had been a miner in the California gold rush, worked upon the
Comstock Lode in Nevada, and then came to Butte, Montana, in
1876 as a silver mining investigator. Purchasing the Anaconda Silver
Mine, he verified his belief that invaluable copper deposits existed
underneath. So sensational was his success that he not only built
a fabulous copper industry but also several towns, a string of banks,
a notable ranch, and the leading newspaper of the state. By 1889,
Montana led as a mining state with an annual output of $41,000,000
in metals, over half of which came from Butte, an overgrown mining
camp of 30,000 people.

Colorado had a revival of silver-mining activity in the late seventies and eighties, centering about Leadville, which was next to
Denver in size. In 1882, Leadville was an unruly mining town of
some 35,000 people and produced over $17,000,000 in bullion. The
foundation of the world-famous house of Guggenheim was laid in
Colorado during this era by a Swiss-American merchant of Philadelphia, Meyer Guggenheim. He reaped a fortune through his
smelting processes rather than by mining itself, particularly through
his large refineries at Pueblo, Colorado, and in Mexico. His seven
exceptionally able sons helped to expand the house of Guggenheim
throughout the mining world. The mineral empire of Colorado
entered the Union in 1876 as the "centennial state," and reached its
mining peak in 1900 when $50,000,000 worth of precious metals were
mined. Then, like Montana and other mining states, its romantic
mining towns were increasingly overshadowed by solid farm and
stock-raising communities.

In 1875, one of the richest gold finds was uncovered in the Black
Hills at Deadwood Gulch in what is now South Dakota. Even the
hostile Sioux whose territory was invaded could not prevent Deadwood from becoming almost overnight a city of 25,000, mostly of
the migratory sort. Although far from unique in its wickedness and
homicidal tendencies among western mining camps, its satanic

reputation and adventurous characters did mark it off from other such towns. Among them was Wild Bill Hickok, who had recently mastered the gunmen of Abilene, only to die, shot in the back by a local thug.

The tale of Virginia City is almost the history of Nevada, and its spectacular rise and fall reflects the wild fluctuations of mining life. By 1880, this town reached its acme with 11,000 people who came from all over the Union and from Western Europe. The silver riches of the Comstock Lode had produced scores of millionaires for San Francisco's elegant Nob Hill. In the streets, one could see well-to-do gentlemen in frock coats and stovepipe hats accompanying women in silk dresses newly imported from Paris. At the glittering opera house, there were seasons when the greatest actors and singers of New York and the European capitals might offer a performance —Modjeska, Edwin Booth, David Belasco, Maude Adams, or Adelina Patti. Hundreds subscribed to the best books and Eastern magazines or attended the club reading rooms or the various churches. The schools seem to have been quite adequate. Virginia City was proud of its newspaper, *The Territorial Enterprise,* and its colorful literary tradition. Best-known of its staff at one time was the red-headed, mustachioed journalist, Sam Clemens, who left a number of un-inhibited articles on fellow-reporters, local politicians, and on prac-tically anything at all. As "Mark Twain," he wrote fantastic hoaxes, burlesqued notables, and satirized the town.

This individualistic era ended with the passing of placer mining. Under this system, gold had been simply panned from the stream beds; very little capital was required for a miner to set himself up in business. As this source of gold declined, corporations came in with expensive machinery and a more scientific knowledge of geology to introduce a new phase of mining history. Engineering feats like Adolph Sutro's four-mile tunnel in Nevada penetrated into the deeply imbedded lodes of precious metals. The corporate en-terprise of Anaconda and Guggenheim reduced the ancient Argo-nauts of the West to wage laborers. Bad labor conditions spread the violence of the I.W.W. through the Western Federation of Miners led by Moyer and Haywood. Violent strikes broke out in

the 1890's like those of Coeur d'Alene, Cripple Creek, and Leadville. Gone were the adventurous miners who had been confident
that they were all going to be millionaires.

While Bryan was campaigning for free silver in the summer of
1896, his arguments for bimetallism struck a snag when in August
gold was discovered along the Klondike River in Canada's Yukon
Territory. Over $200,000,000 in gold came from the Klondike. Within
a few years Alaska, too, came to share in the rich discoveries, especially in Seward Peninsula where the annual output exceeded
$5,000,000 and, in the opening decade of the twentieth century, pro-
duced over $90,000,000 in gold.

Once more the old mining frontier came to life as the tough "sour-
doughs" braved the dangerous mountain passes, the deep snows,
the bitter cold, and the food shortages to camp at primitive Dawson
City on the Klondike, or Anvil City, later Nome, the gold center of
the Seward Peninsula. Men lost their way amid glaciers and even
hardy souls who wandered off the trail feared their minds would
break in this wild Northern territory, whose worthlessness had
hitherto been taken for granted. In 1897-98, at the height of the
gold rush, Dawson City's floating population of several thousand
lived in typically western camp style in frame or log houses, tents,
or a few cheap hotels; the miners floundered about in muddy streets,
drank and gambled heavily, and kept a wary eye for thieves and
gunmen. This individualistic mining era, like its predecessors elsewhere, was shortly to give way to that of the large corporations like
the Guggenheim interests and the mining companies of J. P. Morgan.

One of the gold hunters in the Klondike was Jack London, who
had left San Francisco in 1897 to chance the dangers of Chilcoot
Pass and the Klondike. He got little in gold for his pains and suffered from scurvy, but he carried away vivid frontier images that
became the semi-autobiographical *Burning Daylight* and the primi-
tivistic dog story, *The Call of the Wild*. Not only did he win extraordinary popularity among readers of adventure stories but his books
inspired an entire school of Arctic adventure writers.

Though the Klondike strike turned out to be on Canadian soil,
most of the miners were Americans and in the States San Francisco

and Seattle were heavy beneficiaries. Among the Canadian adventurers who captivated American readers was the English-born bank clerk, Robert W. Service, whose eight years in Yukon Territory helped him to write the ballads of this land, notably in *Songs of a Sourdough, Trails of '98,* and *Ballads of a Cheechako.* No Alaskan and Canadian ballads of this era fascinated so many as did Service's melodramatic poem, "The Shooting of Dan McGrew."

4

Less exciting than the cattle and mining frontiers, but far more stable in settling the Great Plains that had defied Spaniard and Frenchman, was the farmer's frontier. More and more homesteaders came after the close of the Indian wars, such as the Sioux outbreaks of the 1870's. The transcontinental railroads insured an eastern market. With the best lands east of the Mississippi picked over, speculators and farmers were receptive to the siren call of the railroad colonizer offering cheap lands, even if the rivers ran the wrong way and the soil seemed tough for plowing and the plains looked distressingly barren. Generous government laws, especially the Homestead Act of 1862, gave away land almost for the asking. Hostile Indians, homicidal cattlemen, and natural obstacles did not deter the stubborn, and often gullible, pioneers.

On the plains of Kansas and Nebraska the first comers met the timber shortage by cutting makeshift bricks of sod, using wood only for doors, rafters, and window casings. In this sod-house frontier rain often turned the houses into mud heaps and drenched the human beavers. Precious wood was later transported at considerable expense. Fencing, so essential for protection against marauding cattle, sometimes cost three times as much as in the East, amounting to $640 for enclosing a 160-acre homestead; and the cost of frequent repairs of fences was prohibitive for young farm folk. Fortunately the fencing problem was solved first by the use of hedges and then, after 1874, by the use of barbed wire, which cost less than two dollars a hundred pounds in the 1890's. Federal legislation such as the timber culture acts of 1873 and 1878 encouraged large-scale tree-planting on the plains to meet the need of fuel, housing, and shade, and to control the water runoff.

Water proved a far more difficult problem. During the spring the rivers swelled into floods and tore away houses and drowned livestock; then they would relapse into feeble rivulets by late summer, unable to satisfy the dwellers along the banks. Only dogged cultivation and some form of irrigation made large parts of the semi-arid plains inhabitable. Drills for deep wells and windmills to raise the water to the surface were first introduced to this area by cattlemen and railroad men and then were gratefully adopted by the farmers until the entire Platte Valley bristled with the whirling windmills. In dry Wyoming, farmers kept two million acres of land in wheat, oats, and potatoes under cultivation with the aid of 5000 miles of irrigation canals.

Dry farming techniques were developed and improved. Farmers plowed deep furrows to raise the capillarity of the soil. Hardier varieties of wheat, oats, barley, and other crops were needed. From Russia came the famous hard spring wheat, Red Fife, and from the Crimea came the winter wheat seeds that were so well adapted to the plains.

That men could cooperate to make the very deserts bloom was most dramatically illustrated in the Mormon Commonwealth of Utah. Brigham Young's people were determined to build a Utopia free from the persecutions of the "gentile" and deliberately ignored the mining riches of the territory for decades in order to keep the corrupting influence of frontier mining life from destroying the Mormons and possibly costing them their homes. They went ahead, undeterred by the vast areas of salt and alkali lands, the desert near the Great Salt Lake, and the scarcity of timber. Within a few years, they found extensive lands where large-scale irrigation could produce a rich agriculture of cereals, fruits, and vegetables. Under Brigham Young's direction the industrious Mormons built a system of canals and reclaimed the barren hills.

Mormon converts from the farms, the factories, and the mines of England, Scandinavia, and the East—"the poorest of the poor," as Young put it—labored cheerfully to quicken the barren lands into life, measuring out the precious water in the early years, and earning enough to rise in the social scale. "Many and many a man here," asserted Young in one of his early discourses, "who is now able to ride in his wagon and perhaps in his carriage, for years before he started for Zion never saw daylight. His days were spent in the coal mines; and his daily toil would commence before light in the morning and continue after dark at night." Proudly he declared, looking back at 1846,

We came to these mountains because we had no other place to go to. We had to leave our homes and possessions on the fertile lands of Illinois to make our dwelling places in these desert wilds, on barren, sterile plains amid lofty, rugged mountains. None dared come here to live until we came here, and we now find it to be one of the best countries in the world for us.

Gentile women of Salt Lake City campaigned against polygamy, abetted by public opinion all over the country. Mark Twain and others visited the Mormons and caricatured their polygamy as an oriental harem system. Actually about 3 per cent of the Saints, according to a Mormon historian, had polygamous ties, and each wife lived in a separate establishment with her children. Successive federal laws, culminating in the Edmunds Act of 1882, forced the Saints to abolish the practice, thereby opening the road to a statehood that had been deliberately withheld for decades. The Mormon commonwealth proved no backward civilization in the history of the Far West, being noted for its exceptionally high literacy and its advanced public school system, universities, and newspapers.

One of the most stirring events in the farmer's penetration of the Great Plains was the development of Oklahoma, known as Indian Territory. Here the "secesh" Indian tribes who had allowed themselves to be drawn into supporting the Confederacy were punished by being forced to cede much of their extensive lands and by being moved on to permit the resettling of other plains Indians on their property. Covetous white squatters ("boomers"), who gathered in camps along the territorial boundary during the eighties, were held back with difficulty by federal troops. They demanded their alleged rights to occupy the vast empty lands in the center of Indian

Territory. The boomers took their name from their exaggerated
booming of the glorious farming and mining future of Oklahoma.
Middle westerners sympathized with the boomers, believing that
they were the victims of a plot in favor of powerful cattlemen who
had been permitted to graze their animals in the Territory.

Congress yielded to public pressure in 1885 by authorizing the
purchase of unoccupied lands in Oklahoma and President Harrison
designated the time of opening as noon, April 22, 1889. At the signal,
the boomers—with not a few "sooners" preceding them in disregard
of the law—broke into the Territory on horseback, in carriages or
wagons in a wild race to seize the best homesteads. By late fall,
Oklahoma had 60,000 settlers, of whom 10,000 lived in Oklahoma
City, a flimsy metropolis of tents, and 8000 in Guthrie. When President Cleveland opened up the six million acres of the Cherokee
Strip at noon of September 16, 1893, more than 100,000 registered
for land grants and Enid came into existence with an initial population of 5000. As in other new American settlements, the founding
of numerous schools, churches, and newspapers came in a matter
of months. It was not unusual for the pioneers to decide that they
wanted to start off with a complete system of higher as well as
elementary education. In 1891, for example, the Oklahoma Agricultural and Mechanical College was founded by the territorial legislature at Stillwater and the next year the University of Oklahoma was
opened at Norman.

5

The frontier home in those counties isolated from railroad and
stagecoach transportation was likely to be more than ordinarily
humble. Limited local materials determined whether the newcomers
lived in a log house, an adobe brick dwelling, a sod made of turf
blocks, or a crude dugout. Large families often crowded into a single
room, sharing it with chickens, dogs, or pigs. Furniture was homemade and so were clothes—jean trousers, calico and gingham
dresses, and bonnets. With improved transportation and income, it
became possible to buy these things from the store. On the plains,
where wood was scarce, people overcame their squeamishness about

using buffalo or cow chips as fuel. Pioneer isolation meant an ill-balanced diet, stomach ailments, and scurvy. Pork, corn, molasses, and wretched coffee—a diet like that of the poor Southern sharecropper—was supplemented by occasional game or fish. Poor housing led to unhealthful exposure to penetrating blizzards and snowstorms.

The frontier doctor was often a heroic man, but he had to travel hundreds of miles to attend to some of his patients and was ill-supplied with medications. He might have to remove bullets, set broken bones, or operate without anesthetics or sedatives. Too few bothered to pay him and thereby compelled him to develop a sideline of teaching school or selling groceries or liquors. Dentists, if available, were no better off. Housewives acted as midwives, nurses, and doctors and kept their shelves well-stocked with patent medicines, particularly "bitters," liver and stomach regulators, and tonics. They were usually adept at gathering herbs as remedies and forced their ailing children to take sulphur and molasses. As for the men, whisky proved to have the most varied virtues, from curing internal ailments to the snake bite. Finally, there were the numerous supernatural remedies, including charms, amulets, or other cures derived from generations of folklore.

Schools in frontier counties were invariably crude and no better in appearance than the pioneer houses in the community. Still, the pioneers invariably found time away from their own pressing tasks to cooperate in building the schoolhouse. Teachers, who were too often only semiliterate, received, perhaps deservedly, little more than a pittance for their efforts while frontier lawlessness and local bullies made their lot a most wretched one. School terms were very short, for farmers could not afford to allow their children too much time away from home tasks. Rural schools were bad almost everywhere in the United States, but most of all on the frontier. However, Carl Rister notes that on the Southern plains, at least, the schoolmaster enjoyed the prestige of being a community leader and spokesman. After 1880, the advent of more stable communities resulted in better schools. Western farmers usually showed a decided eagerness to transplant Eastern ideas of education to the wilderness at the first opportunity. Once the state governments and local officials were firmly in control, the voters secured more and better schools, teachers' institutes, and normal schools.

The eccentricities of frontier justice and the severity of frontier violence can scarcely be exaggerated. In the sparsely-settled West, where men from all over the world came in search of wealth or escape, it was impossible to provide enough officers of the law and an efficient system of justice. Southerners carried over the tradition of endless feuding to the Southwest. Any personal grievance or property right served as an excuse. Cowmen attacked sheepmen in their isolated camps and stampeded their herds over cliffs or clubbed them to death. In 1883, after cowmen had used barbed wire fences to enclose their cattle on land that was not their own, their victims among the farmers and small ranchmen began a "fence-cutting war." In the mining and cattle towns, the mortality among sheriffs was fearsome indeed. They had to cope with Eastern convicts and shiftless debtors who had escaped to the West, assured of anonymity in a country of strangers. Hired "badmen" like Billy the Kid and well-organized gangs of cutthroats, whose membership sometimes included town officials, terrorized entire counties. To make matters worse, there were too few jails and these were usually rickety buildings.

To deal with desperadoes, horse thieves, and criminals who had escaped through bribing the courts, frontier citizens organized informal vigilante courts and carried out their own judgments. They might take a suspect away from the sheriff or capture the criminal themselves and hold a "necktie party" after a few preliminaries. Tough, straight-shooting sheriffs and marshals like Wild Bill Hickok could subdue an unruly town, but even this law man of Abilene had to be dismissed for killing a man in a feud on his own spare time. In 1874, Texas met a large wave of lawlessness by reviving the antebellum organization of Texas Rangers. This hardy company put down vendettas and range wars, and tirelessly tracked down outlaw bands. Among their celebrated feats was the capture of Sam Bass, the bandit leader. Old-timers afterwards sang these words:

Sam Bass was born in Indiana, which was his native home,
Before he reached young manhood, the boy began to roam,
He first came out to Texas, a cowboy for to be—
A better-hearted fellow you scarce could hope to see.

This "good badman," whom some liked to think was a Robin
Hood who robbed rich moneylenders to pay off the poor widow's
mortgage, needed these myths. He was a reckless gambler with a
fondness for horse racing, spent his money lavishly, especially for
expensive whisky, and robbed at least five trains and two stage-
coaches. Finally, the Rangers trapped and shot Sam Bass and others
of his gang. One of his men had betrayed him and his plan to rob
a bank.

Justice was thoroughly blind in the informal courts of too many
of the justices of the peace. While there must have been innumerable
honest and hard-working local judges, their achievements were
apparently too dull to attract the chroniclers of the West; hence the
illiterate, unscrupulous "J.P.'s" have monopolized the writers' attention. They knew little about law or the statutes, but practiced the
customary law of the frontier. Bribery, intimidation, and ignorance,
too, prevailed among them and the courtroom itself sometimes
doubled as a tavern where the J.P., as the proprietor, could keep an
eye on this larger aspect of his business.

The king of the J.P.'s in the Western tradition was Roy Bean, who
had left his native Kentucky hills as a youth to set himself up finally
as a law officer and tavern keeper on the Rio Grande. His business
sign has become a tourist legend: "Judge Roy Bean, Notary Public—
Justice of the Peace—Law West of the Pecos—Ice Beer." Lacking a
jail, he tied his prisoners to a tree; and he generously expanded his
judicial powers—and fees—by granting divorces. His eccentric ver-
dicts have become western folklore. He adored the popular English
actress, Lily Langtry, whose picture he had seen in the choice
pages of the *Police Gazette*, and he succeeded in having the town
named after her—which thoroughly pleased the English visitor.

Frontier courts at the higher levels also had their shortcomings
and miscarriages of justice. Not until the federal courts were well
established did the situation improve. The jury was an abused

institution in the East, but it was anarchic in the West. Americans retained a decided preference for jury trials in all sorts of suits besides those involving major crimes at a time when England, the mother of the system, was showing definite misgivings about it and was sharply restricting the use of the jury to certain types of cases. Juries, which were made up heavily of debtors in the West, did not always understand the rights of the creditors. Notorious criminals might intimidate the juries by threatening revenge in case of an unfavorable verdict. However, by the turn of the century, the western states were stabilizing the judicial system and building modern courts and stout prisons.

Among the stabilizing influences upon the frontier was the church. In the West, Catholic and Protestant missionaries had often served to keep the peace between Indians and whites. The Methodist circuit rider and the itinerant preacher tried to overcome the handicap that distance put upon religion on the frontier; this had to be solely a labor of love, for there was little compensation in salary. Outlaws and Indians on the warpath made their life a dangerous one. As in earlier frontiers, religion came to the isolated Westerner through the camp meeting revivals. For two weeks or more, just after the harvest had been gathered, farmers and their entire families arrived in their wagons to picnic on the revival grounds and to respond fervently to the exhortations of the shouting preachers. This experience offered a major emotional stimulation in the restricted lives of the people on the plains. Church attendance grew steadily on the frontier, for churches, like schools, were among the first buildings to be constructed. Fundamentalism was strong among these Baptist and Methodist peoples; their preachers discouraged card-playing, drinking, dancing, and horse racing. This was a more difficult ideal farther West in the cattle and mining towns.

Despite fundamentalism, recreation did not differ greatly from the pastimes of the older West. Scandinavians, Germans, and other Europeans brought their traditional ways and amusements to enrich the social life of the community. Frontier ebullience and Old Lutheran fundamentalism sometimes clashed over the drinking and gambling, but the spirit of play could not be enjoined. Fiddlers,

accompanied perhaps by someone with a banjo or guitar, played
the "Arkansas Traveler," "Turkey in the Straw," or "Skip-to-my-
Lou," while callers sang out in nasal rhythm for the square dances:

> Choose your partner, form a ring
> Figure eight, and double L swing . . .
> Swing 'em east and swing 'em west,
> Swing the girl that you love best.

Westerners enjoyed barbecues, fish frys, and candy-pulling parties
for young people. Above all, horsemanship delighted them, whether
in the rodeo, the horse race, or the Southern tournament, where
riders with long lances dashed at full speed at a series of suspended
rings. In the Southwest, despite cultural prejudices, Americans
emulated the ways of their pleasure-loving Mexican neighbors of
old El Paso, San Antonio, Santa Fe, and Albuquerque. Anglo-Saxons,
too, danced the Spanish waltz, the quadrille, and the fandango,
while the Spanish-American elite borrowed the Americanized ball.
Both peoples loved horse racing, gambling, and, to a varying extent,
cockfighting. The pageantry of the Mexican, his Spanish, Moorish
and Indian architecture, and his leather and metal ornamentation
found imitators throughout the Southwest.

6

The stagecoach, with its painful twisting and turning, welcome
though it was as an alternative to walking or riding on horseback
across the inhospitable plains, scarcely answered the need for comfortable transportation. Lack of road-building materials, canals,
or adequate rivers made the coming of the railway the fondest hope
of the Far West. Sectional jealousies and the war itself, as well as
the insuperable financial risks of building a railroad ahead of population and profitable traffic delayed the transcontinental railways until
the late sixties. By that time generous federal subsidies, such as
alternate sections of land and loans, enabled the builders to go
ahead.

Surveyors and armies of tracklayers, attracted by such high

wages as $2.50 a day for laborers, fought off Indians in order to get on with their task. Young John Peter Altgeld of Ohio, son of poor German immigrants, and destined to be a famous Illinois governor and leader of the Democratic party, started as a humble, if well-paid, laborer on the western railroad. The Union Pacific, under the resourceful chief engineer General Grenville Dodge, hired large numbers of Union and Confederate veterans, Irish, Germans, Mexicans, Chinese and a sprinkling of assorted convicts. Encouraged by wage incentives, they worked hard, laying track and driving in the huge spikes, always keeping their firearms stacked nearby for Indian attacks. A maudlin note crept into the sentimental songs of the Irish workmen, "Poor Paddy, He Works on the Railroad,"

> Then drill, my Paddies, drill,—
> Drill, my heroes, drill,—
> Drill all day, no sugar in your tay,
> Workin' on the U. P. railway.

The tracklayers moved a mile a day in the summer, speeding up to ten miles daily as they advanced, sleeping at night in long flat cars on wheels or in tents. Each of the terminus towns was a temporary social center where all the western traits of lawlessness, wild gambling, and heavy drinking found expression in a "hell on wheels," leaving behind improvised cemeteries for men who had died with their boots on. Indians tore up tracks and rails, razed telegraph poles, and occasionally wrecked engines before being driven off. The plains offered too few trees to furnish enough ties and company lumbermen practically denuded the banks of the Missouri to supply wood for the railroad.

East of the Mississippi the railroad builders had located their tracks to serve well-established communities and traffic, but in vast areas of the Great Plains they could arbitrarily build new towns or capriciously relegate others to the limbo of ghost towns. Speculators close to Dodge and Durant of the Union Pacific, to Stanford and Huntington of the Central (and later Southern) Pacific, or to General William J. Palmer of the Kansas Pacific, bought town lots with the assurance of huge profits without undue risk. Cheyenne was the lusty offspring of the Union Pacific and the chief social and political center for the thousands of homemakers who entered empty Wyoming after the railroad arrived. Before Cheyenne was founded only the old trading posts of Fort Laramie and Fort Bridger and a few mining camps existed to suggest civilization. From 1870 to 1890 this territory of cattlemen, sheepmen, and homesteaders grew from less than ten thousand to over sixty thousand people.

Denver, left off the main Union Pacific line for Cheyenne, in which Dodge's friends were financially interested, refused to be ignored. Though Vice-President Durant of the Union Pacific complacently reported that "Denver is too dead to bury," the town's business leaders financed a line to Cheyenne and collaborated with the Kansas Pacific in constructing a direct track from the East to the Southwest, ultimately with outlets to Los Angeles and the Pacific Coast. Tracklayers advanced through blistering deserts, dangerous mountain curves, long tunnels in the heart of the Rockies, deep abysses, and unbelievable canyons like the Royal Gorge in the Colorado Rockies. By the early seventies, after Denver's isolation had been completely broken, the town blossomed into a cosmopolitan city, far more durable and prosperous than the mining towns elsewhere. In one civic campaign its desperadoes and frontier gamblers were expelled as relics of a bygone era.

Los Angeles began its sensational climb in the 1870's, already an irrepressible booster of its climate, though less certain of its tangible economic resources. When the Southern Pacific, then favoring San Francisco, threatened to bypass the city and build directly to San Bernardino instead, Los Angeles granted the heavy railway subsidies desired—about 5 per cent of the assessed value of Los Angeles County plus a free right of way and a sixty-acre lot for a depot, actually not excessive, considering the railroad's costs. Passenger freight rates remained exorbitant until the Santa Fe completed its lines over the historic southern trail to reach San Diego and then Los Angeles by the late 1880's.

In the ensuing rate war between the two railroads, freight charges fell from five dollars a ton to thirty cents, and passengers from

Chicago paid only $10 rather than $55. Cheap passenger fares and highly exaggerated advertising of Southern California drew many thousands to the City of the Angels and inspired a fantastic real estate boom that not only put Los Angeles property on a par with the best in the East but led to the founding of Pasadena, Monrovia, and many other towns. Iowa farmers, mostly younger sons who saw limited opportunity among the high-priced lands at home, began their persistent trek to Southern California. Helen Hunt Jackson, the New England novelist, arrived for her health in the 1870's and joined the boosters who gloried in the climate and the historic mission civilization.

In 1873, a basic agricultural resource of Southern California was introduced at Riverside with the planting and trying out of the so-called Washington navel orange from Bahia, Brazil. The large, sweet, and seedless orange contrasted favorably with the sour, dry, thick-skinned native product, and even took all the first prizes at exhibits over the hitherto dominant Florida orange. Thus began a long rivalry. Once the railroads arrived the California citrus field expanded under irrigation, revealing the genuine richness and adaptability of the soil for agriculture. By the mid-1880's thousands of carloads of oranges and lemons were leaving for the East. That unique cooperative, the California Fruit Growers Exchange, did much to stabilize the business and to popularize its attractive label "Sunkist."

San Francisco, where Nevada millionaires built their homes, seemed the chief beneficiary of the Central Pacific-Union Pacific link across the continent, its magnificent protective harbor inviting the trade of the Pacific. Here William Randolph Hearst, son of a wealthy mining promoter, published the *San Francisco Chronicle* and in his sensational style fought the political tactics of the Southern Pacific Railroad, whose headquarters were in the city. Within a short distance were the two outstanding universities of the West, the University of California and Stanford, the latter beginning with an oversize endowment of $20,000,000 left to commemorate the untimely death of young Leland Stanford, Jr., son of one of the Big Four who built the Central and Southern Pacific.

7

Miners, cattlemen, farmers, and railroad men elbowed aside the Indians of the Far West and took what they needed. The Union Pacific alone stripped a belt of fifty miles across the continent, killing off the game and depleting the scattered trees. Its rivals did much the same thing elsewhere. Miners of Nevada cut down the piñon groves, tore up the sagebrush, and drove the grasshoppers away, leaving the desert Paiutes to beg for a livelihood, like the lowly California Diggers. President Grant added a paternalistic note by staffing the Indian Service with Quakers, but he did not punish his corrupt secretary of war who trafficked in trader concessions at Indian posts. The army, battling the desperate Indians, liked the opinion of General Philip Sheridan who was credited with the maxim, "The only good Indian is a dead one." Still, a conscientious soldier like General George Crook, faithfully carrying out his instructions to crush the Sioux in the Black Hills, admitted that it was hard to fight the Indians, knowing they were in the right.

A misunderstanding arose over the government order of 1875 calling the Sioux and other Plains tribes back to their reservations on penalty of being treated as enemies. Stubbornly, the Sioux concentrated their might at the Little Big Horn River and in the historic episode of "Custer's Last Stand" wiped out the 225 men of General George Custer's Seventh Cavalry. He had recklessly led his men into ambush in his eagerness to win glory without sharing it with the main body of the troops. In death Custer won the glory denied him in life, for his widow led a movement to canonize him in military annals. As for Sitting Bull's Sioux, like others who resisted the disciplined force of federal troops, they were broken and moved to reservations. The heroic resistance of Chief Joseph and his Nez Percé in the Snake Valley, after refusing to stay on their Idaho reservations, ended in inevitable defeat in 1877 after a lengthy chase by the soldiers of Colonel Nelson A. Miles. The Apaches in the Southwest, rebelling against meager rations on their reservations and the attacks of white outlaws, broke out under Victorio and then Geronimo, raiding the settlements during the

seventies and eighties and hiding in hidden canyons and mountain
lairs until trapped by federal and Mexican troops.

In the East, which had once crusaded for Negro rights, two Ponca
chiefs, Standing Bear and Bright Eyes, touched sympathetic audiences with the woes of the Red Man. One of these impressed listeners was the Massachusetts-born novelist, Helen Hunt Jackson, who
became a latter-day Harriet Beecher Stowe in behalf of a racial
minority. Moving to Southern California in 1872 to recover her
health, Mrs. Jackson became absorbed by the culture of the Mission
Indians and the degradation of these scattered tribes. In 1881 appeared *A Century of Dishonor,* a scathing indictment of federal Indian policy, some of it grossly exaggerated for propagandistic effect.
Popular indignation was awakened by this long record of broken
faith. Far more widely read was her picturesque novel, *Ramona,*
which appeared in 1884, the year before her death. This sentimental
and melancholy novel, in the Victorian tradition of Longfellow's
Hiawatha, told the idyllic love story of the part-Indian girl, Ramona,
and her husband Alessandro. Their beautiful world of Spanish-
Indian missions and unspoiled simplicity was violently disrupted
by the American gold seekers. Beneath the weight of the Anglo-
Saxon's lust for riches and his materialism, the old Spanish and
Indian patriarchal life crumbled and Ramona herself broke mentally
and was finally murdered. Although Mrs. Jackson's interpretation
neglected many historic factors, and the love story often overshadowed the wrongs of the Indian, the book did much to arouse
the conscience of the nation. Indian Rights Associations sprang
up in most cities, much to the author's delight, and Congress finally
took action in the Dawes Act of 1887.

The Dawes Act was scarcely a Magna Carta for the Indian, but
it seemed promising at the time. Congress tried to make a settled
farmer out of an Indian nomad and fit him into the Anglo-Saxon
pattern; and, to extinguish the reservation system, which, it was
felt, was pauperizing him, Congress offered a plan for breaking up
the tribal structure and traditions. With certain exceptions family
heads were permitted to choose 160-acre allotments, free from tribal
control, which were to be held inalienable for twenty-five years

before title would be granted. This procedure carried with it the privilege of citizenship.

Unfortunately, this Act, even with subsequent amendments, not only failed to integrate the Indian into western culture but even broke down those traditional elements that gave him some degree of self-respect and stability. Half-educated children were estranged from the inner warmth of tribal life. Unscrupulous land grabbers impoverished the Indians, so many of whom were unprepared for modern farming, and forced them back upon charity and a degraded life. Not until 1934 was a new philosophy of minority rights applied that allowed a more wholesome respect for the best values in Indian culture—too many of them undepicted in the gory "Westerns" of Hollywood.

8

The Far West left an enduring mark on American literature. Francis Parkman told the fascinating story of the Oregon Trail from his own keen observations; and he wrote the history of the French pioneers in the New World and the international struggle for the Canadian forest. In San Francisco, the sympathetic and attractive Western and Central American histories of Hubert Howe Bancroft left a mine of useful, if not always accurate, materials in his thirty-nine large volumes published during 1874–90. Theodore Roosevelt wrote several vivid books during the eighties about his ranch experiences, the history of the early West, and the life of the pioneer Missouri statesman, Thomas Hart Benton. Most writers of American history were to feel the deep impress of Frederick Jackson Turner's theories of the frontier and sectionalism in shaping the institutions and traits of this nation. As a result, a far richer social, geographic, and economic interpretation of American development became possible.

In fiction and travel literature, Mark Twain exploited the West more effectively than any other writer. His native Mississippi Valley and his youth in early Missouri were immortalized in *Tom Sawyer* (1876) and *The Adventures of Huckleberry Finn* (1884), reviving the exciting world of river pirates and village boys' pranks and fancies. *Life on the Mississippi* (1883) had retailed Twain's early manhood as a skilled steamboat pilot and his later visit to the river towns; and *Roughing It* (1872) told of his trip with his brother by stagecoach to Carson City, Nevada, and to the Sandwich Islands. With his friend Charles Dudley Warner he gave a meaningful label to the corrupt speculative and tinsel era following the Civil War in *The Gilded Age*. His keen humor expressed the unconventional West and ridiculed the genteel manners of American Victorianism. As a result, he had a host of followers in San Francisco long before he captured Boston.

Contemporary with Twain but far less gifted was Bret Harte of California, a journalist who was something of a clever parodist and who found his medium in stories of life in western gold-mining camps. While editor of the *Overland Monthly* he wrote *The Luck of Roaring Camp*, based on the sentimental Dickens formula of whimsical humor and pathos and he did another highly successful story in a similar vein, *The Outcasts of Poker Flat*. These California frontier themes, though indifferently received in the West, which sneered at his inaccuracy, won Harte a large enthusiastic audience in the East as did his humorous poem, *The Heathen Chinee*. Kindly social pariahs, sentimental miners, honorable gamblers, and tearful melodrama are touchingly mixed in the fashion attractive to American moralists who liked to find good in human nature, however degraded. But to make a charming idyll of tough mining life was too much for old-timers who recalled the harsh days of the real frontier. Interestingly enough, when Bret Harte went East, and finally to England, encouraged by literary ovations based on his California stories, his fountain of genius turned dry and he proved unable to write successfully with newer formulas.

Also popular was the younger Emerson Hough of Iowa who used his editorship of *Forest and Stream* and his early legal practice along the Rio Grande frontier to learn the West at first hand. His much-read book *The Story of the Cowboy* (1897) captivated Theodore Roosevelt. Just before Hough's death in 1923 he was able to watch an extremely successful motion picture made of his recent novel, *The Covered Wagon* (1922), which captured some of the romance, excitement, and dialect of the early frontier. Of the numerous story-tellers of cowboy life, none perhaps managed so well to establish the romantic stereotype of the cowboy as Owen Wister, a Phila-delphian by birth, who had lived in Arizona and New Mexico. His popular novel, *The Virginian* (1902) furnished later western scena-rio writers with the picture of the courtly rancher, the sinister cattle rustler, and the silent elusive Indian.

Easterners, young men in the cities especially, who experienced a vicarious thrill from the cheap paper-backed wild west stories, idolized the work of Ned Buntline, as Edward Z. C. Judson was known. This New York boy had been a seaman, had fought in the Seminole War, and had served as a fur company man along the Yellowstone. He had an undeniable gift for turning out hundreds of engrossing stories of the thriller variety, being one of the first of the dime novelists. In 1869 he began his tremendously popular series of "Buffalo Bill" stories and easily persuaded the original, Wil-liam F. Cody, to go on the stage in *The Scout of the Plains*—a career Cody never wholly dropped thereafter. Cody's exploits, embellished with the very cooperative aid of the subject himself, had enough of fact in them, including his work as an expert shot, trailer, and pony express rider, to stimulate even lesser pulp writers than Ned Bunt-line.

In the western tradition of dime novels and outlaw ballads were the tales of Jesse James and his brother Frank and their allies, the tough, sharp-shooting Younger brothers. Jesse had so improved upon his education in crime of Civil War days under Quantrell as to startle the nation during the 1870's by his bold robberies of the Rock Island, Kansas Pacific, and Missouri Pacific railways. Westerners, glorifying Jesse James as a chivalrous foe of greedy bankers and railroad barons, refused to cooperate with the law in halting the bandits. Finally, when the governor of Missouri offered a $10,000 reward for Jesse dead or alive, two of his band, the Ford brothers, killed him in 1882 at his home in St. Joseph where he was living under the name of Howard. By this time the Younger brothers, too, were behind bars, having been trapped and shot in an unsuccessful robbery of a bank at Northfield, Minnesota, during which the cashier

was killed. The James brothers who had participated escaped and
Frank James even managed to reach a ripe old age unharassed by
the law. In the popular *Ballad of Jesse James* the refrain expresses
the opinion of his worshippers:

> Jesse had a wife to mourn all her life
> The children they are brave.
> 'Twas a dirty little coward shot Mister Howard
> And laid Jesse James in his grave.

Even as Frederick Jackson Turner spoke of the passing frontier
to the scholars of the American Historical Association in 1893, a
vigorous conservation movement had already begun. The Westerner's tradition of soil butchery and careless exploitation of natural
resources had been encouraged by the scarcity of men on the
frontier and the rich virgin soil, thick forests, abundant fisheries,
and minerals that required only the simplest of working equipment.
This laissez-faire habit was reflected in easygoing or defective land
laws that permitted cattle barons, mineral kings, and timber corporations to acquire the nation's surviving forests and mines at nominal
prices. Besides, the desperate battle for precious water holes in the
arid West and the constant fear of destructive floods suggested to
many that only government action on a large scale could solve such
problems. There were those like Theodore Roosevelt and later
George Norris of Nebraska who foresaw an age of electrical power
in which all of the people rather than the special interests alone
would profit from this fruitful source of wealth. The West was not
yet gone.

· 5 ·

The Urban Impact on Rural Life: Hamlin Garland and Edward Eggleston

---

I

IN 1884, young Hamlin Garland quit the farm for a literary career in Boston. He saw no sense in following his restless father to a pioneer homestead in the bleak Dakotas. Born in 1860 on a Wisconsin farm and raised on the Iowa prairies, he had become disillusioned with the endless chores and the dreary routine of profitless toil. He had no desire to do as his New England ancestors had done—to go West for another home "beneath the sunset." Within a few years after his departure Joseph Kirkland, his literary friend, was to advise him, "You're the first actual farmer in American fiction—now tell the truth about it." He did, after the critical vogue of the newer realistic writers. Few of the multitude that left farms and villages for the city were as articulate as Garland (and many angrily took issue with his view of the farm), but a good number shared his eagerness to give up rural life for the attractions of the metropolis. Already Broadway was exploiting the "hick" as well as the immigrant and the Negro as a subject for skits and later for vaudeville jokes.

The country-to-city movement was only a phase of the Industrial Revolution in Western Europe and America. In Washington's day 95 per cent of all Americans lived in communities of less than 2500 people. By 1880, this proportion had fallen to 71.8 per cent, and twenty years later was 60.3 per cent; thereafter the downward

98

trend continued rapidly. In New England, rural dwellers had already become a minority before this era ended, while the cities expanded. Luther Burbank, the famous plant breeder, gave up his farm at Lunenberg, Massachusetts, in 1875 to join his brothers in California. It is true that rural areas even to this day have never declined in absolute numbers, unlike Western Europe in this respect, but their slow growth despite a high birth rate, especially in the South, reveals the losses to urban centers. Thus in 1870–1910 the rural population increased from 28.6 millions to 49.9 millions, but villages between 2500 and 5000 grew from 1 million to 3.7 millions and towns of 5000 to 10,000 expanded from 1.2 millions to 4.2 millions. This was the trend all the way up to the largest cities. There were only fourteen cities with more than 100,000 people during Grant's first term, but by Taft's era there were fifty. Among those who moved from the farm to the relatively comfortable village were the Garlands. They enjoyed a brief respite in the village of Osage, Iowa, and this made it all the more distasteful for them to go on to the isolated Dakotas.

Rural isolation fostered a strong feeling of local solidarity and suspicion of outsiders and new methods. Farmers had little faith in doctors and stubbornly clung to home remedies. Country folk distrusted the villagers, especially the merchants, and the latter reciprocated by looking down upon the "yokels." Foreigners were apt to be excluded altogether from the neighborhood society. Young Hamlin Garland recalled that he and the other little boys were in constant feud against the Norskies, as the Norwegians were called, and attacked them for no reason at all. Class differences were relatively unimportant in the country, but counted for a great deal among the villagers. In these constantly growing villages a few families would dominate the schools and churches as well as local business.

Garland's escape to the city did not reveal the fact that mechanization rather than urban excitement was beginning to disintegrate rural society and to threaten the dominance of horsepower by the end of this era. In the villages weavers, tailors, and shoemakers lost their trade to mail-order houses and large-scale urban enterprise.

The mechanization of the farm meant that hundreds of thousands were being displaced gradually before 1900 and in wholesale fashion thereafter. Between 1860 and 1900 the value of farm implements and machinery rose from $246 millions to $750 millions; by 1914 even this latter figure had tripled. Before the turn of the century the United States had become the world's leading manufacturer of farm machinery.

The Marsh harvester, which Garland had operated as a boy of sixteen, doubled the amount of grain harvested in the same space of time. John F. Appleby's twine binder (1878) stepped up the harvesting process eightfold. Thousands of patents were issued for threshers, reapers, hay stackers, potato planters, manure spreaders and other machines. Finally in 1901 came the tractor, followed three years later by the caterpillar tread, and in 1905 by the power-operated milking machine. In 1910, there were 1000 tractors in operation; six years later there were 37,000. Productivity in this era tripled for many staples, aided by the doubling of land under cultivation; but farm population fell short of doubling. Land values rose too high for mere subsistence farmers. The railroads, canals, and improved roads broke down the isolation of self-sufficient homesteads and spread the domain of cash farming. Were it not for the fact that farming is a way of life as well as a business, the exodus from rural America would have been far greater than it actually was. As a result of the new commercialized farming, the agricultural map of the nation was sharply divided into a "corn belt," a "wheat belt," and a "dairy belt." Farming had become a highly specialized enterprise in many parts of the nation.

Agriculture offered economic security to those who could afford the investment in large-scale commerecial farming. In the era of 1865–96, declining farm prices resulted in bankruptcy for many thousands and tenancy for others. In the West farm ownership remained fairly stable, but in the Middle West and South tenancy assumed large proportions. In 1880, 19.2 per cent of all Northern farms were operated by tenants; by 1910, the proportion had gone up to 26.5 per cent. Southern tenants cultivated 36.2 per cent of all farms in 1880, 47 per cent in 1900, and almost 50 per cent in 1910. Too many tenants, especially in the South, were pathetic insecure farmers standing at the bottom of the social scale and indifferent to adding improvements or to maintaining the soil or the farm buildings.

But recent studies by Dr. James Malin and others for Kansas and Wisconsin show that farm tenancy there was not exploitative of the soil or even bad social policy; furthermore, tenancy was not necessarily a consequence of falling prices. The system often gave younger people a chance to save enough money to buy farms for themselves—in effect offering an "agricultural ladder" to farm ownership. A large proportion of tenants were relatives of the landlord and hence apt to be treated especially well. In Iowa, for example, Henry C. Wallace of the state agricultural college at Ames, who was the father of the future vice-president, became the tenant of his own well-to-do father. Though he did not prosper overly as a tenant farmer, his family connections assured him of security.

Garland, an unusually squeamish farmer, complained of the farm discomforts during the 1870's, especially in the pioneer communities of Iowa. His family lived in an unpainted, utilitarian square cottage. The children slept upstairs in a low unplastered chamber and on winter mornings they rushed downstairs to dress near the fire. A summer kitchen was used to keep the stove from overheating the house during the warm weather. In winter this was dispensed with and everyone ate and lived in the sixteen-square-foot front room. There was no privacy for anyone under such conditions. Outside was the unsanitary privy with its dangerous potentialities for contamination of the water supply. And Garland never forgot the smells and flies of the barn.

Things were better in the older rural communities, though simple frame dwellings with two rooms upstairs and two down tended to be the norm. Gradually, the farmer disposed of his homemade furniture and bought modern tables and chairs through the mail-order catalog. The kerosene lamp displaced the cruder lard oil or whale oil lamps and candles, but the electrification of the farm lay far ahead. By 1900, many farmers could boast of a sewing machine, a telephone, a piano, and a spring buggy. The well-to-do whose houses were piped for running water might imitate city people by installing a wooden bathtub lined with zinc; otherwise, the farmers would do as the Garlands did: take a bath in a wooden tub that served at other times as a laundry wash tub.

2

Much of the history of the farmer after the Civil War deals with farm organizations and attempts at rural cooperation. The frontier had bred self-reliance, but not anarchic individualism. Nor did farmers have an abiding love for solitude as the facts of their social activities show. When declining prices, heavy mortgages, and foreclosures struck at their existence, they quickly improvised militant collective organizations comparable in strength and purpose to urban trade unions. On occasion, the embattled Grangers, Alliance Men, or Populists might effect a joint strategy with the Knights of Labor and lobby successfully for specific reforms. There were limits, however, to rural radicalism in this country because of the growing hegemony of large-scale farming and the relative isolation of the average farmer. In Europe the farm community tended to live in compact villages, with the farms spread out around them, but in this country the land grant system had fostered scattered rural neighborhoods.

Richard Garland, Hamlin's father, was something of a rebel, proud of his New England abolitionist past, and eager to accept a leader's role within the Grange. This organization had grown out of numerous farmers' clubs that had come into existence after the Civil War. In 1867, Oliver H. Kelley, who had once been a farmer in Minnesota and had studied rural conditions in the South for the Department of Agriculture, organized the Patrons of Husbandry, generally known as the Grange. It was intended as a social and fraternal organization with some of the secret ritual of a masonic group.

Families like the Garlands came to the Grange meetings in the schoolhouse for social activities perhaps twice a month during the afternoon or evening. Members read agricultural and literary essays, debated controversial political issues, and borrowed books from the small Grange library. Young couples danced the square dances or the old-fashioned reels. They might sing their favorite songs, including hymns from the *Moody and Sankey Song Book*. In some places there was no objection to a friendly card game, but gambling and hard drinking was usually taboo in evangelical communities. Fish suppers were popular in Richard Garland's Iowa Grange and the Grange picnic was a big event everywhere.

By 1874, the Grange had over 1,500,000 members, most of them in the Middle West, but many in the South as well. Unfortunately, the Grange became too deeply involved in risky cooperative ventures in elevators and stores and suffered numerous bankruptcies. Richard Garland moved to Osage to supervise Grange interests in a grain elevator. Cooperatives were assailed by competing manufacturers who cut prices until the inexperienced farmers surrendered. Too many farmers were ready to take advantage of these temporary bargains from the anti-Grange stores, even if this meant the destruction of their own cooperative movement. However, the Grange did succeed in operating cooperative grain elevators and after 1900 various farm groups showed a good deal of sound business management in running dairy and livestock cooperatives.

The farmers' clubs, the Grangers, the Alliancemen, and finally the Populists left a significant heritage in the basic legislation and philosophy they sponsored for government regulation of business. Their battle against railroads and other monopolies led to the first major reversal of more than a century of economic laissez faire. The effort to halt extortionate railroad and warehouse rates resulted in state regulatory commissions in state after state to oversee those economic activities affected by a public interest. This meant a revival of half-forgotten common law principles that strengthened the community's "police power" against private monopolies. The culminating victory for government regulation of business on a national scale was the passage of the Interstate Commerce Act of 1887. This set up the Interstate Commerce Commission, destined to grow in strength by successive statutes, to halt railroad rebates and other discriminatory practices; by the acts of 1906 and 1910 their power was extended over other modes of transportation and rate control.

3

In the village's economy and its social structure few outranked the merchant. He might be the local banker (particularly in the South, which lacked banks), the postmaster, and the owner of the general store at the crossroads. The farmer came to his store to stock up on the most varied goods—farm implements, patent medicines, groceries, hardware, harness, clothes, and drygoods. He expected to charge his purchases against the collateral of his future crop while the merchant, too, had to buy from the wholesaler on credit. This meant heavy risks that were reflected in high prices. In addition, the general store could scarcely hope to satisfy the critical farmer who had once tasted the experience of buying in large city stores and was increasingly reluctant to accept substitutes. The Garlands in Osage found the storekeepers hostile to the Grange competition represented by Hamlin's father, who was then an agent for a co-operative.

The general store in its heyday was a social oasis in the dry at-mosphere of rural isolation. Farmers who had traveled ten or fifteen miles to the store and had sacrificed much valuable time made it up by meeting with their cronies around the old box stove as they seated themselves on the flour and cracker barrels. They pumped the merchant dry of local gossip and other news that he had picked up from various customers. Together the farmers would make up their minds on political issues, tell stories, or philosophize on social matters. These country stores were collectively the rural parliament of the nation where decisions were reached that were often trans-lated into law.

Into this bucolic Eden of the general store crept a far more dan-gerous serpent than the inefficient Grangers. This was the mail-order house. The most successful of the early firms to offer mail-order sell-ing was owned by Aaron Montgomery Ward, a former traveling salesman of Chicago who had long sold to farmers and villagers. Montgomery Ward listened to the farmers' complaints of the high prices they paid for manufactured goods and to their denuncia-tion of the middlemen. He proposed a remedy in the mail-order system. His firm was not the first American mail-order house when it was established in 1872, but it was the first large concern to sell a wide variety of goods by mail.

By 1900 another Chicago mail-order firm had caught up with Montgomery Ward and even outdid the older company. Sears, Roebuck and Company, established in 1887, had adopted and even improved upon Ward's merchandising methods. Richard Warren Sears, a Minnesota farm boy, began as a railroad clerk with a sideline of jewelry-selling through station agents—all of whom were already bonded railway employees and hence safe risks for him. Eventually, he turned to the mail-order business on a general scale and showed a genius for writing the type of informal advertising appealing to rural customers in that Victorian era of sentimentality. An audacious merchandiser, he was able to undersell competitors and to popularize the Sears guarantee behind his goods. At least once, it is true, he did stoop to such a dodge for "rubes" as advertising an illustrated roomful of furniture—with the word "miniature" in small letters—for ninety-five cents. Customers were assured that this offer was made solely for advertising purposes. One of Sears's weaknesses was overselling his commodities. His advertising also let the farmers know he was on their side in fighting monopoly, "We are Waging War against Combinations, Associations, Trusts, and High Prices."

In 1895 the mercurial Sears secured capital and an astute stable partner in Julius Rosenwald, a clothing merchant whose father had begun as an immigrant peddler. Together (Roebuck remained a nonentity) they expanded the Sears, Roebuck catalog to cover almost everything under the sun from "perfect fitting corsets" and spring buggies to lurid dime novels and cures for the tobacco and narcotic habits. In isolated farmhouses, especially during the long winters, families read and reread the Sears, Roebuck catalog for its literary value. There were over five hundred pages of it as early as 1894 and one ordered by simply tearing out the advertisement and mailing it in.

Farmers and mail-order houses were enriched by two gifts of the taxpayer—rural free delivery and the cheap parcel post system.

Unlike Europe, the United States tended to look upon the post office as an agency of national development rather than as a source of revenue. A predominantly rural population was scattered over huge fertile lands that could be rapidly developed once the problems of communication and markets were solved. A policy of regular postal deficits made possible first-class mail delivery at two cents an ounce by 1885 and gave rural as well as urban readers the privilege of low rates for newspapers and magazines. That same year the "special delivery" system began. Service improved early in this era with the introduction of the railway postal car and the construction of numerous postal roads. In 1863 city dwellers no longer had to walk to the local post office to look into their family boxes for mail; free delivery had just been established. Within a few decades pressure from smaller cities and towns resulted in similar free delivery service to the very doorstep of the recipient.

But in the fourth-class rural post offices the mail sack was frequently dumped on a table and the farmers or village folk, after traveling some distance from home, had the privilege of fishing for their own letters. Isolated farmers often came ten or fifteen miles only to discover that there was no mail for them. This meant a costly loss of time from farm work. In Europe, where distances were not too great, rural free delivery was already a fact. Only in this country, where huge additional deficits were envisaged by Congress, did decades elapse without action. Village businessmen resisted the innovation, fearful of a loss in business. Eventually, the pressure of the state Granges and other rural groups achieved "R.F.D."

In 1896 experimental rural delivery routes were set up in parts of West Virginia. So successful was this that four years later over 2500 routes were serving more than 1,800,000 persons. The mails now went to the man—unless he was too far out—rather than the reverse. Private mailboxes were protected from thieves by extending to them the federal law forbidding tampering with the mails. The results of R.F.D., aside from the anticipated heavy deficits, were almost revolutionary. The Postmaster-General reported as early as 1900:

Rural free delivery brings the farm within the daily range of the intellectual and commercial activities of the world, and the isolation and monotony which have been the bane of agricultural life are sensibly mitigated. It proves to be one of the most effective and powerful of educational agencies. Wherever it is extended the schools improve and the civic spirit of the community feels a new pulsation.

One Oregon farmer wrote at this time, "Before free delivery was started there were 13 daily papers taken at Turner Post Office. Today there are 113." With the carriers expected regularly, the farmers hurried to remove snow from the roads after a snowstorm and thus transportation of foodstuffs to village and city markets as well as the delivery of the mails was possible at almost all times.

Road-building was stimulated by this development. In 1908 the nation possessed only 650 miles of macadamized roads and no concrete highways. Beginning in the nineties, the use of the bicycle and later the automobile led the states to embark on large-scale road-building programs. With the expansion of R.F.D. and the growth of new markets, the need for better roads became acute. In 1916, Congress passed the Rural Post Roads Act providing large appropriations to aid states in building rural post roads.

4

In the farmer's *annus mirabilis* of 1862, at a time when Southern statesmen had deserted Washington, Congress responded to the Northern agricultural demand for a Homestead Act, the Morrill Land Grant College Act, and the provision for a Department of Agriculture (though without cabinet status until 1882). Scientific aid to the farmer, hitherto almost the sole concern of the agricultural societies and the relatively few state departments of agriculture, thus became a major interest of the federal government. Rural pressure assured that this aid should be much more than "book farming" and should embrace practical demonstration and experiment. In 1887 the Hatch Act was to provide these experiment stations for each area and in 1914 the Smith-Lever Act subsidized college and governmental extension work among the farmers.

Under the Morrill Land Grant Act agricultural colleges were to be endowed by a gift of 30,000 acres of public land for each congressman and senator of the state. About eleven million acres of land endowment were sold, but much of it represented left-over inferior land, disposed of on a low market. The original sponsors were disappointed that the new "cow colleges" did not offer the experts and specialized agricultural curriculum that had been envisaged. Farm papers poked fun at the professors' ignorance of practical farming. Most of the states set up new agricultural colleges; others expanded existing universities. In response to Populist criticism in the nineties the technical work of the land grant colleges was much improved.

Iowa State College of Agricultural and Mechanical Arts at Ames became a great land grant institution in the 1880's under the leadership of President Seaman Knapp. This remarkable agriculturalist wrote the first draft of the Hatch Act and later encouraged scientific farming, especially in rice cultivation, in Louisiana and other parts of the South. At Iowa State College, Henry Wallace and later his son were students and eventually applied their lessons while federal secretaries of agriculture. Another outstanding alumnus of this college was the gentle George Washington Carver, who had been born of slave parents in Missouri and had picked up his preparatory schooling in the most difficult and miscellaneous ways possible. Iowa State College soon forgot that he was a Negro in their admiration of his scientific genius and his talent as a painter. Young Henry A. Wallace acquired from him his earliest interest in plant genetics. Later, Carver directed the department of agricultural research at Tuskegee Institute and won fame for his researches on the industrial uses of the peanut and the sweet potato. His expansion of the market for peanuts was to provide a new profitable crop for innumerable Southern farmers, most of whom scarcely knew that their benefactor was a Negro. Elsewhere, the earliest of the better land grant colleges appeared in New York (Cornell), Massachusetts, Michigan, Illinois, and Kansas.

An ex-Confederate, William Henry Hatch of Missouri, secured the passage of the Hatch Act of 1887 embodying the ideas of Seaman Knapp for federal aid to state agricultural experiment stations.

Successful European applications of the experiment station idea influenced its adoption here. The stations issued bulletins publicizing the results of animal nutrition studies, introduced new crops, and experimented with the insecticides best adapted to the region. They also acted as guardians of the farmers' interest in exposing frauds in commercial fertilizers, quack medicines for cattle, adulterated foods, and inefficient creamery equipment.

In the field of agricultural extension work a prominent place belongs to the Farmers' Institutes, which were modelled after the pattern of teachers' institutes. During the 1880's and thereafter these rural institutes brought to the isolated farmer the scientific benefits of the agricultural colleges, farm boards, agricultural societies, farm periodicals, and the experiment stations. Sessions lasting from two to four days were held each winter, usually under the sponsorship of a county agricultural society, with expert lectures on farming and home economics alternating with a well-rounded rural entertainment program. The entire family arrived in the buggy to enjoy the dramatics, music, refreshments, and speeches of the participants. To encourage community participation in the discussions, a "question box" was put up for interested persons. As one federal government expert put it, "All persons in attendance, the humblest as well as the most prominent, are urged to ask questions upon points suggested in the address and to present related facts gained from personal experience."

The Farmers' Institutes were eventually absorbed by the agencies set up by the Smith-Lever Act of 1914. Under this federal grant-in-aid system, county agents continued the functions of the Institute lecturers in bringing to the rural communities the best of agricultural science. In addition, the Smith-Lever Act financed the agricultural extension work done by the boys' and girls' farm clubs that had come into prominence after 1900. The best-known of these groups were the 4-H Clubs—signifying the development of "head, heart, health, and hands." They were proud to exhibit their choice corn or the things they made in home economics classes. The 4-H Clubs, organized on a state-wide and a local level, encouraged the children to have a good time and to work competitively at their projects.

5

To a large extent the numerous farm services offered by the federal and state governments after the Civil War grew out of similar educational and research functions of the agricultural society. "The agricultural societies," writes Professor Wayne C. Neely, "were the predominant form of association among American farmers of the middle nineteenth century." Nearly every state and county had its agricultural society and sometimes a horticultural society as well. According to an incomplete list of the Department of Agriculture, there were 1367 state, district, county, and township agricultural societies in 1868. Most of them were north of the Mason and Dixon line and were particularly strong in the Middle West. These societies had roots in the English agricultural science of the seventeenth and eighteenth centuries. In colonial America their vogue had been confined to well-to-do gentleman farmers. The era of the common man had popularized the agricultural society and made its activities more understandable to the unlettered farmer. The societies conducted farming experiments, debated new methods, and often published their results in formal "transactions" or in newspapers.

The democratization of the agricultural society led to many new functions for the traditional agricultural fairs. In this annual farm show sponsored by the local society, all farmers, not merely the erudite ones, could easily participate. Farmers were usually glad to compete with their fellows for prizes on the best crops, the best cattle, the fastest horses, or the handiwork of their wives. In this agricultural fair, which reached its golden age by 1850, there was no place for the ivory tower of book farming, which practical agriculturalists have usually detested. Just as the farmers were encouraged to speak up for their pet ideas in the Farmers' Institutes, so they had every incentive at the fairs to parade the results of their knowledge as well as their toil.

Gradually, the horse race stole attention away from the other exhibits. In the Iowa county fair of the 1870's Hamlin Garland and his younger contemporaries enjoyed the horse races most. "Our survey of fat sheep, broad-backed bulls and shining colts was a duty, but to cheer Huckleberry at the home stretch was a privilege." There was also a fascinating "midway" of sophisticated concessionaires of all kinds including patent medicine shows, snake oil exhibits, sledge-hammer contests, and an array of refreshment booths. Baseball became one of the leading fair attractions both North and South after the Civil War. Among the less publicized elements in the fair were enterprising pickpockets, confidence men, and loose women. By the twentieth century the urban influence had so raised the sophistication of the county and state fairs that they came to bear a strong resemblance to city amusement parks. As early as 1888 the *Cultivator and Country Gentleman* (as quoted by Wayne C. Neely) was able to give this report of the Rhode Island State Fair:

He [the farmer] has seen a "grand tournament" of bicycles, a balloon ascension, "a young and handsome couple" married in the balloon and sent off in it, polo games, steeple chasing, football match and racing by wheelbarrows, greased poles, sacks and horses.

Professional horse racing, control by jockey clubs, and the rise of specialized fair managers marked the commercialization of the agricultural fair. The state fair, particularly, emerged as a permanent group of buildings and exhibits involving hundreds of thousands of dollars annually in governmental and private expenditures. Metal structures replaced the tents and crude cattle pens of old. But the educational aspects of the fair did not disappear. Many of these aspects were transferred to specialized livestock, horticultural, and poultry shows, which have continued to be held ever since that time.

6

The little red schoolhouse with its half-educated schoolmaster or schoolmarm stubbornly resisted urban and vocational influences, but important concessions were made long before this era ended. When a former Indiana schoolmaster, Edward Eggleston, published *The Hoosier Schoolmaster* in 1871, native Hoosiers denounced this as a libel on their civilization. Eggleston had drawn on his own teaching experiences and those of his brother, George Cary, during the 1850's, but he reassured his readers that the crudities of the Flat Creek school were a thing of the past. Indiana, in fact, could boast in 1871 of a permanent school fund (including congressional land grants) of nearly nine million dollars and of a school year that averaged 129 days of actual operation. Illiteracy had been almost conquered. Indiana's school system involved the segregation of Negroes, as in the schools of the South, but so did many other public school districts in the North. As for the overgrown school bullies who threatened to beat up mild teachers like Ralph Hartsook, they seemed to have toned down. However, the local merchants who held the fate of the rural schoolmasters in their hands and imposed their own brand of religious or economic orthodoxy upon them were far from extinct in most states.

At the time Eggleston's book was on its way to popularity, the Garland children were attending a desolate schoolhouse in Iowa with a most drab interior of rough plastered walls. The room was usually too hot or too cold. In winter the girls often sat on their feet to keep warm, and small children were privileged to sit near the square stove whose slender legs rested daintily on a pile of bricks. Older communities in the East and Middle West, however, had already built much better schools than this frontier building. After all, the schoolhouse also served as a center for adult community festivities, as a meeting place for Grangers, Populists, and Chautauqua literary societies, and as a revivalist tabernacle.

The schoolteacher had to cope with the arduous task of teaching ungraded classes. This meant going back and forth, practically in tutorial fashion, among children of different educational levels and spending ten or fifteen minutes with each group on an assignment. Illinois, one of the most progressive states in 1900, paid male teachers an average of $60.34 a month and women $52.45. Most schoolmasters gave up this thankless, badly paid profession in which their social status was hardly above that of a hired hand. Long before 1900 the schoolmarms outnumbered the men in the rural schools and the feminine monopoly of elementary school teaching was almost complete by World War I. High schools and short-term normal schools continued to grind out a quota of women teachers who usually quit after four or five years. However, this trend toward women teaching was also true of city schools; the urban systems, too, failed to compensate family men adequately.

As late as 1910, Ellwood P. Cubberley, the historian of American schools, could write for the *Cyclopedia of Education:* "The country school . . . has made little progress beyond where it was a generation ago." Yet he quickly qualified this by pointing out how many states had already graded their schools, standardized their textbooks, and stabilized the course of study. He also emphasized the significance of the growing movement for modern consolidated schools. Beginning in 1889, Massachusetts and Connecticut awakened a general movement to unite several school districts into a central consolidated district in which a well-heated, comfortable school building of three or four rooms could house the pupils of the larger area. Wagons and, later, school buses and interurban trolley cars carried the children of the outlying neighborhoods to school. Roads were improved to accommodate these vehicles. The Middle West, Indiana particularly, quickly followed the leadership of New England in establishing consolidated schools. Only the South lagged behind by making no legislative provision for either consolidation or state funds for school transportation. The new regime usually meant better-paid and better-trained teachers, up-to-date equipment, and a thoroughly graded system. But the inefficient single-room schoolhouse continued to be the norm in rural America.

Rural high schools often grew out of elementary schools simply by the process of adding advanced subjects. But as in all rural schools, growth was hampered by isolated conditions. Courses and staff were both too few. Some communities solved their problem by consolidating high-school districts. Others resigned themselves to a two-year rural program of studies. The curriculum tended to be as similar to the city courses as conditions permitted. In fact many rural parents thought of secondary education as intended to prepare youngsters for city careers.

The opening of the new century coincided with a contemporary

reassessment of rural life and a conscious effort to halt the movement to the city. In 1897, the National Educational Association Committee stressed the need for more agencies to educate rural leaders.
President Roosevelt, fearful of the decline of rural life, selected in
1908 a remarkable Country Life Commission to investigate conditions. Its members included Liberty Hyde Bailey of Cornell, Walter
Hines Page, Gifford Pinchot, and the farm editor Henry Wallace
(grandfather of Henry Agard Wallace). They declared their goal "a
new and permanent rural civilization" which would "supply the city
and metropolis with fresh blood, clean bodies, and clear brains that
can endure the strain of modern urban life." The Commission was
especially critical of the imitative tendency in rural schools:

Everywhere there is a demand that education have a relation to living,
that the schools should express daily life, and that in the rural districts
they should educate by means of agriculture and country life subjects.

Within a few years rural high schools were adding new courses
in agricultural methods, animal husbandry, dairying, horticulture,
and other farm subjects. Normal schools showed a similar tendency,
some of them even maintaining demonstration farms and large experimental plots of land. By the end of this era the normal schools
were adding curricula designed specifically for rural teachers. Rural
pressure was responsible for the addition of courses on "nature"
to the public school curriculum, even in the cities.

7

Not least among rural educational institutions (and to some extent urban as well) was the Chautauqua. This was founded in 1874
in Western New York by a Methodist Episcopal clergyman, John
Heyl Vincent, who had been an innovator in Sunday school teaching methods. In fact, Chautauqua grew out of a Sunday school
teachers' assembly in which several evangelical groups joined. Both
Professor William R. Harper, later president of the University of
Chicago, and his colleague Shailer Mathews added the idealism of
the social gospel to the program of Bible studies,—Hebrew, Greek,

and history—which they directed. Chautauqua devoted many sessions to labor problems, the emancipation of women, social service, religious themes, the peace movement, the creative arts and crafts, and a variety of other literary, religious, and scientific topics. In the crafts program there was the esthetic influence of William Morris, the English advocate of an individualistic kind of socialism. Morris had been shocked by the totalitarian features of Bellamy's socialistic state. He stressed the handicraft ideal of the Middle Ages as a guide to creative self-expression and better living conditions.

Edward Eggleston was a friend of Bishop Vincent and the editor of the *Sunday School Teacher,* a major religious publication. In 1893 he was invited to appear at Lake Chautauqua and felt overwhelmed by the atmosphere of a social and intellectual beehive in this attractive watering place. He watched the bands and processions, the cavalcade of students at the lectures, and the romantic affairs of young couples. Half-seriously, he jotted down his impressions:

You can learn Greek, Latin, Hebrew and for aught I know Choctaw here. You can learn "Americanized Delsarte" and Penmanship and Pedagogy and Exegetics and Homiletics and History and Rowing and Piano Music and fancy bicycling and singing and athletics and how to read a hymn in public and the art of writing family and Business letters and everything else except dancing and whist.

Most rural folk were scarcely likely to know what was going on at Lake Chautauqua, but they became well acquainted with the "traveling Chautauqua." In the summer of 1904 Chautauqua introduced a circuit system of activities among villages and towns of 500 to 10,000 people. These programs usually lasted less than a week and were given in circus tents. Lecturers dealt with public health or social and literary topics. A traveling troupe brought the drama to people who had few occasions to see a play. The Chautauqua band lent an air of excitement to the proceedings while entertainers of all sorts absorbed the attention of the spectators. By 1912, according to John Noffsinger, there were six Middlewestern states with a total of 600 such Chautauquas. Millions of spectators in that generation came to attend this exciting affair. Eventually, the traveling Chautauqua evolved into a tinselled commercialized show with certain features of the city amusement park.

Another offshoot of Chautauqua was the network of summer camps all over the country in which middle-class citizens combined intellectual pursuits with the pleasures of vacationing in a scenic environment. Such summer camps as the one at Boulder, Colorado, were the forerunners of the present-day college summer schools. Still another Chautauqua outgrowth, according to Noffsinger, was the modern correspondence school. This grew out of the desire of many summer school students to continue their studies at home during the winter months. Chautauqua had to develop its own textbooks and methods to serve the extension students. Many villages and towns also had their local society of the Chautauqua Literary and Scientific Circle, which was originated in 1878 and spread even to England. These societies continued the antebellum tradition of self-culture that had been so successfully realized in the lyceum. The members usually met in the schoolhouse.

8

In this era, as in the earlier part of the nineteenth century, the farmer liked to subscribe to an agricultural periodical such as the *American Agriculturist,* the *Rural New Yorker,* and the *Cultivator and Country Gentleman.* There was a tendency at this time to devote space to stories and sketches as well as to instructive articles and advertisements. Iowa had an outstanding farm journal in *The Iowa Homestead,* edited by the Wallaces. Old "Uncle" Henry himself was the owner of a thousand-acre farm, but he could champion the woes of the small farmer—up to a point. In 1896 he voted for McKinley rather than the Populist-Democratic standard-bearer, Bryan.

The Garlands subscribed to Edward Eggleston's *Hearth and Home,* published in New York city. It was in this journal that young Hamlin first read with delight the serial form of *The Hoosier Schoolmaster.* The chief "high class" periodicals they knew were *Godey's*

Lady's Book and *Peterson's Magazine*. Richard Garland liked to read the humorous dialect of Petroleum V. Nasby (David Ross Locke) in the *Toledo Blade,* and to take the political advice of Horace Greeley in the *New York Tribune*. Like other farmers, he bought an almanac regularly. Hamlin and the other boys preferred to read and to trade the exciting dime novels issued by Beadle and Company until 1889. Already in the seventies, Beadle's detective stories like *Old Sleuth* were competing with the frontier heroes in the affections of these Iowa children.

Libraries could scarcely flourish in isolated farm communities but in 1890 began the significant traveling library. Melvil Dewey, New York's state librarian, who is best remembered for his "Dewey Decimal System," introduced the idea of an extension library organization. He lent books to existing rural libraries, local Granges, and farmers' reading clubs. Illinois made the traveling library part of the Farmers' Institutes. Although most of the books were of a light character, a substantial part consisted of tomes on scientific farming. Such technical books usually made up the collections of the agricultural experiment station. In the past, agricultural societies had been the most active in building specialized libraries. In this era, the agricultural universities, like Cornell, Michigan, and Massachusetts, led the way and usually welcomed farmers who came to use their books.

The farmer's sons with literary gifts, like Eggleston and Garland, had to go to the cities where publishing opportunities existed. In New York, Eggleston became a pioneer exponent of rural dialect in literature. He had been influenced by Bret Harte and strongly encouraged by the author of the *Bigelow Papers,* James Russell Lowell. Interested since his youth in studying Hoosier dialect and folkways, he found it easy to agree with Taine that the original artist must work with the materials he finds in his own environment. Eggleston's own background as a Minnesota circuit rider, a Hoosier schoolmaster, and a Sunday school teacher gave his writing a strong saccharine flavor, too often of an exhortatory religious type. He prided himself on the "provincial realism" of his crude characters and drew some of his chief incidents, such as the night robbery by a respectable doctor and his gang, from actual experience. However, characters like the tearful youngster, Shocky, have scarcely existed at any time upon this earth—except in a somewhat more credible form in *Oliver Twist* or *Nicholas Nickleby.* This was still the era of literary romanticism.

Much more realistic was Eggleston's mastery of Hoosier speech, which he defined in 1892 as "the folk speech of the southern part of Ohio, Indiana, and Illinois of forty years ago." He had first attracted Lowell's attention by his newspaper articles on Hoosier dialect. Later he noted the close relationship between the idioms and pronunciation of Scotch-Irish pioneers and those of the Hoosiers. For example, both usually said "wair" for "were" and "air" for "are." An occasional Pennsylvania German word had crept in like "smear-case" for cottage cheese.

Eggleston made little money from *The Hoosier Schoolmaster* because it was pirated outrageously by Europeans in that day before international copyright law, but he could say proudly, "It is the file-leader of the procession of American dialect novels." His later novels, such as *The Circuit Rider, Roxy,* and *The Hoosier Schoolboy,* tried to exploit the same literary vein but without artistic success. He was destined to be a man of one book. An aftermath of *The Hoosier Schoolmaster* was Eggleston's effort as a Brooklyn pastor to translate the novel's idea of a Church of the Best Licks, as suggested to Bud Means, into the euphonious Church of the Christian Endeavor. By the late 1870's Endeavor Clubs had spread from this inspiration of a creedless church, or—as one wag put it—"The First Church of the Holy Ambiguity." It seems likely that these clubs had some connection with the Christian Endeavor movement organized in 1881 by the Reverend Francis E. Clark of Portland, Maine.

In 1871, the same year that *The Hoosier Schoolmaster* appeared, another Hoosier, John Hay, put in his best licks in a group of dialect poems, *Pike County Ballads,* and stimulated others to attempt similar ventures into dialect poetry. Hay was born in Salem, Indiana, and had served as Lincoln's private secretary. Like Bret Harte, Eggleston, and hundreds of his contemporaries who chose Dickens as their model, his work was heavily sentimental and idealistic in the Sunday school manner, but he had a knack for picturing distinctive frontier types. Jim Bludso, in his *Pike County Ballads* is a tough, bigamous, blasphemous steamboat engineer, but with an extraordinary penchant for truth and self-sacrifice. He gave up his life to save the passengers trapped on his burning vessel, *The Prairie Belle*:

> He wern't no saint—but at jedgment
> I'd run my chance with Jim,
> 'Longside of some pious gentlemen
> That wouldn't shook hands with him.

In short, Jim Bludso was worthy of companionship with the most honorable cardsharps and thieves in Bret Harte's mining tales. However, John Hay married the daughter of a rich Cleveland banker, turned increasingly conservative, and showed a deep distrust of organized labor in his social novel, *The Breadwinners*. He was far more creative as a diplomat and as secretary of state under McKinley and Roosevelt.

The man who earned the title of "Hoosier poet" was James Whitcomb Riley. He was born in Greenfield, Indiana, in 1849 and as a boy wandered off to paint signs and barns for farmers, worked in a medicine show, and joined a group of strolling players. His literary career began after 1875 when he wrote verses under a pseudonym for the *Indianapolis Journal*. In 1883, he published his first book of Hoosier dialect poems, *The Old Swimmin'-Hole*. So universal was the sentimental appeal of his nostalgic poetry that he won the affection not only of countryfolk but of city people who recalled their rural youth. Children loved his *Rhymes of Childhood* (1890), especially "Little Orphant Annie" with its delightful refrain about "the Gobble-uns'll git you." His manifest sincerity endeared him to his generation who memorized "When the Frost Is on the Punkin" or "Old Schoolday Romances." Even "Gene" Debs, the Socialist candidate for the presidency five times, was sufficiently true to his Hoosier past to enjoy carousing about town with Riley. In 1915 Indiana celebrated the poet's birthday as Riley Day.

Somewhere between the older romantic writers and the younger realists was another popular Hoosier, the Indianapolis-born Booth Tarkington, who had graduated from Purdue and Princeton to become a solid businessman. In 1899, he wrote a "best-seller" in *The Gentleman from Indiana*, which dealt with an idealistic Indiana newspaper editor in a drab, backward small town. The *New York Times* recognized Tarkington's skill: "The author has produced an exceedingly strong and realistic novel of the middlewest." Even greater laurels came for *Penrod* (1914) and its sequels. These novels of adolescent life in a small town suggested Twain's stories of Tom Sawyer and Huckleberry Finn. In later novels Tarkington was definitely labeled as a cheerful interpreter of comfortable middle-class life in the half-rural towns of the Middle West. Like the romantic genre painters of the mid-nineteenth century who depicted nostalgic views of everyday life, Tarkington offered a literary counterpart of genre realism.

The Hoosier whose novels penetrated into most American homes was General Lew Wallace, the Civil War hero who wrote *The Fair God* (1873) and *Ben Hur* (1880). Though he went far afield from Indiana for his material, he offered his orthodox rural neighbors an antidote to Ingersoll's agnosticism by depicting the great spiritual victory of Christianity in a historical romance of the days of the Roman Empire. Arthur Quinn, the critic, has praised the unusual skill and painstaking effort of Wallace in portraying character, background, and nationalities; he noted that *Ben Hur* had such lasting appeal that it had sold nearly two million copies by 1933.

Much more craftsmanlike than these Hoosiers and more precise in picturing the Middle West was Willa Cather. She was born in Virginia in 1876 but was raised from childhood on a Nebraska farm near Red Cloud. There she saw the vicissitudes of farming, its droughts, storms, and "acts of God," and the drabness of farm villages. But she also felt a kinship with the inner warmth and psychological depth of her Scandinavian, German, and Bohemian neighbors whom she was to depict in *O Pioneers* (1913), *The Song of the Lark* (1915), and *My Ántonia* (1918). Though her best work was yet to come, she had already revealed her chief tendencies. Her rich sense impressions and rural background enabled her to add depth to the literary picture of the prairie country, the corn and wheatlands, but the city emerges in the more favorable light in these novels. Willa Cather was too universal in her sympathies to limit herself to the regional uniqueness of the local colorist. She took seriously the advice of the New England novelist, Sarah Orne Jewett, "One must know the world *so well* before one can know the parish."

Hamlin Garland of Wisconsin and Iowa, as we have seen, broke with the romanticists to tell the story of the prairies as realistically as he could. His rebellious attitude toward the hardships of rural life permeated his stories *Main-Travelled Roads* (1890) and such autobiographical books as his very successful *Son of the Middle Border*. He showed an excellent reportorial skill in most of his writings, though farmers challenged the fairness of his anti-rural view.

In a similar critical vein, Edgar Lee Masters, a rural Kansan who had moved to Chicago, achieved immediate fame for his sardonic verses, *Spoon River Anthology* (1915). In this poem Masters dwelt upon the hypocrisies hidden in a small community and used the device of commenting upon the graves of its local cemetery:

> I loathed you, Spoon River. I tried to rise above you,
> I was ashamed of you. I despised you
> As the place of my nativity.

He saw no culture in this rural world, though he recognized the great lonely souls, the Lincolns and Altgelds, who came from it. *Spoon River Anthology* foreshadowed the later realism of Sinclair Lewis and Sherwood Anderson in depicting the tyrannies and deceptions of small town life and the pressure for social conformity.

From 1865 to 1917 rural America went through the most revolutionary changes in history due to the dynamic pressures of urbanization. The process was often painful and aroused such revolts as those of the Grangers and the Populists. Isolation gave way to increasing integration through the telegraph, the telephone, the early automobile, and the better roads movement. New economic and cultural institutions hastened the process: land grant colleges, experiment stations, the mail-order house, rural free delivery, the parcel post system, consolidated schools, a vigorous rural press, the expanded agricultural fair, the traveling Chautauquas, and the traveling libraries. The direction of this integrating process was increasingly in the hands of the village, the town, and the city. Meanwhile, rural population poured into these urban areas. By 1920, the Census Office recorded for the first time that the population of urban America had outstripped that of rural America. A new era in American history had begun.

· 6 ·

The Urban Impact on the Home:
Era of Frances Willard

I

In 1873, the young Methodist university of Northwestern in Evanston, Illinois, gave the imposing title of professor of English, Art, and Aesthetics, and Dean of the Women's College, to a vigorous daughter of the Puritans. Dean Frances E. Willard had grown up in a strictly Methodist home, but her sensitive spirit had rebelled against her father's ironclad patriarchal ideas. She had envied the fine schooling given her brother but she had had to content herself with the third-rate education considered suitable for the delicate sex at the North Western Female College, a small school then unaffiliated with the University. Though she was a natural leader destined to devote her life to freeing women of their inferior status, she never escaped a certain timidity with men and remained a spinster—but she kept a bittersweet taste of a short-lived romance.

Higher education for women inevitably accompanied the new vocational opportunities generated by the expanding cities and the Industrial Revolution. However, most career-minded ladies of the middle class in Frances' day thought as she did that elementary school teaching was the principal vocation for their sex. Only recently, in 1867, Remington had begun to manufacture the typewriter, an invention of Christopher L. Sholes. This was to open a wide field of livelihood for women. There were jobs for women as clerks and saleswomen at Wanamaker's huge department stores and other merchandising es-

123

tablishments that had come into existence since the Civil War. As for uneducated working girls, they had never been chivalrously excluded from the hardest tasks on the farm and had long been accepted with alacrity into the first factories born of the Industrial Revolution.

Oberlin College, the militant antislavery and Congregationalist school where both parents of Frances Willard had once studied preparatory subjects, had been one of the first colleges to admit women. This precedent had been set soon after it opened its doors in 1833. The normal schools inspired by Horace Mann's leadership in Massachusetts and many new state universities were offering women more and more opportunities to study professional subjects. Mary Lyon's Mount Holyoke Female Seminary, opened in 1836, had yet to develop genuine collegiate standing, but this was not too far off. However, the new women's college of Vassar, founded in 1865, prided itself upon standards equivalent to the best in men's colleges. Such standards were also the specific aim stated by the philanthropic Sophia Smith of Massachusetts in leaving $365,000 in 1870 for Northampton's Smith College, which opened five years later. The year of that bequest, Henry F. Durant, a wealthy Harvard-trained lawyer who had turned revivalist after the death of his son, sought an identical educational goal in founding Wellesley College. Thus the most famous of the women's colleges were coming into existence at the time Miss Willard became dean of the new women's college at Northwestern. A Quaker philanthropist was yet to build Bryn Mawr College just outside of Philadelphia in 1885. By 1894, there were to be as many as 84,000 women attending colleges and normal schools, besides 163,000 girls in American high schools.

While women continued to make up the bulk of the readers of novels, particularly of the sentimental or inspirational type, there was increasing evidence of maturity in reading taste. This is illustrated by the passing of such sentimental magazines as *Godey's Lady's Book* and the *Ladies' National Magazine* in favor of the somewhat more realistic *Woman's Home Companion* (1873) and the *Ladies' Home Journal* (1883). The latter was ably edited by a Netherlands-born journalist, Edward W. Bok, who combined the tradition of orthodox morality with a lively interest in the newer civic welfare and national issues. The *Ladies' Home Journal,* which sold at ten cents a copy, was not only the most widely read woman's magazine, but it speedily became one of the most successful publications of any type in the country.

The educated middle-class woman made her influence felt publicly through a large network of women's clubs like Clio, the Wednesday Culture Club, and Sorosis. In 1868, a group of professional women organized Sorosis, in which Frances Willard became a frequent speaker, and this organization sponsored a variety of welfare and cultural activities. Sorosis and other clubs sponsored in 1889 the General Federation of Women's Clubs, which eventually went beyond its original self-imposed program for a literary, artistic, and scientific culture. Before this era ended the women's clubs were sponsoring committees on public education, home economics, child labor reforms, sex education, and feminist programs.

Women too, just like the men, organized their own fraternal and patriotic orders. Best known were the Order of the Eastern Star (1876), the Daughters of the American Revolution (1890), the Colonial Dames of America (1891), and the United Daughters of the Confederacy (1891). Frances Willard herself joined the D.A.R. as a charter member, though she remained an inactive one. The Daughters of the American Revolution included only descendants of Revolutionary ancestors, but their policies belied this radical origin. They endeavored to hasten the growth of a strong self-conscious nationalist spirit, still lacking in a young country in which one out of every seven was of foreign birth and far more were natives of foreign parentage. Their members did not always keep up with the D.A.R.'s political resolutions, but they enjoyed its social activities and the status it conferred in a land that lacked an hereditary aristocracy. In the ensuing years the D.A.R. acted as the guardian of the pure Anglo-Saxon tradition as they understood it, sponsored Americanization classes for immigrants to facilitate the melting pot process, kept a watchful eye over alleged unpatriotic passages in textbooks, and fostered a flag observance ritual. However, like many other women's organizations, the D.A.R. did not take an active part in those militant feminist causes that were close to Frances Willard's heart.

2

When Miss Willard failed in her efforts to make her Women's College relatively independent in policies, she turned in 1874 to another phase of the woman's movement, temperance and equal suffrage—"home protection," as she called it later. The very year that she left Northwestern, a remarkable phenomenon occurred. In city after city middle-class women waged a "Woman's War" by marching upon the saloons, singing hymns, praying, and pleading with saloonkeepers to give up their traffic in liquor. Wives of the most influential citizens joined this war, closing at least 3000 saloons and inflicting wholesale losses upon thousands of others. Here was the revival of the long dormant prewar temperance crusade. Frances Willard herself upon one occasion joined a woman's marching band in Pittsburgh, and for a few months in 1877 became a colleague of the noted evangelist, Dwight L. Moody, in organizing women's meetings.

Decades later, in 1899, the country was startled by the same technique, far more belligerently applied by Mrs. Carry Nation. She began her crusade to enforce the state's dry law by destroying the saloon in Medicine Lodge, Kansas. After public prayer she clutched a wildly swinging hatchet and smashed beer kegs, whisky bottles, and other saloon property until the United States and even Europe paused to listen to her propaganda for prohibition.

Frances Willard discovered her lifework in building up the Women's Christian Temperance Union, which was founded in Cleveland in 1874, the year of the Woman's War. As her meticulous biographer Dr. Mary Earhart observes, the significance of the W.C.T.U. (which became the World's W.C.T.U. in 1883) lay not only in its propaganda against intoxicating liquors but in its well-integrated state units, which could be utilized to fight for woman suffrage, labor reforms, international peace organizations, and various moral causes. The backbone of the W.C.T.U., despite its nonsectarian philosophy, was the church, particularly the Methodist organization; in fact, Methodist Evanston became its headquarters.

Miss Willard's "white-ribboned women" enlarged the scope of the antebellum temperance movement and the earlier Daughters of Temperance, by going beyond moral suasion and legislative lobbying to a broad strategic attack on many fronts. One of the best weapons of the W.C.T.U. in combatting alcoholism was to persuade most states to make temperance instruction compulsory in the public schools. Public opinion had turned against the distilleries during the Whisky Ring scandals of Grant's second term, which revealed criminal collusion between federal officials, including the President's personal secretary, and the St. Louis liquor interests (among others) to defraud the Treasury of considerable internal revenue. In this early liberal phase of the temperance movement, it was widely believed that the saloon was the chief cause of poverty, the broken home, and corruption in politics. Nationality conflicts also played a role. Dry nativists attacked "wet" German and Irish immigrants on the liquor and Sabbath issues, with the newcomers professing to see a basic issue of liberty involved that was no less important than the principles of 1776.

The all-shattering prohibition offensive came with the powerful Anti-Saloon League, founded by an alliance of temperance societies and church groups at Oberlin, Ohio, in 1893. The League sent out hundreds of agents to attack liquor as the chief foe of the American family. They acquired an enviable mastery of pressure politics in state affairs where they obtained the passage of local option laws or state-wide prohibition. At Washington, the Anti-Saloon League became a powerful lobby, which pressed congressmen to initiate the passage of the Eighteenth Amendment.

Behind the League's agents was the dry sentiment of fundamentalist rural America, besides the important work carried on by feminist allies in the cities. World War I caught the city "wets" off guard and demoralized the distillery and saloon lobby, so much of which was tarred with the brush of German ownership. In the rural South the "drys" used the race issue as a prohibition argument to keep liquor from the Negroes. Wherever the strict evangelical churches were in the saddle, there prohibition had its most belligerent advocates. But even before 1919, when the Eighteenth Amendment was passed forbidding the manufacture, sale, or transportation of intoxicating liquors, many social scientists had begun to consider alcoholism as more often the product rather than the cause of poverty, family disorganization, and mental breakdowns. The desertion of liberals from the prohibitionist ranks left them a far more conservative group than the early followers of Frances Willard.

3

Miss Willard's role in promoting woman suffrage has been almost buried in the history of the temperance movement. The ante-bellum leaders, Susan B. Anthony, Lucy Stone, Elizabeth Cady Stanton, and Wendell Phillips, were not only alive but dominated the emancipation movement with all the weapons of publicity and military organization. Yet Miss Anthony did not underrate the clever strategy of the W.C.T.U. leader and the advantages of working for suffrage within well-organized state and local units. In fact, Miss Willard brought the progressive temper of the organized western feminist movement into a cause that seemed to be turning conservative under the influence of the Eastern organizations. Susan B. Anthony concentrated upon her efforts to convert Congress into initiating a "Sixteenth" Amendment for woman suffrage, but did not live long enough to enjoy victory in 1920, when the Nineteenth Amendment, known as the Susan B. Anthony Amendment, was passed. She came to appreciate increasingly the work of Miss Willard in winning the vote for women in municipal and school elections.

Still, while the head of the W.C.T.U. could hold her followers only by insisting publicly that the vote was a necessary preliminary to the successful drive against "grogshops," the Anthony-Stanton leaders did not conceal their steadfast desire for more far-reaching objectives. They wished the suffrage for both Negroes and women, the protection of women's rights in marriage, the opening of more professions and trades to women, and "equal pay for equal work." This group had patiently suspended their suffragette activities until the Negro had been freed and had been given the vote and civil liberties by the Thirteenth, Fourteenth, and Fifteenth Amendments. The less patient Miss Anthony had been indicted when she insisted on voting under the Fourteenth Amendment. A federal Court in *United States v. Anthony* decided that the states would have to pass specific suffrage legislation before this right could be granted.

The suffragettes gained victory after victory on various fronts, aided by the Grangers, Populists, and labor leaders. A basic factor was the rapid increase of jobs for women, amounting to a *de facto* form of female emancipation. Even the conservative Southern states dropped their severe restrictions upon remarriage after divorce. In 1882, New York courts allowed married women wider rights of property ownership and declared that wives might sue their husbands for damages in the event of brutality. In the progressive decades before World War I wives were conceded in three-fourths of the states their right to own and to control their personal property; two-thirds of the states permitted wives to retain their earnings; and in most states courts allowed wives to sue and to make contracts.

As for the ballot itself, unsympathetic legislators at the state capitols and in Congress found it expedient to yield after the suffragettes had won equal suffrage in numerous localities. Between 1869 and 1900 progressive Western legislatures in Wyoming, Idaho, Colorado, and Utah granted women the right to vote; and before World War I began, eleven states were in the feminist column.

The woman suffrage movement, it must be recalled, was part of a trend common to all countries experiencing the Industrial Revolution and its consequent process of urbanization. It became a literary issue through the much-discussed play of Henrik Ibsen, *A Doll's House* (1879), in which the rebellion of Nora in a man-made society is the leading theme. In most western countries the liberal parties championed the suffragettes. Finland accepted woman suffrage in 1906, Ibsen's Norway in 1913, and Denmark in 1915. The English suffragettes of the twentieth century were far more militant than their American sisters. Before the men decided that they had had enough, the followers of Emmeline Pankhurst and her daughter Christabel had marched in belligerent mass demonstrations, staged hunger strikes, burnt property, smashed windows, and heckled their opponents mercilessly. By 1907, they had won the vote in local British

elections and, a decade later, after women had contributed heavily
to the war effort, older women received the ballot nationally; but not
until 1928 was their aim completely realized.

4

Frances Willard's white-ribboned women devoted a considerable
part of their energies, in common with other feminist reformers like
Susan B. Anthony and Elizabeth Cady Stanton, to destroying the
double standard of morality for the sexes. The campaign for sex purity
was not merely an expression of Victorianism, but was another facet
of the struggle for woman's emancipation. The notion that men had
an exclusive right to sow wild oats had been reaffirmed by social
theorists—male of course—from Montesquieu to James Kent. The
noted New York chancellor cited numerous jurists for the opinion
that the adultery committed by a husband "ought not to be noticed
or made subject to the same animadversions as that of the wife."
While feminists attacked the double standard of morality affecting
marriage and divorce laws, the W.C.T.U. stressed sexual purity. They
widely publicized assault cases in the press and when alleged seduc-
ers or rapists were on trial, Frances Willard's ladies appeared in court
to see that the way of the transgressor was duly hard. To shield
feminine morality and to protect the modesty of the woman prisoner,
the W.C.T.U. introduced the policewoman and the matron. Unmarried mothers and prostitutes were rehabilitated in "rescue homes"
created by the temperance women or the Salvation Army.

While the W.C.T.U. kept the control of their movement in the hands
of women, the older feminist groups were frequently embarrassed by
the eccentricities of certain male allies like Henry Ward Beecher,
organizer of the Equal Rights Association. In 1874, during the very
year that the W.C.T.U. was formed, Theodore Tilton, a journalist-
reformer, brought a suit for $100,000 damages against Beecher for
committing adultery with his wife, Mrs. Elizabeth Tilton. The lady
involved was chairman of the executive committee of the Equal
Rights Association and an editor of its suffrage organ, *Revolution*.
Both Elizabeth and Henry belonged at one time to the radical wing

of the feminists while Theodore Tilton himself had been a devoted
journalistic supporter of the great preacher of Plymouth Church,
Brooklyn. Actually, this talented brother of Harriet Beecher Stowe
had remarkably few abiding convictions and proved an inconstant
supporter of various reforms from abolition to female suffrage. He
loved to move his huge admiring congregation to tears with his dramatic utterances, his theatrical mannerisms, and his sonorous voice.

The Beecher affair proved a great triumph for outspoken journalism in an intimate matter hitherto bound up in the Victorian conspiracy of silence. The journalists who had done most to force Tilton to
take court action against Beecher were two remarkable if eccentric
feminists, Victoria Claflin Woodhull and her sister Tennessee Claflin,
editors of the sensational *Woodhull and Claflin's Weekly* of New
York. They led the extreme left wing of the feminists and lectured on
behalf of greater freedom for women, birth control, eugenics, and the
single moral standard for both sexes. Victoria, herself—unlike Susan
B. Anthony and certain other suffragettes—was unusually pretty. She
was a spellbinder on the lecture platform, and one of the first women
to speak out openly for scientific birth control in the interest of
eugenics, for rational sex education, and for liberal divorce laws. She
was a leader in spiritualist and mental healing circles and even campaigned to elect herself president of the United States with Frederick
Douglass, the ex-slave, as vice-president.

One of the most unrelenting foes of the Claflin sisters, especially
after their shocking Beecher articles, was the most puritanical of all
American moralists, Anthony Comstock. This son of a strict Congregationalist farmer of Connecticut always retained a humorless, fanatical
mien which his Civil War experiences may have worsened. Shortly
after the War, he gave up his drygoods business for professional
reform. In 1868, he felt attracted by the current Y.M.C.A. campaign
against obscene literature and took up their work in prosecuting
the publishers of it. He helped persuade Congress to forbid the
mailing of pornographic literature and birth control information and
was willing to serve as a special agent, even without pay, to bring up
moral questions for the Post Office during several decades until his
death in 1915. Among the institutions he founded was Boston's puri-

tanical Watch and Ward Society. His Society for the Suppression of Vice raided bookstores and even art galleries that displayed unclad figures; he hounded abortionists, gamblers, patent-medicine vendors, and artists who used nude models. His biographers, Heywood Broun and Margaret Leech, portray him as a humorless champion of youthful purity, grimly keeping count of the dozen or more charlatans that he drove to suicide.

5

The fact that divorce increased from 27 to 86 per 100,000 population during 1867–1906 arose from the rapid urbanization of the era and also reflected the liberalization of divorce laws effected by feminists like Miss Anthony and Mrs. Stanton. There were fewer than ten thousand divorces altogether in 1867, when divorce meant social ostracism. Catherine Beecher, Harriet's conservative sister, expressed a prevailing viewpoint of the 1870's when she insisted that it was sinful for a man to remarry while his first wife was still alive. By 1907, more than 72,000 divorces were granted in this country—more in fact than in the rest of the Christian world combined.

In part this trend reflected the loosening of economic and religious bonds by the secularism of the new American city and by the sharp increase in careers open to women (and their children) chafing against the restraints of unhappy marriages. The growing insistence on a single moral standard led legislatures to relax the procedural requirements to establish adultery as well as desertion and cruelty as grounds for divorce. The waiting period for divorces was usually a year, though Reno, Nevada, cut this in half by the new century. Divorces occurred most frequently in the individualistic newer sections of the country, such as the West and the large cities.

Conservative churches like the Roman Catholic and Lutheran tried to check the official divorce rate in the cities, but they could not halt the sensational increase of desertion, "the poor man's divorce," among their following. Desertion was at least four times as common as divorce and seemed to thrive in a footloose society of unemployed or migratory factory hands and broken immigrant homes.

Birth control was still another result of the individualist influence of the metropolis upon the family, particularly among the middle class. Native families in New England and the West showed the most marked decline in the average number of children. Only the huge inflow of millions of immigrants and the persistence of a large birth rate in the rural South kept population totals soaring upward from 38,558,371 in 1870 to 91,972,266 in 1910. Of course the advance made in public health by reducing the death rate was also a major factor in keeping population up. Modern cities, it became increasingly clear, did not reproduce themselves; but the constant movement of rural folk as well as immigrants to the city tended to conceal this fact. The shrinking size of middle-class families, popularly regarded as the biological source of the best national leaders, led President Theodore Roosevelt as well as other prominent men to condemn the tendency toward "race suicide."

Despite the unfavorable legal situation in the United States for birth-control advocates, a determined visiting nurse of New York's East Side, Margaret Sanger, revived the movement in 1914. She argued that the lives of many ailing mothers could be saved if the doctors were empowered to offer birth-control information and guidance. When she tried to distribute her pamphlet on birth control, *Family Limitation*, the police jailed her but only succeeded in strengthening her following. In 1914 she organized the National Birth Control League, which expanded through branches in various states. Thereafter, the movement advanced on several fronts through propaganda and legislation despite organized opposition by religious, particularly Roman Catholic, groups. Birth control, coupled with a declining death rate, was to become an increasing factor in the ever-growing proportion of elderly people in the American population.

6

Most workmen felt undecided whether to treat employed women as fellow workers or as unfair competitors. Enlightened labor leaders, like the officers of the National Labor Union in 1868, welcomed factory women into their locals. Terence Powderly, warm friend of feminism, encouraged women to organize within the Knights of

Labor, whose solidarity was expressed in the slogan, "An injury to one is an injury to all." However, it was difficult to inculcate "job consciousness" in trade union style among so many women who regarded their work as a temporary expedient until marriage brought release. In skilled fields women averaged about one-third as much pay as men, even as late as World War I. However, sufficient progress was made in organizing women to justify the formation in 1903 of the National Woman's Trade Union League to work for the ideal of "equal pay for equal work"—Miss Anthony's slogan—and for better working conditions. At the professional level, women not only completed their monopoly of elementary school teaching but won a majority of high school posts before this era ended.

Long hours and appalling conditions of factory sanitation for women and children persisted under the prevailing philosophy of laissez faire. During 1870–1900, the proportion of children working in industry and commerce sharply increased. Before the Civil War older industrial states had secured some measure of social legislation for children, but these laws were unenforced and by 1890 were largely ignored. "In most states," reported the National Consumer's League for this era, "it was not illegal to send children as young as ten or eight or seven years into a mill and keep them at work unlimited hours." A federal Senate Commission on Industrial Relations summarized the situation:

Time after time in each of these industrial states the sentiment of the public was aroused, organization was effected, and well-drafted bills were introduced only to be killed in committee, emasculated, or killed on the floor of the legislature, or passed with exceptions which rendered them entirely ineffective. Even the attempt to reduce the hours of children below twelve per day was bitterly contested and met by every known trick of legislative chicanery.

Industrial England had passed beyond this stage of laissez faire and parliamentary indifference at least a generation earlier than America; by the nineties other western European countries too, had moved ahead of this country in passing social legislation.

Although Massachusetts and New York manufacturers bowed to the popular demand for reform, Illinois industrialists combined to challenge that section of the factory law forbidding women to work more than an eight-hour day. They hailed their resounding victory in the state supreme court in *Ritchie v. Illinois* (1895). The conservative court declared that it was not impressed by the government's arguments regarding the effect of long hours upon the health of women. Instead, the judges accepted the Spencerian argument that the individual's freedom of contract, guaranteed by the Fourteenth Amendment, had been violated by the restrictions on woman's right to bargain freely for her services. The total result of the Ritchie decision was to discourage similar state laws elsewhere and to keep the United States well behind England, France, Germany, and other countries in social legislation. William T. Stead, English visiting reformer and editor of the *Review of Reviews,* made this observation in his book, *If Christ Came to Chicago:* "Legislative restrictions which even the most reactionary, hard-hearted capitalist in England admits to be indispensable for the protection of labor are unconstitutional according to the state of Illinois."

Governor Altgeld himself was defeated for re-election by special interests, while the vigorous Chief Inspector, Florence Kelley, was dismissed by the incoming governor of Illinois. The ground lost was not recovered until 1908. At that time the United States Supreme Court upheld Oregon's law of 1903 prohibiting industry to hire women for more than ten hours a day. Oregon's counsel, Louis D. Brandeis, convinced the Court, through a novel use of sociological and historical data—the method of "sociological jurisprudence"—that excessive hours had a direct bearing on the health of women and the stability of the family. Hence the state's "police power"—its right to legislate for the health, safety, morals, and well-being of its citizens—was upheld against the individualistic doctrine of "freedom of contract." Even the stubborn individualists were coming to recognize that a contract between a powerful corporation and a prospective woman employee was not one drawn up between equals and did involve paramount community interests. However, the judge made it clear that they were exempting only women from the free contract doctrine and that men still retained their "liberty" to bargain for as long a day as they chose.

7

Urbanization had its advantages as well as its drawbacks for the child. Advances in nutrition and public health did much to check disease. "The American environment," wrote Arthur Calhoun, the sociologist, in 1917, "adds height, weight, and chest girth to the progeny of European stock." Besides, the city, as compared to the farm and village, offered new opportunities for schooling and vocations. Even the sons and daughters of workingmen could look forward to entering skilled trades or well-paid professions. Rural parents often educated their children for careers in the growing cities.

But the problem of urban adjustment was indeed a serious one for children. The Industrial Revolution with its insatiable demand for labor made a mockery of compulsory school laws and child labor restrictions. Even in the Massachusetts of the elderly Emerson and Lowell, there were in 1875 over 60,000 children of school age without any schooling whatever. Juvenile delinquency grew in seriousness as a social problem. In the seventies, for example, New York city debated the question of what to do with an estimated ten thousand homeless boys who wandered about the streets and often moved in gangs and beat up policemen and poorly protected citizens. In 1890, Jacob Riis, a Danish-born journalist of New York, sardonically reported the reform of Hell's Kitchen, "The gang rarely beats a policeman nowadays and it has not killed one in a long while." Gangs usually sprouted in city slums, especially in poor immigrant neighborhoods where adolescents frequently broke from parental control and imitated the worst traits of "Americanized" youngsters. The gang, as Dr. Frederic Thrasher has shown in his book on this urban institution, became a substitute in the disorganized slum community for the home, the church, the school, and the normal channels of recreation. And, while maladjusted boys sought excitement through gang warfare according to the "code," girls turned to individual delinquency.

Prisons were schools of crime where impressionable youths sat at the feet of expert criminals. In 1877, New York State led other states in forbidding magistrates to sentence children under sixteen to jail.

At the same time, the new charter for the State Reformatory for Men at Elmira provided special incentives such as the "indeterminate sentence" for the rehabilitation of young male offenders between 16 and 30. The supervision was entrusted to a strong environmentalist, Zebulon R. Brockway, whose ideal was the "socializing of the antisocial" through physical, vocational, and military training as well as through ethical and esthetic instruction. The indeterminate sentence replaced the fixed sentence by making the exact term within a certain range of years depend upon good behavior and evidence of rehabilitation. Brockway's success in reforming youth made the Elmira experiment the model for other prisons soon thereafter. About this time, incentive systems of probation and parole (based on England's "ticket of leave") were also coming into vogue in the East.

A more positive approach to the problem of the urban delinquent based on the new mental hygiene and psychology came with the juvenile court movement and its underlying philosophy. This apparently began with Illinois' law of 1899, which offered what became in effect the basis of a new code for child offenders:

It proposes a plan whereby he may be treated, not as a criminal or one legally charged with crime, but as a ward of the State, to receive practically the care, custody, and discipline that are accorded the neglected and dependent child, and which, as the Act states, "shall approximate as nearly as may be that which should be given by its parents."

One of the most successful juvenile court judges was Ben B. Lindsey, the first head of the Denver Juvenile Court. He had long fought for honest government and anti-child-labor laws and now he set an example of informal juvenile court technique without lawyers or juries. Children were not charged with any crime but were treated by experts as immature and maladjusted individuals in whose downfall environmental conditions and inadequate parental control were responsible. This clinical approach to understanding the child's personality was strengthened after 1909 by Dr. William Healy and his Chicago associates who set up a juvenile psychopathic institute in connection with the city's juvenile court. Out of this mental hygiene emphasis grew the child guidance clinic. By 1914 there were over a hundred such clinics attached to medical schools, mental hospitals, juvenile courts, and other institutions. So successful was the entire juvenile court movement that western Europe promptly borrowed its techniques and improved them by placing less reliance upon policemen and more on social workers in the handling of children.

Another positive program was the enlightened treatment of neglected and dependent children. Rather ironically, the effective defense of mistreated children had to await the more humane treatment of animals. Henry Bergh of New York, who had founded in 1866 the Society for the Prevention of Cruelty to Animals, decided almost a decade later to sponsor the Society for the Prevention of Cruelty to Children. His society vigorously prosecuted callous parents, removed children from brutal environments, and inspired the growth of similar societies elsewhere. After 1883 a movement began in Illinois to shift dependent children from orphanages and other institutions to private foster homes at the expense and under the supervision of the state. This policy received the enthusiastic sponsorship of President Theodore Roosevelt at the White House Conference on the Care of Dependent Children. Even better than this policy of finding substitutes for the natural home was the movement led by Missouri in 1911 to provide mother's and widow's pensions to support children in their own homes. By 1913, eighteen states had passed such laws. Again, during these progressive years before World War I, President Taft's administration provided a Children's Bureau to act as a research and administrative agency in problems affecting the child; this included the formulation of juvenile court standards and scientific fact-finding regarding child labor conditions. However, the federal law of 1916 to outlaw child labor was nullified by the Supreme Court as a violation of the reserved powers of the states under the Tenth Amendment. Fortunately, many states during the progressive decade before World War I began to introduce more effective child labor laws.

City life meant a revolution in age-old patterns of play. Adults and children no longer joined in common pleasures, except as passive spectators at a commercial amusement park or at a theater. Folk games, folk dances, and husking bees belonged to a vanishing rural past. Supervision of children in crowded neighborhoods, especially when both parents might be working, was difficult. To cope with this situation, social workers and others sought to develop a new technique of supervised play. In 1885 such a group in Boston sponsored sand gardens to serve as free playgrounds for city children. This play movement evolved through a number of stages beginning with small parks, then civic art and welfare centers, and finally in 1915 as a neighborhood organization. Teamwork and interesting recreational programs according to age groups were stressed. From 1905 on, the leadership of the play movement was taken over by the Playground and Recreation Association of America, which stimulated the growth of more children's recreational centers.

British and American experience with youth activities led to a common institutional idea in the Boy Scout movement. Although Sir Robert Baden-Powell founded the Boy Scout organization in 1908 and his sister, Agnes, established the Girl Guides two years later, they had drawn partly from American and Canadian exponents of scouting and woodcraft. Best known was the naturalist and illustrator, Daniel Carter Beard, who taught city boys forest lore and love of the out-of-doors in his Sons of Daniel Boone, later known as the Boy Pioneers of America. The Boy Scouts learned good citizenship, self-reliance, and woodcraft; they were taught by their scoutmasters the techniques of lifesaving, safety-first methods, and the prevention of forest fires. They welcomed into their ranks all creeds and races, immigrants as well as natives. Despite the uniforms they wore, there was little of militarism in their indoctrination.

In 1913, Juliette Low founded the Girl Scouts of America in Savannah, Georgia. Still another girls' group was formed in 1912 by the Canadian naturalist, E. Thompson Seton and his wife and by the Luther Gulicks of the Y.M.C.A. movement. This was the Camp Fire Girls, devoted to "home craft, health craft, hand craft, nature lore, and citizenship." Small children of eight to ten years were organized into an auxiliary group of Blue Birds. Indian names, symbols, and ceremonials gave color to the activities of the Camp Fire Girls and the Blue Birds.

8

The complex needs of the factory and office led to the teaching of
more and more vocational subjects in the schools, a longer period of
education, and a practical shop apprenticeship. Opponents of the
classical ideal in education, especially after 1890, cited Herbart and
other German educators as authority for the belief that the curriculum must emphasize the problems of the everyday world and hence
one must make room for such practical subjects as manual training,
domestic arts and science, typewriting, and economics. By the end of
the century, educators were challenging the prevailing idea that the
purpose of the school was disciplinary, that is, it must train the "powers of the mind." Thorndike of Columbia emphatically denied the validity of any transfer of training from one subject to another except
for "identical elements." His theory encouraged vocational tendencies
by stressing specific skills rather than by assuming that a broad education in a few academic subjects was beneficial and pervasive.

Competing, and sometimes compromising, with the vocational ideas
was the historic progressive tradition of Rousseau as developed by
Froebel, Bronson Alcott, George Bancroft, and finally, John Dewey.
These men rebelled against learning by rote and fostered the movement to adapt the subject-matter to the everyday needs of the child.
Froebel, the founder of the kindergarten, believed that the child must
learn through self-activity, not by memorization and drill, in order to
understand his role in the family and society. The educator must
arouse this voluntary activity by planning games requiring both manual and intellectual facility. Thus in the words popularized by Dewey,
the child would be "learning by doing." Froebel's kindergarten, although introduced to this country before the Civil War, made rapid
progress after 1873, the year that the German Froebel Alliance was
formed in Prussia to spread these ideas. Unlike Western Europe, the
United States integrated the kindergarten into its public school system and its progressive ideals were expected to permeate the school
from the lowest grade upwards. In 1873, Dr. William T. Harris, the
superintendent of the St. Louis public schools, made his system the

first to adopt the kindergarten. Born in Connecticut, he had been reared during the years of New England's crusade for public schools and later studied idealistic philosophy and pedagogy in Germany, as did so many other educators of this era.

Harris was also a leader in the manual training movement of the 1880's. Theoretically, the emphasis upon handwork was a logical application of Froebel's idea of learning by doing, for the progressive educators believed in practical activities as a natural aid for the child to understand and appreciate his society and civilization. However, Harris and too many other educators were led astray by their enthusiasm for vocational education and glorified machine culture and big business. Shopwork invaded the high schools during the eighties and soon captured the elementary grades as well. One after another, as pressure groups dictated, vocational subjects were required, such as domestic science for girls, drawing, agriculture, and applied sciences. Commercial subjects were quickly added.

Vocationalism was nationally organized in 1906 with the formation of the National Society for the Promotion of Industrial Education. Finally, this agitation culminated in the Smith-Hughes Act of 1917, a generous grant-in-aid system by which the federal government cooperated with the states in subsidizing classes in commerce, industry, agriculture, trades, and home economics. Already a vocational guidance movement had begun in 1908 under Professor Frank Parsons of Boston University and was being taken up by the settlement houses.

Urban-industrial pressures encouraged an enlarged curriculum. The public school curriculum expanded until the high school, newly extended to four years, overflowed into the junior college. By 1900, the taxpayers were spending $250,000,000 for public education and $445,000,000 ten years later. In 1870, there were about 500 high schools in the entire nation; by 1915, there were 11,674. The proportion of children of high school age that actually attended was only 2 per cent in 1870 and 20 per cent in 1915. These figures also reflected the victory for free tax-supported secondary schools that had been won by the Kalamazoo decision, which upheld the levying of taxes for such purposes. Greek disappeared from a curriculum originally designed to be a simplified version of the college liberal arts program. However, Latin fought a major rear guard action well beyond this era. The high school, it was tacitly agreed, must serve the demands of college entrance requirements, not merely the needs of those who did not intend to go any farther.

American enthusiasm for mass education was also reflected in the rapid growth of the free tax-supported public library. This development was aided greatly by the volunteer efforts of the American Library Association (1876). Progressive librarians by the end of this era were attempting to raise the mission of libraries from being mere custodians of books to being active agencies of learning. In 1890, the Brookline (Mass.) Public Library introduced a separate children's reading room to serve the special interests of juveniles. After 1905, schools began to build their own school libraries as a part of their program.

9

For the laboring classes, especially among the new immigrants, the worst blight on family life was incredibly bad housing, typified in New York city by the crowded tenement. "The tenements today are New York," wrote Jacob Riis in *How the Other Half Lives* (1890), "harboring three-fourths of the population." The tenement was not a new fixture in urban life. Elderly people of the antebellum generation recalled the frequent fires that used to break out in such firetraps, the murderous rodents that killed babies in their cribs, the dank, smelly cellar that served as an apartment for several families, and the dark windowless interior rooms. For all this, the wretched families had paid high rents to indifferent absentee landlords whose property rights were scrupulously protected by Tammany or other political organizations. Immigrant crowding made the situation unique, although European industrial cities that lacked substantial foreign immigration had similar housing problems of their own. The prevailing spirit of laissez faire hampered reformers everywhere. Only after the terrible cholera epidemic following the Civil War, which carried off thousands in the already blighted East Side, was the Tenement House Act of 1867 passed. As a result, officials compelled the landlords to introduce air shafts and interior windows for ventilation and closed thousands of cellars as unfit for human habitation.

But crowding remained and mortality was fearfully high. In 1880, New York city, with a population of 1,206,299, had a death rate of 25.19 per thousand, and an average of 16 people to a dwelling place. London, a far larger city in comparison, with a population of 3,816,483, recorded a death rate of 21.3 per thousand and averaged less than 8 persons to a dwelling place. Riis describes the typical tenement that he knew in 1890:

It is generally a brick building from four to six stories high on the street, frequently with a store on the first floor which, when used for the sale of liquor, has a side opening for the benefit of the inmates and to evade the Sunday law; four families occupy each floor, and a set of rooms consists of one or two dark closets, used as bedrooms, with a living room twelve feet by ten. The staircase is too often a dark well in the centre of the house, and no direct through ventilation is possible, each family being separated from the other by partitions.

To make matters worse, the immigrant families of New York often converted their apartments into sweatshops where garments or cigars were manufactured amid the most unsanitary conditions. Florence Kelley reported similar conditions in Chicago in 1895. The custom of taking in boarders added to the congestion. Middle-class European visitors were frequently shocked by the housing situation. Little wonder that the English novelist and Fabian Socialist, H. G. Wells, severely condemned the laissez-faire spirit after his visit of 1906.

On the other hand, it is easy to overdo this picture of squalor for all cities. James Bryce, the distinguished Scottish historian and lawyer, who spent considerable time in American cities during the 1880's, thought that the American city, outside of a few like New York, was very attractive by European standards. "In cities like Cleveland or Chicago," he wrote in The American Commonwealth (1888), "one finds miles on miles of suburbs filled with neat wooden houses, each with its tiny garden plot, owned by the shop assistants and handicraftsmen who return on the horse cars in the evening from their work." In the West, living conditions appeared far better than in most European towns.

10

Despite the Tweeds and their imitators in public life, the cities managed to succeed to a gratifying extent in bringing the benefits of the public health movement to their citizens. This was originally a British movement inspired by Edwin Chadwick who had published an epochal investigation in 1842, *Report on the Sanitary Condition of the Labouring Population of Great Britain*. Chadwick had tried to show to what extent disease and filth were factors in producing poverty. Once the germ theory of disease was firmly established by Pasteur and Koch, the sanitary principles of Chadwick swept city after city throughout the western world. By 1900 municipal authorities in this country had gone far in wiping out the tragic epidemics wrought by cholera, typhoid, scarlet fever, and diphtheria. To combat these diseases, doctors and social workers resorted to a new policy of preventive medicine. Thus the National Tuberculosis Association was formed in 1904 to eliminate sources of infection and to suggest means of increasing individual resistance to disease.

One may say without exaggeration that the new scientific principles of the urban age led to a genuine revolution in public health. The story of rapid improvements in urban water supplies (chlorination of water began in 1908) and waste disposal and the numerous municipal agencies for combatting infant mortality illustrate this amazing progress. Pasteurized milk stations, visiting nurses, clinics, dispensaries, and public education in hygiene were all part of this development, especially after 1900. In that year there were 150 clinics of all types in the country—a modest figure, it is true, by later standards.

The record of nursing alone constitutes a major chapter in the history of the public health movement. Dorothea Dix and her hastily-trained Civil War nurses were only the modest precursors of the scientifically educated nurses turned out by the new Johns Hopkins School of Nursing and others. The techniques and principles of Florence Nightingale and the British Sanitary Commission inspired numerous British and American hospitals after the 1860's to adopt modern standardized procedures of nursing. In 1893, Lillian Wald established the famous Nurses' Settlement on Henry Street, New York, to bring the benefits of public health nursing to an entire neighborhood, thus ending the aloofness of the visiting nurse system. Public health nurses offered an organized community service to prevent disease as well as to help the sick; this meant an increasing emphasis upon community health education.

City advantages in transportation made possible a healthful diversity of diet that had been lacking in rural America. After the seventies the urban diet included many more vegetables, fruits, salads, and fresh fish. Although unscrupulous manufacturers adulterated many commercially prepared foods, the new age of analytical chemistry made these tricks easy to detect. Just before World War I chemists began a revolution in the field of nutrition by the discovery of vitamins. Hitherto nutritionists had concentrated on the caloric (or energy-producing) value of the various foods; but just before the nineteenth century ended, European chemists discovered that diet deficiencies were a far more complex matter than the simple counting of calories. In 1912, Elmer V. McCollum of Yale identified Vitamin A as a fat-soluble found in butterfat, egg yolk, lettuce leaves, and in certain other foods. This vitamin was important in the growth of children and young animals, and especially in the development of healthy teeth. Discoveries of other vitamins followed during the succeeding decades, thus adding an entirely new approach to the problem of physical and even mental health.

The laissez-faire principle of "Let the buyer beware" received repeated setbacks in the sale and manufacture of foods and drugs. Some protection against spoiled meat and milk was attained in the 1870's through the various city boards of health that had come into existence. A major victory over laissez faire was gained by the well-organized lobby of dairymen who struck hard at oleomargarine competition in 1886 by securing in the Oleomargarine Act the first federal law on adulterants. Congress was also compelled, despite the bitter resistance of food processors, to do something about food adulteration after a dozen countries banned the importation of pork products and certain other foods. In the Department of Agriculture, Harvey Wiley, chief of the Bureau of Chemistry, set his famous

Poison Squad to work upon food and drug adulterants and publicized the need for effective national legislation.

The "embalmed beef" scandal, involving the alleged sale of chem-
ically-treated, partly-decomposed meat to the American soldiers in
Cuba during the Spanish-American War, shook public confidence in
the meat-packing industry. Muckrakers like Samuel Hopkins Adams
publicized the flagrant abuses in patent medicines. Unwittingly,
mothers quieted their babies with medicines containing morphine or
other opiates. Consumptives relied upon impressively colored medicines that were no more than unadulterated alcohol. The final jar to
confidence in the probity of the Beef Trust came in 1906 with the publication of Upton Sinclair's novel, *The Jungle.* His revelations of filth
and carelessness in the preparation of meat products were enough
to discourage many from buying them; federal investigators did
not think that Sinclair's picture was wholly exaggerated. As a result, the Meat Inspection Act and the Pure Food and Drug Act were
both quickly passed that same year. The latter forbade the shipment
in interstate or foreign trade of adulterated or misbranded goods.
The control of purely intrastate products was still left to the states,
many of which had failed to provide any enforcement for their
health laws. However, these pioneer laws of 1906 against food and
drug abuses were fundamental as a real beginning in the protection
of the consumer's health and eventually led to far more effective
laws.

By 1917, it is clear, the urban impact on the home had gone far
in disintegrating the patriarchal family. The economic opportunities
afforded by the increasing division of labor, the invention of the
typewriter, and the new department stores and offices fostered the
"emancipated woman." Women's colleges offered advanced training, trade unions absorbed some of the female workers, and women's
clubs acted as channels of reform and social protest. City life and
laborsaving inventions made the home a more individualistic institution, in which the common bond was less economical or religious
and more affectional in nature. Birth control limited the size of the
middle-class family, thereby releasing many of the energies of

women from the raising of large families, while divorce released them from unwanted marriages.

Emancipation was further reflected in the battle against the double standard and the passage of feminist laws protecting woman's rights in marriage and divorce. Organized women, led by Frances Willard, fought the saloon as the key to poverty, broken homes, and immorality, and campaigned for the right to vote as an essential prerequisite to further reforms. Settlement-house leaders like Jane Addams, Florence Kelley, and Lillian Wald played a large role in eliminating tenement house abuses, in promoting the public health movement, and in pushing social legislation for women and children in industry. Such accomplishments had to be made in the face of the worst era of political corruption in American history—an urban era in which social dislocation and unassimilated city peoples helped break down the traditional values of a rural society.

· 7 ·

Urbanism and the Church: From
Beecher to Rauschenbusch

[1865-1917]

I

THE growth of the metropolis, with all that it implied in secularism
and anti-traditionalism, gave the churches the greatest challenge in
their history. Yet the foreign visitor was impressed by all the ex-
ternal signs of the majestic victory of religion in America between
Appomattox and Sarajevo. Never had the urban churches, enriched
by the captains of industry, been so crowded; if the modern Gothic
buildings with their expensive organs did not outshine the art of
the medieval cathedrals, it was not for lack of money; and never
before had theological schools, Sunday schools, missions, and church
charities attained such dimensions and prosperity in this country.
Church attendance figures soared in geometrical ratio, despite the
secular world of Charles Darwin, Robert Ingersoll, and Jacques
Loeb.

The shift of immigration sources in this era from Northwestern
Europe, where Protestants predominated, to Southeastern Europe,
with its huge Catholic and Jewish elements, gave the metropolis a
large non-Protestant quality.

Catholics and Protestants, Jews and Gentiles, believers and atheists rubbed shoulders in an intimacy foreign to rural society. If the
Utopian religious cultists of the mid-century had been unable to

148

shield their followers from error through isolated settlements, how could each urban church retain its unique doctrinal differences when denominational intermarriages daily reflected biological rather than religious promptings? *Interdenominationalism* of the Y.M.C.A. type was inevitable under these circumstances.

In the rootless industrial city, workingmen built their dingy homes around their workplaces and factories. They had little leisure left for church affairs. Low wages, sickness, and joblessness were apt to be more real than the fires of hell and the bliss of eternal salvation. Drink, gambling, and prostitution flourished in this environment. To the perplexed, socialism seemed a more convincing panacea than did personal regeneration. To aid in this difficult task of garnering souls, both Protestant and Catholic churches invoked the social gospel, which meant that the social order was to be transformed into a kingdom of righteousness on earth based upon the social teachings of Jesus. To vie with the attractions of gregarious city life as well as to solve the social evils, there arose, especially after 1890, the "institutional church," handsomely outfitted with welfare services, game and club rooms, and classes for the foreign-born.

The urban intellectuals, even more than the workmen, led the trek away from the church. This generation debated over and over again the problem of reconciling modern science with religion and failed to resolve its secret doubts, even while reaffirming the unity of both. Before the Civil War certain German theological schools fostered "scientific criticism" of the Bible. David Friedrich Strauss of Tübingen shocked the orthodox world in 1835 with his naturalistic "higher criticism" of the Bible and of Christ, in his *Life of Jesus*. Revelation, miracles, and the supernatural suffered their most severe attacks since the time of Voltaire. Protestantism, leaning heavily on the doctrine that the Bible was literally inspired and the sole authority for religion, staggered under the attacks of the "higher critics" upon the origin and development of Christian sacred writings. Scholars, armed with vast linguistic knowledge, challenged the accuracy and authorship of various biblical texts, and anthropologists like Edward Tylor and James Frazer in Britain undermined the assumptions of orthodoxy through the new science of "comparative religion." Frazer's monumental work, *The Golden Bough* (1890), a critical collection of religious and superstitious practices and beliefs, stimulated the reader's impression that Christianity consisted of myths analogous to those of primitive religions.

To the Bible literalists, science was definitely at war with religion. Sir Charles Lyell, the geologist, had already disturbed the Bible literalists by showing that the earth was far older than the mere six thousand years or so suggested by clerical calculations of the date of creation. He had pointed out that any analysis of geological processes proved that the earth had a far greater antiquity than the year 4004 B.C. But the greatest blow to the literalists came from Darwin's *Origin of Species* (1859) and *Descent of Man* (1871). Darwin's theory of natural selection gave the *coup de grâce* in many minds to the idea that man was literally created in the physical image of God. Evolution implied that man was an imperfect product that had developed from some humble amoeba. There seemed cold comfort in the impersonal God whom the deterministic scientists had resurrected from the eighteenth century Deists. This concept of God might please secularists, but it offered no attraction whatever to those who believed in the efficacy of prayer and miracles to correct the inequities of life.

Darwin needed all the help of American philosophers like John Fiske and scientists like Asa Gray to reconcile the idea of divine purpose in the universe with the blind determinism implied in his idea that chance biological variations are selected for survival by the impersonal agency of the environment. Even Darwin, who was too optimistic to believe that "this magnificent world," as he put it, could be the product of blind chance, doubted that God was interested in deciding upon what species were to survive. Many of the organic variations were too useless, he felt, to be the result of special design and merely reflected a struggle for existence. To him the philosophic problem of chance versus design was insoluble. Such reasoning may have led William James and the pragmatists to decide that the search for absolute certainties was futile and that it was enough to know how ideas "worked" in concrete situations.

The impact of evolutionary thought on religion led theologians to make several kinds of intellectual adjustment. Among liberal Protestants, Darwinism and the "higher criticism" were the parents of Modernism which looked upon religious truths as evolutionary, adapting themselves to changing conditions, rather than acting as eternally fixed dogmas. Modernism stimulated the growth of liberal Christianity beyond the confines of Unitarianism and Emersonian transcendentalism. Progressive Protestant theologians, interested in solving the urban problems of labor and poverty, were attracted to a "social gospel" based on evolutionary ideas, particularly as implied in the doctrine of the immanence of God in human society. According to the leading exponents of the social gospel, the evolutionists had proved that God was part of a changing cosmic process and that His divine plan was unfolded in the progress of man upward to an ever higher stage. From this idea, it was easy to reach the conclusion that God's design involved the early emergence of a kingdom of righteousness on earth no less than in heaven. Unlike the millennialist, who simply waited for the Second Coming, the social gospeler believed that the kingdom would come through the intelligent planning of religious men.

Catholicism escaped much of the revolutionary impact of secularism, for it had never shared the biblical literalism of orthodox Protestantism, but rested instead upon the teachings of church tradition, spiritual revelations, and miracles. Heresies like Modernism, schisms, and intellectual deviations could be felled at a blow by the spiritual weapons of the Vatican, ranging from doctrinal encyclicals to excommunications. Catholics contended that science, rightly construed, could not possibly challenge religious dogmas. The *Catholic Encyclopedia* held that the human soul, being of a spiritual nature, could not have evolved from that of the brute; and that a distinction must be made between "the theory of evolution as based on theistic principles and as based on a materialistic and atheistic foundation." To the author of the *Encyclopedia* article Darwin's theory of natural selection was open to scientific criticism as well.

Among the liberal Protestants who clung to economic conservatism rather than the social gospel were a number of fashionable preachers of the Gilded Age who minimized the labor problem but exalted the new science. The best-known of these is Henry Ward Beecher, minister of the well-to-do Plymouth Church in Brooklyn. This remarkable brother of the immortal Harriet had steadily lost whatever he may have once had of the prewar tradition of social dissent. During the Panic of 1873, he refused to admit that there was any basic social maladjustment in the existence of millions of unemployed and the breadlines that taxed the resources of urban churches everywhere. However, he was outspoken in his denunciation of unions, strikes, and labor violence. A *New York Times* reporter in 1877 noted these defiant words of the Great Preacher:

The trade union, originated under the European system, destroys liberty . . . I do not say that a dollar a day is enough to support . . . a man and five children if a man would insist on smoking and drinking beer. . . . But the man who cannot live on bread and water is not fit to live.

His biographer, Paxton Hibben, relates that thirty police and a corps of secret service men guarded Beecher during this harangue. While Plymouth Church applauded, critical journalists caricatured him and his $20,000-a-year salary.

This son of strict old Lyman Beecher moved ever farther from the historic Calvinism and ideals of his Congregationalist background. While he clung to the language of the supernatural, his theology became increasingly "liberal" and "humanistic" in the crudest sense, betraying the most flagrant philosophical inconsistencies. His optimistic sermons made "love" their cardinal point, but he did not extend its application to the laboring man. He reassured his wealthy congregation that the Bible must not be taken too literally in its strictures upon the rich man's entering heaven. He could eulogize the militant agnostic, Colonel Robert Ingersoll (whose economic views coincided with his own) and, at the same time, tell his listeners that he could not accept predestination or Hell. Following closely in the footsteps of several prominent Anglican churchmen who, in 1877, had repudiated the traditional concept of Hell, Beecher was able to create a new sensation in the American pulpit—there were many of these "shockers" in his technique—by saying that he could not believe that God could be so malign as to destroy men in the fires of Hell like insects over a fire. In 1882, he publicly explained his convenient pragmatic theology to the Congregational Association:

I gradually formed a theology by practise—by trying it on, and the things that really did God's work in the hearts of men I set down as good theology, and the things that did not, *whether they were true or not, they were not true to me.*

He converted innumerable followers to an early acceptance of evolution and to his Spencerian version of "liberal religion." Religion to him was an adventure in personal well-being—limited to the middle class in its material benefits—and it was simple for Beecher to raise evolution to the status of a spiritual revelation, "God's thought in the evolution of matter." These ideas appeared in his exuberant book, *Evolution and Religion* (1885). He took issue with the "bigoted theologists, ignorant pietists, jealous churchmen," and unintelligent men who ridiculed Lyell's geology and Darwin's biology.

In an age of middle-class complacency, Beecher made a dogma of self-congratulation; at a time when severe social dislocations had been let loose by industrialism and crowded cities, he diverted the Christian doctrine of social responsibility into the irresponsibility of Spencerian laissez faire and the uncritical acceptance of the inevitability of social progress. Science was in effect equated with God and became a popular religion despite its lack of ethical content.

2

Rural Protestants and their orthodox allies in the cities rebelled against the "modernist" liberals and their faith in science as a guide to spiritual values. In many congregations liberals and conservatives quarreled, being too often held together only by their mutual stake in church property. By the twentieth century the conservatives had organized themselves into "fundamentalist" sects wherever it was necessary. In 1910, these religious authoritarians issued a booklet assailing Modernism, *The Fundamentals; a Testimony to the Truth,* which contained an uncompromising statement of fundamentalist views as against heresy. This pamphlet stressed five points of doctrine: the virgin birth of Christ, the resurrection, the imminent Second Coming, the atonement for man's sins by Christ's sacrifice, and the inerrancy of the Bible. As for the Catholic Church, its rejection of Modernism was thorough; papal encyclicals emphatically denounced this as a flagrant heresy to be avoided by the faithful.

Not a few urban intellectuals and working-class radicals espoused a far more anti-traditional viewpoint than Modernism. This was the agnosticism of Robert Ingersoll and his followers. In England, Thomas Henry Huxley, an English biologist whose militant championship of evolution on the public platform won him the title, "Darwin's bulldog," attacked dogmatic theology in the name of "agnosticism." He defined this as a scientific attitude of suspended judgment in which the individual finds a lack of evidence to affirm the existence of God or a life after death. In effect this meant a denial of the historic mission of the Church and a reversion to Voltaire in its militant anti-clericalism.

The amazing popularity of Robert Green Ingersoll (1833-99), dubbed "the great agnostic," suggests the increased tolerance of his generation to an irreligious position hitherto unforgivable in a major public figure. In antebellum times, it is true, radical reformers like Robert Dale Owen and Frances Wright had organized the "Free Enquirers" to oppose organized religion as well as to promote sweeping plans of social reconstruction. A sprinkling of "freethinkers" had always infiltrated American radical thought in previous generations.

However, Ingersoll, like Voltaire, had no intention of assaulting the bastions of economic orthodoxy, for he was the friend and legal counsel of the mighty in business industry. He had broken with the Congregationalism of his minister-father in which he had been reared. Gifted with a flair for spread-eagle oratory, and buttressed by an impressive Civil War record, he became a politician and a wealthy lawyer with a long list of legal victories won before impressionable jurors. Not the least of his laurels was his masterly and successful defense of the defendants in the "Star Route" scandals involving large-scale fraud against the government in the compensation of mail contractors. So orthodox were the views of Ingersoll in politics and economics that he might possibly have reached the highest office had his irreligious views not been a barrier to his "availability." He could bury vital economic issues beneath the most contagious emotional appeals of the "bloody shirt" variety, keeping green the memories of Civil War sectional hates. Best remembered as a service to his party was his nomination of James G. Blaine in 1876 as the Republican presidential candidate. His flattering characterization of the shifty Blaine as the Plumed Knight caught the imagination of his generation.

Influenced by Darwin, Huxley, and the "higher criticism" movement against the Bible's infallibility, he expounded his agnosticism before huge crowds for thirty years, attracting the young lawyer, Clarence Darrow, among many other liberals, to his position. His forceful oratory as well as his heterodox ideas drew audiences for such lecture topics as "Some Mistake of Moses" and "Why I Am an Agnostic." In the latter speech he defined the agnostic, "He gives up the hope of ascertaining first or final causes, of comprehending the supernatural, or of conceiving of an infinite personality." To him the world was without beginning and would be without end; religion and morals were in large part the product of soil, climate, and circumstance. He declared that Shakespeare was preferable to the prophets from a literary point of view and that Darwin and Humboldt were superior to the author of Genesis as scientists. Constantly he attacked organized religion. "With sword and flame, it destroyed the brave and thoughtful men who told the truth. It was the enemy of investigation and reason. Faith and fiction were in partnership." Unlike the agnostics and atheists among the working-class socialists, he avoided any criticism of the churches for conservative economic tenets.

3

The cityward movement challenged the evangelical exhorters who discarded formal theology for a simple emotional appeal to the uprooted semi-literate masses. Foremost among those to retain the soul-saving tradition of the camp meeting, though in a more dignified form, was Dwight L. Moody, once a Boston shoe salesman, but active in city missionary work and Sunday school teaching since the 1850's. He served as secretary of the Chicago Y.M.C.A. and during the Civil War became an active missionary on the field for the United States Christian Commission. Never ordained as a minister and lacking all but rudimentary book learning, he proved nevertheless one of the most effective preachers of all time. To the agnostics and Modernists who found inconsistencies in the Bible, he replied emphatically, "The Bible was not made to understand!"

In 1870, he met Ira David Sankey, a minor revenue clerk who desired above everything to use his powerful dramatic voice in winning souls. Moody and Sankey toured the British Isles as well as the United States and aroused the revivalist spirit wherever they went. The *New York Times* declared in 1876, "A new hope has lifted up hundreds of human beings; a new consolation has come to the sorrowful; and a better principle has entered the sordid life of the day through the labors of these plain men." Moody seemed to be a new John Wesley, eager to inspire religious excitement without the extremes of hysteria or the "jerks." Women often credited their conversions to the effect of a hymn sung by Sankey such as "Hold the Fort," "Watching and Waiting," and "Ninety and Nine." Moody recalled he had heard "Rock of Ages" once a day for six years.

These evangelists avoided the pressing economic questions of the day. Wall Street, like the East Side slums, had souls to save and the advantages of the world to come appeared far too great for quarrels over temporary advantages in this one. The wealthy as well as the poor contributed heavily to Moody's insistent fund-raising campaigns in behalf of his large chain of educational institutions. In 1889, he had built a citadel of evangelical training in the (Moody) Bible Institute for Home and Foreign Missions in Chicago. At his birthplace and residence, Northfield, Massachusetts, he introduced annual conferences of church workers and students. A master of publicity—his critics called him the Barnum of religion—he scattered tons of religious tracts wherever he went. When he died in 1899 the statistically-minded estimated that he had carried his gospel messages fully a million miles, addressed 100,000,000 people, and prayed directly with 750,000 sinners. Admirers insisted that he had reduced the population of hell by a million souls.

Moody's earnest words, spoken in rapid conversational style while he used only the simplest of gestures, deeply affected his listeners and drew masses back to the "Old Time Religion." Sankey sat at the organ, always facing the congregation and eagerly watching their expressions. He played the beloved gospel hymns and sang impressively like a basso profundo of the opera.

In the early twentieth century, evangelism had its most sensational champion in Billy Sunday, a professional baseball player from Iowa. Although like Moody, he came to evangelical work through the Y.M.C.A., there was almost none of Moody's dignity in his pulpit manner, despite the fact that he was actually ordained a Presbyterian minister in 1903. In his Philadelphia pulpit Billy Sunday wound up like a baseball pitcher and exhorted the audience "to put it over the plate for Jesus." But he, too, like Moody, ignored the basic economic and social abuses of his day except for his heated campaign against the saloon. To the fundamentalist, Sabbath-breaking and drink were the chief social problems of the times.

4

The Young Men's Christian Association, which had provided such militants as Moody, Sunday, and Anthony Comstock, had been founded in England in 1844 by George Williams and had been sponsored by men of at least four different Protestant denominations. It was an interdenominational laymen's movement to convert youth, particularly those spiritually adrift in the cities, to religion. The movement took root in America in 1851 with the founding of the Boston chapter and grew into vast national and international dimensions. The Y.M.C.A. did much to promote the religious revival of 1857-58, which penetrated into the financial districts as well as the homes of the humble, and it organized charities for the poor and nursing aid for the sick.

Beginning in 1868, "active" members were expected to be members in good standing of evangelical churches, while others might join as "associate" members, providing they were of good moral character. Each branch centered around the personality of a vigorous secretary. The New York "Y" introduced physical education, thereby giving an important impetus to the adoption of German calisthenics in the public schools of the nation. To rally the youth for religion and to reconcile class and race, the "Y" steadily expanded its Sunday school program to absorb a variety of social activities, such as reading rooms, clubs and classes of all types, as well as gymnastics. During the Civil War the various Y.M.C.A. groups united to form the United States Christian Commission to furnish to the soldiers wholesome books and tracts, both religious and secular. Such services were expanded to include recreation in the Spanish-American War and World War I.

Another such English institution transplanted to New York in 1858 was the Young Women's Christian Association. This, too, had urban as well as religious roots. Originally, women were attracted to the idea of a large prayer group for their sex. Too often they had been frowned upon or discriminated against in the conduct of missionary and evangelical work. The founders, such as Emma Robarts in England, cited their aim in the biblical thought that "thy sons and thy daughters shall prophesy." Their purpose was "to labor for the temporal, moral, and religious welfare of young self-supporting women." In 1887, after William T. Stead had publicized the immorality prevalent among girls who earned a pittance in industry, the London Y.W.C.A. added a strong social program to this limited gospel movement. Out of this grew women's hostels, the Traveller's Aid Society, and the Park Mission.

After 1866, the American Y.W.C.A., like others elsewhere, modeled their organizational structure after the Y.M.C.A. Physical education, schooling in many liberal and applied subjects, and social and recreational activities were added to religious training. The American Y.W.C.A. pioneered with the cafeteria idea in its Kansas City branch. Its main purpose was to reduce food prices for working girls by eliminating as much of the service cost as possible. From Kansas City the cafeteria system moved eastward and became popular both in "Y" circles and outside by 1900. So successful was the Y.W.C.A. in this country that it was able to report in 1910 a total membership of close to a quarter of a million spread over 196 city associations. Many hundreds were enrolled in mission study classes. Troubled immigrant women frequently turned to the "Y" for advice and assistance.

Since the battle for church survival in a secular age depended upon the success of youth programs, Protestants experimented with other institutions besides the two "Y" movements. The leading Methodist denominations forged their instrument in the Epworth League, originating in 1872 in Philadelphia from a group organized by the Reverend T. B. Neely of the Fifty-first Street Methodist Episcopal Church. The most remarkably successful of the religious youth groups was the Young People's Society of Christian Endeavor. In February, 1881, the Reverend Francis E. Clark founded the first chapter at his Williston Congregational Church in Portland, Maine. By 1911, the Society had become an interdenominational movement of nearly 2,700,000 American members while over 1,200,000 more belonged to Canadian and overseas chapters—a grand total of nearly four million young men and women. The Christian Endeavor pledge required each member to promise to apply religion through some concrete service, however small, to society. Their motto was "For Christ and the Church" and their activities embraced missions, charities, and social programs. Among the Christian Endeavor principles was this social-economic platform:

Christian endeavor stands for Peace and Good Will among men, and is opposed to all unjust war and unjust industrial strife, as contrary to the principles of the Prince of Peace. "Arbitration and Conciliation" are two of its watchwords for the twentieth century, and an International Christian Brotherhood and a universal language for intercommunication two of its ideals.

5

In a sense the efforts of Protestants to retain their urban membership may be considered as a militant counter-reformation against
secularism and indifference. The leaders of this movement originated
in industrial England and were the soldiers of the Salvation Army.
This movement, like so many others of this period, was interdenominational and therefore tended to minimize dogmatic differences
among Protestants in order to achieve the experience of Christian
conversion.

The first general and founder of the Salvation Army was William
Booth, who had been reared within the Church of England and had
joined a band of Wesleyan Methodists as a youthful evangelist. In
1850 he became a minister and thereafter embarked as an independent evangelist in London, bringing his remarkable wife, Catherine, to his aid. He labored for the souls of slum dwellers, drunk-
ards, and the human debris of London. His audiences filled huge
tents, theaters, and open fields. "The Christian Mission is the
Salvation Army," he once said and this name became fixed in the
reorganization of 1880. General Booth invoked "councils of war,"
moved his evangelists in "corps," and held meetings in "citadels."
In seaports, evangelists called themselves "captains." Eventually,
The War Cry became the official organ of the movement.

From the beginning the Salvation Army realized that hungry and
homeless men must first be fed and sheltered before they were
ready for a Christian life. Soup kitchens, shelters, and other social
institutions quickly evolved. This strategy of combining social with
spiritual services was stressed in Booth's book, *Darkest England and
the Way Out.* The new and unusually prominent role of women as
evangelists owed much to Catherine Booth, who was aware of the
precedents set by the Quakers in this direction. By 1890, there were
5000 women officers in the Salvation Army, many wearing the distinctive bonnet fashioned by Catherine herself.

In 1880, the very year that the name Salvation Army was formally
adopted, a branch was established in Pennsylvania under Commissioner George Railton and seven women workers from England.

Younger members of the Booth family took charge of the American organization. One of the best known, Evangeline Cory Booth, daughter of the founder, held the leadership for thirty years after 1904 and then became the General of the Army. The Army's militant evangelical methods in the United States and elsewhere have been frankly explained by one of the Booths:

The Salvationist's vision of a rebellious world and of perishing souls seems to justify any and every device, however sharp, striking, or even vulgar for attracting, for compelling, the attention of the hardened and indifferent to whom his appeal is made. . . . The testimony meeting is described as a "free and easy" and the response of "Amen" as a "volley." Many Army services are punctuated from first to last with joyous exclamations, clapping of hands, laughter, or tears.

One of the best conversion methods had to do with the "mourner's bench," which is said to have been borrowed by William Booth from President Charles Finney of Oberlin, the noted evangelist. This was a row of seats in front of the speaker's platform at which sinners kneeled in token of repentance. This version of the "anxious seat" added a keen dramatic interest to the services. Street marches by the "Hallelujah lasses," their familiar guitars, tambourines, and brass instruments, and lively or sentimental tunes from the Salvation Army Song Books were part of their appeal to prospective converts. Many of these songs were secular in origin but were sung with specially adapted salvationist words. By 1900, the Salvation Army had grown in this country to 700 corps of 20,000 privates commanded by 3000 officers. At this time, too, they were conducting an average of 11,000 weekly meetings with an attendance of over two million people.

After 1890, William Booth's plan for a large-scale welfare program began to unfold. The American branch of the Army helped the derelicts through numerous soup kitchens, old clothes depots, cheap hotels, and homes for alcoholics. Destitute families were housed in special shelters, permitted to buy necessities at cheap food stores, given employment, or aided generously through a loan service. Mothers were sent to maternity homes and cared for through public nursing agencies; unmarried mothers and prostitutes were aided through rescue homes. A special prison-gate bureau helped newly released prisoners to start fresh lives. The salvage of human derelicts was a mighty industry with the Army.

This vast program might be stigmatized as consisting of "palliatives" instead of social reform, but to the destitute it meant immediate sympathetic aid until such time as the nation and the municipalities were ready to shoulder the burden in a more scientific way. For the churches, it meant vast recruits of members, and for society, it led to the physical as well as spiritual rehabilitation of a submerged class that normally had no outlets but drink and unbridled sensualism.

In 1896, General Ballington Booth and his wife led a group of secessionists out of the Salvation Army to form an exclusively American movement with a more democratic internal structure, the Volunteers of America. They continued the military paraphernalia on a lesser scale, but avoided direct competition with the churches. In their evangelical work they stressed conversion among convicts and alcoholics. Their Volunteer Prison League enrolled thousands of convicts who pledged themselves to a disciplined Christian life. Ex-convicts were assisted to find secure niches in society where the stigma of their past might not force them back into criminal acts.

6

The long dreary depression eras of 1873 and 1893 and the violent nation-wide strikes associated with them led many thoughtful clergymen to revise their exclusive emphasis on otherworldliness. Besides, the rapid growth of Marxist socialism among laborers during the 1880's and afterwards alarmed churchmen in both Europe and America. Radical clubs ridiculed the clergyman's promises of salvation as "pie in the sky" and in Marxian terms assailed religion as an opiate for the people to divert attention from the class struggle. After 1890, many Protestants and Catholics devoted serious attention to formulating a "social gospel," which taught that the principles of Christianity were broad enough to support a just social order of a cooperative nature. For them, the traditional kingdom of heaven could not be allowed to obscure the hope of a kingdom of righteousness on earth.

Socially-minded critics attacked the orthodox who were only concerned with the problem of personal redemption without realizing that society, too, must be redeemed from its economic abuses. They were dissatisfied with the limited ascetic program of the churches—temperance, Sabbatarianism, Comstockian morality, and persistent campaigns to halt smoking and card-playing. Within the traditional church doctrine of stewardship, churchmen insisted that all wealth is held and administered for the common good. Catholics recurred to the pre-capitalistic Christian society of the medieval guild community with its subordination to the common good—in theory at least—of profits and competitive conflict. Social gospelers also found theological sanctions in the doctrine that God was immanent in human society—a formula that tended to blur the usually sharp distinctions between secular and religious interests.

England directly influenced the social gospel movement and its institutions, for her urban-industrial problems resembled those of the United States in an accentuated form. Within the Church of England a group of clerics and laymen, led by Frederick D. Maurice, took up where Chartism had left off in 1848 to rebel against laissez-faire capitalism and to demand that the economic order conform to Christian ethics within a cooperative system. Best-known of these "Christian Socialists" to American readers was the clergyman-novelist Charles Kingsley, who wrote *Alton Locke* (1850) and *Yeast* (1851) to picture working-class conditions. In England, too, there was the esthetic and individualistic Socialism of William Morris and John Ruskin. These men seldom went beyond plans or experiments for a producer's or consumer's cooperative, but they influenced the gradualist tradition of the Fabian Socialists and the British Labour Party. From England, too, came the settlement movement, which was originated by an Anglican vicar, Samuel A. Barnett, as an experiment in London slum rehabilitation. Barnett founded Toynbee Hall in 1884 to provide university-trained "residents" in a poor district of the East End. Essentially, all these activities were merely middle-class efforts to direct the economic salvation of the working classes. Some groups of the Christian Socialists were even cool to secular trade-union movements and none favored the revolutionary Marxist or anarchist panaceas for the ills of the world.

Much more influential upon the later Christian Socialist movement was Washington Gladden, outspoken pastor of the First Congregational Church in Columbus, Ohio. He insisted that now that slavery had been abolished, the emancipation of labor came next and the social problem was therefore primary. Active in various municipal and social reforms, he expressed his conviction that the laborer's real wages had declined during 1860-86 and were still falling. He was one of the early clerical figures to give the weight of church support to trade unions and the right to strike; his wrath fell upon the abuses of unregulated economic competition. Adam Smith and classical economics, he charged, had come to replace the Bible. His numerous books, such as *Applied Christianity* (1886), popularized the social gospel. In 1891 appeared his challenging exposition of religious Modernism in *Who Wrote the Bible?*

While Gladden offered little in the way of concrete reforms, the developing English movement of Christian Socialism crossed the Atlantic and gave a program to many American social gospelers. One of these American leaders of Christian Socialism was an Episcopal clergyman of Boston, William D. P. Bliss, who named his organization the Church of the Carpenter and even joined the Knights of Labor. Like other radical clergymen, he had been attracted at first by Edward Bellamy's Utopian Socialist book *Looking Backward, 2000-1887* (1888), in which the leading character awakens in the midst of a socialist society that plans almost every phase of daily life. However, the secular nature of Bellamy's Nationalist movement led Bliss and other churchmen to turn away and organize in 1889 the Society of Christian Socialists in Boston, editing *The Dawn,* and attacking plutocracy and economic planlessness in favor of a gradualist program of regulation and control of capital.

The greatest name and influence in American Social Christianity was undoubtedly Walter Rauschenbusch, a Baptist clergyman of Rochester, New York, the son of German liberal Forty-eighters. As a young idealistic pastor in New York city's slums, he had seen poverty at first hand; as a result, his religion was imbued with a strong social quality. He had read sympathetically Henry George's single-tax doctrines, Tolstoy's idealistic essays on personal redemption, and John Spargo's socialist writings. He emerged a Christian Socialist, devoted to the goal of a socialist state based on biblical principles.

To Marxians, however, his rejection of the principles of the class struggle as a cardinal tenet of socialism put him outside the pale of "scientific socialism." Rauschenbusch denounced the jungle philosophy of unregulated competition and proposed a social order in which the profit motive would be replaced by a cooperative ideal. In *Christianizing the Social Order* (1912), written at the height of the Bull Moose movement, he predicted gloomily, "An ever increasing number of people are henceforth to live in a land owned by an ever decreasing number." It was time to turn away from mammonism and corporate control of government and time for all society to experience the exalted sense of personal regeneration that the convert knew.

In his published Yale lectures of 1917, *A Theology for the Social Gospel*, Rauschenbusch formulated the doctrinal basis of Social Christianity. Most popular of all was *The Social Principles of Jesus* (1917). These titles alone suggest the consistent emphasis that he put upon his central tenets of a kingdom of righteousness on earth. Under his leadership Christian Socialists organized the Brotherhood of the Kingdom. More important than this is the fact that, for an entire generation at least, innumerable idealistic young clergymen were profoundly influenced by the social teachings of Rauschenbusch.

No man in the entire Social Christian movement enjoyed so vast an audience as the Reverend Charles Monroe Sheldon of Topeka, Kansas, whose mass appeal as a novelist may justly be compared with that of Harriet Beecher Stowe. A prolific writer of idealistic sketches for denominational papers, this Congregationalist minister knew poverty and unemployment from close observation. In 1896, he published *In His Steps: What Would Jesus Do?* This began with

a story related to a congregation by an unemployed youth whose
wife had died in a New York tenement. The young man challenged
the congregation by asking what Jesus would do if He were a
member of this church. After the youth died the aroused pastor asked
his congregation to live for a year exactly as they thought Jesus would,
regardless of consequences. Thereafter a wholesale transformation
took place as members gave up narrow or harmful activities to
promote better housing for the poor, mission work, and temperance.
So sensational was the success here and abroad of *In His Steps* that
the book sold over 100,000 copies in a year and quickly passed the
million mark and the story was shown on the motion picture screen
in 1936.

The climax of the social gospel movement came in 1908 after
Unitarians, Episcopalians, Methodists, Baptists, and Congregation-
alists had already formed welfare organizations and adopted social
principles going beyond the older restricted notions of charity. In
May, 1908, the Methodist Episcopal Church issued its famous
"Social Creed," which included these principles: industrial conciliation and arbitration; elimination of factory hazards to life and health;
the abolition of child labor; protection of women in industry; abolition of the sweat shop; the "gradual and reasonable reduction of
the hours of labor to the lowest practical point, with work for all";
and the acquisition of "that degree of leisure for all which is the
condition of the highest human life." They advocated a holiday of
one day in seven, "a living wage in every industry," and particularly
"the highest wage that each industry can afford, and for the most
equitable division of the products in industry that can ultimately
be devised."

This ambitious program was implemented that same year by the
formation of the most important interdenominational group in the
history of Protestantism: The Federal Council of the Churches of
Christ in America, eventually representing twenty-seven national
denominations, including both races, and dealing with practically
every problem of human welfare. This organization took over as its
own the Social Creed of the Methodists and set up local and state
councils to assist it in dealing with national and international ques-

tions including evangelical programs, reform of marriage laws, philanthropy, and social legislation. "The Council holds it a Christian duty to make the influence of Christ effective in all human relations," reads a recent semi-official statement; "It draws Christian representatives of management, labor, and agriculture together to consider what light is shed upon their problems by their common Christian commitment." Thus in the twentieth century centrifugal tendencies of Protestantism had been partially checked through such interdenominational forms as the F.C.C.C.A. More and more churches took up the "labor question," investigated strikes sympathetically, or offered their services as labor mediators. The "institutional" church grew after 1890 to include a wide variety of welfare, educational, and recreational activities. Such urban churches often added employment bureaus, charitable relief agencies, kindergartens, gymnasiums, libraries, clubs, dispensaries, soup kitchens, hospitals, and home economics classes. A "Christian sociology" pervaded their philosophy.

7

With the urban emphasis upon interdenominationalism and the social gospel, the birth of new sects became an increasing rarity. One of the most important of the few urban sects that were organized in this period was the Christian Science Church. Appealing to the middle class primarily, it did not take an active role in the social gospel movement. Its emphasis on mental healing, suggesting certain of the therapeutic values of psychoanalysis, seemed well-adapted to uprooted urban culture in which mental adjustments often took physical forms baffling to the techniques of ordinary medicine. This "Church of Christ, Scientist" was chartered in 1879 in Boston by a unique figure in American church history, Mary Baker Eddy, already a woman of fifty-eight.

Mrs. Eddy was born in 1821 on a farm in New Hampshire of a long line of Congregational ancestors. She was largely self-educated, though she had an unmistakably keen native intelligence. Her personal life was not happy, for her first husband died, she divorced her second, and the third, Asa Eddy, whom she loved dearly, died a few years after their marriage. Throughout her early life she had suffered from sudden pains in her spine and chronic invalidism and she had tried the current healing panaceas, including mesmerism and spiritualism. She consulted Phineas P. Quimby of Portland, Maine, regarding her health and thought that she had secured some relief. Quimby used no medicines, but relied upon manipulation and mental suggestion. When he died in 1866, Mrs. Eddy turned to other hopes of cure and became immersed in the idea of the healing mission of Jesus. She had long been interested in the mental factors in illness and hoped to convince the churches to take up her emphasis on faith healing. When this hope failed to materialize, she developed her own church to carry out the principles she had discovered.

In 1875, she published *Science and Health,* which in various revised forms became the textbook of the Christian Science movement. She developed the idea that Jesus came upon earth not only to redeem man from sin, but also from disease. Men must discover "the Christ in us." In one of her most-quoted passages, she said,

There is no life, truth, intelligence, nor substance in matter. All is infinite Mind and its infinite manifestations, for God is All-in-All. Spirit is immortal Truth; matter is mortal error. . . . Spirit is God, and man is His image and likeness. Therefore man is not material; he is spiritual.

This, in a highly condensed form, gave the essence of her teachings. By living the life of a genuine Christian, one might hope to overcome error and unreality, which includes sickness and sin. These cheerful ideas of mind-cure were especially attractive to the optimistic psychology of many Americans. To spread the faith, Mrs. Eddy founded monthly, weekly, and daily newspapers. By 1890, her *Christian Science Journal* advertised the presence of 250 healers, 20 churches, and 90 societies. The phenomenon of a woman at the head of a large church was not new in New England, for Mother Ann Lee had founded Shaker colonies there a century before.

In 1906 a two-million-dollar addition to the Mother Church at Boston was completed. At that time the Boston organization was estimated to have over 40,000 members, and there were at least 25,000 more elsewhere. Two years later the *Christian Science Monitor* appeared; it offered lectures on the faith together with an unusually high level of journalism in which the sections on foreign affairs ranked with the best in the country. It avoided any emphasis on vice or crime and sought to keep a neutral position between capital and labor. In 1910, the eighty-nine-year-old woman who had obviously built up a powerful organization died. Within a few years, her church won many converts in England, Germany, and elsewhere.

8

The American Roman Catholic Church was overwhelmingly recruited from immigrants who found their livelihood in the cities and thus it became predominantly an urban church. Despite the poverty of the newcomers, the hierarchy was able to build parochial schools, churches, colleges, hospitals, and monastic institutions. In addition, the church had to support its own extensive program of charities. Besides the unique Catholic problem of adjusting millions of incoming Irishmen, Bavarians, Italians, Poles, Czechs, Austrians, and others to the American environment, there were also the same problems faced by Protestants: secularism, Marxist socialism, and urban indifference.

In this era the leadership of Cardinal Gibbons was often decisive in Catholic affairs. Without demanding any special status for the large American Catholic population within the Roman Church, he urged the Vatican that the Church must not be stigmatized by Americans as an alien institution. Instead, bishops should be chosen who were in accord with American ideas of democracy. When in 1891 certain nationalistic German Catholics sought a special status for their nationality, the Cardinal successfully fought this "Cahenslyism" as a threat to the homogeneity of American Catholicism. On that occasion a Peter Cahensly had presented a church memorial recommending that each nationality be given its churches, priests, and proportion of bishops according to their respective numbers. Although it had been the practice of the hierarchy to provide each foreign language group with a priest who could speak its language, the Cardinal denounced any effort to segregate each group on a rigid nationality basis.

Next to the Cardinal in influence was the very able archbishop of St. Paul, John Ireland. At one time President Roosevelt even intervened indirectly to help the archbishop get a cardinal's hat—an odd activity for a Protestant! Like Cardinal Gibbons, Archbishop Ireland favored an American policy for the church in this country with special emphasis upon an enthusiastic acceptance of political democracy. However, he tended to minimize the great economic problems of the time except to advocate temperance and conservative trade unionism. In 1903, he publicly declared, "I have no fear of great fortunes in the hands of individuals, nor of vast aggregations of capital in the hands of corporations." His friendships with James J. Hill, railroad magnate, and with President McKinley exposed him to the shafts of progressives. Yet he often expressed strong sympathies for organized labor, even remarking on one occasion, "Until their material condition is improved it is futile to speak to them of spiritual life and duties."

Many Catholic priests and laymen did support radical causes. A particularly significant case was that of Father Edward McGlynn who made ardent speeches in behalf of Henry George and the single tax doctrines. In 1886, the attention of the entire nation was arrested by the news that he had been suspended by his superiors from his priestly duties. When he refused a summons to Rome to defend his opinions, he was excommunicated. However, the decree was revoked by the end of 1892 and he resumed his duties. Father McGlynn's victory encouraged other Catholics to espouse radical labor reforms. The attitude of the American hierarchy may perhaps be inferred from a significant letter in the Baltimore Cathedral Archives. On July 21, 1894, at the height of the disorders of the Pullman Strike, Archbishop Ireland wrote to Cardinal Gibbons:

The Church must be kept before the American people as the great prop of social order and law—all the more so that Catholics are numerous in strikes and riots. Socialistic ideas have gone into our people and into many of our priests. We have been siding with labor in its grievances: The unthinking ones transgress the golden mean, and rush into war against property.

For Catholics everywhere who hoped for a vigorous program of social action to meet the problems of poverty and materialism, a ready-made creed appeared in the famous papal encyclical, *Rerum Novarum*, issued by Leo XIII in 1891. Pope Leo had been an able social reformer while still a young priest; and some years before issuing the encyclical he had directed that social problems be made a part of the training curriculum for priests. An erudite philosopher with a special interest in the teachings of St. Thomas Aquinas, Pope Leo revived Thomism and thereby gave a new vitality to Catholic philosophy in the ensuing decades. The encyclical condemned laissez faire in industry as unchristian, declared that labor was not a commodity to be bought and sold on the market, upheld the right to organize unions, and asserted the principle of the living wage based upon the needs of the family. Class collaboration, instead of class conflict, was the keynote of the encyclical: "Capital cannot do without labor nor labor without capital." *Rerum Novarum* made slow progress as far as adoption in this country is concerned, but there were many militant Catholic advocates of its ideas.

The American Catholic who devoted his life most effectively and brilliantly to the application of the principles of *Rerum Novarum* was a priestly professor of social economics at Catholic University, Father John A. Ryan. Born of Irish parents in 1869 in a village near St. Paul, he had learned his Populist ideas from rebels like Ignatius Donnelly and from the anti-landlord sentiments of *The Irish World* to which his family had long subscribed. Professor Richard T. Ely of the University of Wisconsin, who may have influenced him, wrote an introduction to Ryan's doctoral dissertation, which appeared in 1906 as *A Living Wage*. This book attracted wide interest and almost certainly left an impression on the thinking of innumerable social reformers.

Father Ryan asserted the principle that no employer had any right to take interest on his investment until all his employees had

received a living wage. This he estimated at $600 a year as a mini-
mum subsistence for a family. He later wrote that this book was the
first in English to advocate a legally established compulsory minimum wage sufficient for the decent maintenance of the worker's
family. Unlike certain other Catholic critics of the economic order,
this priest-economist refused to escape to the Middle Ages for a just
social order. He believed that Americans had definitely broken with
European tradition and would seek their solution in terms of their
own experience. "The laborer's right to a living wage," he declared,
"is like all other moral rights, based on his intrinsic worth as a
person, and on the sacredness of those needs that are essential to
the reasonable development of personality." Charity was good, but
no substitute for justice. His wage ideas were developed more
maturely in *Distributive Justice* (1917), which carried the subtitle,
The Right and Wrong of Our Present Distribution of Wealth.
Throughout his life he combined his scholarly interests with active
social work.

The monolithic structure of the Roman Catholic Church made it
relatively simple to escape schisms and to deal with heresies and
secularist doctrines arising out of the new age of science. In 1864,
Pope Pius IX issued the *Syllabus of Errors* to denounce freethinkers,
agnostics, materialists, anticlericals, freemasons, and doctrinal liberals. The papal encyclical *Pascendi* (1907) issued by Pope Pius X
condemned Modernism as a union of faith with a false philosophy.
Inevitably, the cities made some inroads upon orthodoxy, but these
were far more than offset by steady accretions of strictly orthodox
immigrant groups.

Unlike conservative Protestant churches, the Catholic hierarchy
could meet new science uncncumbered by any dogmatic belief in
the literal truth of the Bible; and while very slow to accept Darwinism they were not compelled to stake the validity of doctrine upon
the truth or falsehood of evolution. On the other hand, Protestantism, traditionally consecrated to "justification by faith alone" had
moved over—except for a fundamentalist wing—to a humanitarian
program ever more devoted to "good works" as a way of salvation.
Critics of social Christianity wondered whether churchmen were

competent to solve the complex economic problems of contemporary society or were even well-advised to attempt it. Well-to-do congregations resented clerical meddling in the employer's problems; but the fashionable liberal Christianity of Henry Ward Beecher could only end in altogether estranging the working classes from religion.

The Captain of Industry, the Gilded Age, and Taylorization

[1865-1917]

I

"THE captain of industry," wrote the caustic Thorstein Veblen in *The Theory of the Leisure Class* (1899), "is an astute man rather than an ingenious one, and his captaincy is a pecuniary rather than an industrial captaincy.... The mechanically effective details of production and of industrial organization are delegated to subordinates of a less 'practical' turn of mind—men who are possessed of a gift for workmanship rather than administrative ability." Young Veblen, then an instructor in economics at the new University of Chicago was himself a beneficiary in a small way of several "captains of industry" whose largess made the University possible—John D. Rockefeller, Marshall Field, Charles T. Yerkes, and a host of others. The term itself, popularized after the Civil War, reflected the romantic hero worship and gospel of work preached by Carlyle, the rugged individualism of laissez faire, and the "struggle for survival" as currently discussed by Darwin and Spencer.

Although Veblen drew too sharp a line between the "pecuniary"-minded administrators and the technicians "with a gift for workmanship," he put his finger upon a historic process which too few of his contemporaries understood: *the commercialization of economic and cultural life.* The salesman, the promoter, and the speculator

174

took precedence over the handicraftsman who was solely interested in making good boots according to the proud tradition of the craft guilds. Credit and capital assumed a highly liquid, transferable form; and the marketing of securities offered a more certain and easy road to wealth than technological competence alone. Little wonder that John Pierpont Morgan, Sr., came to epitomize in the popular mind the victory of finance capitalism.

During the early nineteenth century the great private fortunes had belonged to landholding and mercantile families such as the Astors. Thereafter many mercantile houses, like that of George Peabody, evolved into powerful investment banking houses; and transportation and industry gave rise to the multimillionaires, Cornelius Vanderbilt, Carnegie, Duke, Ford, and others. In 1892, according to Professor Lewis Corey, the *New York Tribune* counted 4047 American fortunes over a million dollars, particularly—in the order named—in manufacturing, merchandising, real estate, and transportation. In 1916, there were 6633 persons earning an annual income of $100,000 or more. Western Europe, too, had its Cecil Rhodes, the Rothschilds, and Alfred Nobel, but the multimillionaire tended to be an American more frequently than otherwise.

This new class of business titans grew out of a singularly favorable process in the nation's growth. The steel kings—Carnegie, Frick, and Schwab—were made possible in large part by the insatiable demands of the railway age for steel rails and bridges. The era opened with plank bridges, ferries, costly, inefficient rails, and the pressing need for transcontinental railways. Crowded cities began to build entire traction systems, elevated lines, and eventually steel-frame skyscrapers. In the West homesteaders and cattle barons solved the desperate problem of fencing after 1874 by adopting barbed wire. Before this era ended the invention of the automobile expanded the uses of steel on a larger scale than ever. Industrialization, spurred on by the demands of a huge domestic, as well as a foreign, market, required enormous quantities of iron and steel machines and supplies. European wars such as the Austro-Prussian War of 1866, the Franco-Prussian War, and finally World War I, meant profitable orders for armor plate and other steel weapons.

Production costs fell as technological advances, both European and American, made the Age of Steel possible. In 1856, Sir Henry Bessemer created the basic decarbonizing process to transform molten pig iron into durable steel. No less basic was the fact that Americans had immense resources of iron ores in the recently developed Mesabi Range of northeast Minnesota, and that shipments of these ores could readily move across the Great Lakes to Cleveland or be reshipped to Pittsburgh. Cheap water and rail transportation united these iron ores with the ample coal deposits of the Alleghenies. Still another factor in the story of steel is the influence of the tariff, which did nothing for technological efficiency but a great deal to increase the fortunes of the captains of the steel industry. Even the historically low-tariff Democratic party broke ranks before the advance of tariff lobbyists from Pittsburgh, Cleveland, and Chicago.

Just as the national and international factors behind the Age of Steel produced titans of industry, so similar causes gave birth to semimonopolistic giants like Rockefeller in oil, the Armours, Swifts, and Morris' in meat-packing, the Havemeyers in sugar, the Dukes in tobacco, the Morgans and Schiffs in finance. Significantly, the years 1866-97, when so many of these business giants reached a pinnacle of wealth and power, were marked by a steady decline in prices. Much of this was due to monetary causes, such as those arising from the decline in gold production, as well as the economies effected by the mechanization of agriculture, transportation, and factory production. Industrialists had to combat the downward movement of prices while weighted down with new expensive machinery that became obsolete at an increasingly rapid rate.

Here was a temptation to operate at a temporary loss in order to avoid the costly idleness of machines—in other words to overproduce and to use all possible weapons such as rebates and commercial chicanery to win price wars. Bigness did not always spring from the efficiencies due to large-scale production, but often from the frantic efforts of the financiers to eliminate competition and thus to keep prices up. Captains of industry and their defenders in the press euphemistically explained this process as the masterly reorganization of competitive chaos into an orderly system. For example, Morgan's clients, fearful of a costly steel war between Carnegie and William Rockefeller (among others), importuned him to make peace by consolidation; so was born the first billion dollar company, the United States Steel Corporation. Monopoly was fostered under such economic pressures.

Underlying this accelerated phase of the Industrial Revolution and the Age of Giants was the sharp increase of population, especially in the cities wherever machine industry secured a foothold. Famine was banished in Western Europe, though the chronic economic depression took its place, and mortality declined. In the United States millions of immigrants were welcomed to the factories, the forges, and the shops. As late as 1830 only one city (New York with 202,589 people) had over 100,000 inhabitants and by 1860 there were but nine in this class with a combined total of 2,638,781 out of the nation's population of 31,513,114. In 1910, however, urbanization had moved at so rapid a rate as to put fifty cities in this category with an aggregate of over 20,302,000 people out of 92,406,536. At the same time, farm mechanization, the instability of staple farming, and the attraction of city life drew millions away from farm communities into urban industries. Here were both labor for the machines and consumers for the mass products of these machines.

Another factor making for "bigness" was the prevailing Jeffersonian idea that government must not intervene in business—except for tariffs and other direct benefits. Liberals in their revolt against mercantilism and chattel slavery had gone far in making laissez faire respectable. It was easy to preserve the notion that the state had little power, except as a policeman, to maintain order among competing or conflicting individuals and groups. In this era of trusts competition was extolled as the fulfillment of nature's law—so conveniently formulated by Darwin and Herbert Spencer—of the survival of the fittest. Andrew Carnegie, who declared a lifelong intellectual debt to these evolutionists, never tired of asserting in Darwinist terms the scientific basis for laissez faire, as he did in an article of 1889 for the *North American Review:*

The price which society pays for the law of competition, like the price it pays for cheap comforts and luxuries, is also great; . . . and while the law may be sometimes hard for the individual, it is best for the race, because it insures the survival of the fittest in every department. We accept and welcome, therefore as conditions to which we must accommodate ourselves, great inequality of environment, the concentration of business, industrial and commercial, in the hands of a few, and the law of competition between these, as being not only beneficial, but essential for the future of the race.

John D. Rockefeller, with scarcely more formal education than Carnegie, also knew how to justify bigness and laissez faire in the language of social Darwinism:

The growth of a large business is merely a survival of the fittest. . . . The American Beauty Rose can be produced in the splendor and fragrance which brings cheer to its beholder only by sacrificing the early buds which grow up around it.

Likewise, James J. Hill, builder of the Great Northern railway system, and Chauncey Depew, president of the New York Central Railroad and arch-lobbyist, eulogized the law of the "survival of the fittest" which, by implication, made the captain of industry one of Nietzsche's supermen.

2

A host of business historians have attempted to draw a composite portrait of the captain of industry. Was this elite class of businessmen recruited, as the various business biographies suggest, from an uneducated group of poor, rural, and often immigrant families? This seems to hold, more or less, for men like Carnegie, Swift, Armour, Nelson Morris, Marshall Field, Jay Gould, Cornelius Vanderbilt, Ford, and many others. Recent statistical studies of William Miller, Thomas Cochran, and others suggest that these men are not the typical entrepreneurs of American business and finance of any era. Miller's study, "American Historians and the Business Elite," is based upon the careers of 190 corporation presidents and board chairmen among the leading businesses of 1900-10.

He shows that three-fourths came from old colonial families and that four-fifths were sons of business and professional people; only 2 per cent rose from the working class. Two-fifths had gone to college and another group almost as large had attended high school. Ninety per cent were Protestants, especially Episcopalians and Presbyterians, 7 per cent were Catholic, and 3 per cent were Jews. Only 41 per cent came from rural areas. Most of them had not begun to work as boys and they had attained their present eminence usually in middle age. This was anything but in the "rags to riches" tradition, although it did not disprove the facts of considerable mobility and opportunity in American life.

Of the famous captains of industry who have attracted the lion's share of popular and scholarly biographies, all possessed amazing energy—but almost all of this was devoted to the art of money-getting. Scarcely any of them had been trained in vocations still bound by guild traditions and hence they were psychologically disposed to experiment with new methods and adventurous ideas. Too few, like Rockefeller or Wanamaker, had strong religious convictions, and even these men did not forget that "business is business." They often showed an astonishing knowledge of plant details, but few were actually as expert as Henry Ford was in regard to the problems of production. In many instances these men of the post-Civil War generation earned their original capital as commission merchants during the war.

The best publicized of the ideal captains of industry was Andrew Carnegie. Yet by Veblen's standards his technological contributions were small, though his autobiography gives him credit for introducing the Bessemer process and pioneering in the substitution of wrought iron for wooden bridges. Actually, the facts to the contrary are scarcely controversial. At first he was wont to express hesitation at these innovations, arguing, "Pioneering doesn't pay a new concern: we must wait until the process develops." Besides, Carnegie acted primarily as a promoter and salesman for his various iron and steel companies. He had a gift for telling stories and a warm personality that made him a favorite everywhere. From his residence in New York city he scrutinized production reports and pitted his partners and superintendents against each other. He owed much to the Kloman brothers, the actual pioneers in the industry, whose plants he annexed, together with the Klomans themselves. In the same absorptive fashion he came to acquire technologically brilliant associates like Henry Clay Frick and Charles Schwab. Still, Carnegie must be credited with the knack for surrounding himself with such able men; if he was not among the first to try on the new, he was far from the last to cast the old aside.

In merchandising, Marshall Field, once a Massachusetts farmboy, became the successor of Potter Palmer in Chicago, and continued the tradition of elegance to meet the demands of the fine ladies who admired the frescoed walls, the imported wares, and the courtesy of his carefully selected employees. Many of the merchandising methods that were later adopted in the best department stores either originated or were popularized by Marshall Field. For lower-class customers he had a bargain basement with a cheaper line of goods while the wealthy had access to the most exclusive merchandise on the upper floors. Clerks were strictly forbidden to misrepresent goods and were told to act as if the customer was always right. Especially novel in this era and attractive to upper-class women were the store restaurant, the letter-writing room, and the comfortable rest rooms. Each department had its unique setting to stimulate the interest of the shopper. The Marshall Field windows revealed window-trimming at its best.

One of the greatest of the captains of industry during the early twentieth century was another farm-bred boy, Henry Ford, who belongs to the inventor-producer category of George M. Pullman and Cyrus McCormick. He was beholden to many European and American inventors who had contributed the essential features of the automobile long before his own modest experiments had begun. Germany's gifted mechanics, notably Gottlieb Daimler and Carl Benz, had developed the high-speed internal-combustion gasoline engine for automobiles. The foremost inventors and pioneer manufacturers of the automobile were Frenchmen and their primacy is witnessed by the world-wide acceptance of such French terms as "automobile," "garage," and "chauffeur." As Dr. Keith Sward declares, France was producing 5000 cars more than the United States

1885-1905

"Not at Home," by Eastman Johnson. The interior of a middle-class
home during the Gilded Age. (Brooklyn Museum)

"Harlem" central office in New York in 1897. This was a magneto-type switchboard, serving "hand-crank" telephones. In 1898, it was converted to common battery service, and with this change was probably the first in the city to enable callers to signal the operator simply by lifting the receiver. (New York Telephone Company)

Potter Palmer's mansion, Lake Shore Drive, Chicago, typical of the architecture of the Gilded Age. (Chicago Historical Society)

The Haymarket (anarchist) Riot in Chicago. A dynamite bomb exploding among the police. (Drawing by T. de Thulstrup after a wood engraving by H. Jeanneret, 1886; Bettmann Archive)

The final assembly line at the Ford Motor Company's Highland Park plant in 1913. Bodies were skidded down the wooden ramp and lowered onto the chassis as they moved along below. Crude as it may seem today, production schedules were broken daily. December 10, 1915, saw the 1,000,000th Ford car built. (Bettmann Archive)

"Steerage, 1907," by Alfred Stieglitz. (Philadelphia Museum of Art)

Opposite, top: Chinatown, San Francisco, before the fire and earthquake of 1906. (California Historical Society)

Opposite, bottom: "Cliff Dwellers," by George Bellows. (Los Angeles County Museum)

Primrose & West's Big Minstrel Festival. (Bettmann Archive)

Thomas A. Edison, after five days and nights of work to perfect his favorite invention, the phonograph. (Bettmann Archive)

The Wright brothers. This plane in 1903 stayed aloft for 59 seconds. One of the brothers is on the ground while the other is in the plane. (Bettmann Archive)

"Stag at Sharkey's," by George Bellows. (Cleveland Museum of Art)

Lillian Russell as "Pepita." (Theatre Collection, New York Public Library)

in 1903, the year the Ford Motor Company was founded. In this country, George B. Selden, trained in Yale's Sheffield Scientific School, claimed the basic inventions for the gasoline-driven car. To protect his patent monopoly he organized a patent pool through the Association of Licensed Auto Manufacturers, which Ford was to destroy.

The assembly line, which eventually made "Fordismus" part of the German vocabulary, did not originate with Ford, though his application of this automatic conveyor principle was new in the automobile shop. Armour and Swift had already applied the idea to meat processing, for example. Before 1914, Ford's assembly system produced a car in thirteen hours; by the end of that year the time had been cut to 93 minutes. Like the other highly successful captains of industry, Ford had the indispensable gift for selecting brilliant technicians and business strategists as subordinates, key men like William Knudsen, Walter E. Flanders, Carl Emde, and James Couzens. He himself, like Marshall Field, Pullman, and Swift, kept close to the plant operations and wisely encouraged workers to contribute new ideas and methods. When his assembly line led to sharply increased nervous tension among harassed workmen and a very costly turnover in personnel, he decided to initiate the five-dollar day, then far above going wages. Steadily his unit costs dropped and his motor car came within the purchasing power of millions of Americans. Obviously, Ford was no mere stock manipulator without a gift for workmanship.

However, Professor Keith Sward's analytical study, *The Legend of Henry Ford*, proves that the Detroit manufacturer did not escape altogether the Veblenian weaknesses, from a social point of view, of other captains of industry. Although he helped to break the monopolistic hold of George B. Selden's basic patents over the automobile industry, he often exercised autocratic control over thousands of Ford suppliers and dealers. His individualistic labor bias was no less uncompromising than that of Pullman and Armour, for he continued to fight unionism even after his competitors had ceased to do so. He utilized his five-dollar day and the assembly line to create a unique speed-up system in American industry.

Clever public relations men praised his paternalistic policies and his "profit-sharing through wages," reinterpreting his motives as primarily benevolent rather than expedient. Little wonder that many citizens liked to think of Ford as an ideal candidate for president of the United States.

3

The concentration of wealth in the hands of the captains of industry, so many of whom were unlettered, meant that billions of dollars would be expended not only for luxurious living but, more important, to foster the imitative style of culture that seemed good in their eyes. The cultural result in this era has been invariably characterized by historians in such unfavorable terms as "the Gilded Age," "the Chrome Age," the "Plush Age," the "Great Barbecue," and "Brown Decades," to mention but a few. In that day before the revolutionary income tax and heavy corporate taxes, the huge surplus earned by a thriving industrial society was spent in large part according to the decisions of the agents of the great capitalists and the philanthropic foundations established by them. Between the Civil War and 1900 such capitalists left their surplus funds to education. Schools and libraries seemed the open sesame of opportunity in an individualist competitive world, even to wealthy men who had never stopped long enough from the process of amassing wealth to learn the wisdom of the ages—though willing enough to acquire an honorary degree or two from the colleges they sponsored. Only in the twentieth century did a more enlightened group of philanthropists divert more of their attention and wealth to other basic problems of social welfare.

The social contribution of wealthy businessmen had its best exponent and eulogist in Andrew Carnegie, who in his own lifetime gave away nine-tenths of his $300,000,000 fortune for public purposes. He endowed eight permanent philanthropic foundations of which the largest was the Carnegie Corporation of New York for "the advancement and diffusion of knowledge and understanding." He provided over 2500 library buildings for communities in America

THE CAPTAIN OF INDUSTRY

and Canada that lacked them, and founded such scientific institutions as the Carnegie Institute of Technology at Pittsburgh (1901) and the Carnegie Institution at Washington (1902). Schools for both races benefited greatly from his substantial gifts. To impecunious college professors, unable to amass enough savings to retire with dignity, he offered millions in free pensions through the Carnegie Foundation for the Advancement of Teaching.

Like other philanthropists who hoped to end war through financing peace movements—such as the Nobel Peace Prize and Edwin Ginn's World Peace Foundation—he founded a peace research and publication fund, the ten-million-dollar Carnegie Endowment for International Peace, dedicated to the speedy abolition of war between the so-called civilized nations. He erected a Temple of Peace at the Hague to promote international arbitration and a beautiful building in Washington for the Pan American Union. Wisely, he made his bequests flexible enough to enable administrators to alter his original instructions in order to meet future changing conditions.

Much more articulate than his fellow-millionaires—he had long dreamed of a literary career—he wrote numerous books and articles on his favorite doctrine of the stewardship of wealth. In *The Gospel of Wealth* (1900) he wrote:

This, then, is held to be the duty of the man of wealth: to set an example of modest, unostentatious living, shunning display or extravagance; to provide moderately for all wants of those dependent upon him; and, after doing so, to consider revenues which come to him simply as trust funds. . . .

In his book, *The Empire of Business* (1902), he reaffirmed this doctrine of surplus wealth as a sacred trust and asserted,

It is to business men following business careers that we chiefly owe our universities, colleges, libraries, and educational institutions, as witness, Girard, Lehigh, Chicago, Harvard, Yale, Cornell, and many others.

While Carnegie was probably the second richest man in the country, John D. Rockefeller was the first and was credited with being a "billionaire." By the time of his death in 1937 the oil king had given away well over a half billion dollars to numerous organizations, particularly through the Rockefeller Foundation, which he had founded in 1913. As already noted, the Foundation wrought a miracle of social rehabilitation in the South and abroad by controlling or stamping out hookworm disease, yellow fever, and malaria, and in assisting medical schools. The General Education Board disregarded race lines to raise the level of education and science, especially in the South. John D. Rockefeller, like other wealthy businessmen, looked favorably upon founding theological schools and hoped to make a great Baptist institution of the University of Chicago. However, he did not interfere with its evolution into a great secular institution and, contrary to contemporary charges of interference with academic freedom, left its policies to President William Rainey Harper and his able colleagues. His son, John D. Rockefeller, Jr., devoted his life to the supervision of the Rockefeller philanthropies.

Such huge charitable foundations, usually incorporated under state or federal law and enjoying tax exemptions, were new patrons of the arts and public welfare on a scale undreamed of in the days of Maecenas. Despite grumblings of "tainted money" the trustees usually displayed a high integrity in administration, which stood in pleasant contrast to some aspects of the original process of wealth accumulation. Upton Sinclair's *Goose Step* (1923), which echoed a charge of the "muckrakers" regarding the dominance of wealth over private schools, grossly exaggerated the situation. However, popular fears that the private college was lost to Big Business undoubtedly increased appropriations for state schools. During the Bemis case at the University of Chicago, involving the dismissal of a leftist economics professor by President Harper, progressives argued with more spirit than sound evidence that this was due to direct intervention by the Rockefellers or other financial contributors. That the private university enjoys less academic freedom than the state colleges has never been demonstrated.

4

The captains of industry, whom Veblen grossly libelled as a "leisure class," had tended to devote most of their waking hours to business. However, when, in the twilight of their lives, they embarked upon "culture" in the spirit of keeping up with the Joneses, the result was apt to justify Veblen's mordant characterizations of "pecuniary emulation," "conspicuous leisure," "conspicuous consumption," "pecuniary canons of taste," and "dress as an expression of the pecuniary culture." Thorstein Veblen, himself, had been one of twelve children raised in a poor Norwegian settlement in Minnesota. He looked upon the "leisure class" as predatory and parasitical, deriving prestige—like the Puget Sound Indian who practiced potlatch—from wasteful displays of wealth and status. They liked exploitation, display, and manipulation of the stock market, rather than workmanlike creativeness or the best utilization of productive forces. As evidence of "conspicuous leisure," Veblen cited such leisure-class values as the study of dead languages apart from genuine intellectual considerations, the insistence on expensive dress and furniture, the pursuit of time-consuming and expensive sports such as breeding race horses and pedigreed dogs, the display of decorous manners, and the acquisition of titles and honorary degrees. The connoisseur of food, clothes, architecture, and weapons practiced a time-consuming art that only a leisure class could afford to acquire. One secured high status by "making an invidious pecuniary comparison" with one's aristocratic neighbors by displaying numerous servants in livery, who resided in spacious quarters and specialized rigidly in personal attendance, leaving the more menial household tasks to another category of servants.

Much of Veblen's indictment may be documented—but not all of it. Carnegie and Rockefeller, the richest of them all, lived lives of traditional restraint and scarcely interfered with the institutions or professorial chairs that they endowed. So did Wanamaker and Marshall Field, the store owners. J. P. Morgan, Sr., and William C. Whitney fit only partly into the Gilded Age pattern. Both were generous and intelligent patrons of the arts, though displaying a strong preference for established European masters in the world of painting rather than evincing much interest or understanding for significant contemporary artists. Morgan, enjoying a yacht and mansion, had full acceptance in society and needed no additional display. In 1891, he organized the exclusive Metropolitan Club, known as "the millionaires club," the most resplendent of the various aristocratic clubs set up to imitate the fashionable London dining clubs. The younger J. P. Morgan asserted in 1936, "If you destroy the leisure class, you destroy civilization."

Whitney, who had married the sister of the treasurer of the Standard Oil Company, and had himself amassed a forty-million-dollar fortune within ten years, largely in New York street railways, filled his Fifth Avenue palace with art treasures from Europe and annexed a staircase from a medieval castle. During the 1890's he commissioned McKim, Mead, and White to build an Italian Renaissance palace for his second wife. Above all he loved horses and the excitement of the race tracks in Kentucky and in England. He did much to make horseracing fashionable at Saratoga and, after his wife died, retired from business to devote himself to sport. August Belmont, American agent of the Rothschilds, became president of the exclusive Jockey Club. Horse racing had fascinated Commodore Vanderbilt, but he was too crude for the younger society, which made horse racing and horse shows ceremonial institutions for the wealthy elite after his death.

Charles T. Yerkes, the Chicago traction millionaire who suffered social ostracism for his buccaneering methods of self-enrichment, found compensation in a series of (brief) marriages, the purchase of a gold bedstead belonging to the king of the Belgians, and the acquisition of immense collections of historic European paintings. His office windows gleamed with medieval stained glass. He left to the University of Chicago the impressive Yerkes Observatory at Lake Geneva. Mrs. Potter Palmer ruled over the "Gold Coast" in her huge turreted castle along Lake Shore Drive and entertained regally for titled aristocrats as well as Middle Western parvenus. Marshall Field, absorbed in his myriad enterprises, yielded to his wife's insistence that the Fields build a mansion that would outdo those of their class, one in which elaborate balls and receptions would compare favorably with those of European nobility. Still, Field did not forget Chicago, for he donated $10,000,000 for the world-famous Field Museum of Natural History and millions more for the University of Chicago and other public institutions. Oil and steel millionaires in Rockefeller's Cleveland made Euclid Avenue the aristocratic counterpart of Chicago's Lake Shore Drive and New York's Fifth Avenue.

In a young nation with a parvenu elite, the monied classes saw no attraction in the democratic notions of social equality. While the Constitution cruelly forbade titles of nobility to American citizens, thousands of daughters from substantial meat-packing, steel, oil, and real-estate families acquired status by marrying titled foreigners. Others plotted with the harassed American ambassador to the Court of St. James for the privilege of curtseying to the royal couple after cheerfully enduring hours of waiting in a long anteroom. Exclusiveness was enhanced by the founding in 1887 of *The Social Register* in which a coterie of shrewd journalists published a list of genuine "society" folk, together with the relevant facts of their family background, club memberships, and yacht acquisitions. Genealogy grew as a paid profession under the patronage of those who wished to prove the respectable antiquity of their families as compared to that of certain parvenus.

Even Carnegie had his castle in Scotland and James B. Duke's father liked to parade through Europe's hotels and museums under the status afforded by a misplaced comma, "Washington, Duke of Durham." College fraternities and sororities maintained class distinctions regardless of democratic shibboleths. Princeton's president, Woodrow Wilson, fought vainly to abolish the exclusive eating clubs of the wealthier students.

The fashionable—and even lesser folk as well—liked to read the "Society Page" in which enterprising columnists described the glittering events of the "social season," the expensive clothes worn at the opera, and the vacationing plans of the elite. Among the select affairs of the season was the debut in which Society acknowledged by its presence that a young lady had reached the age when she was ready to consider socially eligible males in marriage. "Serving notice upon the social world that a daughter has become nubile," wrote Wecter, "the debut has immemorial roots which may be traced to coming of age in Samoa and Polynesia." The debut usually involved an expensive round of dances, hotel receptions, and theater parties. Little wonder that the socially negligible Thorstein Veblen tried to explain small families among the elite by arguing that these nabobs could not afford to have many children! Gilded youth with aspirations for social service found an attractive and respectable social outlet in the Junior League, founded in 1901 by a daughter of the railway magnate, Edward H. Harriman. This combination of social work and exclusiveness in membership spread to most large cities.

One of the most amusing tales told by Wecter is the story of the society patronage of opera houses. By the 1880's the choice box seats of opera houses had risen so far in prestige value that the struggle between the wealthy colonial families and the ultra rich parvenus came to a desperate juncture. When the "Golden Horse-shoe" of the New York Academy of Music excluded the Vanderbilts and others of the newly-rich, the excluded parvenus combined to build the more lavish Metropolitan Opera House and to bask in the glory of the new "Diamond Horseshoe" of elite boxholders. How well the operas were presented was necessarily less important, although the expense of imported Italian opera singers must be widely recognized.

This cultural life had its directing spirit in Samuel Ward McAllister, a wealthy Georgia lawyer in antebellum years who had married the daughter of a Georgia millionaire. After observing the impressive traditional ways of European elite, particularly of London's exclusive Almack circle, he resolved to transform parvenu America into the baroque magnificence of the Old World. Ward McAllister moved to the village of Newport and made it into a center of fashion. E. M. Hinton writes in a biographic sketch, "The modest country picnic under his practised hand became a fête champêtre with music, floral decorations, dancing, and exquisitely iced champagne." By the 1860's he had become the arbiter of New

York's "society." In 1872 he broke the ultra-exclusive clique of a few rich families by organizing the heads of the leading city families, both the old Knickerbocker families and the flashy "smart set," as Patriarchs to enlarge the social circle through subscription balls. John Jacob Astor, Jr., a Livingston, and a Van Rensselaer were among the twenty-five Patriarchs.

McAllister apparently coined the term "Four Hundred." According to an oft-told story, Mrs. William Astor—whose family had gradually thrown off in the public mind the crude associations with old John Jacob Astor—found her ballroom too small to accommodate her lengthy list. This predicament was ended by McAllister, who reduced the list skillfully and later asserted at the very fashionable Union Club that there were "only about four hundred people in New York Society." Thus the label of the Four Hundred stuck.

Ward McAllister left a snobbish record of high society in his book, *Society As I Have Found It* (1890), and described the antics of the new multimillionaires of the 1880's with a connoisseur's delight. Veblen may have derived his notion of conspicuous consumption from such a passage:

One was no longer content with a dinner of a dozen or more to be served by a couple of servants. Fashion demanded that you be received in the hall of the house in which you were to dine by from five to six servants, who, with the butler, were to serve the repast. The butler, on such occasions, [did] alone the head-work, and under him he had these men in livery serve the dinner, he to guide and direct them. Soft strains of music were introduced between the courses, and in some houses gold replaced silver in the way of plate, and everything that skill and art could suggest were added to make the dinners not a vulgar display, but a great gastronomic effort, evidencing the possession by the host of both money and taste.

The grand doings on the society page did not always entertain its lower-class readers. During the recurrent depressions of 1873, 1885, and 1893, journalists found much to criticize in calling attention to the millions wasted in leisure-class spectacles and to the dominant position of ill-qualified captains of industry or their wives as patrons of the arts and sciences. During the eighties, when the fashionable

restaurant movement was epitomized by New York's elaborate
Delmonico's, unfriendly reporters injured the presidential hopes of
James G. Blaine by describing an alleged "Belshazzar's Feast" of
the candidate at that restaurant. As for the arts, there could be no
reasonable expectation that the esthetic acumen of Lorenzo de'
Medici or the great Renaissance popes could be found within the
circumscribed horizon of the princes of Porkopolis or the Dukes
of Durham. But the generosity of American philanthropists astonished the world by its lavishness and its keynote of service. The
next generation was to see innumerable small as well as large taxpayers become the new patrons of hospitals, schools, and museums.
Some equilibrium between the philanthropic captains of industry
and the service state had yet to be achieved that would allow the
freest rein to creative democratic development.

5

The social and cultural shortcomings of the captains of industry
in the transition of the United States to large-scale production must
not obscure the fundamental contribution made by their energies
to the unique American standard of living. On a gold basis the
estimated national wealth rose from 20 billion dollars in 1865 to
88.5 billions in 1900 and 186.3 billions in 1912. Manufacturing, mining, transportation, and other industrial activities led the economy
of the nation. Real wages rose ever higher on the whole and the
average day of the non-agricultural worker fell from eleven hours
in 1860 to ten in 1887, and nine by 1917. Shorter hours made far
greater progress among the highly skilled trades. Union members
of the building trades were close to a forty-four hour week at the
outbreak of World War I. Better nutrition and economic conditions
were major factors in the rapid increase of the average expectation
of life during this period. It is no longer necessary to repeat the
official statistics to prove that the 100,549,000 Americans of Woodrow Wilson's day enjoyed a higher standard of living than the
35,700,000 people in practically the same area during the administration of Andrew Johnson.

Decades before this era ended signs appeared that the erratic qualities of the captain of industry were passing in favor of a high degree of rationality in American industry. During the 1880's, Frederick W. Taylor, an engineer of Philadelphia, had developed certain principles of industrial efficiency that would transform existing production methods along the lines of "scientific management." He tried to analyze the reasons why he had become involved in a controversy over output with the workers of the Midvale Steel Company where he had worked as a gang boss. "Throughout American industry," he wrote in later years, "management's concept of a proper day's work was what the foreman could drive workers to do and the worker's conception was how little they could do and hold their jobs." Workers distrusted speed-up ideas that meant layoffs, In those days industry had reached a stage of overproduction and painful competition when it became more essential than ever to cut costs in order to maintain or raise profits.

Taylor aimed to bridge the gap between management and labor by aligning the self-interest of the latter with the employer through higher wages made possible by increased efficiency. He related a clearly defined task of reasonable difficulty under standardized conditions with the incentive of high wages. In 1895, he published the paper, "A Piece Rate System" to explain his ideas of measuring production through a "time study" department in which the stop watch would determine the essential manual operations and help in the fixing of rates for payment. He elaborated these ideas further in 1903 in a paper read before fellow engineers, "Shop Management." Here he forecast the future factory organization with specialized departments of "routing," "a cost and time division," and a central planner, "the disciplinarian," who later evolved into a scientific personnel manager.

In 1908, the Harvard Graduate School of Business Administration, which grew out of the largess of the president of the First National Bank of New York, George F. Baker, started its career with the enthusiastic acceptance of "Taylorization." Industrialists watched scientific management cautiously but after 1911 it became a vogue. This was due to the extraordinary publicity given Taylor

during the Eastern Rate hearings regarding higher railroad rates
demanded by the transportation executives. A manufacturer's counsel, Louis D. Brandeis, argued with considerable detail that the railroads could add millions to their profits and raise wages too on the
same rates by adopting the Taylor system.

Brandeis had long developed a democratic theory of free competitive enterprise. He knew the big industrial corporations well
for he had been a highly paid counsel for many of them and was not
impressed by the prevailing assumption that mere bigness made for
efficiency, lower prices, and better quality. Too many industries, he
felt, had expanded far beyond the point of optimum efficiency per
unit and were concealing their basic weaknesses by monopolistic
devices and tariffs to choke off competition. This was the message
of an essay that attracted wide attention, "The Curse of Bigness,"
which appeared in *Harper's Weekly* and presented a case for "regulated competition" as against "regulated monopoly." He felt disturbed by the growing hegemony of bankers and insurance directors
over the actual operation of factories and in *Other People's Money*
(1914), he questioned the efficiency of the banker-entrepreneur and
the dubious expedients of the investment trust. His arguments were
given point by the current revelations of the gross inefficiency and
high costs of New York's leading insurance firms. Brandeis did
much to convert President Woodrow Wilson to the regulative ideas
underlying the new Federal Trade Commission—that a preventive
technique of penalizing monopoly-fostering practices "item by item"
was superior to the direct but ineffective "trust-busting" method of
breaking up large units into their component parts. Theodore
Roosevelt's emphasis on trust-busting had failed completely.

With Taylorization came other evidences of increased economic
rationality in American business and industry, especially after 1910.
Business planning took on a more objective scientific form with the
general introduction at this time of the public accountant, the
marketing specialist, the consulting engineer, and the business
economist. National advertising integrated the railroad, the automobile, the telephone, and other forms of transportation and communication into a profitable nation-wide market for the products

of mechanized industry such as packaged foods and women's clothes. Mass purchasing power seemed much better realized than ever in the past. The Captain of Industry looked upon these facts and felt confident that his service in multiplying goods made unnecessary the efforts of social reformers in dividing income.

· 9 ·

The Labor Movement from Wendell Phillips to Samuel Gompers

[1865-1917]

I

THE glittering metropolis born of the Industrial Revolution uprooted the village mechanic and handicraftsman and defined more
clearly than ever the sharpening outlines of a working class.
High-priced urban real estate allowed few opportunities for the
laborer to fall back on the resources of truck gardening, poultry-
raising, or keeping a cow or two—although some did even in the
big cities. Rents, groceries, clothes, and urban amusements were all
expensive by rural standards. Severe depressions like those of
1873-79 and 1893-97 revealed the utter dependence of the laborer
upon an urban oasis that had suddenly dried into a desert. The new
railroad system intensified the competition between workers of
hitherto distant towns and cities. At the same time a flood of immigrants, almost entirely unregulated, sharpened the competition
for jobs and led organized labor to demand the restriction of foreigners.

The new machines made handicraft skills obsolete. Entire crafts,
whose methods of production were rooted in guild times and who
were proud of a long tradition of highly skilled independent shops,

gave way to factory production and a minute division of labor. For example, numerous unskilled workers became shoemakers after the invention of the sewing machine for stitching uppers (1852) and the McKay pegging machine (1862). In 1867 the new cigar mold for shaping cigars made their manufacture no longer a highly skilled one-man process but a series of specialized tasks that required only a brief training. Women and boys frequently took over the industrial tasks once considered fitting only for men.

Undoubtedly the long-run effect of urbanization on labor meant a higher standard of living, but in this transitional period between the Civil War and World War I the human dislocations were painful indeed. Antiquated individualistic attitudes and laws, born in a handicraft and rural society, hampered the efforts of reformers to protect workers against insecurity, industrial hazards, and legal obstacles against effective union organization. The era ended without the modest minimum of old age, sickness, and unemployment benefits that Bismarck's Germany and Tory England had granted. Unionization, too, lagged far behind the progress of industrialized Western Europe.

Actually, American trade unions enrolled less than 5 per cent of the laboring classes in the 1870's and did not advance beyond 10 per cent by the outbreak of World War I. Although labor history is usually told of necessity in terms of labor unions, this ignores the lot of 85 to 95 per cent of the working population. Why did the American worker usually ignore trade unions during this era? Why did he prefer to vote for Republican or Democratic candidates instead of supporting a labor slate? The answers require a fundamental analysis of the American labor movement.

First of all must be emphasized the relative fluidity of the American class structure. Despite the increasingly heavy capital required for the new factory machines and their rapid obsolescence, there remained from antebellum days a large group of journeymen and self-employed workers who made the transition from employee to employer and back again not once but several times in their lives. Wendell Phillips, whose humanitarianism embraced labor causes as well as reforms for the Negro and the Indian, explained in a letter of 1874 why the Marxian concept of class war was wholly inapplicable to American conditions:

> There'll never be, I believe and trust, a class party here, labor against capital, the lines are so indefinite, like dove's neck colors. Three-fourths of our population are to some extent capitalists, and again all see that there really ought always to be alliance, not struggle, between them. So me lean chiefly on related questions for growth: limitations of hours is almost the only special measure.

Compared to Europe, wealth was far less concentrated and opportunity greater. In 1900, the richest 2 per cent in Wisconsin owned 57 per cent of the wealth, but the same class in England owned 71.7 per cent. In terms of *income* rather than title to wealth, the lower 65 per cent in America held at least 39 per cent of the rapidly mounting national income (the largest in the world) by World War I. Professor Willford I. King of the University of Wisconsin wrote *The Wealth and Income of the People of the United States* in 1915 and came to the conclusion that wealth and income distribution in America offered a sufficient stimulus to effective work. However, he gave no Pollyanna picture:

> The facts of the case seem to be that, for the young man having the average start in life, the chances are about one to four or five that he will accumulate property worth mentioning and about one in fifty that he will become moderately wealthy.

It must be added that, although the American standard of living led all the rest of the world, social workers found working class standards far from adequate. In 1903, the United States Bureau of Labor made a careful study of 25,000 working-class families and reported that approximately two-thirds received less than $700 annually and nearly one-half less than $600. According to a rather convincing estimate of a budget for a family of five, the minimum of a "subsistence-plus" standard was $700. Even in this group three-fifths of the families studied lived in less than four rooms; one-third gathered their fuel in the streets; only one in six spent anything for the care of their teeth; and "recreation and education were reduced to the lowest terms."

Competition with the immigrant did not seriously hamper the advance of the native to higher status. Immigrants provided an ever-growing consumer's market and thereby stimulated the nation's economy, but they were usually competent only to hold unskilled and semiskilled jobs, leaving the highly skilled and managerial tasks to natives who stepped up the social ladder. Such was the case in antebellum times and the situation was basically the same in the era of Powderly and Gompers.

Individualism was a strong American trait derived in part at least from the self-reliant frontier psychology and the militant Protestant heritage. The middle-class idea that unions and labor parties violated this tradition of freedom found a responsive chord in the hearts of the laboring classes as well. However, frontier individualism had not excluded a considerable amount of self-help and, in 1905, the West helped produce the most militant brand of unionism in the Industrial Workers of the World. The strong tradition of "joining" in this country often opened the way for unions that had the fraternal objectives of a lodge rather than a belligerent worker's organization. Still another factor was the semireligious tradition of utopianism, which looked toward the coming of a cooperative commonwealth in the future. This ideal was often taken up by the early unions, but it militated in practice against any distinct "labor consciousness." Its leaders and programs were usually middle class, reformist, and gradualist.

Finally, the fact that America tended to be a huge "open shop" in this era can be partly explained by the aggressive tactics of many large employers and the devastating effect of the recurrent economic depressions. Labor organizers were frequently blacklisted out of the trade; lockouts wore down labor resistance; Pinkerton spies, police, private deputies, and troops crushed strikes and protected strikebreakers; and the best of lawyers could be employed to invoke against unions the common law doctrines of "restraint of trade" and "conspiracy."

Conservative courts, influenced by the vogue of Spencerian laissez faire as well as by the legal resources of capital, were slow to uphold elementary social legislation but were determined in their defense of the labor injunction and the Yellow-Dog contract in which prospective employees agreed not to enter a trade union on pain of dismissal. In 1898, Congress outlawed the yellow-dog contract in interstate commerce. Ten years later the Supreme Court in *Adair* v. *the United States* (1908) declared this anti-union practice a violation of the "freedom of contract" implied in the word "liberty" guaranteed by the Fifth Amendment. When Kansas attempted to forbid the yellow-dog contract, the Supreme Court declared this unconstitutional in *Coppage* v. *Kansas* (1915), invoking this time the doctrine of freedom of contract as implied in the Fourteenth Amendment. This resulted in the nullifying of similar laws among a dozen other states. In both the *Adair* and *Coppage* cases Justice Oliver Wendell Holmes, Jr., delivered a dissenting opinion, pointing out that the liberty to contract for one's services was meaningless unless the parties to the contract (employer and employee) were equal in strength. Although he had doubts about the value of trade unions, he nevertheless argued that legislatures had the right to act "to establish the equality of position between the parties in which liberty of contract begins."

Employers' associations, beginning with local groups during the Civil War and expanding into national networks thereafter, justified themselves as stabilizing agencies against the interference of unions with production. Sometimes these combined price-fixing with anti-union activities. Sympathizers for such causes were won more readily after the Paris Commune uprising of 1871 when the specter of an international Red revolution first chilled Western civilization. The most powerful of these employers' groups was the General Managers Association, formed in 1886, and representing twenty-four leading railroads aggregating a mileage of 40,933 and a capitalization of well over two billion dollars. Members were assessed for such services as the furnishing of strikebreakers, the circulation of a national black list, the establishment of a general schedule of wages, and the formulation of other employment policies. Committees of the Association, rather than individual railway administrators, met with those workers professing grievances. This affected almost a quarter of a million employees and won the great Pullman Strike for the railroads. In 1895, a federal investigating committee on the Pullman Strike reported,

If we regard its practical workings rather than its professions as expressed in its constitution, the General Manager's Association has no more standing in law than the old Trunk Line Pool. . . .

The Association is an illustration of the persistent and shrewdly devised plans of corporations to overreach their limitations, and to usurp indirectly powers and rights not contemplated in their charters and not obtainable from the people or their legislators.

Better known to the next generation was the National Association of Manufacturers organized in 1895 to promote tariff protection, but shifting thereafter to an attack upon unions and in behalf of the "individual freedom" of the "open shop." In their convention of 1903 the N.A.M. dwelt upon the tyranny of organized labor and declared their policy to be opposed to the recognition of unions. Thereafter, this organization, under David M. Parry, formed the national spearhead of an open shop drive. They launched the Citizen's Industrial Association as the chief agency to promote their cause in the press and in public meetings. The C.I.A. fought the patronage of union-label goods and urged their own supporters to buy goods from those resisting the unions. One of their best-known converts among the educators was President Charles W. Eliot of Harvard who praised the strikebreaker as an American hero, the defender of individual liberty.

One N.A.M. president, J. W. Van Cleve, made St. Louis the leading open shop center. In the notable antiboycott case involving Buck's Stove and Range Company of St. Louis (1906), he secured an injunction against the officers of the American Federation of Labor (who had listed his firm on the "We Don't Patronize" list) forbidding them to discuss the current metal polishers' strike for a nine-hour day. When Samuel Gompers rejected the injunction as illegal he was sentenced to one year in jail (which he never served) and two officers were also punished. This revival of the old conspiracy doctrine of the common law wiped out a substantial part of labor's gains in the courts since *Commonwealth* v. *Hunt* (1842) had legalized trade unions.

2

Two major motivations spurred on the American labor movement despite the fact that recurrent panics like those of 1837, 1857, 1873 and 1893 had wiped out many flourishing trade unions. One was the self-interest of the craftsmen, particularly the printers, carpenters, and cigar-makers, who feared the growing competition of the unskilled and semiskilled workers in an increasingly mechanized economy. They labored jealously to keep down the number of apprentices and exclude rival unions from their "jurisdiction." The other was the piecemeal reformism sponsored by middle-class humanitarians like Wendell Phillips and by the trade union leaders. While the craftsmen were most firmly entrenched in powerful local unions, which aimed at a monopoly of the job, the reformists organized on an expansive national scale, hoping for the millennial advent of a brotherhood of cooperatives. The antebellum faith persisted that men could be saved by replacing the selfish motives of competition with the altruistic impulses of cooperation. Albert Brisbane, American apostle of Fourier's phalansteries, was still alive and deeply absorbed in the labor movement. Phillips and other antislavery men were ready to embark on the eight-hour movement to free men from labor exploitation.

To offset the tendency of transportation to sharpen labor competition over an ever larger market, labor leaders after the Civil War turned to national unions. In 1866, the National Labor Union came into existence in Baltimore as a reformist, Utopian organization. It minimized the usual craft techniques of strikes and immediate shop issues. Instead, the union demanded an eight-hour day, producers' cooperatives, the abolition of convict labor, Chinese exclusion, the sale of public lands only to actual settlers, and the establishment of a department of labor. Both skilled and unskilled, even farmers and suffragettes, were welcomed into the National Labor Union. Their president, William H. Sylvis, represented the strongest labor union in the country, the Molders' International Union.

Sylvis sponsored a number of iron molder cooperatives, which failed like so many similar experiments among unions and Grangers.

The successful example of the British Rochdale cooperative system did not insure success for such movements here. Laborers and farmers lacked "class consciousness" and bought wherever the price was lowest—even patronizing the cutthroat stores that aimed at the extinction of the cooperatives. Credit sources were lacking, dishonesty and inefficiency riddled the cooperatives, and they were tainted with the red brush of communism in the eyes of timorous citizens. The N.L.U. allied itself with the inflationist Greenback movement of the 1870's, despite labor's usual hostility to inflation, hopeful that this farmer-labor alliance would lead to the end of the "wage system." This conglomeration of unions, farmers' societies, and reformist eight-hour leagues finally died in 1872 after a brief experiment in politics as the National Labor and Reform party.

Quite a different kind of union were the "Molly Maguires," the secret ring controlling the Ancient Order of Hibernians in the anthracite coal fields of Pennsylvania. It is doubtful whether the "Mollies" were identical with an older violent organization of the same name in Ireland, but the inspiration was obvious and both had a background of antilandlordism. Although Irish Catholics, they were denounced by the church for their violence and their oaths of secrecy that clashed with the obligations of the confessional. Since the 1860's the Mollies had fought with every weapon against exploitation by gang bosses, foremen, and company stores in the mining villages. Their grievances were genuine, especially in a day when the railroad-controlled mine operators themselves frequently resorted to brutal tactics, but the homicidal "Mollie" methods estranged well-wishers.

One railroad owner decided to end this situation by calling in the new detective agency of Allan Pinkerton whose fame was already nation-wide. This Scottish-born detective had been sensationally successful in exposing a gang of counterfeiters in Chicago in 1850. In 1861, he had thwarted a plot to murder Lincoln and had been so active in war espionage that he has been credited with founding the federal secret service. Just after the war he again won applause for his solution of a $700,000 robbery of the Adams Express Company. Increasingly, his detective agency became intimately linked with the large corporations that were resisting unionization. The worst notoriety came after his death when his sons sent a small army of Pinkertons into an industrial civil war during the Homestead Strike of 1892.

Now, in 1873, Allan Pinkerton promptly responded to the appeal for aid by sending one of his best operatives, James McParlan, whose Irish Catholic background was calculated to lull the suspicions of the "Mollies." McParlan lived among these men, posed as a fugitive from the law, and rose to a key position within the order while he painstakingly gathered evidence. He struck in 1875, incriminating over a score of leaders, which resulted in the execution of ten and the jailing of fourteen for long terms. The Mollie Maguires were smashed and unionism among the anthracite miners ended for a time.

The panic of 1873–78 with its 3,000,000 unemployed aroused defiance in many of the idle men whose families were starving or left to the limited resources of church relief. In turn, the police resorted to harsh repressive measures. The worst incident was the Tompkins Square riot of 1874 in New York city. This involved a large mass meeting under the sponsorship of the socialistic International Workingmen's Association. Shortly before the meeting began, city authorities changed their minds and cancelled the permit, but not in time to notify many people. The police, nevertheless, insisted on immediate dispersal and charged into the crowd, consisting largely of immigrants, and clubbed those who stood in their way. One of these bystanders was Samuel Gompers, who escaped injury by jumping down a cellarway. This experience convinced him that the taint of radicalism was enough to discredit any labor cause. His future American Federation of Labor was to go far in the direction of making unionism respectable to the middle-class citizen.

Meanwhile, a successor to the defunct National Labor Union had been born, the "Noble and Holy Order of the Knights of Labor." Like its predecessor, the Knights were Utopian in outlook, stressed the solidarity of labor, both skilled and unskilled, and preached the cooperative commonwealth. Their slogan, "An injury to one is the concern of all," suggested a far more militant organization. Uriah S. Stephens, who had hoped to enter the Baptist ministry but had become a tailor instead, had made his Garment Cutters' Association the sponsor of the Knights in 1869. He stressed secrecy as essential for the protection of labor and developed a highly intricate Christian ritual with grandiose masonic titles, beginning with himself as Grand Master Workman.

In 1878, the Knights were organized on a national scale, and invited into their membership wage-earners, even former wage-earners, and reformers who had no trade at all. They did exclude "unproductive" professional men like lawyers, bankers, liquor dealers, and stockbrokers. In rural districts members were often gathered on a geographical rather than on a trade basis into local "assemblies." Their program resembled that of the National Labor Union in its inclusion of cooperatives, the eight-hour day, and other reforms. Too, they were hospitable to woman's rights and added the idea of equal pay for equal work and the prohibition of child labor. With the Granger radicals, they preached government ownership of the railroads and telegraph and a graduated income tax. Strikes were minimized in favor of arbitration. In 1879, when Stephens resigned in favor of Terence Powderly, the Knights had more than 28,000 members and were rapidly moving forward.

The Knights were notably shrewd lobbyists. In 1882, they persuaded Congress to pass the Chinese Exclusion Act, a measure long agitated among laborers, especially in the California "Sand Lot" agitation of Denis Kearney's day. "The Chinese must go!" was an old slogan that was finally realized. Three years later the Knights led the unions to another victory, this time securing the passage of the Alien Contract Labor Law to halt the importation of laborers under contract. For decades many thousands of Europeans as well as Chinese had been imported here under a previous contract at wages that seemed high by foreign standards, but were definitely a cut below prevailing wages. By congressional laws of the next few years, alien contract laborers were deported and all soliciting of immigrants was forbidden. Far too much of organized labor's energies was absorbed in this type of anti-immigrant agitation, rather than in more fundamental social legislation in the general interest of all labor.

The Southwest railway strike of 1885, unauthorized by Powderly, was sensationally successful and won thousands of new members for the Knights. In that conflict the universally detested speculator, Jay Gould, now a railway magnate, was compelled to rescind current wage cuts. Meanwhile, membership rose to 700,000—a unique record in American trade-union history. When the tide turned the next year and militant locals plunged the Knights into reckless strike adventures, Powderly counted for less than nothing in settling the dispute.

Finally, the national strikes in behalf of the eight-hour day foundered on the Haymarket Riot hysteria of 1886 and led to a violent public reaction against all unions and the Knights in particular. A half million dues-paying members dropped away in two years and by 1893 the Knights had dwindled to 75,000. With the decay of the Knights, industrial unionism would have suffered a severe setback had it not been for the organizing efforts of Eugene V. Debs in his American Railway Union and the revolutionary Industrial Workers of the World.

3

The Knights of Labor had never tolerated revolutionary violence but its 1886 campaign for the eight-hour day was blamed for the dynamite plottings and terrorism of the anarchist Black International during the Haymarket Riot. Actually, the agitation for shorter hours had had a long constructive history. It represented but the human counterpart of the technological revolution that was reducing the number of labor hours involved in each process of manufacturing and distribution.

In 1840, the earlier ten-hour movement had been so influential as to lead President Martin Van Buren to limit the hours of labor for all navy-yard employees to ten hours. After the Civil War trade-union leaders and reformers moved on to the next battle—an eight-hour day. Its leading exponent was a self-educated Boston machinist,

Ira Steward, fondly called "the eight-hour monomaniac" by his friends and acquaintances. He advocated a "golden law of wages" to replace David Ricardo's "iron law of wages," which had held the pessimistic view that wages could not rise above the subsistence level because of population pressure. Classical economists and captains of industry were directly or indirectly influenced by Ricardo's book *On the Principles of Political Economy and Taxation* (1817) which stated, "The natural price of labour is that price which is necessary to enable the labourers, one with another, to subsist and to perpetuate their race, without either increase or diminution." George Pullman bluntly told federal investigators that wages were determined by "the law of supply and demand," not by philanthropy.

Steward helped organize an Eight-Hour League in Massachusetts and became the leader of numerous such leagues throughout the North. Lobbies were set up in state legislatures and at Washington. Political candidates were pledged to support a general eight-hour law. In 1868, President Andrew Johnson signed an eight-hour bill covering government workers, although this suffered for years from conflicting administrative interpretations. By the end of the sixties at least six states had passed eight-hour laws covering industry, but these were usually nullified by the legal chicanery of harassed conservative politicians. Wisconsin, for example, made eight hours mandatory only "when the contract was silent on the subject or where there is no express contract to the contrary."

One of Steward's friends, Wendell Phillips, took an active part in this political agitation. This Harvard-trained son of wealthy Boston parents had given twenty-five years of his life to abolitionism. After the Civil War he had agitated for an independent labor party and thereafter had helped to sponsor the Eight-Hour League of his state and the new Massachusetts Bureau of Labor Statistics. He contributed money and wrote numerous articles for the eight-hour day, ran for Congress in 1866 and also for governor on the Labor Reform party ticket. During the decade before his death in 1884 he took active part in the Greenback movement. He was not alone among the antislavery fighters who felt that labor reform was the logical successor to the earlier battle for the Negro's freedom.

The shorter hours movement became identified with subversive radicalism in the unsympathetic metropolitan press, particularly in Joseph Medill's *Chicago Tribune*. A small group of German anarchists with an even smaller native following frightened citizens by their terroristic language in behalf of an eight-hour day as a class war issue. Not all anarchists were advocates of the "deed," but their speeches and writings sometimes contained allusions to the dynamite that would be blown up on the always unspecified day of revolution. Such was the case of the radical immigrant editor, August Spies, and his small Chicago paper, the *Arbeiter Zeitung*, which had a circulation of under 3600.

Attention was focused upon the approaching anarchist Haymarket meeting of May 4. This proved to be an indignation meeting with anarchist overtones, all of which obviously referred to a remote future revolution. However, Captain Bonfield of the police decided to have a showdown and marched with a force of 180 upon the meeting. When one disgruntled speaker protested that this was a peaceable meeting, he was suddenly interrupted by a bomb that rose over the heads of the crowd and exploded among the police. Fifty of them were injured, seven of them fatally.

In the subsequent efforts to fix the blame for the bomb-throwing eight men were adjudged guilty of conspiracy by an obviously prejudiced jury and their appeals to the Illinois Supreme Court and to the United States Supreme Court failed. In England, William Morris wrote to his friend Robert Browning, "I am much troubled by this horror." Protest came from William Dean Howells, Annie Besant, George Bernard Shaw, and hundreds of other notables. The governor offered to commute the death sentences of the men to life imprisonment (one committed suicide), but this was refused by all but two. Later, the survivors were pardoned by Governor Altgeld on the ground that the trial had been unfair.

Although the Knights of Labor leaned backward to avoid any association with or sympathy for the defendants, public opinion turned against them anyway and against the eight-hour movement. Employers then cancelled the concessions already made to the strikers. In their gratitude to the police, Chicago businessmen raised large purses for them. Discovering bomb-throwing plots became a profitable activity for the Chicago police officials according to the testimony given by a former chief of police to the *Chicago Daily News* on May 10, 1889:

It was my policy to quiet matters down as soon as possible after the 4th of May. . . .

On the other hand, Captain Schaack wanted to keep things stirring. He wanted bombs to be found here, there, all around, everywhere. . . . After we got the anarchist societies broken up, Schaack wanted to send men to again organize new societies right away. He wanted to keep the thing boiling . . . keep himself prominent before the public. . . . After I heard all that, I began to think there was, perhaps, not so much to all this anarchist business as they claimed.

Samuel Gompers believed that the reaction had set the labor movement back at least a decade. Once more he felt vindicated in his belief that no labor cause could afford the slightest tinge of radicalism. The Knights of Labor had been wrong in assuming that they could overcome the hostility of the metropolitan press. The reaction was the cue for a wholesale return to "pure and simple" trade unionism, divorced from socialist panaceas, cooperatives, labor parties, and militant strikes. In this setting the American Federation of Labor came into existence.

4

Samuel Gompers was born in London's East End in 1850 of Dutch-Jewish parentage and had come to New York with his parents in 1863. He was apprenticed to a cigar maker and later in an East Side tenement he worked alongside his father in making cigars. In the International Cigar Makers Union he had learned to study and to reject socialism and to adopt the "pure and simple" union strategy of Adolph Strasser, the president of the International. The cigar makers successfully fought the contractor's sweat shop, raised wages, reduced the hours of work, and built up a large strike fund by high initiation fees and union dues. One of their techniques was to urge members and sympathizers to patronize only those who displayed the union label.

These ideas became the stock in trade of the American Federation of Labor, which finally emerged in 1886 at Columbus, Ohio, from the union of earlier craft organizations representing some 150,000 unionists. Unlike the Knights of Labor whom they fought for years, the A. F. of L. based its national and international structure on strong local unions united at the upper levels into city and state federations. Each craft jealously preserved its exclusive jurisdiction of a trade, aided by the national Executive Council to avoid dual unionism and jurisdictional disputes. Strike funds were gathered through membership assessments, but in most things the locals enjoyed considerable "states' rights." Radical doctrinaires were discouraged by the Gompers leadership.

In 1885, Adolph Strasser had told a Senate committee of the aim of his cigar-maker's union. "We have no ultimate ends. We are going on from day to day. We fight only for immediate objects and objects that can be realized in a few years." This idea was tirelessly reiterated by Gompers until his death in 1924:

The primary essential in our mission has been the protection of the wage-worker, now; to increase his wages; to cut hours off the long workday, which was killing him; to improve the safety and the sanitary conditions of the work shop; to free him from the tyrannies, petty or otherwise, which served to make his existence a slavery. These, in the nature of things, I repeat, were and are the primary objects of trade unionism.

Labor parties were ruled out, except for occasional forays into the political field in behalf of candidates favorable to labor. "Reward your friends and punish your enemies," was a Gompers maxim. Class consciousness and militancy were discouraged. "There was no point in taking an immovable position for an impossible object," he argued.

The A. F. of L. claimed credit for the subsequent victory of the eight-hour movement, the passage of child labor laws in thirty-eight states, workmen's compensation laws in thirty-five states, numerous compulsory education laws, and laws improving the position of women in industry. Gompers was proud of the labor provisions in the Clayton Act of 1914 for which he had campaigned.

The Clayton Act, in language reminiscent of the papal encyclical *Rerum Novarum* and of the Social Gospel Creed, declared that "the labor of a human being is not a commodity or article of commerce." Section 6, which Gompers called the Magna Carta of Labor, exempted trade unions and their members from prosecution, as conspirators in restraint of trade, under the Sherman Antitrust law, which had been invoked successfully in 1902 by the employers' American Anti-Boycott Association against the United Hatters of America. Labor injunctions were banned unless essential to prevent irreparable injury to property rights for which no adequate compensation existed at law. However, the Clayton Act proved a mirage as far as the unions and trust-busters were concerned. Jurists were to find fatal legal weaknesses in the law during the conservative 1920's. "Government by injunction," labor's complaint since the Debs cases of 1895, continued to plague the unions.

The A. F. of L. policy of immigration restriction, which it shared with other unions, was rewarded in 1917 by the literacy test, which concealed restriction under the guise of selection. This was the third major labor victory against immigration since the Chinese Exclusion Act of 1882 and the Alien Contract Labor Law of 1885. By 1917, A. F. of L. total membership passed the two-million mark, about two-thirds of the entire trade union membership in the United States. The urbane Samuel Gompers, who talked the democratic language of British trade unionism without imitating their cooperative experiments, had gone far in justifying "pure and simple unionism"—though millions of the unskilled remained outside the fold of labor organization.

One militant labor leader who gave Gompers many an uncomfortable hour was Eugene Victor Debs, born in 1855, son of an Alsatian grocer who had emigrated in 1849 to live in the French section of Terre Haute, Indiana. Debs did not go beyond the first year of high school but he was a voracious reader and he developed a rationalistic philosophy that estranged him from his Catholic background. Never a labor doctrinaire, though more radical than most leaders, he followed his lifelong reformist inclinations in behalf of labor, particularly of the railroad workers; he had been a locomotive fireman and knew the hazards of that job. In 1880, he became secretary and treasurer of the conservative Brotherhood of Locomotive Firemen and the editor of the *Locomotive Fireman's Magazine.* Like other labor leaders he was influenced by the writings of the Danish-American socialist, Laurence Gronlund, author of *The Cooperative Commonwealth.* This book advocated the gradual achievement of some form of state socialism. He was also impressed by the theories of Professor Richard T. Ely, particularly by the economist's idea that strict trade unionism no longer met the new conditions of corporate centralization and had to be replaced by a broader labor organization.

Dissatisfied with the narrow self-interest of the Railroad Brotherhoods, Debs turned to a new plan of organizing the lowly engine-wiper and the section-hand as well as the engineer and conductor. This plan was used in the formation of the American Railway Union in 1893, which was based on the principle of industrial unionism to unite various categories of trainmen according to a logical shop grouping, rather than a grouping by crafts. The Knights of Labor had also encouraged industrial unionism, but lacked the unified purpose of the A.R.U. Debs's organization tried to stop wage cuts in that severe depression year, and quickly attracted 150,000 members. So effective was Debs that in the brief Great Northern Strike of April, 1894, the A.R.U. tied up transportation from St. Paul to the Coast and compelled James J. Hill to withdraw 75 per cent of the recent pay cuts.

The A.R.U. next moved on to boycott all Pullman cars during the national strike of 1894. George Pullman and the General Managers Association profited by Hill's mistakes and developed a shrewd anti-strike strategy. The Pullman officers refused to arbitrate while the Managers prepared to fire the heaviest antilabor artillery. Meanwhile, the strike was spreading to twenty-seven states, though no serious interference with mail trains was officially reported.

Attorney General Richard Olney recommended the issuance of a federal injunction against the strike leaders. The labor injunction had long declined in England, the land of its birth, but in the American strikes of the 1880's it had taken on a new lease on life in the name of the "time-honored principles of equity jurisdiction." On July 1 a blanket injunction was issued against Debs and other A.R.U. officials, enjoining any strike activity whatsoever. The A.R.U. rejected the injunction as illegal and blamed the railway officials who refused to forward mail trains unless Pullman cars were attached. While the *Chicago Tribune* attacked "Dictator Debs," the liberal *Chicago Times* denounced the injunction: "Childlike trust in the benevolence and fairness of the employer must be the workingmen's future policy if this injunction be made an effective precedent." The second major weapon was the use of federal troops in the Chicago Strike, despite the fact that the governor was ready to act in sending in state militia but had not been consulted.

The strike collapsed, Debs went to jail for six months on a contempt of court charge, and Gompers urged the men to hurry back to their jobs. The strikers (many were never rehired) later had the moral victory of a sympathetic federal report on the Chicago Strike by the United States Commissioner of Labor, Carroll D. Wright. As for the issue of "government by injunction," this entered the Democratic platform of 1896 and was written by Altgeld. Later, the Clayton Act attempted to outlaw labor injunctions. The issue of federal troops in labor disputes also became a political issue. For the time, Gompers had triumphed in his insistence that the limited objectives of craft unionism alone deserved labor support; and temporarily, industrial unionism fell under a cloud.

One of Debs's most serious errors from any constructive standpoint was his sponsorship in 1905 of the revolutionary Industrial Workers of the World, though he broke with them two years later. So eager was he to promote industrial unionism and integrate it with socialism that he came close to identifying himself with revolutionary syndicalism and its One Big Union based on political rather than trade unionist action. One of the explosive ingredients of the I.W.W. was William D. (Big Bill) Haywood's Western Federation of Miners, which combined trade union tactics with frontier violence. Colorado miners grew more violent in the face of provocative managerial tactics tolerated by absentee mineowners. Transient workers, lumberjacks, and migratory farm workers, who felt no genuine stake

in society, made a religion of the I.W.W. Their songs of social hate
were usually set to the tunes of gospel hymns. In 1912, the I.W.W.
led the hitherto unorganized textile workers of Lawrence, Massachusetts, to a sweeping victory against extremely low wages, long hours,
and poor working conditions. Steel workers, packing-plant employees, and other unskilled men quickly joined until a total membership of 60,000 was reached. They acquired a crusading spirit and
fervently sang such songs as "The Red Flag" and "Hallelujah! I'm a
Bum!" even as they were marched off to jail. Their creed of violence,
though not necessarily practiced by most of them, advocated sabotage as well as strikes and the ultimate overthrow of capitalism by
revolutionary tactics. Many were irresponsible romantics like Haywood. Finally, their refusal to bear arms in any "capitalist war" led
to the destruction of the "Wobblies" during World War I and
immediately afterward.

5

American labor was deeply interested in the Progressive movement under Roosevelt, Taft, and Wilson. The middle-class nature of
this reform movement did not exclude labor whose psychology was
also predominantly middle-class. Trust-busting and other anti-
monopoly programs attracted laborers conscious of the rising cost of
living and the nation-wide combinations of employers, which made
obsolete the old personal relationship between owner and hired
man. Populistic farmers whose ideas were taken up by the major
parties in 1912 had long included labor planks in their statement of
principles. The People's party had favored a graduated income tax
and the abolition of Pinkertons and industrial spies. Gompers supported Bryan in 1908 and Wilson in 1912.

Labor was not unsympathetic to the Progressive party's demands
for "direct democracy" and responsible government—the hoped-for
end of boss rule through the initiative, the referendum, the recall,
the primaries, the direct election of senators, the shorter ballot,
equal suffrage for men and women, and a corrupt practices act.
Unions had long before advocated the party's planks for "Social and
Industrial Justice": industrial safety and health legislation, work-

men's compensation laws, prohibition of child labor, minimum wage standards, the eight-hour day, the abolition of convict labor, the right to organize, and a social insurance system for old age, sickness, and unemployment.

During most of the nineteenth century Anglo-American law used the law of negligence to restrain injured workmen from collecting compensation. This "fellow servant" doctrine meant that employers were not liable if the injury proceeded from the carelessness of a fellow-worker or that reasonable care had not been exercised by the employee. The employer even argued successfully in the courts that the worker assumed the risks of injury inherent in the occupation by accepting employment. Workers could collect damages only through an expensive lawsuit and this was not too attractive in view of the "fellow servant" doctrine and the notion of "assumption of risk." Toward the end of the century the "fellow servant" doctrine was dropped in most American courts. In 1908, the Federal Employers' Liability Act abolished the "fellow servant" rule and the "assumption of risk" doctrine of common law in accidents upon interstate railways. Most states followed this lead in enacting such Employers' Liability laws.

Actual workmen's compensation laws, aside from the principle of liability, began in 1902 with Maryland's legislation, but this was declared unconstitutional. However, in 1911, nine states passed compensation laws and most other states had followed this example by 1917. The old system that compelled injured workmen to go to court for damages was finally replaced by a compulsory system of nearly automatic payments for injuries. Thus the hopelessly inadequate efforts of the trade unions to protect their members from industrial risks were supplemented by an increasingly effective workmen's compensation system.

German paternalistic ideas of state health, unemployment, and old age insurance made little headway here until the 1930's, except for Wisconsin's sickness insurance. Orthodox union leaders like Samuel Gompers preferred to fight for higher wages as the chief solution to the social risks of the workman. Gompers spoke the individualistic language of the average American wage earner of that period:

We must not as a nation allow ourselves to drift upon a policy of excessive regulation by legislation—a policy that eats at and will surely undermine the very foundations of personal freedom. . . . Labor seeks legislation from the hands of government for such purposes only as the individuals or groups of workers cannot effect for themselves. . . . Thus labor asks legislation providing for the abolition of child labor; security and safety in life and work; sanitation in factory, shop, mill and home; workmen's compensation in preference to employers' liability; the regulation of convict labor and the like; the enactment of laws such as the proposed seamen's bill and the labor provisions of the Clayton law already enacted; the regulation of the issuance of injunctions and the trials of contempt cases; these latter work for freedom, for right, for justice.

In this same editorial of February, 1915, in the *American Federationist*, Gompers argued, "Initiative, aggressive conviction, enlightened self-interest, are the characteristics that must be dominant among the people if the nation is to make substantial progress toward better living and higher ideals."

Senator Robert M. La Follette of Wisconsin, ideological leader of the Progressive party, carried to victory the long-agitated union demands for justice to the seaman. For decades the sailor had been exploited by "crimps," usually shipping masters who operated boardinghouses for sailors and thereby won control over their employment. The sailor often sank into heavy debt to the crimp during the period of waiting for a ship and this sum was repaid to the shipmasters on their own terms. Desertion laws remained severe although corporal punishment had been abolished by the White Act of 1898.

At first, the seamen's unions were weak and tended to be suspicious of joint action with landsmen. Finally, in 1913-15 the International Seamen's Union under their able Norwegian-American leader, Andrew Furuseth, secured the aid of organized labor, public opinion, and Congress itself. The La Follette Seamen's Act affected American vessels and foreign vessels when in American ports. Sailors could no longer be jailed for desertion while the ship was in a safe harbor and their liability was restricted to personal property left on the vessel. The crimp system was shaken by the provision that sailors had the right to get half of their unpaid wages in port and their earnings could not be easily forfeited to creditors. In addition, they won a nine-hour day while in port, better food allowances, and various safety measures. The dictatorship of Captain Bligh had ended.

6

Despite major depressions, strikes, and radical panaceas, American labor clung stoutly to the ideal of class collaboration in industry. The unionized minority apparently agreed with Samuel Gompers that labor parties and doctrinaire adventures had no place in a society that offered obvious opportunities for getting ahead. However, labor was suspicious of the efforts of Frederick W. Taylor to cement class collaboration through the efficiency devices of scientific management. The American Federation of Labor fought it tooth and nail after 1910 when the movement seemed to have won many industrial converts. The craft unions saw their dominant position disintegrating before the pressure of automatic machine processes and timesaving techniques. Besides, they could show that many of the early devotees of scientific management thought of it in terms of a ruthless speed-up system rather than as a program that would ease the burden of labor as well as enrich the stockholders. Eventually, more unions appreciated the fact that the "full dinner pail" for millions was far more apt to be achieved and maintained through scientific management and stepped-up production than through legislative efforts or strikes alone.

Louis Brandeis, the disinterested champion of Taylorization, influenced labor philosophy in the direction of class collaboration. His greatest successes were achieved as an impartial arbiter for the International Ladies' Garment Workers Union and as the originator of employer-employee committees that became the model also for the Amalgamated Clothing Workers' Union. In various labor conferences and published statements, he advised labor to seek its true self-interest. Unionism and collective bargaining were essential to bring the industrial structure into harmony with political democracy, but labor must accept certain duties as well as privileges. Unions must strive to raise the earnings of business and not arbitrarily to

limit the production of workers. Union demands must be adapted
to the conditions of a particular business and while efforts must be
made to secure labor's fullest possible share of all business earnings,
capital and management must receive that portion required for their
healthy existence.

He insisted that regularity of employment was a superior goal to
sporadic high wages. A high annual wage and a stable home would
accompany scientific realization of regularized employment. This
would utilize machinery efficiently and reduce unit costs. Excessive
hours beyond the eight-hour day were wasteful of manpower,
caused fatigue, and shortened the worker's productive years. Besides,
he declared, leisure was necessary for the worker's education and
personal development. These ideas were intended to demonstrate
that the intelligent self-interest of the employer coincided with
that of the worker. In the succeeding decades many enlightened
industrialists came to realize that such principles did not involve
distasteful concessions to the strength of organized labor but were
essential for the highest efficiency and for steady profits. Labor
disciples of Brandeis, like Hillman and Dubinsky, led the way
toward class collaboration in industry.

· 10 ·

The Passing of the Old
Immigration:
From Schurz to Veblen

I

In 1910, at a time when Israel Zangwill was acclaimed both here
and abroad for his current play, *The Melting Pot*, which popularized an optimistic term for assimilation, one American in every
seven was foreign born. On the eve of the Civil War this ratio had
been only one in eight, but in 1910 the census takers counted 13,-
345,545 foreign-born among a total population of 92,406,536. Zangwill, an Anglo-Jewish playwright, portrayed the transformation of
a Jewish immigrant into an American. To the hero America was
"God's crucible, where all the races of Europe are melting and reforming." But the author also believed that each immigrant group
had its own distinctive contribution which would inevitably enrich
the melting pot.

The Old Immigration from advanced western European countries
such as Germany, England, France, and the Scandinavian nations
carried with it a high cultural prestige. In contrast with the New
Immigration from Southeastern Europe after 1880, these nationalities were heavily Protestant, relatively literate, and shared to a
large extent the cultural habits of the old American settlers. The
highly cultivated *Illinois Staats Zeitung*, for example, might speculate on whether assimilation to Anglo-American standards was really
worth while and hoped that Puritan America might become Teuto-

America. One aggressive German-American writer, Julius Goebel, castigated Zangwill's play,

> For us German Americans, the teaching of this play is simply a mixture of insipid phrases and unhistorical thinking. . . . The open or secret attempt to do away with our German cultural type—that is to say, our speech, our customs, and our views of life—in the smudge kitchen of a national melting pot has its source in illusion.

In the years preceding our entrance into World War I, Roosevelt and Wilson assailed the "hyphenated" German-American or Irish-American as disloyal, but most of these charges were both unfair and untrue. In the end, assimilation was irresistible for all groups.

America had long been Europe's chief frontier. Population outlets elsewhere had been secondary. Englishmen might like to go to Canada, Australia, and other English-speaking possessions, but they, too, came in millions to the United States. In 1910, there were 1,219,968 British-born Americans (excluding those from Ireland). Irishmen, of course, aside from the Protestant minority, felt no strong affinity for Britain's dominions, though a substantial number did settle in Canada and Australia. Ireland's land crisis continued to be acute and, to the displaced Irish farmers, the high wages in America were very attractive. Germans still came to this country in large annual migrations primarily for economic reasons, though many left to escape the military conscription laws. When the German Empire began to stabilize its economy during the nineties, the heavy emigration came to an end. As for the Scandinavians, they fled from the unremitting population pressure felt in their partly uncultivable countries.

The Industrial Revolution had set into motion an entire train of circumstances and causes that uprooted millions of human beings. Scientific discoveries reduced the death rate, but the additional millions could not easily support themselves with their outmoded farming and handicraft techniques. The surplus population worked on marginal lands that should have been retired from production. Unprogressive European landlords had little to offer except tariffs to meet the sharp competition of Australian wool, American wheat and meat, and similar products from Canada and Argentina. The world had shrunk in size, for the fast steamships and refrigerator cars carried competing products around a new world market and demolished backward rural economies. Britain solved her population problems by total industrialization and free trade. France and Germany shifted from the less productive staple crops and introduced a scientific conservation movement whose effect altered Theodore Roosevelt's America through Gifford Pinchot, a student of German conservation methods. But this process of adjusting to the new technology required time before it could stem the tide of emigration.

One of the great attractions of America for many Europeans in this era of rampant militarism was the certain prospect of immunity from peacetime conscription and possibly from wars altogether. Continental powers, especially after 1870, raised their conscription requirements ever higher to meet new anticipated dangers. High wages in the boom cities of America, democratic freedom and equality, the ease of attaining citizenship—all were part of an enticing image of America. A photograph of the local tenant farmer or laborer who made good, dressed handsomely like a member of the upper classes at home, was enough to offset warnings about hardships, failures, or social discriminations.

2

Of the Old Immigration, the Germans continued to play a major role in the affairs of their adopted land. Before Germany managed to achieve the high economic stability of the 1890's and afterward through a scientific and industrial revolution, emigration took place on a large scale. In 1882, alone, over 250,000 arrived, a record annual total for all time; in fact, the decade of the 1880's showed a far greater German exodus than did the dark 1850's, memorable for the potato blight. But the groundwork of German immigrant institutions had already been laid in the major cities, and the Germanias of Milwaukee, St. Louis, Chicago, New York, and Cincinnati were capable of absorbing and directing the newcomers.

As in antebellum days, the German clubs and newspapers demanded their "Sabbath freedom" and attacked the "Puritan" closing laws and temperance movements, winning many concessions. Catholic and Greek Orthodox laborers, deprived of the numerous traditional church holidays, sympathized with the German (and Irish) efforts to make Sunday a day of lively recreation as well as a day of rest. This issue was highlighted in 1893 when critics demanded (and temporarily succeeded in getting their way) that the Chicago Columbian Exposition be kept open on Sundays.

In 1876, the *National Demokrat* expressed widespread German indignation against the "Puritans":

The nation owes nothing to Puritanism.... The day was an unfortunate one in which New England attained power in the hypocritical role of champion of humanity and could lay its hands, soiled with usury, on the necks of the people.

Too many of the Forty-eighters and other German liberals fell under the magic spell of Bismarck who seemed to have demonstrated, as he said, that the great things of the world were done not by parliamentary majorities—that was the mistake of 1848—but by "blood and iron." An increasing conservatism had set in among erstwhile liberals. A major exception was Carl Schurz, the outstanding liberal leader of the German-Americans. He had served as a major-general during the Civil War and then turned to journalism and politics, editing the *St. Louis Westliche Post,* upon which he employed the able immigrant Joseph Pulitzer. Disgusted with the corruption of the Grant regime, he led the Missouri and Illinois Germans and others into the Liberal Republican party of 1872, even backing Horace Greeley for president despite the candidate's temperance and "Puritan" views. On that occasion Raster's *Illinois Staats-Zeitung* stood with the party, but exacted a price—a "Personal Liberty" plank in the national platform aimed at prohibition and Sabbatarianism. This checked the nativists within the party.

A small but vociferous German minority brought over far more radical doctrines than Schurz's, particularly those stemming from Karl Marx and the anarchist Michael Bakunin. The most responsible of these groups were the Social Democrats, led by the Austrian-German, Victor Louis Berger of Milwaukee, editor of the *Milwaukee Leader*, the chief Socialist paper in the United States. He is said to have converted Eugene Debs to socialism and to have helped him to organize the Socialist party. However, he broke with the revolutionary faction and adopted the moderate Social Democratic program then popular in the homeland. Under his influence, Milwaukee elected a Socialist administration that did little for socialism but a great deal for honest progressive government. During World War I, he sided with the leftist antiwar Socialists, but turned to ever more moderate causes. The Congress that denied Berger his seat in the hysterical days of 1918 and 1920 (he was re-elected in 1922 and thereafter retained his seat) did not realize that his influence upon the Socialist party was for moderate social reform, not subversive class war.

As in the past, German-Americans left a decisive influence upon American music, especially in symphonic, operatic, and choral forms. The Prussian-born youth, Theodore Thomas, rose to eminence as a director of outstanding orchestras in New York and Chicago, and spread the idea of "popular night concerts." He planned his programs in such a way as to educate his audiences in the direction of an increasingly sophisticated taste. He popularized Wagnerian music and left an abiding tradition among his immediate successors, at least in Chicago's Orchestra Hall, which was dedicated in 1904. His hope for America's musical maturity is seen in his early experiments with English opera sung by Americans.

Among the giants who became of lasting importance in the rise of American music were Leopold Damrosch and his sons, Frank and Walter. The father, who was born in 1832 in Posen, had been encouraged by Liszt to forsake medicine for music and after a brilliant career in Weimar and elsewhere in Europe he moved to New York in 1871. He founded the Oratorio Society of New York and the New York Symphony Society and wrote a number of significant musical compositions. A great devotee of Wagner, he persuaded the new Metropolitan Opera Company, founded in 1883, to introduce German opera and he managed the opera's first season.

Frank Damrosch was educated in music by his father and studied at Yale. He achieved a solid career in directing public school music in Denver and was an eminent conductor of both choral and orchestral music in New York and Philadelphia. Walter, like his father and older brother, was associated with the Metropolitan and formed his own opera company to produce Wagner's operas. From 1896 to 1927, he was the well-known conductor of the New York Symphony and a prolific composer of operas and orchestral pieces. He left behind a strong tradition in popular musical education for children and young people.

The German *Turnverein* movement continued to grow throughout this era and German gymnastics became part of the basic American tradition of physical education through the Y.M.C.A., the Naval Academy, and the Cleveland public school system. Faust has described the wide adoption of the picture post card through the New York branches of German firms; he tells of the near-monopoly of toy-making by German firms, including the invention of the "Teddy Bear" in honor of Theodore Roosevelt. In the brewery business German-Americans like Adolphus Busch, owner of Anheuser-Busch Brewing Company, reaped millions and turned to philanthropy on a substantial scale. The American optical business attained high standards after two German opticians organized Bausch and Lomb in Rochester. Among the great technicians were Professor Charles P. Steinmetz, who patented over a hundred inventions in the field of electrical apparatus and contributed valuable theoretical findings in electricity; and John A. Roebling and his son Washington made the magnificent Brooklyn Bridge possible through their development of steel wire cables for suspension bridges.

The optimism of the German-Americans was rudely jarred during the prewar years of 1914-17 when they saw the prospect of war against the Fatherland assume an ever-increasing reality. Not all German-Americans were interested in politics or conceded the justice of the Kaiser's cause, but the prospect of fighting their kinsfolk was a most dispiriting one. Proud of their cultural renaissance and the recent advances toward responsible government, Germans could scarcely accept the picture of the Hun and the widely publicized charges of his calculated frightfulness. German brewers and Irish saloonkeepers financially supported propaganda efforts in the press to keep this country out of war. The German-American press played a large part in this effort and inevitably aroused the dislike of Allied partisans. Ahead loomed the great test of the war years after April, 1917.

3

In the tolerant atmosphere of America, German Jews attained a degree of acceptance within the larger German community that contrasted considerably with their position in Germany. In Chicago, for example, jubilant German-Americans celebrated the Franco-Prussian victory of 1871 by choosing Jewish business leaders to head the procession as Bismarck and Moltke. Local Germania warned Adolf Stöcker, the notoriously antisemitic court pastor of the Kaiser, to avoid his usual tirades against the Jews if he wished to be received. Chicago's famed Germania Club, the center of so many community activities, was founded by a German-Jewish lawyer. Among the Forty-eighters, Carl Schurz had married a German-Jewish girl who had studied with Froebel and introduced the first German kindergarten into this country.

Part of this liberation was due to the breakdown of the spiritual ghetto by the influence of the Enlightenment and Moses Mendelssohn. In the United States the "occidentalizing" leader of Reform Judaism was the Bohemian-born but German-speaking Isaac Mayer Wise, who had been appointed to his Cincinnati pulpit in 1854. Disregarding cries of "apostate," he introduced mixed choirs, gave English sermons on a wide range of secular as well as religious topics, broke down the oriental seclusion of a separate women's section to enable families to sit together in the synagogue, and adopted or introduced other practices of the German Reform movement. This meant dispensing with hats during services, reading most of the prayers in English, dropping the kosher dietary laws, and playing the organ. Rabbi Wise, fortified by his scholarly reputation and the backing of a wealthy congregation, institutionalized his Reform innovations through the organization in 1873 of the Union of

American-Hebrew Congregations. In 1875, he sponsored the Hebrew Union College of Cincinnati, the intellectual citadel of Reform Judaism, where many rabbis of this sect were trained. In 1889, he established the Central Conference of American Rabbis as an authoritative religious body and founded several liberal Israelite periodicals. But he resisted the advance of Theodore Herzl's political Zionism and denied that the Jews were a nationality. Wise was a prolific writer, published several German novels and plays, and delivered sermons before a large following even outside his coreligionists.

Many German Jews, however, refused to forsake orthodoxy and quarreled with Wise, preferring to follow Isaac Leeser, editor of *The Occident,* who was credited with the founding of an American Jewish press. The strength of traditional Judaism revived with the coming of the strictly orthodox East European Jews. In order to bridge the gap between Reform Judaism, which many feared would lead to apostasy, and unyielding orthodoxy, a third group combined limited changes in traditional rituals with modern thought as "Conservatives." To train Rabbis for Conservative synagogues, which attracted an ever-growing proportion of American Jewry, the Jewish Theological Seminary of America was established in 1886.

German Jews left their mark upon American development. The Strauses modernized the merchandising field in the renovated Macy's department store and in Abraham and Straus. Oscar Mergenthaler invented the first linotype machine and thus revolutionized typesetting. The fabulous Guggenheims contributed major smelting processes to the metallurgical world. Simon Baruch of Posen, Germany, father of the noted statesman, Bernard, turned to medicine after fighting in the Confederate Army, and was one of the first Americans to operate for appendicitis; he also pioneered in the field of hydrotherapy. Oscar Hammerstein and numerous other German-Jewish theatrical managers did much to develop the elaborate stage and operatic spectacles of prewar America.

The career of Jacob Schiff is particularly illustrative of the philosophy of good works that increasingly underlay Judaism as well as the Christian socialism of this time. Schiff was born in Frankfort-

am-Main in 1847 of a long line of scholarly ancestors. He came to
New York at fourteen, and after a successful process of self-educa-
tion and shrewd management became the senior partner of Kuhn,
Loeb and Company. He and his firm financed many of the leading
railroads and even backed Harriman in his railroad duel with James
Hill, then supported by Morgan himself. Unlike other captains
of industry and multimillionaires, he accepted unionism and the
right to strike. Like his co-religionist, Julius Rosenwald, he gave
generously to Tuskegee Institute and other Negro institutions. The
list of his major benefactions is unusually long. He sponsored German and Semitic studies in the major eastern universities and
financed settlement houses, free libraries, Jewish charities, seminaries, and publications, and aid to persecuted Jews abroad. His
indignation at Czarist atrocities against Jews led him to refuse a
major loan to Russia. In politics, he was both the friend and adviser
of more than one American statesman.

4

Next to the Germans in number came the Irish. Of the 13,345,545
foreign-born in 1910, over one-sixth, precisely 2,311,085, were German and 1,352,155 were Irish—a figure that had fallen by a quarter
of a million since 1890. The sons and daughters of the Irish of the
Starving Forties had been assimilated and tended to forget the
hatreds felt by their parents toward England and the Orangemen—
although newcomers and the Irish press kept this flame very much
alive. Like the easily-assimilable English, Scots, and Welsh, they
had no serious language barrier to surmount. Even the Irish names
had been modified in spelling and replaced in many instances by
culturally neutral forms. Between 1865 and 1894 the immigration
from the Emerald Isle continued to be substantial, averaging about
50,000 annually; thereafter, as conditions improved at home, their
numbers fell steadily, though never dropping below 25,000 in the
prewar years.

The new Irish immigrants were not much better off in worldly
goods than those of the earlier migrations. They lived in semi-

segregated communities, patronized anti-British papers like *The Irish World* and *The Irish Nation*, and fought competitors for their pick-and-shovel jobs, particularly among the Italians, Greeks, Poles, and others of the New Immigration. Meanwhile, the older Irish-American settlers stepped up the social ladder, often acting as gang bosses or foremen over Slavic or Italian workmen.

Politicians beat the drum of Irish nationalism and the more militant Irishmen even plotted to win Ireland's independence from bases in the New World. For example, many Irish veterans of the Civil War joined the Fenian conspiracy of 1866 and marched into Eastern Canada to seize Fort Erie. The conspiracy failed, but the incident proved a delicate one for statesmen to handle in view of Irish-American emotions on the subject. In some Irish districts the voters defeated politicians believed to be guilty of showing courtesies to England's representatives.

On the national scene the Irish vote often solidified over an anti-British issue. Republicans worked hard and with only moderate success to wean the Irish away from the Democratic party. In 1884, James G. Blaine may have lost the Irish vote, and hence the election, in pivotal New York state, when he failed to check a minister who declared in his presence that the Democratic party was the party of "Rum, Romanism, and Rebellion." Alert Democratic reporters carefully circulated this *faux pas* among the sensitive Irish, with excellent results. Not even the well publicized fact that Blaine had a Catholic mother could save the man from Maine.

In 1888, Grover Cleveland lost partly because of the "Murchison letter" trap designed to alienate the Irish. On this occasion a naturalized Englishman, Murchison, asked an apparently innocent question of the British ambassador regarding the proper way to vote in this election. The English diplomat suggested that Cleveland would best serve England's cause. Republican newspapers promptly published this alleged evidence of Britain's power in America. Twisting the lion's tail had concrete value for politicians anxious to garner the nationalistic Irish vote. Correspondingly, this tactic injured Anglo-American relations during the serious Venezuela boundary crisis, the various Panama Canal controversies, and the neutrality debate before America's entrance into World War I.

The Irish love for boxing and athletics had its greatest exponent in John L. Sullivan. He gave up his trade as tinsmith to appear as a pugilist in William Muldoon's variety show in Boston. Before this audience he offered twenty-five dollars to any man who could knock him down. In 1882, he challenged the national champion, Paddy Ryan, and knocked him out in Mississippi City, Mississippi. For a decade thereafter, this primitive giant unleashed his fury at one challenger after another in Europe and America. The last of his sensational bare-knuckles fights was the battle with Jake Kilrain who lasted seventy-five rounds. The "Great John L." was prodigal with his money, married and divorced a chorus girl, turned temperance lecturer at one time, and finally died in poverty. Vachel Lindsay, the poet, left a warm tribute to him in the verses "John L. Sullivan, the Strong Boy of Boston."

Another Sullivan, more important in American culture, was Louis Henri Sullivan, father of functionalism in architecture, who also was born in Boston; but despite his indubitably Irish manners and appearance, there was little of Erin's culture in his work. Victor Herbert, whose melodious operas were often compared with those of Sir Arthur Sullivan, was born in Dublin but left as a child to study music in Germany, France, and Italy. However, he joined many Irish-American societies and was president before his death in 1924 of the Friendly Sons of St. Patrick and the Sons of Irish Freedom. Another Dublin-born genius was the sculptor Augustus Saint-Gaudens, but his training, too, was heavily Continental rather than Gaelic. The invigorating impulse of the Irish literary revival of Yeats and Lady Gregory came to this country only in small part through the impecunious immigrant.

Ireland's chief cultural influence upon America came through the predominance of Irish priests within the American Roman Catholic Church. Archbishop John Ireland of St. Paul had left County Kilkenny in 1849 as a boy and rose in this era to one of the most influential posts of the Catholic hierarchy. He was one of the founders of the Catholic University of America. At this institution, Father John A. Ryan taught the economics of a "living wage" and became the foremost exponent of the Catholic social gospel. During his youth he had been influenced by the cry for social justice of *The Irish World*, an antilandlord paper. In industry, Michael Cudahy of County Kilkenny became a partner of Armour and Company in 1875-90 and then built his own notable firm, the Cudahy Packing Company. In finance, the second-generation Irishman, Thomas Fortune Ryan, amassed $200,000,000 by combining his excellent Tammany contacts with a shrewd understanding of municipal traction finances.

5

Scandinavia moved slowly from agriculture to industry while her population pressure made the America fever acute. Steamship and emigrant agents felt encouraged to visit the interior rural settlements for prospects. In 1910, there were 1,250,662 Norwegians, Swedes, and Danes in the United States, most of them in the Old Northwest, especially in Minnesota, Illinois, and Wisconsin, though there were substantial colonies elsewhere as well. The landless were eager to take up cheap lands in the remote frontier counties, despite pioneer hardships. It did not take them long to discard their early shanties and cabins for beautiful farmhouses surrounded by luxuriant corn and wheat fields. Religious pressure, especially among dissenters against the state church, influenced many to come here. In 1910, about 60,000 Scandinavian Mormons lived just south of Great Salt Lake, reflecting the huge harvest of souls gathered by Mormon missionaries, especially in Copenhagen. Half of these were Danes, 20,000 were Swedes, and 10,000, Norwegians.

The Norwegian wave of 1820-65 had brought only 77,874, but the second great migration of 1866-73 carried 110,896, and the third between 1880 and 1893 totalled 254,666. The impress of Norway on the geography of Minnesota, according to Professor Theodore Blegen, is marked by no fewer than two hundred names of townships, villages, and lakes such as Haugen, Brandsvold, and Thorstad. Among these immigrants was the rugged carpenter and farmer,

Thomas Veblen, whose son Thorstein deeply influenced American thought. The Veblens had left Norway for a Wisconsin farm and Mrs. Veblen, like so many other Scandinavian women, served as a maid in a native family. Thorstein had no chance in this pioneer community to meet the "leisure class" that he wrote about later, but he may have acquired his challenging, sardonic outlook among these people. He and his eleven brothers and sisters had few opportunities to learn English in their Wisconsin and Minnesota farm homes; in fact, Thorstein had scarcely mastered the language when he entered Carleton Academy at seventeen.

Norwegian and Swedish craftsmen and businessmen sought the cities of the Old Northwest. By 1890, Chicago alone had attracted 22,000 Norwegians, while Minneapolis and St. Paul, the twin cities that flourished in this lumbering, flour-making, and dairy country, grew rapidly as Viking strongholds. Longfellow's *Hiawatha* had immortalized Minnehaha Falls and Lake Minnetonka in the environs of Minneapolis, but the poet—alas!—knew these splendors only from photographs. On the streets, Swedish, Norwegian, and German papers reflected the foreign-born elements in the population. Before this period ended, Minneapolis was the country's greatest wheat market and a leader in the production of flour. In Chicago, Iver Lawson, a Norwegian, climbed swiftly to riches as a realtor and clothing merchant but he was overshadowed in the public mind by the eminence of his son Victor, the proprietor and editor of the *Chicago Daily News,* first penny newspaper in the West. Victor Lawson, a vigorous if puritanical journalist, was a pioneer in the development of a foreign news service.

Along the Pacific Coast, in Alaska and around the Great Lakes, particularly Lake Superior, tens of thousands of Norwegian and Swedish sailors, the Viking heirs to centuries of ocean adventure, eagerly joined the well-paid American crews or became interested in lumbering, fishing, or farming. Norwegians built up the Alaskan herring business after 1890 and introduced a salting process that made it possible to capture the Scandinavian-American market of the Middle West. It was logical indeed that the labor spokesman for American seamen was a Norwegian-American, Andrew Furuseth, who campaigned for the La Follette Seamen's Act of 1915.

While Lutheranism predominated among the Scandinavians, the nineteenth century advance of non-conformist Protestant churches was encouraged by the individualist atmosphere of the West. Thousand of Baptists, Methodists, Mormons, and other sects came with the immigrants, built churches, schools, colleges, and hospitals, and founded newspapers. Like the Germans, the Scandinavians loved huge choral societies, such as their own United Scandinavian Singers of America, and the Norwegians were especially proud of the St. Olaf College Choir, the music of Grieg, their folk songs, and the gospel hymns.

In the field of sport, as Blegen shows with fascinating detail, the Norwegians made a substantial contribution. They brought with them their ancient sport of skiing and found the skis useful in traversing the snow-covered prairies. After 1880, St. Paul was noted for its ice carnivals, ski clubs, and the commercial manufacture of skis. Norwegian ice champions from the homeland, together with Finnish athletes, set the pace for Americans who enjoyed winter sports.

Norwegian-Americans, like others of the Old Immigration, were anxious to keep historical records of their accomplishments and sponsored local history societies and publications. Names like those of Veblen, Lawson, and Ole Rölvaag, the novelist, suggest the high degree of literacy swiftly attained in this era, although these exceptional men are not typical for any ethnic group. The story of the Norwegian-American immigration assumed epic proportions to writers in the homeland as well as to Rölvaag, author of *Giants in the Earth*. Johan Bojer wrote a highly successful novel on a similar theme in *The Emigrants* (1925), and both Knut Hamsun and Björnson visited this country and wrote their impressions of the Norwegian-Americans. The agnostic playwright, Björnson, "Norway's Ingersoll," conceded that the emigrants had become prosperous, but were still uncouth, narrow Calvinists. Sometimes unappreciative audiences threw cabbages and stale eggs at this critic of the clergy, but most of his listeners came in all sincerity to be edified.

The Swedes came from a richer land than rockbound Norway and tended increasingly to outstrip the Norwegians in both literacy and number. They had made Minnesota more Swedish than German or Norwegian by 1905, when they accounted for 12.5 per cent of the state's population of 1,997,401. As in other emigrant countries, the youth of Sweden were aroused by the railroad and steamship agents, newspaper advertising, and "America letters" and hoped to acquire good lands cheaply in the New World. The peak of this migration came in 1882 when 64,607 Swedes left for the United States; the next peak year was 1888 with 54,698. Thus by 1900, there were 571,926 Swedish-born immigrants living in this country.

In many ways the Swedish experience resembled the Norwegian. If the Norwegians brought winter sports to America, the athletic Swedes introduced scientific "medical gymnastics," founded by their poet, Per Henrick Ling, and established the American vogue of "setting-up exercises" and Swedish massage. They, too, loved choral music and organized large male singing societies. Again, like the Norwegians, they shared in the evangelical movement away from their state-sponsored Lutheran Church, and counted thousands among themselves as followers of Dwight L. Moody and other revivalists. Both groups shared in the pietist and Lutheran fundamentalist tendencies of mid-nineteenth century Scandinavia and combatted the heavy drinking that was traditional among many of their members.

Swedes vied with Norwegians in founding colleges, notably Augustana, Luther, Gustavus Adolphus, Bethany (Kansas), and Upsala. Howard Hanson, the noted composer and director of the Eastman School of Music, was born in the Swedish community of Wahoo, Nebraska, and was graduated from the town's Luther College. Many of these colleges, however, were at first scarcely above academy rank and merely served the purpose of training the clergy of the various sects. All were coeducational and, despite their sectarian Swedish affiliations, welcomed students of various faiths and nationalities. In fact, literacy had made tremendous strides among the Swedes after 1842, when their homeland government had introduced compulsory public schools, and therefore these newcomers were among the most literate of the various immigrant peoples.

The Swedes took a decided interest in politics, aided by their highly literate constituency in Minnesota, Wisconsin, and Illinois and by a vigorous press. Although they tended to be conservative Lutherans with a predilection for the Republican party, more and more of them felt the impact of the rising Social Democratic movement in Sweden and showed an affinity for social causes such as the Progressive movement and the militant Non-Partisan League. Charles A. Lindbergh, Sr., father of the aviator, left Stockholm to gain a Minnesota farm and a law education at the University of Michigan, and served as a Progressive Republican leader in Congress for five terms during 1907-17. He proved an unyielding foe of monopolies, sponsored the investigation of the "Money Trust," and, like other Progressives and many other Scandinavians, fought the entrance of the United States into World War I. He probably forfeited his election as governor of Minnesota because of his antiwar activities. His son Charles also antagonized many by his rigidly isolationist views just before World War II.

A second-generation Swede who began as a bootblack but emerged as one of the foremost interpreters of American democracy was Carl Sandburg. He was born in Galesburg, Illinois, the son of a blacksmith immigrant, August Johnson, who later changed his name to Sandburg. Carl tried his hand at various tasks—sometimes as a milk-wagon driver, a barber, and as a hobo roaming over the Middle West and learning the folklore of America. Later he served as a soldier in Puerto Rico during the Spanish-American War. His volume of free verse, *Chicago Poems* (1915), interpreted the aggressive, raw, western spirit of the "hog-butcher for the World" and established his métier as a poet of the people.

6

Of the Old Immigration, no group was so generally reckoned as unassimilable as the Chinese. Yet the unfortunate record of race relations in California stands in glaring contrast to the cheerful story of cultural integration in Hawaii. There the descendants of 40,000 Chinese laborers prospered in the twentieth century without the irritations of segregation and race riots. Part of the explanation lies in the persistent color prejudices in America going back to colonial times, but these attitudes were also heavily economic in origin, for Irish and German immigrants and organized labor raised the loudest outcry, "The Chinese must go!" Senator George C. Perkins of California expressed the widespread anti-Chinese prejudices of his constituency in 1906:

Bringing with them slavery, concubinage, prostitution, the opium vice, the disease of leprosy, the offensive and defensive organization of clans and guilds, the lowest standard of living known, and a detestation of the people with whom they live and with whom they will not even leave their bones when dead, they form a community within a community and there live the Chinese life.

The senator must have labored hard to compress in so few words all the gross anti-Chinese libels of his day.

The 50,000 Chinese in this country in 1860 had grown to over 108,000 by 1880. Two years later, just before the Chinese Exclusion Act cut off immigration, nearly 40,000 more rushed in. Despite abuse and injuries the Chinese had continued to come, much more impressed by the examples of wealthy Chinese-Americans who had made good than by the warnings of the Six Societies that only suffering lay ahead for emigrants. There was never a "horde" of Chinese in the States, but most of them congregated in California, though an increasing number moved to other Far Western states and finally to New York.

The railroads, particularly Governor Leland Stanford's Southern Pacific Railroad, employed tens of thousands of Chinese workmen, many of them as contract laborers hired directly from China, their steamship passage readily guaranteed by their future employers. Their labor at low wages went far to make the financing of the risky western railroads feasible. Elsewhere, the Chinese, often taking jobs rejected by others, became "gap-fillers," such as common laborers, laundrymen, houseboys, gardeners, and fishermen. Employers found them a willing, cheap source of labor and gladly hired them as cigar makers, shoemakers, and even in other crafts where whites—especially Irishmen and Germans—were already intrenched. In 1867, a historian wrote, "The cleanliness, politeness and good behavior of the Chinese was in everybody's mouth and what they contributed saved several counties from bankruptcy."

The segregation of the various "Chinatowns" was not originally due to outside prejudices. As in the case of other immigrant nationalities, the first generation found the linguistic and cultural differences too great to cope with individually, particularly in the difficult task of earning a livelihood in a strange land. But by the time the second generation had reached maturity the psychological walls of Chinatown seemed thicker than ever because of outside discriminations against them in housing, jobs, and schooling in white districts. In San Francisco, Chinatown grew rapidly until, by 1906, it occupied fifteen blocks. There, the Chinese adapted the familiar institutions of the old country to New World conditions. But the outside world knew these Orientals only through the crime news and the sensational Chinatown tours under loquacious and irresponsible guides who selected opium dens and gambling dives with which to shock visitors.

Actually, the Chinese were little different from other immigrant groups in the tendency to assimilate. Their shortage of women led them to intermarry with Indians, Mexicans, and South Europeans until California's law of 1903 banned racial intermarriage with whites. By the eighties native-born Chinese Christians and many foreign-born Chinese had given up the queue and had replaced their baggy trousers with those in the American style. So many adopted Christianity that the traditional temples and other Chinese institutions declined in importance. Ambitious Cantonese, "the Yankees of China," prospered as merchants and restaurateurs, held elaborate parties and celebrations on appropriate days, and demonstrated the fact that they, like others, saw no particular charm in an ascetic life.

Segregated immigrant neighborhoods, where ignorance of the laws and customs of an adopted land is common, have usually been prey to political graft and police extortion in the name of protection. The Chinese were accustomed to graft, known as "squeeze" at home, and proved to be a gold mine to extortionist policemen here. To make matters worse, they had their own professional criminal element among certain tongs—the term in this country means little more than an association—who terrorized the business community, blackmailed the well-to-do, demanded large sums for tribute, and sent expert killers to dispatch informers and other uncooperative individuals. Some of these "highbinders" or "hatchet men" could trace their criminal associations back to old Chinese societies.

The sins of the hatchet men were commonly and erroneously attributed to the conservative Six Societies, actually the Chinese immigrant's equivalent of the ancient village and communal association. These Societies had numerous cooperative and mutual aid functions and, in addition, spoke authoritatively for segregated Chinatown. They maintained lodging houses and cooperative kitchens, aided and supervised immigration, helped the sick, offered cheap burial to the poor, and issued strict rules of conduct for their members.

Even before the Burlingame Treaty of 1868, which had encouraged Chinese immigration to this country, the agitation for exclusion had begun on the West Coast. One of the worst agitators was an immigrant, Denis Kearney, who had come from County Cork in 1847 and arrived in California the year of the Burlingame Treaty. Self-educated, ambitious, and completely opportunistic, he realized his political potentialities in heading the notorious "Sand Lot movement" in San Francisco. The name was derived from the "sand lots" across from the city hall where free speech sometimes degenerated into license. He organized the Workingmen's Trade and Labor Union and called for the elimination of cheap Chinese labor as degrading to all labor and as reflecting "the dangerous encroachments of capital." However, he did not approve of the unprovoked riots against the Chinese in California and in other Far Western states. The anti-Chinese forces sponsored laws to prevent these immigrants from holding real estate in California, but the courts nullified some of these discriminatory acts.

Organized labor, as noted elsewhere, became the prop of this movement. In the shoe industry Irish immigrants faced the strong competition of Chinese; and the Knights of St. Crispin even organized a branch in San Francisco to cope with this situation. Unemployed workers during the great depression of the late 1870's intimidated farmers and industrialists who hired Chinese. Cigar makers and shoemakers labeled their goods with anti-Chinese inscriptions. "These were the beginnings of the trade union label," writes Selig Perlman, the labor historian, "which later became an important factor in the American labor movement." Even some employers, unwilling to meet the vigorous competition of Chinese businessmen, joined the exclusionists. Racialists like the Order of the Caucasians also added their protest. By 1876, both national parties wrote a Chinese exclusion plank in their platforms and subsequently the federal government abrogated the Burlingame Treaty. In 1882, President Arthur signed the Chinese Exclusion Act suspending the coming of Chinese laborers for ten years—this eventually became permanent—and providing for stringent rules of enforcement. Subsequently, this restriction was expanded through the arbitrary definition of the word "laborer" by hostile immigrant authorities and new irritations arose because of the strict application of immigration inspection rules to Chinese students and businessmen.

Meanwhile, as the new century opened, Chinese nationalism had taken on revolutionary proportions that compelled their quiescent government finally to take heed of foreign provocations. Chinese newspapers carried detailed accounts and cartoons of American abuses. A boycott against American goods began, with the tacit approval of the Imperial Government. Nationalists pointed out that while the West always held China to strict accountability for lives and property, as in the Boxer Rebellion crisis, the United States had done far too little to protect Chinese-American rights in California. The fact that certain of California's laws regarding the Chinese were outside the scope of Washington did not seem convincing, especially after it became apparent that President Roosevelt was able to exercise pressure on that state in the interest of Japanese-

Americans. Even the generous remission of the Boxer indemnity to the United States in favor of Chinese education could not entirely offset in the minds of youthful nationalists the persistent anti-Chinese social and economic discrimination on the West Coast. It is a historic fact that American statesmen took serious risks to preserve the Open Door in China and thus to maintain the territorial unity of a nation threatened by complete disintegration from both outside and within. But it is unfortunate that local prejudices against the Chinese-American were permitted to mar an otherwise praiseworthy record.

· 11 ·

The New Immigration:
Hillman and Pupin

[1880-1917]

I

"OLD Americans" like Henry Cabot Lodge and the Daughters of the American Revolution were worried over the fact that since 1880 the bulk of immigrants from Northwestern Europe had begun to decline in favor of the "unassimilable" newcomers from Southern and Eastern parts of the Continent. Surviving Know-Nothing nativists, such as the American Protective Association in the Middle West, disliked the heavily Catholic and Jewish elements in the New Immigration and organized against them. The insistence upon cultural homogeneity has usually been strong in civilized as well as in primitive societies, unless countered by some educative process.

Nineteenth-century America, devoted to the doctrine of laissez faire, fell behind Canada and other large immigrant-receiving countries in providing supervision over the arrivals who in so many cases had left ancestral villages of a backward technological level. Despite this failure to direct the immigrant, old settlers denounced the unbearably congested cities where the immigrants crowded together for understanding and mutual aid in segregated Little Italys, Little Hungarys, Polonias, and Ghettos. Trade unions, ever fearful of economic competition, doubted whether these unskilled workers would ever be more than strikebreakers and a depressing influence

238

upon wages and living conditions. Still another irritant was racialism. By the end of the century European racialist theories encouraged by the advance of nationalism, had acquired the prestige of "science," and had penetrated reputable eastern American colleges. The dogmas of Anglo-Saxon superiority and the survival of the fittest were invoked to classify those of the New Immigration as biologically and morally inferior to the "Aryan" races. Restrictionists had already stopped most of the Chinese immigration on similar economic and racial grounds. The next such movement produced the restrictionist laws of 1917, 1921, and 1924. The end of the traditional hospitality of the United States toward immigration was in sight.

Propagandists from steamship companies, railroads, and state immigration bureaus did not have a difficult time in attracting people living under the wretched circumstances of Europe at that time. They advertised in European newspapers and circulated in pamphlet form translations of American newspaper items illustrating the peace and plenty of the New World. Some stood at Italian church doors, writes Merle Curti, distributing cards with hymns and verses praising the United States. In Greece, agents put up highly colored posters of America to lure the immigrant. Letters from America and well-chosen photographs often did the rest.

A composite picture of the immigrant from Southern and Eastern Europe would differ perhaps only in degree and in certain details from that of earlier immigrants. At first he tended to be a young transient, hopeful of earning enough to aid his family at home and perhaps to provide a dowry for an unmarried sister. Under the guidance of his more experienced countrymen he would go to the cities regardless of his agrarian background and select a factory job or a peddler's business in which fellow-countrymen were already owners or labor agents. Frugality was a necessity in this first stage of adjustment, especially since prices were far higher than he had expected.

Separated by language and customs from the natives, he lived within a detached cultural fragment of his homeland and learned about America through his press (if he were literate) and the numerous mutual aid and recreational societies. Living alone, he might seek the sociability of the saloon or café. Sometimes a married immigrant took another spouse while his wife vainly waited in the homeland for a steamship ticket. He frequently attended theaters, especially the immigrant theater, which he had seldom done at home, and he was not too critical of their amateur acting or crude humor. Eventually, he would save enough money to send a steamship ticket to his wife or brother in the old country; if unmarried, he would try to find a girl of his own nationality. Single men might fall into the maidenly snare of a breach of promise suit in which a cold judge might insist on marriage with the plaintiff as an alternative to paying heavy damages. His neighborhood contacts were largely within his own ethnic group or with neighboring nationalities whose children often carried on a feud with his own.

Though he may have done little newspaper reading in the homeland, he usually became a voracious reader of the foreign-language press. With a babel of over forty languages and dialects in the America of 1917, this press had an important integrative function. Besides, these newspapers seemed far more interesting than the papers in the old country and were completely uncensored in their handling of vital news. They occupied an ambivalent role in the assimilation process. On the one hand, they aided good citizenship by expert discussions of American events and ideals; on the other, foreign language editors often yielded to the natural temptation to prolong their usefulness by perpetuating a strong sense of loyalty to the homeland, sometimes introducing a discordant minority factor in national and local elections and in foreign affairs.

Assimilation, especially when the instruction came from half-educated natives of the poorer classes, was often erratic and not necessarily beneficial. Phillips Russell in his article, "The Americanization of an Alien," wrote half-seriously of the immigrant in the early twentieth century who learned his manners and English from a New York subway guard or a traffic policeman, his sportsmanship from the crowds throwing pop bottles at a baseball umpire, his religion from the emotionalism of Billy Sunday, and his political idealism from Tammany Hall. This, unfortunately, was not entirely untrue.

In the crowded, segregated tenement neighborhoods, where poverty, ignorance, and filth mingled in defiance of paper legislation, there was considerable juvenile delinquency, crime, ignorance, and dependence on charity. Policemen, with negligible sociological training, tended to single out "Dagoes," "Polaks," "Bohunks," "Sheenies," or some other group as inherently criminal despite the fact that investigations in Chicago River wards or dilapidated East Side New York precincts showed a similar state of social disorganization within practically all foreign-born communities and many native ones as well. The children in such communities, rejected by native boys and girls and deprived of wholesome outlets for recreation in the slums, often escaped the traditional moral restraints of their elders without quite absorbing the cultural attitudes of the older settlers. This was the familiar "second generation" problem, but fortunately it never seriously affected more than a minority of any nationality. As the newer immigrants moved in, the older groups rose in the social scale, became foremen or skilled workmen, and showed increased social stability.

The unlettered immigrant, ignorant of the law and fearful of government, was an easy prey for sharpers. Maurice Davie has noted many of their tricks. Runners from the lodging houses met the immigrant at the wharf and often used the stratagem of seizing the baby—if there was one—to compel the protesting parents to follow. Frauds of all sorts in insurance, land, urban real estate, and worthless stock were perpetrated upon the "greenhorns." Cab drivers might take a long circuitous route to the lodging house and charge the newcomer twenty dollars for the ride. One driver even put an immigrant on the Third Avenue Elevated, paid his nickel fare while pocketing several hundred dollars and told him solemnly that this train would take him to Kansas City.

Fellow-nationals often cheated their own countrymen, especially through the unbusinesslike "immigrant banks," which were operated by saloon-keepers, labor agents, grocers, or boardinghouse bosses.

These "bankers" offered a wide array of services, spoke the language of their depositors, offered legal advice and bail, accepted money for safekeeping, transmitted immigrants' remittances abroad, and offered information in the most affable manner on the Old World and on naturalization matters. These banks were sociable, informal rooms, not austere Greek temples, where one might write letters, read newspapers, and chat. But when one of these banks collapsed, the tragedies were very pathetic. Immigrants tended to distrust American banks because these had no government backing. A major event in their lives was the establishment in 1911 of the Postal Savings System; fully three-quarters of its depositors were immigrants until 1921. While the federal and local governments did too little for the immigrant, considerable aid came from private agencies such as the Y.W.C.A., the Travelers Aid, the settlement houses, social agencies, and religious organizations; most important were the innumerable mutual aid societies within each nationality group.

Assimilation was marked by the steady infiltration of English words into immigrant vocabularies until cultured visitors from the homeland showed disgust at the mongrelization of their erstwhile "pure" language. It seemed shocking to note that the German-American or Yiddish past tense of "jump" was "gejumped." Naturalization judges, immigration officials, and business associates hastened the process of name-changing. In 1923, the Cabots of Boston fought bitterly in the courts to prevent the Kabotchniks from assuming their aristocratic name—but unavailingly.

2

The Italians came in far greater numbers than any other nationality in the New Immigration. Between 1881 and 1917 about four million sons and daughters of Italy arrived, although a large proportion were transients and did not stay long before returning home. In 1910, the Italian-born population of the United States was 1,343,070. Their annual influx had been small until the 1880's and only in 1900 did the yearly figure pass the 100,000 mark. Thereafter, these people came in a rapidly widening stream, exceeding 250,000 a year during 1906, 1907, 1913, and 1914. In previous decades they had preferred the sunnier climate of Brazil, Uruguay, or Argentina, but now they turned toward the United States in a concentrated flow from Southern Italy. The industrialization of Northern Italy and a consequent higher standard of living tended to slow up emigration from that section. In addition, Italian consuls in New York were issuing pessimistic reports and discouraging professional Italians, largely in the North, from emigrating.

In Sicily and the southern Italian provinces the miserable struggle for existence at the end of the nineteenth century reflected the inability of the traditional agrarian and handicraft economy to support the rapidly growing population. The abolition of feudalism had been a failure; huge estates, held by a few, were still cultivated by antiquated methods; and absentee landlords represented about one-third of all landowners. Efficiency was drastically hampered by the traditional church holidays, which absorbed half of the possible working days in some provinces. Disease and lack of sanitation took a heavy toll of life. Exploitative leaseholders and agents were too eager to get immediate returns from the ancient land to invest much to preserve its fertility. Tenants and sharecroppers—the predominant classes—had no real incentive to make improvements. Worst of all, the amount of rainfall in the South had declined over the centuries until fresh drinking water became a saleable commodity, too precious to waste on baths and laundry. In some sections the deforestation of centuries allowed the rain to run off into malarial swamps and stagnant pools. Italy was the worst malarial country in Europe. In 1905, 323,000 Italians were ill of malaria and thousands of them died. Diet deficiencies caused anemia and pellagra. The tempo of life never relapsed for too long into bucolic quiet, for periodic earthquakes wiped out entire towns, particularly in Calabria. In Sicily, bandits and the notorious gangsters of the Mafia and the Camorra robbed the countryfolk, undeterred by the police.

To the average South Italian the government was a hazy abstraction, something to be feared or distrusted. His village and his family dealt in their own fashion with the concerns of everyday life. The fact that Italy had become a unified nation might mean a good deal to a North Italian, but to the Southerners the village or province was still the entire world, their dialect took precedence over literary Italian, and extreme localism blotted out nationalism. In the United States these immigrants showed their localistic prejudices by secluding themselves among people of their own district or village and by organizing mutual aid societies on this geographic basis.

Catholicism in Southern Italy was heavily overlaid with pagan survivals, magic, and superstition. Even the priests were not too far above their parishioners in culture and were definitely below the cultural level of the priesthood elsewhere. They frowned at the secularism of the new government schools, which children were required to attend, though few went beyond the third or fourth year. Illiteracy among the South Italian immigrants averaged 53.9 per cent. Peasants and fishermen believed that the evil eye was inherent in certain people, whose glance could cause injury, sickness, or death unless averted by amulets or other supernatural means. Wizards and ghosts seemed as worthy of credence as the saints of the church. Occasionally, American observers reported that Italians in Chicago or New York had stoned a woman believed to possess the evil eye.

Still, the South Italian was lighthearted, generous to the extent of bankrupting himself for his clan and friends, and stubbornly loyal to his social responsibilities. He loved the feast days of the patron saints, with their processions, music, and fireworks. In America, Little Italys continued this pageantry. Italians liked to sing, to play the violin, the tambourine, and even the harp, though Americans associated them with the neighborhood organ grinders accompanied by their ludicrously dressed up monkeys. Young people were expected to support their parents in sickness and in old age, which might be reckoned generously at fifty years. In the United States the Italian poor preferred to avoid the stigma of relief and kept their parents, their invalids, and feeble-minded relatives in their homes. The emotional quality of their lives permeated their culture. In the New World their loud ritualistic wailing at wakes and funerals, attributed partly to the custom of frightening away evil spirits, astonished the native-born Americans.

The Italian flood poured into the cities and industrial towns where unskilled workers were in demand. Like most newcomers they were willing to work for little, to take the place of striking workmen, and to avoid unions. In the great cities they monopolized street cleaning and public construction work like the subways. The rebuilding of San Francisco after the earthquake of 1906 was done in large part by Italian laborers. In New York city, as early as 1890, practically all bootblacks were Italian and so were most of the fruit peddlers. Italian barbers replaced the French, and Italian waiters won preference over the Negroes in restaurants and hotels. In 1892, reported the Italian consul, Italians owned most of the fruit stands in New York; Sicilians imported fruits and wines and many Italians became wholesalers in this line. In New Orleans, Italian hucksters added oysters to their fruit and vegetable business. After 1900, South Italian shoemakers replaced Germans in this occupation and took over much of the cigar-making trade.

Labor agents, the notorious *padroni,* enriched themselves at the expense of the "greenhorns." The *padroni* hired gangs of workmen, charged a heavy commission for the service, and advanced passage money for the journey from Italy, also at a fancy price. They often managed groups of working children, even sending them into the streets to beg. There were other parasites, too. The good, kindly banker from the immigrant's own village also exacted a heavy commission for his services and occasionally absconded altogether. At home, the women tended to age prematurely and many were victims of tuberculosis or pneumonia. They overworked themselves to support their large broods, took in garment jobs and rarely saw the sun as they had done in Italy. When illness came they relied on patent medicines, quacks, or magic for their cures.

Just as the Chinese community was afflicted with its criminal group of hatchet men, so the Southern Italians were beset by the organized gangsters of Italy. During the opening years of the century the Italian government took such vigorous steps to stamp out the secret criminal societies that many of their members emigrated to America. The worst were the Mafia of Sicily and the Camorra centering in Naples; both were specialists in intimidation, blackmail,

bribery, robbery, and murder. They also helped to perpetuate the
vendetta in the feudal style familiar among Kentucky mountaineers.
Free-lance criminals could raise their prestige by decorating
their extortion notes with the Black Hand or Mafia symbols. Black
Hand criminals made a special point of killing their victims at the
very hour previously announced. Terrified witnesses refused to
talk and kinsmen of murdered men sometimes embarked upon their
own revenge according to the Sicilian code. Innocent immigrants,
distrusting the metropolitan police—with some reason—and traditionally opposed to informers, became the helpless prey of gangsters
who bombed their homes and businesses or murdered their relatives
if payment was not forthcoming. The police were complaisant, except for sporadic ineffective drives. In Chicago, the chief of police
airily dismissed complaints regarding Mafia plots in the Italian
district, "Oh, we've always had trouble up there; they never bother
anyone but each other." American newspapers continued to display
an anti-Italian tone for years after World War I on account of the
criminal societies. As one Italian put it, "We often have to say we are
French, or Spanish, or Turks, to hold a job."

An international incident occurred in 1890 over the alleged depre-
dations of the Mafia in New Orleans where Irish and Italians clashed
repeatedly. When the Irish chief of police was murdered, a mob
lynched eleven Italians. Italy protested indignantly and international
tension developed before the State Department effected an adjustment of claims. In New York, in 1910, many of the gangsters were
rounded up in a major drive, the ringleaders were deported, and
others were punished. Such progress was made possible in large
part by the use of special Italian detective squads familiar with the
language and ways of the criminals and their victims. By 1915,
crime in the various Little Italys had been reduced to normal proportions and the Italian immigrant came to show a greater trust in
the justice of the American police and the courts.

In the process of assimilation, numerous defections from Catholic
orthodoxy occurred, but few joined the Socialists, Anarchists or the
various rationalist groups and few became Protestants. In industry

Italians learned to join unions and to strike successfully, as they did in the great Lawrence textile strike of 1912. Italian families were eager to educate their youth through the public schools and to gain for them the prestige of white-collar positions; but they lagged behind other Catholic nationalities in supporting parochial schools, apparently reflecting the contemporary anticlerical trend of the Italian government. They learned to overcome their suspicions of doctors, blood tests, and hospitals. Fraternal and mutual benefit societies like the large national organization of the Sons of Italy did much to soften the humiliating status of "wops" in the cities. They offered a large measure of psychological compensation through the Italian-American program of keeping alive a love for Italy, retaining the Italian language alongside of English, and in stressing Columbus Day as a symbol of solidarity between America and Italy.

In the Italian contribution to America, the gift of song ranks uppermost. Italian opera and Italian singers and music teachers kept the German Wagnerians and symphonic orchestras on the alert. American singers studied in Italy and often affected Italian names. The richness and warmth of Italian vocal music were best illustrated in the great artists of the Metropolitan, Enrico Caruso, the most famous tenor of his day, and Amelita Galli-Curci, a coloratura soprano of unbelievable vocal range and natural tone quality. Caruso was born in Naples in 1873 and began his musical life as a choir boy. In 1903, after international successes in Italy, Russia, and Argentina, he joined the Metropolitan and distinguished himself as Rodolfo in *La Bohème* and in various roles in scores of other operas. Galli-Curci had been born and trained in Milan, but was primarily educated as a pianist, with vocal training largely as an afterthought, something that she had to cultivate by herself. With her glorious voice this proved not too difficult a task. She toured Europe and Latin America with Caruso and Titta Ruffo, the famous baritone. Only in 1916 did she join an American company, the Chicago Civic Opera Company, and four years later, the Metropolitan. Music lovers admired her charming roles of Mimi in *La Bohème* and Lucia in *Lucia di Lammermoor*. Recordings brought the voices of these stars to many thousands of Americans.

3

While four million Italian emigrants left for the United States during 1881-1917, Eastern Europe lost two million Jews. Unlike the Italians, most of the Jews from the very beginning came here to stay. The Jewish population of this country had probably not exceeded 250,000 in President Grant's day, and most of these were Germans; but by the time President Wilson began his second term there were 3,389,000 Jews in the population; three-fourths of these were of Czarist Russian origin and 1,500,000 alone resided in New York city. Aside from the Russian Jews (and these included some Polish and Lithuanian Jews as well), there was one additional group of 300,000 Polish Jews who left the Galician provinces of Austria-Hungary, and another Jewish exodus of about one-fifth this number from Rumania.

In 1881, the relatively liberal Czar Alexander II was assassinated by terrorists and with him was interred the hope of emancipating the Jews from their restricted medieval status. His reactionary successor, Alexander III, revived violent antisemitism under the Romanov banner of "autocracy, Greek orthodoxy, and Russian nationalism." The agrarian depression, liberal propaganda, and imperialistic wars shook the stability of the empire. Though serfdom had been abolished, a few landowners owned more property than ever and the peasants lacked sufficient good land for subsistence. Industrialization had not yet succeeded in displacing the inefficient handicraft system. Under such circumstances the ministers of the Autocrat of All the Russias attempted to channel popular discontent through the usual safety valve of antisemitism, a policy later disclosed and denounced by statesmen of the Duma.

The Czar's officials tightened the hundreds of special laws governing Jewish life in the segregated Pale and deliberately instigated pogroms—combinations of massacres and pillaging—against Jewish communities. Jews who had left the Pale were expelled; village Jews were transferred to certain towns, and their children were restricted, or even barred, from the schools. The ineffectual Nicholas II offered only temporary relief. Russian Jews, once welcomed in mass by the aristocracy as indispensable middlemen for the backward agrarian

villages, were officially attacked as parasites, revolutionists, and heretics. Peasant uprisings against landlords were diverted into such savage pogroms as the Kishinev massacre of 1903, which lasted three
days and aroused the condemnation of many western governments,
including that of the United States. Scores of these inspired pogroms
occurred in areas where Jews and non-Jews had hitherto lived
amicably.

In the synagogues Jews who intonated the traditional prayer of
deliverance "Next year, in Jerusalem," often meant "Next year, in
America." Although the Zionist plan of a homeland in Palestine had
been elaborated in 1882 by Theodor Herzl, orthodox Jews still preferred to wait for the Messiah to end the historic dispersion of the
Jews. Only a handful took an active part in the colonization projects
for Palestine or sought, as Israel Zangwill preferred, a colony in East
Africa or elsewhere. To the tormented, the reality of America out-
shone the dream of a haven in Zion.

Most of the Russian Jews were handicraftsmen. Of the Jewish
emigrants to the United States, 68.19 per cent were skilled workers,
the largest proportion for any immigrant group; half of these workers were in the needle trades. Czarist restrictions in the Pale reduced
Jewish economic life almost to the absurdity of that mythical village
where people earned a livelihood by taking in each other's washing.
Wholesalers, petty shopkeepers, and peddlers dealt directly with the
peasants, but their profits were usually dissipated by paying the
heavy bribes and fines required to escape Czarist regulations, by
paying off the blackmail demanded by inciters of pogroms, and by
keeping the police from pressing nuisance actions against the Jews.
There was every temptation to strike back by mulcting the peasants.
Mary Antin, daughter of a Polotsk shopkeeper who brought his family to America, wrote of the Czar in *The Promised Land:*

There he had us cooped up, thousands of us where only hundreds
could live, and every means of living taxed to the utmost. When there
are too many wolves in the prairie, they begin to prey upon each other.
We starving captives of the Pale—we did as do the hungry brutes. . . .
Such spiritual deformities are self-explained in the step-children of the
Czar.

Money meant survival—to buy permission to travel even for necessary purposes, to avoid arbitrary arrest from officials, to pay fines for relatives who escaped military service, which was made especially burdensome for Jews, and to exist without mob attacks. Ambitious Jews bought their way into the privileges of attending college and entering professions, despite Czarist restrictions. But those who were greatly enriched as merchants tended in the long run to be squeezed dry by this mode of existence. So poor were the Jews who entered the United States, that only 6 per cent possessed $50 or more and 55.33 per cent had no money at all; the average for the Jewish immigrant was $15.50 as against the general immigrant average of $22. Even the incoming Chinese began with much better financial resources. Passage money for these Jews came from relatives in over 67 per cent of all cases as compared with 35.8 per cent for all other non-Jewish immigrants.

In other respects, too, they were handicapped in beginning life anew. Despite an ancient tradition of respect for learning, the Eastern European Jews had been officially excluded too long from schooling to compare well with the literacy average of other groups and they showed an illiteracy rate of 26 per cent. However, this average was partly due to the custom of neglecting the education of women, for illiteracy among males was just under 20 per cent. More significant, as already seen, was the fact that they usually possessed a trade easily adaptable to urban conditions. Once they found employment a rush to the night schools began.

Thousands of Jews poured into the needle trades of New York, Chicago, and other cities. They entered a sweated industry in which long hours, unhealthful conditions, and poor wages obtained. To combat these conditions, Jewish labor leaders who had belonged to Russian unions—these had been underground organizations—experimented with collective bargaining. One of the ablest of these was Sidney Hillman, born in Lithuania in 1887 and educated at one time for the rabbinate. He had turned to the ideas of the Enlightenment, had read J. S. Mill and Tolstoi, had joined the Russian union movement, and was jailed for activity in the revolution of 1905. To escape exile to Siberia, he fled to England in 1907 and shortly after went to work for Hart, Schaffner, and Marx in Chicago.

His fellow tailors and pressers were Jews, Turks, Greeks, Poles and others, united by their grievance of earning less than ten or twelve dollars for a fifty-four hour week. He helped to organize these men, became one of the leaders in the successful strike of 1910, and supported an impartial arbitration plan (initiated by the democratic Schaffner) that became a permanent part of the industry. In 1914, he left for New York and was soon elected president of the newly organized Amalgamated Clothing Workers. Herbert Harris, the labor historian, describes Hillman's conversion to a class collaborationist philosophy that went beyond Gompers' pure and simple unionism: "He urged Amalgamated members to make their organization more than a vehicle for collective bargaining, and to share with their employers the responsibility for improving quality, increasing output, abolishing waste, reducing overhead." By 1916, Hillman had organized the men's clothing industry of New York and had made the forty-eight-hour week general. These gains were soon extended to other large cities.

Within the American Jewish ghettos the semi-oriental village of Eastern Europe came again to life. These ghetto dwellers had only casual contacts with the assimilated and prosperous German Jewish community. There was the plain single-room Jewish synagogue with dilapidated benches, whose Orthodox rabbi not only directed strictly spiritual affairs but also resolved personal conflicts in the community according to Talmudic principles. Visitors stared at the ultra-religious *Chasid* with his flowing beard, long side locks, and traditional gabardine coat. Along Maxwell Street in Chicago, or Hester Street in New York, the unwary Anglo-Saxon shopper might be discomfited by the zeal of the "pullers" who seized the customer's coat lapel and tried to coax him into their shops or to their pushcarts. On the Jewish Sabbath, all business activity ceased, though the younger generation became increasingly indifferent to all the meticulous rules of Sabbatarianism. Gentile immigrants from Eastern Europe, unaccustomed to the American one-price system, liked to patronize the ghetto markets and were ready to haggle with the Jewish merchant or peddler.

In the schools little Mary Antin and her generation of youngsters showed a marked eagerness to earn high marks and acquire the social status prized by every poor immigrant and especially by a persecuted people. There was an unusually large number of immigrant mutual aid and charitable institutions, supported by small contributions from synagogue members as well as by wealthy philanthropists like Jacob Schiff. One of the earliest settlement houses was the Henry Street Settlement of New York, where Lillian Wald embarked upon her sympathetic social work with Jewish immigrants and their foreign-born neighbors of other faiths. Miss Wald stemmed from a German-Jewish middle-class family of Cincinnati, and had been trained as a public nurse. She organized public health nursing within the settlement movement, and was one of the original advocates of the Federal Children's Bureau.

With the heavy influx of Russian and Polish Jews came an increase in the relatively mild antisemitism of the past. Saratoga resorts and exclusive eastern colleges had long hesitated to accept even smooth-shaven assimilated Jews with impeccable American accents. As early as the eighties, Emma Lazarus, the Jewish-American poet of immigrant life, could write:

Even in America, presumably the refuge of the oppressed, public opinion has not yet reached that point where it absolves the race from the sin of the individual. Every Jew, however honorable or enlightened, has the humiliating knowledge that his security and reputation are, in a certain sense, bound up with those of the meanest rascal who belongs to his tribe, and who has it in his power to jeopardize the social status of his whole nation.

On the whole, however, aside from the daily clashes of Jewish boys with boys of other immigrant neighbors, antisemitism was muffled and did not prevent the economic advancement of innumerable Jews. Pogroms were a thing of the nightmarish past.

Russian Jews had their small but creative *intelligentsia*, the products of a cultural stimulation that often takes place when different intellectual traditions come into repeated contact. They were secular in outlook and familiar with the great Russian novels as well as with the literature of the Yiddish writers and Hebraists. Yiddish, a seventeenth-century German jargon with a sprinkling of Hebrew and Slavic words, offered an international language to most Jews. The Eastern European Enlightenment among Jews (the Haskala movement) made Yiddish a challenging literary vehicle to many aspiring Jewish writers.

Abraham Cahan, a Lithuanian Socialist who had learned American journalism as a reporter under the direction of Lincoln Steffens, took over the dormant *Jewish Daily Forward* (founded in 1897) and revived it with an attractive potpourri of stories written in the homely Yiddish vernacular, advice to the lovelorn, and the most intimate news about the East Side. The *Forward* became the rallying point of many able Yiddish short story writers and poets. Cahan himself scored a literary success for his realistic novel of the Jewish immigrant worker and the ghetto in *The Rise of David Levinsky,* which was written in English. Among the Yiddish-American writers whose fame went far beyond the walls of the ghetto were Sholem Asch, who wrote the successful Yiddish comedy, *Mottke the Thief* (1917); he was to win a major following in later years for his novels, *The Three Cities* and *The Nazarene.* From Kiev came Sholom Aleichem (Solomon Rabinowitz) whose twinkling humor and sympathetic insight gave him the critic's applause as the Jewish Mark Twain. Others praised him as the greatest Jewish literary figure since Heine. One Jewish critic, Marie Syrkin, has offered this opinion: "One cannot escape the conclusion that the literary output of Yiddish writers in the United States has reached greater heights than that attained by American Jewish writers, except possibly in the field of the drama." Though Yiddish seemed a crude tongue to exponents of Hebrew and German, it was the literary channel of men who had deep psychological roots in the unique culture and suffering of the Russian and Polish ghettos.

The Jewish immigrant stage like that of other immigrant groups of this era tended to be heavily melodramatic and sentimental, with songs and dances interjected at almost any point in the plot. Jacob Gordon was to introduce stage reforms along the lines of Russian realism, but the advent of the sophisticated Jewish Art Theatre was yet to come. In one important respect the Russian Jews may have acted as the American cultural middlemen for Stanislavsky's theatrical art, which created the Moscow Art Theatre and influenced the Little Theater movement in the United States. These Moscow actors were at first limited to the Third Street Theatre on Manhattan's East Side where Russian-speaking Jews, some of them later active in the English theater, could understand their performances.

America's theaters and music halls were deeply influenced by Jewish entrepreneurs and entertainers. Out of the East European Pale came Louis B. Mayer and Samuel Goldwyn, who rose from humble pursuits to help make the United States the motion picture capital of the world. David Sarnoff left his native Minsk in 1900 to begin his American career which led him to the presidency of the Radio Corporation of America. In 1893, Israel Baline left Russia, destined to make millions sing the compositions he wrote as Irving Berlin. In the Russia of Alexander III and Nicholas II few of these emigrants could have hoped to escape the economic treadmill of the ghetto. Their careers offered additional testimony that the "new immigration" was no less creative than the old.

4

Another of the Czar's stepchildren was the Pole, whose country had become a geographical abstraction ever since the late eighteenth century when it had been carved up among Austria, Prussia, and Russia. The migration of Prussian Poles, like that of the Germans, had been high in the 1880's, but it declined thereafter as the agricultural economy was modernized. But Russian Poland and Austrian Galicia remained inefficient both agriculturally and industrially. Crop failures and textile crises deranged the economy. The introduction of universal military service into Russian Poland in 1876 drove many to emigrate. Even more basic was the pressure of population in this backward peasant economy, and the land hunger of discontented Poles. The aristocratic landlord class owned relatively efficient estates but offered no progressive leadership to these masses and were indifferent to trade and industry. More than half of the Poles who came to America were landless peasants.

Three-fourths of the Poles lived in agricultural villages and tilled small strips of land for themselves or the landlord, using antiquated methods. Wladyslaw Reymont, the great Polish novelist, has left an unforgettable picture of their primitive simplicity in *The Peasants*. In Galicia, 84.4 per cent, according to Paul Fox, owned tiny farms of twelve acres or less and even such holdings were apt to be divided among families with many children. Land taxes were high and transportation was poor, while church holidays, numbering 150 to 200 days annually in many sections, further reduced productivity. In the unprogressive peasant villages families lived in thatched or mud-and-straw covered huts of two rooms, usually reserving one for livestock and poultry. Their diet was simple—cabbage soup (borscht), potatoes, a few other vegetables, eggs, and on special occasions meat and poultry. Life was enlivened by church festal days, hilarious wedding celebrations, village dances, church fairs, and visiting musicians. The Poles remained a gregarious people in the New World.

The education of the people was promoted successfully by neither the landlords nor the predominant Catholic Church. In Austrian Galicia 52 per cent of the men and 60 per cent of the women were illiterate. The Polish peasants, like those of other parts of Eastern Europe and of Southern Italy, mixed a large store of superstition and magic with their religion. To make matters worse, the Czars discouraged the use of Polish and tried to stamp out the historic Polish culture by a crude program of Russification. Polish patriots, hoping to see the overthrow of Czarism, fought these repressive measures and sang the defiant words of their national song, "Poland is not yet lost ..." Under such miserable conditions the simple Polish peasant was often ready to believe that the real source of his misery was the large Jewish class of middlemen, particularly the moneylenders and agents of the landlords. Antisemitism long confused the direction of Poland's economic and social progress.

Over a million Polish-born immigrants from Russian Poland, Austrian Galicia, and German Poland lived in the United States on the eve of World War I. They congregated in the Pennsylvania mining towns, in New York city, Chicago, and Cleveland. Thousands took over declining New England farms in the Connecticut valley and

made these prosper. About one-third of the Poles settled on the
farms of the Middle West, New England, and Texas. But in the cities
few Poles were skilled and hence were glad to accept heavy manual
work, many living on a daily diet of sausage and bread. Few of
this generation entered the professions or white-collar fields, relying
instead upon Polish-speaking Jewish doctors and lawyers.

The Catholic parish was usually the center of the Polish-American
community though the majority of Poles sent their children to public
rather than to parochial schools. The family retained its patriarchal
organization; and its clannish quality was at first unaffected by intermarriage with other nationalities. However, secularism steadily en-
croached on the religious outlook of the Poles. Polish culture, hitherto
repressed, had its outlet in thousands of national halls and Polish-
language schools. In the large Polish-American press anticlerical and
reformist newspapers outdid the conservative papers in circulation.
Nationalists aroused enthusiasm for the future of Poland reborn and
freed of Russian domination. The strongest nationalist agency was
the Polish National Alliance of Chicago, founded in 1880, though
preceded by similar Polish organizations. It avowed a purpose

> to promote the moral and material development of Polish immigrants
> in the United States through the establishment of Polish "homes," schools,
> and benevolent institutions, and through the encouragement of Polish
> industry; to encourage temperance; and to maintain the proper observ-
> ance of national holidays.

Clerical leaders, dissatisfied with the secular nature of the Polish National Alliance enlarged an earlier religious group at the same time
to form the Polish Roman Catholic Union, which combined both religious and nationalist objectives. The solidarity of the Polish-American
community was strengthened by numerous building and loan associations that helped to satisfy the Pole's strong desire to own his own
home.

5

Other Czarist nationalities, the Ukrainians, the German-Russians,
the Finns, and even the White Russians joined the exodus once the
government relaxed its traditional policy of discouraging emigration.

Many were transients, with no intention of staying longer than was necessary to earn enough for a second chance in Russia. The 1910 census showed nearly 58,000 Russian-speaking immigrants of foreign birth, including 13,800 from Austria and 1,400 from Hungary. These figures did not altogether exclude Russian Jews. The next census (there was little immigration during the war years) recorded 392,049 foreign-born Russians in this country. By that time about 700,000 Americans were either Russian or natives of Russian parentage and most of them lived in urban colonies.

Russian immigrants had infiltrated the West Coast back in the fur-trading days when Alaska was a Russian colony. In the 1870's, German-Russian Mennonites from the Volga fled the conscription laws and religious persecution to build communal settlements in Kansas, Nebraska, and the Dakotas. These Volga colonists were descended from the original seventeenth- and eighteenth-century Germans of the Palatinate, whence had come, also, so many of the Pennsylvania Germans. From Lincoln, Nebraska, as a center they moved into the beet fields of that state and harvested the wheat of Kansas and the Dakotas. They introduced a miraculous wheat plant from the old country, the so-called "Turkey Wheat," which was easily able to withstand the frost or drought that periodically destroyed the crop of their American neighbors. Their success led experts from the Department of Agriculture to visit Russia and bring back hardy varieties of seed which eventually brought millions of dollars to the farmers of the Great Plains.

To Slavic cities like Cleveland, Buffalo, Pittsburgh, and others came the illiterate, hard-working mudsills of society from peasant Russia. They loyally supported their Greek orthodox churches and followed the advice of their patriarchal bearded priests, who advised them on the minutiae of everyday life. The Holy Synod in America controlled 169 churches and 100,000 members in 1916. Most of the Russians were conservative in religion and politics; a small minority of political refugees had imbibed the ideas of Marx, Bakunin, or Kropotkin. These former *muzhiks* (peasants) drank heavily, danced the lively polkas, czardas, and other folk dances, and played their native balalaika instruments. The meeting of East and West was signified by

the sharp contrast of broad oriental church domes amid the slender
Roman Catholic and Protestant church spires.

In Pennsylvania's industrial and mining slums Russians were hired
to replace Irish workers. Among them were 3000 Old Believers,
seventeenth-century religious schismatics who had become loyal adherents of the Czar and wished only to pile up a small hoard for their
eventual return to Russia. Their long beards, loose native blouses,
and uncouth habits set them apart. Foremen found the unlettered
Russians to be docile troglodytes as strikebreakers in the mines, steel
mills, and factories. Russian priests wondered audibly why Pennsylvania's laws forbade baseball on Sunday but permitted the seven-day
week in the steel mills. Slums, long hours, and heavy mortality darkened their lives. As one Russian-American newspaper put it, "America is not at all interested in the soul and spiritual life of the Russian
immigrant, only in his muscles." To the average American, all Eastern Europeans looked alike and were often lumped together as "Po-
lacks." Some relief came through the Russian fraternal societies and
charities and from the settlement houses, the Y.M.C.A., and the
Y.W.C.A. The American free school system and the libraries and the
unrivaled economic opportunities offered salvation to the children of
these immigrants.

A small radical press, supported by some 50,000 political refugees,
agitated for the overthrow of Czarism. The most active clubs were
the Russian Revolutionary Society, the Russian Social Democratic
Party, the Bund, and the League of Friends of Russian Freedom.
Apart from the Radical Marxists and Bakuninites were the Ukrainian
Nationalists, conservative socially and economically, but neverthe-
less determined to win the independence of the Ukraine from the
Romanovs.

6

Not at all typical of the various Slavic immigrants were the Bohemians and Moravians within the Austro-Hungarian Empire. They
tended to be a literate, skilled, and even rationalist people; in fact,
their literacy rate was the highest of the various nationalities in the
polyglot Hapsburg empire and their enterprising spirit marked them

off as the Prussians of that nation. To a large extent the Bohemian-Moravian newcomers belonged to the old immigration, for they left in large numbers during the potato blight of the 1840's as well as thereafter. At first they took up farms in the Middle West, but by the 1860's they had turned to the cities in large numbers, making Cleveland a major Czech center and establishing large communities in Chicago, New York, and St. Louis. In 1910, the census reported 228,738 Bohemians and Moravians in the United States and about twice that number if one included Americans of Czech parentage.

Czech workers were most numerous as tailors, small shopkeepers, and cigar makers. "Every Czech a cigar maker" was a popular adage. They played an important part in promoting urban real estate and their exceptionally numerous building and loan associations reflected a keen desire to own their own homes. In 1910, for example, 94 of 197 such associations in Chicago were Czech and represented half of their total assets. Many Czechs, with a successful tradition in making beer, opened saloons, which required little capital. The immigrant saloon, particularly among the Slavs, was more than a place to drink liquor. It was a social center, a lodge, a relief society, and a political meeting place. By the twentieth century the saloon had lost many social functions to the attractive National Halls, gymnastic or "sokol" societies, summer camps, and settlement houses.

While the American environment had a disintegrating, secular effect on the religious communalism of many Central and Eastern European immigrants, its influence on the Czechs was no less than startling. Czech nationalists had long gloried in the rebellious church principles of John Hus and had associated the Hapsburg reconversion of Bohemia to Catholicism in the seventeenth century with the political subjugation of their country. Once they were in America, perhaps 50 per cent of the Czechs fell away from Catholicism and embraced freethinking ideas. The Czech press reflected this rationalist tendency; in fact, one of the leading Bohemian editors even named his son for Robert Ingersoll. In 1903, according to the editor of *Svornost* in Chicago, fully 300 special Sunday schools existed in that city, teaching rationalist principles to about 30,000 Czechs. The leading rationalist group, originally Catholic, was the Bohemian-

Slavonian Benevolent Society, founded in 1854. Their attractive halls were used to foster nationalism, intellectual individualism, and mutual aid services. Clerical papers and organizations struck back at the "infidels" and engaged in a bitter controversy in cities with large Czech communities.

In America the Czechs continued their cultural affinity with the Austrian Germans. Many Czechs spoke German as well as Bohemian. The early immigrants had been guided by the Austrian papers to German-American settlements in Milwaukee, Chicago, and Racine. In fact, wherever Bohemians intermarried, it was usually with Germans. Both groups were highly literate and shared similar tastes.

Despite the difficult spelling of Czech names, the American press could scarcely overlook a number of gifted Bohemians. Best-known to young Americans was the Bohemian-born Rudolf Friml, the composer of *The Firefly, High Jinks, Katinka,* and *Rose Marie.* He had studied music in Prague and had come to New York city as a resident in 1906 after an extensive international tour as the piano accompanist of the renowned Czech violinist, Jan Kubelik. For three years the great Anton Dvořák was director of the National Conservatory of Music in New York city. He had a keen perception of the possibilities of native American music and was an enthusiastic advocate of the use of the Indian, Negro, and cowboy traditions. His best-remembered works are the *New World Symphony* and the piano music of *Humoresque.*

Physical anthropologists in America and Europe rated Ales Hrdlička among their outstanding scholars. Hrdlička, born in 1869 in a Bohemian village, received his scientific education in New York and specialized at first in medicine. In 1910, after considerable experience with anthropological field work in the Southwest, he was appointed curator of the United States National Museum where he had already organized a department of physical anthropology. As an immigrant, it is significant that he later published the study *Old Americans* (1925), which suggested that the seventeenth-century Anglo-Americans were hardly blond Nordics in physical characteristics, but a round-headed, brunette type.

Thomas G. Masaryk, the future founder of Czechoslovakia, knew the United States well as a lecturer at the University of Chicago and elsewhere. Fittingly enough, American Czechs played a major role in the diplomacy and organization of the young democratic republic. In 1914, the American Committee for the Liberation of the Czech People was formed in New York and set up at least 350 branches throughout the country.

7

Things did not go too well economically even for the junior partner of the Hapsburgs, Hungary. As usual, the land problem and new conscription laws were basic. Over half of all farm owners in this predominantly agrarian society owned less than five acres each, while a few landlords held title to one-third of the arable lands. The aristocratic Esterházy family, noted in history for their extravagance and regal splendor, ruled over an estate of 221,241 acres. Altogether, 87 per cent of the people owned less than ten acres—the minimum needed to support a family. To make matters worse, the inefficient, extensive farming that might have been tolerable where land was abundant, continued to be in vogue. So far was feudalism from extinction that innumerable farmers still owed feudal services and contributions to the lord of the demesne. When competitive foreign wheat affected Hungary, the government raised the tariff, but only succeeded in lowering the standard of living thereby.

In contrast with the wretched conditions for the peasantry, the decadent Hungarian aristocracy lived a traditional feudal life, gambling, riding horses, playing the role of the gentleman farmer, even of the cultivated student, and occasionally conceding to the modern spirit by becoming nominal bank directors to lend tone to bourgeois financiers. They kept the commonality largely disfranchised and supported the regime in repressing unions and popular demonstrations. Imperial officials had even less regard for the large Slavic minorities within Hungary. The economic policies of the ruling classes were not the only factors behind emigration; there were also the new military conscription policies which drove tens of thousands to leave Hungary during the nineties and afterwards.

Instead of the bourgeois emigration to America of Louis Kossuth's

day, the new exiles of the end of the century—"Hunkies"—joined
other unskilled groups as manual laborers, miners, and factory hands.
Between 1899 and 1913 over 400,000 Magyars had left for the
United States, reaching a peak in 1907. Part of this migration consisted of Jews who had left primarily for economic reasons; anti-
semitism was mild in prewar Hungary. Two-thirds of the Hungarians
were Catholic and most of the remainder were Lutherans, Calvinists,
and Jews. In America, the proportion of Protestant Magyars gained
steadily at the expense of the Catholics. Total illiteracy was not too
common, for only 11.4 per cent of the Magyars were unable to read
or write.

The chief Hungarian centers were New York, Cleveland, Detroit,
Pittsburgh, and Chicago. Of all Cleveland's immigrants the Hungarians seemed the most in evidence. Their newspaper, *Szabadság*
(Liberty) had a wide circulation in pre-World War I days. This influential paper not only served the immigrant but became a powerful
foe of the Habsburg autocracy at home, and demanded genuine popular suffrage for the peasantry. No Slavs themselves, but Magyars, the
Hungarians fought the influence of Pan-Slavism among their Slovak
brethren from the homeland and persuaded the Catholic hierarchy
to send only Hungarian-speaking priests to their churches. Like other
immigrant groups the Hungarians had numerous benevolent and
cultural societies and nationalistic organizations. They brought with
them the colorful harvest festival, ceremonial feasts, melodic Magyar
and gypsy music, distinctive dishes like chicken paprikash, goulash,
and stuffed cabbage, and lively dances like the Czardas.

8

Often mistaken for Hungarians by immigration clerks and census
takers were the South Slavs of the Habsburg Empire, the Serbs,
Croats, and Slovenes of future Yugoslavia. Some lived in scattered
communities within Hungary itself; most of them resided in Dalma-
tia. The Serbs were belligerently nationalistic, proud of having recovered their independence from Turkey in the 1830's, and of having
created a new state in the freed areas. Like the Russians, they be-

longed to the Orthodox Church, which denied the primacy of the
Roman Pope. They were a sturdy peasant people belonging to a patriarchal and communal society and were almost primitive in their
economy; few could read or write. The Croatians and Slovenes were
largely Roman Catholic and somewhat higher than the Serbs in literacy; Croatians often spoke German or Hungarian as well as their
local speech.

These Yugoslavs left for the usual reasons: landlordism, agrarian
blights, and military conscription laws. Most of them were fit only
for manual work; Serb women even worked in the fields though
Croats and Slovenes did not like to have their women work outside
the home. Tens of thousands arrived during the 1890's and the early
years of the twentieth century. They gravitated toward the heaviest
jobs in the steel mills around Chicago and the mines and mills around
Pittsburgh. Like other Southeastern immigrants, they came at first as
transients, lived in male cooperative settlements, and steadily adjusted themselves to permanence. They adopted most of the economic, cultural, and recreational agencies that other groups had
used to reorient themselves to America.

One of the most remarkable though least typical of this Yugoslav
immigration was Nikola Tesla, son of a Croatian Orthodox priest.
After being educated at the University of Prague, he became interested in electricity, and worked for the Austrian government as an
engineer. In 1884, he came to the United States, joined the Edison
Company at West Orange, New Jersey, and thereafter in New York
devoted his life to research. Four years after his arrival he patented
an induction motor based on his principle of a rotary magnetic field.
He invented a system of arc lighting, generators of high-frequency
currents, and a transformer. He developed the great Niagara power
system and a system of transmitting electric power without wires.
His eightieth birthday in 1936 was the occasion for an international
celebration.

Even better known to Americans than Tesla was another genius in
the field of electricity, Michael Pupin, a Serb whose parents were
illiterate but intelligent. He spent part of his early manhood as a farm
worker and a herdsman. Encouraged by his mother and several

American visitors, he determined to educate himself as far as possible in the Imperial schools, but finally sold his belongings for a steamship ticket to the United States. He arrived in New York in 1874 with five cents in his pocket, attended the Bowery Mission for its cheap soup, and worked in a cracker factory. At night he studied in the library of Cooper Union and pursued his interest in mathematics and science. Finally, he won a scholarship at Columbia, earned high honors, studied at Cambridge and Berlin, where he took his Ph.D., and returned to teach electromechanics at Columbia thereafter.

He showed his genius in solving basic technical problems connected with the long-distance telephone, especially in correcting the attenuation of electrical current conveying speech. After the invention of the X-ray in 1895 he was the first American to construct an X-ray tube and to secure an X-ray photo. Eventually, he secured thirty-four patents in the electrical field. He built himself, in Norfolk, Connecticut, a medieval style Serb home with the traditional inner court, gave away money for Serbian cultural projects, and took an active part in diplomacy leading to Yugoslavia's independence. Always, however, he remained an enthusiastic American, appreciative of the democratic institutions of his adopted land. His widely-read autobiography, *From Immigrant to Inventor* (1923), one of his numerous writings, received the Pulitzer Prize. He was one of the original sponsors of the American Mathematical Society and the National Research Council and left the bulk of his estate to Columbia University. In his thinking were blended native genius and a fervor for democratic idealism that he had acquired in the anti-Habsburg movement among the Serbs.

9

The tardy Greek emigration, pressing hard upon the Italians and others of the new immigration, began slowly in the 1890's and reached large proportions only in the decade before our entrance into World War I. Only a thousand came in 1891, and the total Greek population was less than 9000 in 1900; however, the subsequent rush brought a peak of 46,283 in 1907 alone and a total Greek-American population of 184,907 by 1910.

These Greeks came largely from primitive farm districts, were heavily illiterate (about 25 per cent), and lived at a low subsistence level. The Eastern European agrarian crisis was accentuated in Greece by the local depression, due to French competition, in the important Greek currant market. Primitive farm implements and methods, the hundreds of holidays of the Greek Orthodox Church, and poor internal transportation kept the standard of living down. There were 180 fasting days in the Greek religious year. In the cities industrialization had only begun and the workman's family usually lived in a single room and rarely enjoyed the luxury of eating meat, butter, eggs, or milk. Breakfast was likely to consist of black coffee and bread, luncheon of black olives, a tomato, or some grapes with bread; and supper was little more than rice boiled with wild greens, together with olive oil and bread. As elsewhere, two years of military service awaited each youth. To make matters worse, Rumania and Bulgaria began to discriminate against Greek immigrants and seasonal farm workers and laborers; this cut off an important safety valve for overpopulation.

Under such circumstances the steamship agents and other propagandists had little difficulty in drawing thousands away from their ancient villages and towns. Greek-Americans awed the peasants by sending pictures and clippings from the foreign-language press. Villagers gasped at the elaborate wedding celebrations of ordinary Greek immigrants only recently sunk in the poverty of their homeland. Padroni, as among the Italians, often bought the steamship tickets for youths under a camouflaged labor contract. They posed as fathers or uncles of the bootblacks and messenger boys they sent to America. In the Greek towns padroni had long dominated the bootblack business and knew all the tricks and evasions needed in their exploitative business.

The arrivals were unskilled workmen and were directed by their experienced fellow-countrymen to factories and stores in New York, Chicago, and Lowell. Greek businessmen, heirs to the ancient commercial traditions of the Eastern Mediterranean, hired the newcomers as clerks in their confectionery, fruit, and candy stores. With a little capital the immigrant learned from his countrymen how to peddle candy, fruit, and flowers, eventually giving up his pushcart for a dignified, neat retail store. The Greek "Ice Cream Parlor" and the "Shoe Shine Parlor" became distinctive urban institutions and reflected the ingenuity of the Hellene in attracting customers. Chicago led in the number of Greek confectionery stores and counted 400 of them in 1912 together with some 600 to 800 Greek restaurants and cafés. The humble Italian bootblack stands gave way to the Greek's mirrored shoeshine parlor with their tobacco stands and their side rooms for pool playing. Some of these establishments were worth from ten to twenty thousand dollars and enterprising Greeks often owned more than one. Greeks took over much of Coney Island's concession business aggregating millions of dollars, and others turned to service trades such as barbering, cobbling, and tailoring.

Thousands of Greeks went to work on the western railroads, living cooperatively in the boxcars, and sleeping in bunks along the sidings. In separate boxcars Bulgarian, Rumanian, Croatian, and Italian workers lived apart in their own little colonies. During the idle winter these Greek laborers poured into Chicago and other western cities and played cards in the Greek cafés. Many more of the unskilled workers were directed by Greek labor agents to the large Greek colony in Lowell, Massachusetts, where they worked for low wages in the mills, and lived in ill-ventilated, overcrowded tenements. At first they did the most menial jobs, such as sweeping the mills or handling heavy equipment. By 1913, Anglo-Saxon Lowell was partly an Eastern European town with Greeks, Poles, and Italians competing successfully against the older French-Canadian, Scandinavian, and Irish workers. Clashes between the newly-arrived Greeks and the French-Canadians and Irish broke out from time to time. Unlike the heavy-drinking, brawling factory workers of other groups, the Greeks usually came to work sober on Monday mornings and worked patiently and methodically at their assigned tasks.

As the Greeks gave up the idea of returning home and brought their families to America, community life became stabilized. Divorce was infrequent, morality strict, and the oriental seclusion of women persisted. At Greek family picnics they roasted entire lambs over a spit as in the old country and danced to the ancient familiar tunes. On Good Friday night the Greek stores were draped in purple and black, and a procession of men, carrying lighted candles and chanting hymns, filled the streets; they were watched with deep curiosity by immigrants of other nationalities. Community life tended to center upon the sociable Greek cafés or coffeehouses. There the men might talk and smoke all day, read the newspapers, sip thick, sweet Turkish coffee, and play cards—usually for small stakes. In this informal atmosphere collarless waiters and proprietors served them in shirt sleeves.

Greek children, once they escaped the peonage of bootblack parlors or other such work, proved eager, bright students, ambitious to rise in the world. In the churches, the Orthodox priests reigned subject to the intervention of critical laymen through parish committees. The Orthodox Church helped to unite the community as a social as well as religious unit. There was also the usual large quota of mutual aid societies to strengthen the Greeks economically. The most important nationalist group was the Pan-Hellenic Union, organized in 1904 and embracing 150 branches by 1912. They had the immigrant function of public relations, the perpetuation of cultural ties with the homeland, and the support of tradition. Striving toward a similar goal the Greek-American press kept the flame of Hellenism alive and offered valuable information for the growing import business in Greek hands.

IO

The New Immigration, despite its solid cultural and economic contributions, seemed too alien a strain to Old Americans to pass without challenge. Among the restrictionists, aside from the trade unions, who feared the competition of cheap labor, was a successor of the Know-Nothing party of the fifties, the American Protective Association. This originated in the Middle West corn belt and offered a program of tighter naturalization laws including longer periods of residence, the exclusion of illiterates and Europe's "pauper labor," a boycott of Catholic political candidates, and the abolition of parochial schools. On several major occasions in Illinois and Wisconsin, Catholics and Lutherans joined forces to save the parochial schools from A.P.A. laws. Germans, Scandinavians, and others fought A.P.A. efforts to halt the use of foreign languages as the chief medium of instruction.

Social scientists, then influenced by the racialist thinking inspired by western European scholars, often taught the Teutonic origins of American institutions and Nordic superiority. These ideas offered a pseudo-scientific basis for restrictionism and influenced the organization of the Immigration Restriction League in 1894 with John Fiske, the historian, as one of the first presidents. The League lobbied successfully for the literacy test, which finally passed Congress in 1917 despite the vetoes of Cleveland, Taft, and Wilson. To the latter, literacy was a test of opportunity, not fitness. Thus the earlier policy of selection (except for the exclusion of the Chinese and, to some extent, the Japanese as well) was replaced by one of outright exclusion, though under the guise of a literacy test. Previously, the laws had either protected newcomers from exploitation or barred the unfit—alien convicts, prostitutes, the insane, contract laborers, polygamists, paupers, and the diseased. It is true that the first test of political beliefs in American history had been added shortly after the assassination of McKinley by the anarchist, Czolgosz; thereafter immigrants were expected to disavow anarchist principles. Informal immigration restriction had also been practiced by the federal immigration bureaus who were made responsible to the new Department of Labor after 1913.

The beginnings of the formal restrictive policy owed much to Senator Henry Cabot Lodge of Massachusetts, representative of the Old Americans, who had urged this cause since the early nineties. Lodge's committee on immigration in 1911 issued a forty-two-volume report to Congress on the Old and the New Immigrants in regard to their qualities of assimilation. Its report had been strongly adverse and its charges had been less than objective or scientific, concluding with the need of restricting "undesirable immigration" through a literacy test. This would obviously hurt mostly the more illiterate Catholic, Greek Orthodox, and Jewish influx from Southern and Eastern Europe.

The New Immigration, as Edward G. Hartmann declares, had its staunch native friends among the well-informed—the social workers, educators, and liberal journalists. They challenged the thesis that these immigrants were unassimilable and argued that the real danger was the uncritical absorption of the worst features of American life in the eastern slums. What was needed was to preserve the influence of immigrant parents over their children, as the neighborhood social centers were trying to do, and to blend the better features of immigrant culture with American traits.

Much less scientific in their methods were the uncritically assimilationist efforts of the National Society of Colonial Dames of America (founded in 1891), the National Society of the Sons of the American Revolution (1889), and the Daughters of the American Revolution (1890). These hereditary patriotic societies were particularly concerned with the purity of Anglo-American culture. They had apparently forgotten their own revolutionary origins and considered (especially in later years) the various movements of social protest as suspect if not disloyal. They took an active role in the Americanization movement at the opening of the century and sponsored immigrant education through scholarships, special textbooks, foreign-language pamphlets, public lectures on American history and citizenship, and the training of immigrant teachers. As yet, the patriotic societies had not embarked on the narrowly chauvinistic policies that some of them adopted during the 1920's and 1930's.

Historians and sociologists tend to feel that the Americanization movement of the prewar years possessed more enthusiasm than thoroughness or scientific purpose. Undoubtedly, it helped innumerable immigrants, as is clear from so many autobiographical accounts; but the uncritical emphasis on unity fell short of the social workers' aim of respecting the integrity of immigrant social and ethical values. But in this age of rampant nationalism in Europe as well as in America, little more could be expected. Scarcely any large immigrant-receiving countries showed great enlightenment in dealing with mass immigration. In the offing lay the exclusionist immigration policies of 1921 and 1924 and the National Origins Act.

The remarkable achievement of the United States, especially in this era, was its ability to absorb so overwhelming an alien influx without serious damage to its internal democratic structure. Both primitive and civilized societies have been marked by an insistence upon cultural and racial homogeneity. This had been worsened by modern nationalism and colonialism, which had widened the gulf between cultural majorities and "lesser breeds without the law." Scarcely any nation has been able to absorb huge immigrations without serious conflict, for the result has usually been that large undigested masses of newcomers have existed within its boundaries.

Since the New Immigration brought with it heavy Catholic, Jewish, and Greek Orthodox elements whose culture contrasted greatly with that of early Americans, the difficulties of adjustment are easily understood. More important has been the fact that despite the weaknesses of the Americanization process, millions of Europe's displaced people were accommodated within a democratic framework. Those who came here, especially in the New Immigration, were of the very poorest classes, scarcely emancipated from medieval paternalism and feudal habits. Yet they and their children usually became good democrats, believers in the American messianic hope of world democracy; and in the process, they contributed overwhelmingly to the economic strength of America and to a richer cultural diversity.

· 12 ·

Invention and Urban Recreation: Edison and Belasco

[1865-1917]

I

ONE DAY in 1876 newspaper reporters gathered at Menlo Park, New Jersey, to see the new laboratory of Thomas Alva Edison and expected the Wizard of Menlo Park to conjure up at least a few minor miracles for their benefit. That was the year when the Philadelphia Centennial Exposition was displaying to the world Bell's telephone contraption, powerful electric arc lamps supplied by current from a dynamo, Baldwin locomotives, and many other revelations of America's material and cultural progress since the Declaration of Independence.

Already, Edison had made a number of significant inventions that affected urban life considerably. He had sold his invention of the mimeograph machine to the Chicago manufacturer, A. B. Dick, who was to make it a universal instrument for office work. After Carlos Glidden and Christopher L. Sholes of Milwaukee invented the typewriter in 1868, Edison made basic improvements (as in the type bar) before the Remingtons, who were gunsmiths of Ilion, New York, decided in 1873, to manufacture typewriters. In the pioneer field of multiple telegraphy Edison introduced the *diplex* system of sending two messages over the same wire and at the same time. He improved both transmission and reception and speeded up the

271

rate of sending messages. He invented and manufactured stock tickers and even constructed a good vote-recorder for Congress—only to be blocked by the filibustering members who preferred more leisurely methods of counting votes.

In 1876, Edison, like Alexander Graham Bell and Elisha Gray, had his own telephone invention. Though he generously conceded the credit to Bell, his own improvements were to make the crude, noisy toy into a clear, practical, instrument for transmitting the human voice. The Western Union Telegraph Company under Jay Gould and his successors acquired Edison's telephone patents and fought the New England Bell Telephone Company for primacy. Although the Western Union was defeated in 1879 and agreed to stay out of the phone business if the Bell Company kept out of the telegraph field, they secured substantial royalties from Bell on the basis of Edison's patents.

Had the Western Union won, it is quite possible that the progress of the telephone might have been delayed for years in order to expand the uses of the telegraph. As it turned out, the Bell Company under the very able management of Theodore N. Vail, raised the efficiency of the American telephone by insisting not only on high standards of service but by introducing standardized equipment, leased rather than sold to the patron. This avoided the confusing diversity of telephones that existed in France. By 1900, there were 800,000 phones in use and nearly 6,000,000 in 1915, the year that long-distance service between New York and San Francisco was established.

Edison did a great deal to provide the bright lights of the city that beckoned to so many rural and immigrant newcomers. Before the Wizard went to work upon electrical illumination, gas-lighting was used on the streets and in the homes of most city people. The idea of electricity was of course no new thing; it dated back to ancient European traditions as well as to the eighteenth and nineteenth century experiments of Franklin, Sir Humphry Davy, and Michael Faraday. In 1879, Charles F. Brush of Ohio—among a number of rival inventors in the field—popularized his arc lamps, which operated on a single wire. That year Cleveland's Public Square shone brilliantly with the glaring and hissing carbons of his lamps. Edison and his associates soon produced better arc lamps and provided the first American central power plants in lower Manhattan, and cheaper modes of electrical power transmission.

Best-known and perhaps most laborious of Edison's work was the invention in 1878 of the soft glow or incandescent lamp, using the vacuum-sealed glass container and a bamboo filament. Successive experiments and world-wide searching for a workable filament material had led to the desired result. A few years later various enterprising spirits introduced electrical lighting in churches, theaters, and for outdoor electric signs. One of the first theaters to forsake gas for electricity was the Bijou in Boston, which made the change in time for its performance of a Gilbert and Sullivan operetta. In a major enterprise to advance his electrical interests Edison incorporated his own firm, which was soon absorbed in 1889 by a syndicate under Henry Villard known as the Edison General Electric Company.

The laments of the gas companies did not last long, for they still monopolized cooking and heating. Even in the field of cheap home lighting they retained their leadership for decades after 1885 when the Viennese inventor, Dr. Auer von Welsbach introduced the Welsbach burner, using a conical mantle which helped give forth a bright but well-diffused light. Besides, the gas companies frequently bought out the municipal electric companies and thus softened the impact of electrical competition. Some of them enlisted the aid of bipartisan councilmen in machine-run cities like Chicago, New York, and Philadelphia. Cheap and better lighting not only stimulated outdoor recreation but it also provided more opportunities for indoor sports and games. It also encouraged overtime and nightwork by making possible the continuous operation of many factories.

Edison was especially proud of his invention of the phonograph—a remarkable achievement, particularly for a man with his defective hearing. In 1877, he succeeded in developing his "speaking phonograph" and displayed it to Senator Roscoe Conkling and other notables by recording solemnly "There was a little girl who had a little curl right in the middle of her forehead." Newspapers were excited by Edison's latest marvel and, despite the crudeness of the early recorded sounds, public interest steadily increased. Edison himself saw in the device vast possibilities for education, commercial application, and entertainment. Before this era ended he applied the phonograph idea to a dictating machine, known as the Ediphone, and thus once again, as in the case of the mimeograph, affected office procedures.

Edison and his associates went beyond a host of European pioneers of motion pictures by developing the "kinetographic camera" and the kinetoscope. This camera mechanism utilized a practicable celluloid roll film that had first been developed by George Eastman in 1880. Once a series of photographs had been made by the kinetograph, the pictures were exhibited through the "peep-show" aperture of the kinetoscope—the machine that is still a fixture among the penny arcades of the nation. After 1895 a projection machine on the "magic lantern" principle was devised, together with a screen. From this inventive stage the next step was the construction of a motion picture studio, a darkened wooden shack with a movable roof to provide sunlight. This was the famous Black Maria. An Edison cameraman, Edwin S. Porter, later produced the first feature-length story in 1903. By 1912, Edison had developed the kinetophone as a synchronization of sight and sound. This forecast the subsequent development of the talking motion pictures and the end of the "silent" films—long before they had reached their peak of success.

2

In outward physical appearance the city was changing, too. Downtown, congestion was intensified by the new all-steel frame skyscraper, which appeared in 1883 when Chicagoans built the Home Insurance Building. Up to this time (and since the 1850's) the pressure for ground space had been partly met by thick-walled and poorly-lighted masonry skyscrapers with limited height possibilities. The steel frame and later the electric elevator changed all this by permitting thinner walls, more floor space, better lighting, and soaring heights. While Chicago had become an oasis for architects since the great fire of 1871, New York quickly outstripped the pretensions of the city on Lake Michigan. By 1912, New York's fifty-seven-story Woolworth Building—then the tallest in the world—was completed. Four years later New York took the leadership in the movement for zoning buildings in the interest of lighting, air, and safety from fire. City planning, aided by home rule urban charters, was emerging from mere decorative "city beautiful" ideas to broad development schemes controlling traffic as well as appearance and eventually other phases of urban well-being.

Just as skyscrapers both relieved and then intensified urban congestion, so did the coming of the electric surface railway, the elevated railway, and the subway. The cable car was introduced in 1873, and it proved especially valuable in conquering the steep inclines of San Francisco's streets. Electric streetcars spread in the 1880's and led to a rapid decline of the slow-moving horse and cable cars. These railways became of primary importance in interurban transit and fostered the growth of suburbs, though they did not wholly break the centripetal force of the metropolitan downtown area. Subways, which had already appeared in London and Budapest, came to Boston in the latter 1890's and to New York in 1904.

Far more decentralizing in effect than the electric interurban railway was the automobile. French pioneers had already gallicized the name of this revolutionary invention and had added such terms as garage and chauffeur. The Germans, Daimler and Benz developed the high-speed internal-combustion engine; and in this country, George B. Selden, a patent lawyer, claimed most of the basic inventions for the gasoline-driven car. Henry Ford and Ransom E. Olds made possible a cheaper car for the people through the assembly line system, which meant quantity production and standardization. The unique American emphasis on mass production went back to Eli Whitney, inventor of the interchangeable parts rifle, and to the Yankee mechanics who were concerned with the problem of conserving labor costs in a land blest with rich natural resources and opportunities that outstripped the labor supply. Trained mechanics produced by the carriage and bicycle business were available to direct the new machines. Detroit, once a bicycle manufacturing town, became the center of a group of booming automobile cities such as Cleveland, Youngstown, Akron, and others. By 1915, over 2,500,000 automobiles were registered in this country.

The automobile, itself a major form of recreation, set into motion a series of urban changes. Neighborhoods became more mobile than ever, thus creating problems of education, crime, traffic, and recreation. New satellite cities grew up in a metropolitan frame-work, reflecting a more intensive regional division of labor. Suburbs sprang up rapidly with their attendant housing booms. The city planning movement was further stimulated by the need to restore order and balance amid the chaotic growth of streets, neighbor-hoods, and urban institutions. Vast highway projects were initiated and, as the speed of the automobile grew, the regional barriers between East and West, North and South, partly broke down. The new automobile highways became a major instrument for the spread of urban culture.

3

Just as the modern city was the great miracle of man's ability to organize on a high technological plane, so city amusements grew out of this penchant for organization. Congestion had swallowed the large open fields and space was held at a premium. Spectator recrea-tions multiplied and tempted businessmen to invest heavily in com-mercialized entertainment. While schools and settlement houses tried to foster an urban neighborhood spirit conducive to natural recreational opportunities, this type of neighborhood was at best a synthetic version of the community kinship feeling of village and rural life. Urban mobility was too great for stable traditional ties. Adults too rarely joined the children as they did in the folk dances and games of rural society; recreations were organized more strictly by age groups—athletic clubs, professional sports clubs, Boy Scout troops, and children's playground groups.

But the city provided in profusion daily opportunities for recrea-tion, and the steady decline in working hours gave increased leisure time to more people. The appetite for recreation must have been whetted by the New Immigration, which included peasant peoples of Southeastern Europe who had enjoyed as many as one or two hundred church holidays a year. Even before the New Immigration, Germans, Irishmen, and other groups had done much to abolish many Sunday closing laws that prevented workingmen from enjoying the only free day in the week.

The Anglo-American tradition of competitive sport had been largely amateur, but urban conditions led to a high degree of professionalization and commercialization. Such was the story of baseball, already well organized into urban clubs and playing schedules in the decade before the Civil War. This sport became so popular that country fairs, North and South, as well as sand-lot nines of the city took it up enthusiastically. However, the Gilded Age saw the rapid growth of professionalism and a particularly rank growth of gamblers who bribed players to "throw" the game. The intermediary stage between amateur and professional baseball was the semi-professional game, in which the players did not play for a living but were hired for occasional games.

In 1871, the National Association of Professional Baseball Players was organized in New York to set up a circuit of rival teams from the large cities. A quarrel over gambling scandals and contract-breaking led seceders to form the National League of Professional Baseball Players. Thereafter, a rival American League emerged and after a quarrel over rules and hiring practices—the Baseball War of 1901-3—the leagues stabilized their relationship. The American League could boast of the championship-winning Connie Mack who had left the Pittsburgh Pirates and the National League to join the Philadelphia Athletics in 1901. The Nationals kept John J. McGraw, star third baseman and manager of the New York Giants, who competed several times for the "world championship" with Mack's Athletics. This "world series" had been firmly established by 1903 as a final contest between the "pennant" champions of each league. It had evolved from a series of post-season games frequently held in the years after 1884.

Thus, before this period ended, professional baseball emerged as a highly organized activity involving heavy expenditures, detailed rules of operation, player contracts, and an intricate system of club agreements. Minor leagues—the "bush leagues"—served smaller cities and became the recruiting ground for the big leagues. Baseball diamonds were surrounded by expensive stands as well as "bleachers," so-called from the exposure of that outer section of seats to the sun. Colleges liked amateur baseball, but the awkward college calendar practically eliminated the summer season and therefore gave an advantage to football. However, the amateur spirit was deeply imbedded in the innumerable boys' teams scattered throughout the villages and cities of the nation.

Although boxing had strong amateur followers in the schools—Theodore Roosevelt was a boxing enthusiast—it lent itself easily to professionalization and urban promotion. Prize fighting had long been popular among slaves and freed Negroes in antebellum times. Professional boxing gradually lost its stigma as an underworld sport, especially after the general introduction of the Marquis of Queensberry rules. These barred certain blows, limited each round to three minutes, required a count of ten for boxers knocked down, and introduced the five-ounce padded gloves. The doughty John L. Sullivan, exhibitionist that he was, proved circumspect enough to establish fighting with large gloves; his earlier contests were with bare knuckles. His day of wild slugging (although Sullivan himself had some boxing skill) ended after his defeat in 1892 at New Orleans by "'Gentleman Jim" Corbett, a scientific prize fighter who had been trained at the gymnasium of San Francisco's Olympic Club. Boxing skill was even more in evidence with Bob Fitzsimmons whose "solar plexus" blow knocked out Corbett. The victory of a Negro "world's champion," Jack Johnson, in 1910 was reminiscent of the primacy of Negro prizefighters in antebellum days. However, the highly profitable era of boxing came only in the 1920's when promoters like Tex Rickard made the sport respectable for spectators of all classes and both sexes.

Horse racing could not long be monopolized by the fashionable jockey club members and horse fanciers like August Belmont, Leland Stanford, and William C. Whitney. Gamblers and "bookies" centered their livelihood about the races, despite the fact that by 1900 every state had passed laws forbidding race track betting.

Anthony Comstock, self-appointed arbiter of American morals, issued in 1904 his pamphlet, *Race Track Infamy: or, Do Gamblers Own New York State?* Despite the efforts of reformers like Governor Charles Evans Hughes of New York, who did drive the race track gamblers out of the state for two years, the gamblers always returned. Still, there were vast crowds who came largely to enjoy the spectacle of carefully-bred race horses winning the Kentucky Derby or the Belmont Park "classics." August Belmont, the financier associated with the Rothschilds, owned the stables that produced Man O' War, sire of famous race horses. He did much to give New York State leadership in horse-racing matches.

Eastern "ivy colleges" like Harvard, Yale, and Princeton took the lead in keeping the competitive amateur spirit alive, particularly in intercollegiate boat races, football, and the indoor sports. Football dated back to the ancient plebeian sport of kicking the ball, which English immigrants had brought over in colonial times. Aristocratic English public schools had transmuted the baser sport into the respectable ball-carrying game of Rugby. Early in the post-Civil War era Rugby football was taken up by the eastern universities and the contemporary form of the American game came into existence. Urban limitations reduced the size of the playing field and the number of players.

However, massed plays and rough tackling led to so many casualties, even deaths, that the major colleges were on the point of abolishing football when President Roosevelt, ever the advocate of the "strenuous life," intervened to save the sport in a White House conference. Thereafter, particularly under the leadership of Walter Camp (Yale, '80), football assumed a less brutal and more scientific form with new distinctive American plays such as the forward pass. Camp established the custom in 1889 of publicly selecting all-star elevens—the "All-American" team. Football became increasingly the outstanding spectator sport as the expert few thrilled the many sedentary thousands who were content to watch the game. It proved so profitable as to pay the way for lesser college sports.

The only major sport of wholly American origin was basketball, invented in 1891 by Dr. James Naismith, a former Canadian theological student who had become an athletic instructor for the International Y.M.C.A. Training School of Springfield, Massachusetts. Naismith solved a Y.M.C.A. winter problem by developing an exciting indoor game to keep athletes in condition between the football and baseball seasons. The "Y," which had become the national leader in physical education, quickly popularized it both here and abroad. Girls' colleges like Smith as well as the men's colleges played basketball within a few years of its invention. The game had the advantage of teaching specialized skills and a cooperative spirit. Another "Y" teacher originated volley ball as a less strenuous indoor sport to attract other gymnasium students. This, too, had its enthusiasts in the Y.W.C.A. as well as the men's organization.

Altogether, the professional development of physical education, based on German and Swedish principles, took its chief impetus from the Y.M.C.A. (and Y.W.C.A.) which originated so many techniques as well as games. The "Y" combination of religious and athletic objectives, which Charles Kingsley had once called "muscular Christianity," flourished despite certain evangelical criticism and had an obviously beneficial effect upon American youth. One of the Y.M.C.A.'s most remarkable physical education directors, Dr. Luther H. Gulick, who had helped Naismith devise basketball, introduced "Y" principles while he was director of physical training for New York city's public schools. He developed new child hygiene methods and organized the Camp Fire Girls. During World War I he directed the expansion of Y.M.C.A. services to the armed forces; at this time, too, he wrote his best book, *The Dynamic of Manhood* (1917).

For the urban masses there still remained, albeit in a commercialized form, many older forms of sport, social gatherings, and spectacles. Sleigh-ride parties, ice skating, and coasting carnivals persisted; but the introduction of roller skating from England about 1876 transformed many warehouses into commercial roller skating rinks. Croquet, which reached epidemic proportions in 1866, was the leading Victorian sport. It had originated in France but came here by way of England. Within a short time croquet became a highly organized sport with national as well as local clubs.

The bicycling craze of the seventies swept the country despite the obvious pitfalls for unskilled riders in being thrown over the handle bars because of the high front wheel. A major bicycle industry sprang up, aided by the numerous bicycle clubs. During the nineties a revival of the bicycle craze began together with a national movement for better roads. Soon, workingmen were bicycling to their factories and postmen were delivering their mail from bicycles; young couples tried the "bicycle built for two"; even doctors and clergymen did not think it too plebeian to use this new mode of transportation before the automobile replaced it. New York and other large cities imitated the British after 1889 in encouraging such public spectacles as the six-day bicycle race.

By the eighties the middle classes were increasingly attracted by golf and sponsored large private and municipal golf links. Polo, tennis, hockey, and private athletic club activities allured the well-to-do and the "dudes" while billiards and bowling had their followers among all classes.

City children found outlets for their energies in the supervised play movement after 1900 and in the back-to-nature activities of the Boy Scouts, the Girl Scouts, and the Camp Fire Girls. After 1873 came a rapid expansion of zoological parks based on English and German models. Urban needs led to the large-scale planning of public parks, especially in the 1890's, resulting in such achievements as Chicago's beautiful Lincoln Park along the lake front and the metropolitan park systems of Boston, Cleveland, and other cities. Circus entertainment under the indefatigable improvisation of P. T. Barnum and his successors reached into more towns than ever because of rail transportation. This meant millions in profits for "the greatest show on earth." Commercial amusement parks like Coney Island attracted millions during this era to the Midway panorama of cheap exhibits, freak shows, games of chance, and spectacles of all sorts, as well as to the beer gardens and beaches. The traditional family picnics were apt to be held in the grounds adjacent to the amusement park exhibits. Mammoth urban fairs like the Philadelphia Centennial of 1876, the Chicago Columbian Exposition of 1893, and the St. Louis Fair of 1904 drew visitors from the entire world and gave millions a good excuse for pleasurable traveling. These fairs offered both entertainment and education while advertising the wares of the exhibitors. All these public spectacles tended to secularize the Sabbath despite the resistance of church groups.

This era witnessed a swift increase in fraternal societies, both Masonic and non-Masonic, especially at the turn of the century. The rapid expansion of women's organizations and immigrant societies contributed to this tendency. In 1910, business and professional men organized service clubs in the "luncheon club movement," beginning with the Rotary Club. This combined the "booster spirit" of business with high ethical and philanthropic aims.

4

Urban commercialization kept the theaters crowded and prosperous, especially by the nineties, when a centralized "booking" organization and highly advertised "star" system gave fabulous salaries to the few and a certain modicum of security and regularized employment to the many. Yet, as Henry James pointed out in 1875, there was no intimate relation between the stage and "the general cause of American civilization." This gap between life and the theater partly reflected the trend toward greater commercialization, but it also was part of the Victorian "genteel tradition" in literature then championed by James Russell Lowell. Worse yet, the best American writers, including Mark Twain, either ignored playwriting or failed to master its intricacies. "The misfortune hitherto of American dramatic literature," wrote Brander Matthews, the critic, in 1877, "has been that those who make plays did not make literature and that those who made literature did not make plays."

There were exceptions, of course, and actors had the opportunity of exhibiting their art in the highly creditable, native plays of Bronson Howard, Augustin Daly, and William Vaughan Moody, whose *The Great Divide* (1907) was the Great American Play of its time, although producers usually found it more profitable to rely on mere clever dialogue and pretty scenery or on the prestige of well-established European plays than to risk their investment on the mediocre output of most of the playwrights of the period. The blood and thunder acting tradition of Kean and Forrest was dying. Edwin Booth, perhaps the greatest actor of his day, had temporarily retired after his brother had killed Lincoln, and he emerged somewhat subdued in style. After the eighties and nineties a new generation of polished technicians like Richard Mansfield was undertaking the interpretation of Shakespeare or introducing the problem plays of Ibsen, Shaw, and Pinero as well as the comedies of Oscar Wilde and the sentimentalities of Rostand's *Cyrano de Bergerac*. Famous acting families like the Drews and the Barrymores (related by marriage) emerged under the appreciative sponsorship of Daly and Frohman, and were ready on occasion to attempt "variety" as well as "legitimate" drama.

Four Jewish-American impresarios, Charles Frohman, Abraham Lincoln Erlanger, David Belasco, and Oscar Hammerstein lent lavishness and enchantment to the stage through their gift for theatrical organization and promotion. In 1915, when Frohman was drowned on the *Lusitania,* he was already acknowledged the "Napoleon of the stage" and the sponsor of a "star factory," which included John Drew, Maude Adams, William Faversham, and Ethel Barrymore. Through the winsome and sprightly Maude Adams he introduced the plays of Sir James M. Barrie and profited from the subsequent vogue for *The Little Minister* and *Peter Pan.* His Empire State Theatre became a shrine in the history of the reviving American stage.

Frohman, born in Sandusky, Ohio, had become acquainted with another Ohio theater owner, Erlanger, and together they organized a syndicate in 1896 to centralize the nation's "booking" of theatrical talent. One of the costly inefficiencies of the day was the recurrent unemployment of road companies in some areas while theaters in many cities suffered from a lack of good performers. A centralized system of booking, serving as a clearinghouse for actors and managers, was intended to cure this situation. However, the monopolistic grip over the theaters was widely resented and fought by independents and artists like Sarah Bernhardt who was even willing to act in a circus tent rather than submit to the dictation of the "trust."

The syndicate finally broke down when the key firm of Klaw and

Erlanger proved unable to offer sufficient talented performers for the expanding theatrical business. Erlanger continued to be a dominant theatrical figure with a large national chain of theaters renowned for "legitimate" drama and vaudeville. But booking and the star system had definitely brought the guild tradition of the theater into decline, for the old stock company that partook of the cooperative guild organization of the past was no longer dominant. Actors tended less than ever to select and manage their own plays and routes in equalitarian style and divide the receipts among themselves. The Frohmans, Erlangers, and Belascos had inaugurated a new day of a highly organized and commercially-integrated theater.

By 1900, another Frohman associate, David Belasco of San Francisco (1853-1931), was fast becoming a legendary figure of the theater, gifted, as he was, not only as an actor and playwright but also as an outstanding producer. Though George Jean Nathan scoffed at him as a "Broadway Rasputin" who had achieved "the canonization of the simple humbug," there was little doubt of his unique ability as a showman and creator of highly successful plays of the French "well-made" type, popularized by Sardou. He ignored social significance for romantic comedy or melodrama and was a wizard of technical perfection in creating illusions through stage effects. His greatest achievement as a producer was his development in 1890 of Mrs. Leslie Carter whom he starred in a play of his own, *The Heart of Maryland*. Possibly, as some critics suggested, Mrs. Carter was only a fairly competent actress, but Belasco built an aura about her in which he was aided by the sensational facts of her recent divorce trial. In 1911, he wrote *The Return of Peter Grimm*, a story of life after death, for his actor protégé, David Warfield, and again demonstrated his keen judgment of what constituted a success. To many in a later nostalgic age, the name of David Belasco became synonymous with the theater at its zenith.

Against the advance of the highly solvent theater of Broadway and its imitators there developed a rebellion of idealists who clung stubbornly to the guild tradition. They were not overly impressed by the new glittering theaters and the profitable long runs made possible by the great promoters and central booking agencies. Long runs prevented diversity of experience and the crowded theaters promoted by the shrewd impresarios required too many artistic concessions to the least common denominator of mass appreciation. This rebellion was part of a larger international movement of realistic actors in Paris and Moscow who rejected the contemporary emphasis on stage carpentry, extravaganzas, stage stereotypes, and mere story-telling. Constantine Stanislavsky founded the Moscow Art Theatre in 1890 and recruited amateurs rather than professionals to interpret the realistic themes of Chekhov, Gorki, and Shakespeare. One of this group, Paul Orlenov, brought his troupe to New York in 1905. To an American interviewer Orlenov declared,

I hear that in America all plays must have a joyful ending. I should be sorry that I came if I thought it true that seven out of ten plays must be ruined by the necessity of a happy ending. It would be a satisfaction to make suffering fashionable.

His players stressed a sensitive interpretation of character and an almost morbid quality of introspection. When they performed *Czar Feodor,* their expressions conveyed a stark quality of realism with only a few words spoken in an entire act—the tense murder scene. Orlenov introduced New York to Dostoevski's novels as adapted to the stage, particularly *The Brothers Karamazov* and *Crime and Punishment.* He gave, in Russian, Ibsen's *Ghosts* and Strindberg's *Countess Julie.* Here was the essential artistic material for the Little Theater.

In 1909, a movement in defiance of the theatrical syndicate began in New York's New Theater under Winthrop Ames. This was soon followed by others. Some have dated the movement from Maurice Browne's pioneer experiments in 1912 with eager amateurs in Chicago's Little Theatre. Within a few years there were such experimental groups as the Provincetown Players, the Neighborhood Playhouse, and the Washington Square Players. Out of the latter was eventually to emerge the Theatre Guild, which combined professional competency with an experimental realism. Harvard, Yale, and other colleges joined the rebels. George P. Baker, an English professor at Harvard, trained a remarkable group of playwrights and stage directors in the new realistic techniques through his "47 Workshop." Thus his influence on the Little Theater both in the colleges and elsewhere was considerable.

Related to this revolt in behalf of theatrical realism was that of the American ballet artists against formalism and saccharine romanticism. The rebels followed the leadership of Sergei Diaghilev of the Ballet Russe, Anna Pavlova, the classical expressionist and ballerina of the Mariinski Theater of St. Petersburg, and of the magnificent, if mentally unstable, Nijinsky. All of them appeared on the New York stage at various times before World War I. In this field the United States had its proud artistic export in Isadora Duncan, born in 1878, who left an unappreciative American public in her youth to struggle for years in London and Paris before winning recognition as one of the foremost interpretive dancers of her time. Painstakingly, she studied the Greek vases in the Louvre for authentic suggestions about the natural flowing motions of classical dancing as distinct from the formal techniques of the ballet. She influenced Diaghilev and other famous contemporaries in Russia and elsewhere on the Continent and later American dancers as well.

5

The theatrical caviar for the masses, especially during 1890-1910, was the popular-priced melodrama. Back in Napoleon's day, France had evolved the typical features of this sensational and often maudlin stage spectacle. English and American playwrights, as Dr. Lewin Goff has shown, had quickly adapted the melodrama to the more unsophisticated audiences, although offering restrained versions in the expensive theaters. The stock characters were, of course, the mustachioed villain clad in a black cloak and doomed after a brief triumph to be defeated in his plot against virtue; the honest, hardworking hero, courageous protector of the innocent; the beautiful, frail heroine, persecuted unbelievingly, tearful, and subject to fainting; and a supporting cast of homeless waifs, defenseless old parents, and some comic relief characters.

Seated in judgment in the ten- and twenty-cent seats of the gal-

lery were the uninhibited arbiters of the play who not only hissed
the villain or cheered the hero, but often extended unsolicited advice to the stage characters caught in the toils of some new struggle.
A really good villain could get himself hissed whenever he appeared.
The playgoers in the better seats were more docile than those in the
gallery, but they also muttered their imprecations and sneered back
at the villain. The orchestra's soft slow music could elicit tears of
pity for the heroine or its fast tempo might build up the mood of
suspense.

Stories of city life and the background of the slums and sweatshops were very common. To please working-class audiences who
liked to see honest poverty triumph, it was desirable to put a top-hat
on the villain and thus make it patent that he came from the idle
rich. Among the popular stereotypes of the melodrama was the
sinister Chinese "highbinder," as in *Chinatown Charlie, the Opium
Fiend* in which the heroine had to escape from underground opium
dens, secret passages, and other everyday furnishings of Chinese
life. Versatile stage carpenters furnished innumerable scenes for
each play to depict the necessary earthquake, trainwreck, fire, or
sylvan landscape.

Owen Davis, a Harvard graduate who kept promising himself that
each current melodrama of his would be the last, was the leading
playwright in this medium, especially after 1905 when he formed a
highly remunerative partnership with Al Woods in New York. He
could turn out a long play within a week and grind out one after
another on the usual formula. Audiences liked his *Edna, the Pretty
Typewriter* and *Nellie, the Beautiful Cloak Model*. In the plot of
Nellie, the villain makes improper advances to the virtuous girl and
pushes her under a descending elevator in the first act, throws her
off Brooklyn Bridge in the second, binds her to the elevated train
tracks before an onrushing locomotive in the third, and climbs into
her bedroom window in the fourth. When these courting tactics
fail, the puzzled villain asks reproachfully, "Why do you fear me,
Nellie?" This play ran for a year before crowded houses.

After 1910 the incoming motion pictures plagiarized the melodrama so thoroughly that the more expensive "legitimate" theaters

gave up the unequal struggle. A decade before, these theaters had gone through the usual monopoly stage when the Stair and Havlin Circuit set up a centralized booking system controlling over 150 theaters of their own. In their operations, Stair and Havlin resembled the dominant theatrical syndicate and were fully as influential within their own sphere of the popular-priced theaters. But the movie camera had unlimited resources for illusion and sensation, and was far superior to the tricks of the stage carpenter. In the succeeding decade or so, movie audiences did not always give up their prerogative of hissing the villain, cheering the hero, and weeping for the imperiled heroine. But the old rapport between audience and stage was gone.

6

The inexpensive minstrel show reached its greatest mass popularity during the seventies and eighties and thereafter fought for its life by every device and concoction of entertainment against vaudeville, burlesque, and finally the motion pictures. Its characteristic form, as Carl Wittke points out in *Tambo and Bones,* had been established by the noted E. P. Christy Minstrels. Just before the performance a street parade and band, led by a fancy-dressed drum major, ushered in the minstrels who wore long Prince Albert coats and silk hats and carried twirling canes. White men in blackface make-up of burnt cork (there were some Negro minstrel groups like those of W. C. Handy) arranged themselves in a semicircle. A pompous "interlocutor"—the straight man—announced the songs and exchanged observations with the end men, "Mistah Tambo" or "Mistah Bones" who usually bested him by wit or entertained the audience with instrumental music and song. The second part of the "olio" was a variety bill of dances and various skits. Although the minstrels seemed to be under the impression that they were depicting the actual American Negro with all his foibles (and theaters sometimes even hired a few ex-slaves as performers to heighten the reality), they presented little more than a persistent stereotype of the happy-go-lucky, sentimental, and superstitious Negro. Later, Al Jolson and Eddie Cantor continued this tradition in musical comedy.

But the minstrel show was doomed and nothing could save it, not even the burlesque shows, slapstick comedy, and Irish acts that were incongruously grafted upon it. By the 1890's the number of touring minstrel companies had fallen from over thirty to only ten. Vaudeville proved to be its most formidable rival and carried off its talented performers. Minstrel joke books and vaudeville blackface acts perpetuated the memories of the antebellum minstrel show. However, the music of Stephen Foster, which had been such an intimate part of the show, proved to be indestructible and there remained the amateur minstrel show, which continued to be popular for lodge and charitable benefits.

Vaudeville was America's version of England's "variety" show with its potpourri of unrelated acts; it showed some of the marks of its minstrel past, though it lacked the integration of either minstrelsy or the old burlesque performances. Beginning with a silent act of acrobats, the show would develop with more engrossing numbers. By the nineties, its overwhelming popularity with the public had eclipsed other stage entertainment. Its predecessors had included such mid-nineteenth-century "variety" as the Mississippi "showboat" with its floating troupes, which had visited the river towns and the Louisiana bayous during the 1860's and 1870's. Among its less re spectable ancestors and contemporaries were the crude burlesque shows of the hard-boiled Tenderloin districts, which offered suggestive pantomime, sex jokes with double meanings that were not too difficult to perceive, and high-kicking girls. Their audiences were nearly all male.

To lure the family audience in that Victorian Age, vaudeville managers like Tony Pastor and Benjamin F. Keith kept the acts "clean." Tony Pastor, who had once been a child musical prodigy at Barnum's Museum and a circus ringmaster, had established a variety show in New York and introduced the beautiful Lillian Russell who appeared about 1880 in the role of Josephine in *H. M. S. Pinafore*. Lillian was even better known as the friend of the fabulous "Diamond Jim" Brady, the Broadway *bon vivant* and millionaire, but she became increasingly bored with stage life and even entered politics, running for the mayor's office in Pittsburgh.

Tony, himself, liked to sing *The Strawberry Blond* (*The Band Played On*) and became a central figure on the Broadway stage.

The tradition of polite vaudeville and the continuous performance became a multimillion-dollar business in the hands of two former circus "spielers," Benjamin Franklin Keith of Boston and his partner Edward F. Albee. These men rapidly accumulated a chain of vaudeville houses in a circuit that covered the entire nation. Following the example of Erlanger, they joined forces in 1905 with several theater magnates to centralize booking in vaudeville. This brought into existence the monopolistic United Booking Company as an official clearinghouse to standardize contracts, to regulate conflicts, and to arrange employment for actors. Outspoken critics denounced this step as the birth of a trust. Keith, according to Douglas Gilbert, had to pay Erlanger off heavily to keep that aggressive theater owner out of the vaudeville monopoly.

7

Vaudeville harbored the proverbial viper in its bosom when it patronized the movies. The shadow of events to come could be seen in 1900 when vaudeville theater owners broke an actors' strike by turning to the crude movies of that day as a substitute for live talent. Ingenious French, British, and American photographers and Thomas Edison, inventor of the kinetoscope, had laid the basis for a new art. The penny arcade continued the vogue of Edison's kinetoscope by presenting pictures whose subjects scarcely changed in the decades thereafter. The still-famous names of Lumière, inventor of the cinematograph, Pathé, and Gaumont suggest the extent of indebtedness to France. From that country also came the development of clever camera tricks that at once affected such slap-stick comedy as Mack Sennett's bathing beauty pictures and influenced drama thereafter. At the opening of the twentieth century the movies were simple, brief, and flickering pictures of prize fights, news stories, other short themes, which served as "chasers" between vaudeville acts. The great commercial possibilities became clear in 1903 after Edison's cameraman, Edwin S. Porter, produced a continuous-story film of some length in *The Great Train Robbery,* a lively melodrama. In two years the "nickelodeon era" of five-cent shows had begun. Gradually the nickelodeon gave up its shabby home in stores and warehouses to enter pretentious theaters illuminated outside by bright electric lights.

The early themes were either melodramatic, with a sentimental regard for the victory of the poor and virtuous, or quite risqué. In that first stage of laissez-faire pictures, almost any vulgarity passed. Some cities attempted censorship, including Mayor Newton D. Baker's Cleveland. There, in 1913, the censors reported that they had cut approximately 10 per cent of the reels they had seen for such things as scanty costumes, details of a jail break, portrayal of police graft, prize fights, and scenes devoted to crime.

By this time the motion picture industry had become a mighty national business with fabulously expensive stars and equipment. The small studio was no longer able to begin business with only five or six hundred dollars in cash and produce a picture for a few hundred dollars more. In 1909 the inevitable trust movement began with the Motion Picture Patents Company, which even included the two leading French cinema firms, Melies and Pathé. They attempted to monopolize the supply of raw film and the rental of pictures. So vigorous was the resistance of the independent producers, especially William Fox, and the exhibitors, that the monopoly failed. Finally, the Sherman Antitrust Act was successfully invoked in 1914 to force the dissolution of the trust. One major result of this film war was that many independents fled the subpoenas of the trusts by moving to Los Angeles, not too far from the safety of the Mexican border, which explains the genesis and location of Hollywood.

American motion picture directors, like the French, showed vast ingenuity in exploiting the potentialities of the camera. The most famous of these was the Kentuckian, David Wark Griffith, the son of a Confederate officer and a person reared in the romantic tradition of the Lost Cause. He selected idealized types of feminine beauty and character, such as Mary Pickford, Dorothy Gish, and Blanche Sweet, and introduced them in the sentimental roles the audiences loved. In technique, he developed such graphic devices for the camera as the close-up, the fade-out, and various suspense-building techniques. These were sensationally successful in his feature film, *The Birth of a Nation,* which appeared in 1915. One factor of movie-making disturbed Griffith: the social aspects of the themes he used. In adapting *The Birth of a Nation* from *The Clansman,* he retained its glorification of the Ku Klux Klan as the defender of white civilization and depicted Negroes as lustful, degraded beings. Liberal white editors as well as Negroes were angered over this portrayal of race prejudice, as well as bad history, on the screen. Griffith replied by defending freedom of expression, but he had learned his lesson and attempted to make amends in later films.

The motion picture industry attracted an unusual group of entrepreneurs who were able to adapt themselves to the rapid tempo of the infant giant of the theater. There was Carl Laemmle who perceived the possibilities of the star system for the movies; Adolph Zukor of Hungary who joined with the Frohmans to import the best of the French classics; and Jesse Lasky (a vaudeville producer), Cecil B. De Mille, and Samuel Goldwyn who organized the Jesse Lasky Feature Play Company to present famous plays. From Italy and other European countries came a vogue for spectacles such as *Quo Vadis* (1913), which were eagerly taken up by the producers. So great was the success of the motion picture by 1914, as Lewis Jacobs declares, that America was making more than half of the world's pictures. Three years later, with the war forcing many European studios into bankruptcy, this proportion had swelled into a near-monopoly.

8

The pattern of the post Civil War American burlesque was determined by the extraordinary success of *The Black Crook,* an extravaganza of 1866-67 that was frequently revived, and by the reception given to the English troupe of Lydia Thompson and her British Blondes in 1869-70. Theater managers took close note of the fact that audiences had sat through five hours to watch the elaborate spectacle of *The Black Crook,* whose kicking girls clad in revealing flesh-colored tights were to be imitated over and over again. Lydia

Thompson's rather Amazonian blonde girls also set a standard for burlesque entertainment. According to the press, they included "the cancan in its lewdest form" in their repertoire and exchanged bawdities with the largely male audience. Even San Francisco newspapers professed to be shocked, although their comments merely increased the crowds. The San Francisco Minstrels, very popular in New York as well as in their own city, burlesqued the peroxide vogue introduced by the British Blondes on Broadway, *The Siege of the Blondes or, 'Tis Sweet for Our Country to Dye*.

Although the burlesque stage managers did not all become disciples of Lydia Thompson or *The Black Crook*, one segment of this group moved to the slum areas as a frankly bawdy show with no serious pretentions to wit or art. Elsewhere, the burlesque stage continued its older tradition of imaginative pantomime, clever parody, and ballet. Until vaudeville thinned the ranks of genuine burlesque stars, these theaters had their own distinctive brand of entertainment to offer. One of the most popular subjects for burlesque were the plays of Gilbert and Sullivan, in fact, the plays themselves were repeatedly pirated because they lacked copyright protection in this country. Weber and Fields, as already noted, developed the possibilities of social satire in burlesque in their Music Hall by 1900. In the related field of the Broadway musical revue, Florenz Ziegfeld began what was also intended to be a light commentary upon the passing show. His *Ziegfeld Follies of 1907* was the first of an annual musical vogue with the "glorified American girl" of the chorus, the highly ingenious stage settings, and the lavish costumes. Aside from the successful musical revue, burlesque was moribund, its puckish qualities of satire absorbed by vaudeville and later by Hollywood. Only the stupid pornography and crude acting of Tenderloin burlesque and the American invention of the strip tease remained in the post World War decades.

9

American music in this era was still largely derivative, and the leading American musicians were in great measure Europeans.

Middle Western cities escaped a provincial musical life by the influence of German, Bohemian, and Scandinavian musicians and the choral music of German and Scandinavian organizations. Chicago boasted of the noted Wagnerian conductor Hans Balatka of Moravia who headed its Philharmonic orchestra. He introduced certain works of Beethoven, Haydn, and Schubert hitherto unknown to American audiences even to those quite familiar with these masters. Soon he had to compete with the gifted German-born Theodore Thomas whose influence for good music left a permanent tradition in Chicago. He had directed Cincinnati's mammoth German musical festival of 1873 and his successes elsewhere had inspired the wealthy Major Henry Lee Higginson in 1881 to give his own city an outstanding orchestra, the Boston Symphony Orchestra. A group of fifty Chicago businessmen guaranteed to Thomas in 1891 to make up the deficits that might arise from his orchestral experience in that city. At the Chicago Fair of 1893 he introduced a summer musical festival and invited American composers to submit their work for a competition. In that day of unchallenged European supremacy his repertoires were unusually generous in including American compositions though he made no concessions to second-rate work regardless of its origin.

Leopold Damrosch and his sons dominated the Metropolitan Opera House and other concert halls supported by the lavish contributions of wealthy captains of industry. Oscar Hammerstein, with a mania for building opera houses and producing these musical spectacles, added to the music as well as the drama for the middle class. Damrosch the elder introduced the great Russian composer Peter Ilich Tschaikovsky to America in 1891. At the new Carnegie Music Hall the Russian enchanted his audience by directing his own concerto and completely lost his previous misgivings about the musical tastes of Americans. He wrote an excited letter home:

My concerto went magnificently. The enthusiasm was far greater than anything I have met with, even in Russia. I was recalled over and over again; handkerchiefs were waved, cheers resounded—in fact, it is easy to see that I have taken the Americans by storm.

Newspaper critics vied with each other in praise, ranking the Russian as "one of the first" of modern composers or at least "the first of modern composers after Wagner."

Among other noted European visitors, Anton Dvořák was connected with American conservatories during 1892-95 and gathered his impressions for the beautiful *New World Symphony* with its recurrent American refrains. Influenced by the contemporary folklorist movement, he looked into the American experience for an original indigenous theme and advised native composers to study the Negro, Indian, and cowboy traditions. One of those who followed his advice was Arthur Farwell, a student of Indian and Negro music who founded the Wa-Wan Press in 1901 to publish such native themes. Later he lectured on music at various schools and took a leading part in encouraging music in city parks and playgrounds. Better known among the Dvořák-influenced nativists was Charles Wakefield Cadman, who recorded the songs of the Omaha Indians and composed many Indian pieces for orchestra, piano, and even for opera. Americans were to sing over and over again his romantic songs, *The Land of the Sky Blue Water* and *At Dawning*, and the Metropolitan Opera House presented his Indian opera, *Shanewis* in 1918.

While most American composers of this era were overshadowed by the prestige and ability of their European contemporaries in this age of Wagner, several won a wide following in their day and continue to be popular. The best known was the romantic Ethelbert Nevin (1862-1901) whom the music historian John Tasker Howard has compared with Stephen Foster, though Nevin was a far better trained musician. Like Foster, he was born in the Pittsburgh area and his music had much of the nostalgic charm of the older man's. When he moved to Italy in 1895 he wrote the very melodic suite, *A Day in Venice;* but overwhelming popularity came for his smaller pieces, *The Rosary, Mighty Lak' a Rose,* and *Narcissus* (from his *Water Scenes*). More academic, but not too far from the romantic tradition, was Edward MacDowell (1861-1908). His leaning toward native American themes in the Dvořák manner is expressed in his sonatas, such as *The Woodland Sketches* (1896), which included the perennial favorites *To a Wild Rose* and *To a Water Lily*. MacDowell later suffered deep disappointment in his brief years as a professor of music at Columbia University. There he quarreled with the new president, Nicholas Murray Butler, over the organization of a broad comprehensive fine arts department.

An American music, whose mass patronage would eliminate the deficits of the opera house or the concert hall, evolved through the growth of an Afro-American musical idiom expressed in the "blues" and "ragtime." There are suggestions that jazz evolved from African music, perhaps by way of French adaptations as known in New Orleans, but these are mere hypotheses. In the improvised manner of a folk art, Negro musical expression in slavery days had not only been influenced by Africa, but by British folk songs and hymns, Irish jigs, military marches, West Indian slave songs, and Latin-American rhythms. The rich spirituals of the Fisk and Hampton singers charmed white audiences with their improvised elements of Negro folk music. Within the complex origins of the plaintive "blues" were original Negro variations of the European scale and harmonic principles developed in work songs enriched by gestures, syncopated dance music, "barber shop" harmony, and the play of "vocalized" brass instruments by Negro musicians unfettered by classical rules of harmony. They retained the folk art motif of constant improvisation, using trumpets, trombones, and clarinets rather than fixed-tone instruments. In New Orleans and Memphis, Negro brass bands and Negro minstrel shows impressed white bands who borrowed the eccentric rhythms during the nineties. Chicago cafés of 1914 derided this music as "jazz," a word of uncertain origin but quite possibly of obscene derivation.

The "father of the blues"—if this product of many ancestors can be said to have had a father—was William Christopher Handy, born in Florence, Alabama, in 1873. He knew Negro music well from his wanderings throughout the South and as a manager of a Negro minstrel show and band. To assist Boss Edward H. Crump of Memphis in his political campaign he originated the "Memphis Blues" in 1912 and quickly won recognition. The words sung by Handy's band were not necessarily flattering, for they concluded bluntly,

"Mister Crump can go and catch hisself some air." Better known was his "St. Louis Blues," written two years later, with its familiar theme of unrequited love. Using in part a tango rhythm, now attributed to the African-derived habañera accented with the improvised "breaks" of jazz, Handy set these words to *St. Louis Blues:*

> I hate to see de ev'nin' sun go down
> Hate to see de eve-nin' sun go down
> Cause my baby;—he done lef dis town. . .
> St. Louis woman wid her diamon' rings
> Pulls dat man roun' by her apron strings
> 'Twant for powder—an' for store-bought hair
> De man I love—would not gone nowhere.

Thus Handy and his noted trumpet blared forth the birth of a new musical expression derived from Negro folk themes and decades of improvisation by fellow-Negro musicians. "I took the humor of the coon-song," he declared, "the syncopation of ragtime, and the spirit of negro folk-song, and called it blues." Jazz was welcomed in a frenzied age of urbanization and swift tempo.

Negro syncopation, involving the "ragging" of popular songs, gave birth to ragtime. Soon white composers were adapting the sentimental songs of the nineties as well as the dance tunes to ragtime rhythm. Among the most successful of these composers was a Russian-born youth, Israel Baline, who had adopted the name of Irving Berlin and earned his living as a singing waiter in the Chinatown and Bowery cabarets of New York. In 1911, a year before Handy's "Memphis Blues" appeared, he published "Alexander's Ragtime Band" and "Everybody's Doin' It." These songs were so successful that Berlin opened a music publishing business in Tin Pan Alley, as New York's popular music publishing district came to be called. Ragtime revolutionized popular dancing by changing and speeding up the steps on the dance floor. Public dance halls, ever more lavishly built, sprang up in the cities by the end of this era and forecast the "jazz age" of F. Scott Fitzgerald. In the 1920's syncopation became increasingly "respectable" through the work of George Gershwin and Paul Whiteman.

Music for the urban masses was varied indeed. In the streets one heard German street bands and Italian organ grinders; in the parks, military bands played the stirring marches of John Philip Sousa and others; and in the social halls of the immigrant groups were innumerable choral societies and music of the various homelands. Above all, American audiences loved operettas. Gilbert and Sullivan musicals absorbed simple Deadwood as well as sophisticated Broadway for months at a time. Victor Herbert, the gifted and prolific Irish-American composer who had been educated for much more serious music, left perennial light favorites in *Babes in Toyland* (1903), *Mlle. Modiste* (1905), *The Red Mill* (1906), and *Naughty Marietta* (1910). He tried to use his considerable Continental musical training in writing grand opera, particularly *Natoma* (1911) and *Madeleine* (1914), but these were not successes. Far more in the spirit of the times were the lively musical scores he wrote for the *Ziegfeld Follies*.

Although American popular tastes in music seemed deplorable to Europeans, there was hope for the future in the increasing development of music in public schools and colleges in the tradition of Lowell Mason. Besides, there were the potentialities of the phonograph, which Edison had invented during the late 1870's and was steadily improving in tone quality. Even those who could not afford to attend the best concerts and operas might hope to hear some of their favorite pieces on the phonograph.

It is unnecessary to belabor the point that commercialized recreation in the form of highly organized sport and entertainment was inevitable under urban conditions. Moreover, the result was often magnificent and more adequate in personal satisfactions than the limited recreations of many isolated rural areas. But there was every danger that the wholesome quality of spontaneity and neighborliness implicit in rural pleasures might be lost amid the casual contacts of commercial amusement parks, theaters, and sport spectacles. To some extent, neighborhood agencies like the Y.M.C.A. and the settlement houses sought to remedy this difficulty through social clubs, gymnasiums, and group affairs. Thoughtful critics viewed apprehensively the invasion of the impersonal corporate spirit of economic life into the arts. Actual trusts reigned at various times over the drama, vaudeville, melodrama, and the motion picture industry.

Thorstein Veblen, inveterate foe of the new commercialism, attacked what he conceived to be the predatory quality of sport and recreation for the "leisure class." In *The Theory of the Leisure Class* (1899) he denied that sport necessarily produced the noble traits of self-reliance and good-fellowship; rather it tended to breed truculence and clannishness and to exalt the martial spirit and the desire to display warlike prowess. "It has been said, not inaptly," he wrote sardonically, "that the relation of football to physical culture is much the same as that of the bull-fight to agriculture." The predatory traits fostered were only an expression of the modern competitive spirit, he thought. College sports seemed to him the product of clannish fraternities and a leisure class desire for "conspicuous consumption" and make-believe.

Veblen's indictment, exaggerated as it was, had some substantial grains of truth. Woodrow Wilson of Princeton, like college presidents elsewhere, had his hands full in a futile attempt to curb the undemocratic spirit of the fraternities. Captains of industry, as previously noted, did find a vicarious expression of power in financing the new lavish opera houses of New York. The nouveau riche fought the older aristocratic families over conspicuous family boxes in the "Golden Horseshoe" of the elegant Academy of Music and when they failed, constructed the "Diamond Horseshoe" of the even more elaborate Metropolitan Opera House. The story of fashionable resorts like Saratoga, Belmont's Jockey Club, the extravagant comingout parties, and the aristocratic receptions of the Gilded Age would also give point to Veblen's indictment. However, the dour Norwegian-American scholar failed to prove that the total picture of urban recreation was actually cast in the image of a parasitical leisure class. The amateur spirit, despite grave exceptions, still survived as an expression of good sportsmanship and youthful energy that was far from "predatory" in psychology.

· 13 ·

Darwinism, Pragmatism, and Scientific Determinism: Era of William James

I

IN 1868 William James wrote to his brother Henry:

The more I think of Darwin's ideas the more weighty do they appear to me, though of course my opinion is worth very little—still, I *believe* that that scoundrel Agassiz is unworthy either intellectually or morally for him to wipe his shoes on, and I find a certain pleasure in yielding to the feeling.

Thus James, like so many other intellectuals, chose Darwin as his guide rather than the distinguished anti-evolutionist, Louis Agassiz, the Swiss-American naturalist at Harvard. James had only recently idolized Agassiz and gladly joined him as his assistant in 1865 on a zoological expedition in Brazil. Ever since Darwin's *Origin of Species* had appeared in 1859, Agassiz had opposed the theory that new species originate and survive through the selective influence of the environment, that is, by the process of "Natural Selection." He held to the prevailing idea that all species were immutable since Creation. Only a few American scientists of any repute, like his botanist colleague, Asa Gray, cared to take open issue with the erudite Agassiz before his death in 1873.

William James and his brother Henry, the future novelist, had been born in New York city, but their peripatetic father, the elder Henry, did not leave them too long in one place, taking them to Europe and finally settling in New England. The father, fortunately endowed with a substantial legacy, was never, as he boasted, "guilty of a stroke of business," and after his rebellion against orthodoxy cost him the opportunity of becoming a Presbyterian minister, he turned to his free-lance interests as a philosopher. The sons were raised in an atmosphere filled with the mysticism of Swedenborg, the social reformism of Fourier, and the transcendental idealism and individualism of Emerson. They knew the great intellectual spirits of Brook Farm who came to their home. Thus the James family was stamped with the culture of transcendentalism, that earnest faith in the inherent goodness of man and his freedom to will a better society if he only dared to trust himself. William James spent his life in attempting to mediate between this optimistic Emersonian world of the free individual and the determinism—sometimes pessimistic—of the new scientific world. He never ceased to believe that man was the captain of his soul, the master of his fate. But the conflicts within his mind almost cost him his sanity at one time.

Even before the *Origin of Species* appeared, the scientific impetus furnished by the Industrial Revolution had completely altered the predictable, Newtonian world of the James family. Evolutionary ideas did not begin with Darwin. During the Enlightenment of the seventeenth and eighteenth centuries, philosophers had popularized the idea of the gradual, continuous progress of society and had even specified the various "stages" of development. This notion of development was the essence of the idea of *social* evolution that dominated the thinking of the social scientists of the late nineteenth century. The Greeks had considered but laid aside the social evolutionary idea of progress in favor of a belief in cyclical change, the recurrent rise and fall of civilizations. Christian doctrine apparently had added the optimistic idea of man's upward development through spiritual regeneration to the goal of perfection.

As far as evolutionary biology is concerned, the Greeks did not go very far beyond the idea of fixed species; and orthodox Christians concurred in this belief. But before the eighteenth century ended, evolutionary concepts had penetrated into botany through Buffon, Lamarck, and Charles Darwin's own grandfather, Erasmus Darwin. Therefore, by the time that the *Origin of Species* was published, the well-educated reader knew something of the possibilities of biological evolution and, also, through Herbert Spencer particularly, the optimistic doctrine of inevitable social progress from the simpler to the more complex stages. By this time, too, the misleading assumption had spread widely that the laws of nature and the laws of cultural change followed the same pattern of continuous organic growth by stages to a higher and more satisfying form. Darwin, like others of his day, accepted these optimistic social evolutionary beliefs, but his unique contribution was to raise evolutionary speculation of all kinds to such high prestige through his natural selection idea that he set into motion a fresh revolution in thought comparable only to that of Isaac Newton.

Darwin wrote that biological evolution consisted of the "accumulation of innumerable slight variations." He explained, "According to the theory of natural selection, an interminable number of intermediate forms must have existed, linking together all the species in each group by gradations as fine as our existing varieties." Nature selected those variants best able to survive the conditions imposed by the environment, whether it was heat, cold, conflict, or other factors. The implications were, of course, staggering. Just as Copernicus and Galileo had deprived the earth of its traditional central position in the universe, so Darwin and other evolutionists had reduced man's godlike status by linking him closely with the animals. Social evolutionists, reasoning by analogy, went on to reduce men's ideas and institutions to mere evolutionary products, still imperfect, but destined to evolve toward perfection. In still another direction, "Social Darwinists" applied the ideas of the survival of the fittest in crude jungle style to the justification of acquiring empire from "backward nations" or to the defense of economic monopoly over less efficient business rivals. As for the

evolutionary "law of progress," Americans had long felt encouraged
by their material successes to believe that progress is inevitable.

2

Among the Americans who did most to strengthen the technical
structure of Darwinism was Professor Othniel C. Marsh of Yale
(1831-99) whose fossil discoveries helped to recover certain "missing links" of lost animal forms intermediate in the process of evolution. He had been encouraged by his Yale teacher, James D. Dana,
the noted geologist, to take up paleontology and to concentrate upon
evidences of fossil life. Americans as far back as Franklin and Jefferson had been fascinated by the skeletal survivals of ancient extinct species. Marsh carried on the hunt for fossils in Kansas and
Colorado with the financial assistance of a wealthy uncle, George
Peabody, whom he also persuaded to establish well-equipped natural museums in Cambridge and New Haven. In 1890, Marsh was
ready to publish his discovery of a transitional form, the extinct
toothed birds, as a definite link between reptiles and modern birds.
Darwin expressed his gratitude in a letter to Marsh, saying, "Your
old birds have offered the best support to the theory of evolution
[since the Origin of Species]."

Even more significant, as Bernard Jaffe relates in *Men of Science
in America*, was the remarkable work of Marsh in reconstructing the
evolution of the horse. The Spaniard had introduced the modern
horse to America, but even by that time the tar pits of La Brea,
California, and elsewhere showed evidence of a truly indigenous
animal. The ancient horse had evolved from an animal about the
size of a fox, with four toes, then three, and finally, only one. Huxley, who visited Marsh in 1876, declared in his exuberant fashion,
"I believe you are a magician. Whatever I want, you conjure it up."
Shortly before his death in 1899, Marsh published his findings regarding the evidences of prehistoric animals he had discovered in
the sandstone lands of Colorado, *Dinosaurs of North America* and
Vertebrate Fossils of the Denver Basin. He combined the Greek

words *deinos* (terrible) and *sauros* (lizard) to coin the word dinosaur.

At Harvard, Asa Gray and John Fiske were ardent supporters of Darwinism, while William James was among the first to offer a course in evolution in 1877-78 under the title of comparative anatomy and physiology. Darwinism dominated James's early courses in psychology and philosophy through the textbooks of that ardent evolutionist, Herbert Spencer, who dealt with mind as a function evolving with the organism and adapting itself to the physical environment.

Evolutionists focused attention upon the nature of heredity in the process of organic development. Darwin himself believed that the characteristics acquired by an organism in the process of adaptation were definitely inherited. However, the long-obscure work on inheritance by the Augustinian monk, Gregor Mendel, was publicized and elaborated by Hugo de Vries and others at the turn of the century. Darwin's critic, August Weismann, had denied the inheritance of acquired characteristics and had taught that the germ cells alone determined what traits would be inherited. Father Mendel developed the laws of heredity for plant life and showed the existence of sharply contrasting determinants in the germ cells. Those characters that prevailed in most of the plant offspring he called "dominant" and those largely suppressed, "recessive."

At Columbia University (and previously at Bryn Mawr) Thomas Hunt Morgan developed a distinguished school of geneticists and applied to animal forms the Mendelian laws derived from plant life. Morgan experimented with the prolific fruit fly, *Drosophila melanogaster*, to discover the mechanism of heredity. He described "genes" within the chromosomes as basic determinants of heredity and explained the transmission of certain sex-linked characteristics. Among his famous works of this era were *Heredity and Sex* (1913) and *Mechanism of Mendelian Heredity* (1915). All these findings had invaluable applications for human, animal, and plant genetics. The aristocratic implications of the new emphasis on heredity came in the individualistic 1920's.

Popular attitudes toward heredity—and scientific ones, too—were

influenced by the work of the sociologist, Richard L. Dugdale, employed by the New York Prison Association. In 1875 he published his
classic study of the Jukes, a fictitious name for an actual family, and
showed a close link between the descendants of the Jukes and
crime, degeneration, and insanity. Not until the 1930's did it become
clear that families like the Jukes and the Kallikaks had lived for
generations under the worst economic environment and that the
explanation of their degeneracy was not necessarily in the field of
genetics. Meanwhile, Dugdale's readers often cited his study to
bolster theories of racial and family superiority. Those who believed
themselves to belong to an hereditary elite thought that their success
stemmed from the survival of the fittest. The new company of the
elect did not hark back to Calvin but to the inexorable laws of
heredity, which revealed themselves in the captains of industry and
their counterparts in the Anglo-Saxon world.

Many biologists were converted to scientific determinism and
materialism by the brilliant physiologist, Jacques Loeb, who came
to this country from Germany in 1891 and worked successively at
Bryn Mawr, the University of Chicago, the University of California,
and the Rockefeller Institute of New York. His most famous explanation was that of "tropism"—the reflex action of attraction or
repulsion by lower animals and plants in response to heat, light,
moisture, and other factors. The work that excited most popular attention and conjecture was his development of the egg of the sea
urchin without fertilization. Newspapers promptly concluded that
science was about to reproduce life by artificial means. Loeb's original researches into animal psychology gave America leadership in
this branch of psychology and strengthened Darwin's evolutionary
idea of an affinity between the human and animal minds. Loeb did
not stop with his laboratory researches, for he constructed an entire
deterministic philosophy, of which he wrote in *The Mechanistic
Conception of Life* (1912). Though he believed that human existence
was the plaything of chance, not divine purpose, and the end
product of chemical mechanisms, he argued that a humane ethics
was still possible. Hereditary instincts compelled us to struggle
for justice and truth. "Economic, social, and political conditions or

ignorance and superstition may warp and inhibit the inherited instincts and thus create a civilization with a faulty or low development of ethics." Thus Loeb conveniently substituted his own optimistic idealism for the pessimistic implications usually associated with scientific determinism.

It was indeed unsettling in this era to reconcile the new mechanistic physical science with the traditional view of the universe. The logic of the steam engine had given birth to the science of thermodynamics with its revolutionary laws of the conservation and degradation of energy. The second law of thermodynamics states that energy tends to move from a higher to a lower level and implies that eventually the universe will run down to a dead level of intense cold. Pondering the lesson of this law, James wrote, "This world may indeed, as science assures us, some day ... freeze." But he was too optimistic to allow this hypothesis to affect his belief in a cheerful universe that gave a central position to man. Successive discoveries revealed an atom-built universe and "electrons" that moved within the invisible atom like planets within the solar system. Scientists were using a spectroscope to detect such elements as helium in the sun and to identify other elements in the heavenly bodies with those on earth.

Albert Michelson and E. W. Morley, in 1887, upset prevailing ideas of the "ether" surrounding the earth by obtaining results that suggested that the absolute motion of the earth through the ether is not measurable, a perplexity finally solved through the Einsteinian theory of relativity. Michelson, who joined the faculty of the new University of Chicago in 1892, received the Nobel Prize in physics in 1907. At Yale, Willard Gibbs, professor of mathematical physics, was laying the basis for physical chemistry and won acclaim both here and abroad for his book, *On the Equilibrium of Heterogeneous Substances* (1876). Though his work was too abstruse to affect popular attitudes directly, he revolutionized current concepts of the behavior of matter and energy in its application to at least a half dozen scientific fields. Little wonder that the challenge of the new physics should inspire Henry Adams, the historian, to speculate at length upon the possibilities of writing history in terms of the new concepts of energy and the dynamo as symbols of our civilization. Like Gibbs, he too wished to write a "Rule of Phase," but to apply it to history.

3

Darwinists like William James hastened the secession of psychology from philosophy and led the psychologists to clamor for the dignified position of a natural science. The "psyche" was no longer the "soul" that Aristotle and the scholastics talked about, but a biological process evolving with the animal form and adapting itself to its environment. In Germany during the 1870's Wilhelm Wundt inaugurated a new experimental physiological psychology and opened his famous laboratory at the University of Leipzig, which became the mecca for aspiring American psychologists. A new laboratory science had been born, anxious to forget its early affinity with philosophy and phrenology.

Shortly after (or perhaps even before) Wundt opened his Leipzig laboratory, James established the first psychology laboratory in America by simply setting aside classroom space for experimental work. Although he disliked actual experiments, he recognized their necessity and value, particularly if they were closely integrated within a set of philosophical principles. James's significant textbook, *Principles of Psychology* (1890), was no mere editing of European ideas but an original synthesis, studded with several striking theories of his own, which influenced the future course of American psychology. The work was enriched by his flair for striking language and the impress of his eager personality.

Literary people like James Joyce, Gertrude Stein, and John Dos Passos, as well as the psychologists, were later influenced by James's original conception of "the stream of consciousness" described in the *Principles of Psychology*. Unlike Wundt, who tended to break down the adult consciousness into separate components that were mechanically integrated, James described a dynamic process of constant change in which a stream of consciousness reflected a series of "states of mind." No mental state once gone could recur; the new state could not be identical with that which was before.

One felt and perceived things differently according to mood, age, health, and season, despite the sameness of the object. Within this stream of consciousness were "fringes," "psychic overtones," and other factors determined by the selective factor of the self. This notion that the consciousness was a changing and cumulative configuration of impressions over which the individual exercised some selective influence shows James anticipating the later school of Gestalt psychology.

Another of James's contributions to psychology was a theory of emotion, the so-called James-Lange theory. He wrote that "particular perceptions certainly do produce wide-spread bodily effects by a sort of immediate physical influence, antecedent to the arousal of an emotion or emotional idea." In his paradoxical way he popularized this to mean, "we feel sorry because we cry, angry because we strike, afraid because we tremble." He explained that there are certain reflex adjustments of the nervous system to emotional stimuli that lead to bodily changes and that their perception *is* the emotion. However, this theory was later challenged and modified.

James's distinguished disciple, G. Stanley Hall, was born on a Massachusetts farm and had been educated in theology and philosophy before his reading of the evolutionists and the works of the higher criticism movement deflected him from the ministry. He studied psychology with Wundt as well as with James and was invited in 1881 to lecture in psychology at the new graduate school, Johns Hopkins, opened in 1876 through the $7,000,000 gift of a Baltimore merchant. Here, in 1883, he opened the first regular psychological laboratory in America (dwarfing the informal experimental arrangements that James had introduced almost a decade before at Harvard) and founded a host of pioneer psychological journals, institutes, and associations. Among these were the *American Journal of Psychology* (1887) and the American Psychological Association (1892). Later, as president of another graduate school, Clark University, founded in 1887, he continued his work despite administrative duties.

He left his mark not only as an organizer, but as an original scholar

William James (1842-1910), psychologist and philosopher.
(From a photograph by Alice Boughton, February, 1907; Bettmann Archive)

A humorous penciled sketch of Dr
Oliver Wendell Holmes, physician and
litterateur. (Boston Medical Library)

Louisa May Alcott, author.
(Bettmann Archive)

Jack London, writer. (*Cleveland Plain Dealer*)

Trinity Church, Boston, designed by H. H. Richardson. (Bettmann Archive)

World's Columbian Exposition, 1893, Court of Honor. (Chicago Historical Society)

Boston Public Library, designed by Charles F. McKim. (Boston Public Library)
Cathedral of St. John the Divine, New York, designed by Ralph Adams Cram.
The exterior as it will look from northeast corner. Architect's sketch. (Cathedral
of St. John the Divine)

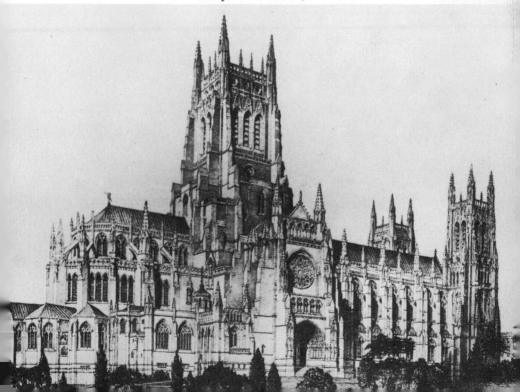

"The Gulf Stream," by Winslow Homer. (The Metropolitan Museum of Art)

"Autumn Oaks," by George Inness. (The Metropolitan Museum of Art)

"Checkers — up at the Farm," by John Rogers. These statuette groups were very popular after the Civil War. (Essex Institute Collection)

'Death Staying the Hand of the Sculptor," by Daniel Chester French. (The Metropolitan Museum of Art)

Orlando, Lloyd George, Clemenceau, and Wilson at the Versailles Peace Conference. (Bettmann Archive)

Goodbye to his big brother. Doughboys leaving Kansas City, Missouri, during World War I. (National Archives)

with an impressive following, particularly in the field of child psychology. His most influential work, partly based on his novel use of the questionnaire method (originated by Francis Galton, Darwin's cousin), was *Adolescence* (1904). This study contributed greatly to the prevailing tendency to raise the status of the child in society, though Hall leaned heavily upon conservative ideas of chivalric honor, obedience to authority, and mechanical drill. To an unusual degree he frankly examined the sex factor in adolescence and recommended sex education as well as conventional moral and citizenship training. His followers were to stress his ideas of a child-centered curriculum with special attention to the gifted child and heredity rather than to the creation of a democratic school environment.

Among the educational leaders who adapted the methods of the exact sciences to the new psychology and pedagogy was Edward Lee Thorndike of Columbia. Like Hall, he emphasized the roles of the gifted child, heredity, and eugenics. His monumental work, *Educational Psychology* (1913), tended to make the subject an applied science and won a wide following for him among American educators. His famous learning theory of identical elements challenged the prevailing idea that there was a transfer of training from one discipline learned to a new subject, i.e., that facility in mathematics led to facility in Latin or English. He concluded that only identical elements in the two learning situations could be transferred. His critics, especially Merle Curti, have pointed out that this theory led to an emphasis on the idea that training must be for specific ends; hence a greater emphasis was laid upon narrow technical, vocational, and scientific subjects at the expense of the broad liberal studies. Thorndike's emphasis on innate mental differences also had aristocratic social overtones favorable to the perpetuation of a stratified society. The American enthusiasm for mental testing, derived partly from Binet, was directed into conservative channels by the followers of Thorndike, Hall, and other leading psychologists. The individualistic generation of the 1920's was reared in large part upon the pedagogical theories of Thorndike and his disciples.

4

The abnormal personality as well as the healthy mind absorbed the interest of William James and led him to sponsor the mental hygiene movement. In 1909 he wrote to Rockefeller in an effort to solicit funds for the prevention and cure of mental disease:

> During my life as a "psychologist" I have had much to do with our asylums, and I have had so painfully borne in upon me the massiveness of human evil which the term "insanity" covers, and the inadequacy of our arrangements for coping with it, that I long ago registered a vow that if I myself, by Heaven's grace, should ever be able to leave any money for public use it should be for "insanity" exclusively.

The crusade for the insane led a generation before by Mann, Dorothea Dix, and others had fallen upon evil days. Faith in education and hospitalization as a remedy for insanity had given way to disillusionment and apathy. A few state administrators like Altgeld of Illinois reversed the pendulum and tried to eliminate the prevailing brutalities toward mental patients. He brought in Adolf Meyer, the Swiss psychiatrist, and had him lecture to the staffs of the Illinois institutions on the newer techniques of mental therapy. Meyer taught the value of case histories and personality studies in his work at Cornell and Johns Hopkins and is credited with coining the phrase "mental hygiene movement," which implied preventive action. Illinois' leadership in this movement is suggested by its early adoption of the juvenile court and the child guidance clinic.

James gave his enthusiastic support to the leader of the mental hygiene movement, Clifford W. Beers. He helped him get a publisher for the startling book, *A Mind That Found Itself*, sent him a gift of a thousand dollars, and assisted him in the organization of the National Committee for Mental Hygiene in 1909. Americans were shocked by the revelations of Beers's autobiographical book, particularly by those concerning the brutalities that Beers and other patients had suffered at the hands of callous attendants. Thenceforth, public opinion rallied to the demand for the use of trained psychiatrists in hospitals, prisons, clinics, and courts.

That same year before his death, James showed a hospitable attitude toward Freud and psychoanalysis. "I hope that Freud and his pupils will push their ideas to their utmost limits, so that we may learn what they are.... They can't fail to throw light on human nature; ... " However, his personal impression of Sigmund Freud was that he was obsessed with fixed ideas, especially in his dream theories and interpretation of symbols.

In 1909, President Stanley Hall of Clark University invited Freud to lecture on psychoanalysis before academic psychologists. Freud paid his respects to a colleague, Dr. Josef Breuer, who had used hypnosis as a cathartic procedure to cure a woman of an hysterical condition resulting in paralysis. Instead of continuing with the hypnotic technique, Freud had developed a method of "free association" by which the patient cooperated with him in recalling a chain of recollections that led to the disturbing "repressed" factor kept back by a "censor" in a vast unconscious life. Dreams, rightly construed, afforded a method of probing the unconscious, for through them one could observe the gratification of repressed wishes at a time when the censorship of the "ego" is largely withdrawn and the basic drives of the "id," especially the sexual impulses, are revealed. These lectures and other works of Freud were made available in American editions beginning that year; by 1913, *The Interpretation of Dreams,* written in 1900, had been translated for American readers. Later Freud commented upon the American characteristic of strong sexual repressions which, he felt, could be examined through psychoanalysis.

American newspapers widely publicized Freud's visit and his scholarly audience seemed impressed, although certain leading American neurologists, like Morton Prince of Tufts and Harvard, the outstanding figure in abnormal psychology, remained among Freud's persistent critics. Prince himself founded the *Journal of Abnormal and Social Psychology* in 1909 and published the most striking cases of multiple and dual personality, suggestive of the fantasy that Stevenson had related in 1886 in *Dr. Jekyl and Mr. Hyde.* He used hypnosis rather than "free association" as a tool of analysis in solving emotional conflict and he rejected Freud's notion of the unconscious and his emphasis on sex.

From 1910 on, books on Freud appeared by the score and encouraged the faddists after World War I to develop their own vulgarization of Freud. It was still too early to grasp the philosophical implications of Freudianism and its challenge, especially in its early dogmatic form, to the primacy of human reason. Here lay the ingredients for a cult of the irrational with the animality of man uppermost. Man was scarcely the captain of his soul—if he had a soul—for his free choices were again whittled down in this age of scientific determinism. On the other hand, the advent of Freud inspired the mental hygiene movement with an optimism regarding the treatment of psychoneuroses that had been lacking in the generation after Dorothea Dix.

5

American philosophers and educators were reared in the optimistic idealism of Emerson and Whitman based on the triumphs of a pioneer people in conquering natural obstacles. Like philosophers elsewhere, they had to come to terms with the new scientific naturalism of Darwin and Spencer, which challenged their supernatural beliefs, but they clung to a faith in human intelligence and purposefulness in the universe. The old dilemma that had to be resolved anew was one of determinism versus free will and chance versus design. From Europe came the positivist philosophy of August Comte (1798-1857) and his successors who rejected both theology and metaphysics in favor of scientific fact-finding, called positivism. Experiment and trial-and-error methods—the method of the "empiricists"—were increasingly preferred to the search for truth by the logical deductive methods of the "rationalists."

William James had spent his boyhood in a home where his father met with idealists like Emerson to discuss enthusiastically the high destiny of man, his intuitive insights, Swedenborgian mysticism, and the vast possibilities of nature beyond the finite limits of human experience. This was an exhilarating atmosphere in which one was assured of a coherent, purposeful universe and an all-pervasive divinity. To be part and parcel of God was as high a destiny as man could wish. For young James, suddenly plunging into biology and psychology at a time when new scientific hypotheses were over-turning the Emersonian world, the inner conflict was most disturb-ing. About 1872 he struggled through a period of uncertainty and near melancholia but was saved by the renewed optimism he derived from reading Renouvier's philosophical justification of free will: "the sustaining of a thought *because I choose to* when I might have other thoughts." James wrote, "My first act of free will shall be to believe in free will."

The philosophical bridge that James built between the idealistic world of his father and that of the new science was the doctrine of pragmatism. In 1878 one of his former Harvard classmates, Charles S. Peirce, had described the idea of pragmatism in an essay, "How To Make Our Ideas Clear." To clarify ideas, Peirce argued, it was necessary to show their consequences in action. The difference be-tween one idea and another was expressed in the differences that would be involved in their practical application to concrete situa-tions. James took this as a point of departure in his famous Lowell Institute lectures on pragmatism in 1906.

Pragmatism, he asserted, was both a method and a theory of truth. It was "empirical" and therefore at war with the logical pre-tensions of rationalism, and it sought to settle "metaphysical dis-putes that otherwise might be interminable."

A pragmatist turns his back resolutely and once for all upon a lot of inveterate habits dear to professional philosophies. He turns away from abstraction and insufficiency, from verbal solutions, from bad *a priori* reasons, from fixed principles, closed systems, and pretended absolutes and origins. . . . You must bring out of each word its practical cash-value, set it at work within the stream of your experience.

Ideas, he remarked, became true "just in so far as they help us to get into satisfactory relation with other parts of our experience." Furthermore, he added,

If theological ideas prove to have a value for concrete life, they will be true, for pragmatism, in the sense of being good for so much. For how much more they are true, will depend entirely on their relations to the other truths that also have to be acknowledged.

This pragmatic view explains his argument in *The Will to Believe* (1897):

> ... we have a right to believe the physical order to be only a partial order; ... we have a right to supplement it by an unseen spiritual order which we assume on trust, if only thereby life may seem to us better worth living again.

James went far to justify the pragmatic value of religion in his Gifford lectures at the University of Edinburgh, published as *The Varieties of Religious Experience* (1902). He dealt sympathetically with Christian Science, conversion, saintliness, and mysticism:

> Ought it to be assumed that in all men the mixture of religion with other elements should be identical? ... If an Emerson were forced to be a Wesley, or a Moody forced to be a Whitman, the total human consciousness of the divine would suffer. The divine can mean no single quality, it must mean a group of qualities, by being champions of which in alternation, different men may all find worthy missions. ... So a "god of battles" must be allowed to be the god for one kind of person, a god of peace and heaven and home, the god for another. ... If we are sick souls, we require a religion of deliverance; but why think so much of deliverance, if we are healthy-minded?

It is not surprising, in view of this hospitality to such a variety of religious experiences, that James himself was impressed by psychic phenomena and even accepted the presidency of the Society for Psychical Research and wrote several articles on the subject. However, he was quick to detect fraud among its practitioners, though believing in its potentialities.

It was easy to vulgarize pragmatism in a commercial age when success was too frequently identified with virtue. To say that an idea was true if it worked for the individual was to ignore the philosophic tests of workability that James had in mind. As a Darwinist, he believed that ideas must meet the selective test of their environment to survive, but he was too much the scientist and too strongly a religious, ethical person to allow this test to be anything but rigorous. James's unfortunate propensity for striking phrases like "cash value" gave the impression of crude Yankee materialism, but the colorful phrase is obviously misleading. Among the vulgarizers, fascists like Mussolini later cited the arguments of pragmatism to reject democratic values and to teach a crude national expediency instead. But Machiavellianism was not invented or advocated by James and he would have denied that the self-interest of a single nation was enough to justify militarism or totalitarianism. Fascists and imperialists who frankly avowed pragmatism liked to attack the intellectuals by citing the pragmatic argument that thought without action was sterile. This resulted in an intolerant nationalism that James could not have admitted for a moment. Undoubtedly James had overstated his case in the effort to free his generation from the bonds of absolutism on the one hand and the dangers of agnosticism and blind determinism on the other. He offered a philosophy of action that proved congenial to the American temperament, though academic philosophers usually dissented from his iconoclastic method.

James was especially happy in the victory of pragmatism under the guise of "instrumentalism" at the University of Chicago where John Dewey taught philosophy and the new pedagogy during 1894-1904. Dewey, like James, had begun with philosophic idealism and moved toward empiricism, which emphasized experience as the sole reality. Noting the revolution in philosophy evoked by Darwinism, he could paraphrase James and say, "Philosophy foreswears inquiry after absolute origins and absolute finalities in order to explore specific values and the specific conditions that generate them." Like James, he was a voluntarist, believing in the power of the human intelligence to remake man's environment and hence in his ability to escape wholly deterministic influences.

While James retained considerable social conservatism and only occasionally entered the arena of reform, despite his activitist philosophy, Dewey devoted his life to social causes as well as to their philosophy. He influenced American educational theory more deeply than any other man and tried to make the school an instrument to build a democratic social order: "To improve our education, to ameliorate our manners, to advance our politics, we must have recourse to specific conditions of generation," he asserted. At the new children's school of the University of Chicago he experimented with the principles that constituted "progressive education." In 1904 he continued this work at Teachers College, Columbia.

Like Froebel, Dewey believed that the school was not merely a preparation for life but was actually the life of the child. In this process of adaptation the curriculum and its subject matter must be adjusted to the "instinctive, impulsive attitudes and activities of the child." Genuine problem-solving and meaningful projects, including manual work, were intended to displace mere memorization and artificial assignments. Dewey had no desire to accelerate the trend toward vocationalism that urban conditions were fostering, but to make handwork a means of self-expression. He rejected the traditional leisure-class or classical theory of education, which stressed the ability to talk and write about things rather than the doing of them. His "learning by doing" was another famous phrase, which, like those of William James, was destined to be misunderstood and abused in practice. Unlike Thorndike, Dewey intended that the child-centered curriculum should serve the democratic end of achieving a cooperative society rather than the aristocratic one of promoting the exceptional child and the competitive individual. Too many progressive educators were to cater to the selfish, anti-social whims of their charges rather than to their cooperative qualities. Dewey's own emphasis was upon the growth of the child as a good citizen in a democratic society.

Dewey's progressive principles for elementary education had their counterpart in the field of higher education under Charles W. Eliot, president of Harvard (1869-1909). Eliot had been influenced by his former philosophy teacher, Ralph Waldo Emerson, whose ideal of a liberal education included a place for vocational subjects in "the development of every faculty that can add accomplishment to the noble being." Eliot's "New Education" replaced the formal required curriculum by an "elective system." As he explained at his inaugural in 1869:

The elective system fosters scholarship, because it gives free play to natural preferences and inborn aptitudes, makes possible enthusiasm for a chosen work, relieves the professor and the ardent disciple of the presence of a body of students who are compelled to an unwelcome task, and enlarges instruction by substituting many and various lessons given to small, lively classes, for a few lessons many times repeated to different sections of a numerous class.

By 1906, Eliot reported, "All the American colleges have now adopted the elective system of studies, tho not all to the same degree or extent." There were inevitable abuses: students often selected the easiest subjects or those subjects offered at the most convenient hours; sometimes, the result was a chaotic mass of unrelated subjects. Worst of all, as in the case of abuses of Dewey's "learning by doing," the door was left open to pure and simple vocationalism devoid of any larger philosophical motive. However, it was also inevitable that the bookish classical curriculum isolated from everyday life would yield to the practical demands on the colleges that commerce and industry were making. The pragmatic spirit of the times called for adaptation to a world that prized action above contemplation. Eliot carried his revolution into the professional schools. His law school dean, C. C. Langdell, introduced in 1870 the casebook method of study—a pragmatic approach to concrete cases —to replace the formal textbook system. Within a generation this system was accepted in American law schools.

In looking over the philosophical field at the end of the century, Dewey noted "a recrudescence of absolutistic philosophies" as well as the antitraditional theories. While the James-Dewey school were attempting to reconcile voluntarism with the scientific view of a constantly changing universe, philosophical idealists like Josiah Royce were combatting the emphasis on the Darwinist idea of change and constant adaptation. Royce had been born in 1855 on the western slopes of the Sierras where his pioneer parents crossed into California. He was educated at the University of California, Johns Hopkins, Yale, and finally in Germany among the Hegelian idealists. James had befriended Royce and arranged for him to teach at Harvard.

To Royce this was a universe of order, of God's eternal will, and of the Absolute, but he rejected the Hegelian effort to subordinate man to the absolute state. As a pioneer-bred idealist he tried to combat the centralizing tendency of urban society "to discourage individuality, and to approach a dead level of harassed mediocrity." He dwelt particularly upon an ethics founded on a strong sense of loyalty, involving self-sacrifice and cooperation by men living in a community of free individuals. His best-known books were *The World and the Individual* (1901) and *The Philosophy of Loyalty* (1908).

Darwin and Spencer had no more unreserved admirers and popularizers among the philosophers and historians than the erudite John Fiske. His prolific pen and persuasive platform style did a great deal to reassure the laity that Darwinism could be reconciled with the traditional view of a divinely ordered world, and won for him the personal friendship and praise of Darwin, Spencer, and Huxley. Proudly he wrote Darwin about his own modest footnote to the theory of evolution, which was later published as *The Meaning of Infancy* (1883). His central theme was that the long period of human infancy determined the civilizing character of mankind. Prolonged infancy led to a stable family life in order to protect and educate the infant. It fostered the development of a gregarious instinct that led to altruism instead of selfish jungle traits. Whichever direction Fiske looked, he came up with the most comforting optimism for those who wished to keep a foot in both camps of Darwinism and liberal religion. The American faith in inevitable progress received its most enthusiastic sponsorship in his writings and speeches.

14

Social Evolution and the Social Studies: Sumner and Holmes

I

THE faith in science of this Darwinian era led scholars to make a renewed effort to create a science of society, the dream of Francis Bacon, Comte, and a host of other philosophers. No man advanced this goal as much as Herbert Spencer, who tried to borrow the tools of the natural sciences for the use of the social sciences. Born in Derby, England, in 1820 and largely self-educated, especially in engineering and economics, Spencer joined the editorial staff of the *London Economist* and wrote free trade articles from an extremely individualistic viewpoint. Even before Darwin's *Origin of Species* (1859), he published his evolutionary ideas in *Social Statics* (1850), which offered a mechanism of social evolution that he derived largely from the new physics, rather than from biology alone. The principle of the "conservation of energy," which posited the idea that matter and energy are never destroyed but are constantly changing in form, served him as an explanation of the evolutionary process of the redistribution of matter from unstable homogeneity to a more balanced heterogeneity. Applying this to society, he came to the conclusion that these evolutionary forces would achieve a stable social equilibrium and a state of maximum human happiness.

From Malthus and his pessimistic social theory that population tends to outstrip food supply, Spencer developed his famous phrase, the "survival of the fittest"—so often attributed to Darwin, who quoted Spencer's phrase in his *Origin of Species*—and intensified his own extreme individualistic philosophy of the struggle for existence. By the time the *Origin of Species* was published, Spencer had already developed his central evolutionary ideas except, of course, for the principle of natural selection. He wrote in *Social Statics* and in later works that society would achieve the desired equilibrium only after the state had stripped away its functions, even including the postal service, tax-supported schools, poor relief, and public sanitation. Implicit in his thinking was the eighteenth-century faith in a world ruled by natural law and in the corollary of laissez faire: none must interfere with the laws of nature by hampering the activities of the individual. Seldom had the ethics of the jungle been so persuasively presented.

In his three-volume *Principles of Sociology* (1876-96), Spencer employed his amazing general erudition as well as his social evolutionary ideas in constructing the long-awaited science of society. He not only pictured a universal evolution of society as an integrated whole in ever more progressive forms, but also traced the evolution of separate aspects of culture—religion, industry, property, marriage, and so on. Thus he (and especially Lewis H. Morgan) formulated the basic idea of social evolution that influenced the sociologists and laymen of his day, the idea of uniform stages through which a social institution might progress: Marriage, for example, would evolve from the promiscuity of the herd to group marriage and finally to monogamy.

Of the American academicians who took up enthusiastically the social Darwinism of Herbert Spencer, none went farther in making it the heart of his teachings than William Graham Sumner, an economist and later sociologist of Yale. Sumner was born in 1840 in Paterson, New Jersey, the son of a thrifty English laborer. Before becoming an Episcopalian minister he had studied classical languages at Yale and philosophy in Germany. This, in the judgment of Yale's president, Noah Porter, qualified him for a post in political economy in 1872. The subject was nebulous enough to include almost anything, but Sumner seemed safely orthodox. Before long, however, he was reading Herbert Spencer to his classes and showing leanings toward agnosticism.

His early writings bore the unmistakable imprint of Spencer's social Darwinism; and on the lecture platform he assailed reformers, the income tax, and even government regulation of monopoly. His essay, "The Forgotten Man" (1883), referred to the middle-class citizen who had to pay the cost of state social services, tariff protectionism, the eight-hour day, and trade union demands. This was scarcely the sense in which the phrase, "forgotten man" was used by the progressive Walter Hines Page or in later years by Franklin D. Roosevelt. He denied that men were entitled to "natural rights"; they had only those rights obtained in the struggle for existence. Above all, he was almost a complete scientific determinist. He stated flatly his fatalistic philosophy in an essay, *The Absurd Effort To Make the World Over* (1894):

Everyone of us is a child of his age and cannot get out of it. He is in the stream and is swept along with it. All his sciences and philosophy come to him out of it. Therefore the tide will not be changed by us.... The things which will change it are the great discoveries and inventions, the new reactions inside the social organism, and the changes in the earth itself on account of changes in the cosmical forces.

Sumner's reputation rests largely upon his book *Folkways* (1907), one of the most influential works in American sociology. This book marked the beginning of a definite Sumner school of sociologists. "Folkways" were conceived to be group habits that grow out of chance products of adjustment to the social environment. When they are believed to be indispensable to the group they are "mores" (such as monogamy) and become informal agencies of social control. "The mores can make anything right and prevent the condemnation of anything." Ethical relativists were especially pleased to read that the mores were more apt to be products of chance than of rationality and that notions of right and wrong varied according to time, place, and custom. *Folkways* did offer many useful concepts to sociologists—including in-group, out-group, and ethnocentrism—but its implications were not only relativistic but most rugged in their individualism.

However, Sumner was entering the Progressive Era during which other sociologists and social workers spoke a more popular language of cooperative action. The year following the publication of *Folkways*, the Protestants had formulated their *Social Creed* and had organized the Federal Council of Churches. Catholic leaders, following the doctrine of *Rerum Novarum*, had rejected social Darwinism. Among those who dreamed of a science of society without the Spencerian bias of laissez faire was Professor Lester F. Ward of Brown University (1841-1913). He had spent forty years of his life in the federal civil service without acquiring any fear of "bureaucracy." In religion he was a rationalist and had edited *The Iconoclast*. His social ideas reflected the originality and sympathies of a self-educated person born in frontier poverty. He, too, like Spencer, borrowed from the new energy concepts of physics as well as from biology, but his evolutionary doctrine in *Dynamic Sociology* stressed the role of mind in directing social progress and in resisting the competitive abuses in society. "Is not civilization," he asked, "with all it has accomplished, the result of man's not letting things alone, and of his not letting nature take its course?" To him, the goal of society should be "the scientific control of the social forces by the collective mind of society." This meant that equality of opportunity should be afforded to everyone, regardless of race, sex, or class. "Every true legislator must be a sociologist," he asserted.

In the reformist tradition of Lester Ward, though less erratic, was another influential founder of sociology, Albion W. Small, the head of the sociology department in the new University of Chicago, and the first editor of the *American Journal of Sociology*. His idea of synthesizing the social studies into a special discipline was free from Spencerian laissez faire. Sociology's mission to him was not to escape to an ivory-tower, but to pursue gradual social reforms based on Christian ethics. Small had been trained in a theological seminary as well as in the German universities, but, unlike Sumner, he retained his early idealistic sympathies. He left his influence upon the significant school of sociologists at the University of Chicago.

Among the early anthropologists who examined similar cultural problems with the sociologists was Lewis Henry Morgan, a lawyer of Aurora, New York. He had befriended his Indian neighbors on the Seneca reservation and they permitted him to study their customs. In his *Ancient Society* (1877) he utilized his study of kinship systems to show that culture passes through the same stages everywhere. For example, he held that the matriarchal organization preceded the patriarchal system. His materialist interpretation of history won him the acclaim of Marx and socialist groups. But his more solid contribution of social interpretation in studying kinship groups strongly influenced the development of anthropology in both Europe and America.

2

Pragmatism had its greatest triumph in "sociological jurisprudence," although its final victory was not clear until the mid-twentieth century. In the light of Newtonian physics and the eighteenth-century "laws of nature," law had been thought of as based upon immutable certainties and "discovered" only through court precedents. Even the revolutionary decisions of John Marshall in defining the nature of contracts, commerce, and the state were believed to belong to an old legal tradition, which he and his colleagues had merely applied. The American doctrine of judicial review, which many Progressives detested, had given the courts a unique position of superiority over the popularly-elected legislatures and had strengthened the reverence for "judicial statesmanship" and the idea of a fixed body of law. Supreme Court Justice Stephen J. Field, who had been frightened by the threat to property represented by the Paris Commune of 1871, succeeded in converting the Court by the eighties to the opinion that the Fourteenth Amendment protected corporations from unfriendly state regulation. "Freedom of contract" was one of the immutable principles of the law that American courts relied on more and more after 1890 in their rejection of shorter hour laws for both men and women and of statutes forbidding "yellow-dog" contracts.

Sociological jurisprudence was the outcome of the pragmatic method applied to law with important ideas contributed by Europeans. To jurists like Oliver Wendell Holmes, Jr., the foremost representative of this school, law was not an unchanging, self-sufficient system resting upon a pedestal but a social institution that could be improved by conscious effort. Law must adapt itself to a changing social environment and for this purpose the practical experience of legislators was superior to the *a priori* abstractions of jurists. This process of legal adaptation was furthered to some extent by the revolution in law-school teaching methods fostered in 1870 at Harvard by Dean Christopher C. Langdell. His new "casebook system" discarded the traditionally heavy reliance upon ancient textbook maxims and drew primarily from actual cases reflecting the world of experience.

Holmes was born in Boston in 1841, the son of the outstanding medical authority and littérateur who was best known for the sprightly sketches of *The Autocrat of the Breakfast-Table* (1858). Like his father, he was a social conservative, critical of reformers and the current commercialism, but, like so many of his generation who had fought in the Civil War, he believed that all life was a struggle and that battle was the destiny of man. He was raised in the Boston circle of Theodore Parker, Wendell Phillips, and William James and educated inevitably at Harvard where he began his brilliant career as a legal scholar. In 1881 he published a series of lectures as *The Common Law* in which he expressed his pragmatic belief that the life of the law had not been logic, but experience:

> The felt necessities of the time, the prevalent moral and political theories, intuitions of public policy, avowed or unconscious, even the prejudices which judges share with their fellow-men, have had a good deal more to do than the syllogism in determining the rules by which men should be governed.

During 1882-1902 he served on the Supreme Court of Massachusetts and thereafter until 1932 upon the United States Supreme Court bench. As in the case of William James, pragmatism enabled Holmes to be tolerant of unorthodox or reformist ideas that he could not possibly accept for himself. As early as 1873 he had shown his Darwinian tendencies in the comment, "The more powerful interests must be more or less reflected in legislation; which, like every other device of man or beast, must tend in the long run to aid the survival of the fittest." His method of reconciling social conservatism with pragmatism is clear from an observation of 1900:

> While I think the strike a lawful instrument in the universal struggle of life, I think it pure phantasy to suppose that there is a body of capital of which labor as a whole secures a larger share by that means. . . . I think it lawful for a body of workmen to try by combination to get more than they now are getting, although they do it at the expense of their fellows, and to that end to strengthen their union by the boycott and the strike.

After President Roosevelt appointed Holmes to the conservative Supreme Court he frequently found himself writing dissenting opinions couched in the language of pragmatism. Though he disappointed the president in 1904 by dissenting against the majority opinion that held the Northern Securities Company must be dissolved, he usually resisted the tendency of the court to nullify popular laws. Thus in the noted Lochner case, involving the constitutionality of New York's ten-hour law for bakers, he disagreed with the majority who rejected it on the ground that it violated "freedom of contract." Holmes argued:

> The liberty of the citizen to do as he likes so long as he does not interfere with the liberty of others to do the same, which has been a shibboleth for some well-known writers, is interfered with by school laws, by the Post Office, by every State or municipal institution which takes his money for purposes thought desirable, whether he likes it or not. The Fourteenth Amendment does not enact Mr. Herbert Spencer's *Social Statics*.

Holmes' chief contribution was in the field of free speech—"freedom for the thought that we hate," as he put it in 1928. The best-known of these opinions was his dissent in *Abrams* v. *U. S.* (1919), involving the distribution of several leaflets attacking Wilson's intervention in Russia and calling for a general strike in protest. Here, he expressed his pragmatic philosophy in its clearest form:

> . . . But when men have realized that time has upset many fighting faiths, they may come to believe even more than they believe the very foundations of their own conduct that the ultimate good desired is better reached by free trade in ideas—that the best test of truth is the power

326 SOCIETY AND THOUGHT

of the thought to get itself accepted in the competition of the market, and that truth is the only ground upon which their wishes safely can be carried out. That, at any rate, is the theory of our Constitution. It is an experiment, as all life is an experiment. . . . While that experiment is part of our system I think that we should be eternally vigilant against attempts to check the expression of opinions that we loathe and believe to be fraught with death, unless they so imminently threaten immediate interference with the lawful and pressing purposes of the law that an immediate check is required to save the country.

The greatest success of sociological jurisprudence before World War I was the "Brandeis Brief" used in the case of *Muller* v. *Oregon* (1908), involving shorter hours for women. In this suit, Louis Brandeis won a decision for the state by hiring several social workers to amass data for him showing the evil consequences of long hours upon the health of women. He convinced the judges that the "police power" was far more relevant here than the principle of freedom of contract. Brandeis' disciple, Felix Frankfurter, continued this sociological technique in related cases. The most scholarly expositor of sociological jurisprudence was Roscoe Pound, a Nebraska-born law professor who taught at the University of Nebraska, Northwestern, and Chicago before coming to the Harvard Law School in 1910. In fact, he may have coined the term "sociological jurisprudence" as well as popularized the concept directly or indirectly among a large younger generation of lawyers and statesmen some of whom were to occupy key posts in the New Deal and upon the Supreme Court of the 1940's and 1950's. To this school, the pragmatic test to determine truth and justice seemed far more important than the tradition of the law's certainty whose principle could only be "found," not made.

3

Old George Bancroft, the historian—he was born the year Jefferson was elected president—was pleased to receive an appointment in 1867 as minister to Germany. There the historian met Professor Leopold Von Ranke of the University of Berlin, the leader in the new school of "scientific history" who was teaching the research techniques of the seminar method to a crop of young American historians. Ranke enthusiastically praised Bancroft's *History of the United States* whose tenth and last volume was to appear in 1874 and remarked that it was the best work from the democratic point of view.

The realistic German must have been well aware of the shortcomings of Bancroft's generation of idealistic historians—their faith in unlimited progress and in the "general laws" of the universe and their liberal nationalist bias. Bancroft had prided himself on his use of innumerable sources, but his volumes, as one critic observed, continued to "vote for Jackson." He had neglected economics and social history to prove that the United States, guided by providence, was the world leader in the democratic battle for religious liberty and humanity. His volumes were filled with naïve optimism and continued to please American readers of the seventies and eighties.

The literary historians who had dramatized the past and glorified the great man in the style of Emerson and Carlyle were dying off and few cared to take up the tradition of romantic history. Prescott and Irving had both died in 1859, and Motley, who lived long enough to adopt Darwinism, had only indifferent success with his final history of the Netherlands. Motley's world was based on immutable principles of reason in which freedom and authority were neatly blended into a Whiggish system of constitutional government, nationalism, and conservative economics. Like Bancroft, Charles Sumner, James Russell Lowell, and others of his day, he raised the "law of progress" to an eternal principle and was not disturbed by the implications of Darwinism:

> To be created at once in likeness to the Omnipotent and to a fantastic brute; to be compounded thus of the bestial and the angelic, alternately dragged upward and downward by conflicting forces, presses upon us the conviction, even without divine revelation, that this world is a place of trial and of progress towards some higher sphere.

In short, he saw eye to eye with John Fiske, the philosopher-historian, who asserted that evolution was another evidence of divine purpose and the optimistic law of progress.

After Motley's death there still survived among the literary historians Francis Parkman who combined original research with the vivid first-hand impressions of the terrain described. Despite a condition of near-blindness and nervousness, Parkman recovered sufficiently to write his imaginative studies of the French and Indians in early Canada and the West. He showed skill in depicting character, but retained the prejudices of the white man in evaluating Indian culture, together with the preconceptions of the Anglo-Saxon Protestant in dealing with the French Catholic regime in Canada.

As late as 1880 college history teaching was still in embryo. Only eleven professors taught history in the entire nation; many academicians gave incidental history courses alongside their specialties in philosophy, theology, or the classics. All this was soon to change under the pragmatic influence of the new sciences. The techniques of the natural sciences were mulled over to serve the practical needs of history in an industrial-commercial world. Diplomacy, wars, politics, and palace intrigues dealt only with a small facet of human history, it was now realized. New sources, local historical societies, as well as historical seminars were marshaled into service in order to understand man in his everyday life. Young historians studied in the German seminars of Ranke and his disciples in Europe and America. England offered the living models of John Richard Green and Henry T. Buckle whose concept of social history gave attention to the conditioning influence of the environment such as the forces of geography, soil, and climate—not merely the unfolding of an immutable law of progress as expressed in ideals.

Among those who took Buckle to heart was the largely self-educated businessman, James Ford Rhodes, who retired in 1885 to devote himself to history-writing. His seven-volume work, *History of the United States from the Compromise of 1850* (1893-1906) was relatively non-partisan by the Bancroft standards and gave more attention than usual to economics. But he neglected the West and retained the older moralizing quality of his predecessors. At Princeton, an engineering professor, John Bach McMaster, turned his admiration of Buckle to even better account than Rhodes did, for he

drew copiously upon newspapers and pamphlets to write the fullest
and most interesting American social history to date. His *History of
the People of the United States* (8 vols., 1883-1913), despite a
Whiggish-industrial bias and numerous errors, and occasional lapses
into rank plagiarism, had a wide following and influence. Like
Bancroft, he glorified the American destiny and mission and exuded
excessive optimism about the present state of national affairs. His
accounts of everyday plantation life (his father had been a Louisiana slaveholder), country fairs, and city incidents retained their
interest long after the political and diplomatic works of his contemporaries ceased to attract readers. The ideal of McMaster had
been anticipated in 1880 by Edward Eggleston who had written his
brother:

I am going to write a series of volumes which together shall constitute
a History of Life in the United States—not a history of the United States,
bear in mind, but a history of life there, the life of the people, the sources
of their ideas and habits, the course of their development from beginnings.

In 1870 the brilliant and erratic Henry Adams began teaching
medieval history and later American history of the Jeffersonian
period. This direct descendant of presidents and diplomats pondered
over the lessons of history and eventually decided that Clio had
no answers worth noting. Still, his nine-volume *History of the United
States during the Administrations of Jefferson and Madison* (1889-
1891) was indeed magnificent in its interpretation, style, and attention to social as well as political history. Carl Becker praised its
"clarity, tight construction, and sheer intelligence." Adams later
occupied himself with speculations regarding a completely materialistic history based on the second law of thermodynamics and introduced these ideas in his highly imaginative works, *Mont-Saint-
Michel and Chartres* (1913) and *The Education of Henry Adams*
(1918), written in the third person. He thought of the Middle Ages
as dominated by the "force" of the Virgin and of modern times as
energized by the dynamo. His private letters reveal the strong sub-
jectivism and eccentricity that the imaginative style of his later
books conceal, such as his belief that contemporary politics is to be

understood by studying the alleged omnipotent power of Jewish financiers.

Frederick Jackson Turner and Woodrow Wilson were among the many distinguished historians and political scientists who studied in the German-inspired seminar of Herbert Baxter Adams at The Johns Hopkins University. Adams stressed the German "germ theory of politics," which looked upon American institutions as an evolutionary product derived from primitive German origins. He was also one of the founders of the American Historical Association in 1884.

Turner, who had been raised in frontier Wisconsin, declared rebelliously, "Too exclusive attention has been paid by institutional students to the Germanic origins, too little to the American factors." But he too was a social evolutionist, for he described the frontier as a social process of successive stages beginning with the Indian and the hunter and culminating in the manufacturing organization of the city. Political sections were the unique products of this frontier evolution and their special regional qualities grew out of this experience. "Whatever be the truth regarding European history," he wrote, "American history is chiefly concerned with social forces, shaping and reshaping under the conditions of a nation changing as it adjusts to its environment." The frontier, he felt, had promoted a composite nationality for the American people through a crucible of nationalities welded together by common dangers and isolation from England. It gave the American intellect its most striking characteristics:

That coarseness and strength combined with acuteness and inquisitiveness; that practical, inventive turn of mind quick to find expedients; that masterful grasp of material things, lacking in the artistic but powerful to effect great ends; that restless, nervous energy; that dominant individualism, working for good and for evil, and withal that buoyancy and exuberance which comes with freedom—these are traits of the frontier, or traits called out elsewhere because of the existence of the frontier.

But Turner was troubled by the current movement of Populism and Free Silver and feared that the free lands that had made democracy a fact had also bred a selfish, intolerant form of individualism, lax in matters of business honor and currency.

Professor Turner, who moved from the University of Wisconsin to Harvard, raised so many significant questions that an entire generation of frontier historians sprang into existence, especially in the Middle West. There they organized the Mississippi Valley Historical Association in 1914. Disciples probed the Turnerian significance of the role of sections in American history and the various conditioning factors in western history. Later critics insisted that Turner ignored the existence of social classes in his concern for geographic sections—a charge that is not true of his later work; that he had done harm by emphasizing the uniqueness of America—as if Bancroft and his nationalist generation had not already done that!—and that the frontier was never, as Turner's disciples implied, a safety valve for Eastern labor. Many of these critics ignored Turner's own modifications of his theories and attacked the straw man of crude geographic determinism. In this era, however, Turner's march was a triumphant advance in which his ideas were hailed by Woodrow Wilson and Theodore Roosevelt.

The new scientific history was not always born of the detached laboratory spirit, although the flavor of science was consciously sought through dry monographs upon fragmentary subjects. Often the historian seemed unconscious of his bias or underlying assumptions, for he achieved an imaginary objectivity by adopting the positivistic technique of piling one fact upon another. In the new field of Southern history, revisionists North and South asserted their scientific temper by overturning the verdict of abolitionist historians. The result was an anti-Negro and anti-Carpetbag interpretation that coincided with the concurrent decline of civil rights for Negroes in the courts and "demagogue"-run Southern legislatures. In 1907, reviewers were usually laudatory in discussing Professor William A. Dunning's *Reconstruction, Political and Economic*. The author defended the Black Codes with their limitations on Negro testimony in the courts as "justified by well-established traits and habits of negroes...." Reconstruction was "a social and political system in which all the forces that made for civilization were dominated by a mass of barbarous freedmen." As for the humanitarian Radical, Charles Sumner, said Dunning, "He was the perfect type of that narrow fanaticism which erudition and egotism combine to produce, and to which political crises alone give the opportunity for actual achievement." Here was the revisionist pattern of the Dunning school, which, through its Columbia seminar and elsewhere, changed a substantial part of the history textbooks during the succeeding decades, until the ideological ground lost by the South as a result of the Civil War and Reconstruction was partly regained.

A much more valuable result of historiography was the development, at Columbia, of the New History by James Harvey Robinson and a group of young cultural historians including Charles A. Beard and Carlton J. H. Hayes and elsewhere by Carl Becker and Preserved Smith. They had been directly or indirectly influenced by the German historian, Karl Lamprecht, who believed that an integrated form of social and intellectual history was needed to understand the collective psychology of an era and its evolutionary development. In 1911, James Harvey Robinson published *The New History,* which transferred the German emphasis upon *Kulturgeschichte* to America. Robinson called for the historian to equip himself with the tools of the related social sciences, especially anthropology, sociology, economics, and psychology. Together with Charles Beard he popularized this total view of man's historical past through numerous school textbooks. Most of this school accepted Robinson's view that history was an instrument of social action, not merely an encyclopedic view of the "past everything" as deriders called the New History.

Charles Beard won a considerable progressive following in these years for his iconoclastic researches into the founding of the nation, particularly in *An Economic Interpretation of the Constitution* (1913) and *Economic Origins of Jeffersonian Democracy* (1915). In the first book he took issue with Fiske's idea of a "critical era" during 1783-87, which allegedly led to a spontaneous popular demand for a new constitution to replace the Articles of Confederation. He cited contemporary treasury records to show that most of the framers of the Constitution held government securities that would rise in value with the ratification of the new document. A few pressure groups, he contended, had put through the Constitution over the objections of a possible majority. Although Beard later admitted that he had overstated his case, he stood by his guns against a host of academicians and others who were shocked at this application of economic motives to a revered document.

4

The line between history and the fields of political science and economics was far more distinct after World War I than before. Many an eminent political scientist or economist began with his Ph.D. in history. But the trend toward specialization resulted in a number of academic splinters that became separate studies and departments. Political scientists devoted themselves to practical studies of "actual government" (to use Albert B. Hart's book title of 1903) and of governmental devices such as the initiative, referendum, and recall, the commission system of government, city home rule, and the short ballot. Woodrow Wilson, president of the National Short Ballot Organization, formed in 1909, regarded this movement as the key to the "restoration of popular government." Wilson, as already noted, believed that government was something organic, not static in the sense of the checks and balances system. "It is accountable to Darwin, not to Newton," he wrote in *Constitutional Government in the United States* (1908). "It is modified by its environment, necessitated by its tasks, shaped to its functions by the sheer pressure of life. . . . Living political constitutions must be Darwinian in structure and in practice." Here was the political theory of the welfare state, though Wilson had only begun to see its implications in practice.

In economics, the pragmatic revolt against idealism took the form of a general rejection of abstract classical theories. This quest for greater realism led to historical and analytical studies of the economic behavior of actual human beings and evolving economic institutions such as banking, trade unions, business cycles, and the mechanisms of the distribution of wealth. Here again the leadership among these "institutionalists" came from Europe, especially from

Germany, where Sombart and Weber were studying the origins of capitalism and its interaction with religious thought, and others were examining the cyclic nature of economic crises.

The most famous of the institutionalists was Thorstein Veblen, author of *The Theory of the Leisure Class* (1899) and *The Theory of Business Enterprise* (1904). His extremely critical view of business enterprise as a parasitic exploitative process that dominated all phases of culture has already been noted in considering the rise of the "captains of industry." There remains to be added the fact that Veblen considered economics to be an evolutionary science which could use, as he did, ethnological and psychological techniques to study the interaction of human instincts and the environment.

While academic economists had a strong core of economic conservatives among them, there were influential radicals outside the universities. No American academician, not even Richard T. Ely, the social economist, had more disciples than Henry George, author of *Progress and Poverty* (1879) and exponent of the single-tax idea. "Political Economy has been called the dismal science," he observed, "and, as currently taught, is hopeless and despairing." While accepting evolutionary science and the pessimistic second law of thermodynamics, he called for an optimistic assertion of human will in controlling society:

The laws which Political Economy discovers, like the facts and relations of physical nature, harmonize with what seems to be the law of mental development—not a necessary and involuntary progress, but a progress in which the human will is an initiatory force.

For Henry George the association of poverty with progress was the challenge of the times. Largely self-educated, he came to a conclusion favored by few universities. Labor and capital, the real producers of wealth, were paying tribute to land monopolists in the form of unearned rent increment due to artificial and speculative land scarcity. The solution lay not in land confiscation, but to "appropriate all rent by taxation ... to abolish all taxation save that upon land values." This became the burden of his crusading message for the single tax.

Though few adopted this idea, his analysis inspired a host of progressives to take up the cudgels for economic reform. Mayor Tom Johnson of Cleveland, who admitted he had once been an industrial monopolist, said that he had felt the first stirrings of conversion to reform after reading George's *Social Problems* (1883). Johnson's close aide, Newton D. Baker, wrote: "I am inclined to believe that no writer of our times has had a more profound influence upon the thinking of the world." John Dewey is said to have rated George among the ten greatest world philosophers. Tolstoy almost idolized Henry George as the man who had opened the road to an immediate solution of the Russian land problem. George's work, he insisted, stood "alone in the literature of science," and by demolishing "the whole scientific web of Spencer-Mill" enlightened the conscience of mankind.

Darwinism stimulated the social sciences and rearranged them into a neat pattern. Each social science eagerly adopted the approach of the social evolutionist who looked upon human institutions as organic things adapting themselves to an ever-changing environment. From this idea it followed that institutions, like biological organisms, evolve upward by stages in a purposeful direction —though some social scientists disliked the supernatural flavor in the idea of purpose. The symmetry of pattern left by Darwinism upon the social studies has been noted in detail. Psychology, for example, became a laboratory science and studied the mind as an evolving organism or habit-system. In the New Pedagogy of Dewey, the child was adapted to democratic living through a flexible curriculum and cooperative school institutions intended to encourage both self-expression and a socialized sense of responsibility. In philosophy, the pragmatist sought to discover truth by seeing how it survived the test of conflict with other truths, leaving the fittest to emerge victor. This idea was clearly expressed by the phrase of Oliver Wendell Holmes, Jr., the "free trade in ideas," and in the rise of sociological jurisprudence, which treated law as an evolving set of practices—not fixed axioms—adapting themselves to a changing world.

Everywhere the social evolutionist made his mark—in sociology, anthropology, history, political science, and in other fields. Religion, too, as noted in an earlier chapter, had its evolutionary advocate in the Modernist who liked to think of dogma as an evolving body of religious ideas and in the Beecher type of liberal who carried evolutionary science directly into the church. But the next generation of anthropologists after Lewis Morgan and Sumner showed that human institutions did not "evolve" in uniform stages everywhere and thus they drove the social evolutionists back upon a defensive position. Nevertheless, there still remained the Darwinist victory over the Newtonian concepts of fixed natural laws as they were applied to the social sciences in the eighteenth and early nineteenth centuries. Twentieth-century man was far less confident than Jefferson and the classicists that the "self-evident" laws of nature ran the affairs of society. Like the ancient Sophists, he was certain only of change.

Social evolution apparently gave aid and comfort to laissez-faire individualists like Sumner and other disciples of Herbert Spencer; but it also enheartened social planners like John Dewey, Lester F. Ward, and Henry George. These two camps differed largely by their contrasting emphasis upon the role of organized intelligence in directing and controlling the social order. The social planners rejected the Darwinist fatalism of their opponents and pinned their faith upon the power of scientific experiment to achieve the good society. On the whole, these Progressives clung to the traditional human values and defended them from Spencerian doctrines of the survival of the fittest by asserting the capacity of man to control his social environment and to choose his human destiny. Progress to them was inevitable only if men made it so.

15

Toward Literary Realism and the New Journalism: Whitman, Dreiser, and Pulitzer

---

I

"NEVER was there, perhaps, more hollowness at heart than at present, and here in the United States," wrote Walt Whitman dejectedly in 1871 in his chief prose work, *Democratic Vistas:*

> I say that our New World democracy, however great a success in uplifting the masses out of their sloughs, in materialistic development, products, and in a certain highly-deceptive superficial popular intellectuality, is, so far, an almost complete failure in its social aspects, and in really grand religious, moral, literary, and esthetic results.

It was easy for a sensitive observer of the era of Grant and Jay Gould to forget that creative literary spirits and an appreciative reading public still existed in the 1870's. Whitman himself had been dismissed in 1865 from his humble post in the Department of the Interior because the Secretary was shocked to learn that the unconventional author of *Leaves of Grass* was on his staff. Friends published the poem, "The Good Gray Poet," in his defense and the public responded by showing a sudden interest in Whitman's poems. Hitherto, only a few had recognized Whitman's poetic genius; but in 1882 the Philadelphia edition of *Leaves of Grass* was so profitable as to ease the final years of paralysis and tuberculosis for him.

In *Democratic Vistas* Whitman did more than attack the vulgarity, corruption, and complacency of contemporary American democracy. Fundamentally an optimistic disciple of Emerson, he reiterated his faith in the future of his land. Like Emerson in *The American Scholar*, he urged Americans to create an original culture distinct from the aristocratic and clerical European traditions. But American individualism, he felt, would not be narrowly chauvinistic but capable of cosmopolitan sympathies, thus "making the races comrades."

Mark Twain, whose intellectual and psychological roots were as thoroughly American as Whitman's, felt some constraint in the presence of the still-living great—Emerson, Lowell, Holmes, and the Boston circle, but his best work appeared during the seventies and eighties. Readers reacted enthusiastically to *The Innocents Abroad*, (1869), *Roughing It* (1871), *Tom Sawyer* (1876), *Life on the Mississippi* (1883) and *Huckleberry Finn* (1884). They expressed the expansive, optimistic mood of Victorian America. Even later realistic critics preferred these books to his subsequent pessimistic stories. Thus the chief co-author of *The Gilded Age* (1873), a term he helped to fasten upon his own day, could hardly complain of a lack of appreciation, however much he might have wished to write in a more uninhibited and skeptical vein.

Still, New England culture lacked the intensity of the years when Emerson and Lowell spoke with the fervor of social and literary rebels. Van Wyck Brooks is probably correct in referring to this period of Brahmin culture as "Indian Summer," a term Howells had once used as a title for a book. Lowell and Longfellow had turned with nostalgia to the remote past and were now captivated by Dante more than by the indigenous American themes of ante-bellum times. Emerson was failing in health, but promising young Boston intellectuals were ready to continue the Puritan intellectual tradition—Howells, Henry James, William James, Charles Eliot, and Oliver Wendell Holmes, Jr., to mention but a few.

It seems cruel to apply George Santayana's tag, "the genteel tradition" to this post-bellum atmosphere, despite the social evasions of the *Atlantic Monthly* and the *North American Review*, which were usually in the hands of traditionalists like Thomas Bailey

Aldrich who sniffed at the newer realism from continental Europe.
During the 1880's Aldrich tried to make the *Atlantic* the arbiter of
good taste and polished diction. This archconservative disliked the
alleged vulgarity of dialect in literature, despite the literary quality
of the local color school. The latter were highly competent regionalists of the romantic tradition, including Bret Harte, Joel Chandler
Harris, George Washington Cable, and Edward Eggleston, who
tried to add an element of verity through dialect, though they
usually ignored the deeper truthfulness of character analysis and
social-economic interpretation. They represented a transitional link
between the antebellum romantics and the early twentieth-century
realists. Altogether, their work constituted much of the better literary
efforts of the post-bellum decades.

2

Before Aldrich became editor of the influential *Atlantic* in 1881,
William Dean Howells, Ohio printer and journalist, had held this
distinguished post for a decade. He pleased Lincoln in 1860 by
writing a campaign biography for him and received the consular
office at Venice at a time when literary men were rewarded with
political posts. English, French, and Russian realism attracted him
more and more, and eventually occupied a central position in his
literary theory. In his *Criticism and Fiction* (1892), a collection of
essays written much earlier, he expressed a conservative preference
for the realism of the "divine Jane" Austen, author of *Pride and
Prejudice* and *Sense and Sensibility:* "Realism is nothing more and
nothing less than the truthful treatment of material, and Jane Austen
was the first and the last of the English novelists to treat material
with entire truthfulness." Elsewhere, he had remarked, "Fidelity to
experience and probability of motive are essential conditions of a
great imaginative literature." But he refused to adopt for himself the
frank naturalism of Zola, creator of the decadent prostitute, Nana.
He argued that the Anglo-Saxon novel was not so prudish as asserted, but a faithful representation of modern life "in dealing with
love that was chaste, and with passion so honest that it could be

openly spoken of before the tenderest society bud at dinner." American and English novels, unlike the French, were written for young girls as well as married people, and hence, he reasoned, a strong literary rule of decent restraint was needed.

There was far more of Jane Austen than Tolstoy in *The Rise of Silas Lapham* (1885), the story of a rustic self-made millionaire whose family attempted to adjust itself to the aristocratic society of upper-class Boston. Within his self-imposed literary restrictions Howells achieved a high level of verity and craftsmanship in this novel. He set a standard for realistic portrayal by minimizing the accidents of plot, even descending to commonplace situations in order to direct his focus upon character development. But his optimism steadily declined with the years. His sensitive social conscience rebelled against the contemporary injustices to labor and the execution of the Haymarket anarchists for a crime that had not been proved. By this time he had read Turgenev and Tolstoy. Of the first he wrote fervently:

Life showed itself to me in different colors after I had once read Tourguenief; it became more serious, more awful, and with mystical responsibilities I had not known before. My gay American horizons were bathed in the vast melancholy of the Slav, patient, agnostic, trustful.

For Tolstoy, his "literary passion" knew no bounds:

As much as one merely human can help another I believe he has helped me; he has not influenced me in aesthetics only, but in ethics, too, so that I can never see life in the way I saw it before I knew him.

Tolstoy's religious mysticism and humanitarianism, with their emphasis on self-regeneration rather than political action appealed to the gentle Howells.

His rebellion against labor abuses led him toward a collectivist utopianism after reading the work of Lawrence Grönlund on an ideal socialist commonwealth. Grönlund was a Danish-American immigrant who had been converted to socialism shortly after his arrival and who, then, in turn, had converted others, among them Eugene V. Debs. There was also the socialistic influence of Edward

Bellamy's *Looking Backward* (1888). The picture of a socialist utopia along such lines appeared in Howells' later novels, *A Traveler from Altruria* (1894) and its sequel *Through the Eye of the Needle* (1907). But these were far from his best books.

Far more sophisticated and sensitive in the art of realism, though less concerned with economic injustices, was the remarkable Henry James, brother of the Harvard philosopher. Both had spent much of their youth in European places and Henry later became one of a distinguished band of expatriates who found Western Europe and England especially more mature intellectually and esthetically than their homeland. In his generation the expatriates included Whistler, and among the younger ones, Ezra Pound and T. S. Eliot. But Henry James was no escapist, for he preserved his American connections in the "international theme" of his novels. In *The Ambassadors* (1902), he depicted a New England expatriate who rebelled against the materialism of his industrial section and found fulfillment in the Old World charm and traditions of Western Europe. His novels frequently centered around the life of American expatriates. Yet James had his largest audience in the years that he was close to America (he left in 1876), especially for the novelettes, *Roderick Hudson* (1876), *The American* (1877), *Daisy Miller* (1879), *The Portrait of a Lady* (1881), and *Washington Square* (1881). By the mid-twentieth century a group of sensitive American critics, particularly F. O. Matthiessen, rediscovered the neglected genius of Henry James.

This American novelist who had more awareness than most of his compeers of the esthetic principles of the novel, drew his inspiration in part from the French realists, Flaubert and Balzac, and in part from the Russians. When he met Turgenev in Paris in 1875 James felt deeply impressed by the Russian's outlook and later wrote, "Our Anglo-Saxon, Protestant, moralistic, conventional standards were far away from him, and he judged things with a freedom and spontaneity in which I found a perpetual refreshment." To him Tolstoy's art was perfection itself in its depiction of the inner life. "The perusal of Tolstoy—a wonderful mass of life," he wrote, "is an immense event, a kind of splendid accident, for each of us." He, too, aimed at the realism of uncovering the human soul rather than at the embellishments and tricks of plot structure.

3

Darwinism and the new physics had left their deterministic impact upon the novel by the nineties through naturalism. This clinical approach to man and his experience frequently portrayed him as a helpless pawn of circumstance, as an organic product of an all-determining environment. It was futile for the human insect to struggle against his fate. Pessimism was inherent in this treatment, but many of the naturalists were too thoroughly committed to social action to be consistent in their fatalism. The French naturalistic writer, Émile Zola, and the Russian, Dostoevski, gave this new school of novelists their principles of scientific detachment and clinical observation. Man could be studied frankly as an animal motivated by his appetites. Above all, the naturalist must not shrink from portraying the sexual life of his subject. The long-forgotten frankness of such earlier English novelists as Defoe, Smollett, and Fielding was resurrected and extended despite the objections of the older realists. Painters had won the right to portray human beings in undress, the naturalists argued, then why not novelists? Many of the naturalists began their careers as newspaper reporters and knew life best from the vantage point of a city slum. The urban atmosphere permeated their novels.

By the nineties, Howells was sufficiently sympathetic to naturalism for him to rescue Stephen Crane, one of the first American naturalists, from utter despair and to find a publisher for him. This twenty-four-year-old youth had already (under a pseudonym) written a novel that had been a flat failure, *Maggie: A Girl of the Streets* (1892). Crane was the son of a strict Methodist minister of New Jersey, but he had been weaned away from orthodoxy by his reading of the French naturalists and his experiences as a New York reporter and free-lance writer. Under the obvious inspiration of Zola he wrote a thoroughly naturalistic novelette with the setting in the New York slums and a plot depicting the degeneration of human character, somewhat reminiscent of *Nana*. Maggie, after being deserted by a bartender' lover, was driven into the streets by her drunken mother and vicious brother. Thereafter, as a prostitute, she sank steadily lower and finally drowned herself in the East River.

The realism of this story was heightened by its effective use of slang. More important from the standpoint of naturalism, Crane had taken a plot that Americans could have enjoyed as melodrama, had he given it the proper happy ending or at least a well-pointed moral, but he had refused to inject any sentimentality into the story. Life was like that and to describe it was all one should expect of a novelist. However, the readers and critics were not yet ready for this kind of Zola-esque pessimism and reacted indignantly. To a friend, Crane had written an inscription upon his novel, "It is inevitable that this book will greatly shock you, but continue, pray, with great courage to the end, for it tries to show that environment is a tremendous thing and shapes lives regardlessly."

The novel that seemed so promising to Howells and his friend, Hamlin Garland, was *The Red Badge of Courage* (1895), a Civil War novel. Crane had not yet begun his career as a war correspondent, but he felt that war was a futile display of heroics. In this story, he pictured a frightened, untrained soldier who had run away in panic on the battlefield and was wounded not by the enemy but by a comrade. He decided to live up to the mistaken reputation he had earned as a hero and revived his courage. Critics have pointed out that this type of Civil War naturalism, which depicted the unheroic and weary routine of life in war camps, had already been developed in the Civil War novels of John W. De Forest. However, Crane had developed a high order of craftsmanship by the use of an impressionistic technique, a kind of "stream of consciousness" view of bright successive images. He had excelled his predecessors in the analysis of fear. Crane's naturalism was also skillfully expressed in a truly great short story, "The Open Boat" (1898). This is a story of a shipwrecked crew adrift in a dinghy. Although the men were in sight of land and covered by the darting rays of a nearby lighthouse, they seemed doomed to death by drowning or by man-eating sharks. Nature, fate, life seemed unbelievably indifferent to them! Crane interjects the comment:

When it occurs to a man that nature does not regard him as important, and that she feels she would not maim the universe by disposing of him, he at first wishes to throw bricks at the temple, and he hates deeply the fact that there are no bricks and no temples.

Frank Norris continued the vogue of naturalism, being won to Zola and Flaubert after a romantic enthusiasm for Robert Louis Stevenson and Rudyard Kipling that he never quite discarded. As the son of a wealthy man, he had been reared in comfortable San Francisco society, attended a fashionable preparatory school, and studied art in Paris. He acquired a lasting interest in Darwinism while attending the lectures on evolution of Professor Joseph Le Conte at the University of California. At the same time he fell in love with Émile Zola. He took this naturalist as a model for an ambitious trilogy on the story of American society, an epic of wheat, *The Pit, The Octopus,* and another volume that he did not complete before his death in 1902. *The Pit* centered upon Chicago's wheat speculators and their rout by circumstances. *The Octopus* dealt with the California wheat raisers who fought against exploitation by the railroads, but Norris allowed his naturalist creed to overcome his sense of injustice by explaining the railroad executives, too, as a product of impersonal forces of "supply and demand" rather than as deliberate instigators of evil. The central idea of the trilogy was deterministic. "Men were naught, life was naught, *force* only existed." Still, Norris was too much the optimistic disciple of Spencer to give up a fervent belief in the "law" of progress and ultimate justice. Even Zola, the champion of Dreyfus, had held similar beliefs, These naturalists were still romantics at heart.

There was even more of Zola, especially of his theme of human degeneration and primitivism, in Norris' strongly naturalistic novel, *McTeague* (1899). This is the story of a brutish, lustful San Francisco dentist who acquires his degenerate qualities from an alcoholic father. McTeague marries an avaricious woman whose increasing niggardliness provokes repeated quarrels and finally her murder. His utter degeneration and death follow. This novel dealt with two naturalistic qualities, the determinism of heredity (rather than environment) and the primitive instincts of the brute. More of Norris' primitivism, in a very direct form, appeared in his posthumous novel, *Vandover and the Brute,* in which the central figure degenerates into an animal-like creature.

When Norris took his McTeague manuscript to the "dean of American realists," Howells, he received a strongly sympathetic reception, though the older man had misgivings about the reception the novel would get from American women who constituted so much of the novel reading public. Norris felt impatient with the prevailing attitude of reticence on sex in literature. During his career as a magazine editor, he denounced the prudishness of the American magazine reader and remarked of the current journals of 1895, "They are safe as a graveyard, decorous as a church, as devoid of immorality as an epitaph.... It is the young girl and the family center table that determine the standard of the American short story."

The greatest of the literary naturalists was Theodore Dreiser of Indiana, the son of a very strict Catholic father who had emigrated from Germany. The family suffered from poverty during their long residence on Chicago's shabby West Side. Economic salvation came finally through the eldest son, Paul (who spelt his name Dresser), a successful composer of popular songs, notably *The Blue and the Gray,* a hit of the Spanish-American War, and *On The Banks of the Wabash Far Away.* Theodore became a newspaperman and later as a novelist often drew his plots and characters from the press.

Zola came late into Dreiser's life, but Balzac's realism had a decisive influence upon his work. While he was a young reporter on the *Pittsburgh Dispatch,* he read Huxley and Spencer and lost the final shreds of the Catholicism in which he was reared. Spencer's *First Principles,* he later recalled, "quite blew me, intellectually, to bits." His concept of man as the very center of the universe and the aim of all creation was replaced by the naturalistic view of him as "an infinitesimal speck of energy." Life was expressed in the elemental terms of physics and biology. Love to him was simply a result of chemical affinities.

His first novel, *Sister Carrie* (1900), was partly inspired by an attempt to understand his own sister's rebelliousness in a household where the father could only comprehend that she was a "bad girl." Carrie was an impressionable country girl, fond of pretty clothes and determined to rise in the world. After her first sex adventure she became the demanding mistress of several men and married another only to bankrupt and finally divorce him. While she succeeded in finding a career on the stage, her former husband, who had once been a wealthy businessman, committed suicide. This novel was read enthusiastically in manuscript by Frank Norris, then consultant for Doubleday, Page, and Company, and accepted for publication. However, when Mrs. Frank Doubleday read the novel and noted its utter frankness on sex she was shocked. As a result, the publishers decided that their contract called for publication but not selling, and they stored hundreds of volumes of *Sister Carrie* in their basement or warehouse. Years elapsed before Dreiser succeeded in issuing the novel.

There was much of the determinism of *Sister Carrie*, but also a larger measure of pity, in *Jennie Gerhardt* (1911), another story of a girl who escaped poverty through sex liaisons. The influence of the Darwinist struggle for existence and the Nietzschean will-to-power appears even more in *The Financier* (1912) and *The Titan* (1914). Dreiser combed the Philadelphia and Chicago press files and interviewed the surviving associates of Charles T. Yerkes, the ruthless traction magnate, in order to portray the amoral financier, Frank Cowperwood. This character was interpreted as the product of a crude acquisitive society and as a magnetic personality who pursued money, power, and attractive women with equal intensity and social irresponsibility. Dreiser's own sentimentalism prevented his mechanistic philosophy from destroying the tragic human substance of his stories by a consistent emphasis on determinism. In the end the human will counts for a good deal. Still, Dreiser's agnosticism and pessimism left him with no abiding conviction that life had a purpose. At times he shared the Spencerian faith in progress, at other times he could see only aimless change and constant adaptation to change.

Karl Marx as well as Darwin and Spencer shaped the naturalism of Jack London, the gifted storyteller of the Alaskan frontier. This son of a poor San Francisco family had once been arrested for Socialist harangues in the streets and he had marched in 1894 with an unemployed army from the West that joined Coxey's famous advance upon Washington. But the jumble of ideologies in his perplexed mind also embraced Nietzche's doctrine of the Superman and an obvious feeling of awe for human brutes endowed with ruthless power and energy. In *The Sea Wolf* (1904) he recreated the predatory struggle for survival in a story of life on a sealing schooner and pictured the dominance of the Superman in Captain Wolf Larsen's crude and amoral will-to-power. While most of his tales were not marred by his ideological turmoil and absorbed the attention of innumerable readers, he did attempt a doctrinaire socialistic novel, *The Iron Heel* (1908), which dealt with a dictatorship of the Right, and he wrote many essays along Marxian lines. Side by side with his faith in a socialist state was a contradictory belief in the triumph of Anglo-Saxon imperialism over the globe. The artist who could capture so well the combative spirit of the primitive Northwest in *The Call of the Wild* (1903), *Burning Daylight,* and *Martin Eden* (1909) had tried to reach beyond his grasp for the new complex world of deterministic science.

4

"America demands a poetry that is bold, modern, and all-surrounding and kosmical, as she is herself . . .," wrote Whitman in *Democratic Vistas.* "Like America, it must extricate itself from even the greatest models of the past, and, while courteous to them, must have entire faith in itself, and the product of its own democratic spirit only." This prediction of 1871, spoken with the optimistic faith of Emerson, was to be realized only after the poetical renaissance beginning in 1912 with the rise of the New Poetry. Until then, there were the great transitional poets, Sidney Lanier, Emily

Dickinson, and Whitman himself. Emily Dickinson, a cloistered Massachusetts mystic of limited schooling, left an astonishingly perceptive and sensitive revelation of her inner life. Not until after her death in 1886 could the public begin to realize her gifts, for the first of her work appeared in 1890 and later volumes were published over the period of an entire generation. Her introspective spirit is suggested in the verses:

> The bustle in a house
> The morning after death
> Is solemnest of industries
> Enacted upon earth. - -
> The sweeping up the heart
> And putting love away
> We shall not want to use again
> Until eternity.

In her passionate lyrics and ecstatic moods, she plumbed the depths of a love experience that may have had no reality but in her own warm imagination. For the artificial "genteel female," the "brittle lady" of her day, she had only contempt. Life was far richer than such starved souls could imagine. So Emily Dickinson who "never saw a moor" and "never saw the sea" could experience these and much more because of the keen inner perception of her mind.

Whitman's realistic images, though clad in romantic phrases, and his experimental use of free verse forecast the birth of the New Poetry. By 1912, as revealed in one anthology, *The Lyric Year,* a large number of talented American poets were already experimenting with realism in verse. That same year Harriet Monroe of Chicago secured a special publication outlet for these efforts in her magazine, *Poetry.* Encouragement and direction came from local supporters and from a group of American expatriates like Ezra Pound and his school of English and French "Imagistes," as they called themselves. Pound, an eccentric literary genius who had given up his native Hailey, Idaho, for the rich culture of southern and western Europe, was deeply impressed by the verse technique of Provençal and early Italian poetry. His anthology of imagist poetry, *Des Imagistes* (1914) spread the technique of the new poetry of T. S. Eliot (who decided to move to London in 1914), Amy Lowell of Boston, and a number of Middle Western poets. Pound's dogma called for "pure images," "unrhymed cadence"—or free verse—and precise language.

A formal statement of the Imagists in 1915 began with the principle, "To use the language of common speech, but to employ the *exact* word, not the nearly-exact, nor the merely decorative word." Furthermore, "To create new rhythms—as the expression of new moods—and not to copy old rhythms which merely echo old moods. We do not insist upon 'free verse' as the only method of writing poetry." Above all, the mission of the New Poetry was: "To present an image . . . poetry should render particulars exactly and not deal in vague generalities, however magnificent and sonorous."

American exponents of this realistic spirit in poetry startled readers accustomed to the unfailing rhymes of popular poets of past centuries. Before conventional readers had quite recovered from Whitman's "barbaric yawp," they had to pass judgment on Carl Sandburg's uneven lines dealing with urban and frontier democracy. His *Chicago Poems* (1915), with its apostrophe to the crude city of the stockyards seemed to be prose if the printer had chosen to set it thus: "Hog butcher for the world, tool maker, stacker of wheat, player with railroads and the nation's freight handler; stormy, husky, brawling city of the big shoulders." Emerson had forecast the immense creative potentialities in the everyday and the "vulgar," but only the elite were quite prepared for the realization of this formula.

Just as Sandburg learned his Lincolnesque ideas of democracy by wandering through the villages and cities of the land, so (Nicholas) Vachel Lindsay, a poet and painter, learned the American saga by turning wandering minstrel and exchanging his verse for bed and board. Lindsay had once gone to college to study theology and he never lost a certain fundamentalist and mystic quality. In 1912 he published *General William Booth Enters into Heaven,* indicating that it was to be sung to the tune of "The Blood of the Lamb" with bass drums, banjos, flutes, and tambourines. This was a touching picture that might easily have aroused ridicule in less skilled hands, especially at the point where Booth met his Master face to face. His keen sense for musical rhythm was so successful in the drum sequences of *The Congo and Other Poems* (1914) that the poet felt overwhelmed by the incessant demands of admirers that he recite the jungle refrain. No poet paid a higher tribute to the humane John P. Altgeld than Lindsay did in *The Eagle That Is Forgotten:*

> Sleep softly . . . eagle forgotten . . . under the stone
> Time has its way with you there, and the clay has its own.
> Sleep on, O brave-hearted, O wise man that kindled the flame—
> To live in mankind is far more than to live in a name,
> To live in mankind, far, far more than to live in a name!

In Boston, the energetic and expressive Amy Lowell propagated the New Poetry with such fervor that contemporaries mistook her for the originator of this art form. This daughter of the colonial New England family combined the experimental technique of free verse with a feeling for clear imagery and the music of sound. Of such a quality was her deservedly popular poem, "Patterns" (1915), which dealt delicately yet frankly with the sorrow of a bride-to-be whose lover has been killed "In a pattern called a war." From Maine, a twenty-year-old girl, Edna St. Vincent Millay, suddenly attained national recognition after 1912 when her poem "Renascence" appeared. Like Lindsay and Lowell, she felt intensely the gospel of beauty that the Imagists preached and told in these verses her mystical sense of conversion and exaltation amid the deeply-realized beauties of God and nature.

Edwin A. Robinson of Maine was closer to the nineteenth-century tradition of the great Victorian poets than to the experimental Lowell-Sandburg school, yet he was a part of the deterministic school of literature. Beginning in the nineties with some striking verses showing keen insight, he continued to develop for a generation as a poet of national stature. His characters might have appeared in a naturalistic novel—the prosperous, envied Richard Cory who suddenly "went home and put a bullet through his head"; and the quixotic Miniver Cheevy, "born too late" who "missed the medieval grace of iron clothing," cursed the commonplace, but "called it fate, and kept on drinking." The theme of frustration and suicide in *The Children of the Night* (1897) recurred in his somber, introspective, verses.

5

Nearly nine out of ten Americans could read and write by 1900, but the reading tastes of the masses called for neither realism nor naturalism. Free public schools produced a nation of voracious readers but the resultant literacy was scarcely of the sophisticated, discriminating kind. The sentimental themes of the melodrama on the contemporary stage, and later on the screen, furnished the staple of cheap novels, newspaper features, and magazine fiction. Henry Adams and other observers insisted that women made up most of the novelreading class and left the inference that the relatively sheltered life of the middle-class woman determined the standards of the novel. Technological changes drastically cut the price of printing and paper and made the cheap paper-backed novel available for little more than ten or twenty cents—especially among the "thrillers" for which a vast market existed. Besides, until 1891, when an international copyright agreement was signed, the works of foreign authors could be legally printed here without the payment of royalties.

The vogue for romantic historical fiction, obviously escapist in nature, reached mountainous proportions in 1894-1902. Elegant aristocrats, dashing heroes and beautiful ladies, and thrilling romantic episodes were furnished to the millions in Anthony Hope's oft-reprinted *The Prisoner of Zenda* (1894) and his *Rupert of Hentzau* (1898). The Indiana newspaper editor, George Barr McCutcheon, won innumerable readers for his Gothic romance, *Graustark* (1901); the following year he was also to do well with his light comedy, *Brewster's Millions.* Another Indiana author of perennial romantic favorites was Charles Major, of Indianapolis, who made a huge success of *When Knighthood Was in Flower* (1898) and *Dorothy*

Vernon of Haddon Hall (1902). In most of these books the reader could usually count on the triumph of daring youth and trusting beauty.

Another type of popular theme for the millions was the idealistic, semireligious story built of artificial characters and sermonizing, sentimental dialogue. A Civil War chaplain, Edward P. Roe, combined this type of moral story with the absorbing interest of a "rags-to-riches" hero. According to Frank L. Mott's *Golden Multitudes*, the Roe books have attracted at least four or five million readers. The next generation knew Harold Bell Wright's works even better. This ailing minister had gone to the Ozarks for his health and used this experience to write *The Shepherd of the Hills* (1907), an idealistic tale of a city preacher who came to the Ozarks and discovered an informal, personal religion of ethics. This and many other "best-sellers" such as *The Winning of Barbara Worth* (1911) eventually reached over ten million readers, mostly of the middle class. Combining the attractions of the religious novel and the historical romance was Lew Wallace's *Ben Hur* (1880) which, as already noted, sold more than two million copies within the half-century following its publication.

The adventure story, especially the western, was nearly always among the best-selling books. Beadle and Company issued an avalanche of paper-backed dime novels of adventure and melodrama. This enterprising house sold over four million of these books during the Civil War years alone. Jack London's Alaskan and Klondike tales fascinated all; both young and old were among his devotees. Rex Beach, of Michigan, probably made a profitable change by giving up law to write such light favorites as *The Spoilers* (1906), and *The Barrier* (1907). As for Zane Grey, the Ohio-born dentist, his occasional visits to the West enabled him to launch an entire library —over fifty titles—of cowboy and badman tales. Not only boys, but their male elders felt the excitement of Grey's *Riders of the Purple Sage* (1912) and *The Lone Star Ranger* (1915). Before this period ended, the prolific Edgar Rice Burroughs had issued *Tarzan of the Apes* (1914) and its numerous sequels.

Boys did not usually complain that most of the 135 titles of Horatio

Alger, Jr., were but minor variations on a single theme: the rags-to-riches progress of a bright, self-reliant rural boy who usually saved the old homestead by going to the city and finding a career. Horatio Alger was formerly a practicing Unitarian minister who had graduated from Harvard in 1852. Much of his own life had consisted of frustrations, but his books did catch on, especially titles like *Struggling Upward* and *Strive and Succeed*. By the time of his death in 1899 he had sold 800,000 copies, according to Mott's estimates, and posthumously over sixteen or seventeen million of his books filled boys' libraries. Public librarians eventually decided that the Alger books did not deserve a place on their shelves, but the vogue went on. Alger was but Carnegie with the philosophy of individualism translated for youngsters.

Girls, and many boys too, read and reread the sentimental but inspiring tales of Louisa May Alcott whose father, Bronson, had been ahead of his time in applying the ideas of progressive education for children. The perennial poverty of the Alcotts was relieved by the striking success of *Little Women* (1868). Louisa never married, but at her readers' insistence she married off her chief character, the self-reliant Jo, in a sequel. The idealistic charm of the Alcott books lingered well into the mid-twentieth century among a nostalgic generation and furnished the themes for several successful motion pictures. In this tradition, though on a far lesser level, was Eleanor Porter's *Pollyanna* (1913), a story of an amazingly cheerful and good little girl; a host of imitators sold millions of Pollyanna-style books.

6

The magazine, reflecting technical advances in reproducing illustrations, became a more attractive literary form, notably among such leaders as the big three of the late nineteenth century: *Harper's Monthly, Century Magazine,* and *Scribner's*. The enhanced status of women, as already noted, was signified by the shift from *Godey's Lady's Book,* a fashionable boudoir journal, to Cyrus Curtis' more civic-minded *Ladies' Home Journal*. This was founded in 1883 and brought to national leadership after 1889 by Edward W. Bok, its editor. Intellectuals usually read the *Atlantic Monthly*, the revived *North American Review*, *Lippincott's Magazine*, or *The Nation*. *Harper's Weekly* enjoyed a crusader's reputation, especially after its cartoonist, Thomas Nast, caricatured the Tweed Ring mercilessly in its pages. Nast is credited with the invention of the tiger symbol for Tammany, the elephant for the Republican party, and the donkey for the Democrats. Although Nast could have become a wealthy man by halting his attacks on Tweed and other corrupt politicians, he preferred his own integrity.

In 1865 an Anglo-Irish immigrant, Edwin L. Godkin, founded *The Nation* as a journal of opinion and established a national tradition for independent, intellectual journalism. Godkin had a gift for trenchant phrases—such as the "chromo civilization" for the age of Grant—and a forthright literary style. Though he was a strong force for honesty in politics and backed the merit system in the civil service, his social philosophy was definitely conservative along the lines of Spencerian individualism. He did not perceive the new social forces behind trade unions and Populism and was unwilling to propose anything more radical than free trade. Nevertheless, he made *The Nation* (and also the *New York Evening Post*) a dominant force in the field of literary and esthetic criticism. One of his chief successors on *The Nation* and the *Evening Post* was the liberal Oswald Garrison Villard, whose connections began during Godkin's final years. With Villard began a reversal in social policy toward the dissenting tradition of his abolitionist grandfather, William Lloyd Garrison.

One of the most important events in magazine history of this era was the rise of "muckraking," the journalistic phase of the Progressive Movement. This represented in part the attitude of social protest in literature that was strong during the 1890's and early 1900's. It was also an incident of the revolutionary economies in publishing achieved through the new technology. The nineteenth-century magazine, as Louis Filler explains, had to use expensive drawings, costly woodcuts, and steel engravings for illustrations. With the development of cheap photoengraving in the nineties, a revolutionary cut in costs was effected. In 1893, Frank Munsey announced that *Munsey's Magazine* would sell at ten cents instead of twenty-five. Others had to follow Munsey's lead. This change in price meant a shift to include a lower-income readers' market and a corresponding change in social outlook. It was natural, therefore, that enterprising magazine publishers like S. S. McClure, Hearst, and others as well as Munsey, should eventually turn to popular articles on the abuses of corporate monopolies and urban politics. At the opening of the century *McClure's Magazine*, founded by an Irish immigrant, employed Ida Tarbell to write exposé articles on the Standard Oil Company and she reached a far larger audience than Henry D. Lloyd had found for his brilliant *Wealth against Commonwealth* (1894) on the same topic.

Lincoln Steffens, who was managing editor of *McClure's*, muckraked the rottenness of urban politics in startling articles that were republished as books in *The Shame of the Cities* (1904) and *The Struggle for Self-Government* (1906). Steffens liked to emphasize the fact that the boss system was partly due to bribery by otherwise honest citizens who desired business advantages denied them by the law. Also on the staff of *McClure's* and the *American Magazine* was Ray Stannard Baker, who dealt with labor racketeering and other themes. Baker became closely identified with the peace movement of Woodrow Wilson, and as the president's close friend he acted as his biographer and literary executor. In those days, too, the conservative Republican journalist, Mark Sullivan, was a muckraker for *Collier's* and attacked the patent medicine frauds.

Upton Sinclair, the socialist writer, was able to get published in *Collier's* only a small part of his revelation regarding conditions in meat packing, but he made up for this setback by publishing *The Jungle* and getting the attention of the entire nation from President Roosevelt down to the humblest citizen who felt revolted to read about the filth of the stockyards, which affected the food he ate. Sinclair's book goaded reformers to pass the Meat Inspection Act in 1906 while other muckrakers and government reformers particularly Harvey Wiley, at the same time promoted the passage of the

Pure Food and Drug Act. The exposé articles of David Graham Phillips on "The Treason of the Senate," attacking the corrupt alliance of industrialists and senators, undoubtedly had much to do with the passage of the Seventeenth Amendment providing for the direct election of senators. It was the unkindest cut of all when the future standard-bearer of the Progressive party, Theodore Roosevelt, culled from Bunyan's *Pilgrim's Progress* a derogatory term for these reform journalists: "muckrakers." Although the muckraking journals were in so many instances more concerned with revenue than radical reform, Roosevelt feared that the movement might get out of hand.

Among the conservatives who tried to reply to the muckrakers was Elbert Hubbard, editor of *The Philistine,* a "bohemian" magazine influenced by the romantic handicraft ideas of William Morris. *The Philistine* reached a circulation of 225,000 and Hubbard branched out into other ventures. However, Hubbard was no follower of Morris' socialist ideas, nor did he thoroughly understand the implications of his revolt against machine culture. Instead, he dwelt upon the success pattern of the American businessman and the philosophy he represented. Industrialists were happy to circulate among their employees an estimated 40,000,000 copies of Hubbard's essay, *A Message to Garcia* (1899), which used as an object lesson the story of Rowan who was sent by President McKinley to make contact with the Cuban rebel leader, García. The fact that Rowan went ahead and did not ask McKinley, "Where is he at?" was to Hubbard the crucial point. Employees, Hubbard lamented, had no such initiative as Rowan and they must be weeded out to bring out "the survival of the fittest." This type of failure who asks the boss to take his own message was a firebrand of discontent. "He is impervious to reason, and the only thing that can impress him is the toe of a thick-soled No. 9 boot." Hubbard continued his eulogy of the businessman in *Loyalty in Business* (1921), a work posthumously published (he went down with the *Lusitania* in 1915). Like other conservatives who took Darwin and Spencer to heart, he subscribed to the doctrine that nature had selected a favorite élite to rule the masses.

7

This optimistic generation, which believed that science was already opening the door to untold riches and happiness, liked to put the adjective "New" before almost any of the social studies, literary movements, and sciences. It was therefore highly appropriate to speak of the New Journalism. This development arose from technological and urban factors. Americans had long been a nation of newspaper readers, but the fullest potentialities of circulation among the poor and semiliterate had not yet been tapped. The mass newspaper had appeared before the Civil War through the penny press, but its existence was assured by such technological changes as the conversion of woodpulp into newsprint during 1875-1900. This meant that an essential cost factor was reduced by nine-tenths. The linotype machine (c. 1886) permitted speedy typesetting by eliminating the laborious and costly hand-setting process. Typewriters affected the speed and efficiency of editorial offices and helped create a vital role for the "rewrite man." Reporters became ever more intrusive in their news coverage, aided by the telephone and improved transportation. The speed of telegraphic news made it advantageous to create a separate afternoon and evening edition or an entirely new newspaper in order to satisfy the curiosity of readers for the latest despatches. In fact the expanding telegraph services had an enormous influence on the newspaper. Foreign news, especially war news, could be wired by staff reporters or special war correspondents. Since this was too expensive for any single paper, syndicated news services arose, among them the Associated Press, which held a monopolistic position during most of this era. In 1907, Edward Wyllis Scripps, the democratically-minded journalist, led a group of rivals to organize a competing news agency in the United Press.

The mechanized press was a big business itself and tended increasingly to be conservative in basic philosophy, especially under the pressure of large advertisers. On the other hand, the penny and two-penny newspaper had to scrutinize sharply the social and economic makeup of its subscribers. It might be very profitable to beat the drum for an antibusiness crusade, as Hearst and Pulitzer did for a time. Another approach to mass circulation was to emphasize sensationalism for its own sake—"yellow journalism"—and to add engrossing features and pictures. All these factors, technological and commercial, help to explain the increase of daily newspapers during 1850-1900 from 254 to 2226, representing a circulation increase from 758,454 to 15,102,156. By 1900 an integrating process set in, and the absolute number of newspapers increased slowly to 1910 and thereafter began to decline while the circulation figures continued to climb. Thus, in 1900-10 the number of daily newspapers grew only from 2226 to 2600, but the circulation rose from 15,102,156 to 24,211,977.

Personal journalism was far from dead by the end of this era, despite the tendency toward bigness in newspapers. It is true that old James Gordon Bennett of the *New York Herald* died in 1872, but his son of the same name continued the vigorous personal tradition and financed Henry Stanley in his trip to darkest Africa to search for the missionary, David Livingstone, amid endless columns of publicity for the paper. Horace Greeley of the *New York Tribune* died about the same time as the elder Bennett, and his liberal pro-labor policy was sharply reversed by his successor, Whitelaw Reid, but the new editor dominated policy through his own uncompromising personality. The perpetuation of the personal tradition might have been costly in circulation had these papers not adapted themselves to popular tastes by adding features of sensational interest. Editorials were less assured of readers than before.

The pattern of the New Journalism was largely set by Joseph Pulitzer, though he added no single element that had not been used to some extent by antebellum newspapers. Pulitzer had been associated with the responsible and intellectual Carl Schurz in St. Louis journalism, but he had also risen by the rough-and-tumble methods of the Missouri frontier. In 1878 he had bought the bankrupt *St. Louis Dispatch* and combined it successfully with another paper as the *St. Louis Post-Dispatch*. Pulitzer did very well with his crusading technique against political corruption, but his chief editor antagonized local public opinion by shooting (in self-defense) a lawyer who had resented the slurs against him in the paper. After this, the owner decided to go East and buy the *New York World* from Jay Gould. The principles of the New Journalism that he laid down to his staff emphasized the resourceful reporting of the colorful and unusual. He also repeated in these early years that the *World* would serve as a prolabor paper, demanding a tax on luxuries, inheritances, incomes, and corporations, and calling for a low tariff, a merit system in government, and anticorruption laws.

In his dynamic way Pulitzer created an unusually able staff, built up sensational reporting stunts in the best Bennett manner, and increased the use of headlines, pictures, sketches, and human-interest stories. When Hearst appeared as a competitor in 1896, Pulitzer cut his price to one cent and his staff resorted to the tactics of yellow journalism—scare headlines, lurid sex and crime stories, more stunts, and cartoons. Although the *New York World* was scarcely behind Hearst in demanding war against Spain, Pulitzer tried to oppose militarism and imperialism. He became blind by the nineties, but attempted to keep his control over the paper. In 1903 he left $2,000,-000 to Columbia University for a new school of journalism, and for the Pulitzer Prizes "for the encouragement of public service, public morals, American literature, and the advancement of education."

William Randolph Hearst, son of a millionaire miner, had bought the *San Francisco Examiner* in 1880, and had experimented with Pulitzer's methods. But this became too tame an enterprise for the young man's ambitions and he left to buy the *New York Journal* in 1895 and to battle the mighty Pulitzer himself. Conveniently provided with a vast fortune, Hearst threw in his money recklessly to outdo Pulitzer, copying the prolabor policy and the sensational features. He hired away key members of the *World's* staff, including Arthur Brisbane, the Sunday editor, who was given a fabulous salary to popularize the glib wisdom associated with his name. The term "yellow journalism" was a product of the Hearst-Pulitzer battle and apparently arose from the yellow sheets in the feature section.

The story of Hearst's amazing efforts to bring this country into the Spanish-American War has often been told. This attack upon a weak foreign country, which might have been persuaded to make all the concessions demanded by Cuban patriots, was only in part an incident of a circulation war between Hearst and Pulitzer. It must be pointed out that Hearst had merely seized on a long-smoldering popular issue and that he was able to get war editorials written by such a humanitarian as Governor Altgeld of Illinois. Though Altgeld and the liberal Democrats wanted to free the Cubans, they also fought, later, against imperialism and expansionism. During the war both the *Journal* and the *World* advanced their circulation beyond a million a day and finally to a million and a half. "How do you like the *Journal's* War?" ran the masthead of Hearst's paper. Other newspapers, though not all, followed this lead. Hearst entered the Chicago field and founded the *Chicago Evening American* and the *Chicago Morning Examiner*. Competitors, appalled by this invasion, hired thugs to drive the paper off the streets, but Hearst struck back in kind with his own hirelings. Urging popular causes, which endeared him to Democratic leaders like Bryan, Hearst was a formidable candidate in 1904 for the Democratic presidential nomination. Seldom had the power of the New Journalism been so startlingly displayed as in the case of this newspaper giant.

A far greater exponent of the New Journalism without its sensationalism was Adolph Simon Ochs (1858–1935). Ochs had been born in Cincinnati and was married to the daughter of the American leader of Reform Judaism, Rabbi Isaac M. Wise of that city. Like Wise, Ochs remained non-Zionist, regarding Judaism as a religion rather than a national culture. His father, a Union veteran, had settled in Knoxville, Tennessee, and the son began to work as a newsboy, rising rapidly in the newspaper business until he was able to buy the *Chattanooga Times* in 1878. Under his policy of responsible journalism, this Southern paper rose to national eminence.

When Ochs purchased the *New York Times* in 1896, it was practically bankrupt and hopelessly adrift in a world that seemed to demand only sensationalism. Former editors had already established a reputation for integrity, civic consciousness, and a cosmopolitan outlook, but Ochs had to solve the problem of keeping this type of

paper alive in the day of blatant yellow journalism. His reply to
the sensational Hearst-Pulitzer formula was his masthead slogan,
"All the News That's Fit to Print." He insisted on genuine news, not
merely the synthetic "human-interest" story, a wide coverage of
foreign news by experts, political non-partisanship, and the exclusion
of fraudulent advertising. He took the adventurous step of cutting
the price to one cent, showing his faith in the existence of serious
reading interests among low-income groups. Cautiously, he kept a
middle-of-the-road political policy—perhaps a little right of center
—and made the editorial opinions of the *Times* widely respected
among all classes and its news reports extensive and exceptionally
reliable. From the standpoint of American journalism, he was influential in stemming the advance of crude yellow journalism and
in showing that there were readers who would patronize serious
newspapers, perhaps even one without a comic strip.

Out of the English immigration came a remarkable family of
journalists of integrity and social idealism, the Scrippses. Edward
W. Scripps was born on an Illinois farm, the son of a London book-
binder. His elder brother James became the publisher of the *Detroit
Tribune* and gave him his start through a loan. In 1878, Edward
Scripps began the *Cleveland Penny Press* (now the *Cleveland Press*)
and introduced his liberal ideas favoring labor and combatting
municipal boss-rule. By 1892, there was a chain of five Scripps
papers, the nucleus of the thirty or more that existed at his death
in 1926. With a colleague he set up the Scripps-McRae Press Association in 1895 as a news-gathering agency to compete with the
Associated Press; Hearst entered this field in 1906 with the International News Service. Some of these Scripps publishing interests
were merged as the United Press in 1907. Beginning in 1902, his
Newspaper Enterprise Association offered a syndicated service to
newspapers both outside and within his chain, including cartoons
and feature articles. This was a novel step in the direction of syndicated journalism, a tendency that meant a higher standard of
journalism but a more impersonal tone. Frequent interference with
local journalistic independence and spontaneous expression at the

"grass roots" arose with the advent of chains, especially those in the hands of men less responsible than E. W. Scripps.

American literary realism owed its inspiration to Europe, but native writers did not apply the realistic formula slavishly. Whatever philosophic confusion existed in the minds of the novelists and poets came in large part from the conflict between the idealized traditional world and the experimental iconoclastic spirit of the new scientific era of Darwin. The city and the industrial machine generated the uprooted feeling of the contemporary readers of Howells, Norris, James, and the young Dreiser. Poetry entered the ranks of literary realism through Imagism—another imported movement—which stressed the language of common speech. Imagism disappeared as a vogue but realism remained. However, Whitman had already shown the way to poetic realism.

Popular reading tastes remained, as in the past, escapist in nature, distant from the realities of historical events, the West, adolescence, and city life that the paper-backed books professed to describe. Some marked improvement did appear in many of the stories for children, as in the Louisa May Alcott books, which had more resemblance to reality than the sermonizing Rollo books and their rivals of antebellum days. Women's reading tastes reflected the gradual emancipation of the feminine sex, as is clear in the shift from fashion magazines like *Godey's* to the more socially-aware *Ladies' Home Journal*. Most important as a realistic influence in the field of periodical literature was the muckraking movement with its critical awareness of social problems. As for the New Journalism, it is true that technology created a more impersonal and syndicated press, but the necessity for reaching a mass market led to a greater emphasis on the urban problems of labor, municipal corruption, and industrial monopoly, as well as upon gross sensationalism.

16

Toward Realism in the Arts: Louis Sullivan and Winslow Homer

[1865-1917]

I

In 1873 the severe economic depression cost the seventeen-year-old Louis Sullivan his position in a Philadelphia office of architects. Like many other aspiring architects, he left for Chicago where the Great Fire of 1871 had so demolished the city that unlimited opportunities existed for builders. Fire insurance made possible the rapid reconstruction of Chicago. Sullivan then assisted in making drawings for the popular Victorian Gothic buildings, "Gothic in pantalettes" as he afterwards called it. His utter contempt for the crude imitativeness of this era of architecture possibly exceeded that of any other man—at least so it seemed in later years when he wrote about it in a most sardonic style.

From the Civil War to the Philadelphia Centennial Exposition of 1876, wealthy American businessmen toured Europe and brought back a liking for the pretentious and ponderous Victorian Gothic of England, the lavish French Renaissance style of Louis Napoleon's Second Empire, or the semimedieval half-timbered mixture known as the Queen Anne style. The fondness of parvenu aristocrats for the permanence implied in massive medieval castles with turrets, huge stones, and innumerable arches was too often served by unskilled native builders.

England's Gothic Revival had appeared during the middle eighteenth century, long before John Ruskin and William Morris rationalized it in the nineteenth century as an expression of the creative instinct in man. The English-born American, Richard Up-john, had introduced English Gothic principles in 1839 when he designed the new Trinity Church of New York city in place of the old colonial-style building. This marked the beginning—at least as a sustained movement—of the American Gothic Revival. Ruskin's *Stones of Venice* focused architectural taste upon the North Italian variety of Gothic but Morris' handicraft ideal was too often vulgarized as the shapeless, uncomfortable furniture of the mid-century. In the United States, where architectural technique and public taste lagged behind that of Western Europe, the result was an over-decorated style in houses and furniture that shocked the discriminating. The Victorian Gothic home was recognizable by its towers, gambrel roofs, projecting bay windows, and decorative cast-iron dogs on the lawn. The irregularly-spaced windows failed to keep the rooms and long narrow halls from somber darkness. Worse yet were the cluttered-up furniture, the vogue for horsehair or plush, the ponderous walnut bedsteads, and the bric-a-brac of all kinds set against a background of garish wallpaper.

Queen Anne's architecture was an eclectic potpourri derived from contemporary English country house styles. Within the mixture were usually Jacobean gables, tall Tudor chimneys, imitation half-timbering, and a sprinkling of baroque ornamentation. Far more popular than the Queen Anne style and easily the strongest competitor of the Victorian Gothic was the French Renaissance style of the Second Empire. The Empress Eugenie had already provided American women with the fads in hats and crinoline dresses associated with her name. Empire furniture, elegant home interiors, and fine ironwork exteriors had been freely imitated here since the antebellum decades. At the same time, American architects applied the French mansard roof, the cupola, and other details of the Gallic Renaissance styles to innumerable homes, churches, and commercial buildings. The prewar craze for brownstone front buildings prevailed in the well-to-do neighborhoods and was often associated with the Second Empire style. A later generation in Washington Square, New York, or the Michigan Avenue Gold Coast of Chicago wondered at such exaggerations as the extremely high ceilings, the high narrow windows and doors, and the marble fireplaces. There seemed a naïve reliance upon distorted versions of approved European styles rather than upon the common-sense promptings of comfort and good taste. The colonial functionalist ideal of adapting architecture to the needs of its occupants was dead. The Philadelphia Centennial Exposition of 1876, as seen in retrospect, certainly showed no improvement over the architecture of the Revolutionary era; quite to the contrary, it gave the impression of artistic retrogression and sterility. Lewis Mumford has called this era "The Brown Decades," implying a dominant atmosphere of decay.

The most facile and sophisticated exponent of the French Renaissance style was Richard M. Hunt, a Vermont-born architect who served the Vanderbilts, the Belmonts, the Astors, and others of the commercial aristocracy. Hunt was one of the first Americans to study architecture at the École des Beaux-Arts in Paris; this experience of 1854–57 marked the beginning of an increasing class of expert Paris-trained architects in America. In New York, Hunt made his studio a school for American architects—a novel institution—and was one of the founders of the American Institute of Architects which originated in the office of Richard Upjohn in 1857. An eclectic in taste, Hunt provided wealthy Americans with French Renaissance mansions or, as in the case of William K. Vanderbilt's Fifth Avenue home, a French chateau done in his most meticulous and restrained fashion. He left behind him such varied buildings of note as Harvard's Fogg Museum, New York's Lenox Library, and that city's *Tribune* Building.

For the urban masses, of course, both Victorian Gothic and French Empire styles were out of the question, except as remote models to be copied in the most attenuated form. New York city was largely a conglomeration of tenements, marked by the distinctive dumbbell shaped ground plan. Crowding, as already noted in the discussion of immigration, produced no aesthetic fruits in housing. The Civil War photographer, Mathew B. Brady, has left detailed photographs of Southern cities like Richmond and Charleston, but these show plain though substantial two-story buildings with an architectural mediocrity and monotony exceeded only by the "popular-priced" houses of mid-twentieth century real-estate promoters. One of the factors in the American standard of living that has lagged behind all others is housing at the lower income levels.

2

With the advent of Henry Hobson Richardson American architecture emerged from the eclectic chaos that had existed since the decline of the Greek Revival before the Civil War. Richardson had been born in 1838 at the Priestley sugar plantation in Louisiana. His father had been a prosperous businessman who usually took his family to New Orleans to spend the winters. The boy would have liked to go to West Point, but his speech impediment disqualified him, and he went, instead, to study engineering at Harvard and later, like Richard Hunt, attended the École des Beaux-Arts. Although this famous Paris academy was officially devoted to classicism, Richardson was too original an architect to borrow any style without adding his own personal characteristics. He fell in love with the great arches and vast interiors of the Romanesque buildings in Auvergne and Northern Spain and not long after his return to New York in 1866 he rebelled against the "stupid Victorian classic," the "Ruskinian Gothic," and the other current styles.

During the early 1870's Richardson designed his most famous building, Trinity Church on Copley Square, Boston. Scholars later discovered that this French Romanesque building was no mere archaeological variant of the Middle Ages, but an original "Richardsonian Romanesque," a definite American style. Like the medieval church-builder, he called in all types of artists, not merely competent artisans, including the gifted painter, John La Farge, the sculptor, Augustus Saint-Gaudens, and later the Ruskinians, Sir Edwin Burne-Jones and William Morris, who collaborated in planning or executing the best of the Trinity windows. Burne-Jones, like Morris, belonged to the Pre-Raphaelite Brotherhood of painters who sought to interpret life in a manner to convert people to the higher ideals of unsophisticated beauty as it existed in Italy (so they thought) among the "Primitive" late medieval painters before Raphael. Richardson and his assistant, Stanford White, felt inspired by a picture of the Cathedral of Salamanca in Spain to develop the tower and certain parts of the basic structure of Trinity. The plaster walls of the interior were painted to recapture the glowing colors characteristic of Romanesque churches. Altogether, this was a fitting building for one of the greatest spiritual leaders of the nation, Phillips Brooks, best remembered today for his Christmas hymn, "O Little Town of Bethlehem." For the Protestant Episcopal Church to which Brooks belonged, Trinity Church served its ritualistic tendency well by its rich, partly Byzantine decorations and the massive dignity of its interior.

Richardson adapted his art to industrial as well as ecclesiastic needs and he showed the interest of a functionalist in modern problems. "The things I want most to design," he once said, "are a grain elevator and the interior of a great river steamboat." With a keen eye for serviceability as well as esthetics he did numerous railroad stations, libraries, and other public buildings, including part of the Harvard Law School. One of his most successful commercial structures was the Marshall Field Wholesale Building in Chicago, which showed a functionalist's regard for ample lighting and space. Louis Sullivan, who acknowledged Richardson as a master, wrote this enthusiastic evaluation:

Four-square and brown it stands, in physical fact a monument to trade, to the organized commercial spirit, to the power and progress of the age, to the strength and resource of individuality and force of character; spiritually it stands as the index of a mind large enough to cope with the things, taste them, absorb them and give them forth impressed with the stamp of a large and forceful character; artistically it stands as the creation of one who knows well how to choose his words, who has something to say and says it as the outpouring of a copious, direct, large and simple mind.

Critics have disagreed on whether Richardson was the first modern American architect or merely a reformer belonging to the traditional historic schools. In a broad sense he was a functionalist like Sullivan in understanding that a building must be a natural part of its environment and the culture of the time. But he lacked interest in new materials such as the developments in metal, which functionalists stress. Masonry was his forte and he seemed content to cling to it. Within these limitations he gave vital impulse to the imitative architecture of the Gilded Age and raised the general standard. Unfortunately, his uninspired imitators abused his principles until they quite extinguished the Richardsonian vogue during the decade after his death in 1886.

3

During the nineties the pendulum swung back from medieval romanticism in architecture to academic classicism and Italian Renaissance styles. This tendency was popularized through a former associate of Richardson's, Charles F. McKim. In New England his noted firm of McKim, Mead, and White built some of the most distinguished structures of the decade. Fittingly—or challengingly— they designed the classical Boston Public Library (1895) just opposite Richardson's Romanesque Trinity Church and, like him, invited the leading sculptors and painters to aid in the decoration: John Singer Sargent, Edwin A. Abbey, Daniel Chester French, Augustus Saint-Gaudens, and Puvis de Chavannes. Among their chief commissions were Madison Square Garden (1891) and the monumental library building (among others) of Columbia University. They even undertook certain modifications of the classical University of Virginia in order to bring out more of certain neglected architectural ideas of Jefferson. McKim's interest in architectural education—his own office was an eagerly sought-after school— led him to sponsor and partially to finance the American Academy in Rome, intended as a training center for American architects.

The Chicago Columbian Exposition of 1893 under the direction of Daniel H. Burnham of Chicago went far toward establishing the vogue of the Classical Revival. Burnham and his partner John Root represented one of the most successful architectural firms that had sprung up in Chicago after the Great Fire. Their Masonic Temple, built in 1890, was acclaimed the tallest building in the world and they were even credited with the origin of the term "skyscraper." Alert to the uses of the new metals, they had been quick to adopt the completely riveted steel frame for their tall buildings. However, as Burnham became financially successful, he delegated more and more of his work to subordinates and developed a fondness, according to his critic Louis Sullivan, for what was the tallest and the biggest. To Sullivan—and quite unfairly—Burnham was merely a "colossal merchandiser." His chief sin in the eyes of the father of American modernism was his readiness during the World's Fair to allow Eastern architects like McKim to fasten the Classical Revival upon America through the contagious example set by the Fair buildings. Sullivan, addicted to scornful phrases, wrote that these "classic and Renaissance merchants" had spread the "virus of the World's Fair" for a "bogus antique." The visitors to the Fair, he said, "saw, but an imposition of the spurious upon their eyesight, a naked exhibitionism of charlatanry in the higher feudal and domineering culture, conjoined with expert salesmanship of the materials of decay."

While it is doubtful whether the World's Fair set back the cause of modern architecture as far as Sullivan believed, it proved to be the most impressive spectacle since Americans had begun copying and improving upon the English and French public exhibitions of the mid-century. On the Fair grounds landscape gardening showed the high degree of maturity it had reached under landscape architects like Frederick Law Olmsted, who converted the sandy and marshy wastes of Jackson Park into a fairyland of park, lagoons, islands, and beautiful flowers. The seventy-year-old Olmsted had once been nationally known for his books on the antebellum South such as *The Cotton Kingdom* (1861). Since then he had designed Central Park in New York and Prospect Park in Brooklyn. He and his son, Frederick, Jr., were pioneers in city planning and the organization of state and national parks.

The gleaming whiteness of the Fair buildings, which enhanced the illusion that ancient Rome had come back to life, was achieved by simply whitewashing the exteriors with a squirt gun. Thus Chicago became the White City—however incongruous this flattering color seemed for the "Hog Butcher for the World." Crowds were impressed by the classical architectural atmosphere, the concerts of Theodore Thomas, the displays of new machinery, the world congress of religions, and the fascinating concession stands along the Midway. A half century later elderly men and women looked back with nostalgia upon this experience as one of the most exciting of their lives.

4

Louis Sullivan was the greatest rebel against mere architectural "revivals" divorced from any context with the modern environment and experience. He was born in 1856 in Boston of an Irish father and a Swiss-French mother and shared their volatile emotional temperament. He learned much as a draftsman in the Chicago office of Major William Le Baron Jenney, the first to adopt the steel skeleton in the construction of tall buildings. During 1874 Sullivan studied at the École des Beaux-Arts, but his entire life was a rejection of its classical tenets. Richardson, as we have seen, influenced him and he made no secret of his indebtedness to the functionalist element in the Richardsonian style. Chicago, where Sullivan and his partner Dankmar Adler did most of their work after 1879, was a stimulating place for architects and offered many opportunities for experimentation. In designing Chicago's Auditorium Building Sullivan drew upon the inspiration of Richardson's Marshall Field Warehouse Building to apply his ideal that "form follows function"—that the purpose of the building must be faithfully expressed in the architectural façades as well as in the interior details. At the World's Fair the rebellious Sullivan made his Transportation Building a decided exception to the rule adopted by the architects of classical dominance.

However, his chief importance in the field of architecture was as a teacher, a propagandist, and a prophet of modernism. His book,

Autobiography of an Idea (1924), published the year of his death, shows a fervent belief in functionalism. Darwin, Spencer, and evolutionary thought had been revelations to him. He derived from them the functionalist notion that buildings, like living biological organisms, must adapt themselves to their natural environment. Besides, the scientific evolutionists and pragmatists encouraged him to break with the absolute represented by historical styles and to embark upon experiments to discover the relationship of buildings to modern living needs. To superimpose a foreign design, whether it be classical, Romanesque, or Gothic upon a modern factory, hotel, bank, or home ignored the intimate relationship of art and life. Thus the skyscraper, which Sullivan admired, must be interpreted in its relation to the urban environment and its feature of tallness must be accentuated through simple vertical lines. Besides, its steel construction imposed the need for vertical continuity of design. It must look "like a proud and soaring thing." The Gothic style was wholly inappropriate to achieving this effect. Thus, in the hands of Sullivan and his followers the skyscraper became an original American contribution to architecture.

Sullivan, who continued to be active and successful for many years after McKim and the Fair had revived classical architecture and a chaos of eclecticism, eventually saw his ideal of the functionalist skyscraper expressed in Eliel Saarinen's uncompromisingly modern design for the Chicago Tribune Building, which won only a second prize, it is true, but was widely acclaimed as a masterpiece by discerning architects. Like Emerson and Whitman, he preached against the suicidal imitation of alien aristocratic ideas. He called for a new architecture that could express the individualist, democratic, and optimistic facts of American life. America, he thought, had no need for the static and aristocratic classicism of the École des Beaux-Arts, which ran counter to the invigorating American faith in progress and the experimental spirit.

Sullivan's chief disciple, Frank Lloyd Wright, had worked in the office of Adler and Sullivan and was fully as uncompromising as Sullivan and even more articulate in his theories of modernist architecture. Disliking the crowded city and its offshoot, the sky-scraper, he preached decentralization and designed the home in its relation to living comfort and the contour of the landscape. Historical styles were anathema to him. His "prairie houses," which stressed low horizontal lines and projecting eaves in keeping with the level land, won him a wide reputation even in the prewar years. A German architect "discovered" him in 1908 and publicized Wright's work so widely that Europe eagerly adopted him and made his ideas an important part of the International Style. Japan praised Wright in 1915–16 when he designed the Imperial Hotel in Tokyo. But Americans were not quite ready—not until the late 1920's in fact—to take their own prophets too seriously. Neo-classicism was still in the saddle.

5

Scarcely less vehement than Sullivan and Wright as a critic of classicism and eclecticism was the neo-medievalist, Ralph Adams Cram (1863–1942). He came from a small New Hampshire town but eventually settled in Boston and organized the firm of Cram, Goodhue, and Ferguson to specialize in church architecture. Though his father was a Unitarian minister, the youth had been converted—partly through the surviving English "Back to Rome" movement—to a very High Church Anglicanism. This orientation gave him a strong sympathy for Ruskin, Morris, and the Gothic ideal. Richardson had impressed him with his original application of medieval architectural forms to modern conditions. He developed a basic thesis derived from Catholic and Anglican sources that Gothic architecture was the only appropriate expression for Christian culture and that classicism was the art of paganism. As for the Renaissance, it was only a classical derivative, "a brazen affectation of all the vices and evils of paganism." Only in the Middle Ages, he thought, did man achieve a unity in his religious, artistic, and economic life. Cram felt only contempt for the individualism rampant since the Reformation. In *The Gothic Quest* (1907), he declared:

Realism, naturalism, impressionism, eclecticism, are really but the results of the powerful influence of the contemporary spirit on art, exactly as agnosticism and rationalism are its consequences in another direction, as democracy and the competitive system and mammonism are its results in yet other fields.

However, he was willing to concede that even Colonial art and Jeffersonian classicism were not wholly divorced from the culture of their day. But since the rise of the masses in 1830—taking the form of Jacksonian democracy—all taste had degenerated. Even the Gothic Revival did not please him because it was essentially eclectic and crude rather than a true continuation of the historical development of Gothic arrested by the Renaissance and the Reformation. In later years he attacked modernism as devoid of tradition and merely monotonous.

Cram's neo-medievalism professed to be as functionalist as Richardson's Romanesque, but more authentic in its relation to Christian civilization. His best ecclesiastical work was in connection with the vast Cathedral of St. John the Divine which was entrusted to his firm for completion in 1911. He liked to cite as an example of his theory the design for Rice Institute, Houston, in 1910. The administration building, he declared, was faithfully adapted to the materials and climate of its Southwest environment:

A special rose-hued brick, with a wonderful rose-and-dove-coloured marble we found in Oklahoma; red Texas granite, many coloured marbles for columns and sheathing, from Greece, Italy, Switzerland, Vermont, and Tennessee; glazed, iridescent tiles, green bronze—everything we could think of to give richness, variety, and a certain splendor of effect.

He also converted the United States Military Academy at West Point into a Gothic citadel.

Though Cram was admittedly out of step with the pragmatic spirit of American thought, he attracted the traditionalists who looked for permanence behind the world of change. His aristocratic ideal of a cultural elite was at variance with the current democratic faith in the potentialities of the plain people. The nostalgia for the Middle Ages, so apparent in the later writings of

Henry Adams as well, reflected the intellectuals' search for absolute certainty that science seemed to deny its devotees.

Gothic was enthusiastically patronized by the captains of industry. Upton Sinclair's *Goose Step* satirized the poor natural lighting and discomforts of John D. Rockefeller's Gothic buildings at the new University of Chicago. In later years Chicagoans gaped as they walked past the huge turreted castle of the Potter Palmers along fashionable Lake Shore Drive. Oscar Wilde offended citizens of this metropolis by his cruel comments on the tastelessness of their intricate Gothic water towers. Whitney imported a medieval staircase from Europe and Charles Yerkes even fitted his business office with medieval stained glass. Gothic apparently symbolized power, permanence, and strength to the parvenu millionaire anxious for status. Its aesthetic value, as Veblen observed, was secondary to their desire for "conspicuous consumption" and personal repute.

6

Painting, like architecture, could not escape the atmosphere of urban industry and Darwinian science, though traditionalists fought to continue the forms of art that had grown out of a social order that had died long before. At the end of the century art rebels denounced the classical academic principles of the École des Beaux-Arts and searched for realistic forms that could interpret modern life just as faithfully as did the works of the literary realists and naturalists. Meanwhile, the postbellum decades were dominated by the pleasant romanticism of the "genre" painters who usually tended to be nostalgic in their treatment of what were intended to be pictures of everyday life among the lowly.

Still another vogue was that of the equally pleasing landscape artists—"the Hudson River School" of Bierstadt and others, which was maturing far beyond the naïve technique of Leutze and the original Düsseldorf group. Winslow Homer, George Inness, and other rising painters departed from the studied pastoral simplicity of Cole and Durand to raise American landscape painting to a subtle, realistic, and experimental art. The millions of dollars that the captains of industry poured into the paintings of the Old European masters did very little for creative young artists, although they enabled countless Americans to enjoy and study the masterpieces. Many of these famous paintings were secluded in elegant mansions and kept as a safe monetary investment whose value was not likely to decline too much at the dealer's auction. In those decades few American artists could hope to earn a livelihood from their paintings—a condition that has improved only to a moderate extent today.

Gothic religious art and Japanese aestheticism attracted both American and European painters. In the 1850's, while Ruskin and the Pre-Raphaelite Brotherhood were rediscovering the organic beauty of medieval Gothic styles, Commodore Perry opened unknown Japan to the world. One cosmopolitan American artist, John La Farge, was deeply absorbed in these stimulating influences. He was born in 1835 in New York, the son of well-to-do French parents, and was educated in American Catholic colleges and French art schools. At his Washington Square studio he experimented with light and shade, read Ruskin and Morris, and wrote books on Japanese art. He learned about Japan and the South Seas at first hand in 1886 when he went off on a vacation with Henry Adams to the Far East, hoping to get some inspiration for a mural that he planned for New York's Church of the Ascension. In 1876, at a time when the art of murals had scarcely developed in America, La Farge had responded nobly to the challenge of Richardson when that great architect invited him to decorate Trinity Church in Boston. His feeling for spiritual and aesthetic expression made his painting, "The Ascension," the most brilliant mural work of his day.

La Farge's absorption in the Middle Ages led him to invent opaline glass for stained-glass windows, creating a new art and industry. Aided by a Brooklyn immigrant, a glassmaker, La Farge devised an opalescent stained glass which, through refraction, cast delightful nuances of light and color. The brisk demand for the glass both here and abroad and the many honors showered upon him for this work partly compensated for the lack of public patronage for his paintings, though he left many exquisite flower subjects and imaginative religious paintings. Henry Adams, who loved him as an artist and close friend, liked to say that La Farge was not only at home in the twelfth-century cathedrals, but even felt a sort of ownership over them.

Daring American painters of the postbellum era in Paris were often fascinated by the latest French rebellion against the formalism of the Academy—impressionism. Since the 1860's, a group of these impressionists led by Édouard Manet, Claude Monet, and Paul Cézanne had been experimenting with a new form of visual realism derived in part from the principles of optics. Instead of securing brightness of color by merely mixing colors they painted separate colors side by side in such a way that they combined brilliantly at a distance on the retina of the spectator. At close quarters these impressionistic paintings seemed a shocking blur to laymen and academic painters. Impressionists liked to stress the subjective qualities in a painting and called their works by such titles as "Impressions of a Sunrise" and "Impressions of a Forest."

The most gifted American impressionist was the expatriate, James Whistler, who had been loud in his defense of Manet in 1861. Whistler was born in Lowell, Massachusetts, in 1834 but had been raised as a child in Russia, where his father directed a railroad engineering project for the Czar. Although he returned to this country for a time and studied engineering for three years at West Point, his bohemian tastes drew him to France and England, where he remained until his death in 1903. He sniffed at the American tariff against modern foreign paintings, which he thought was a confession of artistic inferiority. In France he admired the vogue for Japanese patterns and silhouettes and applied this technique to his own work. His impressionistic style suited his own particular art creed—"art for art's sake," the independence of aesthetics from morals, or from the necessity of telling a story or teaching a lesson; more than that, his philosophy meant the exclusive competence of the artist rather than the critic to judge the meaning of the painting.

Academicians were angered by his subjective and impressionist titles; he even called his famous "Whistler's Mother" picture "An

Arrangement in Gray and Black." His love for combat led him to sue John Ruskin, the traditionalist, for his disdainful comments on Whistler's paintings in an exhibit. Said Ruskin, "I have seen and heard much of Cockney impudence before now, but never expected to hear a coxcomb ask two hundred guineas for flinging a pot of paint in the public's face." Whistler won the case, though he received but a farthing in damages. Most significant in this Ruskin case is the public expression of the art-for-art's-sake principles and the triumph of the assertion that the artist alone rather than the critic or the public can properly evaluate his own work. Like other Europeans whose aestheticism owed much to the American writer, Edgar Allan Poe, Whistler could say, "As music is the poetry of sound, so is painting the poetry of sight, and the subject-matter has nothing to do with harmony of sound or of color." The story-telling tradition that Howells had minimized in his literary realism Whistler often ignored in art. At the Ruskin trial he shocked traditionalists by saying, "As to what the picture represents it depends upon who looks at it." His etchings, particularly, were such masterpieces of subtle workmanship and delicate handling of light and shade that they influenced other outstanding etchers and gained early recognition. He has been compared with Benjamin West as a great expatriate painter with a considerable European following.

Within the tradition of Whistler and the impressionist school, the Cincinnati-born John Henry Twachtman developed an originality and vigor that set him off from many other Americans who had studied art abroad. His "Snow-Bound" revealed his experimental technique and a keen sense of aesthetic harmony in landscape interpretation. In a similar impressionist mold derived from Manet and the Japanese prints, Mary Cassatt of Philadelphia achieved something far more than mere competence. She preferred idealized motherhood subjects but she could handle these with exquisite skill and a feeling for warm colors. Other Americans too, like Theodore Robinson and Childe Hassam, turned at various times in their careers to the techniques of impressionism. By the time impressionism gave way to postimpressionism and more radical forms American visitors to the galleries became more tolerant and decided that this style might be something more than an unfortunate conglomeration of blurs on the canvas.

To those who looked for a native American art, Winslow Homer (1836–1910) seemed a very promising hope. Homer acquired his rudiments as an apprentice to a Boston lithographer and became a successful magazine illustrator. He garnered a store of rich impressions, such as the incidents of the sea and country life, from his native Massachusetts. These he transmitted faithfully to his canvas. The continuing vogue for genre paintings and for scenes of the American landscape made his subjects immensely popular, as in such works as "Maine Coast," "New England Country School," and "The Gulf Stream." In the latter, he depicted a Negro stranded in a wrecked boat with huge ravenous sharks about him. What was especially realistic about it was the complete resignation and indifference expressed on his face. Homer usually painted only what he saw and knew thoroughly. He achieved his best effects through his skill with water colors in depicting background.

Another major figure among the realists was Thomas Eakins (1844–1916), whose stature in the critics' estimates has risen with the years. He had studied (and later taught) at the Pennsylvania Academy of the Fine Arts in Philadelphia and in Paris. His best-known genre paintings, "Between Rounds," "The Surgical Clinic of Professor Gross," and "The Agnew Clinic" are meticulously descriptive, even to the blood on the surgeon's hand. Boat races, prize fights, as well as portraits are among his work.

Modern critics have been enthusiastic in their evaluation of Albert P. Ryder (1847–1917), who worked obscurely in a New York garret. This opinion was not the general verdict of the nineteenth century. Whether he is merely "the last of the Romanticists" because of his mysticism and symbolism, or one of the greatest American realists of the spirit seems to be a question resolving in favor of the latter. His somber shades and melting forms suggested the mystic that he was; some have called him an impressionist in style though others have compared him with Cézanne in his feeling for firmness of object. Like Melville, he seemed to dwell on poetical symbols and inner experiences of an unworldly nature. Such appeared to be the characteristics of "Toilers of the Sea" and "Death on the Race Track"—the latter a skeleton riding horseback symbolizing the death of a waiter who had committed suicide over a betting loss.

Rebels among the genre realists, led by Robert Henri, assumed an attitude of open defiance toward the conventional academicians in 1908. This Revolt of the Eight—which included Henri's pupils and associates, John Sloan, George Luks, Everett Shinn, George W. Bellows—reflected the attitude of a group who not only stressed native subject matter but wished to deal frankly with the city slums as well. Some of them spoke the language of economic radicalism and socialism, insisting on social consciousness and the rejection of the idea of art-for-art's-sake. Enemies derided them as urban extremists of the "Ash-Can School."

Henri himself had been trained at the Pennsylvania Academy of the Fine Arts and at the École des Beaux-Arts. He was an inspiring teacher and an artist of considerable spontaneity and visual honesty. His pupil George Bellows, like others of this group, was immensely impressed by the satiric social realism of Goya and Daumier. Bellows studied the crowds at Tom Sharkey's place to depict a prize fight (in later years he did a popular picture of the Dempsey-Firpo match) and drew from observation children playing in the street and prayer meetings. Sloan painted a number of East Side scenes such as the evening crowds around the Third Street Elevated. Genre painting had come a long way in frankness of subject matter and treatment since Eastman Johnson's sentimental "Old Kentucky Home" of 1859. Since then, Johnson himself had developed in satiric sense as well as in craftsmanship.

Before Americans had overcome their prejudices against impressionism and the realism of the Eight, they were exposed to another shock—the Armory Show of 1913 in New York with its display of French postimpressionism and other phases of "Modern" art. The sponsors included a secessionist group of artists who called themselves the Association of American Painters and Sculptors. The Eight were not only in their ranks but furnished several of their typical genre paintings to the exhibit. Ryder, Homer, Twachtman, and La Farge were represented. Leading American sculptors also offered their work. Americans now were no longer ashamed of placing their creations for what might be an invidious comparison with the work of the great European contemporaries. Hundreds of thousands came to see the Armory Show while conservative critics raged at its alleged extremism and aesthetic indecency.

Among the various French heretics whose style angered the critics were Paul Cézanne, Vincent Van Gogh, and Pablo Picasso. Cézanne, the leader of the Modern School of Paris who had "wished to make of Impressionism something as solid and durable as the old masters in the museums" secured stability and depth for his landscapes through the use of geometric shapes. His obiter dictum that things tend to take the shape of cones, spheres, and cubes had inspired Picasso and others to embark upon cubism as a form of art. These abstractionists—Picasso and his group—were denounced as "wild beasts"—les fauves—by the French academicians. Some of them painted pictures that were practically devoid of subject matter in the usual sense except for colored geometric forms. Visitors must have asked themselves whether the abstractionists were madmen or the painters of the future. Painting seemed completely stripped of all meaning.

7

American sculpture as compared to European evolved slowly from the mediocre classicism and sentimental idealization typified by Hiram Powers whose "Greek Slave" could be seen throughout the century in innumerable American homes at the head of the stairs or in the parlor. After the Civil War a rash of statues of generals on horseback, admirals, and local heroes broke out in the public squares and parks of American cities and towns. This type of subject called uniformly for patriotic emphasis and idealization, though gifted sculptors could occasionally achieve originality by individualistic variations within the patriotic formula. American sculptors continued to go to Italy to derive their neo-classic technique even after Auguste Rodin (1840–1917) had given France leadership in modern sculpture.

John Quincy Adams Ward of New York, a completely American-trained sculptor, was among the few who escaped the mid-Victorian pseudoclassic and overidealized tradition. His generals and politicians were vigorously interpreted and given a high degree of plausibility. When the planners of Central Park decided to add sculpture to its attractions, Ward was the first man invited. One of these park statues that he executed most successfully was "The Freedman," a seated Negro looking at the shackles that had just been thrown off. Ward had no lack of admirers in his day and was an active organizer among American sculptors.

His most distinguished pupil, if one may regard a month's training as sufficient to establish such a relationship, was Daniel Chester French. He had learned something about drawing from the Paris-trained Louisa May Alcott and the Massachusetts Institute of Technology (for a year) as well as about sculpture from Ward by the time he executed the famous "Minute Man" for Concord, Massachusetts. In the centennial year Lexington and Concord had commemorated the first battle of the Revolutionary War by commissioning French to do the figure, one well known to present-day Americans whose World War II posters for government bond sales carried his version of the Minute Man. He was so faithful in his bust of Emerson that the poet exclaimed humorously, "That is the face I shave." Although French studied in Italy and Paris, his style remained American and his work showed originality and poetic feeling, particularly in the high quality of his interpretation of "Dr. Gallaudet and His First Deaf-Mute Pupil" and "Death Staying the Hand of the Sculptor." Visitors still admire his seated bronze statue of John Harvard in front of University Hall, his Abraham Lincoln statue at Lincoln, Nebraska, and, above all, his Lincoln at the Lincoln Memorial in Washington. His style remained unaffected in its simple idealism and hence clear to the multitudes who loved his work.

But the giant of his day was Augustus Saint-Gaudens. He was born in Dublin in 1848 of a French father and an Irish mother and was brought here as an infant. During his youth he secured an invaluable experience for a future sculptor as a stone-cameo cutter before studying at the École des Beaux-Arts and in Italy. His most realistic work came in 1881 when he completed "Admiral Farragut" for Madison Square Garden and gave a convincing interpretation of an admiral standing on the quarter-deck of his ship. To make his figures as true to life as possible, he read the biographies of the statesmen that he reproduced in stone. Henry Adams chose Saint-Gaudens for the difficult task of expressing in sculpture the bereavement and sense of tragedy that he felt at his wife's suicide. The sculptor responded imaginatively in "The Adams Memorial," which secured abstract somber effects and tremendous power by the use of heavy draperies about the tragic figure of Mrs. Adams. Chicagoans were especially proud of his standing figure of Lincoln in Lincoln Park which conveyed the nobility of the subject. He was enormously productive in creating highly competent public monuments, busts, and portrait tablets. Although he did not join the radicals who assailed the classicism of the École des Beaux-Arts and the Academy at Rome, he was tolerant toward the newer trends arising before his death in 1907 and distinguished himself as a teacher of sculpture and as an articulate leader among American artists.

The revolutionary Rodin influence and inspiration arrived toward the end of this era, though most cultured Americans seemed familiar with his bronze figure, "The Thinker." Rodin expressed the fresh quality of naturalism in sculpture by his imaginative use of successive hollows and projections to achieve light and shadow as well as muscular expression. Among those who followed in this new direction of psychological realism was George Gray Barnard. He had studied amid personal hardships while attending Chicago's Art Institute and later the École des Beaux-Arts. His earliest indication of promise came with a marble-carved version of two contending figures in an allegory entitled "I Felt Two Natures Struggling within Me." After 1894, when he made his debut in Paris, he was acclaimed a leader among sculptors.

8

For the masses, who could not afford original paintings and statues, there were the enormously popular plaster group miniatures of John Rogers of Salem. He had worked for years as a machinist and then had decided to go to Paris and Rome for a few months' training as a sculptor. At first he peddled his bric-a-brac from house to house but after he had exhibited such favorites as the humorous "Checkers Up at the Farm" and the pathetic scene, "The Slave Auction," he was ready to go into the manufacturing of these miniatures—the tallest was twenty inches high. The various expositions and fairs in Paris, Philadelphia, and Chicago had Rogers group exhibits such as the popular Civil War series, which included Lincoln seated at a council of war or the dramatic series with the character actor Joseph Jefferson as Rip Van Winkle. Homely humor, unashamed sentiment and pathos, intrinsically interesting situations, and always a quality of sincerity marked these works. No sophisticated taste was needed to appreciate a Rogers group and although art critics tended to be condescending about this vogue by the nineties, connoisseurs a half century later hailed these miniatures delightedly as the products of a forgotten folk art. In 1876 those who liked the Rogers group—100,000 of them were sold —could order them from his catalogs at moderate prices ranging from five dollars to fifty.

Even better than the continuing vogue for the romantic lithographs of Currier and Ives and the stiff photography of most professionals who served the rising popularity of albums was the rise of amateur photography. New European and American inventions such as the wet collodion process and the dry plate made the daguerreotype obsolete. In 1888, George Eastman invented the Kodak, an inexpensive small camera that could be held in the hands of any amateur photographer. This introduced a new esthetic experience for ordinary folk who could not hope to do much with an artist's brush or a sculptor's chisel. Mass patronage assured the unusual prosperity of the new Eastman Kodak Company formed in 1892. The average American also enjoyed a richer pictorial experience in his daily life through the profusely illustrated magazines, especially in the nineties, when cheap photoengraving processes replaced the costly and cumbersome woodcuts and steel engravings.

In the nineties, too, Alfred Stieglitz of New York raised amateur photography to a highly sophisticated, technical, and subtle art. He experimented with three-color techniques, edited the *American Amateur Photographer,* and founded *Camera Work.* He and his enthusiastic followers liked to catch the spirit of New York's life as expressed in its streets, such as the wet pavements at night. Because of this characteristic, short-sighted critics caricatured the Stieglitz circle as "the Mop and Pail brigade." But the followers of this prophet had opened a new era in camera realism that made nineteenth-century professional photography seem but a mechanical and unimaginative trade.

Between 1865 and 1917 the gap in art experience between Western Europe and America narrowed considerably. The crudities of Victorian Gothic had given way to Richardson's original applications of Romanesque styles, the craftsmanship of McKim's Classical Revival, and finally, the Modernist challenge of Sullivan and Wright. Cram and Goodhue had begun to introduce a more profound version of the Gothic than those who followed a slavish archaeological model of old Gothic buildings. A growing sophistication marked the tastes of the captains of industry who commanded the services of the architects. Parvenu garishness yielded to the cultural restraints of the younger industrial-commercial patrons. Mass housing, of course, failed to share in this evolution, except for utilitarian improvements in tenement light and air shafts and in plumbing.

The impact of Darwinism upon architecture resulted in the Sullivan-Wright theory that buildings were organic things adapting themselves to an environment through local materials and forms that revealed the function of the edifice. This theory considered architecture as an organic harmonious part of a total human culture. Such a formula meant a break with recurrent "revivals" of historic European styles and the natural growth of distinctive American architecture, since it would be based strictly on environmental factors. In painting, the role of Darwinism was less pronounced, except in the realistic philosophy of the impressionists, the urban rebels such as the Eight, and the modernists. Since realism and naturalism usually gave emphasis to the impact of the environment upon the individual and society, Darwinism influenced the social theories of painters, especially among the naturalistic followers of Robert Henri. Landscape painting and the genre type of work evolved from rural sentimentality to a realistic stage where they reflected the facts of a changing, urban-industrial world.

Patronage in painting and sculpture, as in architecture, reflected the improvement in taste among the businessmen who bought artwork and brought about the gradual passing of a parvenu era. But the Whitneys and Yerkeses were scarcely Renaissance princes in the discrimination or perception of their taste in art. When Veblen wrote in 1899 of the leisure class, he thought that he was describing a contemporary process of "conspicuous consumption" as far as art tastes were concerned among the captains of industry. The foreign label on a painting or statue conveyed prestige and represented a settled reputation with a secure investment value. Correspondingly, native artists, especially those with experimental or original tendencies like Albert P. Ryder, had limited patronage and a low price tag attached to their work. Ryder, naturally, lived in a garret.

For the lower middle class and the laborers, the art experience had to be both inexpensive and easily grasped. The photoengraving process of the nineties made available cheap, well-illustrated magazines selling at ten and fifteen cents. Newspaper pictures and photographs replaced the vogue for Currier and Ives lithographs before the end of the century. Eastman's Kodak made possible a greater degree of mass participation in art since every man might aspire to be his own photographer. In the sculpture of the parks and in public monuments, the taste of the masses determined that the subject matter in many instances be idealized versions of Civil War generals, admirals, and heroic soldiers. The cheap plaster casts of the Rogers groups were easily available and expressed a homely humor and sentimentality that the more academic art was attempting to escape. The rural psychology of Rogers was easier to understand than the realistic American painters who were inspired by the social satire and humor of Daumier and Goya. Above all, the millions of England and America (and elsewhere as well) were firmly wedded to the storytelling and didactic tradition of art. Impressionism, postimpressionism, and abstract art belonged to another world. "Whistler's Mother" obviously was important to ordinary folk because it expressed a sympathetic family relationship, not because it was an "Arrangement in Gray and Black."

· 17 ·

Imperialism, Pacifism, and the War To End War: Mahan and Wilson

I

ASIDE from confirmed pacifists like the Quakers, Mennonites, and Christian non-resistants, innumerable Americans liked to think of themselves as knights-errant courageously fighting the battles of civilization against tyranny everywhere. Tom Paine loved peace, but first he had to "rescue the world from bondage" in two major revolutions. American Jacobins were restrained with some difficulty from aiding the French revolutionists in the battle of all peoples against all kings. Public opinion had followed sympathetically the Latin-American revolutions, the Greek struggle for independence, and the liberation war of Louis Kossuth's Hungary. William Lloyd Garrison as well as the less doctrinaire members of the peace societies had given up the arguments against war in the abstract when the anti-slavery crusade culminated in Civil War. At the end of the century, American humanitarians forced a reluctant president to embark upon a war to free the Cuban people. And Wilson's war against Germany and her allies was in part a popular crusade against militarism.

While men like Jefferson believed that America had a mission to spread democracy by showing the world how peace could be blended with freedom and justice, others had more grandiose ideas of the American mission. To seventeenth-century religious rebels,

the Manifest Destiny of the American continent was the establishment of the New Jerusalem forecast by the Bible. To secular minds
of the Enlightenment, America was destined to be a great experiment in democracy where the Noble Huron and the Natural Man
thrived in an unspoiled wilderness and escaped the decadence of
Europe's aristocratic institutions. Here, they believed, men discovered the true virtue inherent in human nature once it was freed
from the decayed aristocracies and established churches of the Old
World. By the nineteenth century, frontier nationalists spoke of
America as morally unique among nations and endowed with a
Manifest Destiny for territorial expansion. War Hawks declaimed
in this vein on the eve of the War with England in 1812; and
newspapers and politicians rationalized their land hunger for the
Floridas, Texas, and the Far West by spinning the theories of
Manifest Destiny.

By 1865, these annexationists had evolved an entire library of
imperialist writings. They argued that pioneer farmers had rights to
the soil that were superior to those of backward nomadic peoples;
that the Anglo-Saxon benefited mankind by introducing everywhere
democracy, civilization, and regeneration; that geography determined the eventual annexation of nearby undeveloped areas by
powerful states; and above all, that American expansion was not
selfish in a colonial sense, but offered equality to all peoples under
the flag. Such patriots could plainly see that their nation had a
glorious mission to spread the blessings of civilization to mankind.

2

In the 1880's and 1890's, the extreme exponents of Manifest Destiny, Anglo-Saxon superiority, and other doctrines useful to expansionism became feverishly active. European examples in imperialism
in Africa and Asia offered some inspiration. By this time, too, expansionism was encouraged by the fact that the frontier was gone and
by the alleged need of outlets for the rapidly growing cities and
factories. But businessmen were still too absorbed by the highly
profitable domestic market to risk capital upon uncertain overseas

investments. Even by 1900, American investments abroad did not exceed a half billion dollars; but by 1914 the total was over 3.5 billions and the United States Steel Corporation alone could boast of 268 agencies in over 60 nations. At the same time, this country moved from the colonial status of a debtor nation to the world position of a major creditor country. Belatedly, business journals came around to the expansionist views of naval strategists, politicians, missionaries, and Darwinist scholars.

Nationalism, social Darwinism, and racialism added the most combustible fuel to imperialism. Chauvinism and racialism became substitutes for religion in this secular age and their strength was enhanced by commercial, military, and colonial rivalries. Folklorists, who had rediscovered the personality of their nation in primitive legends and customs, fed the vanity and egotism of nationalists. Blood rather than mere culture alone was the new touchstone. All Slavs were brothers; all Teutons were brothers; all Anglo-Saxons were brothers; but Slavs, Teutons, and Anglo-Saxons were not related in the slightest. Differences based on color were emphasized despite the continued invocation, from force of habit, of Christian precepts. In 1899, Rudyard Kipling added currency, though not novelty, to the doctrines of Anglo-Saxon superiority and imperialism when he published "The White Man's Burden" in *McClure's Magazine*. This was widely reprinted on the front pages of leading American newspapers. No more flattering euphemism for imperialism and colonialism had been discovered than Kipling's apostrophe, "Take up the White Man's Burden." This sounded much better than the "survival of the fittest" without giving up the happy thought of racial superiority.

The early expansionist propaganda of the missionary leader, Josiah Strong of Ohio, influenced imperialist theory as well as church history. While secretary of the Congressional Home Missionary Society, he wrote the widely read book, *Our Country* (1885), a brief for the plantings of church missions all over the world. He used social Darwinist ideas to argue that population pressure would compel the Anglo-Saxon to struggle for existence against other races and to dispossess weaker peoples. "It is manifest," he asserted, "that the Anglo-Saxon holds in his hands the destinies of mankind, and it is evident that the United States is to become the home of this race, the principal seat of his power, the great center of his influence." But he believed that this process would benefit everyone by spreading the blessings of civil liberty and "a pure spiritual Christianity." Strong's imperialism did not exclude a fervent belief in the Social Gospel and a dislike of concentrated wealth and labor exploitation. However, his views, broadcast in 170,000 copies of *Our Country*, represented a most extreme application of the missionary slogan of 1900, "The Evangelization of the World in This Generation."

John Fiske, a Darwinian like Strong, also believed in expansionism; and his chauvinism led him to demand immediate immigration restriction. In 1885, the very year that Strong's book appeared, Fiske published an article, "Manifest Destiny," in *Harper's Magazine*, which dwelt upon the ideas of Anglo-Saxon superiority and the mission of conquest in language every whit as enthusiastic as the missionary's. Fiske repeated this idea in innumerable lectures upon "American Political Ideas." He predicted grandly, "The day is at hand when four-fifths of the human race will trace its pedigree to English forefathers, as four-fifths of the white people of the United States trace their pedigree today." Other scholars, too, mixed Darwinism with Anglo-Saxon or Teutonic superiority. One of the most influential of these professors was John W. Burgess, political scientist and historian of Columbia. He was an aggressive exponent of the theory that parliamentary institutions had evolved out of the primitive Teutonic forest tribes and he believed in the superiority and manifest destiny of the "Nordic" peoples. Although Burgess later criticized America's colonial policy as undemocratic, he had already in 1890 laid down his imperialist doctrines of expansion.

No one could excel Captain Alfred Thayer Mahan in shaping imperialistic dogmas in their most plausible and "realistic" form. He was born in 1840 at West Point where his father taught in the military academy, but he chose the United States Naval Academy for his education. During the Civil War he served in the Gulf and Atlantic naval squadrons and in 1886 became president as well as a naval lecturer at the Newport War College. By this time he had dropped his original objection that colonies were too costly and was teaching his classes an aggressive interpretation of the potentiality of sea power. These lectures became the basis for the very influential books, *The Influence of Sea Power upon History, 1660–1783* (1890) and *The Influence of Sea Power upon the French Revolution and Empire, 1793–1812* (2 vols., 1892). His central thesis has become familiar to an entire generation:

> The due use and control of the sea is but one link in the chain of exchange by which wealth accumulates; but it is the central link, which lays under contribution other nations for the benefit of the one holding it, and which history seems to assert, most surely of all gathers itself riches.

He argued that sea power depended upon a nation's economic productivity, its trade, colonies, merchant marine, and navy. Naval bases were essential for oceanic operations and a state of preparedness must constantly prevail. A grim "realist" in the sense usually attributed to German "machtpolitik," he portrayed international relations as a naked struggle for power in which control of the sea was the most indispensable factor. In an article of 1900 he contended, "Self-interest is not only a legitimate but a fundamental cause for national policy, one which needs no cloak of hypocrisy. . . . Governments are corporations, and as corporations have not souls."

In 1893, when President Cleveland reversed Harrison's decision to annex Hawaii, Mahan wrote a significant article for Walter Hines Page, editor of the *Forum*, "Hawaii and Our Future Sea Power." He argued that Hawaii in unfriendly hands endangered the Pacific Coast and trade, but in ours it was an impregnable bulwark against invasion. In this and successive articles he emphasized the need for an Isthmian Canal and Caribbean control as essential to communications between East and West. In his "geopolitical" concept—the term was not yet current—the United States was a vast continental island and needed a two-ocean navy and England's friendship for its security. Mahan argued that our naval policy should be an ex-

pansionist one in which the superior culture of the United States
would enrich backward nations.

Before the twentieth century began, Mahan's ideas had galvan-
ized the big navy men into action. Admiral Tirpitz, leader of the
aggressive German naval school, circulated Mahan's first book as
a basic work for naval men. The Kaiser himself held Mahan in awe.
Japan translated the same work and used it as a textbook. France
and England as well as Germany and Japan altered their tactical
naval dispositions to conform with Mahan's precepts of a striking
naval force. In the United States leading statesmen became his
ardent converts: Theodore Roosevelt, John Hay, and Henry Cabot
Lodge. Roosevelt, the apostle of "virility," "strenuousness," and
other terms suggesting his fear of softness and decadence, made
Mahan's ideas almost his entire stock-in-trade of foreign policy.
"I suppose I need not tell you as regards Hawaii," Roosevelt wrote
as early as 1897, "I take your views absolutely as indeed I do in
foreign policy generally. If I had my way we would annex those
islands tomorrow." As president, Roosevelt carried out the Mahan
policy by a belligerent Panama policy and the aggressive Roosevelt
Corollary to the Monroe Doctrine which made the United States
the policeman of Latin America.

Mahan's rejection of international arbitration had an unfortunate
influence on Roosevelt and Lodge, if not upon the entire world.
Considerable progress had been made by the peace movement in
the field of arbitrating major disputes between nations, especially in
the settlement of the *Alabama* dispute with Britain in 1872 over the
building by England of Confederate cruisers for raids upon Union
commerce. When Russia called the Hague Conference of 1899,
American peace organizations hoped that something might be done
to regularize the arbitration of really vital questions and perhaps to
introduce disarmament as well. Mahan, who was a member of the
American delegation, made his opposition to arbitration clear at that
time and subsequently. He put his argument upon the highest possible plane of an absolutistic ethics and drew upon the American
ideal of the "higher law" or natural moral law for his chief support.
In conflicts between nations, he believed, one could arbitrate only

if the dispute involved no moral principle. No nation could permit compromise upon a matter of conscience. If man-made law, such as international law or the judgment of an umpire, conflicted with moral law then the latter must prevail. This effectively eliminated arbitration upon questions most likely to lead to war.

Mahan believed in the Darwinian idea of the survival of the fittest and he was not far from the brutal doctrine that might makes right. He could make war sound attractive and conciliation appear mean by the dictum that "even the material evils of war are less than the moral evil of compliance with wrong." While his undubitable genius as a great naval strategist strengthened the defenses and military potential of his country, he definitely weakened the peace movement and fostered a nationalistic philosophy of international problems that swelled the armory of imperialism. It is true that Mahan, as an orthodox Episcopalian, deprecated war and based his reasoning on the most absolute moral standards, but his "realism" in analyzing power politics led to such strategic doctrines of expansionism as were involved in the German geopolitics of the twenties and thirties when the Teutonic nationalist, Haushofer, hailed him as master. The Mahan doctrine of aggressive sea power had its obvious counterpart in the Haushofer doctrine of militant land power.

The most uninhibited exponent of Anglo-Saxon racialism, especially in the Roosevelt-Lodge-Mahan circle, was Senator Albert J. Beveridge of Indiana. The senator's imperialism reached its apogee in 1898 when he paid a tribute to Grant at a Boston club, which revealed much more of Beveridge's ideas than it did of the former president's:

> He never forgot that we are a conquering race, and that we must obey our blood and occupy new markets and, if necessary, new lands. He had the prophet's seer-like sight which beheld, as a part of the Almighty's plan, the disappearance of debased civilizations and decaying races before the higher civilization of the nobler and more virile types of men.

Beveridge reasoned that American factories and farms were producing more than Americans could use and hence we must build a powerful navy and merchant marine and acquire large self-governing colonies. Anglo-Saxon solidarity would mean a "people's league of God for the permanent peace of this war-worn world." As for imperialist expansion, he declared, "It is God's great purpose made manifest in the instincts of our race, whose present phase is our personal profit, and whose far-off end is the redemption of the world and the Christianization of mankind." Here was a neat combination of altruism and self-interest. One may easily infer Beveridge's personal message to Roosevelt in 1899 after the senator had returned from the Philippine Islands. On that occasion the Rough Rider wrote to his friend, Lodge, "His views on public matters are almost exactly yours and mine."

The Spanish-American War, as previously noted, did not grow directly out of imperialist pressures but was in large part a product of the desire of humanitarians to rescue the Cubans from Spanish mistreatment upon our very doorstep. Hearst and Pulitzer, it is true, sold millions of newspapers by promoting the war but even they could not create a war out of nothing, though they made it difficult for McKinley to consider the sweeping concessions of Cuban autonomy that Spain was willing to offer this country in an effort to stave off war. Once hostilities began, and Hawaii, the Philippines, Puerto Rico, and Cuba came within the American orbit, the idealistic interventionists fought against annexation. Bryan and Altgeld tried to make the election of 1900 a mandate against imperialism but the defeat of the Democratic party did not prove that most voters were converted to imperialism. Other issues confused the electorate. Symbolically, Altgeld's last speech made a few minutes before a fatal attack of cerebral hemorrhage was a denunciation of imperialism in South Africa and elsewhere.

Correspondingly, the expansionists felt encouraged by their seeming victory at the polls. Beveridge, Mahan, Roosevelt, and Lodge carried forward the new doctrines of the White Man's Burden. Even the Supreme Court majority prepared to remove the constitutional obstacles in the way of building an American empire. In *Downes* v. *Bidwell*, involving the status of Puerto Rico, the majority opinion read,

A false step at this time might be fatal to the development of what Chief Justice Marshall called the American Empire. Choice in some cases, the natural gravitation of small bodies towards large ones in others, the result of a successful war in still others, may bring about conditions which would render the annexation of distant possessions desirable.

For a time it seemed as if the traditional American doctrine of a union of equal states, which had been established by the Northwest Ordinance of 1787, might be completely sacrificed to the imperialistic idea of a dominant people ruling over "lesser breeds without the law." The final victory of democratic equality in all areas under the American flag did not become clear until the 1930's when Philippine independence was assured and Puerto Rico (later) was raised in self-governing status. By then Americans had completely lost interest in emulating the imperial glory that was Rome.

3

The democratic American tradition of self-determination that won the contest with imperialism was deeply rooted in the historic belief that men should be ruled only with their consent. Wilson made this doctrine his cardinal policy. Old-fashioned American democrats expressed their anti-imperialism in newspaper articles, poetry, and essays and used every device of satire and exhortation. Mark Twain, who had been for intervention in Cuba on humanitarian grounds, satirized the imperialists all over the world in his essay, "Greetings from the Nineteenth to the Twentieth Century,"

I bring you the stately nation named Christendom, returning bedraggled, besmirched, and dishonored, from pirate raids into Kiao-Chou, Manchuria, South Africa, and the Philippines, with her soul full of meanness, her pocket full of boodle, and her mouth full of pious hypocrisies. Give her soap and a towel, but hide the looking glass.

When the Philippines were annexed, he told young Winston Churchill, even then the proponent of empire, that now we were "kin in sin." About that time he wrote his sardonic essay, "To the Person Sitting in Darkness," and observed, "The Blessings-of-Civilization Trust, wisely and cautiously administered, is a Daisy.

There is more money in it, more territory, more sovereignty, and other kinds of emolument, than there is in any other game that is played."

Twain loved peace but he was no pacifist, for he justified at various times the use of force in ending chattel slavery, French Bourbonism, Czarist tyranny, and Cuban exploitation. Although his ideas were not always consistent, he hated what he regarded as hypocrisy in invoking God to bless the nation's arms in times of war. His most terrible indictment of this attitude was written during the Russo-Japanese War as "The War Prayer,"

O Lord our God, help us to tear their soldiers to bloody shreds with our shells: ... help us to lay waste their humble homes with a hurricane of fire; help us to wring the hearts of their unoffending widows with un-availing grief; ... help us to turn them out roofless with their little chil-dren to wander unfriended the wastes of their desolated land in rags and hunger and thirst ... we ask it, in the spirit of love, of Him Who is the Source of Love.

Another widely read opponent of imperialism was the Irish-American journalist, Finley Peter Dunne, managing editor of the *Chicago Journal*. Dunne's hatred of imperialism grew out of his own sense of justice and his Irish opposition to England's colonial policies. He knew well the Irish immigrant of Chicago's West Side and created his "Mr. Dooley" as a loquacious bartender dispensing satiric comments along with drinks to his unfailing customer, Mr. Hennessey, who was somewhat slower in comprehension and wit. On the annexation of the Philippines, Mr. Dooley had this to say, "Whin we plant what Hogan calls th' starry banner iv freedom in th' Ph'lippeenes ..., an' give th' sacred blessin' iv liberty to th' poor, downtrodden people iv thim unfortunate isles—dam thim—we'll larn them a lesson. ..." For Hennessey's benefit he simplified McKinley's plea to the Filipinos: "'We can't give ye anny votes because we haven't more thin enough to go around now, but we'll threat ye th' way a father shud threat his childher if we have to break ivry bone in ye'er bodies. So come to our arms,' says we." He could be more subtle too: "Tis not f'r thim wretched an' degraded crathers, without a mind or a shirt iv their own, f'r to give lessons in politeness an' liberty to a nation that mannyfacthers more dhressed beef thin anny other imperyal nation in th' wurruld."

Roosevelt and the most influential American statesmen were regular readers of Dunne's column at the time he published this witticism: "We're a great people," said Mr. Hennessey, earnestly. "We are," said Mr. Dooley. "We are that. An' th' best iv it is, we know we are." As for Teddy, the irrepressible Mr. Dooley remarked, "a lot iv us likes Teddy Rosenfelt that wudden't iver be sispected iv votin' f'r him."

Among the anti-imperialistic poets, the most stirring was William Vaughn Moody. He, too, like the others, felt the exalted sentiments of the Spanish-American War and then turned upon those who would convert an altruistic act into one for national and personal aggrandizement. In 1900, he tried to revive the idealism of Civil War days in "An Ode in Time of Hesitation," which was inspired by Saint-Gaudens' bronze statue of Robert Gould Shaw. This hero had been killed while leading the first enlisted Negro regiment in an attack. The reality of their sacrifice seemed endangered by the war of 1900 to subjugate the Filipinos under Aguinaldo:

> Tempt not our weakness, our cupidity!
> For save we let the island men go free,
> Those baffled and dislaureled ghosts
> Will curse us from the lamentable coasts
> Where walk the frustrate dead.

4

The Civil War, as Merle Curti shows in *Peace or War*, dealt the well-organized peace movement a severe blow from which recovery was a gradual process. Vigorous English, French, and Scandinavian peace organizations cooperated with the reviving American Peace Society in pressing for arbitration treaties, a league of nations, an international court, and a reduction of armaments. These peacemakers had something to do with the fact that the recurrent crises between Britain and America did not ignite into war. Quakers and other nonresistants continued to work actively for peace. President

Grant even staffed the Indian service in part with Quakers in an
effort to end the perpetual state of war in the West. A new militant
organization, the Universal Peace Union, arose in 1866 under the
leadership of Alfred Love and Adin Ballou. It campaigned for immediate disarmament, arbitration, anti-imperialism, and the abolition of military training in the schools and colleges. Feminists in
large numbers, including Frances Willard and the W.C.T.U., joined
the Universal Peace Movement. Labor organizations, hitherto skeptical of the middle-class peace movement, showed increasing interest
in the cause of arbitration and disarmament. From Europe, especially by the turn of the century, came the socialist propaganda line
that modern war was only the product of capitalist greed, imperialist adventures, and the sinister efforts of munitions makers. French
and German socialists pledged themselves never to engage in war
against each other. Businessmen and industrialists from Carnegie to
Henry Ford denounced war as an anachronism in an efficient
orderly universe. Carnegie, the maker of naval armor plate among
other varieties of steel, and Alfred Nobel, Swedish manufacturer of
dynamite, gave many millions away for education and research to
promote peace. Business journals disliked the popular crusades for
war, such as the Spanish-American War, because, among other
things, they disrupted trade. The belief spread in many circles that
modern inventions in communication and industry would break
down regional misunderstandings and promote internationalism.
Besides, it was often argued that the new military inventions, such
as the Gatling gun and dynamite, would make war so terrible that
militarists would refrain from provoking hostilities. Implicit also in
the American faith in progress was the idea that the moral sense of
man would steadily advance from a predatory stage to the altruistic
level and thus eliminate wars.

Some of the social Darwinists argued that war was necessary to
eliminate the unfit, but most of them recognized that modern war
exposed the strongest physical types to destruction. Charles Darwin
declared in 1871 that war acted as a harmful interference with the
process of natural selection. Spencer, Fiske, Ward, Sumner, and
William James believed in the gradual evolution of a peaceful

society. Herbert Spencer sympathized with the peace movement and his apostle, Sumner, was an outspoken foe of imperialism.

Arbitration was the most prominent phase of the peace movement after the Civil War, and it marked the shift away from the vague and mystical generalities regarding the wickedness of war. Here-after, the concrete machinery and institutions of peace would absorb the attention of American and European organizations. In 1872, a Geneva Tribunal arbitrated the *Alabama* claims of the United States for damages sustained during the Civil War by reason of England's building of vessels for the Confederacy. Britain promptly paid the $15,000,000 awarded by the tribunal to the United States. In the Senate, Charles Sumner introduced a hopeful resolution on behalf of the peace societies:

... that in the determination of international differences arbitration should become a substitute for war in reality as in name, and therefore coextensive with war in jurisdiction, so that any question or grievance which might be the occasion of war or of misunderstanding between nations should be considered by this tribunal.

Peacemakers helped to arouse public opinion during the nineties against the Harrison-Blaine policy in Chile, which seemed to be heading toward war. They did support the administration's Pan-Americanism and its ideas of arbitration, reciprocity, and the codification of international law. However, the Pan-American movement lagged until Wilson's time when the president and Colonel House attempted to create a Pan-American League that would be based upon a mutual guarantee of the independence and territorial integrity of every member. But existing Latin-American suspicions of the Colossus of the North and the coming of World War I killed this project.

Ironically, the peak of pacifist activity came during the decade before World War I. Edwin Ginn, the textbook publisher, set aside a million-dollar fund for world peace and founded, in 1910, the World Peace Foundation to spread information on international affairs. Its work was directed by a persistent pacifist, David Starr Jordan, president of Stanford, and it furnished lecturers for women's clubs and labor organizations. Andrew Carnegie's plans were far more ambitious. He built the Peace Palace at the Hague and provided a ten-million-dollar fund in 1910 for another educational and propagandistic agency intended to influence articulate groups such as professors, journalists, reformers, and students. This was the Carnegie Endowment for International Peace, headed by President Nicholas Murray Butler of Columbia. Carnegie became the president of the large New York Peace Society and urged a strong policy of arbitration and collective action by the powers against disturbers of the peace. He took a very active part in the British peace societies and advocated a union of English-speaking peoples as a force for international peace. This, he declared, would mean a "Reunited States—the British-American Union." The pro-British bias of the Carnegie sponsorship practically nullified its peace efforts during 1914–17. Besides the efforts of the philanthropists, there was the organized might of the Christian churches for peace. The Federal Council of Churches, representing the collective strength of nearly 20,000,000 Protestants, set up a vigorous peace committee that fought the propaganda for war with Mexico in 1916 that Senator Albert Fall, Hearst, and the oil interests had fomented.

In the more significant literature of peace, the influence of the Englishman, Norman Angell, is especially important. In 1910 this thoughtful journalist issued a masterly indictment of war in a popular work, *The Great Illusion,* which tried to prove the futility of conquest even from the standpoint of the militarist. He demonstrated "the great illusion"—the unprofitableness of colonies and other fruits of war. He joined the Garton Foundation in England to explore the economic and sociological results of war. That same year William James published an essay on war which the peacemakers publicized widely, "The Moral Equivalent of War." He began bluntly:

The war against war is going to be no holiday excursion or camping party. The military feelings are too deeply grounded to abdicate their place among our ideals until better substitutes are offered than the glory and shame that come to nations as well as to individuals from the ups and downs of politics and the vicissitudes of trade.

Modern war, he said, was too expensive to be profitable and therefore its support has come from an innate pugnacity, a love of glory, and an emotional idealism. "Let public opinion once reach a certain fighting pitch, and no ruler can withstand it. . . . The pliant politician, McKinley, was swept away by their eagerness, and our squalid war with Spain became a necessity." To make war horrible would not eliminate it. Horror means a thrill and hence might attract rather than repel the average citizen. Some substitute, a moral equivalent for war, was necessary. His proposal called for the conscription of youth for a certain number of years to enlist in a productive campaign against nature. Hard, constructive projects in the public interest would help this group to "get the childishness knocked out of them, and to come back into society with healthier sympathies and soberer ideas." Thus we would achieve "toughness without callousness," a high emotional intensity, and a desirable psychology of cooperation and social purpose. Here was a fresh approach to the causes of war, one that eschewed sinister conspiracies and the theory that devils are the sole warmakers.

5

The United States entered World War I at the height of the peace movement and with a member of the American Peace Society in the White House. Woodrow Wilson appeared to be the very antithesis of Alfred Mahan in rejecting the cold realism of the naval strategist regarding the dominance of national self-interest and power politics in foreign policy. "It is a very perilous thing," declared President Wilson in his Mobile Address of 1913, "to determine the foreign policy of a nation in the terms of material interest. It not only is unfair to those with whom you are dealing, but it is degrading as regards your own actions." But like Mahan, he displayed a rigid ethical absolutism that made compromise difficult. Yet, it must be noted that Wilson kept the nation out of World War I until April, 1917, while his opponents, Roosevelt and Charles Evans Hughes, assailed him for temporizing with Germany at the expense of the national honor of this country.

Wilson was not as unyielding a pacifist as his Secretary of State Bryan, but like him drew upon a strong religious background for his ideas regarding peace. Both men believed in the millennial advent of peace through the moral progress of mankind. Wilson, a fervent moralist, always held that nations, like men, were moral persons and for such responsible beings one must consider wrong-doing and guilt to be personal things. In his war declaration against Germany, he observed,

We are at the beginning of an age in which it will be insisted that the same standards of conduct and of responsibility for wrong done shall be observed among nations and their governments that are observed among the individual citizens of civilized states.

Only special circumstances in 1918–19 prevented Wilson from obtaining the "war crimes trial" for the Kaiser and his associates that he wished. For the moralist, peace could not be considered the sole end of mankind. "I will not cry 'peace' so long as there is sin and wrong in the world," he once declared. This was the moral substance of his war declaration:

But the right is more precious than peace, and we shall fight for the things which we have always carried nearest our hearts,—for democracy, for the right of those who submit to authority to have a voice in their own Governments, for the rights and liberties of small nations, for a universal dominion of right by such a concert of free peoples as shall bring peace and safety to all nations and make the world itself at last free.

As a historian, Wilson had criticized American aggression in the War of 1846 with Mexico and even spoke critically of the Spanish-American War as a "war of impulse." As president he denounced imperialism, rejected Dollar Diplomacy, supported the Bryan Conciliation treaties, and insisted on the most meticulous regard for our pledges to England in the Panama Tolls Controversy. Even when he sent marines into the Caribbean states he was obviously impelled solely by what seemed to be unavoidable strategic needs to defend the Panama Canal rather than by pressures of financiers or oil concessionaires.

Wilson had an almost mystical belief in the basic pacifism of the plain people as compared to their rulers. Thus he set the later pattern for distinguishing between the Mexican people and the Huerta government, between the German people and the Kaiser's clique, and still later between the Russian people and the communist rulers. "I sometimes think," he said in 1916, "that it is true that no people ever went to war with another people. Governments have gone to war with one another." This type of thinking gave added substance to the liberal Jeffersonian belief in the doctrine that government rests only on the consent of the governed. A world in which democratic "self-determination" exists, therefore, can only be a universe of peaceful, cooperative peoples. Wilson could have profited more from his study of history or from reading William James's "Moral Equivalent of War."

One of the fruits of this faith in the pacific nature of the common people was Wilson's reversal of the historic American doctrine of recognition of new governments. It was not enough for him that a new government should show itself capable of maintaining control. He insisted that revolutionary regimes must reflect the honest choice of the people, and he applied this test even to dictator-ridden countries like Mexico. In this case Wilson came close to embroiling the United States in war, but he did help the liberal forces in Mexico to inaugurate a much-needed agrarian and labor program. Oil concessionaires would have preferred the old dictatorship which granted favors with a lavish hand, but Wilson chose to consider the interests of the ordinary Mexican laborer and peasant. This application of Golden Rule diplomacy seemed quixotic and dangerous by "realistic" standards, but it represented a kind of knight-errant interventionism that was familiar to American thinking. Behind this was the recurrent belief that America had a mission to spread democracy all over the world.

The logic of Wilson's theories and his interest in peace organizations led him to make the realization of a strong League of Nations the final effort of his life. He was no innovator here, for the machinery of peace had been studied for centuries by antiwar groups. Alfred Lord Tennyson had awakened widespread response in 1842 when he wrote in *Locksley Hall* of "the Parliament of man, the federation of the world." Taft's League To Enforce Peace, organized in 1915, was probably the direct ancestor of the League of Nations. Wilson became converted from an early belief in peace enforcement through moral sanctions to the unswerving position that nothing less than military as well as economic sanctions by all members against aggressors would preserve the peace. The later history of the League of Nations proved that his "realistic" foes had less understanding of realities than did this latter-day prophet. There was much more than copybook morality in his refusal to accept a watered-down league that gave the dangerous illusion of security without actually achieving it. Idealist though he was, Wilson also believed that men must be ready to defend by force the governments and ideals that they regarded as just.

Most samples of public opinion in 1919 suggest that Americans favored a league of nations. A poll of senators indicated an overwhelming majority for the League. As early as 1916 a referendum of the members of the United States Chamber of Commerce showed that a large majority endorsed the plan of the League To Enforce Peace and were ready for military as well as economic sanctions. The explanation for the failure of this country to enter the League belongs to the history of domestic politics.

6

The American social pattern of World War I was partly shaped by the experience of the Civil War as well as by the war practices of European nations. In resorting to conscription the administration and Congress were aware of the New York Draft Riots of 1863, but hit upon the stratagem of turning over the recruiting machinery to civilians instead of soldiers. On June 5, 1917, about ten million young men between the ages of twenty-one and thirty-one registered at polling booths for possible military service just as if they were preparing to vote. The last draft registration occurred on September 12, 1918, and with those that preceded furnished a pool of nearly 13,400,000 men between eighteen and forty-five years of age. Altogether over 2,700,000 were chosen for army duty under the Selective

Service Act. The list of exemptions allowed in the first draft was especially generous, including most men with dependents, those skilled in essential industries, postal employees, certain elected officials, theological students and ministers, and religious pacifists. A boom in marriages resulted from the rush to secure military exemption. In addition, over 330,000 "slackers" evaded the draft, many of them escaping to Mexico.

Fears that the large American population of German descent (an estimated 13 per cent) might forcibly resist the draft did not materialize. Antiwar protests were indeed common at first but most of these came from radical groups. Socialists in the cities and the agrarian Non-Partisan League in the Dakotas held peace meetings and public demonstrations, but they were quickly squelched by federal and local officials as well as by self-appointed mobs. Some small resistance took place among Oklahoma tenant farmers and others elsewhere who felt suspicious about the intentions of the registration officials. Thus the romantic volunteering system, which even England had dropped, was replaced by the draft, not only to provide ample manpower but to put the "right man in the right place." England had found that volunteering drew off the best-trained college students and left a disproportionate group of unskilled men for later military service. The exemption policy together with the "work or fight" order had the effect of protecting the supply of skilled war workers as well as guaranteeing the total of servicemen needed.

Just as in the Civil War, government officials granted exemption to religious objectors to military service, but were very reluctant to protect non-religious "conscientious objectors," especially those who also refused non-combat war service. While army officials eventually recognized 3900 as conscientious objectors, they treated the 450 men who refused substitute service as cowards or traitors. These men were usually sent to federal prisons for terms averaging ten years. In later years revelations appeared of the amazing brutalities perpetrated by callous guards upon the "conshies," including beatings and various forms of torture.

The compulsions of modern war also led to a regime of "war

socialism." Industry was regimented under Bernard Baruch's War Industries Board, which sought to protect military and civilian needs through indirect price controls, priorities, and various measures designed to prevent waste in factory production. Despite the protest of railroad owners, President Wilson acted in December, 1917, to bring about the unification of all railroads under the direction of his Secretary of the Treasury, William G. McAdoo. In this way the federal government felt assured that military consignments, even if unprofitable from a revenue standpoint, would take precedence over civilian traffic. A similar fate of socialization overtook the telephone and telegraph systems and the leading express companies.

Federal and state fuel boards imposed sweeping controls over coal and oil uses. "Heatless Mondays" and certain "lightless" nights were ordered by the federal fuel administrator. The successful European experiment of "daylight saving" was adopted in 1918 to conserve coal and electricity and to promote efficiency. Herbert Hoover as Food Administrator used a volunteer staff and managed to avoid compulsory rationing in his drive to convince the public that food conservation would help win the war by supplying our Allies. He ordered "wheatless" and "meatless" days, cut down the use of scarce foodstuffs in restaurants and bakeries, licensed and controlled wholesale food dealers, and encouraged farm production. Congress, pressed by antisaloon lobbies, used the food control program to forbid the manufacture and sale of intoxicating liquors. Thus prohibition crept in as a conservation measure. It also seemed patriotic to strike at the German brewers in this way. Permanent, nation-wide prohibition came in 1920 with the Eighteenth Amendment.

In a war for democracy it was necessary to distribute the financial as well as the military burden among all classes. Wilson, who favored a heavy draft on wealth and a philosophy of taxation according to ability to pay, found the new income tax law indispensable. He pressed for the payment of war costs through unprecedented excess profits taxes and income taxes on corporations as well as individuals. However, the bulk of revenue had to come from the small taxpayer, especially in the form of innumerable excise taxes and income taxes. Most of the cost of war was met by public borrowing through the sale of Liberty and Victory bonds. The various bond drives were reminiscent of the pioneer publicity methods introduced by the Civil War banker, Jay Cooke, in reaching a mass market. Cooke had been convinced that the small investor was a far better source of cheap loans than the large banks. In World War I the official Committee on Public Information sponsored the greatest bond-selling campaign in history and employed motion picture stars and "four-minute" men as salesmen in various cities and small communities.

Labor gained measurably in status as a result of war needs. Even in the prewar year of 1916 President Wilson decided to throw the support of the administration to the demands of the four railway brotherhoods for an eight-hour day without reduction in wages. "The eight-hour day," he declared, "is an established policy of the country." Thus a nation-wide strike was averted, but conservatives condemned Wilson for a gross betrayal of the public to labor's threats. When the war began, the soaring cost of living stimulated numerous strikes and led Wilson to set up the National War Labor Board under former President Taft and Frank P. Walsh. The Board proved aggressive enough to force its solutions, usually impartial ones, upon labor and capital. Unionization advanced at an unprecedent rate under the favorable conditions of wartime scarcity. The American Federation of Labor added two million more to its membership during 1917 and 1920.

Negro migration northward and to the cities now moved at a fast pace. Wartime necessity opened to them new occupations hitherto restricted to whites. Tens of thousands found well-paid work in steel mills, auto factories, and packing houses. In the industrial centers of Chicago, Detroit, Pittsburgh, Cleveland, and St. Louis, Negroes crowded into cheap slum neighborhoods, segregated by real estate covenants. Competition for jobs and houses worsened racial antagonisms. East St. Louis, Illinois, where the Negro influx had been very great, was shaken by a violent race war in 1917 when thirty-nine Negroes and eight whites were killed and many more injured.

Encouraged by Secretary of War Newton D. Baker, a Southern-

born liberal, Negroes broke through some of the army's racial restrictions and won hundreds of commissions as officers. The navy,
however, kept Negroes in menial positions, and the marines scarcely
made any concessions. Despite interracial conflicts in the army
and a very serious race riot in Houston, Negro troops maintained
a high morale and resisted the German propaganda that stressed
the lynchings and racial prejudices in the South. The bravery of
the Negro soldiers was recognized by innumerable distinguished
citations from the American and French governments. Frenchmen
gave the Negroes a cordial welcome and the Negro musicians in
turn taught their hosts the intricacies of syncopated music. When
the Negro troops returned to America, they were enthusiastically
cheered by crowds of both races.

The most powerful civilian agency for the war was the American
Red Cross. Since 1905, Clara Barton's famous organization had developed as a large-scale semiofficial agency of the government with
the president of the United States as its head. When World War
I broke out in 1914, the American Red Cross quickly went to the
aid of the wounded and starving of both sides. After 1917 it had
to confine its assistance, except at the hospitals, to Allied soldiers.
To carry on its numerous activities the Red Cross campaigned for
funds through publicity of all kinds, parades, billboards, speeches,
school drives, church appeals, and other channels. Eventually they
collected $400,000,000 in successive drives.

They set up a Home Service to offer relief to soldiers' families
who had failed to get allotments, and to help locate missing men.
"We keep your home safe while you fight to keep the world safe,"
said their placards. In addition to its far-flung system of hospitals,
the Red Cross set up a Sanitation Service for the army cantonments
at home, organized a Junior Red Cross in the schools to render
assistance in making relief goods and to collect needed material
from house to house, and they put women to work knitting clothes
for the soldiers. Sometimes army men fumed at the amount of
valuable wool used by the determined knitters in creating surpluses
of socks and sweaters, but it was finally concluded that this activity was as good for the women's morale as it was for the soldiers'.

In Western Europe—and elsewhere later—the Red Cross provided innumerable canteens, including "kitchens on wheels," to dispense coffee or soup to men behind the lines. Red Cross huts provided concerts, dancing, and other forms of recreation. Special services dealt with the enormous problem of aiding uprooted refugees and with child welfare. Before long, the Red Cross covered a multitude of services not at all connected with the hospitals, nurses, and ambulances that were more readily in evidence.

During the Civil War the Y.M.C.A. had organized the United States Christian Commission. This agency had provided the Union soldiers with reading matter, both secular and religious. In 1917 the "Y" undertook an even more ambitious war program on behalf of the soldiers and began with a successful fund drive for $50,000,-000. Y.M.C.A. huts were built in this country and in France, with lecture halls where one might learn French, and watch movies or well-known stage entertainers; canteen rooms provided hot coffee, food, and sociability. Even near the fighting lines there were underground "Y" huts; staff members arranged for relatives to see wounded men at the army hospitals; and "Y" doctors and social workers labored to stamp out venereal and other diseases. Altogether, the Y.M.C.A. was almost an official part of the armed forces. In fact, General Pershing put the "Y" in charge of the entire army post exchange system. On a lesser, but still highly useful scale, the Y.W.C.A. set up white or Negro hostess houses in the United States to permit soldiers to spend their leisure hours with friends or their families. Soldiers also remembered with gratitude the other volunteer agencies, the Knights of Columbus, the Jewish Welfare Board, the Salvation Army (whose free doughnuts and coffee were ubiquitous), the American Library Association, and the War Camp Service.

7

The Civil War had left an unfortunate set of precedents for the violation of civil liberties in wartime. Wilson himself was too aware of these mistakes to imitate them, but public opinion showed a tendency toward a hysterical fear of traitors and even of mere critics.

The President expressed his liberal philosophy in 1917 at the time of the passage of the Espionage Act, "I shall not expect or permit any part of this law to apply to me or any of my official acts, or in any way to be used as a shield against criticism." His attitude seemed a commonsense one in a country that was as physically secure as the United States was in 1917–18.

While Wilson permitted his Attorney General and Postmaster General to overstep the usual limits of state intervention in civil liberties even for wartime, he tried to discourage censorship. He turned for assistance to the former editor of the *Rocky Mountain News*, George Creel, who had shown energy and idealism in his 1916 campaign propaganda for Wilson. Creel's slogan, "Expression, not repression," made him seem a highly desirable person to organize the Committee on Public Information. Creel urged voluntary censorship by the newspapers themselves and concentrated upon positive democratic propaganda to shape the opinion of Americans and even Europeans. He carried the Wilsonian program of war aims to the world and used every device of publicity to raise the effectiveness of the war effort.

Creel's division of historians under Professor Guy Stanton Ford of the University of Minnesota did not resort to inventions of enemy atrocities, but gave the American slant to their pamphlets and books. For example, they dealt with *How the War Came to America*, *America's War Aims and Peace Terms*, and *American Interest in Popular Government Abroad*. Occasionally, they did issue a lurid pamphlet like *The Kaiserite in America* of which 5,500,000 copies were distributed. The Committee of Public Information also created a film division which thoughtfully provided Hollywood with such patriotic themes as *Wolves of Kultur* and *The Beast of Berlin*. They marshaled popular artists under Charles Dana Gibson, originator of the pompadoured Gibson Girl, to illustrate posters for war bond campaigns. Best remembered are two posters of James Montgomery Flagg, "Tell That to the Marines," and (a recruiting poster) Uncle Sam pointing directly toward the spectator, "I Want *YOU* for the United States Army." The Committee's numerous divisions stimulated community singing for morale purposes, encouraged labor to believe that the postwar world would bring far better economic conditions, and even fomented revolutionary propaganda in Germany.

Meanwhile the intolerant war spirit had far outstripped the efforts of George Creel. Mobs sometimes demonstrated their patriotism by painting the porches of German-Americans a bright yellow. The German language, which had been the most popular foreign tongue taught in the schools, was so completely eliminated from the curriculum that it never recovered the same status thereafter. German music was held suspect and even humble sauerkraut became Liberty Cabbage. To make matters much worse, the sudden eruption of Lenin and the Communist Revolution in Russia added the violent ingredient of a Red scare to the anti-Prussian sentiment. Sober judges, reflecting this atmosphere, revived doctrines of repression that had been dormant since the era of the Alien and Sedition Acts in 1798. The Espionage Acts of 1917–18 were sufficiently broad in their provisions for Postmaster General Burleson to exclude journals from the mails if, in his judgment, they had been at any time critical of the government. As a result, two leading socialist journals, *The Masses*, and the *Milwaukee Leader*, among others, were suppressed. He and the federal judges might regard as objectionable any criticism of England's policy in Ireland, or a suggestion that more money should be raised by taxes rather than by loans, or sympathy for the Russian Revolution.

The states had their own sweeping espionage acts. Under Minnesota's law a man went to jail for telling women knitting for the servicemen, "No soldier ever sees these socks." One could be imprisoned for declaring that war was contrary to the teachings of Christ or saying that a referendum should have preceded our declaration of war. In a federal district court Rose Pastor Stokes, a socialist, was sentenced to ten years in a federal prison for saying, "I am for the people and the government is for the profiteers." This court judgment was later reversed. In an unfortunate symbolic title for a federal case, *The United States* v. *"The Spirit of '76,"* it was held that a motion picture which depicted the British unfavorably in a historical film of colonial days violated the Espionage Act.

Eugene Debs, attempting to rally the antiwar sentiment in the badly split Socialist party, delivered a speech in June, 1918, which attacked the war in thinly veiled terms. However, he spoke only of the evils of war in the abstract and condemned it as the product of "the master class." As a result, Debs went to prison and remained there until President Harding pardoned him in 1921. A group of New York radicals who distributed pamphlets condemning Wilson's military intervention in Russia were sentenced to twenty years' imprisonment though they pointed out that their pamphlet had also denounced German militarism. This was the notable Abrams case that inspired Oliver Wendell Holmes in 1919 to write his classic dissenting opinion in behalf of freedom of speech:

Only the emergency that makes it immediately dangerous to leave the correction of evil counsels to time warrants making any exception to the sweeping command, "Congress shall make no law . . . abridging the freedom of speech."

As a pragmatist he believed that the best test of truth was by "free trade in ideas" and the "power of the thought to get itself accepted in the competition of the market." (Brandeis concurred with Holmes.) The limiting factor, as he also pointed out in the case of *Schenck* v. *United States* was "whether the words used are used in such circumstances and are of such a nature as to create a clear and present danger that they will bring about the substantive evils that Congress has a right to prevent." In the Schenck case, involving the act by a Socialist party secretary of distributing leaflets to draftees attacking conscription, Holmes had delivered the majority opinion declaring that here was an instance where a man had transgressed the right of free speech. "The most stringent protection of free speech would not protect a man in falsely shouting fire in a theatre and causing a panic," he declared. This was a case involving "a clear and present danger."

8

The World War offered little to the cause of American culture, except where it was bound up directly with the war effort. Scientists were coordinated within the new National Research Council for war services. The peacetime emphasis on scientific theory yielded to the wartime pressure for concrete practical applications. Certain aspects of medicine relating to the enormous battlefront experience, such as the developments in surgery, gained substantially. Psychologists also profited from the vast opportunities for applying the theories of mental testing to hundreds of thousands of men. It was reported that 25 per cent of the members of the American Psychological Association and a majority of the research students were in some form of war service. Despite a certain amount of confusion in the concepts of native intelligence versus learned behavior, wartime psychologists added much to the understanding of personnel testing and helped the army in discovering the right man for the right place.

Writing war propaganda was not an adequate intellectual expression for the social scientists, while the chauvinistic hysteria discouraged many. Columbia University forced two professors to resign for criticizing America's entrance into the war and the University of Nebraska put a number of professors on trial for their beliefs. Research funds for nonwar purposes were often curtailed. All education suffered from the exigencies of war. While college youth was conscripted, high-school boys left the classroom to take well-paying jobs. During 1918 the high cost of living and better opportunities elsewhere drove thousands of teachers out of the profession and few returned. Ohio alone reported a shortage of 2500 rural teachers. Inexperienced and incompetent teachers had to be drawn upon. Inroads were made upon classroom time by the wartime tendency to use the school as a channel for military cooperation between government officials and civilians. Liberty loan drives, food conservation programs, "Victory food gardens," and new patriotic activities were discussed and planned in the classroom.

Readers showed a decided preference for more fiction but fewer critical works. The war novel seemed to have reached a saturation point even in 1918. "It has been impossible to write serious novels," wrote one critic, "without introducing the war, yet war motives have been already too thoroughly exploited." Escapism was a common literary tendency, although there was an increase in the number of books dealing with world organization and education. Architecture was blighted by the embargo put upon most building enterprises. There was less construction of houses in 1918 than in any year since the Civil War. A painful housing shortage was in the making. Some innovations in planning mass housing were achieved in the numerous government projects for war workers. Many painters were diverted to military camouflage work or to work on posters for war bonds and recruiting. However, the art exhibits continued to attract public interest. The major war exhibit, the Allied War Salon show, was held in New York in December, 1917, to display painting subjects dealing with war. George Luks, one of the Eight, exhibited a very popular picture "Blue Devils of France on Fifth Avenue" and George Bellows won praise for his realistic lithographs. But on the whole, the artists and scholars seemed to be marking time, waiting for the dawn of peace.

· 18 ·

Postwar Reaction, Racialism, and Immigration Restriction: The Twenties

I

WARTIME nationalism extinguished the progressive impulse of the Roosevelt-Taft-Wilson era. The pendulum that had swung in the direction of social reform, away from laissez-faire individualism, was now reversed. This process of change would undoubtedly have come even without the war, but the fear of an enemy at the gates, either Teuton or communist, led to an hysterical reaction. It was compounded of a Red scare, chauvinism, racialism, and a middle-class fear that organized labor was plotting revolution. In Europe the postwar upsurge of communism had given Red Russia a temporary satellite in Hungary and had prompted nationalists in Italy and Germany to seek anticommunist insurance by organizing fascist parties. Even England, shaken by severe unemployment, yielded to the "Red Letter" panic that led to the defeat of the Labour party at the end of 1924. Wilson took a very grave view of the communist peril, while certain of his subordinates fell prey to the mass hysteria, but he adopted the sound policy of expanding food relief in Europe to halt the spread of communism.

The year 1919 opened with a bewildering outbreak of strikes, which newspapers hastily attributed to communist origin. Actually, the causes for labor's unrest were far more obvious. Postwar inflation had sharply increased the cost of living while the end of overtime pay made it hard for laborers to support their families at the same standard as before. Unions that had been born during the war when labor scarcity was great fought for their existence against the open shop drive of the National Association of Manufacturers and their followers. The issue of union recognition was often as important as the demand for higher wages and shorter hours. It did not prove difficult for conservatives to liquidate the small radical wing of labor; and when the partisan smoke had cleared away by the middle twenties it became clear that the unions had lost much of their membership and a good deal of their effectiveness as bargaining agencies. During 1920–23 union membership fell from 5,000,000 to 3,500,000.

The continued failure or unwillingness of the American Federation of Labor to organize the unskilled in the mass production industries encouraged the revolutionary Industrial Workers of the World to carry their propaganda among the unorganized longshoremen, lumbermen, miners, migratory farm hands, and textile workers. Their militant unionism had resulted in repeated successes in negotiations with employers for higher wages and better conditions. However, their ultimate revolutionary objectives tended to discredit the causes to which I.W.W. leaders attached themselves. Public opinion invariably turned against a strike, even if the objectives seemed reasonable, once the unions had been tinged with red. The I.W.W., whose membership had reached 100,000 in prewar days, disintegrated beneath a hail of federal blows against it. The antiwar propaganda and violations of the Espionage Act by the I.W.W. made it vulnerable. Its headquarters were raided, its leaders were jailed or deported, and its membership was heavily fined. In December, 1919, a mob attacked an I.W.W. hall in Centralia, Washington, and wholesale arrests were made of radical leaders.

The great steel strike of 1919 illustrates the manner in which orthodox unions became tarred with the brush of communism. In 1918–19 the Chicago section of the American Federation of Labor had delegated William Z. Foster, then considered a regular trade unionist rather than a revolutionary, to organize the steel workers behind the slogan of an eight-hour day. Ever since the Homestead Strike of 1892, when Carnegie's executives had defeated steel unionization, half of the labor force continued to work the twelve-hour day and all employees averaged a work week of nearly sixty-nine hours. Unionization had been prevented by combining a company welfare program with intimidation. In this strike Old World hatreds were deliberately fanned by supervisors in an effort to divide Italian workers against Serbs. One nationality group would be told that their rivals were deserting the strike to get the jobs of the others. Judge Gary of the United States Steel Corporation favored the policy of discharging union men and refused to confer with their leaders. He insisted that there was no issue except communism and the confiscation of property. His position was backed by other executives in the mass production industries. It was clear that the unionization of steel would open the way for unions in the rubber, automobile, and other assembly line plants.

Despite the pleas of Wilson and Gompers that the steel strike be suspended, Foster went ahead with his plans and eventually called out over 340,000 men in Pennsylvania, Ohio, Indiana, and Illinois. The companies replied by the use of every device of industrial warfare. Their full-page newspaper advertisements, aided by friendly editorial opinion, labeled the strike leaders as Reds. Local police officials broke up union meetings. In Gary, Indiana, Negro strikebreakers were called into the steel plants; when the strikers rioted federal troops moved in to establish martial law. Under these circumstances, defeat was almost inevitable. There was a moral victory, however. The Industrial Relations Department of the Interchurch World Movement thoroughly investigated the strike, supported the steel workers, and revealed the rough tactics of the steel companies. Within a few years these church leaders were able to win an eight-hour day for the strikers through pressure upon President Harding and Judge Gary. But unionization of the basic industries—the true issue—had to await the New Deal era. As for William Z. Foster, he emerged shortly as a militant communist leader.

In New England, reaction was fed by the native resentment

against Italian and Irish immigrants and the growth of radical doctrines among them, especially in Boston. The loss of textile leadership to the South and of much of the shoe industry to the Middle West shook the economic fabric of that section. Strikes by hundreds of thousands of textile workers, telephone operators, and others made 1919 a critical year. Worst of all was the Boston police strike, which came as a result of the city's failure to remedy a low salary scale that began at $1100 a year. At the same time, local officials refused to allow the police to organize a union or to strike. The police felt that they had no alternative but to strike and did so, leaving the city without protection. Public opinion turned against the strikers and even President Wilson denounced the strike as "a crime against civilization." When the men tried to return to their posts they were locked out. Governor Calvin Coolidge declared in a politically astute reply to Samuel Gompers of the American Federation of Labor, "There is no right to strike against the public safety by anybody, anywhere, anytime." This statement was so widely acclaimed that it helped to bring Coolidge to the White House.

New England had its Dreyfus Case in the Sacco-Vanzetti affair. In 1920, in South Braintree, Massachusetts, a factory paymaster and guard carrying a payroll were murdered by two armed men who escaped with others waiting in a car. Shortly afterward, two suspects, Sacco, a shoemaker, and Vanzetti, a fish peddler, were arrested and convicted. Subsequently, the defense attorneys claimed that one of the chief prosecution witnesses who identified the men was a professional criminal who was obviously trying to get the prosecuting attorney to drop the charges then pending against him. Grave doubt was also cast upon the alleged expert testimony regarding the ownership of the guns used in the murder. Finally, a gangster, then being held for other crimes, confessed that he had taken part in the Braintree affair and that Sacco and Vanzetti had not been involved. The defense attorneys demanded a new trial, but they were refused by Judge Webster Thayer, who declared that the confession was clearly fabricated. Subsequent appeals, according to state law, could only review the law but not the facts of the case.

Meanwhile, the trial and various court appeals, which dragged on until 1927, aroused international attention. The hue and cry against Sacco and Vanzetti, it became clear, was partly due to their Italian origin and to the fact that they were confirmed—but obviously naïve —radicals of the philosophical anarchist school. Italians, feeling that their community was under attack, came to the rescue of the two men by contributing to their legal fund. So did many liberal and radical organizations. Conservatives and those who disliked foreigners defended Judge Thayer. William Allen White, editor of the *Emporia Gazette* in Kansas, wrote, after a visit to the state: "Until I went into Massachusetts, into the homes of my ancestors in fact, I had no idea that men could let their passion so completely sweep their judgment into fears and hatreds, so deeply confuse their sanity." Professor Felix Frankfurter attacked the evidence offered at the trial and charged that the jurors represented a conservative element in the community. He was assailed in undignified terms by the learned dean of the Northwestern law school, Dr. Wigmore. A convention of the American Federation of Labor charged that Sacco and Vanzetti were "victims of race and national prejudice and class hatred." In Europe, where the case assumed the highest symbolic importance for democratic thought, demonstrations in front of American embassies occurred. The aging novelist, Anatole France, wrote a touching appeal to the "People of the United States of America":

> Listen to the appeal of an old man of the old world who is not a foreigner, for he is the fellow citizen of all mankind.
> In one of your states, two men, Sacco and Vanzetti, have been convicted for a crime of opinion. . . .
> Save them for your honor, for the honor of your children, and for the generations yet unborn.

But nothing could save the condemned and they were executed in 1927. Uneasy consciences were able in 1939 to change the law governing appeal procedure so that prejudiced trial judges would no longer be able to prevent a new trial. An entire Sacco and Vanzetti literature arose. Upton Sinclair told the story in the novel

Boston (1928) and Maxwell Anderson in the play, *Winterset* (1935). John Dos Passos in *The Big Money* (1936), James T. Farrell in *Bernard Clare* (1946), and other leading writers drew upon this material for their novels and stories. The American sense of justice had been shocked by what seemed to be a gross national sin that had to be expiated by repentance.   ·

A rather unbelievable episode of the postwar years was the whole-sale deportation of alien radicals, "the deportation deliriums," as the Assistant Secretary of Labor called it. On December 21, 1919, the "Soviet ark" *Buford* left New York with 249 Russian aliens aboard. Some of them were known extremists like Emma Goldman and Alexander Berkman; most of the deportees were guilty solely of membership in a radical Russian labor federation. Billy Sunday, the irrepressible evangelist, shouted his opinion of this matter to his congregation, "If I had my way with these ornery wild-eyed Socialists and I.W.W.'s, I would stand them up before a firing squad and save space on our ships." These deportations were the after-math of a series of bombings of the homes of American officials, including that of Attorney General A. Mitchell Palmer. Explosives had been discovered in the mails but the guilty were never dis-covered. Palmer's night raids on radical Russian meetings uncovered no helpful clues, though they provided a net with which to catch radicals for deportation. Radical sympathizers were arrested as guilty by association. Liberals criticized the violation of established legal procedures involved in the hasty arrests and in the hearings being conducted without benefit of counsel for the accused. Non-resistant Tolstoyans were arrested in Chicago together with extreme anarchists. Finally, Assistant Secretary of Labor Louis F. Post, sup-ported by his superiors, critically reviewed the orders for arrest and deportation and saved thousands from expulsion. The American Legion and some congressmen demanded Post's impeachment, but President Wilson and leading American jurists upheld him as a vigorous, patriotic official.

Much of the Red scare has become a familiar part of the history of 1919–21; radical newspapers were suppressed; Victor Berger, the Socialist congressman-elect from Milwaukee, was denied his seat by Congress; five Socialists were expelled from the New York State Assembly; and antisubversive statutes, both state and federal, multiplied. The conservative wartime trend in the courts, narrowly construing civil liberties, continued. Legislators, anxious to prove their own loyalty, voted to require teachers to take a loyalty oath to the Constitution and passed innumerable laws controlling textbooks and the curriculum. In 1917, California even required "home teachers" to visit the families of pupils in order to teach patriotic principles of citizenship. Despite the hue and cry regarding disloyalty among educators, thirty-two states reported in 1924 that in seven years no teacher had been charged with disloyalty. As for independently minded teachers, too few dared to exercise their constitutional privileges of criticism among the citizens of their community.

2

Although the Red scare ended by 1921, the decade continued to foster chauvinism and intolerance. In fact the postwar hysteria brought about an amazing revival of the Ku Klux Klan. In 1915, Colonel William J. Simmons, who had been reared in the nostalgic atmosphere of the Lost Cause and the allegedly chivalric tradition of the old Klan, dedicated the organization in a fiery torch ceremony at the top of Stone Mountain near Atlanta. The current popularity of the motion picture, *Birth of a Nation,* with its glorification of the Klan offered generous publicity for Simmons' Invisible Empire. However, it was not until 1920 that the Klan really expanded on a large scale, growing from a few thousand to 100,000 and then, by 1924, to an estimated 2,500,000 members. By that time Simmons had enlisted the unusual promotional abilities of Edward Young Clarke. To inquisitive congressmen, Simmons explained that the Klan was purely a fraternal and patriotic organization; violence, he insisted, was done by outsiders usurping the hooded splendor of the Klan.

Despite the secrecy of the hooded order, reporters discovered a good deal about their program. Unlike the early Klan, the followers of Simmons and Clarke aimed at a national organization with powerful political ties. Much of the membership was middle class and clearly analogous to European fascist groups. Even in the South, it was found desirable to offer something more than an anti-Negro program. Latter-day Klansmen kidnapped and beat Southern labor organizers or punished immoral women. In the East and Middle West, they absorbed the anti-Catholic sentiment of the old Know-Nothing Movement and the American Protective Association. In California and Oregon, they expanded their anti-Catholic program by exploiting anti-Oriental, anti-Semitic, and antiforeign prejudices. In Oregon, the Klan backed a compulsory school law aimed at the parochial schools, hired "escaped nuns" to spread stories of priestly immoralities, and lynched some of their foes in "necktie parties." Fundamentalist groups were sometimes attracted by their prohibition campaign or the idealistic language the Klansmen spoke. Small townspeople and villagers were especially drawn to the thrilling adventure and pageantry of the K.K.K.

With the Klan capturing entire counties and even state governments, as in Indiana, the practical politician often thought it was a good idea to carry a Klan membership card. Klan nightriders intimidated critics, and whipped, tarred and feathered, or mutilated opponents. The *New York World* published an exposé in 1920–21 of the Klan in the South and revealed four murders, two mutilation cases, twenty-seven tar-and-feather parties, forty-one floggings, forty-three cases of individuals being warned to leave town, and one case of branding. Oklahoma, the paradise of the Klan, seemed complacent over the 2000 outrages that took place over a two-year period. While some Klansmen were satisfied with merely parading, others apparently were not. In Texas the Klan was strong enough to secure a law forbidding Negroes to vote in the Democratic primaries, thus in effect disfranchising the Negro. However, this action was challenged by the Supreme Court in *Nixon* v. *Herndon* (1927) which declared that exclusively white primaries violated the equal protection clause of the Fourteenth Amendment.

The Klan of the 1920's was obviously an instrument of ambitious men who rose to power by marshaling the hatreds and fears of the old native white population against Negroes, foreigners, Catholics, and Jews. Some members preferred to harass labor organizers.

Others, as in Texas, used their peculiar methods of persuasion to keep Negro cotton pickers satisfied with a low rate of payment. Local Klan organizations enjoyed considerable choice in deciding upon what "evils" they wished to clean up. Some of the impetus was merely the traditional "joining" spirit. All sorts of secret fraternal societies had long flourished in this country, especially since 1880 and over six hundred fraternal orders of all kinds existed in 1924.

3

An important ingredient in the intolerance and extreme individualism of the 1920's was the "eugenics cult," an illegitimate offspring of scientific eugenics. Although men as far back as Plato have speculated about the creation of a perfect race through scientific principles of breeding, the modern eugenics movement began with Darwin's cousin, Francis Galton, and with Darwin's son, Leonard. In 1908 they helped to organize England's Eugenics Education Society and stimulated a similar movement in the United States under C. B. Davenport. As a rule, the orthodox geneticists did not go beyond advocating the segregation or sterilization of defectives. In *Buck* v. *Bell* (1927), Justice Oliver Wendell Holmes delivered a majority opinion for the Supreme Court upholding Virginia's law that provided sterilization of state institution inmates who were affected by hereditary insanity:

It is better for all the world, if, instead of waiting to execute degenerate offspring for crime, or to let them starve for their imbecility, society can prevent those who are manifestly unfit from continuing their kind. . . . Three generations of imbeciles are enough.

The dangers inherent in this type of reasoning did not become wholly clear until the days when Hitler's doctors adopted a unique eugenics program of their own. Meanwhile, there had already arisen an extremist wing of eugenicists who were convinced that the Anglo-Saxon or Aryan "race" alone deserved to perpetuate their kind or at least to rule over lesser peoples. Such racialism owed much to Count Joseph Arthur de Gobineau who had published his *Essay on the Inequality of the Races of Man* in 1854. This Frenchman had advocated a theory that race determines history and that races differ mentally and physically. He praised the superior role of the "Aryans" in history. A proslavery scientist of Louisiana had edited the English translation in 1856 and enthusiastically endorsed the work. In 1915, a New York publisher issued a fresh English edition. A naturalized German, Houston Stewart Chamberlain, who had married the daughter of the German nationalistic composer, Richard Wagner, wrote another such racialist work which appeared in English as *The Foundations of the Nineteenth Century* (2 vols., 1911). From the racialism of Gobineau and Chamberlain to that of Adolf Hitler the step was short indeed.

In the United States the eugenics cult took up these doctrines of Aryan or Nordic superiority. Madison Grant in *The Passing of the Great Race* (1916) popularized the Gobineau idea that race is the decisive factor in civilization and that the Aryan race alone has created a great civilization. He held that in racial intermarriage, offspring always reverted to the "lower" type; thus the result of a white-Negro crossing would be a Negro, and of an Aryan and Jewish crossing, a Jew. This line of reasoning was later adopted in Nazi pamphlets. Grant's assertions were given greater prestige by his warm supporter, Professor Henry Fairfield Osborn of Columbia, who wrote in a preface, "Race implies heredity and heredity implies all the moral, social, and intellectual characteristics and traits which are the springs of politics and government."

Among the eminent psychologists who lent themselves to the Nordic propaganda was Professor William McDougall of Harvard, author of *Is America Safe for Democracy?* (1920). He tried to prove that "the upper social strata, as compared with the lower, contain a larger proportion of persons of superior natural endowments." Though he rejected crude racial prejudice, he endowed the Nordics with superior qualities. He disposed of the fact that gifted Negroes exist by arguing that they had a large proportion of white blood. This was a familiar argument in the proslavery South. Two other popular Nordicists who issued alarmist messages were Lothrop

Stoddard, author of *The Rising Tide of Color* (1920) and Professor Edwin M. East, geneticist of Harvard, who wrote *Mankind at the Crossroads* (1923). They believed that the "inferior" races had far greater fertility than the Nordic peoples and hence threatened the population with deterioration. These theories were useful to the immigration restrictionists. Another Nordicist of considerable influence was Professor Ellsworth Huntington, a specialist in "human geography," who added fresh, attractive illustrations for the idea that superior races and superior cultures go together.

The most disturbing critic of the Nordicists, one whom they liked to dismiss as a member of an inferior race, was Professor Franz Boas of Columbia, leader of the "Boas School" whose complete victory came later, in the 1930's. In his best-known work, *The Mind of Primitive Man* (1911), Boas did not seem to go as far as his disciples did in stressing the approximate equality of races, but this was due to his caution of expression. He denied that any proof existed that the physical differences between races were matched by a corresponding cultural or mental gap. In his *Anthropology and Modern Life* (1928) he had this to say to the eugenic cultists: "Eugenics should ... not be allowed to deceive us into the belief that we should try to raise a race of supermen, nor that it should be our aim to eliminate all suffering and pain. ... Eugenics is not a panacea that will cure human ills; it is rather a dangerous sword that may turn its edge against those who rely on its strength." Always he emphasized that race and culture were independent of each other and that aggressive nationalistic indoctrination ran counter to the internationalism fostered by modern technological progress. He deplored the "modern enthusiasm for race superiority" and declared that while the idea of nationality has been a creative force it could only be important if it carried ideals of value to mankind. Boas was not alone in combatting Nordicism. He had many "Nordic" allies of distinction such as Robert H. Lowie, editor of the *American Anthropologist* and Raymond Pearl, professor of biology at Johns Hopkins University. But the atmosphere of the 1920's favored their opponents.

4

The national immigration policy of the twenties was a hybrid of dubious parentage. While it seemed obvious that the prewar flood of unrestricted immigration would sooner or later be curbed in response to economic pressure, the unscientific ideas behind the new immigration laws are significant. Members of the eugenics cult acted as "experts" to congressional committees dealing with restriction. Senator Henry Cabot Lodge of Massachusetts, representative of the old native families and an aggressive nationalist, had held the leadership of this restrictionist movement since 1890. He lived to see his literacy test, aimed at the New Immigration, survive the vetoes of Cleveland, Taft, and Wilson and emerge triumphant as law in 1917. Patriotic societies, especially the hereditary organizations, joined the restrictionists. Not a few labor organizations, including the American Federation of Labor, were outspokenly restrictionist, though they were concerned only with the economic competition of cheap foreign labor. A generation of debate and propaganda culminated in the nationalistic 1920's in a series of anti-immigration laws. However, the immigrant had his friends, too. Jane Addams, Grace Abbott, and other social workers took up their pens to demonstrate the cultural and economic contributions of the immigrant. Naturalized Americans like Jacob Riis and Mary Antin wrote effective books in behalf of the newcomers.

However, war propaganda had cast doubt upon the loyalty of "hyphenated Americans" and the Palmer Raids had initiated an orgy of deportation that obviously strengthened antiforeignism. Many employers who might have favored a generous immigration policy in their own self-interest were shaken by the Red scare and tended to suspect that the latest immigrants were radicals and revolutionaries. The amazing growth of the Klan in the North revealed the existence of strong anti-Catholic, anti-Semitic, and antiforeign sentiments. These were largely directed against the New Immigration.

The Johnson Act of 1921, which set up the quota system, was passed in spite of Wilson's hostility to it and was signed by Harding.

According to this Act the number of aliens admitted each year from any particular nation could not exceed 3 per cent of the number of persons of such nationality resident here in 1910. This was a temporary device intended not only to halt an anticipated flood of immigrants from stricken postwar Europe but to favor northern and western nationalities—the Nordics. Much more important was the Immigration Act of 1924, which replaced the Johnson Act. The legislators tried to reduce the volume of immigration further by cutting the quota percentage from 3 to 2 per cent and they attempted to increase the Nordic content by changing the basic quota date from 1910 to 1890, a year when the New Immigration was still weak.

Especially interesting in the law of 1924 was the national origins clause, which was planned to keep the population as homogeneous as possible and to reduce immigration still further. This clause was intended to go into effect in 1927 but did not actually do so until 1929. It fixed the total annual immigration at 150,000 and directed that quotas for each nation should be calculated according to the proportion of *descendants* of each nationality resident here in 1920. Since each person presumably had two parents, four grandparents, and a horde of earlier ancestors, it would take rather expert genealogists to determine the national origins of most Americans. However, the Nordic advocates were undeterred by such puzzles.

Under the quota system those nations needing emigration outlets usually failed to get relief while the relatively stable Northwestern nations often left their quotas only partly filled. The objective of excluding Southern and Eastern Europeans was partly successful; but, since the nations of the Western Hemisphere were exempted from the quota law the Nordic restrictionists must have been appalled by the huge numbers of Catholics who filled the gap left by the labor shortage: Mexicans, French-Canadians, Puerto Ricans, and those from the American dependency of the Philippine Islands. The movement of Negroes to the urban-industrial areas was likewise accelerated by the immigration laws, which cut off a large source of unskilled labor. Another result of these immigration laws and their stringent application was the separation of families coming from Southern and Eastern Europe. Desperate men had every incentive to attempt illegal entry and risk the chances of deportation.

5

Not only did the drop in the New Immigration leave a shortage of unskilled labor, but the change in the American diet from an emphasis on cereals and meats to more fruits, vegetables, and dairy products created a great demand for cheap produce workers along the Pacific Coast. Mexicans, Filipinos, and Japanese toiled patiently in the sun to harvest the crops of fruits and vegetables. Without these pickers the perishable crops would have rotted on the ground. The Mexicans were the most numerous. In 1910 there had been only 381,000 Mexicans in this country; by 1920 there were over 701,000, and a decade later 1,423,000. They usually came from backward rural communities and villages where mortality was high, illiteracy prevalent, and the standard of living far below the minimum subsistence level. To them, American wages seemed fabulously high.

There was a constant flow back and forth across the border of Mexican laborers who followed the harvests as migratory workers. In the cotton fields of Southern and Western Texas they took jobs that would have gone to Negroes and acted as a human barrier for a time against the westward movement of the Negro. In the Imperial Valley of California, Mexicans picked cantaloupes, lettuce, cotton, and grapefruit. During the cantaloupe season they might earn as much as five to seven dollars a day, but this was far above the typical wage of Mexican laborers. Farm communities usually preferred the Mexican farm hand because he seemed content to remain in this status rather than to become a landowner in their midst. Before the decade ended they were replacing Negroes in Northern steel mills, auto plants, stockyards, and railroad construction yards. Mexican colonies sprang up in Chicago, Gary, Pittsburgh, Kansas City, and Detroit. In the Southwest there were entire Mexican communities around the Plaza of Los Angeles and the industrial section of San Antonio.

Segregation and cultural differences set the Mexican colony apart. Their children attended segregated schools; dark-skinned Mexicans were frequently denied entrance to hotels; and many found it expedient to insist that they were of pure Spanish descent. They consoled themselves that they belonged to *La Raza*—the "race" of Mexican people. Heavy mortality and disease accompanied their low economic standards. In their communities they learned to cooperate in numerous mutual aid societies and social clubs. Primarily a peasant people, they resembled the Southern Italian in some of their folkways and religious practices. Their Catholicism was a compound of Spanish Catholicism, Indian beliefs, and folklore. They emigrated at a time when the Mexican government was campaigning against clericalism and religious schools; hence a good deal of indifference toward active church life existed in some quarters. Besides, American Catholicism seemed to lack the thrilling pageantry of the old Mexican Church with its colorful street processions and native traditions like the fiesta of the Virgin of Guadalupe. In the industrial colonies, young Mexicans sometimes joined the I.W.W. or similar radical organizations that were willing to accept them as equals. The American Federation of Labor seemed slow to absorb the Mexican workers.

The Mexicans loved music and many a family sacrificed enough from their meager income to buy a phonograph even if they had to live in a bare shack. At festivities, including saints' days, they hired a small orchestra or a piano. A minstrel sang the old ballads, strummed on his guitar, and played American dance music. With a strong folk tradition for improvising new words to old music, they composed songs dealing with their coming to the United States, their current successes, or with the crooked labor contractors who duped them. The younger Mexican-American generation, remarked Manuel Gamio, the Mexican sociologist, thought that the songs of their parents were too sentimental or silly. They preferred "I Love My Baby" to the ballads, and thought that music was something restricted to dancing. In the cheap Mexican eating places electric pianolas played the familiar tunes over and over again. Their dishes, enriched with varied meats in the more affluent

American environment, included chicken or beef enchiladas, tacos, chili, tamales, tortillas, beans, and rice. American restaurants in the Southwest offered these delicacies to both native and Mexican customers.

6

Overcrowded Japan had obvious reasons for emigration. At first the emigrants went to Hawaii where they had no serious problem in being accepted in the mixed community. As late as 1900 only 10,000 Japanese resided on the mainland of this country. Yet that very year anti-Chinese leagues sponsored the first Japanese exclusion meeting. In the beginning, the alert, courteous, and hardworking Japanese were welcomed to California, but this cordiality wore off after the victory of Japan over Russia in 1905 and an attitude of suspicion spread. In San Francisco a corrupt city government tried to stay in power by playing up the Japanese menace. Although there were only ninety-three Japanese children in the city, the administration, in 1906, ordered that they be segregated in separate schools. Japan protested vehemently. Previously that same year, when the great earthquake and fire demolished the city, hoodlums had singled out Japanese stores and property for destruction.

The Hearst press campaigned for years against the "yellow peril" while the American Federation of Labor denounced the competition of cheap Japanese labor. An international crisis was averted when President Roosevelt persuaded California to suspend her pending anti-Japanese laws. At the same time he concluded the famous Gentleman's Agreement of 1907 by which Japan promised to refuse passports to her laborers bound for the United States mainland. Mob attacks continued along the West Coast. Although most of the charges against the Japanese had been leveled in the past at other immigrant groups and were demonstrably false, the racialist factor intensified the degree of prejudice. The real yellow menace at the time came from the yellow press. For example, the irresponsible newspaper campaign in 1913 to keep the Japanese from owning land broke out at a time when the total amount of land held by them was only 12,726 acres distributed among 331 farms. California

under Governor Hiram Johnson was as stubbornly opposed to
federal advice on race relations as any Southern state.

Exclusionists thwarted the attempt of the Japanese to import
women through the "picture bride" system. Yet family life was
essential to stability in a disproportionately male community,
especially in a state that forbade racial intermarriage. The newspapers grossly exaggerated the child-bearing qualities of the
Japanese and never tired of raising the specter of a yellow menace.
As a result, the so-called Ladies' Agreement stopped the issuance
of passports to brides after February, 1920. In various laws, California closed the remaining doors open to the Japanese. A land law
of 1920 forbade the leasing of land by "aliens ineligible to citizenship" and prohibited Japanese from obtaining contracts as sharecroppers. Other Southwestern and West Coast states followed
California's leadership. Fortunately, American-born Japanese were
protected by the Fourteenth Amendment from legal discriminations.
The worst blow to Japanese pride came in 1924 with the passage
in Congress of the Japanese Exclusion Act despite the opposition
of Secretary of State Charles E. Hughes. By this time the fear of
Japan had increased and the stereotype of the cunning Oriental
was widely current. Secretary Hughes pointed out that Japan would
be satisfied with a mere token immigration and that the quota
would actually limit Japanese immigrants to only 146 a year. However, Lodge and the nationalists were convinced that Japan had
threatened this country by using the phrase "grave consequences"
in its formal statement of protest; these extremists demanded—and
secured—nothing short of total exclusion. Meanwhile, in 1925, a
West Coast community loaded Japanese sawmill workers and their
families on trucks and drove them out of town. Such incidents
made it easier for Japanese militarists to win support at home for
their aggressive ideas of world power.

The Japanese on the West Coast scarcely displaced any substantial group by taking up farm work in the sugar beet, fruit, and
vegetable industries. Wherever they were permitted to cultivate
the soil they often reclaimed waste lands and converted them into
green fields and abundant crops. In Japan they had learned the art

of utilizing a thin soil on a crowded, irregular terrain, and now they added materially to the agricultural wealth of their adopted country. Japanese fishermen introduced the abalone to American homes as a delicacy. When West Coast laws forced the Japanese off the land, they returned to the cities and became very successful merchants of fruits and vegetables in Los Angeles, Stockton, Portland, and Seattle. "Little Tokyos" sprang up as segregated but thriving Japanese communities.

One of the reasons for the amazing successes of the Japanese-Americans under adversity was their unusual cooperative spirit and the communal organizations that they formed after the home-land patterns. Japanese cooperative associations lent money to farmers in distress and aided those who were dispossessed by whites. Their stores advanced credit liberally while community agencies helped to locate employment for their members. Their literacy was exceptionally high by any standard. At the end of this decade the Issei (or Japanese-born Americans) averaged eight years of education in Japan and the Nisei (or native-born Americans of Japanese ancestry) usually were high-school graduates and often college students. Japanese-language schools and Buddhist temples existed on a large scale in this era due to segregation and the im-migrant's early desire to perpetuate the culture of his native land. Christianity made rapid inroads, aided by the fact that it appeared to offer social acceptance within Western culture. Methodist and Presbyterian missionaries gained innumerable Japanese converts but they were unable to stop the practice of segregating the Orientals in separate churches. Restrictive racial laws, of course, did not apply to the Nisei and their future seemed bright until World War II.

7

The Filipinos were latecomers among the migrant farm workers and laborers along the West Coast. Since the Philippine Islands had become an American dependency, there were no serious bar-riers to immigration unless Congress chose to set up restrictions. In 1920 only 5600 Filipinos lived in the United States, but by 1930 they had increased to 45,000 and congressmen were proposing total exclusion. About nine-tenths of the Filipino arrivals were young unmarried men who had left rural and often primitive island homes where poverty had been the rule. Culturally, they seemed as diverse as possible, for the Philippines were far from national or cultural unity. Many had been reared in the Oriental custom of squatting on the floor while eating their meals or sleeping on mats. Centuries of Spanish and Catholic rule had given a language, a faith, and a way of life to most, but not all. Island isolation preserved diverse pagan and primitive customs and languages. American Protestant missionaries and officials were now adding a new cultural influence.

Filipinos had come in small numbers to Hawaii and the American mainland before World War I. Many hundreds found work in the navy yards or as houseboys. In Eastern Washington large numbers could be seen during the harvest season working in the beet fields, picking apples, or digging potatoes. They found little competition as farm hands in the rapidly expanding lettuce and carrot industry. They were excellent gardeners and proved to be such efficient domestic help that they were preferred to the middle-aged white couples who did this work. In the West Coast cities of Los Angeles, San Francisco, Stockton, and Seattle they became busboys and cooks in restaurants, elevator boys in hotels, and manual workers. Many employers liked them because they were clean, had pleasant manners, and appeared anxious to please. Hundreds of Filipinos went to work in the canneries along the Coast, rubbing shoulders with Portuguese, Mexican, and Italian workmen. In this era of labor scarcity Filipinos were making a definite economic contribution.

However, the current anti-Oriental and anti-Mexican prejudices were soon applied to them. As a largely male community, the Filipino areas showed considerable social instability. Thousands were forever on the move, traveling from one job to another. Journalists and busybodies exaggerated their delinquencies and spoke resentfully of their successes with white women. West Coast laws against intermarriage, borrowed from the Old South, hampered non-Caucasians, though Filipinos often convinced the justice of the peace that they were not among the races covered by the ban. Their crowded houses of this era were typically slum dwellings. Yet the Filipinos knew enough of mutual aid organization rarely to become a public burden. The Y.M.C.A. and other agencies proved helpful in adjusting the Filipino to American urban conditions and in finding recreational substitutes for the taxi dance halls, poolrooms, and gambling houses that seemed inviting to lonely unattached males.

But organized racialist groups, supported by chauvinistic and fraternal societies, demanded by 1930 that the Filipino immigration cease. The decade ended with occasional attacks against Filipino farm hands and their property in Washington and California. Although the avowed causes seemed economic, the underlying factors were racialist and psychological. Concrete evidence that the Filipino was no threat to the livelihood of the American proved unavailing against bigots. Racialist and cultural antipathies provoked the mob spirit and influenced the naïve-minded.

8

Anglo-Canadians and French-Canadians poured over the border in an increasing stream across a broad belt from New York State and New England along the northern American states to the Pacific Coast. About one-third of the Canadians were from the French-speaking eastern provinces of Canada. The Anglo-Canadians of this decade increased from 104,000 to 274,000 and the French-Canadians grew from 40,400 to over 91,000. It may be noted that immigration directly from England also rose in these years from 111,000 to nearly 160,000. Nearly 80 per cent of the Canadian immigrants lived in American cities and towns rather than in the rural areas. While the Protestant Anglo-Canadians, like the English immigrants, were too similar in culture to the old American group to be easily indentified and studied as a compact society, the Catholic French-Canadians stood out as a definite minority group. Their settlements had been contiguous across the New England border and large numbers could be found in Massachusetts factories and New Hampshire

farms. Many lived in Michigan and California. During the 1880's
and 1890's their arrival had aroused a storm of controversy but
this had subsided since then.

Well over a third of the French-Canadians found work in the
factories and competed with the Irish, Italian, Greek, and other
newcomers for the better posts. For centuries in French Quebec they
had maintained their culture and the conservative traditions of the
France of Louis XIV. Their Catholic churches had never been
secularized in the fashion of the Gallic church abroad since the
French Revolution. Liberalism did not conquer in France until
long after their ancestors had left. Nearly one in ten could not speak
English and their communities continued as of yore to be patriarchal
and conservative with families that were larger on the average than
was the case in most American homes. Like other immigrants, they
were well supplied with mutual aid societies offering life insurance,
sick benefits, and loans. A central federal organization of such local
French-Canadian societies existed at Woonsocket, Rhode Island.

9

The decline of immigration opened new vocations and opportunities for the Negro, although in the North and West he had to
compete with the Mexicans and Orientals. At the same time, unskilled Negro laborers pushed the older Europeans into skilled and
semiskilled positions. In the South, where Negroes also moved into
the cities, they found themselves forced to retreat along the economic
front by the concurrent movement of rural whites to urban centers.
These whites drove Negroes out of trades and service jobs that had
been considered "nigger work" since slavery days. Not only were
the Southern Negroes almost eliminated from the white trade as
barbers and waiters, but they lost out as carpenters and even as
garbage collectors. As in the past, race conflicts stirred up Southern
communities and kept able Negroes from doing new kinds of work.

In the North several factors interfered with the rapid advance of
Negro well-being. Unions jealously excluded them from the
highly skilled positions while the competition of the machine and

the new technology injured the status of the unskilled Negro worker. Negroes who aspired to become doctors might, if they were fortunate, enter the few Negro medical schools, but those who were able to gain admission into white medical colleges were often handicapped fatally by the inability to receive an internship in a white hospital. Nevertheless, the Negroes found innumerable positions, some of them at a better-paying level, in steel, meat-packing, rubber, and auto plants. Open-shop employers welcomed Negroes because they seemed immune to unionization. New white-collar positions at good salaries were available in the federal and local civil service. During this decade the federal government alone doubled the number of Negroes in its employment. Especially impressive was the continued growth of Negro businesses, although their efforts to exclude white competitors from their colored trade strengthened segregation and race consciousness. Negro banks, insurance companies, newspapers, retail stores, and factories came into existence on a substantial scale. Booker T. Washington, had he lived, would have been happy to see the efflorescence of the Negro business movement that he had sponsored. The statistics for Negro home-owning, however modest by white standards, showed a comforting increase in well-being. The high mortality rate among Negroes declined markedly as the standard of living improved.

At the same time, this decade continued the prewar gains in Negro education. The school year in the South was lengthened from 120 to 131 days for Negro schools. Although Southern legislatures were still reluctant to keep expenditures for Negro education up to that for whites, the South could boast that it had built more high schools for Negroes during the 1920's alone than during the entire past. By 1930, the Negro elite included about 15,000 college graduates of whom forty were Ph.D.'s and sixty-five had been elected to the Phi Beta Kappa society.

The future of the race was partly secured by the growing political strength of the Negro communities in Chicago and in New York's Harlem. Chicago's colored South Side was able to elect a Negro congressman and to win concessions in local civil service employment and social welfare. Even the uneducated Negro voter knew

far better what was good for him than those Southerners who tried
to withhold the ballot from him. Despite race riots by vicious
gangs, interracial attitudes improved. Leading Southern writers
more than ever showed sympathy and understanding in dealing
with the Negro. The Southern literary renaissance of the twenties
produced such fine novels or plays about Negroes as DuBose Heyward's *Porgy* and *Mamba's Daughters*, Julia Peterkin's *Black April*
and *Scarlet Sister Mary*, and Paul Green's *In Abraham's Bosom*. So
unusual was this tendency to substitute real Negroes for the Uncle
Tom and Uncle Remus stereotypes that readers often assumed that
Heyward, Peterkin, Green, and certain other Southern writers were
Negroes. Heyward, a descendant of a signer of the Declaration of
Independence and of the old South Carolina aristocracy, once arrived to lecture at a large university and found himself described by
local publicity as "not only a member of Harlem's intellectual colony
but a Southern Negro of the old tradition."

The gains did not come without serious setbacks. As the postwar
Negro communities grew rapidly in the North, and to some extent
in the South as well, interracial conflicts grew in the large cities.
Klansmen and racial chauvinists added fuel to the fire. The year
of 1919 in Negro history was the "red summer," not because of the
communist scare but because of violent attacks upon the Negro.
However, Negroes had acquired during the war a greater awareness
of the meaning of democratic principles and showed a disposition
to defend themselves that made mobs pay a price for their sadism.
The worst race riot in American history occurred in Chicago, where
109,000 Negroes lived. Bad housing conditions, especially the over-
flow of Negro neighborhoods into white districts, and poor recreational facilities were among the basic causes of the riot. A bathing
beach dispute led to a wholesale attack upon the Negro South Side.
For thirteen days hoodlums whipped, stoned, and even killed on a
purely racial basis. When order was restored there were twenty-
three Negroes and fifteen whites dead, hundreds of both races
injured, and about a thousand Negro families left homeless. Even
the capital of the nation saw a serious race conflict. Southern cities
and towns had their own experiences of racial conflicts at the same

time. Altogether, about twenty-six race riots seared the country in 1919.

The eugenics cultists made their own contribution to racialism in the South. They led twenty-nine states, mostly Southern, to tighten the guardianship over racial purity by enacting the so-called "racial integrity" laws. Fears that individuals with some Negro blood were "passing" as whites led to a legal definition of a Negro that resembled the later Nazi Nuremburg laws regarding Jews. Eleven states forbade a white to marry anyone with an eighth of Negro blood. Alabama, Georgia, and Virginia went even farther, considering a man to be a Negro if he had the slightest trace of Negro ancestry. This racial program was part of a general campaign for white supremacy.

Patient Negro leaders felt encouraged to note the sudden drop in the number of lynchings. In 1919, at the height of the Negro "red summer," there were seventy lynched, according to Tuskegee Institute figures; but in 1924, the figure had fallen to sixteen and in 1929 to seven. Southern states showed a greater determination to protect their prisoners against lynchers. The young N.A.A.C.P. reported some successes in advancing Negro rights, as in the case of *Herndon* v. *Nixon*, which nullified the Texas white primaries. They did manage to put a federal antilynching bill through the House of Representatives, but it was killed by a Southern filibuster in the Senate.

The naïve and the discouraged were attracted for a time to the African Zionism of a Jamaica-born Negro, Marcus Garvey, who had created a New York branch of the Universal Negro Improvement Association in 1916. Garvey encouraged the Negro to develop a strong pride of race and to give up the hope that American whites would ever concede the rights of the Negro. His solution lay in a "Back to Africa" movement, the founding of an American Negro state on that continent, and the building of Negro enterprises. He collected about ten million dollars between 1919 and 1921 and used one million of it to buy and outfit the Black Star Steamship Line. His followers wore fancy uniforms and were fed on extravagant hopes. Garveyites with obvious exaggeration claimed four or five million members, but they may have had as many as five hundred thousand. Finally, the leader was imprisoned for swindling and, after serving part of his sentence, was deported as an undesirable alien. So ended the strange career of Marcus Garvey. There were other attractive messiahs in that day. George Baker, known as Father Divine, began in 1919 to attract wealthy sponsors, including some white followers, for his vague ideas of transforming earth into heaven and of achieving perpetual peace. His followers were admitted to generous feasts and celebrations at his various "heavens" and "Peace Missions." Father Divine developed his social-religious movement along interracial lines and his pleasant eccentricities did not usually disturb the police.

10

In 1927, a prominent rabbi declared pessimistically of the status of the Jew in America, "We seem to have gone backwards. Conditions are not nearly so bright as forty-five years ago." Familiar with Jewish history, he did not regard the current economic advances made by Jews as a criterion of group acceptance or security. The bitter national controversy over the New Immigration had encouraged the eugenics cult and other intolerant groups to spread anti-Semitism, especially since the 1890's. In reply, Jews organized national defensive societies such as the American Jewish Committee (1906) and the Anti-Defamation League of B'nai Brith (1913). They were stirred in 1915 by the sensational Leo Frank case, when a Jew was hastily convicted of a murder and sex charge and then lynched by a Georgia mob.

Although the Soviets liquidated the Jewish middleman in Russia and oppressed Jewish religious groups together with those of other faith, the anti-Semite of both Europe and America spread charges that the Jews had instigated the revolution and now dominated it. Old anti-Semitic libels were carefully collected by the staff of Henry Ford and published serially in *The Dearborn* (Michigan) *Independent*. These included the Czarist propaganda of the obviously forged *Protocols of the Elders of Zion*, purporting to be a record of a Jewish world conspiracy. In later years the Ford articles reappeared under Nazi auspices as *The International Jew*. Ford himself publicly disavowed these articles, but they were translated and perpetuated by anti-Semites in Europe and Latin America as late as the 1940's.

The Klan also expanded its anti-Semitic appeal during these years and even the colleges and professions reflected the increased animosity to Jews. Ludwig Lewisohn, the German-Jewish novelist who had come here in 1890, described these racial discriminations that the colleges practiced in his autobiographical works, *Upstream* (1922) and *Midchannel* (1929). The medieval *numerus clausus*, or quota system, had been widely revived to restrict the number of Jewish students. Hotels and summer resorts persisted in a policy of racial discrimination which included Jews among the proscribed classes.

The war also left a heavy financial burden upon the American Jewish community because of the fact that Eastern European Jewry had been impoverished during the years in which their towns and villages had been part of the battlefield. In consequence, the Joint Distribution Committee was organized and gave efficient large-scale relief and rehabilitation opportunities to millions of people. Another consequence of the war was the Balfour Declaration of 1917 by which England committed herself to a Palestinian homeland for Jews. Wilson and other American leaders expressed a deep sympathy for this step, which might have saved hundreds of thousands of Eastern European refugees had the project been promptly executed. Despite the disillusionment that followed the attempts of England to modify her obligations under the Balfour Declaration because of Arab hostility, a fresh symbol of hope was given to the Zionists. While Reformed Jewry, largely German, and the Yiddish-speaking labor movement insisted that "America is our Zion," the attractions of political nationalism to a rejected group resulted in a rapidly increasing number of Zionists. At first, English and continental Jews like Chaim Weizmann (he had been born in Russia) took the leadership under the Balfour Declaration, but the final decisions and support depended upon the preponderant American Jewish community now that the communists had forced Russian Zionism underground.

· 19 ·

A Business Civilization:
Era of Henry Ford

[1919-1929]

I

IN GERMANY the new word "Fordismus" summed up the great American achievement in industry. German technicians came to study Henry Ford's assembly line and the efficiency of scientific management as taught by Frederick W. Taylor. Lenin and the Soviet leaders conceded that Ford's assembly methods and Taylorization were among the very few things that they admired in bourgeois American society. By 1921, Ford was building a million cars a year. He had been tempted, but had refused, to accept a billion-dollar offer to sell out his Detroit business. His high wage policy had enabled him to reduce the costly turnover of laborers. Workers had hitherto rebelled against being automatons on the assembly line but the opportunity of earning five dollars a day reconciled them to the monotony. Ford needed only three-fifths as many men as in prewar days to make the same number of cars. Though Ford did not keep up his wage scales during the twenties, he was still ahead of his competitors in output. He and his two chief rivals, General Motors (a du Pont-Morgan firm), and the Chrysler Corporation, produced four-fifths of all automobiles made in this country. In 1927, Ford made the necessary concession to the fact that Americans, if they could afford it, preferred some esthetic variations from the simple, standardized Model T car. Hence he introduced the more attractive Model A amid huge advertising fanfare. Ford idolized the cult of efficiency. He had been partly influenced to send his famous Peace Ship in 1915 to "bring the boys home by Christmas" after reading of the waste of thousands of soldiers' lives in a futile campaign that left the battle lines unchanged.

Labor's hostility to Taylorization had declined during the favorable era of World War I. Thereafter, increased industrial competition and a narrower margin of profit led employers to intensify the application of scientific management to the most efficient use of materials, labor, and machinery. Billions of dollars were saved by industry through the processes of "standardization" and "simplification." Secretary of Commerce Herbert Hoover, an engineer by training, was a leader in the movement to eliminate waste and costly duplication. Millions were spent every year in industrial research. The successful businessman gave up his rule of thumb methods for the utmost rationality in planning, production, and distribution: cost accounting, business forecasting services, personnel management, inventory control, advertising, sales promotion departments, and marketing bureaus.

In this race for efficiency, more than eight thousand manufacturing and mining firms disappeared within a decade while the remaining corporations greatly increased in size. The resulting advance of bigness in industry, trade, and finance was also marked by the expansion of chain stores and branch banking and by the domination of the power industry by ten groups of holding companies. In 1929 half of the corporate wealth of the nation was held by two hundred corporations. This accelerated trend toward monopoly even affected the international scene in the form of cartels. Government itself recognized the trend by relaxing the enforcement of the antitrust laws and by encouraging the trade association movement among businessmen. Not all of this trend toward bigness was due to the search for reduced production costs, but it was a major factor. The theory of competition had to be substantially modified in practice. In the highly competitive automobile business, for example, the National Automobile Chamber of Commerce, which included all but Ford, issued monthly reports of sales and pooled the new patents in their common interest. Railroad executives, who fought government operation of the trains, nevertheless wished some kind of government price-fixing in order to keep minimum rates at a profitable level.

The prestige of the businessman rested upon the undeniable prosperity of this era after 1921 except for weaknesses in staple farming, mining, and a few other industries. The automobile, the real estate boom, and the public utility business led the procession of prosperity. The value of furniture, clothing, and other personal articles of consumption far outstripped the rising cost of living. Real wages gained substantially and the number and size of savings accounts rose rapidly. Americans could boast that their national wealth was almost equal to that of all Europe. Over 23,000,000 cars were on the highways and millions looked upon the automobile as part of a minimum standard of living. Installment selling of retail goods reached the unprecedented total of $7,000,000,000 in 1929 and made available more automobiles, radios, and furniture than ever before.

Never before had American businessmen and economists been so confident that the erratic fluctuations of the business cycle had come under control and that severe depressions were a thing of the past. The slogan of that era was "Stabilization of business" and Hoover believed that the end of poverty was in sight. Will Hays, Republican national chairman, popularized the businessman's slogan, "Less government in business, more business in government." Income taxes were cut, war debts were largely retired, a scientific budget and accounting system was introduced into government, and statesmen were elected who believed that the real initiative and leadership in American society belonged to the businessman. Party differences did not seem too acute to the millions who ceased to go to the polls. Regulatory agencies born during the trust-busting era were allowed to atrophy. Protective tariffs and subsidies went to the businessman, but few favors were accorded the farmer.

As long as prosperity continued, the "booster spirit" of Kiwanis, Rotary, the Lions, and other luncheon and service clubs prevailed and the solidarity of businessmen was affirmed. Individualism was the keynote of this business civilization and its counterpart in foreign affairs was isolationism, though private investments abroad of $13,000,000,000 in 1927 showed that capital itself was not isolationist.

Labor's surviving militancy declined after the disastrous Railway Shopmen's Strike of 1922 and the concurrent upswing of business conditions. The employer's "open shop movement" had weakened the unions. One aspect of this drive was the sponsorship of company unions that were little more than recreational clubs. By 1926 there were over 400 company unions covering over 1,300,000 employees. Under the new science of personnel management, there was a tendency to reduce the labor turnover by group insurance plans that terminated when the employee left or through old-age pension programs. Factories often enjoyed such frills as cafeterias, free clinics, glee clubs, plant baseball or basketball teams, and other attractions. Many companies encouraged their employees to buy stock in the firm by offering them shares at low prices. Rarely did employee ownership come even close to majority control, but here was another incentive device to insure labor cooperation. Thus "welfare capitalism" made palatable the revival of the labor injunction and the yellow-dog contract (which the courts upheld) and hastened the decline of prewar industrial unionism. As for the craft unions, they remained content with the progress made by the bricklayers, the carpenters, the printers, and others in the skilled trades and were often complacent when labor racketeers moved in to control a local. Although Samuel Gompers of the American Federation of Labor took the unusual step in 1924 of supporting the Progressive party, he died that year and his conservative "pure and simple" unionism was continued by William Green of Ohio, a former member of the United Mine Workers. Gompers and Green were as ruggedly individualistic as Coolidge and Hoover.

2

The continued growth of cities and the birth of the numerous metropolitan areas intensified the economic and moral individualism fostered by the triumph of business ideals. Farm families, as before, migrated at a rapid rate to the villages, towns, and cities, although the trend sharply declined between 1925 and the Great Depression. A net emigration of nearly six million people left the country for urban homes during this decade. The Negro from the rural South made up much of this migration. As the youth left for the city, many rural counties, especially in New England, seemed to consist of old people.

Farm mechanization eliminated the need for millions of marginal farmers, particularly in the staple crop sections, though tobacco and many non-cereal crops prospered. However, farm life steadily improved on the whole for the families who remained on the land. Millions of farmers bought automobiles, radios, and modern furniture, and installed telephones. The number of farms that were wired for electricity almost doubled.

Although rural migration to the city may have had certain conservative stabilizing effects upon the metropolis, urbanization continued to break up the traditional and patriarchal tendencies of the family. The term "emancipated woman" was becoming old-fashioned, but the process of independence for that sex moved at a more rapid pace than ever. In 1920 the Susan B. Anthony woman suffrage amendment, once planned to be the Sixteenth Amendment to the Constitution, became at long last the Nineteenth. Thus the electorate was doubled and women were encouraged to participate in far more decisions than those concerning "children, cooking, and church-going." As yet there was the tendency to rely upon the husband's political judgment, but innumerable women's clubs and leagues arose to challenge the politician and to initiate valuable social legislation. In 1921, for example, women's lobbies succeeded in forcing through the federal Shepard-Towner Act, which set up bureaus of child hygiene and prenatal centers. State lobbies of women promoted similar child welfare legislation and political

devices to secure honest government. In 1922 the Cable Act raised
the status of women by giving citizenship to otherwise eligible
married women regardless of whether their husbands were citizens
or not.

There were far more careers open to women than Frances Willard
or Susan B. Anthony had ever dreamed of. To be self-supporting
gave a young woman a chance to decide upon a mate more according to the prevailing ideas of romantic attachments. About 10 per
cent of married women were employed outside the home during
these years. The delicatessen, the bakery, and labor-saving devices
in the kitchen made more leisure available to housewives. Compulsory education and nursery schools took the children off the
hands of the parents during much of the day.

Middletown (Muncie, Indiana), according to the Lynds, revealed
many weaknesses in the marital structure. Too few couples enjoyed
real companionship or shared common enjoyable activities, except
possibly for the bridge games. On Sunday morning, the husband
escaped to play golf or to go hunting with his cronies. Divorces had
increased six times since 1890 and were usually acquired by using
a subterfuge like non-support or cruelty. "Anybody with $25 can
get a divorce," asserted one citizen. The syndicated newspaper
column of Dorothy Dix, who was closely and approvingly read by
at least half the married women, expressed this individualistic
viewpoint:

Probably men are as good husbands now as they ever were, but grand-
mother had to stand grandpa, for he was her meal ticket and her card
of admission to good society. . . . We see that no good purpose is achieved
by keeping two people together who have come to hate each other.

For the country as a whole, divorces increased from one for every
seventeen marriages in 1887 to one for every six in 1924.

American children had always seemed a bit "spoiled" in the eyes
of European visitors, but they had become "problems" in this age of
the "flapper" and of "accent on youth." Middle-class families, both
Protestant and Catholic, practiced birth control and lavished more
affection on the child or two that they had. There was the example

of adult women who used cigarettes, bobbed their hair, drank cocktails, and wore short skirts. In Middletown, school children put their "old-fashioned" parents in their place by the man-to-man type of criticism and went on unchaperoned dates that often lasted until midnight. Questionnaires revealed that petting parties were general among high-school youth and that half of them spent no more than four evenings a week at home. The teen-age boy was expected to call on his girl in a car and the two usually went off to dances or to see sexy movies. *True Story* was a popular magazine for these adolescents.

The twenties were characterized by a greater frankness about sex. In the larger cities, especially in the hotel apartment areas, there was a trend toward extra-marital relationships. Judge Ben Lindsey of Denver, the noted social worker and judicial reformer, caused a sensation when he proposed that society recognize the existing trend by adopting a plan of "companionate marriage" for a trial period before marriage. Freudianism in a vulgarized form gave the sophisticated a pseudoscientific patter regarding sex repressions and inhibitions. It even became advantageous for authors of books or plays to have them banned temporarily or condemned as salacious. Bootleg gin, roadhouse parties, and fast automobiles added their synthetic thrill to this era.

Rural America had long attempted to stem the tide of hedonism through prohibition, but the cities had resisted such legislation. Even after 1920, when the Eighteenth Amendment was ratified, the urban population effectively sabotaged its enforcement. In fact the battle over prohibition raised the issue of whether the nation's respect for law was being undermined. President Harding himself set no inspiring example when he drank liquor in the White House. Immigrant groups, to whom moderate drinking of beer or wine had been part of the order of nature, protested the infringement on their "liberty." European cartoonists pictured the Statue of Liberty with a long list of "Thou Shalt Nots."

The clash between legislation and urban opinion led to an intricate structure of law evasion. Chicago gangsters, profiting from a central position in the national "bootlegging" business, acted as bodyguards for the rival manufacturers and distributors of illicit gin and beer and protected the small "alky cookers" for a price. Often they acted as heads of bootleg rings and fought bloody battles for a monopolistic position. Criminals who had eked out a mere living hitherto from extortion and kidnapping now turned to the riches inherent in evading prohibition. Opponents were taken for a "one way ride" or, as in the case of the Valentine Day Massacre of 1929, a rival gang was lined up against a wall and mowed down by machine guns. City and county governments were corrupted by the easy wealth flowing from the coffers of criminals. Honest policemen were not always certain that their integrity protected them from dismissal. The Capones, O'Bannions, Gennas, and O'Donnells were in the saddle.

In that day before reliable crime statistics, it was difficult to prove that the decade was unique in the annals of crime. Newspapers often devoted the best part of their pages to crime news and murder cases like that in the Hall-Mills affair; and the killing of Bobby Franks by Leopold and Loeb might fill entire pages, not merely single columns. Gangsters and "racketeers" in the liquor and service trades did flourish on a unique scale. The use of machine guns and automatic pistols made murder a simple matter for gangs; and the swift automobile gave criminals a new and frightening mobility. Whatever the precise facts might be regarding the criminality of the twenties, it seems clear enough that this generation believed that they lived in an era when gangsterism was dominant. If this observation is correct, then it follows that they shared the guilt of tolerating a grossly immoral situation.

3

Urbanism continued to take its toll of religious life. Sunday golf, baseball, motoring, and hunting conflicted with church attendance. Visiting nurses and case workers reduced the pastoral visits of the minister. The word "sin" disappeared from many pulpits in the large cities. In Middletown, about one out of nine men went to church, though one out of five women did so. About 5 or 10 per cent of all families, according to the ministers, still continued daily prayers at home although somewhat more read the Bible daily. But Sunday school was still a dominant institution for the young, and most adults who were questioned seemed to believe in God and to think about heaven occasionally; businessmen were more doubtful about the existence of heaven and did not think that there was a hell.

Denominational differences declined under urban influences. Among the liberal Christians, the Federal Council of the Churches of Christ in America, representing about twenty Protestant sects, published and circulated widely *Christian Ideals in Industry*. This assailed the monopolistic trend and called for social security and the rights of trade unions. They worked systematically to combat anti-Semitism and Jim Crowism and propagandized against war. Also in the liberal camp were the five leading theological seminaries. A poll of their students showed that four-fifths denied that heathens and infidels would be damned. Only 11 per cent believed in an actual hell, and still fewer, about 8 per cent, thought that the Bible was divinely inspired; 4 per cent believed that the Bible was "wholly free from legend." Only 25 per cent wrote that they believed in the Virgin Birth. Modernism had indeed made vast inroads among divinity students. Three-fourths of the New York University students who were polled in 1928 said that they believed in God and 25 per cent conceded a life after death. Nearly half of them were members of church organizations. Catholics, despite their urban background, continued to be steady churchgoers and relatively orthodox.

Fundamentalism often went hand in hand with economic orthodoxy and therefore was not wholly out of step with the times. Its unyielding emphasis on Bible literalism led members to conduct an antievolution campaign throughout the country, especially in the rural South. William Jennings Bryan, a lifelong fundamentalist who believed ardently in the Old Time religion and prohibition, lobbied for antievolution laws in one Southern state after another. By 1925 five of them forbade the teaching of evolutionary ideas in the public schools. Support for fundamentalism came that year from the San Francisco convention of the International Walther League, a large

Lutheran youth group. They passed a resolution condemning "Modernism, Liberalism and evolution, and radicalism." They also demanded that the teaching of evolution be forbidden in the public schools.

It was fitting that Bryan himself should champion fundamentalism in the sensational Scopes trial at Dayton, Tennessee, and defend the antievolution law against the biology teacher who had violated it. Bryan had long distorted the doctrine of evolution to suit the mentality of the simple rural folk that he addressed. "They can't make a monkey out of me!" he shouted to enthusiastic audiences. The trial was actually a test case entered into voluntarily by John T. Scopes, the defendant. His liberal supporters chose an avowed agnostic, Clarence Darrow, and two lawyers representing the Civil Liberties Union to defend the biology teacher. Newspapers, recognizing that the news value of the Scopes trial ranked with that of a Dempsey-Firpo match, played up the testimony of that trial while fundamentalist Baptist and Methodist farmers sat in the jury box. Intellectually, the trial made no contribution to religion or science. Bryan simply affirmed the fundamentalist belief in the literal truth of the Bible, the creation of the world in six days, and the genuineness of miracles. Darrow harassed the dignified former secretary of state with the questions and arguments familiar to the Ingersoll type of religious skeptic. The trial exhausted Bryan and hastened his death. For a time newspaper readers debated evolution in the same arid spirit that Darrow and Bryan had shown at Dayton. Almost forgotten was the central issue of whether the taxpayer had the right to impose upon the schools any style of orthodoxy that he thought fitting.

4

If universal literacy was the goal of education, then the United States came much closer than ever to achieving it during the twenties. Almost 90 per cent of those of school age were enrolled in school, and even a high-school education became the rule. The nation was spending nearly three billions a year for education and existing public school property was valued at five billion dollars.

Even these large sums did not provide decent salaries for teachers, for the men deserted a profession that paid an average of only $1260 even in the cities. Since married women were usually discouraged by their school board from continuing as teachers, spinsters filled the ranks. Teachers too often felt bored by their classroom routine and heavy extracurricular duties for there was little challenge in such a regimented system.

In the small towns the local board was apt to disqualify foreigners, Catholics, and Jews as teachers; very often they forbade teachers to smoke and women teachers to bob their hair, go on dates, wear short skirts, dance, or become engaged or married. Conformity was also demanded of them on political and community issues.

Under such circumstances social indoctrination along conservative lines was the rule. Legislatures strengthened this tendency by requiring ultra-patriotic textbooks and more history of the chauvinistic variety. Thus in 1924, New Jersey forbade public schools to use any book which

belittles, falsifies, misrepresents, distorts, doubts, or denies the events leading up to the Declaration of American Independence or any other war in which this country has been engaged ... or belittles ... the deeds and accomplishments of noted American patriots, or which questions the worthiness of their motives or casts aspersions upon their lives.

Wisconsin and other states had similar laws. In Chicago, Mayor Thompson even hinted that he might have his library board make a bonfire of pro-British books. One book was censored for omitting the phrase, "We have met the enemy and they are ours." Another schoolbook was denounced because it contained a reference to "Patrick Henry, a gay, unprosperous and hitherto unknown country lawyer." The *Chicago Tribune*, which followed a consistent anti-British position and carried on its masthead, "My Country Right or Wrong," demanded the dismissal of unorthodox teachers and pacifists.

The results of this teaching situation may be inferred from the reaction of Middletown high-school students to a social study questionnaire. Most students wrote "Yes" for such propositions as, "The

white race is the best race on earth," "The United States is unques-
tionably the best country on earth," and "Every good citizen should
act according to the statement, 'My country, right or wrong!'" The
responses regarding free speech and economic reform reflected a
similar conservative orientation, with the girls showing a far greater
conservatism than the boys. As for the adult community of Middletown, it put a high value upon conformity and even encouraged the
Klan to enforce it.

The march of vocationalism was accelerated by the extraordinary
expansion of industry and commerce. Since the taxpayer often determined the curriculum, he usually insisted on the addition of "practical" subjects like manual arts, printing, machine-shop work, typing,
bookkeeping, and home economics. Besides, the Smith-Hughes Act
of 1917 provided considerable federal and state funds for the teaching of vocational subjects and thus expanded the curriculum still
more. To some extent, the influence of John Dewey's progressive
theories of education added to the growing list of applied subjects,
though Dewey would have made them part of a rounded educational program very far from crude vocationalism.

During this era Dewey's ideas won enthusiastic disciples at home
and even in Asia, Europe, and Latin America. He continued to
stress "learning by doing" as a natural method of developing an
independent individual capable of living successfully in a democratic society. There were inevitable abuses, in this individualistic
era, such as making some progressive schools serve the gifted child
alone rather than the ordinary pupil. Others, as already noted,
might distort Deweyism into mere vocationalism. But Dewey's
unswerving faith in democratic values and his rebellion against the
separation of the school from society had wholesome implications
that offered philosophic direction during an era when school boards
demanded indoctrination for social conformity and regimentation.
Unfortunately, Middletown had too little in common with Dewey.

Henry Ford (1863-1947), automobile manufacturer.
(Brown Brothers)

Ford Motor Company, Lincoln-Mercury Division, St. Louis, Missouri, designed by Albert Kahn Associated Architects & Engineers. An example of functional architecture in industrial building. (Hedrich-Blessing Studio)

Frank Lloyd Wright's functionalist house, Taliesin, at Spring Green, Wisconsin. (Frank Lloyd Wright)

Frank Lloyd Wright, leading American modernist in architecture.
(Frank Lloyd Wright)

Closing of the Jerome Evacuation Center for Japanese-Americans, Denson, Arkansas. (National Archives)

Mexican laborers training hop vines in California. (Brown Brothers)

A football "classic." The Navy-Notre Dame game of November 5, 1950, showing a Navy forward pass. *(Cleveland Plain Dealer)*

Major league baseball. Keltner of the Cleveland Indians slides home in a pre-season game with the New York Giants. *(Cleveland Plain Dealer)*

"Daughters of Revolution," by Grant Wood. (Associated American Artists; Edward G. Robinson, owner)

"Employment Agency," by Isaac Soyer. (Whitney Museum of American Art)

"Arts of the West," mural section of "The Arts of Life in America," by Thomas Hart Benton. (Peter A. Juley photograph; Whitney Museum of American Art)

"Why Not Use the El?" by Reginald Marsh. (Whitney Museum of American Art)

The Security Council considers report of Chinese Communist intervention in Korea. *Left to right:* Yakov Malik, U.S.S.R.; Sir Gladwynn Jebb, U.K.; Warren Austin, U.S.A. Lake Success, N. Y., November 8, 1950. (United Nations)

The General Assembly stands in silent tribute to the fallen United Nations forces in Korea. Paris, December 2, 1951. (United Nations)

5

Urbanism, prosperity, and indifference to social reform led to an extraordinary upswing in sport and other recreational interests. The metropolis, even more than the nineteenth-century city, encouraged the commercial organization of recreation. This meant, of course, an unusual expansion of spectator sports, but those who had cars and could afford the time had numerous forest preserves and parks where there was good fishing, boating, hunting, and hiking. Stuart Chase, estimating the annual expenditures of Americans for all sorts of diversions, including motoring for pleasure, came to the startling conclusion that over $21,000,000,000 was spent for such purposes. Although this total was obviously excessive, it suggested the large role that recreation played in American life.

So strong was the competition of the various sports and recreations that even the great American game of baseball, which drew over 40,000,000 admissions a year, according to Chase, grew only moderately during the decade of the 1920's. However, a star like George Herman (Babe) Ruth, who hit sixty home runs in 1927, added a million dollars a year to the receipts of the American League. The application of modern advertising methods to sport by gifted promoters who carried on the tradition of Barnum, attracted millions of people to boxing, wrestling, and football. George (Tex) Rickard, the boxing promoter, kept a secure hold upon the first pages of newspapers when he publicized the "Battle of the Century" in 1921 between Heavyweight Champion Jack Dempsey and Georges Carpentier of France and netted gate receipts well over a million dollars. The Chicago championship fight of 1927 between Dempsey and Gene Tunney earned over $2,600,000. Another noted promoter, C. C. Pyle, familiarly known as "Cold Cash Pyle," did very well indeed in publicizing Miss Suzanne Lenglen, the French tennis star, and "Red" Grange, the University of Illinois football idol who turned professional. Grange not only earned a million dollars in a professional football season, but he added thousands to his income by selling the use of his name to manufacturers of sweaters, shoes, and candy bars.

Colleges, despite generous gifts obtained in this era before the income tax seriously interfered with private fortunes, depended partly upon football not only to support the lesser sports but to contribute to other collegiate expenses. As a result, there was every incentive to build lavish stadiums and to hire expert coaches—and sometimes players as well—at handsome salaries well exceeding mere professorial earnings. Thus football was an amateur sport only in a figurative sense. Stuart Chase heard a retired football coach remark, "I will guarantee any first-class high-school player that I can get him through any one of a half a dozen good colleges with board and tuition paid and no one pressing him for payment of his 'loans' afterwards."

Recreational life was greatly stimulated by the coming of the radio. In 1920, Station KDKA, a Westinghouse Electric Company affiliate of Pittsburgh, broadcast the results of the Harding-Cox election. Thereafter began an era of homemade crystal receiving sets and "fans" who stayed up into the morning hours hoping to hear a few faint sounds from some distant station. Prize fights and baseball games were now available for many who were hitherto unable to attend them. Invalids, the sick, the blind, and even the partly deaf might escape utter boredom and isolation by tuning in their favorite station. Illiterates found an easy substitute for the printed page and many became more effective members of their communities.

The phonograph and piano suffered during these years from the rivalry of radio. Good music, although driven on the defensive by syncopated tunes, was available at certain hours. But repetition speedily wore out music and greatly shortened the vogue of popular melodies. Children could hear Walter Damrosch's popular symphony concerts for young people and adults selected operas, concerts, and recitals at the mere turn of the dial. Altogether, the radio of the 1920's tended to bring recreation back to the home.

The radio had other effects, too. It diffused urban attitudes and tastes among isolated farms and villages and thus broke down regionalism. Distinctive dialects, diction, and pronunciation were modified in favor of a standard form. But the high hopes for worthwhile education at a mass level were slow to materialize. Listeners could easily turn off a lecture to hear a soap opera while commercial advertising sponsors were reluctant to pay for an educational program when the bulk of listeners were known to prefer a certain jazz orchestra, a popular comedian, or a mystery story. There were important exceptions of course such as the university Round Table discussions. Public enlightenment was often served by the new opportunity given statesmen to explain their policies to a constituency over the air. Governors Alfred E. Smith and Franklin D. Roosevelt of New York used the radio to defend their legislation. During the Hoover-Smith election of 1928 both parties together spent $2,000,000 to broadcast radio speeches. Though the propaganda possibilities of radio were immense, so were its potentialities for good. On the other hand, public lectures and the last of the lyceums and Chautauquas declined rapidly in the face of the new competition. Middletown tolerated short talks of the light inspirational or "practical" variety, but had no great interest in thoughtful, independent analysis from the platform or pulpit. For the most part the radio seemed to be another force promoting social conformity.

The automobile, like the radio, did a great deal to cast American culture into a uniform mold by breaking down regionalism. Ambitious state governors outdid themselves in building motor highways on a lavish scale. While the radio gave the home a greater stake in recreation, the automobile offset this by opening up opportunities for travel all over the country. Life increased in mobility now that one could do so many more things in a single day. The motor car stood as godfather to innumerable suburbs and satellite cities around the metropolis. It made possible the great Florida and California real estate booms. It helped to bring the benefits of modern education to rural communities through the consolidated school and the buses that served it. On the other hand, the new mobility was an unsettling experience, too. Neighborhoods and streets had to be reorganized or planned to meet the changes wrought by the automobile. There was a heavy price to pay for this progress in the many thousands of fatalities and injuries on the highway—about the equivalent of losses in a major war. Crime, too, attained a new mobility, for gangsters, "hijackers," and kidnappers speeded across county and state lines beyond the reach of local officials. This made it inevitable that the federal government should add national policing to its growing functions.

The motion picture was still another recreational agency that helped to standardize American attitudes, habits, and clothes. Chase estimated that 50,000,000 admissions to movies were paid each week. Many attended twice and even three times weekly. They were usually fed extravagant spectacles like *Ben Hur*, which cost $6,000,000, stories with a definite sex emphasis such as the Valentino and Clara Bow films, and simplified versions of novels. The court testimony of innumerable juvenile delinquents shows that the youngsters were often inspired to depart from the straight path by watching a Hollywood badman at work. Apparently, they had been less impressed by the reiterated moral conclusion that crime does not pay. The level of presentation was seldom above the fourteen-year-old level and despite the current tendency of movie censors to allow sexy films, the motion picture almost never violated the tenets of economic orthodoxy.

Hollywood had not only to please American audiences but foreign peoples as well for it was now producing about nine-tenths of the world's films. It unwittingly gave foreigners the impression that America was a land of immorality, violence, fabulous riches, and sheer wastefulness. Though the movies avoided controversy wherever possible, they left an unfortunate impression by picturing Negroes offensively or as Uncle Tom or minstrel show stereotypes. Heroes were usually tall, blond Nordics, while villains were short or stout brunettes. Still, the movies offered a genuine recreational or emotional experience that lent cheer or vicarious excitement to many drab lives. More adventurous German, Russian, and French motion picture producers, less weighed down by the vast financial burdens facing Hollywood, often introduced motion pictures of high artistic worth. From time to time Hollywood, too, could produce such effective pictures as *The Big Parade,* an antiwar story, and

The Covered Wagon, based on Emerson Hough's tale of the westward movement.

A new era in the history of the motion picture began in 1927 when Warner Brothers presented the first serious all-talking picture, *The Jazz Singer,* featuring Al Jolson, which was very enthusiastically received. "Talkies" intensified the qualities of illusion for the motion picture and helped to drive the "legitimate" theater farther into the background. Only the New York stage could flourish against such competition; the others lost out steadily. This opened the way to an era of lavish musicals in film, though the stories did not change much. But "silent" stars whose voices could not qualify were driven into oblivion and thousands of musicians in movie theaters were left unemployed.

6

Many of the entertainment ideas and performers for Hollywood came from Broadway and the music from Tin Pan Alley, as the music publishers' district was called. In the ornate Broadway theaters the influence of Florenz Ziegfeld and his *Follies* made the musical revue the dominant form of entertainment. Ziegfeld hired Irving Berlin, Victor Herbert, Rudolf Friml, and other distinguished composers to write his music. In his shows the leading stars at various times were Eddie Cantor, Marilyn Miller, Bert Williams, Fannie Brice, W. C. Fields, Charles Winninger, and the cowboy humorist, Will Rogers. Ziegfeld's *Follies* centered about elaborately dressed, pretty chorus girls, character actors, and popular singers against a dazzling background of extravagant stage settings. Those who preferred something even less subtle and more crudely risqué went to the *Passing Show* at the Winter Garden, which the Shuberts promoted along the old burlesque lines.

Audiences never tired of sentimental operettas and musical comedies. In the tradition of Victor Herbert and the Viennese composers, the Bohemian-born Rudolf Friml wrote *Rose Marie* and *The Vagabond King.* Sigmund Romberg, who came here from

Hungary, wrote some perennial favorites in *Maytime, Student Prince, Blossom Time, Desert Song,* and *New Moon.* Somewhere between the Viennese tradition and that of jazz was the work of Jerome Kern, who wrote the music for Edna Ferber's story, *Showboat,* which became a highly popular operetta.

Among the leading writers of musical comedy was George Gershwin, a Brooklyn-born musician who eventually won international acclaim for his original symphonic interpretations of jazz. He wrote the music of *Lady Be Good,* which starred the dancers Fred Astaire and his sister Adele, *Girl Crazy,* and, in 1931, *Of Thee I Sing.* Gershwin first attracted attention by his musical scores for *George White's Scandals.* Much more lasting were his symphonic jazz compositions *Rhapsody in Blue* and *Piano Concerto in F.* Although there were some predecessors in this field, Gershwin went farther than anyone else in opening up a new, more serious, aesthetic dimension in jazz music.

Popular music poured out in a carefully regulated flow from the offices of Tin Pan Alley such as those of Irving Berlin, Incorporated. Berlin's sentimental, melodious music seemed to have universal appeal despite the competition of thousands of songs. Especially well liked were his *Always, Remember, Blue Skies, A Russian Lullaby,* and *All Alone.* Many popular songs of the day were obviously imitative and constructed according to a well-worn formula of melody or syncopated rhythm. Sometimes they were simply lifted from the masters. Chopin received no royalties for his contribution to *I'm Always Chasing Rainbows;* nor did Puccini profit from *Avalon,* which Al Jolson sang; and Schubert provided posthumously much of the popular *Song of Love.* This decade was also fond of eccentric words to accompany equally eccentric jazz tunes. Among the very popular were *Mister Gallagher and Mister Shean, Barney Google, You've Got to See Your Momma Every Night, Yes! We Have No Bananas, Collegiate,* and *Yes, Sir, That's My Baby.*

The nineteen twenties is best remembered for its transmutation of ragtime music into jazz and the successes of Paul Whiteman and Vincent Lopez in making jazz respectable. Jazz orchestras, whose members were now clad in the formal dress of symphonic musicians, often played in halls hitherto consecrated to Bach, Beethoven, and Haydn. Devotees of "classical" music struck back at the jazz invasion and denounced the invaders as crudely imitative and vulgar. Thus war raged between "classical" and "popular music" with notable defections made in the ranks of the traditionalists. Jazz, of course, was inseparable from the extraordinary vogue of commercial ballroom dancing. The Charleston, the Black Bottom, and other eccentric dances captured the youth of the nation.

The Jazz Age was also dubbed an era of "flaming youth" by Samuel Hopkins Adams, who used this as the title of a popular novel. Its sensualism was undisguised. The "flapper," the "gigolos," the "shimmy" dancers, and the "accent on youth" were part of this pattern. Prohibition contributed the unpoliced "roadhouse," "bathtub gin," the "bootlegger," and the "speakeasy." The gaudiness and suggestive pantomime of the musical revues added its ingredients to the new cult of hedonism. Although the United States was somewhat larger than New York city, the attitudes of Broadway and Tin Pan Alley had penetrated even Middletown.

7

Journalism reflected the craze for sensationalism of the cities and the trend toward bigness of the leading business enterprises. Frank Luther Mott has attributed the consolidation tendency to the preference of advertisers for the larger circulation of huge newspapers, to the economies effected by combining morning and evening papers, thus running a plant on a twenty-four-hour basis, and to the costly overhead expenses that came from operating the new machines and services of the newspaper business. Frank Munsey and William Randolph Hearst led the procession of consolidation. Munsey, who reaped a fortune of $20,000,000 in journalism, merged entire groups of papers in the search for profitable exploitation, sometimes wrecking a paper in the process. Best known of his mergers is the combination of two historic papers as the *New York Herald-Tribune*. When Munsey died, William Allen

White, editor of the *Emporia* (*Kansas*) *Gazette* and nationally famous as the representative of the old independent journalism, had this satirical obituary ready:

Frank Munsey, the great publisher, is dead. Frank Munsey contributed to the journalism of his day the talent of a meat packer, the morals of a money changer and the manners of an undertaker. He and his kind have about succeeded in transforming a once-noble profession into an eight per cent security. May he rest in trust!

Although White later felt that he had been too cruel, he explained in a letter of January 6, 1926, to President Nicholas M. Butler of Columbia his opposition to the current consolidation and standardization:

I would rather have the press as it was in John Milton's time, or Benjamin Franklin's time, when a man with the proverbial shirttail full of type could express himself, air his views, and get it off his chest, rather than to have the mass production of newspapers owned by investment bankers and filled full of stupid syndicate matter and conventional opinions as they are today.

A good deal of the worst of the old personal journalism as well as the evils of the new was perpetuated by the newspaper empire of William Randolph Hearst. By 1922 he had bought so many newspapers and related interests that he owned twenty dailies, eleven Sunday papers, the International News Service, Universal Service, King Features (the largest of the syndicates), a half dozen magazines, a newsreel company, and other large-scale enterprises. As in prewar days, he demanded sensationalism of his editors, not the "merely important" (as he once put it) and carried on the type of crusades, crime news, and feature articles that appealed to the millions of the less educated in the large cities. He continued his chauvinistic approach to international affairs and hammered away at the yellow peril, Bolshevist intrigues, and the League of Nations.

Among the more beneficent mergers were those of the Scripps chain. Robert P. Scripps continued the socially-minded policy of his father, E. W. Scripps, who died in 1926, and added eighteen newspapers to the family enterprises. He acquired the *Pittsburgh*

Press, the *Akron Times,* and eventually (in 1931) brought about the merger of the *New York Telegram* and the *New York World.* Altogether, chain journalism reached its peak, rising from twelve chains in 1910 to sixty in the 1920's, and controlling over one-third of the total daily circulation of the country.

The twenties gave birth to the blatant tabloid, an idea that the English publisher, Lord Northcliffe, had already developed. Although the small-format newspaper was dominant in colonial times, it now had the added virtues of gross sensationalism and the necessary compactness that subway and streetcar riders needed during the crowded early evening hours. Joseph Medill Patterson, an heir of the old *Chicago Tribune* dynasty, adopted the tabloid form for the *New York Daily News,* which appeared in 1919. It offered engrossing "human interest" pictures, crime, scandals, divorces, the exploits of society playboys, and other such facets of life. Nothing was done to tax the reader's intelligence. By 1924, Patterson reported a daily circulation of 750,000 and competitors were already entering the field. Hearst established the *New York Daily Mirror* while the well-publicized physical culture faddist, Bernarr MacFadden, began the *New York Daily Graphic.* Other cities followed New York. No extravagance seemed too much for these merchants of salacious "news" and even libel suits did not stop the journalists from raking up old scandals as well as discovering new ones. The remarkable fact about the tabloids is that they reached their stupendous circulations without seriously reducing the number of readers of the older papers. An entire semiliterate sector of society had been discovered, people who could read the pictures at least.

Newspapers desiring to keep up with the tabloids in gutter journalism purchased syndicated material on love, seduction, murder, divorce, and similar topics. Middletown youth stated that the comics were their favorite diversion and such readers helped to make millionaires of Bud Fisher, creator of Mutt and Jeff, and Sidney Smith, who portrayed the trials of Andy Gump. Middletown was not alone in a strong preference for the sprightly advice to the family by the much-syndicated Beatrice Fairfax and Dorothy Dix. Arthur Brisbane, Hearst's editorial writer, aired his prejudices on domestic and foreign affairs across the continent. This growth of syndicated news and features and the influence of the advertiser made the newspapers appear far less partisan than they had been a generation before, but this conformity was achieved at a price that honest critics like William Allen White thought too dear. Fortunately, the power of the press was increasingly tempered by the competition of radio, though this vehicle, too, seemed to be on the side of social conformity and conservatism.

8

In many ways the popular magazine held up a mirror to America far more faithfully than did the newspapers. Most self-consciously American was the *Saturday Evening Post,* oldest of all national magazines. Since George H. Lorimer had taken over the editorship in 1899, the *Post* had become the fascinating organ of a business civilization, emphasizing middle-class stability and economic conservatism. One family in ten read the *Post.* Where else could one receive such a bargain of generous reading matter for a nickel? In its pages were the entertaining stories of Booth Tarkington, Scott Fitzgerald, Kenneth Roberts, and Emerson Hough; the political articles of Calvin Coolidge, Herbert Hoover, David Lawrence, Mark Sullivan, and Al Smith; and sports commentaries by Alonzo Stagg and Jack Dempsey. Even the copious advertising matter vibrated with the American gospel of success. Lorimer campaigned for economy and the prompt payment of the war debts owed the United States. He and his contributors warned of the danger of unrestricted immigration, especially from Southeastern Europe, and did a good deal to insure the passage of the Immigration Act of 1924. Regardless of political opinion, almost everyone seemed to read the *Post;* even intellectuals shamefacedly admitted themselves to be quite familiar with its contents. Frequently the articles and stories were of a high order, though they avoided strong social dissent.

The *Literary Digest,* founded in 1890, had many ideal qualities for a mass magazine of the 1920's. Though it was neither literary nor a digest, but a scissors-and-paste job, as James P. Wood observes, the *Digest* offered a careful selection of newspaper and magazine items and cartoons. Educators liked its presentation of the pros and cons of national issues. Journalists, politicians, and historians drew upon the results of its public opinion polls, then a novel device. In these years the *Literary Digest* influenced public opinion considerably—although it would be hard to say in which direction.

Sophisticated cosmopolites read *The New Yorker,* first published in 1925 by Harold Ross and filled with gay, satirical articles by Alexander Woolcott, Robert Benchley, and Dorothy Parker. Even more blatant in its sophistication was the new version of *The Smart Set,* which had originated in 1890 as a society journal and "a magazine of cleverness." After a period of decay it had been revived by William H. Wright as a magazine "to provide lively entertainment for minds that are not primitive." Long before Wright turned to a more profitable career as "S. S. Van Dine," author of the *Canary Murder Case* and other detective thrillers, he brought to the staff of *The Smart Set* two remarkable journalists, Henry L. Mencken and George Jean Nathan. They became the chief editors during 1914-23. Through *The Smart Set* Americans were enlisted in Mencken's war on Puritanism—a term that came to comprise almost anything that he disliked—and on philistinism. Readers were introduced to such European masters of naturalism as James Joyce, D. H. Lawrence, and George Moore. Mencken and Nathan then founded an even more influential magazine for the intelligentsia, *The American Mercury.* Its editors were no aimless iconoclasts, but men of literary taste, though Irving Babbitt referred to Mencken's criticism as "intellectual vaudeville." Sometimes they exalted pygmies, but more often they affirmed the sterling worth of new writers: Theodore Dreiser, Sinclair Lewis, Eugene O'Neill, Scott Fitzgerald, and Joseph Hergesheimer. Their rebellion was reminiscent of the yellow nineties of Oscar Wilde and the art-for-art's-sake school. Believing, as they did, in the biological superiority of the intelligentsia, they had little interest in mass movements and social reforms.

Definitely among the minority, but keenly perceptive of national trends and social values were the liberal journals of opinion. During 1918-33 Oswald Garrison Villard as editor of *The Nation* continued the dissenting tradition of his family and the discriminating judgments on aesthetics of Godkin's old staff. On his distinguished roster of literary critics were the Van Dorens, Carl, Irita, and Mark, and the perennial rebel against injustice, Heywood Broun. Competing with *The Nation* for a similar select group of readers was the *New Republic,* which Herbert Croly had founded in 1914. Croly is best remembered for his philosophy of social planning as expressed in *The Promise of American Life* (1909) and continued in the editorial policy of the *New Republic.* Despite its very small circulation (like that of *The Nation*), its chief contributors were among America's intellectual leaders: John Dewey, Walter Lippmann, Robert Morss Lovett, and Bruce Bliven. The influence of these two liberal journals was due to the professional and intellectual make-up of its readers, including novelists, artists, college professors, and adherents of various social action camps. For them the business civilization of the 1920's was not the true emanation of the idealistic American spirit, but a temporary triumph of a pecuniary culture.

Critics of this era of Henry Ford observed that the American achievement was impressive in quantity, but less so in quality. So said Irving Babbitt in his *Democracy and Leadership* (1924). He quoted, though making some allowance for obvious exaggeration, the opinion of a foreign critic:

What must one think of a country . . . whose most popular orator is W. J. Bryan, whose favorite actor is Charlie Chaplin, whose most widely read novelist is Harold Bell Wright, whose best-known evangelist is Billy Sunday, and whose representative journalist is William Randolph Hearst?

Babbitt denounced the confusion of standards, the vulgarity and triviality of the contemporary scene in America:

There is confusion of standards . . . when we are so impressed by Mr. Henry Ford's abilities as organizer and master mechanic that we listen seriously to his views on money [Babbitt might have added, on politics and race also]; or when, simply because Mr. Edison has shown inventive genius along certain lines, we receive him as an authority on education.

Babbitt's own standards, as will be noted, were no less confused in their expression than those he criticized. But there was a modicum of truth in his indictment of the twenties and of certain American tendencies mirrored in the *Saturday Evening Post*. The high development of rationality, as symbolized in the assembly line, had not been transferred to other aspects of American society. Provincialism, Babbitry, intolerance, and crude commercialism survived. Businessmen, sounding the praises of perpetual prosperity, enjoyed the prestige of leaders who had apparently mastered the complex modern economic apparatus and eliminated forever severe economic depressions. Their way of life, so they believed, was the American way.

· 20 ·

The "Lost Generation"
and Henry L. Mencken

I

"You are all a lost generation," said Gertrude Stein, the literary expatriate, to another exile in Paris, Ernest Hemingway, and he had thought the comment so apt that he wrote it on the flyleaf of his novel of disillusionment, *The Sun Also Rises* (1926). To the young novelists and poets like Hemingway, John Dos Passos, and others who had served in a war to end war only to find that power politics and cynical materialism still existed in the world, life had lost all purpose and direction. Gone were the grand certainties of the Populists, the Progressives, and the champions of the New Freedom. The enthusiasm for a just social order had waned and in its place came an intense preoccupation with self rather than with the common good. Society was past redemption and no group was as important as the individual. The men of the Lost Generation, like Narcissus of the Greek legend, were absorbed in contemplating their own image.

No man typified this individualistic affectation more than Henry Louis Mencken, "the bad boy of Baltimore." His remarkable career and influence reveals the fact that the intellectual roots of the Lost Generation went far deeper than the postwar malady of disillusionment. In prewar days his magazine *The Smart Set* and his articles for the *Baltimore Sun* had already expressed the irresponsible Narcissus attitudes of the Lost Generation. He had leaned heavily upon the moral relativism of the art-for-art's-sake school of James Whistler and Oscar Wilde. According to this view, the artist had no responsibility to teach a lesson, to uphold a moral view, or even to please the public or the critics. It was enough that he and perhaps two or three others liked his work.

Mencken popularized the doctrine of the elite that he found in the writings of the German philosopher, Friedrich Nietzsche. Although he often seemed to be mocking Nietzsche—Mencken rarely was completely serious—he liked the idea that nature was evolving a race of supermen who were destined to rule the human herd. Nature's true aristocrat was not bound by Christian morality or the Philistine's urge that everyone conform to mediocrity. Mencken explained the "Bible Belt" of fundamentalists in the South as the low human residue of small minds remaining after the Civil War had exterminated the Southern elite. Like many of the intelligentsia of the 1920's Mencken believed in the extreme ideas of heredity taught by the eugenics cult. He was even ready to argue that the superiority of many Negroes to poor whites was due to partial descent from the blue-blooded Southern aristocracy. Such ideas led him to reject democracy, to ridicule the "homo boobiens" and the "mob," and to cite triumphantly (and mistakenly) the results of the Alpha mental tests given to the recruits during the war as proof of the inherent inferiority of the plain people. Democracy, he said, offered the impossible alternative of rule by plutocrats on the one hand and a rabble of demagogic reformers on the other.

Collegians and other adolescents who enthusiastically adopted Mencken's *American Mercury* as their guide admired the constant war that the Baltimore editor waged upon "Puritanism"—Mencken arbitrarily expanded the definition of this abused word to include almost all kinds of personal inhibitions. The extraordinary vogue for Freud (as he was vulgarized) in the twenties made it easy to believe that self-discipline and "repressions" were necessary evils. Mencken's sophisticated aphorisms in the successive volumes of *Prejudices* (1919-27) delighted that era. "Love," he would assert, "is the delusion that one woman differs from another." Mencken championed individual rights against moral and political censorship, Boston book bannings, the Klan, prohibition, fundamentalism, and the police raids of Anthony Comstock. His attack on Christianity as a "mob religion" resembled that of Nietzsche. Mencken amused himself sometimes by stealing Gideon Bibles from hotel rooms at Christmas time and sending them to friends, inscribed "With the regards of the author." Actually, as a more sober generation realized during the Great Depression, Mencken was fundamentally conservative on many matters. He was intolerant of economic reformers, lampooned women's rights, and even in his agnosticism, had no desire to interfere with churchgoing habits. His literary judgments were often shrewd and his successful battle against censorship in behalf of Theodore Dreiser saved that novelist from utter discouragement. The academic critics, Stuart Sherman of the University of Illinois and Irving Babbitt of Harvard, felt exasperated by his flippant judgments, but even respectable journals came to regard Mencken as worthy of serious attention and even admiration. Mencken's incorrigible sophisticated patter, partly modeled after the prefaces of George Bernard Shaw, enchanted his generation.

While Mencken strengthened the grip of an individualistic naturalism upon literature, Irving Babbitt led a group of "neo-humanist" critics to decry literary determinism and emotionalism and to exalt the classical heritage of restraint, poise, and balance. He ridiculed Dreiser's view of life as merely "rearranging chemisms" and disliked the current tendency to "humanize" great men by "debunking" them. The contemporary naturalistic novel, he wrote, had gone so far in its effort to escape the tyranny of taboos and inhibitions that the result was confusion and a clutter of psychological terms. He blamed Rousseau, father of romanticism, for the modern tendency to substitute emotionalism for the classic virtues of discipline and decorum, "the law of measure," and the "ideal of the gentleman." To him, as we have seen, Mencken was merely a purveyor of intellectual vaudeville. Neither Mencken nor Babbitt showed a profound understanding of his era. Mencken's wisdom was partly culled from a correspondence school, and Babbitt's ideas reflected an ivory-tower detachment.

From Germany came Oswald Spengler's pessimistic philosophy of history, translated as *The Decline of the West*, which predicted the eclipse of western civilization. Urban culture, he thought, was breeding disintegration by spreading antitraditional ideas. Spengler, an ardent believer that history moved in recurrent cycles of development, tried to show that western culture, born about A.D. 900, had now reached a point analogous to that of the century of Greek decay after Pericles. Walter Lippmann, impressed by the Spenglerian analysis of decay, wrote an appeal for a humanistic faith that would be more solid and modern than Babbitt's "neo-humanism." This was the burden of Lippmann's *A Preface to Morals* (1929). He professed an intellectual debt to his Harvard professors, William James and George Santayana. Apparently he had read sympathetically the pragmatic argument for religious belief in James' *Varieties of Religious Experience,* though he wished to discover a "religion of the spirit" that would be less relativistic than the faith espoused by his teacher. Pessimists like Clarence Darrow, who were not certain that life was worth living, had their coterie in Mencken's America, but their influence was limited in a hard-headed nation that had produced the assembly line and scientific management.

While Lippmann, like so many other prewar Progressives, had left his early reformist views for more traditionalist ways of thinking, an appreciable minority of critics stood fast by the standard of the social rebels of prewar days. At the University of Washington, Professor Vernon Louis Parrington clung to his democratic values derived from Jefferson's agrarianism and faith in the common man. Shortly before his death in 1929 (one volume appeared posthumously), he issued his magnificent three-volume work, *Main Currents in American Thought* (1927-30). He probed the social ideas of American novelists, poets, historians, orators, and pamphleteers and attempted the hazardous task of evaluating these men according to whether or not they belonged to the true Jeffersonian tradition. Sometimes, as in the case of the Puritans, Parrington was hasty in his condemnation but his huge task made such failures inevitable. Colleagues in literature criticized his neglect of the aesthetic contributions of the men he discussed and his overemphasis upon economic factors. But Parrington's social-economic approach had raised far more fundamental questions of human motivation than earlier historians of American literature had done. Literature was not to be assessed hereafter in a social vacuum, except at the writer's peril. The succeeding decades corrected the details of his broad canvas, but also borrowed a good deal of his method.

2

The desire of the naturalistic novelist to study man almost in a clinical way was stimulated by the vogue for psychology during the twenties. Theodore Dreiser in prewar years had emphasized the economic environment as a major conditioning force in determining the behavior of the individual. While he continued to be concerned with economic factors, he now showed a more sensitive psychological technique suggestive of Dostoevski. This was notably the case in his very successful novel, An American Tragedy (1925). The indecisive central character, Clyde Griffiths, is the product of a degrading slum background in Kansas City. Clyde acquired a country girl, Roberta, as a mistress, but his sensual nature leads him to add still another female conquest. Meanwhile Roberta becomes pregnant and in desperation at Clyde's coolness, threatens to expose him. In a series of events, only partly the result of intention, Clyde is driven to drown Roberta and is arrested. Dreiser attempted to explain Clyde as an ordinary boy whose tragedy is largely the product of a situation not of his own making. Sex motivations, a sordid urban environment, and chance are among the ingredients of this human tragedy, as Dreiser saw it. Though Puritan and Irish-Catholic Boston banned An American Tragedy, the book was a success and won Dreiser a wider following than ever. Mencken had correctly measured the potentialities of the Middle Western novelist whom he had long championed.

Of the Lost Generation, Ernest Hemingway of Illinois led in the adaptation of the naturalistic technique to the novel of disillusionment. He had volunteered to fight alongside the Italian Arditi shock troops and had seen the shattering defeat and collapse at Caporetto when officers shot down their own men to stem the panic. These experiences became the gist of his autobiographical novel,

A Farewell to Arms (1929). To many readers his novel *The Sun Also Rises* (1926) was the last word in naturalism because of its frank discussion of sex motives; the book marked the nadir of post-war despair, frustration, and disillusionment. Another Illinoisan of the Lost Generation was John Dos Passos. Once a Harvard aesthete, he had also seen the brutality of war and questioned the meaning of contemporary life. His successful novel, *Manhattan Transfer* (1925) annoyed Irving Babbitt and other academic critics because of its kaleidoscopic technique, its unrelieved pessimism, and the hopeless futility of the life depicted in the American metropolis. To Dos Passos the individual seemed lost in the chaos of a society that lacked idealism and meaning.

No other novelist succeeded as well as F. Scott Fitzgerald in expressing the spirit of the Jazz Age, notably in *This Side of Paradise* (1920). Recent critics and motion picture producers have rediscovered his novelette, *The Great Gatsby* (1925). This is the story of a rather refined, wealthy bootlegger whose unbelievable morality is in direct contrast to the hypocrisies and evasions of his utterly self-centered, philandering guests whom he has invited to his palatial home. Fitzgerald told his sophisticated story easily and absorbed the reader's interest. The fundamentally pessimistic note that he struck belonged to the familiar naturalistic outlook of his friends among the Lost Generation.

Another of the novelists whom Mencken vigorously endorsed was Sinclair Lewis who also came, like Fitzgerald, from Minnesota, but from a small town rather than a city. Lewis joined with Mencken in satirizing the Philistine, the standardized culture of the day, and the commercially-minded booster. But unlike Mencken, whom he admired in his way, he retained a strong idealistic frame of reference. Rotarians and Kiwanians were angered by such satiric novels as *Main Street* (1920) and *Babbitt* (1922). Somewhat given to caricature, Lewis presented an artificial black-and-white picture of small town materialism, smugness, and intellectual intolerance. Americans might well tremble for the future of their country if *Main Street* mirrored the life of the small town and if *Babbitt* was a faithful representative of our business civilization. *Arrowsmith*

(1925) attacked a society that rewarded exclusively the commercial applications of medicine and offered the most meager payment and incentive to original scientific research. *Elmer Gantry* (1927), apparently written with an eye upon the extraordinary Los Angeles evangelist, Aimee Semple McPherson, showed how the crude booster spirit, the dubious ethics, and high pressure methods of commercial life had penetrated religion. Lewis was of course thinking of no collectivistic solutions. Like the literati of his day, he was concerned with the problem of the free artist and creator caught in the toils of a commercialism and herd instinct that demanded social conformity to false standards.

Less given to, and even opposed to, the naturalistic formulas of *The Smart Set* and the *American Mercury* were three remarkable women who clung to the older ideals of realism and literary craftsmanship. Edith Wharton of New York, Ellen Glasgow of Virginia, and Willa Cather, also of Virginia, though considerably different in many ways, rejected the gods of Freud, Nietzsche, James Joyce, and the Lost Generation. Naturalistic critics might think that Edith Wharton was too genteel for their company, but those who enjoyed the delicacy and objectivity of Henry James could easily appreciate the carefully constructed and realistic novels and stories of Mrs. Wharton. In 1911 she had portrayed the tragedy of rural decay in the novelette, *Ethan Frome,* and had shown herself a master of psychological insight. Among her numerous works, *The Age of Innocence* (1920) stood out in its well-integrated, dramatic view of New York middle-class life in the 1870's.

Ellen Glasgow fulfilled her prewar promise of honest realism. Though her view of rural decay was not quite the same theme of degeneracy suggested by Mrs. Wharton's *Ethan Frome,* she had the art of a social historian in tracing the large movements of Southern social classes. Such was *Barren Ground* (1925), one of her best novels. She also viewed critically the hedonism of the postwar era in *The Romantic Comedians* (1926).

As for Willa Cather, whom some ingrained naturalists might dismiss as a starry-eyed romantic, she continued as in prewar times to depict skillfully the neglected non-materialistic side of the American pioneer tradition. Among her various novels, which many thousands enjoyed, was *Death Comes for the Archbishop* (1927). Like the luminous canvases of the contemporary painters of the Southwest deserts, her novels pictured sympathetically the beauty, uniqueness, and local color of the Indian and the Spanish Catholic heritage.

As in the past, popular taste (and frequently Pulitzer prize committees as well) preferred a larger margin of illusion than the literature of the elite allowed. Booth Tarkington in his Indiana novels of adolescence, as in the *Penrod* series, continued to write about a pleasant small town world that contrasted sharply with the world of the Lynds in *Middletown* or of Sinclair Lewis in *Main Street*. There was the nostalgic atmosphere of lavender and old lace as well as strong characterization in *Alice Adams* (1921) which won the Pulitzer Prize. Pleasantly optimistic too in her treatment of the American past was the very popular storyteller, Edna Ferber of Michigan. Her *So Big* (1924), a Pulitzer Prize winner, *Show Boat* (1926), and *Cimarron* (1929) continued the well-established romantic interpretation of the West that millions loved to read about or to see on the stage.

The detective story had declined in quality since the days of Edgar Allan Poe, but a revival set in during the twenties among readers of all classes for the sophisticated thrillers of "S. S. Van Dine." Willard H. Wright, who had raised the standards of *The Smart Set* and had brought Mencken into his circle, had long been a keen literary and art critic and an able magazine editor. His future career suddenly was cut out for him with his enthusiastically received publication of *The Canary Murder Case* (1927) and *The Bishop Murder Case* (1929). The detective character, Philo Vance, became the unfailing model for a host of detective story writers. As "S. S. Van Dine," Wright proved imperishable and his books became staple fare in the drugstore libraries. Another perennial favorite among mystery story readers for a much longer period of time was Mary Roberts Rinehart who had been born in Pittsburgh. *The Red Lamp* (1925) alone sold over a million copies in a year and her love stories and mystery plays, such as *The Bat,* were the literary preferences of multitudes.

The English novelist, Mrs. Edith Maude Hull, attracted over a million readers during this era for her romantic desert stories of adventure and uninhibited sex passion. So popular was *The Sheik* (1921) that it was followed by a sequel and Hollywood found in it an admirable vehicle for the sensuous interpretation of the matinee idol, Rudolph Valentino. Mrs. Hull had innumerable American imitators who were also in the "best-selling" class.

Although O. Henry (William Sydney Porter) died in 1910, his cheerful stories with their trick endings and sentimentalism continued to be highly popular and to be reprinted in special editions and magazines. The naturalists, too, experimented with the short-story form, often with considerable success. Such was the case of Sherwood Anderson of Ohio who suddenly gave up his family and a flourishing paint factory to begin a literary career. Like Sinclair Lewis, he had been raised in a small town and had rebelled against its smugness and hypocrisy. His writings also showed that he had been absorbing Freud and looked upon life in the psychoanalytic terms of repressions, psychoses, and frustrations. Like the Freudian naturalists, he gave sex motivations a leading role in behavior. This technique made his sketches of *Winesburg, Ohio* (1919) unusually bitter, though tinged with pity. The characters of this book are almost Dostoevskian in their primitive introspective qualities. There is the frustrated village boy who angrily strikes the sophisticated town reporter whom he secretly admires and would like as a friend. A gentle German schoolmaster is falsely charged by a half-witted boy with being a sex pervert and is brutally beaten and kicked by a saloonkeeper as a preliminary to a lynching, which, however, does not come off. Winesburg has its peeping Tom minister and a variety of embittered, lonely individuals. Throughout, Sherwood Anderson implied that this ugliness reflected a standardized, tyrannical mammonistic civilization that was faithfully mirrored in the small town. To conceal one's worth-while desires in deference to the demand for social conformity merely inspired frustrations and intellectual dishonesty.

3

The American drama, aside from the usual frothy Broadway spectacles and borrowed themes, showed genuine maturity during the twenties. Patronage had not been lacking in prewar years, but too few American playwrights possessed more than mere competence. A new day dawned with Eugene O'Neill, three times winner of the Pulitzer Prize during the decade. He had studied the art of the playwright with the remarkable Professor George P. Baker of Harvard whose noted "47 Workshop" had trained a number of leading American dramatists. O'Neill's father had been an actor and had raised his son in the atmosphere of the theater. Eugene O'Neill knew drama and life not only from the classics and the great dramatic masterpieces of Ibsen and Strindberg, which influenced his technique, but from many months of rough seafaring life, a brief experience as a gold prospector, and a career as a newspaper reporter.

O'Neill's plays were hailed enthusiastically by the theatrical critic, George Jean Nathan, the outspoken counterpart (and editorial associate) of Mencken for the stage. The dramatist's use of unusually frank dialogue as in *Anna Christie* (1922) was no mere concession to sophisticated Broadway audiences, but one phase of his naturalism. Many of his plays, like *The Moon of the Caribbees* (1919), *The Long Voyage Home* (1919), *Emperor Jones* (1920), and *The Hairy Ape* (1922) expressed the emotions and deeds associated with primitivism: violence, insanity, suicide, and prostitution. In the *Emperor Jones,* a Negro-American lawbreaker becomes a dictator over a primitive people, but he breaks down under the strain of fear and reverts to the primitive psychology of his African ancestors. Charles Gilpin and Paul Robeson were the most successful interpreters of this role. Another venture into the primitive, *The Hairy Ape,* attained great popularity through the convincing role taken by Louis Wolheim. Something novel on the American stage arrived in 1928 with O'Neill's *Strange Interlude,* which used psychoanalysis through the revival of the "aside." It consisted of nine acts and required a long intermission for dinner. Its Freudian license on matters of sex led to its banning in Boston, but helped to give it over four hundred performances in New York.

Maxwell Anderson, with degrees from the University of North Dakota and Stanford, and with experience as an English teacher and newspaperman, found his métier after the war as a dramatist. While on the staff of the *New York World* he collaborated with a fellow editorial writer, Lawrence Stallings, on the antiwar play, *What Price Glory?* (1924). Its realistic "doughboy" dialogue was still novel on the stage and its note of postwar disillusionment struck a popular chord. Out of the South, whose literary revival of the twenties attracted wide attention, came Paul Green's sympathetic plays of the Negro and the sharecropper. His *In Abraham's Bosom* (1927) deservedly won the Pulitzer Prize.

While the commercial stage reigned supreme, the prewar Little Theatre movement and its creative amateur ideals made rapid progress in the colleges. On the professional stage the Theater Guild of New York kept the best of Euripides' masterpieces before discriminating American audiences. Eva Le Gallienne, daughter of the distinguished English essayist and poet, Richard Le Gallienne, combined her talent as actress and theatrical director to present the Civic Repertory Theater to New York. Instead of encouraging the artistically debilitating "long runs," she changed bills nightly. She directed and appeared personally in many plays by Ibsen, Chekhov, Shakespeare, and Barrie. Here was another challenge to pure commercialism in the theater.

4

Although contemporary critics have felt that the poets of the twenties were merely talking to themselves rather than reaching a wide audience, there is little doubt that poetry flourished during this period of T. S. Eliot and Edna St. Vincent Millay. Middletown preferred the platitudes and sentimentality of Edgar Guest, but the best work came from rebels who rejected the materialistic values of the day. Expatriates like Ezra Pound had long since washed their hands of the American scene. In this group of sensitive poets was Thomas Stearns Eliot, who had been born of cultured middle-class parents in St. Louis, was educated under Irving Babbitt and George Santayana at Harvard, and then left in 1914 to reside in London. In 1927, he became a British subject and thereafter joined the Anglo-Catholic fold. Classical values and religious traditionalism attracted him increasingly. In 1922, he published *The Waste Land*, which some critics have regarded as the greatest poem of the twentieth century. Addressed to both British and American readers, it struck a common chord of experience: the futility of modern civilization. *The Waste Land* consisted of episodes arranged almost in kaleidoscopic fashion and contrasted stable ancient civilizations with the meaninglessness of the Jazz Age. He pictured mothers who feared to have children, crude sex experiences without love, and "hollow" men and women who had nothing meaningful to say.

In this era when the bohemianism of New York's Greenwich Village deeply infiltrated American urban culture, Edna St. Vincent Millay joined the rebels among the attic dwellers. Her intense love poetry and hedonistic style were epitomized by one of her oft-quoted lines, "My candle burns at both ends." In 1923, her book of poems, *The Harp Weaver*, won a Pulitzer Prize and three years later she wrote the libretto for *The King's Henchman*, an opera composed by Deems Taylor and produced by the Metropolitan Opera Company. Among the outstanding narrative poets, Stephen Vincent Benet told an American epic in sweeping, fascinating verse of real intensity in his *John Brown's Body* (1928).

Living in semiretirement near Monterey, California, was the scholarly misanthrope, Robinson Jeffers. In his poetry were the influences of Spengler's philosophy of decay, of Freudian symbols, and of the medical lore he had studied. Recognition finally came through his *Tamar and Other Poems* (1924) and *Roan Stallion* (1925). In these feverish verses he dealt with violence, incest, sex frustration, and pessimism. Nature semed far more important than man, who was hastening his own destruction through science.

Gertrude Stein, the expatriate, attempted a rebellion in poetry and prose that attracted very few followers. She had studied psychology with William James and had experimented with automatic

SOCIETY AND THOUGHT

writing, a kind of word sequence determined by mental associations. Like her friend Picasso and the abstractionists in art, she wished to create a "pure" art without storytelling. To this end she wrote "Tender Buttons" in 1914. Her later poem, "Susie Asado," puzzled the uninitiated with such lines as: "Drink pups drink pups lease a sash hold, see it shine..." If this was the product of automatic writing, such a gift for "natural" expression had been vouchsafed to few.

Harlem, which had suddenly grown into a vast Negro city within Manhattan, developed a notable intelligentsia among whom were gifted poets. Paul Laurence Dunbar of Ohio, who had established the tradition of Negro lyric poetry depicting everyday life, died in 1906 but his influence affected the Harlem poets. Of Dunbar's generation was James Weldon Johnson, a Jacksonville lawyer who went to New York city in 1901 and became a successful composer of musical comedies and even wrote the English libretto for a Metropolitan opera, *Goyescas*. Traditional in outlook, he was admirably fitted to write Negro spirituals. In 1927, he wrote *God's Trombones: Seven Negro Sermons in Verse*. In this he depicted a Negrolike, personal God who created the world with the words, "I'm lonely— I'll make me a world." Among the younger Harlem poets who admired the lyricism of Dunbar and Johnson, but added a more rebellious philosophy were Langston Hughes and Countee Cullen. Both made no attempt to conceal their intense race consciousness. Hughes had been born in Joplin, Missouri, was raised in Cleveland, and was educated at Columbia and Lincoln University. He had a melodic feeling for blues and ballads that he displayed in *The Weary Blues* (1926). Cullen was a native Harlemite, a graduate of New York University. Of Dunbar he had written feelingly in *Caroling Dusk* (1927):

> Pride kept his twisted lips apart
> In jest, to hide a heart that bled.

5

The writing of biography and history did not escape the new intellectual tendencies of the twenties. As one might expect of an extremely individualistic decade concerned with psychology as a key to life, a vogue for biography spread rapidly. In England, Lytton Strachey had depicted the lives of eminent Victorians in frank terms that broke away from the hero worship usually associated with those figures, but he often resorted to fictionizing the thoughts of his characters. Biographers in England and America chose Strachey as their model. In New York city William E. Woodward, a businessman and writer, popularized a new term, "debunking," for biography and applied his skeptical attitude in writing about the lives of Washington and Grant. The extraordinary popularity of Woodward's books obviously reflected the antitraditionalism and hedonism of the twenties. To find that America's national idols had feet of clay was reassuring to those eager to cast off moral or ethical restraints. Other biographers borrowed a lesson or two from Freud to explain the lives of Catherine the Great, Elizabeth, and even Joan of Arc in terms of sex motivations.

Among the scholarly biographies Albert J. Beveridge's monumental *Life of Marshall* (1916-19) not only won the Pulitzer Prize but received the enthusiastic endorsement of law school deans during the twenties. The economic conservatism of John Marshall was too much in keeping with the times to be "debunked"; and Beveridge's strong bias against Jefferson was perfectly understandable in a decade when Hamilton was held to be a model for statesmanship. Although Beveridge professed great sorrow that he had to reduce the stature of a great man in his *Abraham Lincoln, 1809-1858* (2 vols., 1928), it was timely indeed for this debunking age to portray the Great Emancipator as a shifty, opportunistic Illinois legislator. It is true that the biographer declared to Professor William E. Dodd that he expected to picture Lincoln as a great president in a future volume, but Beveridge's death prevented his readers from discovering the "other Lincoln." A solid contribution to biography began to come off the presses in 1928, when Allen Johnson and later Dumas

Malone edited the twenty-volume *Dictionary of American Biography*. Over 2200 specialists cooperated in this gigantic task modeled after England's respected *Dictionary of National Biography*.

The tendency of "scientific history" to strip the social studies of moral judgments was transmitted to a receptive generation during the twenties. Thus the "objectivity" of the William A. Dunning school of Southern historians not only led to the discarding of abolitionist interpretations of the Civil War and Reconstruction but it buried equalitarian ideals of race beneath allegedly incontrovertible economic and social facts. It remained for a popular writer, Claude G. Bowers, to express the fullest implications of the position taken by the revisionists in his *The Tragic Era: The Revolution after Lincoln* (1929). Bowers not only followed the direction of Dunning in denouncing the Radicals but he portrayed the early Klan, the Red Shirts, and the planter class in a friendly spirit. Among the able historians who did not yield to the flood of such "revisionism" was William E. Dodd, a staunch Wilsonian Democrat who had been born in North Carolina and had taught history during 1908-33 at the University of Chicago. Dodd's small but influential volume, *The Cotton Kingdom,* was one of the best books in the *Chronicles of America* series (1918-21). It pictured the antebellum South as aristocratic and showed the author's distrust of the planter civilization. Negro historians, unhappy over the Dunning trend toward revisionism, attempted to correct this tendency and to point out that the Negro was no mere pawn in the events of the Civil War and Reconstruction. To this end, Dr. Carter G. Woodson, a Washington, D. C., educator, had founded *The Journal of Negro History* (1916-).

The vogue of cultural history, forecast in prewar times by James Harvey Robinson's New History, made some headway during this era, although there was little of the note of social protest and reform that had once been associated with this school. American specialists in European history such as Carleton J. H. Hayes, Carl Becker, Harry Elmer Barnes, and Preserved Smith stimulated an American *Kulturgeschichte*. In the writing of American cultural history, the most ambitious work was the large cooperative series, *A History of*

American Life (1927-   ) edited by Arthur M. Schlesinger of Iowa and Harvard and Dixon R. Fox of Columbia. This series was usually descriptive rather than integrative or analytical, though several contributors did achieve an integrating interpretive quality by stressing such concepts as urbanism.

One of the most ambitious and brilliant efforts to integrate practically all phases of the American past was *The Rise of American Civilization* (1927) by Charles and Mary Beard. As in prewar times, Beard's basic integrating factor was the economic motive in history. Cultural life reflected the class structure and the economy of the times. Believing as he did that an historical situation was usually the product of contending economic pressure groups, he explained the writing of the "due process" clause of the Fourteenth Amendment as motivated by the desire of businessmen to secure special protection against unfriendly popular laws in the state legislatures. The Beards divided American history into two phases; the first was agrarian dominance, the second, the industrialist's hegemony. *The Rise of American Civilization* appeared simultaneously with Parrington's *Main Currents in American Thought,* but although both were written from an economic viewpoint, the moral values of Parrington were far more explicit and less constrained by an economic determinism. With such notable exceptions, the historian of the twenties had divorced himself from the prewar mood of social protest and Progressivism.

6

Psychology rated with Darwinistic biology as the popular science for the laity. The Narcissus complex of this individualistic era encouraged numerous charlatans as well as scholars to set themselves up in business as psychologists or psychiatrists. Amateur Freudians, as previously noted, used the terminology of psychoanalysis in novels, plays, and the sophisticated conversation of the smart set. In prewar days, when Progressivism was in flower, the sociologists (except for Spencer's disciples) enjoyed the prestige of a reformist era intent on the salvation of society. Now that the dominant motif was a narrow individualism, psychology and the "psychological approach" triumphed over sociology. A special contributing factor for this victory was the wartime success of psychological testing and propaganda techniques in helping to win the war. Mencken and the eugenics cult believed that the Army mental tests had demonstrated that the masses truly belonged to the "booboisie." However solid and worthwhile the study of psychology might be, it served the twenties as a scientific excuse for a moral holiday and, together with eugenics, as a rationale for an aristocratic elite.

Sharing the limelight with psychoanalysis was behaviorism. Its aggressive exponent, Professor John B. Watson of the New School for Social Research, had long been active in the field of animal learning and had borrowed certain ideas of environmental conditioning from the Russian psychologist, Ivan P. Pavlov. The Russian's famous experiments with a dog had proved how an animal that had secreted saliva at the sight of food that had been incidentally accompanied by a certain sound would eventually be "conditioned" to respond the same way when the sound occurred without the presence of food. Such experiments showed that glandular and muscular responses may be conditioned by new stimuli. Thus the "conditioned reflex" and the "conditioned response" entered psychology.

Developing these ideas, Watson published his pedagogical applications of them in *Psychology from the Standpoint of a Behaviorist* (1919). He appeared ready to revolutionize psychology by dropping "consciousness" as its subject matter and forsaking the introspective method of analysis for a pure "stimulus and response" psychology. Behaviorists would not deal with such independent entities as desire, sensation, and instinct, but regarded man as an organism responding automatically to specific stimuli. The brain was a mere switchboard of connections. From these principles Watson was ready to derive the most extravagant claims for the possibilities of conditioning any child to become whatever the educator wished: rich man, poor man, beggar man, or thief. While totalitarian leaders believed that this type of indoctrination was indeed possible and desirable for millions of subjects, Watson eventually decided to limit the applications of his "conditioning" ideas to the more American art of mass advertising. Behaviorist extremists soon discredited their own theories, but the naturalistic philosophy underlying behaviorism attracted thousands of that era.

Psychology and even psychoanalysis left their imprint upon the study of political science, law, and other social studies. It was easy to discern the spirit of the times in the emphasis placed upon the existence of irrational elements in politics, judicial statesmanship, and group reaction to propaganda. One way of escaping moral responsibility for a hedonistic decade was to deny Aristotle's dictum that man is a rational animal. Instead, man could be understood by naturalists as a helpless pawn of circumstance, as a product of glandular or muscular responses, as the plaything of determinant sex motivations, or as the amoral agent of economic interest and political pressure groups. Walter Lippmann, a thoughtful observer of political behavior, stressed the factor of irrationality in politics in his popular book, *Public Opinion* (1922) by explaining that men substituted "stereotypes" or nearly automatic non-rational mental images for the objective view of a situation. The mass appeal of fascism, communism, or Klan bigotry rested upon the uncritical acceptance by the individual of the fact that his distorted stereotypes corresponded to the actual world.

The role of propaganda in shaping men's minds absorbed many of the political science department of the University of Chicago and elsewhere. Charles Merriam, the Chicago chairman, edited an entire series of propaganda books covering a number of major countries, including fascist Italy and communist Russia. These dealt with the achievement of civic loyalty through conditioning by propagandist devices. One member of the staff, Harold D. Lasswell, applied a Freudian technique in his very original studies, *Propaganda Technique in the World War* (1927) and *Psychopathology and Politics* (1930).

Economic conservatism prevented the victory of sociological jurisprudence over the traditional philosophies based on the certainty of the law that could be "discovered" but never created. Holmes and Brandeis, pioneers of the prewar philosophy of a changing law constantly adapting itself to a world in flux, dissented from the conservative opinions of the Supreme Court majority with almost monotonous regularity. However, in many law schools, particularly at Harvard and Yale, prospective lawyers who were to play a major role in the New Deal learned a good deal of the philosophy of sociological jurisprudence.

Although sociology seemed to be partly obscured by the scintillating claims of psychology and biology, its practitioners adjusted themselves by placing a psychological emphasis upon social behavior. Much of the vigor and direction came from the University of Chicago school of sociologists. Under the leadership of Robert Park and Ernest W. Burgess, a host of advanced students developed the implications of the "ecological" approach to the problems of society. The term had been borrowed from the biological field of plant studies and it stressed the idea that the geographic environment was a major determinant in the development of the organism. Sociological ecologists applied this concept to the growth of "natural areas" or neighborhoods in the city. Out of the ensuing University of Chicago studies came books on Chicago's Gold Coast and slums, the Ghetto, "hobohemia," and other urban culture areas. Robert S. Lynd, later professor of sociology at Columbia, collaborated with his wife, Helen, in the exceptionally successful application of the social survey method, *Middletown: A Study in Contemporary American Culture* (1929). Their devices of measurement, combined with sociological observations showing a high order of insight, enriched all students of social history and behavior. Laymen, too, were fascinated by this scientific appraisal of an American city, later revealed as Muncie, Indiana. When the book appeared, Mencken outdid himself in reviewing it for the *American Mercury* under the caption "A City in Moronia," and angered Muncie people by his comments on their "unbelievable stupidities."

Finally, the progress of professional social work during this decade merits attention. Jane Addams, Florence Kelley, Grace Abbott, and Lillian Wald were leaders in the expansion of the early settlement houses into laboratories and agencies for urban rehabilitation. The American Association of Social Workers, begun in 1921, marked the achievement of an independent professional status for its members. Although social workers tended to break away from earlier affiliations (if any) with sociology, they frequently adopted the newer psychological and psychoanalytical teachings. This became an era of innumerable child guidance clinics, alienists, juvenile courts, policewomen, and of expert social workers skilled in psychiatry, the techniques of dealing with delinquency, family disorganization, vocational needs, and, of course, the problem of poverty.

7

Although the American art experience, like other phases of cultural life, showed a continuity from prewar years, there was added a decided quality of hedonism and restless individualistic experimentation. The bohemianism of the Paris Latin Quarter and of Greenwich Village seemed admirably suited for the anti-intellectualism and meaningless "Dadaism" that infected the more sophisticated studios. Less than ever did the artist feel himself to be an organic part of society, for the pure aestheticism of art for art's sake seemed again dominant. Like the Menckenites in literature, too many abstractionists, surrealists, and cubists took a condescending attitude toward the herd and offered their fantasies as a revelation into the true nature of things—or they offered no excuse whatever for any aberration that appeared on the canvas.

Georgia O'Keeffe, a Wisconsin-born muralist and landscape artist who married the great photographic artist, Alfred Stieglitz, earned high recognition for her New Mexico desert scenes and later for her symbolic abstractions. Sometimes the qualities of an abstract painting were fused with objective art as in Charles Sheeler's interpretation of skyscrapers and trains. Especially arresting were the original, partly abstract scenes in the water-color paintings of John Marin. His seemingly hurried strokes appeared to the layman to be the careless untutored work of a child, but experimental artists admired the unique rhythms and intensity of mood that he expressed.

The Revolt of the Eight (actually only a few had been rebels against economic injustice) was now definitely subdued, for galleries no longer discriminated against the paintings of Robert Henri, John Sloan, George Bellows, and others of this circle. The note of social protest that some of them had sounded in 1908 had been considerably softened. As for the younger art rebels, their path was still a thorny one. Museums kept only the masters in their permanent collections while offering temporary exhibits to postimpressionists and other experimenters. There was now a greater awareness that American art had come of age, judging from the appearance of a number of sound histories of American painting, sculpture, and architecture. Suzanne La Follette wrote an unusually well-integrated history of American art in its social-economic setting in *Art in America* (1929).

To the art world prosperity meant primarily that the well-to-do spent over two hundred million dollars for art objects from abroad and far less for the work of native artists. It is true that hundreds of artists did earn a steady income from teaching art in the high schools and colleges, which had awakened to the role of aesthetics in education; but only the commercial artists belonged as a class to the upper ranks of the well-paid professional men and women. The heavy demands of advertisers for attractive or eye-catching drawings, such as those that depicted a girl in a bathing suit smoking a well-known brand of cigarette, guaranteed that a competent commercial artist would not have to starve in a garret.

The death in 1924 of Louis Sullivan, father of functionalism in architecture, reminded sympathetic critics how little progress had been made toward his ideal. That year, Sullivan issued his vehement appeal for modernism in a book devoted to his personal history and art, *Autobiography of an Idea*. He had the satisfaction of watching the striking advances toward modernism made by the Finnish architect, Eliel Saarinen, whose functionalist design for the *Chicago Tribune Tower* won the enthusiastic acclaim of discriminating critics, though it received only second prize in the *Tribune's* international competition. Saarinen came to the United States during the latter twenties and helped to found the Cranbrook School at Bloomfield Hills, Michigan. Although the winners of the *Tribune's* first prize and the contract itself were the highly competent designers, John Mead Howells and Raymond Hood, they superimposed Gothic details upon the impressive lines of the skyscraper, thus violating the functionalist canons of Sullivan and Saarinen.

The true successor to Sullivan was Frank Lloyd Wright whose "prairie houses," with their functionalist, horizontal lines and open interiors, seemed beautifully adapted to the level terrain of the Middle West. Elsewhere, as on the Pacific Coast and in Japan, he had also left a distinctive regional interpretation. In 1923, Wright had the satisfaction of knowing that his exquisite Imperial Hotel in Tokyo had been so ingeniously planned that it was able to survive the terrific earthquake of that year by absorbing the sharp tremors through its flexible foundation and structure. Wright was even more articulate than Sullivan in championing functionalist ideas. His break with historic styles and non-organic architectural theories was complete. He built from the inside outwards, considering primarily the living needs of the occupants, rather than superimposing an alien pattern on the internal structure.

Young Lewis Mumford, a brilliant lecturer at the New School for Social Research, stimulated architectural and city planning theorists by his organic approach to the aesthetic aspects of American civilization. His *Sticks and Stones* (1924) and *The Golden Day* (1926) traced the conflict of American pioneer utilitarianism with the older values of a cosmopolitan culture. "Beneath the organized vivacity of our American communities," he charged, "who is not aware of a blankness, a sterility, a boredom, a despair?" Metropolitan civilization was a failure because the city had become dehumanized. Even the promising city planning movement had not yet emerged from the superficial "city beautiful" stage, i. e., externally decorative but not at all concerned with better living conditions. He felt that city planning must be integrated within a broad social philosophy of human needs in order to make life itself an aesthetic experience. But Mumford's voice was still that of the prophet in the wilderness, for this decade had little enthusiasm for his dream of community planning.

There was however, considerable city planning of a limited type during the twenties. Traffic congestion compelled new adjustments in street construction and complex traffic rules. The construction of skyscrapers and other urban buildings on a large scale required a complicated machinery of zoning ordinances to save the metropolis from utter chaos by restricting certain types of buildings to definite districts. New building codes came into existence to keep the gigantic skyscrapers from completely darkening the streets and nearby buildings. The new skyscraper began with a relatively broad base and narrowed in width by successive setbacks until, as in many instances, it culminated in a narrow tower. Occasionally community planning took the form of "garden cities," model suburban towns to draw off the crowded population of the metropolis. The park and playground movement of prewar times expanded in the cities and enriched the variety of recreational opportunities for millions.

A decade distinguished by such creative men as Eugene O'Neill, John Dewey, T. S. Eliot, Walter Lippmann, Theodore Dreiser, and Sinclair Lewis cannot be dismissed as a futile era. One must of course discount the posturing and affectations of the Lost Generation, Greenwich Village, and those painters and writers who made experimentation an end in itself rather than a means to achieve truth and beauty. Narcissism and a lack of social idealism obstructed the path of many novelists, poets, artists, and popular writers, but it was probably a worthwhile experience for men to assert the artistic potentialities of the individual when freed from the conformities demanded by society. There was obvious therapeutic value in the attacks of the Mencken circle upon the sins of the raucous Booster spirit, small town intolerance, and pure commercialism. Not until the Great Depression and World War II did the shortsighted individualism and undemocratic assumptions of Mencken and his followers reveal themselves. By then it became clear that the real Lost Generation consisted of the youths frustrated by the sudden collapse of economic security and delegated to correct the mistakes of their elders by sacrifice upon the battlefield.

· 21 ·

The Impact of Depression and War Upon The Social Structure

I

"WE have not yet reached the goal," declared Herbert Hoover in 1928, "but given a chance to go forward with the policies of the last eight years, and we shall soon, with the help of God, be within sight of the day when poverty will be banished from the nation." Distinguished economists such as Thomas N. Carver of Harvard and Irving Fisher of Yale shared this optimism. Textbooks, echoing the faith in prosperity, taught the idea that violent fluctuations of the business cycle had been eliminated by the automatic controls of the Federal Reserve Bank system and other modern economic institutions. Business leadership in American society had apparently brought the nation by 1929 (except for the Florida real-estate crash and certain weaknesses in several sectors of the economy) to the very gateway of the promised land. Prosperity gave high prestige to the entrepreneur and his slogan of the twenties, "Less government in business, more business in government."

Then came the worst economic debacle in American history. By 1932 the national income had fallen below that of 1912 when the population was less by 30,000,000 people. Our unemployment in proportion to population almost doubled that of Britain and exceeded that of Germany, two countries that we had considered in fundamental decline since World War I. As the depression deepened, communists and fascists were not alone in glib manifestoes that capitalism was doomed. Americans who had counted upon the

489

wisdom and initiative of the dynamic businessman were rudely
shaken by Senate revelations that too many bankers and industrialists had shown neither wisdom nor integrity in the role they played
in the events leading up to the great crash of 1929.

Hoover had hitherto been considered a progressive because of
his humanitarian activities and his insistence upon stabilizing business through cooperation between government and the businessman.
He had been a pioneer in the depression of 1921 in his demand that
government use public works and private expansion programs to
stave off depressions. But like most people of the early thirties, he
underestimated the severity of the crisis and moved too slowly to
stop the downward spiral of economic life. Nevertheless, he reversed
the social pendulum away from the "rugged individualism" that
he had so often praised toward a larger measure of collective action—
something more than the "collective self-help" that he had recommended. Most important were the Reconstruction Finance Corporation as a huge stabilizing agency and his expansion of public
expenditures for construction and relief to unprecedented levels.
Even the liberal Democratic presidential nominee of 1932 criticized
Hoover for failing to balance the budget. As for fundamental reforms, neither employers nor the craft unions of the Hoover era
looked beyond the goal of recovery for any radical scheme of social
reconstruction.

The deflation of business leadership was completed even before
the election of Roosevelt. Breadlines, Hoovervilles, marches of
unemployed men, the spectacle of people grubbing over garbage cans
for food, and the obvious frustration of youth—the true Lost Generation—all contributed to the general disillusionment. But while
Europeans yielded to extreme nationalistic panaceas and even dictatorship, Americans overwhelmingly elected leaders who declared
their purpose to "save capitalism" while experimenting with large-
scale federal aid and stricter regulation for the sick economy.
Franklin D. Roosevelt was a Wilsonian liberal, but with an upper-
class background that was untouched by proletarianism. Although
he lashed out at "economic royalists," and embarked upon uncharted
social experiments, he did not wander so far from the recognizable

form of private enterprise as to justify the labels of "socialist" or "communist" hurled at him by angry conservatives. But no president, including Theodore Roosevelt and Woodrow Wilson, had so defiantly challenged the wisdom of historic business leadership in directing American life.

Actually, the businessman had enjoyed sufficient prestige in 1933 to be offered a senior partnership in the New Deal, particularly in writing the National Recovery Act of that year. The law was born in the United States Chamber of Commerce and blessed by the president of the General Electric Company. Dominant corporations wrote the "codes" that fixed prices intended to stabilize business. In effect, immunity from antitrust laws was conferred upon these firms, just as Theodore Roosevelt had granted similar immunity to the United States Steel Corporation during the panic of 1907. However, as the NRA turned out, the unions were the ones that profited from the key Section 7A effectively guaranteeing collective bargaining free from employer intimidation. Thereafter the shrunken power of labor swelled to such proportions that employers found little that was good in the New Deal.

An intellectual history of the businessman must note his ideological transformation in these years. The Federalist-Whig-Republican tradition of Hamilton, Marshall, Webster, and John Bingham had stressed nationalism and political-economic centralization. Tariffs, railroad subsidies, and other forms of government aid had been accepted by business with no thought that these ran counter to free-enterprise axioms. The Jeffersonian liberal doctrine of less government, which most agrarian Democrats had prized at one time, had already been borrowed during the 1920's by Republican businessmen. With a populistic—they said socialistic—regime in Washington, business spokesmen added the Jeffersonian theories of states' rights and "strict construction" of the Constitution to the "less government" doctrine as a practical defense against New Deal nationalism. If they were inconsistent in borrowing laissez-faire principles from an old agrarian order to serve modern industrialism, so also, it might be said, was President Thomas Jefferson who on occasion abandoned strict construction to help the land-hungry westerners to acquire Louisiana or retreated from his free-trade principles to support tariff aid on behalf of urban employment. Men have usually been far less consistent in purely political philosophy than in social-economic doctrines. Thus it happened that conservative Republicans joined with equally conservative Democrats in Congress to halt the nationalist advance of Roosevelt's urban-labor-consumer coalition.

New Deal philosophers naturally preferred the nationalism of another Democrat, Andrew Jackson, to the decentralization theories of Jefferson. Like the spokesmen for business, they were pragmatists who selected the most advantageous precedents from history for their own purposes. Critics, forgetting the bankruptcy of so many contemporary economic theories, have assumed that the New Dealers broke with time-tested doctrines to embark on a rudderless voyage of crude pragmatism and sheer expediency. Roosevelt, like Hoover, rejected the advice of rigid academicians who suggested that a do-nothing policy would lead to the natural revival of prices to profitable levels. However, Roosevelt was far more adventurous in experimenting with unorthodox monetary theories, some of which turned out to be failures, but his objectives and personal values did not represent a historic departure from accepted American traditions.

Professor F. S. C. Northrop, the noted philosopher, has been severely critical of New Deal pragmatism and believes that much of the Roosevelt technique was merely experiment unfortified by sound theory. Still, he makes a major exception for the administration's adoption of the theoretical principles of John Maynard Keynes, the English economist. These ideas involved a method of stabilizing the business cycle by striking a balance between spending and saving in the economy. During boom times, the government would increase taxes to reduce spending and it would build up savings. When depressions or recessions came, the process would be reversed and governmental spending would stimulate the economy. Hoover's idea of stabilizing business through deferring public works in good times for periods of depression had been defeated by business resistance; it remained to be seen whether taxpayers would be willing to endure higher taxes in prosperous times for a remote economic contingency; war crises belonged to another category.

Depression and reform weakened the historic importance of the captain of industry. One of the most illustrious parts he had played was that of a Mycaenas—a latter-day patron of the arts, sciences, and social services. However, the fortunes for such purposes were cut down not only by the depression, but also by the increasing income and corporate taxes, capital gains taxes, inheritance taxes, and other levies that beset the path to the huge fortunes of an earlier period. Private colleges and charitable institutions that had piled up endowments of hundreds of millions in the past from Rockefeller, Carnegie, George Baker, and others faced the danger of eclipse if not destruction at the hands of tax-supported institutions and colleges. Inevitably, the power of the state grew as federal funds went to agriculture, education, health, housing, cheap electrical power and flood control, and relief.

Businessmen chafed at the numerous New Deal regulations for recovery and reform which led some of them to complain that their privacy had been ruthlessly invaded and that hereafter (as J. P. Morgan once said) business must be conducted in glass houses under constant public scrutiny. New Dealers argued that the regulation of banking, investment, and labor relations would strengthen, not weaken, capital. The cost of social security and minimum wage and hour laws should pay for themselves in a more stable economy and a more efficient working force. Yet there were those who argued that the quest for social security was un-American because it destroyed the quality of adventurousness that had built this country. Roosevelt, tirelessly reiterating his purpose to preserve capitalism, reminded his listeners that most of his "revolutionary" changes were much milder than England's social reforms that had long been approved even by British Tories. Some of his social legislation, such as the Social Security Act, was timed to take the wind out of the sails of Huey Long's share-the-wealth scheme, Townsend's extravagant old-age pension plan, and irresponsible communist proposals.

Actually, the New Deal did not arrest the long term trend of American business toward consolidation involving the decline of price competition among the industrial giants. Bankruptcy overtook many thousands of factories, banks, and retail establishments. A desperate battle for survival led to a wholesale merger of weaker companies and to the adoption of labor-saving machines, scientific management, and strict economies. There were obvious incentives to evade price competition by both legal and extra-legal devices. At the end of the decade Congress' Temporary National Economic Committee uncovered startling evidence that monopolistic tendencies had been accelerated by the depression. Huge corporations, capitalized at $5,000,000 or more, held the assets of 93 per cent of all transportation and public utility businesses, 78 per cent of the financial houses, 66 per cent of all manufacturing companies, and 65 per cent of the mining and quarrying activities. Corporations produced 92 per cent of all American manufactures. A few tobacco, chemical, and rubber concerns owned from 80 to 92 per cent of all assets in those fields. In 1937, there was only one aluminum corporation in the entire country; three auto firms produced 86 per cent of the output; three cigarette firms did four-fifths of the business; and three companies made over 60 per cent of all the steel manufactured here. Of the 308 life insurance companies, five owned 54.4 per cent or $14,279,000,000 of the total assets. Concentration was far greater in the field of industrial insurance in which Prudential and Metropolitan alone did nearly three-fourths of the entire business.

The TNEC went on to show how monopoly had been accelerated by well financed lobbies through special legislation. Forty-three states legalized "resale price maintenance" which fixed prices on certain products for retailers. "Fair trade" laws, pushed through under the depression-inspired psychology that it was necessary to prevent prices from falling below profitable levels, remained to hamper the competitive system with its fixed price structure that was far from the "just price" ethics of the medieval guild society. States used their taxing or quarantine powers to keep out oleomargarine, chain stores, and peddlers. Health and safety codes were often manipulated to destroy independents who could not afford the expensive equipment required by law. The list of monopoly-fostering devices was long.

As for the social implications of intensified monopoly, they were staggering. Even the vigorous Department of Justice under confirmed antimonopolists like Francis Biddle and Thurman Arnold could not reverse this tendency—if they had any such hopes. Other New Deal regulatory agencies, also staffed by ardent believers in free competition, could scarcely hope to do more than eliminate the more flagrant violations of the competitive principle and the antitrust laws. Public opinion, including expert opinion, was critical but reluctant to go back to the ineffectual trust-busting policies of Theodore Roosevelt. Popular books on the alleged power of "America's Sixty Families" and similar themes interested many thousands of readers but converted few outside the Left to any sense of urgency in combating monopoly. Americans still had faith in the reality of the ballot and their ability to elect a president and Congress of their choice despite the obvious and overwhelming opposition to reform candidates of the metropolitan press as well as of those who might be readily classified among the Sixty Families.

The businessman could do little to halt the rise of a rival power in industrial unions like the C.I.O. which used political as well as economic weapons against him. Unreconstructed captains of industry like Henry Ford or Thomas Girdler of the Republic Steel Company might bitterly resist unionization by converting their plant police into an armed industrial force or by using spies, but they were fighting a losing cause. Enlightened industrialists such as Myron Taylor, chairman of the board of the United States Steel Corporation, accepted the new order without necessarily subscribing to all its reformist principles. Henry Ford eventually decided to give up his stubborn (and sometimes violent) resistance to unionization and his young grandson, Henry Ford II, eventually took over the vast enterprises in a far more cooperative spirit than the founder had shown.

By the end of the decade the businessman was ready to concede a much larger sphere to the state than he had ever before thought to be fitting. Federal intervention within certain limits in social security, education, housing, and health, seemed to be accepted by the business press with a declining amount of criticism about their socialistic implications. American businessmen as a class, unlike their counterparts in Germany and Italy, did not seek insurance against unionism and communism by sponsoring home-bred dictators or extreme nationalistic movements. And American labor, despite the heat of conflict engendered by its bid for power, did not actually lose its confidence in the unique entrepreneurial ability of the businessman. Socialism was not a genuine issue at any time during the capital and labor conflicts of this decade.

The extraordinary production record of American industry during 1940-45 revived the prestige of the businessman. That President Roosevelt's seemingly impossible demands for 50,000 planes did not remain mere rhetoric was due to high industrial statesmanship as well as to vast resources of skilled labor, materials, and modern tools and techniques. Before World War II ended, a new ideology of business leadership had arisen superior to the old slogans of less government in business, though these had not disappeared. Even the leftward-leaning Vice-President, Henry Wallace, spoke of his ideal as "democratic capitalism." Far more pleasant to conservative minds and much better than the familiar but shrill protests of chambers of commerce and the National Association of Manufacturers was the best-selling book of Friedrich Hayek, *Road to Serfdom,* published in 1944. Almost as uncompromising as Herbert Spencer, Professor Hayek suggested that any concessions to collectivism led directly to the loss of personal liberty as in Nazi Germany. Disregarding, as J. K. Galbraith points out, the extensive cooperative experiments in democratic countries like England and the Scandinavian states, he reached the conclusion that freedom and unrestricted individual economic enterprise were indivisible. This line of reasoning brought the concept of government back to the suspect role it had held in the simple agrarian days of Paine and Jefferson.

2

The most arresting phenomenon of these years is the rise of organized labor from virtual impotency to the position of an undisputed social, economic, and political power. During 1920-29 the

American Federation of Labor, which accounted for most organized workmen, had already declined from nearly 4,000,000 to 2,750,000; by 1933, another 400,000 members had been lost. At the same time, employers had developed "welfare capitalism" through company unions comprising over 2,500,000 members. The open-shop movement was stimulated in many industries by the expedient of shifting plants to the unorganized South. Independent unions were too weakened by a decade of paternalism and narrow craft objectives to respond effectively to the challenge of the worst depression in history. Men ceased to pay dues or attend meetings, and even faithful union men understood that in practice union wage scales were only nominal. Little remained but an undignified struggle for the remaining jobs in the jungle spirit of survival at any price. Younger men took the places of those over forty and machines displaced men in the race for economy and efficiency. Technological unemployment was a reality in these depression years, for the stagnant economy failed to absorb the displaced workmen elsewhere. In addition, the unions seemed helpless to check the depression tendency of hard-pressed employers to ignore labor legislation and to introduce crude speed-up methods.

Nothing in the craft philosophy of the late Samuel Gompers and his successor, William Green, had prepared labor for the bewildering changes that occurred after 1933. Even social security had been largely relegated to "welfare capitalism" because the unions believed that high wages and shorter hours would solve most labor problems. Labor had never been a close confidant of government and the secretary of labor had usually been chosen from among retired union men who had never been a real power in the ranks of organized labor. The labor strategy of the New Deal was at first devised by intellectuals rather than by the Greens and the Lewises. Once collective bargaining had been insured by Section 7A of the NRA and by the Wagner Act, labor recovered its voice and its organizing energies. When the A.F.of L. right-wing leaders held back in the drive to organize the mass production industries, John L. Lewis led the secession of militants into the Committee of Industrial Organizations. After 1935 the industrial unionists organized steel, which had been held captive by the open-shop movement since the Steel Strike of 1919; this was followed by similar victories in the auto industry, textiles, rubber, transportation, and some large white-collar organizations. By 1938 the C.I.O. reported 4,000,000 members and claimed parity with the A.F.of L. Their victory had not been an easy one, despite the aid of the National Labor Relations Board and kindred New Deal agencies. Strikes, including "sit-downs" and "wildcat" outbreaks, and occasional bloody conflicts with plant policemen, as in the Little Steel Strike, broke out on a large scale in that decade. Girdler of Little Steel and Ford did not yield to unionization without a bitter struggle.

The advent of the C.I.O. and industrial unionism was more than a checkerboard move in labor's struggle for power. When industrial unionists insisted that entire industries or shops must be organized as a unit regardless of the special claims of well-recognized crafts, the principle of labor solidarity was affirmed. It was a short step from this to the decision of the C.I.O. to contribute financially to New Deal campaign funds and to organize the Political Action Committee to advance prolabor and pro-New Deal candidates. David Dubinsky of the powerful International Ladies' Garment Workers' Union and Sidney Hillman of the Amalgamated Clothing Workers became devoted allies of the Roosevelt Democrats.

Especially significant in the impact of the C.I.O. upon the social structure of the nation was its modification of racialism in the South. While A.F.of L. locals had shown little enthusiasm for Negro workers in their midst, the C.I.O. leaders convinced white Southerners that their economic bargaining power would remain weak unless all workmen regardless of race were part of a militant union. Jim Crow segregation within the unions could not easily be eliminated, but surprising progress in that direction was made. Southern C.I.O. unions frequently held biracial affairs in their social halls while alternately white couples and then Negro couples danced to the band tunes. Thus the unions had made more real progress toward racial amity than the dual school system of the South—or even the educators of the North. Well-meant exhortations were no substitute for practical equalitarian day-to-day contacts on the job. Inevitably the

A.F.of L., too, felt the influence of the new unionism and eased its racial restrictions.

The status of labor and unionization advanced during World War II. Union leaders on the whole carried out their "no-strike" pledge, though they were unable to halt numerous unauthorized or "wildcat" strikes. They managed, with the aid of President Roosevelt, to retain the basic forty-hour week that they had won under the New Deal. When the war ended, over 14,000,000 men and women belonged to unions and even more were directly affected by labor contracts. Industry, too, had come to recognize that union contracts insured stability and prevented costly delays due to strikes; and nearly all responsible labor leaders recognized the hazards of not living up to their promises.

3

The staple farmers, who had scarcely had five prosperous years during the entire 1920's, were not at all prepared for the Great Depression of the thirties. Extremely low prices bankrupted hundreds of thousands of marginal farmers and threatened thousands more with the foreclosure of their farms. Some legislators, imitating the radicalism of Daniel Shays in 1786, tried to stop foreclosures by passing moratorium laws. Desperate dairy farmers overturned milk trucks and tried to halt marketing in the so-called farm holiday movement. In the South, where living standards had always been low, five-cent-a-pound cotton beggared many tenants and sharecroppers. Altogether, farm income, estimated at $7,708,000,000 in 1929, fell to nearly a third of that figure in 1932. In the West, Professor M. L. Wilson of Montana State College proposed compulsory crop restriction and benefit payments to farmers for cooperation in this program, but President Hoover rejected this as unconstitutional and unwise.

By 1933, Professor Wilson's idea of "equality for agriculture" in sharing the national income was realized in the Agricultural Adjustment Act. This was intended "to re-establish prices to farmers at a level that will give purchasing power ... equivalent to the purchasing power of agricultural commodities in the base period [1909-14]."

So began the history of "parity prices." To critics it seemed revolutionary and dangerous for the government to attempt even indirectly to underwrite the farmer's alleged share of the national income. Defenders replied that the only alternative was a prolonged depression for all classes.

The small farmer, the tenant, the sharecropper, and the farm hand were caught in the inexorable vise of an accelerated technological revolution. Mechanization and scientific agriculture were reflected in a shrinking farm population. While the national population rose from 92 to 131 millions during 1910-40, the number of farm people declined from 32 to 30 millions. Productivity per farm worker had increased 28 per cent during the thirties. The disappearance of the horse in favor of the tractor and similar motor-drawn machines had eliminated the need for extensive feed crops. Between World Wars I and II farmers had shifted about 50,000,000 acres from feed crops to general crops. New scientific plant developments such as hybrid corn seed raised productivity by many millions of bushels annually. Specialized poultry and dairy businesses added further to productivity.

A close view of the most productive farmers showed that they were highly trained businessmen and producers. In fact, less than one-third of the farms raised more than two-thirds of the total American output, as J. Clyde Marquis declares. One-third of American farms were unimportant as crop producers, being little better than subsistence farms. Yet when World War II began, the American farmer performed a production miracle analogous to that of the industrialist and city worker. Americans and some of their allies were adequately fed from record-breaking harvests, regardless of the fact that the total farm population was the smallest since Civil War times. Mechanical corn pickers, cotton pickers, combines of harvester-thresher machines, commercial fertilizer, scientific breeding, and other innovations made this possible. The mass production techniques and corporate organization for which Americans were world-famous had gone far to capture the farm.

All this had not been accomplished without paying a heavy price in social dislocation and human suffering. For decades there had been a heavy rural movement to the city; now there were wholesale evictions, clashes between sharecroppers and planters, and a growing but unprosperous class of marginal producers who clung to the farm (when it was possible) as their home even when their activities as commercial farmers had become negligible. Only a novelist could do justice to this picture of an uprooted people. Such was the burden of John Steinbeck's *Grapes of Wrath*, which described the troubles of evicted Oklahoma farmers who were beguiled by California labor-recruiting posters to become fruit pickers, only to suffer from the low-paid, irregular occupations and the hostility of local communities to the invasion of the "Okies." Much of the New Deal farm program was devoted to salvaging some of the derelicts of farm mechanization and the Great Depression. Generous federal loan terms enabled many tenants and other classes to buy farms or to move to productive soil. Rural electrification was also sponsored to raise the farmer's and villager's standard of living.

The Tennessee Valley Authority, for example, brought modern agricultural science to a backward section and furnished cheap electricity to many rural areas that did not seem to be a sound business risk to the established public utility companies. While the power companies and the partisan press denounced the TVA as a socialist venture, it brought a new day to millions of farmers in Tennessee, Mississippi, Alabama, Georgia, and Kentucky. During World War II, TVA easily justified itself to the taxpayer by its vast contributions of munitions and power to the war effort. Less spectacular was the significant fact that the Valley was buying electrical appliances at a faster rate than any other part of the country. New beef, dairy, and fruit industries were coming into existence with the aid of huge farm refrigerators and cooperative freezing lockers. The TVA did not continue the depression practice among local businessmen of advertising low wages, docile Anglo-Saxon labor, and tax exemption in order to entice factories away from other communities.

4

How did the American family react to the Great Depression? The Lynds sought the answer when they went back to Middletown in 1935 to learn what had happened since their former stay a decade earlier. They noted that the businessmen were whistling in the dark and feigning optimism, but were frightened by the downward economic trend. Those retailers hurt worst were the sellers of jewelry, building materials, new cars, candy, and household goods. Men's clothing stores felt the pinch, but women's apparel sales actually increased. Sociologists elsewhere, too, concluded that women's clothing demands were far less responsive to business declines than were men's. Also indicative of relative American values was the fact that the number of filling stations doubled during the early depression years. Newspapers complained in more than one American city that families arrived in their "jalopies" to collect relief checks. The automobile was the last evidence of status for many individuals even when they did not know where to turn for food.

Savings were wiped out and men walked the streets no longer hopeful of finding work. The word "unemployable" gained currency to describe those who had been so long unemployed that a psychological "rust" had set in and an unfavorable attitude toward disciplined work had developed. It was easier for a man to go on relief in cities like Middletown where a certain amount of anonymity existed than in rural areas. Poor families were given small vegetable gardens on vacant lots. Hoboes slept in the basements of courthouses until federal transient camps were set up. Despite anti-New Deal sentiment among Middletown businessmen, they readily accepted all the relief funds that they could get for the town. Nobody starved, but malnutrition took its toll in health. In some cities the poor lived on bread, potatoes, and beans. Social organizations and churches were helpless to meet the huge burden of distress; they gladly turned their clients over to federally supported agencies. Most families apparently gave up the task of caring at home for their own mentally ill, for an unprecedented number of such cases now flooded the state hospitals. This factor, rather than a rapid increase in mental breakdowns, may explain the crowded situation in such institutions.

Among the lower middle class there was more drinking than before and a general breakdown of morals. Suicides increased among businessmen. Both marriages and divorces temporarily declined, but desertion, "the poor man's divorce," increased. Reno, Nevada, ever on the alert to protect its basic industry of divorce, helped to reduce the state residence requirement from three months to six weeks. Under these economic circumstances families came to dread the coming of more children and the birth rate declined to such levels that the effects were felt in school and college enrollments for over two decades. Women and children went to work, if there was any to be had, to supplement the meager family income. Married women teachers, however, were frequently dropped from employment and there was a similar tendency in some businesses to refrain from hiring married women.

Federal aid went far to stabilize the American home caught in the greatest crisis of its history. The government offered relief employment on public projects, white-collar research positions, cheap housing, recreation, rural electrification, low-interest loans, social security legislation, maternity and health benefits, and minimum wage and maximum hour laws. In the slum-infested areas of New York, Chicago, Atlanta, Cleveland, and other large cities, federal projects leveled entire neighborhoods unfit for human habitation in order to provide such low-rent developments as the Jane Addams House on Chicago's West Side, the Ida Wells project in the Negro area of the same city, The Techwood Homes in Atlanta, and the innumerable projects in New York's East Side and Harlem. Although the amount of federally sponsored housing was substantial, it fell far short of closing the gap left by the comparative inactivity of private construction during the depression. While families doubled up in badly crowded housing, hundreds of thousands of rental units remained vacant for want of tenants able to pay. Cries of socialism and fears of losses to existing housing property discouraged any effort to launch a large-scale building crusade and insured the acute housing crisis of the forties and fifties.

The depression greatly reduced the rate of population growth. In

1940 the census recorded 131,669,275 persons within the continental United States as compared to 122,775,046 in 1930, a relatively modest increase of only 7.2 per cent as compared to the 16.1 per cent growth of the twenties. As a result of a sharp drop in the birth rate and a steady advance in the expectation of life, the average age of the population grew rapidly. These factors, together with the depression, led to an intense interest in old-age pensions, adult education, and ideas of security. Many thousands of retired men and women moved to the mild climate of Southern California and joined Dr. Francis E. Townsend of Long Beach in his national campaign for pensions of $200 monthly for all retired people over sixty. Thus, while cities like Philadelphia actually decreased and San Francisco on the West Coast remained stationary in size, the population of the city of Los Angeles, which had been less than 577,000 in 1920, grew (only in part from annexations) to 1,238,000 in 1930 and to 1,504,000 a decade later. New York city continued to grow but at a much slower rate than before. In 1940 it held 7,455,000 people, an increase, it is true, of 524,500 over 1930, but the twenties had outstripped the previous decade by over 1,300,000. With the war years the birth rate and urban growth were once more moving upward. By the end of the war the internal migration of population westward had become a mass movement. As for foreign immigration, little accretion came from that source due to the immigration laws and stiffening regulations as well as to depression and war conditions.

5

The depression and the New Deal philosophy of social planning focused renewed interest upon the consumer rather than upon the competitive businessman. With the revived popularity of Thorstein Veblen who held that the profit motive was the sole incentive in modern society, there came a demand for more consumer protection through legislation. Since the days of Theodore Roosevelt's pioneer legislation on pure food and drugs and on federal meat inspection, the pendulum had swung back to laissez-faire and the adage "Let the Buyer Beware." This policy had had obvious disastrous conse-

quences in the investment market where irresponsible companies
had issued false prospectuses regarding their offerings. A new group
of muckrakers wrote books and articles to attack misleading advertising and misbranding. Among the most effective of this literature
were Arthur Kallet and F. J. Schlink's *100,000,000 Guinea Pigs*
(1933), Ruth Lamb's *American Chamber of Horrors* (1936), and
various magazine articles. Public reaction led both government and
private agencies to embark upon new measures to protect consumers. The Food, Drug, and Cosmetic Act of 1938 strengthened
the laws of 1906 by providing more adequate tests for new drugs,
sharper definitions of adulteration and misbranding, and heavier
penalties for false labels. The federal government issued a *Consumer's Guide* and private groups published Consumer's Research
and Consumer's Union pamphlets to classify various commodities
according to price, quality, and other factors. To guide consumers,
labels of approval for certain products were issued by the American
Medical Association, *Good Housekeeping* magazine, and other well-
known groups. Economists gave college courses on consumer education while women's clubs sponsored lectures on the subject.

6

The Lynds, trying to discover whether the churchmen of Middletown were offering leadership during the crisis, came to an unfavorable conclusion. Ministers who rashly demanded specific
economic changes received little encouragement from their congregations and considerable abuse from the press. Middletowners
looked upon the church as a spiritual refuge rather than as a place
where their economic salvation would be won. Those religious
bodies that stressed ritual rather than militant sermons, like the
Episcopalian, the Roman Catholic, and the orthodox Jewish, retained
the greatest stability. No one objected to vague platitudes on behalf
of justice against "want in the midst of plenty," but beyond that
point the social gospeler advanced at his peril.

Thousands of discouraged churchmen, as a national questionnaire
of 1934 shows, felt sufficiently critical of capitalism to declare for

some form of "cooperative commonwealth," even for socialism. Leftism and pacifism made deep inroads into conventional church doctrines. For a time, the erratic Father Coughlin of the Shrine of the Little Flower enjoyed a radio audience estimated as high as 13,000,000 listeners of all faiths. As long as he spoke in generalities about "driving the money changers out of the temple" he had an enthusiastic following. However, his political adventure of 1936 and his anti-Semitism estranged most of his early supporters and led numerous priests and high Catholic churchmen to denounce his public utterances.

Urban misery and unrest led men to minimize doctrinal differences and to accept interdenominationalism at an even more rapid rate than in the past. The Methodist Church, split since the schism over slavery, felt encouraged to bring together its four major wings, despite certain variations in the rituals of each, into a single national church of 8,000,000 members. This merger occurred at the Uniting Conference of 1939 in Kansas City, Missouri. Separate conferences were held for Negroes, who accepted segregation in order to get a full share of bishops. There were Methodists, however, who protested any concession to racial segregation within the church. On the eve of war, pacifism made considerable inroads among the Methodists; when war came they ranked next to the Quakers and Mennonites in furnishing conscientious objectors. However, the total number of such Methodist pacifists was a negligible fraction of those church members who fought on the battlefield.

7

Negroes were among the first racial and ethnic groups to be forced on relief by the severity of the depression; food riots took place in Harlem, while thousands of Negro farm tenants were evicted in Arkansas, Missouri, and Oklahoma. They migrated from the South at a faster rate than previously, moving into Northern and Western urban centers; within the South rural Negroes also removed to the cities. During 1930-45, under the stimulus of depression and war, more than 3,000,000 Negroes moved northward and westward. Los Angeles soon became one of the major Negro cities of the nation, while the colored communities of Chicago, Detroit, and New York also grew rapidly. The early depression bore down with disproportionate force upon the Negro; he became a major beneficiary of the Roosevelt reforms because he was already living at a marginal level. Thus, while relief, low-rent housing, and minimum wage laws might not affect most whites, they had a direct influence upon Negroes, who were apt to be at the bottom of the social scale. As a result, Negroes transferred their traditional political allegiance from the Republican to the Democratic party. In the contemporary rise of the C.I.O. and industrial unionism, as already seen, the Negro was also a primary beneficiary although tensions beset his advance toward better types of employment and supervisory positions.

The greatest migration of Negroes into the cities came in 1940-45 when the war plants gave them unusual economic opportunities. Efforts to discriminate against Negroes in employment evoked such protests from their leaders that President Roosevelt issued a sweeping executive order forbidding racial discrimination in industries engaged upon war contracts. A Fair Employment Practices Committee was also set up to deal with racial discrimination. In wartime Detroit, where the Negro influx had been heavy and the housing shortage was acute, white working-class families tried to expel Negroes from a federal housing project intended for colored families. Southerners and East Europeans were angered over the upgrading of some Negroes to supervisory posts in the Detroit plants. So great were the tensions behind the incident that they provoked the race riot of June, 1943, and federal troops had to intervene. About twenty-five Negroes and nineteen whites were killed; hundreds were injured. Similar racial outbreaks occurred in Philadelphia and elsewhere.

Despite these conflicts the Negro made rapid progress. By moving into Northern and Western communities he automatically gained political power through the suffrage, thus enabling him to better his racial conditions as far as his ballot could do so. The Negro vote could not be ignored by politicians in the urban areas. Educational progress continued with over 53,000 Negroes attending college by the end of World War II. Negro teachers in Southern tax-supported schools were enabled by Supreme Court decisions to secure salaries comparable to those of white teachers. Lynchings dwindled to the smallest number in over a generation, though the year 1933 was unusually savage, with twenty-four lynchings reported.

In World War II, much more than in the previous war, the Negro played a major role that reflected a far greater degree of racial equality. There were 920,000 Negroes in the army by the end of the war with 7768 Negro officers—a unique fact in racial history. Navy officials relaxed their quotas for Negro personnel and set up large training camps for the colored sailors at Great Lakes Training Center, Illinois, and at Hampton, Virginia. The marines also modified their traditional policy of exclusion. At the front, where Negroes continued to operate in segregated units, the record for bravery, as in World War I, was distinguished. The Ninety-Second Division (Negro) alone suffered 5752 casualties. When the war ended, Southern Negroes showed a greater determination to assert their rights of citizenship, despite a resurgent Ku Klux Klan, and thousands went to the polls in the South defying the intimidation of local bigots.

8

One evidence of more enlightened thinking on race relations is the passage of the Wheeler-Howard Act of 1934, "the New Deal for the Indians." America's oldest minority group, the Indians, may have been as populous in 1934 as three or four centuries previously, but their lot could scarcely be considered a happy one by any stretch of the imagination. The Indian crusade of the eighties, associated with the name of Helen Hunt Jackson, had culminated in the Dawes Act of 1887 and the Burke Act of 1906. These laws were intended to assimilate the Indians into American society by encouraging them to break up tribal lands into individual farms and thus become self-supporting homesteaders and citizens. Instead of achieving this result, the Indian's helplessness had become increasingly patent and shrewd whites had absorbed the larger part of the best native lands. Since 1887, Indian landholdings had fallen from 138,000,000 acres to 48,000,000 acres, nearly half of it arid or semiarid. During the era of Secretary of the Interior Albert B. Fall, the administration of Indian lands became involved in such scandals that an American Indian Defense Association was organized under the leadership of an unusually effective crusader, John Collier. For a decade this organization, aided by various sympathetic magazine writers, propagandized for justice to the Indian.

Substantial reforms began with the Hoover administration, but did not reach fruition until 1933 when President Roosevelt made Collier the Commissioner of Indian Affairs and supported the Wheeler-Howard Bill. Collier had a high respect for the values of Indian culture and recognized that the unplanned assimilationism of the Dawes Act had merely broken the Indian's self-confidence and tribal unity without making him a part of the white man's world. He encouraged the Indian to develop his own religious expression, his language, and his arts. In the Indian Reorganization Act (the Wheeler-Howard Act), for which Indians were allowed to vote, a major effort was launched to revive the power and prestige of tribal life. No longer (it was hoped) would it be possible to alienate the Indian lands easily by sale or lease to white men. In addition, vocational education was encouraged through special loans and a revolving fund of $10,000,000 for economic development loans. Indians also were to set up tribal constitutions covering those rights of self-government granted to them. Altogether the law awakened the initiative of many tribes and encouraged renewed interest in the study of Indian cultures and Indian problems. Professor Randolph Downes, a specialist on Indian affairs, has speculated ". . . had the Wheeler-Howard Act been passed in 1887, the American Indians might by 1934 have been ready for the Dawes Act." During the war, Americans read with interest that 25,000 Indians were serving in the armed forces and winning the highest awards for bravery. Unfortunately, local prejudices against the Indians remained strong in the Southwest and their civic rights were not always freely granted by those states.

9

The greatest tragedy of minority relations in modern America was the plight of the Japanese-Americans during World War II. Like other marginal groups, they had had their difficulties in earning a living during the depression because of the discrimination on the West Coast. But these problems had been overcome with the cooperative spirit that characterized them. Cultural assimilation had gone rapidly forward, perhaps more rapidly than among many other immigrant peoples. The Nisei, or native Americans of Japanese descent, eagerly took up the habits of other native youths and with a far smaller delinquency rate than other second-generation groups. In high schools and colleges they won high grades and popularity, being elected to the student councils, even to class presidencies; and the boys developed an enviable skill in baseball. At home, the oriental ways of the Issei, the Japanese-born immigrants, were being cast aside. Even mothers cut their hair in American style instead of tying it in tight knots at the backs of their heads, and wore American-style dresses instead of the traditional kimonos. Brothers and sisters among the Nisei aroused much head-shaking by their indifference to the patriarchal customs in which the male's role was central and the women were always submissive and self-sacrificing. Nisei youth rebelled against the custom of having their marriages arranged by their parents. Most of them were increasingly indifferent to and ignorant of the Japanese language and culture. As for their economic aptitudes and skills—now largely urban—few outsiders questioned them, but many envied or feared their competition as farmers, merchants, and professional men. Even those bigots who liked to prefix their pet hates with the adjective "dirty" had to admit that the Japanese-Americans had few lessons to learn in the use of soap and the habits of cleanliness. Despite all rebuffs and prejudices, it was clear to unprejudiced laymen that the Japanese-American was intensely eager to be accepted as an American. As for the Issei, more isolated from the assimilationist process, they had the usual doubts of newcomers regarding a strange land, but they worked hard to educate their children, encouraged by the fact that even oriental ancestry did not disqualify any native-born person from enjoying the privileges of citizenship.

It is ironic that Americans who had long shared the sorrow expressed in Longfellow's *Evangeline* for the exiled Acadians should have re-enacted the story on a far worse scale in World War II. The surprise attack upon Pearl Harbor, the wild charges that a Japanese-American Fifth Column was operating in Hawaii and on the West Coast, and the hysteria of wartime explain some of the motives for the decision to evacuate 110,000 men, women, and children from the West Coast to relocation camps in the interior. However, recent writers like Bradford Smith and Carey McWilliams have shown that older bigotries, ordinary greed, and racialism of the fascist variety brought more sinister pressures to bear upon otherwise well-meaning statesmen. Along the West Coast, especially in Southern California, selfish farm interests, Hearst newspapers, American Legionnaires, Native Sons of the Golden West, and other anti-Oriental or exclusionist groups apparently utilized this war-sent opportunity to expel the Japanese once and for all. Despite the fact that all major charges of sabotage and disloyalty had been definitely refuted by the secretaries of the army and navy among other high authorities, the exclusionist elements had their way. General John De Witt, whose testimony carried considerable weight with congressmen on this subject, showed a naïve belief in racialist principles. He asserted to a congressional committee, "A Jap's a Jap. It makes no difference whether he is an American citizen or not." Protesting voices were overwhelmed in the general preoccupation with a major war in which it was feared that enemy submarines, ships, and planes might attack the West Coast on a large scale and then proceed with the aid of Fifth Columnists to take over the country.

By 1942, all West Coast Japanese residents (Hawaii shared only partly in this hysteria) were sent to wait for months in hastily improvised and uncomfortable assembly centers surrounded by barbed wire and guarded by soldiers. Thereafter, they were transferred to relocation camps under a relatively enlightened administration which tried to do the best it could under the sorry circumstances. By including the Nisei, and thus overlooking the rights of a large group of American citizens, an unfortunate constitutional precedent was set. Most Western states, except Colorado, shared the wartime suspicion of the Japanese-Americans. Inevitably, some minor conflicts and strikes broke out in the relocation camps which were distorted in the press. Nisei were in conflict with Issei and families split over the question of retaining their American allegiance. The desire of Nisei to prove their American loyalty was emphatically expressed in their unique, fanatical battle record against the enemy, even against the Japanese foe.

One of the revolutionary changes wrought by the War Relocation Administration was the policy of finally dispersing Japanese-American evacuees throughout the country. This seems to have been decided because of the fear of widespread disorders and renewed discrimination if these people returned to their West Coast homes in large numbers. There was also the belief that the policy would lead to their rapid assimilation. However, the human cost of this experiment was great indeed. Few had capital with which to begin life anew. Isolation and loneliness for scattered people, not yet socially accepted and bearing the onus of war hatreds, were worsened when they had to face the outside world without the psychological warmth of Little Tokyos or equivalent institutions that nearly all immigrant peoples have adopted on the road to assimilation. From a long-run point of view this decision undoubtedly speeded up assimilation and in cities like Chicago and Cleveland the experiment proved successful. Civil rights groups, supported by the Truman administration, tried to persuade Congress to indemnify the evacuees for the losses they had suffered.

The Japanese contribution to American culture was aesthetic, scientific, and intellectual as well as economic and social. In 1899, Hideyo Noguchi left his home in northern Japan to study bacteriology at the University of Pennsylvania. Later he joined the staff of Rockefeller Institute and attracted international note for his Noguchi test which accurately diagnosed syphilis. He investigated yellow fever, of which he himself died a martyr in 1928. A namesake, Yone Noguchi, was a distinguished poet who lectured here and at Oxford on Japanese poetry. In 1911 he wrote a book on the American writer, Lafcadio Hearn, who had come to love Japan's exotic aestheticism while he taught English in its schools, had married a Japanese woman, and had published several interpretative books on the tradition and psychology of Nippon. Still another remarkable Noguchi, Isamu, showed striking originality, modernism, and a monumental quality in his sculpture. Among the younger artists who ranked with the leading American painters was Yasuo Kuniyoshi, who left Okayama in 1906 at the age of thirteen and rose through his own efforts to win a Guggenheim Fellowship in art; his outstanding paintings were displayed at the Metropolitan Museum of Art, the Chicago Art Institute, and other leading museums. In Chicago a philosophic Nisei, S. I. Hayakawa, who taught English at the Illinois Institute of Technology, won national praise for his original exposition of semantics in *Language in Action; a Guide to Accurate Thinking* (1941). And there were many more Japanese-Americans who made their contributions to America, including men who had rebelled against Japanese militarism and had escaped here to continue their struggle for freedom. Too few Americans appreciated the rich diversity behind the relatively unimportant physical differences between themselves and the new Americans. "A Jap is a Jap!" repeated the spiritually blind.

While the Japanese-Americans were segregated in evacuation camps, California and other Southwestern states admitted new minority groups to solve the critical labor shortage of wartime. Mexicans, Negroes, Filipinos, and Italians joined native Easterners and Southerners in working in the war plants and reaping the West Coast harvests. The federal government, at California's behest, tried to aid the fruit and vegetable growers in replacing the Japanese-Americans by importing (at the taxpayers' expense) about 30,000 Mexican farm workers. But bigots in the mushrooming Los Angeles area speedily became allergic to Mexicans, regardless of whether they were citizens or not. Newspapers publicized reports of attacks upon native American couples by Mexican-American gangs, disregarding the fact that the worst gangs had no Mexican members whatsoever. Young Mexican boys, deprived of wholesome recreational opportunities by poverty and social discrimination, found outlets in gang life; many set themselves apart by the fad of wearing "zoot suits," long coats and baggy trousers with narrow cuffs. In June, 1943, a reign of terror began when over a thousand servicemen and native American youths invaded the Mexican-American neighborhoods and beat up those they could find. Many were injured before the police managed to restore order. Here were more contradictions during a war aimed at fascist racialism.

· 22 ·

The Impact of Depression and War upon Mass Education and Recreation

---

I

THE school was an easy victim of the depression. Practically every state had the same discouraging story of drastic economies that crippled education by discharging teachers and overcrowding classrooms. Terms were shortened, equipment was reduced to bare essentials, progressive theories were discarded, and, in general, the clock of educational growth was turned back. Private schools collapsed like a house built of cards. Unemployed youths remained in high school and college to escape a demoralizing idleness and to mark time until prosperity returned. Vocationalism, fed by federal and local subsidies and demanded by the taxpayer, did thrive under the expanded Smith-Hughes Act and the WPA. Universities pushed independent business schools to the wall by setting up colleges of commerce which offered typing, shorthand, and other non-academic courses.

In Middletown, the Lynds found that educators were totally incapable of asserting real leadership during this crisis. Middle-class fears of radicalism led local patriotic societies like the Daughters of the American Revolution to sponsor compulsory high-school courses on the Constitution and to demand the dismissal of "pink" schoolteachers. Middletown newspaper editorials warned teachers who advocated our joining the World Court to forget controversial issues and to let the taxpayer decide upon what should be taught in the schools.

But conventional Middletown was not the entire United States. In the larger cities rebels denounced the meek Griselda role of the schools. At Columbia University, John Dewey and his outspoken colleagues, George S. Counts and William H. Kilpatrick, urged that educators lead the way to a just social order based on cooperative principles rather than on jungle competition. They advocated frank indoctrination of these ideas in the classroom. In 1934, the Commission on Social Studies of the American Historical Association declared that a new age of collectivism was emerging and that students and teachers must be equipped to deal with the problems of economic insecurity, racial understanding, academic freedom, and cooperative values.

New Deal agencies, particularly the Emergency Educational Program, re-employed 44,000 teachers to teach 1,700,000 students and to stimulate the entire field of labor education. Innumerable public schools were kept open by federal funds. The Public Works Administration replaced defective or obsolete school buildings and recreational centers with modern structures. The National Youth Administration gave needy adolescents a chance to continue higher education and to get work experience on school clerical staffs, libraries, research laboratories, health clinics, and other places. Unemployed youths from families on relief secured healthful, productive work in conserving national resources through the Civilian Conservation Corps; many were also taught trades in addition to forestry. All this meant much for frustrated young men; in Germany and Italy they were then being channelized into goose-stepping organizations devoted to ultimately destructive ends. Educators recognized the need for federal aid to local schools, but they felt concerned over the possibility that the American tradition of locally controlled education might be destroyed. The National Education Association, leading organ of the educators, went on record as favoring federal financial assistance and a certain amount of leadership from Washington, but opposed any effort to set up and maintain a federal system of education at the expense of local control.

The President's Committee on Education reported pessimistically in 1936, "The education that can be provided at present in many localities is below the minimum necessary to preserve democratic institutions." They pointed out that the most backward states had the largest birth rate and hence were bound to lower the cultural standards of the rest of the country. The census of 1940 showed that 10,000,000 adults had so little education as to be practically illiterate and that 3,000,000 children were not attending school at all. Large-scale federal aid to education was clearly destined to become a major political demand in the ensuing years.

Hardly had the schools recovered from the depression before they were faced with the crisis arising from the extraordinary defense program of 1939-41 and finally with the war itself. Once more, as in World War I, but on a far greater scale, teacher shortages developed and high-school students neglected classwork to earn the high wages paid in local stores, offices, and factories. Colleges, of course, were almost stripped of male students, except for those who came to take officers' training courses. War demands stimulated the long-run trend toward vocationalism at the expense of the liberal arts.

In 1944 the federal government was actually spending as much money for wartime education as the localities were devoting to elementary, secondary, and college education. Congressmen seemed ready to extend huge sums for public and private schools all the way up to the colleges, but hesitated to run into a religious issue over aid to Catholic and Lutheran parochial schools. On such occasions the issue of the separation of church and state was sure to be raised.

When Americans came to take an inventory of their educational resources through the Selective Service examinations, the results were not too encouraging. Even the pressing need for technical men could not be quickly met despite decades of vocationalism; only 15 per cent of those inducted had had technical training. Many thousands were rejected as "functionally illiterate" because their schooling was not good enough to enable them to read simple instructions. Worse yet, one out of three had to be rejected for physical, mental, and educational deficiencies. While this record was probably better than that of other countries, it struck a blow to national pride and suggested the difficulties that lay ahead for American education. Formal education, it is true, was exceptionally high by the standards of other armies, but the level of social intelligence was disappointing and the comprehension of international issues left much to be desired. A Gallup Poll taken among veterans in 1946 showed that 51 per cent of them thought that Hitler did Germany "a lot of good" during 1933-39 and 22 per cent even justified the Nazi persecution of the Jews.

2

During the early years of the depression the sharp drop in newspaper subscribers handicapped the nation at a time when common consultation and discussion were so necessary. Newspaper bankruptcies and mergers speeded up the process of concentration; the war continued this tendency; and by 1946 it was estimated that 90 per cent of all cities that still had dailies could boast of having only one. Weeklies did increase, especially in smaller places and among Negro communities, but the labor press made only modest gains during depression years. Federal tax laws helped to trim down powerful chains like those of Hearst and Scripps-Howard. The increasing trend toward more syndicated materials resulted in breaking down the colorful regional quality of many city papers, though it often raised the caliber of column writing. Practically every major city, including Middletown, was familiar with the columns written by Drew Pearson, Walter Lippmann, Dr. Morris Fishbein, Walter Winchell, and Dorothy Dix. Staff newspapermen turned to purely local news and even there they faced the restrictions imposed by advertisers and the possibilities of libel suits. The trend toward greater centralization and conservatism was hastened by the influence of national advertisers and distributors.

The great newspapers that survived the depression, the war, and the process of concentration became ever more conservative in outlook, reflecting the financial pressures that bore upon them. A single holding company dominated by bankers might own competing papers in the same city. It is not surprising, therefore, that the American press was overwhelmingly anti-New Deal. Publishers, as employers, resented the encouragement that New Deal laws gave to the unionization of the traditionally individualistic—and poorly paid—reporters and other newsmen. The Newspaper Guild resorted to trade union tactics that angered those who believed that unions threatened the freedom of the press and the independence of the journalist. Owners were also wrathful over the efforts of New Dealers to abolish the hiring of under-age newsboys, under the terms of the child labor laws. A survey by *Editor & Publisher* of three-fourths of all newspapers, representing nearly 90 per cent of the total circulation, showed that only 38.7 per cent of the dailies supported Roosevelt in 1932, 34.5 per cent in 1936, 20.1 per cent in 1940, and 22 per cent in 1944. These were the election years when Roosevelt rolled up imposing majorities. Apparently the power of the press in a day of radio, unions, and better communications was less than commonly believed.

The newspaper with the most circulation of any in this country was the sensational tabloid, the *New York Daily News*. It was edited by a one-time Socialist, Captain Joseph Medill Patterson, grandson and namesake of the famous *Chicago Tribune* editor. Patterson drew most of his readers from the poorest classes and kept his paper in the New Deal column at first, but eventually, like his cousin who edited the *Chicago Tribune*, he joined the foes of Roosevelt. At times the *Daily News* reached a total circulation of 3,400,000 readers.

Second to the *New York Daily News* in circulation was Colonel Robert R. McCormick's *Chicago Tribune*, which was read by at least a million people daily and many more on Sundays. Those who contended that the days of personal journalism were over usually forgot the unique opinionated personality who ruled a vast journalistic empire from his office in the *Tribune* Tower. For years the Colonel (he fancied himself a keen tactician on the basis of a brief World War I experience) preached an anti-British variety of

American chauvinism and carried the slogan, "My Country, Right or Wrong" on the *Tribune* masthead. His paper also carried the modest subheading, "The World's Greatest Newspaper." McCormick probably outdid even Hearst in his crude journalistic war on the New Deal. Not satisfied with unyielding editorial attacks on most Roosevelt measures, which he usually identified with communism, he invaded the news columns themselves to slant the stories against the "crackpot theorists" in Washington. *Tribune* cartoons were unique in their vilification of the Democratic administration and of internationalism. Even during the war the *Tribune* sometimes printed confidential information that was widely regarded as dangerous to security.

It is a safe inference that the *Tribune's* success against such able rivals as the *Chicago Daily News* and Marshall Field III's *Chicago Sun* had little to do with the political vagaries of McCormick. His paper was attractively printed and enriched by outstanding features, some of them the best in the country. It excelled in the women's pages, the sports section, the financial page, the literary page, and the comic strips. Although critical observers pointed out that "Little Orphan Annie" at times expressed a philosophy that was closer to fascism than to democracy, other papers were eager to reprint this strip.

The press distinguished itself just before and during World War II in its unusually accurate and detailed foreign news. So complete was the coverage of the great news-gathering agencies that nothing short of the iron censorship of the Soviet and fascist dictatorships could thwart the alert newspapermen. Telephoto, first by wire and cable, then by wireless, brought immediate pictures of outstanding events to the breakfast table. During the war nearly all newspapers cooperated so well with the Bureau of Censorship that a voluntary censorship proved sufficient. One serious wartime problem was the severe paper shortage that hampered newspapers and led to voluntary rationing.

That the depression did not seriously interfere with the habit of escapism in magazine reading is witnessed by the popularity of *True Story* and various "confession" journals. By the end of the decade the most popular magazines were the *Saturday Evening Post, Life, Collier's,* and *Liberty,* each with a circulation of well over 2,000,000 copies. *Life* magazine introduced a wide vogue of attractive picture journals in 1936; comic strip books, dissatisfied with the juvenile market, invaded the adult reading field. A phenomenon of this era was the unusual success of the pocket-size *Reader's Digest.* It had begun almost inconspicuously in 1922 as a Greenwich Village magazine, but it exceeded the 2,000,000-reader mark in 1937. Despite a rigid policy of no advertisements, De Witt Wallace and his wife, the editors, converted it into a financial success. Busy Americans who liked "serious reading" that made no real demands upon their attention found the *Digest* indispensable. Finally, the intermittent prewar crises and the war itself led millions to read detailed weekly news magazines regularly such as *Time, Newsweek,* and *United States Weekly.* Henry R. Luce, the resourceful editor and publisher of *Time,* had been one of its chief founders in 1923. In 1930 he established the informative and beautifully illustrated magazine *Fortune* for an upper-class clientele. The attractive weekly picture magazine *Life* was also part of his magazine empire.

3

Radio, like the press, showed a good deal of conservatism derived from its advertising sponsorship and corporate ownership. Newspapers tried to meet the competition of radio by wholesale purchases of radio stations. By 1937, over a fourth of all commercial radio stations were dominated by newspaper corporations. New Deal agencies, particularly the Federal Communications Commission, sought to arrest the decline of radio independence and urged a greater emphasis on public service programs instead of excessive commercialization. To Roosevelt and Truman the radio offered a most effective way to offset newspaper hostility to the New Deal and the Fair Deal. Roosevelt's Fireside Chats over the radio were undoubtedly instrumental in winning many supporters.

Like the press, radio greatly expanded the time and attention devoted to news. During 1930-45 the proportion of radio time given to news broadcasts rose from 5 per cent to 20 per cent. Among the ablest news analysts were Elmer Davis, Raymond Gram Swing, and Clifton Utley; perhaps the most heavily sponsored and popular commentators were Lowell Thomas, H. V. Kaltenborn, Gabriel Heatter, and Boake Carter. Even Walter Winchell diversified his Broadway gossip by including "exclusives" not only about "blessed events" of which he had the earliest information, but also concerning foreign news. Soap operas (daytime serials), variety shows, and quiz programs gained at the expense of both classical and popular music. The potentialities of radio for propaganda were clear enough not only from examples in totalitarian countries but from the radio speeches of Father Coughlin. Self-policing by the radio industry itself went far to mitigate the evils of irresponsible propaganda. Radio time was so carefully apportioned among politicians that even Earl Browder, the Communist presidential candidate, had an opportunity to use the radio for his cause.

One of the most serious radio conflicts of this era was the war against the American Society of Composers, Authors, and Publishers (ASCAP). Encouraged by favorable court decisions and by successful European efforts to protect copyrighted music on the air, ASCAP demanded new royalty contracts in 1940 that would have doubled payments to members. However, the National Association of Broadcasters rejected this demand and organized its own system of copyrighted music as Broadcast Music, Incorporated. Until a compromise was reached, the radio listener was deprived of his favorite music.

4

The depression drove away about a third of the usual motion picture audiences and tightened the control of bankers over Hollywood. Some of the larger concerns combined production, distribution, and exhibition by purchasing hundreds of theaters throughout the country. The monopolistic practice of "block booking" compelled independent exhibitors to accept entire groups of pictures, including mediocre films, as a condition of renting any. To stimulate attendance, theaters resorted to giving away dishes, prizes, and cash awards in lottery drawings. Double features (sometimes even triple features) and prices as low as twenty cents were offered to moviegoers. Hollywood met the vogue for double features by classifying pictures as A or B, depending on their cost, and tried to pair the two among exhibitors. In Europe, Hollywood fought for its shrinking market while nationalistic and totalitarian countries began to discriminate against American films. To avoid giving offense, the industry usually offered stories without social messages, except the most innocuous ones.

Thus it happened that Europeans as well as Americans came to see celluloid America as a land of lust, violence, divorce, lightheadedness, and life at the penthouse level. Parents often complained of the sophisticated ideas to which their children were exposed; sociologists protested the false moral standards which encouraged delinquency; and finally, Catholic leaders organized the Legion of Decency to boycott pictures they considered immoral and at the same time to encourage the more suitable themes. Hollywood itself hastened to set up an internal censorship office under an Irish Catholic to meet public criticism. Prosperity soon returned to Hollywood. By 1937, about 85,000,000 persons were attending movies each week and at the end of World War II the weekly total was not much under 100,000,000. However, in the shadows lurked television, waiting for the commercial exploitation that some believed might even give the *coup de grâce* to the two-billion-dollar motion picture industry.

It was easy to caricature Hollywood—and many writers did—but its amazing achievements in technology, artistry, and picturization of fascinating themes continued to give it international leadership. Though the industry was basically conservative in social outlook, its leaders appeared far more friendly to the New Deal than did the press and the radio. It was possible to produce on occasion such themes of social protest as John Steinbeck's *The Grapes of Wrath,* dealing with the dispossessed Okies, or an exposé of Welsh mining conditions like *How Green Was My Valley;* and in *Dead End,* the story showed the influence of bad housing and environment on delinquency. Critics singled out as exceptionally fine such pictures as *The Life of Emile Zola, Goodbye, Mr. Chips, Rebecca, Mrs. Miniver, Random Harvest, Wilson,* and *The Lost Weekend.* The roster of talented actors and actresses was long and impressive. Scarcely behind the radio in educational features, the motion picture world issued *The March of Time* to explain significant international and national issues in a simple, absorbing way. In technology Hollywood enchanted youngsters all over the world with Walt Disney's animated cartoons, beginning with *Snow White and the Seven Dwarfs.* Musicals, always popular, were given a new dimension of appeal through the technicolor process and its rivals. Outside of Hollywood, federal film agencies were achieving marked success with the "documentary" pictures, factual but dramatic accounts of contemporary problems. Best-known of the documentaries were Pare Lorentz' *The Plough That Broke the Plains* and *The River,* both of them dealing with man's cooperative struggle against drought and floods.

5

Most of Broadway's theaters were darkened during the early depression years; outside of New York, bankruptcies converted innumerable theaters into motion picture houses. As for the actors, employment had never been too certain even in good times. Now they looked about for any sort of livelihood and regarded the new Federal Theater Project begun in 1935 as a Godsend. Inevitably, many incompetent amateurs joined the federal stage projects (there were 12,000 actors hired), which weakened some of the performances. However, the successes of the Federal Theater are much more significant. Project directors experimented with living themes that Broadway had long evaded. When Sinclair Lewis wrote the anti-Fascist play, *It Can't Happen Here* (1936), eighteen units of the Federal Theater Project promptly produced it. They also gave a better than competent presentation of Robert Sherwood's *Abe Lincoln in Illinois,* an idealistic interpretation of the early Lincoln. Often the federal actors staged plays of social protest and angered conservatives who felt that the themes should be as socially neutral as Broadway's. Anti-New Deal congressmen attacked the administration by making the Federal Theater a scapegoat and charging it with communist tendencies. As a result, the sponsors of the theater gave up any hope of converting the Federal Theater into a permanent state theater after European models.

Shortly before the decade ended, Broadway and the legitimate stage elsewhere retrieved its customary splendor. At first the commercial theater was hampered by the shortage of talented experienced actors. To attract audiences for long runs, theater managers hired Hollywood "big names." The traditionally close relationship between the American and English stage became very intimate during these years. Actors and authors frequently counted upon having substantial audiences in both countries. Quite unlike the theater of the 1920's, Broadway seemed more willing to experiment with themes of social protest, antifascism, and controversial philosophic ideas. Among the leftist themes were those of Clifford Odets' early plays, especially *Waiting for Lefty*, a militant prounion story, and *Awake and Sing*. Robert Sherwood's *Idiot's Delight* excoriated war; and Maxwell Anderson's *Winterset* revived the memory of the Sacco-Vanzetti case. Among the best of the numerous anti-Nazi plays was Lillian Hellman's absorbing story, *Watch on the Rhine*. Even the unusually outspoken indictment of race relations presented in Richard Wright's novel, *Native Son*, was adapted for the stage. Art-for-art's sake appeared thoroughly dead.

The "greats" of the twenties returned to the stage by the mid-thirties. Katharine Cornell, the versatile actress who had begun her career with the experimental Washington Square Players, was enthusiastically received when she played Juliet to the Romeo of the noted English actor, Maurice Evans. A few years later she demonstrated that she could be a delightful comedienne as well. Alfred Lunt and his wife Lynn Fontanne were indisputably the finest acting couple of these years. They visited the Moscow Art Theater to study the sensitive techniques of that renowned institution. Their best roles were in *Strange Interlude, Pygmalion, Idiot's Delight,* and *Amphytrion 38*. Few stage stars lived their roles so completely as the Lunts.

Operettas and musical comedies eclipsed their former popularity and quality by the 1940's. Even the prewar operettas of Strauss, Lehar, and Herbert could be seen almost any season. Cole Porter, whom Hollywood honored with the usual fictionized biography, achieved new popularity with his rhythmic music to *Anything Goes, Dubarry Was a Lady, Panama Hattie, Something for the Boys,* and *Mexican Hayride.* Irving Berlin showed that he had not relapsed into a stodgy Tin Pan Alley executive when he wrote the sparkling *This Is the Army* for the soldiers of World War II, many of whom were not even born when he had written a similarly successful musical about army life during World War I. In 1937, music-lovers were saddened by the death of young George Gershwin at the height of a brilliant career. He had collaborated with George S. Kaufman in *Of Thee I Sing,* which had been awarded the Pulitzer Prize; and much more important, his melodic music for *Porgy and Bess* had blended magnificently with the libretto of Du Bose and Dorothy Heyward. Gershwin had raised the blues and other jazz forms to symphonic proportions and had revealed the aesthetic potentialities of such music. To him, also, Hollywood paid the honor of presenting a biographic film, with selections from the best of his music. This era, too, saw the meteoric rise of the gifted New York composer, Richard Rodgers. He collaborated with Lorenz Hart and then with Oscar Hammerstein II in numerous musical successes. One of the most effective was *Oklahoma!,* based on a Western folk play by Lynn Riggs.

Among the leading American playwrights with a flair for subtle humor was George S. Kaufman, who was born in Pittsburgh in 1889. Good-naturedly he ribbed the WPA in *You Can't Take It with You,* and advised the world to relax despite the depression and to take such humble pleasures as presented themselves. In *I'd Rather Be Right,* which starred the aging but still Puckish George M. Cohan as President Roosevelt, the New Dealers came in for some more mild satire. These two plays among other highly successful ones were written in collaboration with another outstanding playwright and librettist, Moss Hart. Kaufman and Hart produced one of their cleverest satires in *The Man Who Came to Dinner,* which caricatured the sophisticated journalist writer and radio wit, Alexander Woollcott. Other successful comic plays of this era vastly amused audiences by dwelling upon the foibles of middle-class life.

6

The social consciousness of the 1930's left a strong impact upon recreational life although the dominance of commercial interests remained. Once the havoc wrought by the depression upon most recreational institutions had been cleared away, there was a tendency to emphasize communal and cooperative interests instead of purely competitive and individualistic aims. Taxpayers supported municipal golf links while the private country clubs declined. In the schools a growing emphasis on intramural sports as a benefit to everyone began to displace the old enthusiasm for exclusively intercollegiate spectacles. More recreation could be found in the home, especially in the vogue for jigsaw puzzles, stamp collecting, bridge, ping pong, and amateur carpentry.

Most indicative of the new social spirit was the popular support given to the New Deal recreational program. Hundreds of millions were spent by the federal government for new playgrounds, parks, swimming centers, and tennis courts. Especially impressive was the expansion of both federal and state parks. Numerous fish and game sanctuaries were constructed in the expanding national forests. Among the most active states in the park recreation movement was California, which set up seven new state parks in 1933. Once the worst of the depression ended, millions visited the national and state parks annually in record-breaking crowds. Private industry, of course, continued to contribute to popular recreation. The Union Pacific Railway developed the magnificent Sun Valley, Idaho, for the tens of thousands of visitors who came each year. New England winter festivals and snow trains were stimulated by the railroads of that region. Unusually low railway and bus fares made traveling possible for many more people than ever. Transcontinental buses competed with the railroads for passengers. Bicycling was revived as a popular sport on the largest scale since the 1890's. All this showed an increasing participation by the average person, especially in the cities, in healthful recreational activities.

As for the spectator sports, both amateur and professional, these eventually recovered most—but not all—of their former eminence of the 1920's. In boxing not even the great Joe Louis, the "Brown Bomber," and his extraordinary manager-promoter, Michael Jacobs, were able to surpass or even come close to the gate receipts that the Dempsey-Tunney fight had won a decade before. Yet Louis fought twenty-three sensational title defense matches in this era, a unique record for a champion, and knocked out all but two of his challengers, usually in short order. Baseball completed its recovery by 1936 and gave its chief laurels to the New York Yankees, who won five World Series championships during 1937-43. Of the Yankee heroes, Lou Gehrig and Joe Di Maggio seemed most securely established on a pedestal by the fans. Professional football astonished those who had assumed it would never rival the college sport, for it actually became a formidable competitor. College football stars eagerly joined the professionals after graduation, especially the Chicago Bears, the New York Giants, the Washington Redskins, and the Green Bay Packers. Another new development was the sudden enthusiasm for basketball after 1937 when changes in the rules of the game, especially in eliminating the center jump, speeded up action so enormously that it drew crowds of devotees to fill large stadiums. This American sport, which emphasized teamwork rather than the prowess of a single individual, was enthusiastically played by European teams, even in the Berlin Olympics of 1936. However, World War II, by drawing off the best youth into the armed forces, had a temporarily depressing effect on these sports.

The Great Depression and World War II did not reverse, except temporarily, the continuing impact of the metropolis upon American culture. Hard times did deflate the prestige of the businessman and put the reins of national leadership in the hands of consumer-minded reformers. As a result, American economic individualism yielded to more collectivist tendencies, and the philosophy of social security and mass unionism replaced the adventurous competitive spirit of the nineteeth century. The new regulated economy, especially in wartime, gave the federal government a senior partnership in determining the rules of the game. As for the New Dealers, they believed that they were rescuing capitalism from a cul-de-sac rather than destroying it.

From the vantage point of the mid-century it is clear that the long-run social trends had not been terminated by the depression or the war. For example, the tendency toward economic concentration grew in both industry and agriculture. Industrial unionism was but the logical counterpart to the highly integrated financial-industrial-commercial structure. Although banker control affected the newspapers, the radio, and the movies, and although these agencies were frequently out of step with public opinion on social issues, the will of the people was seldom before so energetically expressed at the ballot box. The battle against economic collapse and the war for survival against fascism awakened fresh idealism and a new social consciousness as compared to the hedonism of the 1920's. Minority problems such as those of the Negro, the Jew, and the Indian showed genuine progress; but wartime friction worsened the lot of Japanese-Americans and Mexicans. The faith in mass education continued despite certain disillusionments; it was largely the conflict over the separation of church and state that prevented the federal government from putting its enormous resources behind an unprecedented program of school expansion. America had not become a socialist state, as ultra-conservatives charged, but it had almost closed the gap of a generation between the activist state of Western Europe and the semipassivity in social-economic affairs of the nineteenth-century American government. Freedom, according to the new order, was no longer a negative, individualistic concept but a positive philosophy involving considerable social control for its realization. "Necessitous men are not free men," said its foremost exponent in the White House.

· 23 ·

Social Consciousness during the
Depression and War Years

[1929-1945]

I

HENRY L. MENCKEN awoke during the Great Depression to find that he had suddenly become obsolete as an American institution. He had still much to say about philistines and puritans, but the times were out of joint for individualists of the Smart Set. "Sing a Song of Social Significance," ran a humorous chorus from *Pins and Needles,* which was produced by the socially conscious International Ladies' Garment Workers' Union. Mencken had spent too much time belaboring the "herd" to admire the social significance in the renewed emphasis upon the common man. During the early depression years a shrinking number of devotees still read Mencken's outbursts in *The American Mercury, The Nation,* and the *Baltimore Sun,* but his ideas had become "dated" and too few were in the mood for nostalgia. Fortunately for Mencken's peace of mind, he had never had too high an opinion of the human race and he waited patiently for the New Deal to run its course while he cast his vote for Landon.

To millions of plain people in Europe and America, nothing seemed so urgent as survival in a world of unemployment, war, and economic collapse. Communist propaganda hammered away at the line that only in the Soviet Union did full employment exist and men were not afraid of being displaced by the machine. While democratic writers stood unnerved by this onslaught, Italian fascists and German Nazis joined the attack on capitalism and noisily promised security and military glory. Both communists and fascists alike sang the tune of democratic decadence. Little wonder that so many American novelists and critics turned for a time to the certainties of the "proletarian novel" and the literary clichés of class consciousness. Mencken, Babbitt, Freud, and even Henry Ford offered no abiding principles to cope with the perplexities of the 1930's. The affirmations of Marx, particularly the economic interpretation of society, seemed convincing at the time to intellectuals like Hemingway and Dos Passos, and, to some extent, to James T. Farrell and John Steinbeck.

The current ideological struggle against totalitarianism led to a rediscovery of traditional values, the "usable past" that could be adapted to modern conditions of insecurity. Many Europeans, reduced to despair by economic depression and thwarted nationalism, were ready to accept the confused semantics of totalitarianism—that tyranny was freedom, that dictatorship was direct democracy, and that enslavement was liberation. The more hopeful climate of American thought, encouraged by vigorous democratic leadership, made possible an emphatic reassertion of historic human rights that were finally defended on the battlefield. Dadaism and the posturing of the Lost Generation were dead.

Not all of the leading novelists and playwrights fitted into the category of socially conscious writers approved by the critics of the *New Republic, The Nation,* and the *New Masses.* As a matter of fact the bulk of popular writings, as in the past, tended to be escapist or romantic in nature. Even at the higher levels Willa Cather continued her romantic view of the past and the unique peoples who had helped to make America. Eugene O'Neill, hailed as the nation's greatest playwright, delved even deeper than before into Greek tragic symbolism for abiding human values and the theme of personal frustration and implacable fate.

Economic determinism and collectivism crowded out the aestheticism and Narcissus-complex of the twenties but the vogue of naturalism continued in the form of "hard-boiled realism." There was a difference, however, in the new mood of literary naturalism. The aesthetic naturalist of the 1920's like Dos Passos was fatalistic in his fears that life had no larger meaning than sheer sensualism. To the social naturalist of the Farrell-Steinbeck school (and the new Hemingway and Dos Passos) there was usually implicit a rebellious note that left a wide margin of free will. Man could, by taking thought and summoning his courage, change this sorry scheme of things. Instead of idle self-contemplation after the manner of the lyric poets of the twenties, the newer writers often contemplated the American scene in one of its regional facets—the agrarian Middle West, the sharecropper South, the urban slums, and the Far West of Steinbeck and Robinson Jeffers. Thus regionalism, which had already had a vogue during the twenties as mere local color, now assumed a critical social aspect with strong regional schools established in literature, painting, and sociology.

Fleeing Nazi and fascist fanaticism, a remarkable intellectual elite of refugees came to the United States and left an influence comparable to that of the Huguenot exiles in seventeenth-century Europe and America. This influx mattered far more than the return of so many of the Lost Generation to this country. America was no longer a cultural province of Europe as in the days of Henry James and Whistler, but now, thanks to the atavism of Hitler and Mussolini, it acquired many intellectual figures of world eminence. The Nobel prize winner, Thomas Mann, and his gifted children, Klaus and Erika, left Nazi Germany to work for the rebirth of a civilized "other Germany." In his American exile Thomas Mann published *Joseph and His Brothers, Joseph in Exile,* and other novels. Franz Werfel had moved from his native Prague to Vienna after serving in World War I and had reached the pinnacle of literary success with his exciting novel *The Forty Days of Musa Dagh,* written just as Hitler was consolidating his power. As he wandered dispiritedly through France during his flight from the Nazis, he felt inspired by the story of the saintly Bernadette of Lourdes, a simple peasant girl whose religious visions and miraculous healing powers had made a shrine of her village. This tradition became the essence of his reverent, imaginative novel, *The Song of Bernadette,* which he published in the United States; he lived long enough to see it become a successful motion picture. In the same tragic exodus was Lion Feuchtwanger, well known to American as well as European readers for his fascinating novel, *Power.* He, too, spent a brief exile in France before it was overrun by the Nazis, and then came to this country to renew his arrested literary career.

Hitler also drove George Grosz, the leader of German expressionism in art, to an American exile. Grosz, whose painting stimulated American experimenters, was a bold critic of both militarism and economic injustice, but his satirical paintings of postwar Germany offended chauvinists while his ultra-modernism was relegated to the gallery of "degenerate art" by the Nazis. Even more direct in his impact upon American art was the exiled Walter Gropius, founder of the famous Bauhaus school of architecture in Weimar. He had gone far toward developing in architecture a striking functionalism that was enriched by experiments in new uses of glass, metals, and other materials. Thus he strengthened the functionalist tendency to make art a partner of science and technology. In 1937, Chicago became the site of his New Bauhaus, where the original Weimar program was considerably expanded; the next year Harvard invited him to teach in its School of Architecture (he later became chairman of the department). It had taken generations to produce a Frank Lloyd Wright; now the cultural suicide of Germany added Gropius and others to enrich the American architectural tradition.

In music the Nazi regime gave Paul Hindemith, a leading modernist composer, to this country where he was made a professor at Yale, and a leader of the noted Berkshire Music Center. Bruno Walter, the idol of the Vienna State Opera, failed to meet the tests of Nazi racial purity but was enthusiastically received as a guest conductor for the Metropolitan, the New York Philharmonic, and other distinguished orchestras. In the same category of racialist exclusion was the noted physicist, Albert Einstein, who was stripped of his property and citizenship by Hitler. Princeton University invited Einstein to continue his researches at the Institute for Advanced Study. Probably more influential in their impact upon American culture were the thousands of lesser professional figures whose contacts with students and the general public was much more direct. By the forties the level of American professional studies had so risen that aspiring artists, musicians, scientists, and writers were usually able to secure the most thorough training without crossing the Atlantic. Although shortsighted local medical and other professional societies were fearful of the European invasion and secured stricter licensing laws to bar competition, they could not prevent the fruttifying impact of the refugee elite.

2

Aside from the pulp writers who offered the usual sugar-coated fiction of escapism to the millions, the leading novelists reflected a new social consciousness. This literature of social protest had its historic roots in the Progressive era of Theodore Roosevelt and even much earlier. Few novelists actually studied or mastered Marxism and it was obvious that the American "proletarian" novel fell far short of the approved Soviet models. Behind the candid camera realism of the thirties lurked the idealism and nostalgia of an earlier optimistic America. There was no summons to the barricades, but an exhortation to build a just social order within the traditional framework.

John Dos Passos, once an aesthete of the art-for-art's-sake school, had shown a social awakening in the late twenties when he joined a picket line demonstrating in behalf of Sacco and Vanzetti. For this impulsive deed he had gone to jail. He was no longer interested in writing novels of postwar disillusionment as he had done in *Three Soldiers* (1921), but reached out to draw up a savage indictment of the course of American society since the imperialistic days of 1898. In a trilogy, *USA*, he used a very effective impressionistic technique to portray vividly the failures—he omitted the successes—of his country. The reader felt absorbed by the novelist's ingenious use of news items, catchwords, popular songs, and the camera eye (the author's own point of view). Dos Passos mercilessly satirized the American dream of opportunity and individual success and the ideals of an acquisitive society. In his panoramic pages were word-pictures of overcrowded slums, unemployment, Sacco-Vanzetti, Debs, and the impersonal, inexorable advance of mechanization and the concentration of wealth. If his books did not exactly agree with the verdict of the objective social historian, they expressed the bitterness of an uprooted, frustrated depression era. However, Dos Passos did modify his radical judgments when prosperity returned.

Another familiar figure of the Lost Generation, Ernest Hemingway, experienced a similar conversion to social consciousness. In 1937 he published *To Have and To Have Not* which used the theme of a smuggler's rise and fall to illustrate the collectivist truth that even the most uncompromising individualist cannot stand alone. During the Spanish Civil War, Hemingway left to help the Loyalist cause against Franco. Out of his actual observations grew his best novel, *For Whom the Bell Tolls* (1940). His hero, Robert Jordan, is symbolically the idealistic grandson of a Union officer of that other civil war for freedom. He gives up his college teaching for the Loyalists as a dynamiter and, when he is surrounded by fascist troops, Jordan sells his life dearly by killing as many of the enemy as possible. Hemingway's collectivist emphasis was directly expressed in the title and inscription from John Donne, "No man is an Iland, entire of it selfe; . . . any man's death diminishes me, because I am involved in Mankinde; And therefore never send to know for whom the bell tolls; It tolls for thee." While Hemingway often shocked readers by his blunt realism, which some critics called obscenity, he was also a gifted story teller, especially in the short story of which he proved master. Hollywood found an admirable motion picture theme in his tense short story, *"The Killers"* as well as in the novel, *For Whom the Bell Tolls.*

Regionalism served naturalists and romantics, bitter social critics and nostalgic storytellers of the lost past. Millions apparently preferred the pageantry of the Old South in Margaret Mitchell's *Gone with the Wind* (1936) to the current ventures in hard-boiled realism. Yet Miss Mitchell was duly critical of the cynical speculators who fattened themselves upon the misery of the Confederacy and knew no loyalties; but she continued the stereotype of the helpless, un-

intelligent Negro and in effect justified the early Klan. Altogether
her book, which received the Pulitzer Prize, was a pleasant antidote to depression worries, and earned a fortune as one of the most
popular (and extravagantly produced) motion pictures of the
decade.

Southern regionalists of the naturalistic school seemed very
remote in outlook from the Georgia-born Margaret Mitchell. Yet
certain romantic agrarian beliefs were shared by Caldwell, Stribling,
Faulkner, and others with the author of *Gone with the Wind.* All
felt a sense of Southern decay since antebellum days and looked
upon the coming of industry as an intrusion upon the unspoiled
innocence of the Old South. Lillian Hellman, a leftist playwright
who had been born in New Orleans, developed such a theme in her
play, *The Little Foxes* (1939). This portrayed a postbellum commercial class of money-mad individuals who lacked the traditional
ethical restraints of the old planters.

The same theme of Southern decay, expressed in the most re-
volting passages of modern literature, appears in the naturalistic
novel, *Sanctuary,* by William Faulkner. This rural Mississippian
had been raised in the traditions of the Lost Cause and had even
joined the Canadian Air Force during World War I to avoid serving
with Yankees. He had been influenced by the grim naturalism of
Dostoevski without the Russian's deep spirituality. The decay of
Southern aristocracy and victory of an exploitative new industrialism
had been the underlying motifs of his novel *Sartoris* (1929); and
his later novels were indebted to the tradition of Poe in their qualities of horror, decadence, and morbidity.

Erskine Caldwell of rural Georgia, who had worked in a Southern
mill and had attended the University of Virginia and the University of Pennsylvania, combined the theme of Southern decay with
a poignant sympathy for the sharecropper, the Negro, and the mill
worker. He could blend pity and laughter in depicting Jeeter Lester,
the shiftless no-account descendant of an old Southern family of
landowners. In *Tobacco Road* (1932), Jeeter and his degenerate
family flounder about helplessly in rural squalor and ignorance,
unable to make any constructive decision. In the Lesters, the tragedy

of Southern poverty is arrestingly told by means of comic exaggeration. Caldwell's *God's Little Acre* (1933), which was sometimes dismissed as grossly obscene, gave a similar picture of backwardness, particularly in the animalistic sexualism and economic hopelessness of the chief characters. This novelist, no less than the other leading Southern writers, loved the South but he served his neighbors by retaining a critical attitude and working for better conditions among sharecroppers and the victims of race hatreds.

The Southern theme of aristocratic decay can be further exemplified in a number of leading novels, plays, and poetry. Thomas S. Stribling of Tennessee wrote such an interpretation of the South in a trilogy, *The Forge, The Store,* and *Unfinished Cathedral.* His realistic novels centered primarily around the Southern small town and the rise of the new commercialism. An entire group of Southern poets, novelists, and non-fiction writers, led by Allen Tate, an English professor, editor, and poet of Nashville, declared their utter rejection of modern industrialism in *I'll Take My Stand* (1930). The leaders were obviously influenced by the aristocratic traditionalism of T. S. Eliot and sought their values in the remote agrarian past of Jefferson and the premachine civilization of the eighteenth-century small farmer. They stated a nostalgic mood rather than a concrete social program that had the remotest chance of fulfillment.

On the West Coast, where Upton Sinclair and Lincoln Steffens (who died in 1936) continued their lifelong protest against social injustices, the most effective literary critic of contemporary society was John Steinbeck, a native of Salinas, California. He had studied at Stanford, where he had been particularly absorbed by marine biology and writing. At various times in his robust career he had worked his way East on a freighter, had been a New York newspaper reporter, had picked fruit in the California orchards, had worked as a chemist, and had persisted in his efforts to be a novelist. These experiences gave a convincing naturalness to successful regional novels.

His familiarity with the itinerant farm hands and their social problems was shown in *Tortilla Flat, Of Mice and Men,* and much later in *Cannery Row.* But his international reputation rested on

The Grapes of Wrath, a portrayal of the impoverished migratory workers, the Joads, who had left the ruined Dust Bowl when their Oklahoma farm had been taken over by a banking syndicate. The Joads were misled by California advertisements regarding high pay for fruit pickers and made their way in a battered car only to encounter irregular employment and petty tyrannies of the local police. *The Grapes of Wrath* has been compared in propaganda value to *Uncle Tom's Cabin,* for it aroused an entire nation to a sense of economic injustice in a land where such undemocratic conditions had been thought impossible. Steinbeck was no mere propagandist, but a sensitive observer of the social consequences of farm mechanization and the increasing impersonality of agrarian life. And he was a literary artist, not a caricaturist. *The Grapes of Wrath* also made a very impressive motion picture despite the inevitable change that novels usually suffered in transference to the screen.

To this regionalist tendency toward merciless agrarian self-criticism, the urban novelists and playwrights added an assault upon the slums. These city writers also stressed the naturalistic theme of human degradation and decay. James T. Farrell of Chicago could easily match the "hard-boiled" naturalism of the Southern writers in depicting human degeneracy, predatory sex exploits, and sodden sensibilities. His ambitious trilogy, *Studs Lonigan,* traced the decay of a gang of South Side boys, brutalized by a loathsome environment and doomed to cruel frustration and defeat. Studs and his gang are finally beaten by the Great Depression, disease, and hopelessness. Farrell once knew this life as a minor member of the gang. Like Zola he planned a long series of novels and other works to describe microscopically the decay of a group, though his emphasis was upon environmentalism rather than heredity or fatalism. He had learned much in technique from Dostoevski, Flaubert, and James Joyce. Farrell had a substantial European following, for his novels appeared in numerous translations and foreign editions.

Somewhat similar use of the slum-and-degeneracy theme marked the bitter Chicago novel, *Native Son* (1940) by Richard Wright, a Negro who had been born near Natchez, Mississippi, and had risen to literary success from miscellaneous employment as porter, ditch-digger, and clerk. His warped central character, Bigger Thomas, who is almost devoid of redeeming qualities, is explained as a product of the rat-infested Negro South Side where slums and racial blind alleys block the path of normal youthful aspirations. In its leftist philosophy the novel reflected the early Marxian phase of Wright's career.

In poetry, the Toryism of Ezra Pound and T. S. Eliot had a decided influence despite the social consciousness of this epoch. Pound lived in Italy after 1924 and became so enamored of Mussolini's fascism that he wrote the antidemocratic work, "Jefferson and/or Mussolini." During the war he broadcast fascist propaganda for which he was later condemned as a traitor. Far more humanistic in personal values was his conservative disciple, T. S. Eliot, who had become an ardent Anglo-Catholic and traditionalist. For a year Eliot taught poetry at Harvard and was cordially received after his long absence from the United States. His message to a depression-ridden and war-torn world was for more spirituality and dogmatic certainty. In this vein he wrote *Ash Wednesday, The Rock,* and the play of Thomas à Becket's life, *Murder in the Cathedral.* He influenced the nostalgic idealism of Allen Tate's "Southern Agrarian poets" and captivated for a time Archibald MacLeish and other leading contemporary poets.

MacLeish broke with his early aestheticism and became a severe critic of the economic order, especially in *Land of the Free* and *America Was Promises.* "Promises," he asserted, "are theirs who take them." When Hitler's armies appeared to be overrunning western civilization while Americans seemed lethargic in attitude, MacLeish penned a noteworthy essay, "The Irresponsibles" to attack the post-World War I intellectuals who had disarmed democracy by their pacifism and the sheer defeatism that grew out of cynical creeds. President Roosevelt appointed him head of the Library of Congress and during the war MacLeish directed the ideological attack upon fascism as Director of the Office of Facts and Figures. Among the other outstanding poets who deserted the hedonistic lyricists of the twenties to assert a greater social consciousness was

Edna St. Vincent Millay. She condemned the Franco dictatorship in
Say That We Saw Spain Die and called for aid to imperilled Britain
in 1940 with *There Are No Islands Any More*. Her Greenwich Village
period was definitely over. In similar apostrophes to the new spirit
of social reform were the democratic affirmations of Carl Sandburg,
particularly in *The People, Yes*.

3

The Great Depression left painters, sculptors, and architects with
little patronage until the federal government itself became a patron
of the arts. Congress was cool to any such European idea as a
Ministry of Fine Arts, but tolerated the existence of a painting and
sculpture section within the Treasury Department. By 1939 the
various federal arts projects were employing 5000 artists in some
forty states and producing innumerable works of art that public
institutions gratefully accepted. Many of these products, of course,
were mediocre, but this was far from the rule. Most of the better
sculptors, for example, were on the relief rolls and this fact inevitably
raised the quality of the work done. As business conditions improved,
private enterprise resumed its role as art patron, particularly in
connection with magazine advertisements. In 1944 the Pepsi-Cola
Corporation encouraged innumerable artists by fostering a national
art competition that resulted in the purchase of many contemporary
paintings for calendar pictures and traveling exhibits. *Life* magazine
used its elaborate photographic processes and attractive pages to
bring art to the people. The *Encyclopedia Britannica*, newly installed at the University of Chicago, collected many contemporary
American paintings for reproduction.

Hard times gave the artist a keen social sensitivity that pushed
the proponents of "pure art" into the background. In self-defense,
abstractionists and surrealists had to insist that their work, too,
was socially conscious. Among the leftists who enjoyed unusual
prestige was William Gropper of New York who illustrated the
New Masses and many books with sardonic caricatures of contemporary life. One of his often-reproduced paintings, "The Opposition,"

pictured the Senate in which a member waves a document triumphantly before his dozing colleagues. The naturalized Russian-American painter, Peter Blume, used the startling surrealist techniques
popularized by Salvador Dali to portray "The Eternal City," a
bitterly antifascist view of Mussolini's Rome. From Mexico came
the radical interpretations of Diego Rivera who was rediscovering
the communal and revolutionary spirit of the Indian. Rivera and
José Orozco were commissioned to execute murals in the United
States but their leftist emphasis sometimes made their patrons regret
the invitation. However, as a result of the Rivera-Orozco stimulus
and generous New Deal patronage, mural painting was widely
popular in this country.

Regionalism in art was another expression of social consciousness,
though local landscapes could be depicted from a conservative,
nostalgic viewpoint as well as a radical one. Artists in this genre
gave the Middle West a new importance in the field of aesthetics
although the primacy of New York city as the art capital of America
was never threatened. In rural Ohio, Charles Burchfield had moved
away from his former romantic landscape art to a realistic handling
of dilapidated farmhouses and barns. Like the literary naturalists,
he sought a theme in the decay and disintegration of traditional
life. Among his most successful disciples was Thomas Hart Benton
of Missouri, who had been trained at the Chicago Art Institute and
in Paris. While Benton lacked depth and intellectual consistency
in his social interpretations of the American scene, he developed a
technique of linear distortion that gave his work considerable
fascination. Best known are his murals for the Whitney Museum
of American Art, "The Arts of Life in America," which depicted
cowboy life, the backward rural South, and urban facets of the
national scene. For Missouri's capital he portrayed the state's history in a series of controversial mural subjects that included Daniel
Boone and the Kansas City political machine.

More profound than Benton among the regionalists was Grant
Wood, a native Iowan who taught art for a time at the University
of Iowa. He interpreted rural life with a realism enhanced by
applying the techniques of the old Dutch and Flemish primitives.

Professor Northrop in *The Meeting of East and West* (1946) wrote this personal estimate of Wood's painting:

More recently, Grant Wood in "American Gothic" and especially in "Daughters of Revolution" made us look at our blankish Protestant souls with all their rigid ethical virtues, but devoid of a hearty, human spontaneous expression of feeling, compassion, and the emotions.

Wood's friend, John Steuart Curry of Kansas, was another remarkable regionalist who interpreted the life of the Middle West. Curry was born in rural Kansas, the son of a stockman; he won national attention for his murals in several government buildings at Washington and in the Kansas State capitol. His "Baptism in Kansas" caught the monotonous quality of the Middle Western landscape and the religious fundamentalism of the farm folk who arrived at the ceremony in their store-bought clothes. Together with regionalism came unmistakable manifestations of a national awareness in art, such as the tendency to raise the evaluations of American art reputations of both the colonial and national periods. Albert P. Ryder and John H. Twachtman, particularly, rose in this process of upward reassessment. As a result, many more native artists than ever were represented in the great art galleries and museums.

Architecture was arrested in its development during the early depression years by the simple fact that so little building was being done. While architects did not have to go on relief to secure government patronage, they were heavy beneficiaries of the emergency revival of government-sponsored construction. When Congress belatedly decided that this country needed a permanent depository for its valuable records, there was a magnificent opportunity to design the huge National Archives building with the most modern details of construction. Post offices and federal housing projects were among the largest architectural commissions. The numerous federal projects included the mass housing developments that replaced part of the Brooklyn slums with modern structures allowing ample exposure to the sunlight the year round. Frank Lloyd Wright, hostile to the congested city and the skyscraper that worsened this crowding, urged that the unhealthful and monotonous slums be replaced by parklike urban areas. However, the new government projects, because of their monumental proportions, tended to perpetuate urban congestion.

Modernism in the functionalist American tradition of Louis Sullivan and Frank Lloyd Wright continued to advance. Wright's ingenious houses, some of them designs of sheer fantasy, continued to delight those who could afford them. Thus at Bear Run, Pennsylvania, he constructed a house covering several ground levels to blend with the background of a waterfall and the sloping land. However, Wright's friends were indignant in 1933 when Chicago overlooked him for Raymond M. Hood in planning the structures of the city's modernistic World's Fair, the "Century of Progress." Hood's modernism, they felt, was not functionalist, but eclectic. Yet Hood, who had designed the Chicago Tribune Tower, also was commissioned to design the *New York Daily News* building and, above all, in collaboration with Harvey Corbett, to plan John D. Rockefeller, Jr.'s gigantic Radio City project in New York. Manhattan also sounded the keynote of modernism and machine culture in New York's World's Fair of 1939. On the other hand, San Francisco's Fair of the same year chose to fall back upon the indigenous Spanish and Indian culture as its dominant architectural note.

Industrial architects rebelled against the skyscraper design in favor of single-storied, naturally-lighted buildings sprawled over large areas. Among the internationally-famous American architects of office and factory buildings was Albert Kahn of Detroit who had left Germany as a boy of twelve and eventually became the leading architect in the automobile and aircraft industries. Russia invited him to design some of its most important industrial structures. Other significant European-born experimenters in modernist forms of architecture were Richard J. Neutra of Berlin, who set up the Experimental School at Los Angeles, Walter Gropius of the Bauhaus movement, and Mies van der Rohe of Czechoslovakia.

4

Historians, however much they might like to think of themselves
as disciples of Ranke who merely wished to tell objectively "how
it actually happened," could not long remain detached from the
seething events and partisan emotions of the thirties and forties.
Popular writers were the first to attempt a more socially critical
history. Thus Matthew Josephson revived the antimonopolistic
tradition of Gustavus Myers in *The Robber Barons* (1934), which
cruelly portrayed the post-Civil War crop of millionaires as predatory businessmen more concerned with pyramiding their holdings
than with raising the nation's standard of living. *The Politicos* (1938)
pictured the politically obverse side of this picture of the "robber
barons" by showing how these men corrupted political life. Ferdi-
nand Lundberg's *Imperial Hearst* (1936) and *America's Sixty
Families* (1937), both best sellers, continued the theme of financial
monopoly and concentrated power. There appeared a host of critical biographies of Rockefeller, Mellon, the Guggenheims, Armour,
and other entrepreneurs. More friendly biographies of American
businessmen came from academic historians rather than from
journalists and free-lance literary men.

Charles Beard, who had ceased in 1917 to be a professor of
politics at Columbia University, found himself once more accepted
as an unsparingly critical prophet of American life. His *America in
Midpassage* (1939), written in collaboration with his wife Mary,
was a severe arraignment of the impact of the profit motive on
almost every aspect of our culture. He considered the dominance of
finance capitalism so complete in such fields as the stage, radio,
and the motion picture industry as to leave little room for a humanistic culture. On the whole, however, he was then a supporter
of the administration and praised Franklin D. Roosevelt because
"he carried on the tradition of humanistic democracy which from
colonial times had been a powerful dynamic in the whole movement of American civilization and culture..." In other writings
Beard refuted any suspicions of Marxism by pointing to his consistent record as a disciple of James Madison's economic realism,

especially as expressed in the Tenth Number of the *Federalist Papers.* He stressed the idea that self-interest was a predominant human motivation and even advised that foreign investments be discouraged in order to avoid creating any material stakes by big business in a foreign war. This suspicion of finance capitalism even gave his later writings a definite isolationist hue and contributed to what many historians have regarded as his most unfortunate volume, *President Roosevelt and the Coming of the War 1941* (1948).

History-writing benefited from the patronage of the New Deal. In order to provide work in occupations not directly competitive with private industry, the administration poured many millions into white-collar research and literary projects. Among the WPA activities was the Federal Writers' Project, which produced many local histories and guidebooks covering the entire nation. The Historical Records Survey sent out WPA investigators to locate historical documents in courthouses, private collections, and other depositories. The head of the Reference Division of the new National Archives directed a series of regional projects in the Survey of Federal Archives to locate historical materials in post offices and other federal agencies. WPA workers gave invaluable assistance to historical libraries in cataloguing hitherto unclassified and hence almost inaccessible materials.

Historians and other social scientists, now faced with the need for social action to cope with domestic and international emergencies, felt more aware than ever that the steady march of specialization had handicapped them in the current search for a total view of the world they lived in. Each academic specialty had been divided and subdivided into new specialties until professors of separate departments had difficulty in communicating with each other on any but the most superficial terms. Each discipline regarded itself as an autonomous field of study and guarded its domain jealously against invasion by academic rivals. The specialist often tried to solve current problems with an utter indifference for the techniques of even allied departments.

This situation was sufficiently urgent to lead to certain remedies.

Scholarly agencies like the Social Science Research Council of New York and the American Council of Learned Societies fostered many interdisciplinary studies and projects for retraining social scientists along broader lines. Edwin R. A. Seligman and Alvin Johnson edited a magnificent fifteen-volume *Encyclopedia of the Social Sciences* to help the various social studies to find common ground. Philosophers, literary professors, and historians sought new insights into cultural integration through such developments as the study and teaching of social and intellectual history. In American history valuable social and cultural materials were made available by the completion of the pioneer "History of American Life Series," edited by Arthur M. Schlesinger and Dixon R. Fox. American specialists in European history shared in this revival of the New History—for the movement among historians was largely in this direction. Thus William L. Langer of Harvard edited "The Rise of Modern Europe Series," which attempted to integrate all phases of human activity in such a way as to show the common motivating factors behind them at a given time.

5

No field of scholarship could escape the direct influence of these times by retreating into antiquarianism or affecting complete detachment. Political scientists took cognizance of the enormous expansion of government activities by giving numerous courses in public administration and preparing more students than ever for civil service careers. In the conflict with totalitarianism the political scientist turned to a renewed emphasis upon political theory. This was not merely, as in the past, a history of political philosophers studied descriptively in a chronological setting, but an attempt to prove the validity of various ideas as guides to social action. The war and the peace brought into existence many new courses in the field of international relations. College professors, now increasingly intent upon results in a pragmatic way, reserved their scorn for "merely academic" issues. The atmosphere of leisurely scholastic speculation had disappeared.

If political scientists were in a hurry, economists were even more so. The Great Depression demolished some proud reputations and forced the leisurely type of economist to enter the partisan melee. Both Hoover and Roosevelt had to break with the orthodox economists who counseled little beyond free trade theories. A symptom of the times was the extraordinary revival of Thorstein Veblen's ideas, which were so critical of finance capitalism. Even more arresting was the temporary success of an extreme disciple of Veblen, Howard Scott, who developed a system of "technocracy" as a substitute for the contemporary "price system." Taking as a point of departure Veblen's book, *The Engineers and the Price System*, Scott proposed to create a society dominated by an elite of industrial engineers in order to reach the fullest potentialities of modern technology. For a time many social planners were tempted by the glittering promises of Technocracy.

The research staff of the Brookings Institution offered some radical implications in their noteworthy studies of *America's Capacity to Produce* (1934) and *America's Capacity to Consume* (1934). They proved what World War II and the postwar era were to demonstrate sensationally: that even the great boom years of 1927-29 had only tapped the country's productive capacity and had left unsatisfied the larger part of the population. These observations encouraged the New Deal proponents of large-scale social planning to aim at something more than the modest goal of recovery alone.

Even before the Temporary National Economic Committee in Congress had startled the country with revelations that competition no longer existed in a substantial part of the economy, the economist had either dropped or modified the competitive theories of neo-classicism. Instead of assuming a normal situation where competition usually prevailed, economists now tended to speak of "imperfect" or "monopolistic" competition as the norm. Following Veblen, academic economists showed greater tolerance toward the idea that economic behavior was a product of many noneconomic factors of a social, cultural, or even wholly irrational nature.

The sociologist and social worker also came into unusual prominence because of the impact of depression problems. Social workers, trained to deal with personal maladjustments, were overwhelmed by the flow of able-bodied, normal men and women who were destitute through no fault of their own. Federal aid, social security, public projects had to replace the limited facilities of private social agencies. The current interest in regionalism led sociologists to follow the leadership of the University of Chicago, Columbia, and the University of North Carolina in using regional studies as preliminary to social planning. This "ecological school," which had developed during the twenties and now assumed a dominant position among sociologists, examined the impact of environmental influences upon social behavior, normal and irrational. The Lynds, as already seen, continued their urban case history of Muncie as *Middletown in Transition* (1937), an invaluable approach to a direct total view of an American community during the depression years.

With the rise of Nazi racialism, anthropologists in this country as well as in other democratic nations turned toward a renewed study of race. Franz Boas and his students who had fought the eugenics cult during the 1920's pressed further their studies into the alleged mental and psychological differences between races. By this time, environmentalism was so firmly in the academic saddle that there were few responsible scholars to contest the verdict of Jacques Barzun and others that racialism was merely an expression of modern superstition.

6

At the height of the New Deal era of social experimentation, philosophy seemed more tightly bound by the assumptions of pragmatism than in the days of William James. The frontier distrust of book learning and theory had long encouraged a cult of the practical at the expense of philosophic integration. It did not require more than a vulgarized form of John Dewey's "instrumentalism" for American educators to regard thought as a mere instrument of action and to discard the contemplative life as an ideal. The pragmatists' suspicion of "pure reason" and intellectualism led them often to assume that men deceived themselves into believing that they had reached their conclusions by independent thinking;

actually it was widely held, they tended to "rationalize" their desires, interests, and emotions as true. Many, if not most, lawyers called to staff the key New Deal agencies subscribed to that form of pragmatism known as "legal realism" or "sociological jurisprudence." The overwhelming reliance upon case law encouraged the tendency to separate applied law from legal philosophy and theory. However, the academic philosopher, F. S. C. Northrop, who was most critical of this tendency, in *The Meeting of East and West* (1946) admitted that the New Deal had shown an increasing awareness of the need for a stable theoretical structure as a basis for experiment and practice. Northrop's criticism of Thurman W. Arnold's book *The Folklore of Capitalism* (1937) as revelatory of the least desirable aspects of New Deal pragmatism, actually overlooked the ideals implicit in the argument of the former Assistant Attorney General. Arnold had analyzed the uncritical economic "folklore" of those who invoked outworn axioms to obstruct essential social adjustments to new problems. Although Arnold liked to use the bold language of the pragmatists, he shared the liberal values of Jefferson and Paine. With these men, he believed that it was folly for the past to rule the present from beyond the grave. "The greatest destroyer of ideals," he wrote, "is he who believes in them so strongly that he cannot fit them to practical needs."

The ideological opposition to totalitarianism led to a revulsion against the cruder kinds of pragmatism, of which fascism was an extreme variety. In 1946, while Northrop assailed the pragmatists, Brand Blanshard, a philosophical idealist, asserted overoptimistically, "Pragmatism is dying." He saw a decided trend away from the ethical relativism that had dominated the social studies during the 1920's and 1930's. Ethical relativists, especially the disciples of William Graham Sumner who stressed the idea that right and wrong were relative to place, time, custom, and circumstance, continued to question the existence of universal values. Now the lessons of Hitlerism caused men to re-examine their views in a new perspective and to search for more enduring certainties. "I will not give my life for a mere 'frame of reference,'" asserted a philosophical idealist at the University of Chicago.

Even the college elective system of Harvard's Charles Eliot, which had thrived upon the pragmatic belief that education must be primarily concerned with adapting the individual to a changing world, was severely criticized by philosophical idealists. At the University of Chicago, President Robert M. Hutchins aroused national controversy by attacking the "service station idea of education"—the notion that the purpose of a university is only to serve the health and wealth of the community. In his book *The Higher Learning in America* (1936) he called for a return to the speculative spirit of the medieval university and even advocated a revival of the medieval curriculum of the trivium and the quadrivium. Against the disintegrating effect of positivism and its end products, factualism and skepticism, he proposed a revival of the intellectual unity of the Middle Ages. He revised the University of Chicago curriculum to focus study upon the integrating of ideas and tried to spread an enthusiasm for the Great Books not only as a guide to contemporary problems but also as an intellectual pursuit for its own sake. Libraries all over the country set up Great Books programs under the direction of Hutchins and his associates. In many colleges, especially after World War II, the list of elective courses was shortened to require a core of certain basic humanistic subjects. Interdepartmental programs of study attempted to achieve intellectual unity and understanding by breaking down the isolation of academic departments.

The Hutchins group at the University of Chicago had taken an idealistic position that, on its theological side, had been long germinating among the Catholic neo-scholastics. In France the brilliant philosophers Jacques Maritain and Étienne Gilson had strengthened the neo-scholastic movement begun by Pope Leo XIII a generation before and based upon the writings of St. Thomas Aquinas. By making reason a godlike quality governing moral and social action, the neo-scholastics attracted intellectuals (many of them religious converts) to their banner. They regarded the separation between the intellectual and the spiritual as the chief sickness of modern society. Out of this chaos they believed had come the

modern worship of the state and the selfish ethics of economic individualism. Father John A. Ryan of Catholic University spread
the Christian labor philosophy of the papal encyclicals and other
Catholics showed greater militancy in sponsoring labor organizations. These progressive tendencies gave the church new vitality
during this era of crisis. While the Hutchins group (including both
Protestants and Catholics) felt that secularism was too strong to
permit ethical unity for the world through religion, they looked to
an idealistic philosophy to secure this goal.

Protestants, too, rebelled against pragmatism and liberalism in
favor of authoritarian doctrines. Even the fundamentalists showed
remarkable vitality, judging from the sensational growth of the
evangelistic "holy cults." At the more sophisticated levels of Protestant thought, liberals were driven upon the defensive by the
influence of the Swiss theologian, Karl Barth, who rejected the
humanistic doctrines that made man a part of the very substance
of God rather than sharply distinguishing between the two. The
liberal social gospelers had made God "immanent" in human society and thus gave religion a direct stake in the economic order;
but in so doing, the Barthians contended, they had confused the
transcendent nature of God with the secular character of the
universe.

Once American Protestants shifted their attention from the depression to the menace of totalitarianism, many felt attracted to the
absolutistic dogmas of Barth. The most important convert to this
"neo-orthodoxy" was the former liberal theologian, Reinhold Nie-
buhr, whose new ideas were expressed in a series of published
lectures, *The Nature and Destiny of Man.* Though still a democrat
and antifascist in social convictions, he was no longer optimistic
regarding the lasting results of social panaceas. Man was driven
to sin by his sense of psychological insecurity derived from a feeling of his inconsequence in an infinite world. Against this powerful
sinful drive, man must struggle all his life by putting his faith in
God. Thus the theological pendulum was swinging back to traditionalism if not exactly to original sin in its literal meaning.

7

Scientific thought and technology was too organic a part of society to escape current social changes. The depression spurred on the large industrial laboratories to discover cheaper processes and better materials. Industrial chemistry paid its way many times over by such technological contributions as those in the field of plastics; synthetic substitutes were particularly welcome in a society that feared an emergency shortage of wood as the forests dwindled. "Chemurgy" cheered up staple farmers by its discovery of new industrial uses for farm products. Tray agriculture, which grew foodstuffs in water basins containing certain chemicals, forecast revolutionary possibilities in alleviating the world-wide struggle for food and raw materials. Medicine, as a beneficiary of the great American chemical industry since World War I, reported a succession of far-reaching discoveries, including sulfa drugs, new vitamin concentrates, and new specific vaccines for epidemic diseases.

The continued mechanization of the farm, a process accelerated by the depression and war, brought in a variety of revolutionary inventions, such as the mechanical cotton picker and corn picker, and advances in poultry-raising and animal-raising techniques. Engineering produced one of its greatest triumphs in the development of air-conditioning, which promised a more efficient use of the summer months, particularly in the South. Among the other arresting developments that were expected to change social habits were the trailer cars, television and radio frequency modulation (FM), whose commercial uses had to await the end of World War II, fluorescent lighting, the inexpensive prefabricated house, and innumerable "gadgets" like the candid camera, the auto radio, and others. All this was readily conceded to be "progress."

Social workers and New Dealers who were influenced by Britain's experiments in making medical science available to the millions fought over a decade to secure federal aid for more hospitals and medical services. The Federal Public Health Service (according to the Beards) investigated the state of public health during 1935-36 and discovered that on any winter day over six million people were ill and more than 40 per cent of these had chronic ailments. Eighty per cent of the sick belonged to families whose average income was less than $1500. To make matters worse, about two-thirds of the population lived in small communities with no hospital facilities whatsoever. Efforts to initiate a public health crusade to provide federally subsidized medical care and hospital facilities met the stonewall resistance of conservatives who denounced "socialized medicine." The American Medical Association at first condemned both voluntary and compulsory systems of health insurance. Opponents of medical reform held that there were enough free dispensaries and other health services to take care of practically all poor families. They also stressed the fact that the United States led the world in the number of physicians per capita. As a result, national health proposals were buried in congressional committees from year to year.

Undoubtedly the greatest scientific discovery since Darwin's theory of natural selection was the sensational development of atomic power by the nuclear physicists. During the early thirties, Professor Harold C. Urey of Columbia had earned a Nobel Prize for his researches into "deuterium" or heavy water and this had stimulated many "atom-smashers" (both here and abroad) who used deuterium particles in their efforts to discover the properties of the atom nucleus. The most arresting step in the field of nuclear fission was made in 1939 when German scientists split the uranium nucleus and tapped its unbelievable potentialities of atomic energy. German refugee scientists transmitted these results to a Copenhagen physicist, Professor Niels Bohr, who thereafter left for the United States to consult with Albert Einstein, J. A. Wheeler, and Enrico Fermi.

By this time the United States was actively involved in World War II and Einstein used his prestige to help convince President Roosevelt that Nazi experiments with an atomic bomb required that this country enter the race at once or face disaster. American, British, and Canadian statesmen agreed to pool their scientific resources in this venture. As a result, over 125,000 scientists, techni-

cians, and other types of workers embarked upon the greatest
cooperative venture in scientific history, the "Manhattan Project."
They spent $2,000,000,000 in a desperate effort to achieve within
three or four years what might well have required thirty or forty
under normal circumstances. The first bomb was secretly exploded
on July 16, 1945, at the Alamogordo Air Base in the desert of New
Mexico. On August 5, an atomic bomb was dropped with devastating effect on the Japanese munitions center, Hiroshima.

The first reaction to the atomic bomb was partly one of horror
despite the fact that it led Japan to surrender within a matter of
days and probably saved the lives of over a million Allied soldiers.
Only an effective system of international control, or fears on the
part of friend and foe alike of an atomic war, could prevent wholesale annihilation. Blackmailing governments, armed with an atomic
stockpile, might possibly achieve what Hitler had failed to secure.
Subsequent experiments suggested the doom of infantry and naval
weapons of war. Optimists stressed the peacetime potentialities of
atomic power as a creator of electrical energy and as a curative
agent. Possibly coal and other fuel shortages could be eliminated
once atomic energy was properly shielded to prevent the escape of
dangerous radiation, and if certain other technical difficulties were
overcome. Cancerous tissues, it was believed, could be treated and
cured through the increased production of radioactive isotopes by
means of uranium fission fragments. In any event, the United States
was now committed to the most portentous atomic experiments.
Oak Ridge, Tennessee, became a vast center of research and training in the field of nuclear physics.

The United States had been first to introduce the atomic bomb
and upon its shoulders rested much of the burden of world defense
against any resurgence of communism. It was commonly understood even in 1945 that the "secret" of the atomic bomb could not
be kept beyond a few years and that other countries would soon
begin to produce their own atomic stockpiles. Never, it was felt,
had there been such a test of whether man was able to prevent
science from destroying him. Americans, whose historic optimism
had been partly based on the fact that science would inevitably

build a better world, were stunned by this atomic challenge to their faith in technology. Would social and moral intelligence be hopelessly outstripped by the precocity of machine man? It was a melancholy fact that generations of advance in transportation and communication had not made the world kin in spirit but had allowed the growth of violent nationalism and totalitarianism. Science enabled minorities to dominate majorities through modern weapons and propaganda. However, the example of the thousands of co-operative scientists and technicians who invented the atomic bomb suggested the possibility of a cooperative social science and a higher level of statesmanship in enabling mankind to survive and to profit from the newer scientific discoveries. Meanwhile, it was not a new experience for men to live in the shadow of destruction —whether from earthquakes, epidemics, or atom bombs. Even the horrors of bacteriological warfare need not overcome the marvelously adaptive power of human beings to survive and to master their environment.

· 24 ·

The Cold War: Two Worlds
in Cultural Rivalry

I

ALTHOUGH Henry Wallace's goal of "Sixty Million Jobs" proved easy of fulfillment in the postwar years, Wendell Willkie's "One World" did not. Within the United Nations, the United States and the Soviet Union became rival centers of polar attraction among the members, for these two nations were the acknowledged first-rate military powers of the world. The demise of Germany, Japan, and Mussolini's Italy left a vacuum that power politics abhorred. Postwar chaos, world-wide poverty, and Asiatic nationalism played into the hands of astute communist propagandists. In the cultural field as well as in the military, political, and economic spheres, the two great powers confronted each other in a world increasingly divided between democracy and totalitarianism.

Actually, the Russian communists took as few chances as possible in the competition of ideas with the West, for the Soviet Union and her satellites, "people's democracies," tolerated only to a very limited extent a cultural interchange of scholars and ideas with the outside world. The Soviet Union refrained from joining strong international agencies for cultural cooperation such as the United Nations Educational, Scientific, and Cultural Organization (UNESCO). Fantastic communist charges of Wall Street spy rings and sinister militaristic plotting served as a pretext for closing American libraries, educational services, and religious organizations abroad. The Russian satellites and communist China tended to

556

imitate the police measures of the Soviet Union where entrances and exits had always been doubly barred and where there was little tolerance for ideological neutrality whether it concerned a novel, a symphonic composition, or a theory of plant genetics. In this warfare of ideas the communists denied there was any inconsistency in their simultaneous use of nationalist and internationalist appeals. But communist novelists and poets who struck too emphatically a note of internationalism could be ruined by semiofficial Marxian critics who might accuse them in vitriolic terms of being "homeless cosmopolitans."

American statesmen learned after World War I that only hunger and despair, not weaknesses in democratic philosophy, were the real sources of communist victories in Europe. But combatting communism in Asia was more difficult, for their ideas of free enterprise and civil liberty had only tenuous roots while a renascent nationalism identified the West with historic imperialism and racialism. Communists were quick to single out American shortcomings in race relations as a telling argument among the colored peoples of the world. They omitted, of course, any mention of the rapid progress that Americans were making in improving the lot of minority groups by voluntary action. The Soviet Union, which prided itself upon a policy of racial equality, had been far from successful in extirpating the age-old hatreds of minorities; Hitler's armies discovered this when they invaded the Ukraine and recruited innumerable anti-Semites and regional separatists for the Nazi cause.

The great test for America during the Cold War was not only to resist the advance of Russian power over the globe, but to preserve intact her own democratic heritage of civil liberty and individual opportunity. Public-opinion polls and election results during these postwar years showed a widespread belief in a "get tough with Russia" policy and revealed a critical attitude toward the alleged "softness" and even loyalty of the State Department. Politicians at Washington and in the state legislature won votes by calling for ever stronger "loyalty oaths" and investigations among civil service employees and educators.

The Red scare of 1919 seemed destined to be repeated and per-

haps surpassed. In those days communist Russia was relatively weak
and offered no threat to the United States. Now the Russians were
the only military rivals left and they seemed bent on a policy of
communist expansion. To make matters worse, American communists apparently adopted the new international line that the chief
threat to peace was American "imperialism" and that in any war
with the Soviet Union true communists would not fight for the
United States. This implied the existence of a Fifth Column and
sabotage. Paul Robeson, the Negro singer who had never disguised
his admiration for Russia, asserted that in any war with the Soviet
Union, Negro-Americans also would not fight. This assertion was
emphatically rejected by leading Negro spokesmen, but it added
to the tension. The valor of Negro-American troops fighting in Korea
gave the lie to Robeson's remark.

More serious, of course, were the actual facts of the international
situation: the communist advance in eastern Europe and Asia, the
forcible conversion of eastern Germany to communism, the Berlin
blockade, the discovery of a group of atomic spies serving Russia
in this country, and finally, in 1950, the North Korean communist
invasion of South Korea. Though Russians cited Lenin, Stalin, and
other high authorities for the axiom that capitalism and communism
could coexist peaceably upon the globe, the total picture of the
international chessboard was not reassuring.

To attain national security without hysteria, the FBI and other
federal departments worked smoothly and efficiently, but the newspapers demanded ever greater tests of loyalty for men in government
or academic service. Rather dismaying to the supporters of civil
liberties were the sweeping charges of Senator Joseph McCarthy
of Wisconsin intended to impugn the loyalty of the State Department
and its advisers. In 1950, this senator aroused a sensation by his accu-
sation (made behind Senate immunity to prosecution for libel) that
there were 205 communists or fellow travelers within the State Department and that one Far Eastern expert, Professor Owen J. Lattimore of Johns Hopkins University, was a top Soviet espionage agent.
The subsequent hearing uncovered mere hearsay and the charges fell
flat but Lattimore had to draw heavily upon his limited financial

resources to clear himself. The Senate Foreign Relations Committee sustained Lattimore 9 to 2 and castigated the senator, "We have seen the technique of the 'Big Lie,' elsewhere employed by the totalitarian dictators with devastating success, utilized here for the first time on a sustained basis in our history." Lattimore later observed in his book, *Ordeal by Slander:*

The standards that the witch-hunters are trying to impose on us are the standards of propaganda, of mob-thinking, and of thought control. . . . Within our own country our traditional freedoms are being paralyzed by fear fostered by organized pressure groups which are hard at work to deepen the intimidation and make paralysis more rigid.

He warned that "McCarthyism" and incipient fascism would intimidate experts on communism and discourage the necessary study of Marxist theory and tactics at a time when objective thinking was desperately needed in the complex task of halting Russian imperialism.

2

Postwar America of the latter forties and early fifties was a far stronger nation than in the years following World War I. Once more the population curve was moving rapidly upward despite the early pessimistic predictions that we would reach relatively stable numbers by mid-century. During the decade of the thirties the population increase had been only 7.2 per cent, an all-time low ratio, but the forties experienced a sudden spurt in the birth rate, an increased immigration, and a lengthened span of life, altogether a growth of 14.5 per cent during the decade. The 1950 census reported nearly 151 millions living in the continental United States. This expansion was greatest in the Far West, particularly in California which added nearly 3.7 millions to her population. Los Angeles alone went forward from 1.5 million to nearly 2 million. Four other states that expanded by over a million persons were New York, Texas, Michigan, and Ohio. While industrial cities continued to gain rapidly, there was a marked tendency, thanks to the automobile, to disperse the urban population over a vast suburban area at the expense of the older section. Industry, oil discoveries, and government projects accounted for the extraordinary growth of cities in Texas and other parts of the South. Baton Rouge multiplied by 257 per cent, Corpus Christi, Texas, by 88.6 per cent, Phoenix by 61.2 per cent, and Fort Worth by 55.9 per cent.

Fear of an atomic bomb attack upon the highly centralized American industrial centers led experts to demand the dispersal of factories and population. Such an "industrial dispersion policy" was announced in August, 1951, by President Truman. The National Security Resources Board pointed out that since the war some 18 billion dollars had been spent annually for new plants and equipment largely in areas already highly industrialized. To encourage dispersal of the new plants, the administration expected to provide a variety of incentives such as tax concessions, the allocation of critical materials, defense loans, and defense contracts. So revolutionary an idea seemed too sweeping and expensive for acceptance without a partisan conflict.

These postwar years saw unusual progress in public health. In 1900 the average life expectancy was only 49 years, but those born in 1950 could hope to reach an average of 67 years of age. Increasing interest was now focussed upon "geriatric" treatment, dealing with problems of aging and chronic degenerative ailments. "The era of quick death from wholesale epidemics is over," wrote Dr. Leonard A. Scheele, Surgeon-General of the United States, "The slow killers are now the nation's outstanding health enemies." These were chronic illness, heart disease, and cancer. Poliomyelitis, known as infantile paralysis, did show a disquieting growth to over 41,000 cases in 1949. The campaign against this disease had already assumed national proportions in the thirties, beginning with President Roosevelt, who himself was a victim of the malady.

The most striking example of a successful cooperative effort against disease was the postwar campaign against tuberculosis. Officials of the National Planning Association asserted that this disease could be wiped out in ten years, using medical knowledge that science now possessed. Negroes were particularly susceptible to tuberculosis; their death rate from it was over three times as great as that of the whites. A characteristic of tuberculosis is that it strikes at people during their most productive years, fifteen to forty-four. Once the call to battle was sounded, state and federal agencies joined with private groups in seeking out the enemy. Mobile X-ray bus units took chest surveys of entire communities. Incipient cases were detected and advanced illnesses checked by means of such new drugs as streptomycin and its derivatives. The results were gratifying. During four years of campaigning, the number of deaths from tuberculosis fell from 41.3 per 100,000 population in 1944 to 31 in 1948. So successful was the current movement in public health that it was indeed fitting that the United States Health Service was assigned a major role in President Truman's "Point Four" program for technical aid to underdeveloped areas abroad. This meant the export of the highly developed public health techniques to the world on a far larger scale than ever before.

Half of all hospital beds were occupied by mental patients and this problem, particularly in its preventive aspects, attracted an unusual amount of attention during these years. Not only did the study of psychiatry, psychoanalysis, and abnormal psychology grow rapidly during this period but Hollywood arrested the attention of millions of laymen to the problem of mental health by such effective motion pictures as *The Snake Pit* and *Home of the Brave*. In 1946, Congress passed the National Mental Health Act, which set up a National Institute operated by the Public Health Service. The law envisaged a national grant-in-aid system to deal with mental cases outside of community institutions by correcting the behavior disorders of children and by preventing psychiatric illness among adults. Funds were made available for such purposes to universities, hospitals, laboratories, and individual doctors. Another important step forward came in 1950 with the merger of the four leading mental health organizations into a single, more efficient national society, the National Association for Mental Health. This absorbed the old National Committee for Mental Health that Clifford Beers had helped to found in 1909. It was hoped that it would now be possible to strengthen the treatment of mental ailments by a broad basic program of prevention.

3

Despite fears of a "recession" in 1949 these were indubitably prosperous years in every major economic sector. Industry and the farm were called on to fill deferred wartime needs, defense orders, and Korean War orders, as well as the normal economic demand. "Full employment," with minor exceptions, was the rule. As a result of government orders, the national economy was not compelled to meet the test of converting from high wartime productivity to the restricted demands of normal peacetime consumption. Only inflation and a severe housing shortage remained to plague the average citizen.

The businessman's prestige had revived considerably since the dark days of the thirties and there was a tendency to stress laissez-faire ideas of free enterprise as the democratic antithesis of totalitarian socialism. Economic individualism and religious orthodoxy were often coupled together as a basic bulwark against communism. However, Britain's shift to socialism, which was not wholly repudiated even by the Tories, and the spread of collectivist ideas elsewhere—apart from communism—offered a perplexing obstacle to those who wished to export the contemporary American version of free enterprise.

Organized labor was far stronger than in the 1920's and it fought much more effectively to keep up wage levels threatened by inflation. However, the nation-wide coal strike of John L. Lewis' United Mine Workers and the widespread railroad strike antagonized public opinion in 1946 and led Congress to enact an antistrike bill, which President Truman vetoed. State after state passed antistrike laws or other restrictive legislation aimed at labor. In the ensuing reaction against unions, Congress enacted the Taft-Hartley Act of 1947 over the President's veto. This amended the Wagner Act, which Senator Taft had long denounced as a one-sided law strengthening labor at the expense of management and making the National Labor Relations Board judge, jury, and prosecutor. Although this act cannot be accurately summarized here, it should be noted that it made unions suable in court, revised the labor-management procedure to ban certain labor practices deemed to be unfair, provided a federal injunction against illegal strikes, outlawed the closed shop, and permitted more frequent plant elections (which unions argued had an injurious effect on their stability). Although union leaders denounced this law as a "slave labor act" and subsequent court cases showed it handicapped collective bargaining in a good number of instances, organized labor apparently had lost none of its real strength. The communist issue, which had ruined so many unions in 1919-20, was skillfully handled by the C.I.O., the A.F.of L., and most of the great independent unions. As a rule, union officials dislodged known communists without falling into the trap of replacing them by safe but ineffectual unionists. Certain communist-led unions survived but they were forced into the open.

These years marked great victories for the principle of social security. Walter Reuther of the United Automobile Workers (C.I.O.) led the way to sweeping labor contracts that provided for company-paid pensions of $100 a month (aside from federal social security) for workers over 65 years of age with thirty years of service. In 1950 the federal government itself strengthened the movement by making eligible for old-age insurance benefits ten million more employees, including those employed in non-profit institutions. The trend was definitely not back to the individualistic 1920's.

4

While the public schools began to fill up as a consequence of the high birth rates prevailing on the eve of World War II, the colleges were crowded by returning veterans subsidized by the GI Bill of Rights. Teacher shortages did not disappear with the end of the war, for there was little inducement to return to a notoriously underpaid profession while industry and commerce were paying so well. In fact, even by 1950 when a general upswing took place in teachers' salaries, they tended to fall below the general average for all employed persons.

As after World War I, the communist issue played a large role in the schools, particularly in the colleges. The National Education

Association, representing most public school educators, agreed in 1949 to ban communists from teaching. By that year twenty-five states had already adopted loyalty oaths for all teachers and more states were planning to enact similar laws. Teachers generally regarded the oaths as unnecessary, discriminatory insofar as no other class of professional people had to sign these oaths, and obviously intimidating in effect. Besides, they argued, actual communists would not hesitate to sign them. The University of Washington dismissed three faculty members as communists while the University of California was prepared to discharge a large number of professors who refused to sign a loyalty oath; however, a California court decision nullified the California oath as a violation of the state constitution. In that state, where the Tenney Committee had been zealous in detecting the slightest evidence of radical sympathies, particularly in the schools and in the movies, the Red scare was much more severe than elsewhere. Former Attorney General Francis Biddle, commenting on a new book dealing with the Tenney Committee, spoke of:

. . . the creeping fear, the obsession with Russia distorting and confusing our purpose and our direction, the resort to methods usually identified with Star Chamber and the Inquisition. All these things mark an immature mind that lives in a world of terrifying phantoms.

At a time when there were genuine spies and saboteurs to deal with and an unusually effective Federal Bureau of Investigation existed, certain minor politicians preferred to play detective and win votes by chastising educators as Reds. Academic freedom was one of the most difficult concepts for the average voter and taxpayer to understand.

This situation existed throughout the civil service. State and federal committees on un-American activities succeeded in securing loyalty laws that expelled government employees who were "security risks" or found "guilty by association" with subversive persons. Such doctrines had been rejected by Wilsonian liberals like Louis F. Post in 1919-20, but were now revived as justified by a grave communist danger. The increasing threat to academic freedom was underlined in 1949 when a Georgia congressman, John S. Wood, chairman of the House Committee on Un-American Activities, ordered a probe of school textbooks for evidences of radical ideas. However, this step was condemned widely and protested by five of this nine-member committee.

An important chapter in education was opened with the passage of the Fulbright Act by the Seventy-ninth Congress. This set up an educational exchange program "to further goodwill and understanding between the United States and other countries through the exchange of students, teachers, lecturers, research scholars, and specialists." The funds were derived from the foreign currencies credited to this country by governments abroad for the purchase of United States Government property left there at the close of the war. There were no communist countries in the list of nations participating in the Fulbright benefits. Such a program promised to tighten the intellectual ties between the United States and the rest of the free world. Under this and other auspices, about 16,000 American students, mostly at the graduate level, were studying in foreign universities in 1949 and 26,000 foreign students came to study in American schools of higher learning. The scope of student exchange activities was broadened further under the Smith-Mundt Act.

American technical knowledge was marked for export to underdeveloped areas as part of the famous Point Four program stated by President Truman in January, 1949. He condemned the old imperialistic spirit of exploitation and added,

... we must embark on a bold new program for making the benefits of our scientific advances and industrial progress available for the improvement and growth of underdeveloped areas.

This, as already noted, included public health aid. It was another manifestation of a closer intimacy between American culture and the world, a process that the communists distorted as "cultural imperialism."

5

In the field of popular education and recreation, the most arresting innovations were the commercial applications of frequency modulation (FM), which was a static-free type of broadcasting, and television. Frequency modulation was patented in 1933 by Edwin H. Armstrong, a professor of electrical engineering at Columbia University. Its large-scale development began after World War II. By October, 1946, there were 540 FM stations, but most of them were owned by the regular AM stations and about 40 per cent of the FM organizations were controlled by newspaper publishers. It was believed that FM, with its superior sound fidelity, would replace AM and encourage improved musical programs. The United States, which had pioneered in this field, did not quite achieve the results expected. FM programs tended to duplicate AM programs and only exceptional FM station managers offered consistently high-grade instruction and entertainment.

Television swiftly captured the nation's fancy after the war despite the high cost of receiving sets and the early technical imperfections. Only 170,000 television receivers existed in the entire country as late as 1947, but three years later there were 7,200,000 sets, while 107 television stations served 58 metropolitan areas. Educators felt disappointed with the results of commercial dominance of television and the vulgarization of most channel broadcasts. Grunting wrestlers, including lady wrestlers, toiled with ludicrous effect over their opponents; prize fights, ball games, and auto races were frequent features; old motion pictures, especially "Westerns," appeared daily; and variety entertainment ranked among the highest in popularity. On the favorable side were many worthwhile plays, vital discussions of important questions, and frequent offerings of symphonic classics. Colleges demanded a larger share of TV channels for educational programs, though the Ford Foundation, a multimillion-dollar philanthropic agency, appeared willing to promote educational objectives through commercial as well as non-profit channels.

Technical instruction proved a major beneficiary of television. Military instructors and industrial technicians combined illustrations with oral explanations. In atomic research, where radiation was harmful, technical processes could be watched safely through television; anywhere, in fact, where it was impractical or unsafe for persons to observe technical activities, TV became almost indispensable. With the aid of color television, doctors and medical students could observe surgery in its most natural aspect.

The invention promised to bring the citizens and their government into greater contact. One of the most engrossing events in television history came in 1951 when millions watched the Kefauver Senate Committee cross-examine powerful gamblers and gangsters; this was a probe into the national ramifications of gambling and related forms of vice. Although the public learned a good deal about the corruption of local government by nation-wide vice syndicates, usually with headquarters in Florida, there was no unusual demand by the citizenry that something drastic be done about protected vice. But certain remedial measures did come about from this public exposure. Another result of this new dimension of sight in communication was an accelerated tendency, already fostered by the radio and the automobile, to break down regional differences in American culture.

Television emptied many motion picture houses and reduced the attendance at televised sports events. Hollywood had had its financial worries before this. In an economy drive the producers tried to save money by soliciting for the free films made by the various federal agencies, especially by the military services. The usual result of incorporating hundreds of feet of such film into major features was to eulogize every branch of the government and to produce a plethora of war movies.

Perhaps Hollywood's greatest social contribution in these years was its unwonted frankness in dealing with genuine social issues, particularly with minority problems. Even Southern audiences, except where local censors banned the films, were willing to see the new cycle of pro-Negro films. At first the cautious producers restricted themselves to mere peripheral problems of race such as Negroes "passing" as whites, notably in *Lost Boundaries,* in which a Negro doctor passed as a white man in New Hampshire and won high community respect until discovered. In *Pinky*, another white-appearing Negro, a nurse who had passed for years as white in the North, returned to her Southern home and suffered humiliating discriminations. *Intruder in the Dust* was unusual in its frank treatment of the lynching spirit that captured a Southern town. Such pictures indicated that the familiar minstrel stereotype of the Negro was going out in favor of an interpretation in which minority persons could be treated as individuals.

The wide diffusion of automobile ownership after World War II stamped American culture as a "centaur civilization" with the long-hoped-for advent of two cars in every garage much closer than ever. Postwar cars were laden with more gadgets than Sinclair Lewis' Babbitt had ever dreamed of, and they offered greater ease in driving, handsome upholstery, and attractive streamlining and color designs. As the art of walking for pleasure declined among drivers, new institutions sprang up to serve them: drive-in theaters, drive-in restaurants, drive-in banks, etc. Public transportation systems, deserted by millions of car owners, staggered under the burden of financing city-wide and interurban travel for declining numbers of passengers. Public buses replaced streetcars and attempted with difficulty to serve a growing metropolis whose boundaries were being rapidly extended by the influence of the private automobile. This situation was reflected in a mushroom growth of suburban areas that outstripped previous movements. Municipal institutions, schools, libraries, and traffic systems had to be constantly adapted to this America on wheels. It was tempting, but still premature, to speculate on the effects on the American mind of television, with its bewildering wealth of stimuli, and of the automobile, with its ubiquitousness. But speculation itself seemed out of place in this "centaur civilization."

6

Europeans in 1865 would not have found it hard to believe that in the mid-twentieth century their Old World descendants would look to America as a fortress of individual freedom. Many Protestant dissenters had sought for generations for a New Jerusalem on this side of the Atlantic free from state coercion. Workmen and farmers escaped the tyranny of class and caste by moving to Europe's frontier overseas and thereafter by rising according to their abilities. To millions of immigrants and their kinsfolk abroad, the image of the United States was a blend of freedom and economic opportunity. There was also the persistent eighteenth-century myth of the New World as an unspoiled wilderness inhabited by the Noble Savage and Natural Man. Widely held, also, was the idea that this country had a beneficent mission to spread liberal ideals throughout the world. This had been preached by Jefferson, Paine, La Fayette, and Kosciusko; and it was to be reaffirmed by Louis Kossuth of Hungary and Thomas Masaryk, founder of Czechoslovakia. Movements to liberate Ireland, Hungary, Poland, Cuba, Russia, and Czechoslovakia had deep American roots.

Few nations had been compounded of so many elements of religious, political, and economic dissent. The vast frontier had encouraged self-reliance, equality, and tough survival traits to strengthen a people to whom freedom was a treasure earned by vigilance, perseverance, and an optimistic faith. No worship of the state could easily take root where the individual counted for so much.

In the ideological battle for the soul of the world, the implacable critics of this country harped constantly upon the themes of American imperialism, Negro discrimination, and philistinism, without mentioning the striking advances made in almost every direction. By proving that the United States was unfit to act as a world leader, totalitarian critics could win half the battle. To counteract this, the federal government used the Voice of America program to broadcast facts regarding the United States to the countries behind the Iron Curtain. Western Europe and other parts of the world came into closer contact with this country through UNESCO, the Marshall Plan, and a freer exchange of scholars, journalists, students, and technicians. In this process the export of American ideas and methods proceeded on the largest scale in history.

In 1902, William T. Stead, a critical but essentially friendly English editor, had published a book with a title revealing the new role of the United States as a patron rather than a client: *The*

Americanization of the World. He was thinking primarily of the impact of American industry and commerce upon Europe. The tradition of mass production, going back to the days of Eli Whitney and the interchangeable parts rifle, had given American toolmakers and technicians a leading place in the world of industry. By 1920, American manufacturers had been able to cut costs and prices while improving quality for automobiles, sewing machines, industrial equipment, and other products through standardization, simplification, and scientific management. The assembly line fascinated German and Russian engineers who came here to study American methods. Germany's "rationalization" movement to modernize her industrial plant utilized American principles, while Soviet Russia's dream of "catching up with and surpassing America" was expressed in a persistent effort to emulate Henry Ford's system. Even in Stead's day the names of Edison, Westinghouse, Singer, Bell, and Cyrus McCormick were familiar labels on industrial equipment all over the world. Europeans readily took to the latest American inventions, which were usually retailed cheaply—phonographs, sewing machines, vacuum cleaners, safety razors, fountain pens, telephones, typewriters, incandescent lamps, innumerable labor-saving gadgets, and cheap American adaptations of European inventions. To mid-twentieth-century Europe, America came to epitomize machine civilization. With the reaction against the dominance of the machine, this country was bound to suffer in the European mind.

Stead could have broadened his idea of the Americanization of the world by including the export of ideas, institutions, habits, recreations, and art to the world. His own country stood in a unique cultural relationship to her one-time colony. America's debt to British culture appeared so overwhelming that few noted that the relationship was far from one-sided. As already seen, American novels, poems, histories, and magazines sold in the millions during the nineteenth century, particularly such books as *Uncle Tom's Cabin.* American expatriates like Henry James, T. S. Eliot, and Ezra Pound rated among England's greatest literary figures of the early twentieth century. In painting, Benjamin West and James Whistler made their particular styles dominant among large groups of contemporary artists. The British, who had some well-founded objections to the influence of sensational American journalism upon English newspapers, forgot that United States journalists had learned the art of exploiting police reports from early English papers and that Lord Northcliffe had been our mentor in developing the modern tabloid. Besides, American journalism did contribute better newsgathering methods, frankness of presentation, and a much fuller picture of the state of public opinion. The enterprising *New York Herald-Tribune* and the *Chicago Tribune* established overseas editions for European readers. Those patriots who feared for the purity of the English tongue must have been dismayed to hear Prime Minister Neville Chamberlain entitle himself "a go-getter for peace"—it was bad enough that the statement was not even true. H. L. Mencken, author of the rather substantial work, *The American Language,* declared in his 1936 edition that Englishmen were yielding more and more to American forms in vocabulary, ideas, spelling, and pronunciation.

The impact of this country upon Britain has been carefully analyzed by Richard H. Heindel who includes almost every level of cultural contact in the broad sense of this term. In the realm of law, where the Anglo-American bond was intimate, English jurists cited the authority of Story and Kent and of American interpretations of maritime and international law. Americans had once borrowed heavily from John Howard and other English prison reformers, but in turn they exported their own modifications and inventions: the indeterminate sentence, the juvenile reformatory, the juvenile court, the use of medical men on prison boards, and such prison improvements as better food, communal dining, and more visiting hours.

Dr. Halvdan Koht, the Scandinavian scholar, has stressed the close cooperation of British and American reformers and religious leaders; often the initiative and innovating influence began here. American prohibitionists originated the "local option" system. American pacifists and suffragettes were especially resourceful in inventing methods of organization. Christian Science, born in the United States, attracted numerous English converts. The Salvation Army, the Y.M.C.A., the Y.W.C.A., and the Student Volunteer Missions were

Anglo-American institutions. Moody and Sankey carried the American evangelical spirit to thousands of Englishmen just as Wesley and Whitefield had done in this country over a century before. American industrial unionism, particularly in the militant form of the I.W.W., led England's labor leaders, also, to agitate for the reorganization of unions on a shop rather than a craft basis. Barnum's Tom Thumb, the minstrel show, the cowboy and wild Indian stereotypes, and large American commercial exhibits attracted Englishmen everywhere. As for Hollywood's influence, this was so great as to disturb many Britons. English audiences, like American ones, imitated the clothes, manners, speech, and attitudes of the screen.

Beginning with the Venezuela crisis of 1895, which might easily have resulted in an Anglo-American war, peacemakers worked for a closer bond between the two countries. Carnegie was not alone in his labors for a union of English-speaking peoples. Viscount James Bryce, English historian who later became ambassador to the United States, devoted his energies to cementing Anglo-American friendship. His *American Commonwealth* (1888) not only offered keen insights into national institutions and habits but encouraged many Englishmen to begin a serious study of American history. In 1912, Oxford established a lectureship in American history, a subject hitherto neglected. Other colleges quickly followed and this tendency was encouraged in the forties by the Fulbright grants. Quite a few Englishmen celebrated the Fourth of July and even the royal family gave the impression that they rejoiced that America had resisted in 1776. The experience as allies in two world wars led Winston Churchill and many more British leaders to believe that the English and American democracies had a common duty to preserve free society.

Within the English-speaking world, isolated Australia moved closer in sentiment to the United States, and the greatest intimacy existed between Canada and this country. Commuters crossed daily between such key points as Buffalo and Toronto or Detroit and Windsor. Even the heavy tariff barriers did not lessen the reality of "the unfortified frontier" stretching across a continent. In the 1930's about a third of those of Canadian stock in this hemisphere lived south of the border and some 800,000 of American descent resided in Canada. Under the circumstances, two neighboring English-speaking countries, one of 150,000,000 persons and the other a mere 13,000,000, were inevitably drawn into a cultural relationship of patron and client.

In 1951 this unique situation was pessimistically reported on after two years study by the Canadian Royal Commission on the National Development of the Arts, Letters, and Sciences. They reviewed gloomily the extent to which American films, radio programs, books, and magazines had captured the country. "We must not be blind to the very present danger of permanent dependence," declared the Massey Report, prepared under the direction of Chancellor Vincent Massey of the University of Toronto. While the Commission praised the worth-while American contributions to scholarship, literature, and music, they feared that Canadian cultural institutions had been debilitated or neglected. "Our use of American institutions or our lazy, even abject imitation of them has caused an uncritical acceptance of ideas and assumptions which are alien to our tradition." Canada's arts and sciences had suffered, and its libraries and museums rated far below those of the "States." To correct this tendency, the Commission recommended heavy subsidies to cultural agencies and that government control over radio be extended to include television as well. This, it was hoped, would curb the "alien" influence of pulp magazines, soap operas, and certain types of movies.

Not all Canadians agreed with the Massey Commission. Professor Frank H. Underhill of the University of Toronto, writing for *The Canadian Forum*, dissented emphatically from the Commission's interpretation of the facts of Canadian-American cultural relations. "The way to become mature," he reasoned, "is not by cutting yourself off from older people who are more mature than you are." He declared emphatically:

If we allow ourselves to be obsessed by the danger of American cultural annexation, so that the thought preys on us day and night, we shall only become a slightly bigger Ulster. The idea that by taking thought, and with the help of some government subventions, we can become another England—which, one suspects, is Mr. Massey's ultimate idea—is purely fantastic.

Underhill went on to state what seemed to be the crux of the entire matter:

The root cultural problem in our modern mass-democracies is this relationship between the mass culture, which is in danger of being further debased with every new invention in mass communications and the culture of the few. . . . What we need, we, the minority of Canadians who care for the culture of the few, is closer contact with the *finest* expressions of the American mind.

It was clear that educated Canadians, like the educated groups of other countries, including the United States, suffered because of the tendency of modern commercialization to seek the profitable mass market of "the least common denominator" in the cultural sense. Mass mediums of entertainment and instruction might raise the standard of the least literate, but there was also the danger that a general cultural debasement of the best values would take place wherever the profit motive alone determined what the standards should be. Whether government subsidies could halt the process of debasement remained to be seen. Sooner or later, it was generally felt, the taxpayer would succeed to the role of patron of the arts (as in WPA days) once held by the church, the aristocracy, and the captains of industry.

7

France had long been the mentor of the United States in the arts and critical of the soulless quality of the machine civilization allegedly typified by this country. Yet in the years following World War II, French readers as well as French novelists and poets showed a keen appreciation of contemporary American literature. They liked its hard-boiled realism and vitality, though they doubted whether the American writer was not a propagandist rather than an artist. André Gide, who had insisted in 1920 that America had no soul and lacked the psychological depth that came of suffering and experience, now recognized a new United States that had ceased to make a religion of material progress. Yet the sophisticated French symbolists and surrealists had long acknowledged Edgar Allan Poe as their master. Poe's esthetic principles of criticism and writing, through the ardent championship of Charles Baudelaire and others, had become the starting point for the symbolist poets and even those who affected the weary spirit of "decadence" and "dadaism." The mystery and horror stories of Poe had also inspired many French imitators. France remembered the charm and wisdom of Benjamin Franklin, the idealism of Thomas Paine, the revolutionary bond of La Fayette, and the experience of being an ally in the two world wars.

The current Soviet effort to lessen American influences in communist countries makes the history of Russian-American contacts of unusual interest. Before 1945 the totalitarian Czarist and Soviet regimes had left a substantial margin for economic and cultural intimacy with the United States. Czarist writers had frequently made the point that Russia and America were astonishingly alike in geographic features and that both shared the frontier stage of development. Yankee mechanical ingenuity fascinated nineteenth-century Russian leaders almost as much as Ford's assembly did Soviet technicians. During the 1840's, Nicholas I had invited the American engineer Major George W. Whistler, father of the famous painter, to help industrialize Russia by supervising the construction of roads and railways. In 1860, Russian engineers visited Cleveland and other cities along the Great Lakes to study small water craft and tugs. Even during the Civil War, American factories were filling Russian orders for reapers and mowers. By 1900, Russia was absorbing one-third of our entire farm machinery exports. American engineers built the locomotives and rails for the strategic Russian-dominated Chinese Eastern Railway. In St. Petersburg, the giant Nevsky Works operated with American tools and giant lathes and George Westinghouse built a huge electrical plant for the city. German technical competition was overcome by American engineers and technicians in Russia. One well-informed contemporary, referring to the "Americanization of Russia," declared:

Strangely enough, if Russia ever becomes even in a limited degree a manufacturing nation, which does not seem possible, she will owe the development of her mines largely to American machinery, and the release of myriads of muzhiks from slavery of the soil to take their places in factories and workshops entirely to the labor-saving devices that America sends to till her fields and gather the abundant crops.

The Russian intelligentsia, including such diverse men as Alexander Herzen, Tolstoy, Ostrogorski, and Constantine Pobyedonostsev, admitted a keen interest in American ideas. Tolstoy and other Russian social idealists idolized Henry George, father of the single tax, because his theory of land nationalization seemed to offer a solution for the Russian land problem. The great Russian novelist and religious mystic was especially influenced by Adin Ballou, the Christian Socialist and pacifist who had published *Christian Non-Resistance* and had founded the Hopedale Community near Boston. Not only did Tolstoy correspond with Ballou, but he translated and circulated two of the latter's tracts. In Tolstoy's first chapter of *The Kingdom of God Is within You,* Ballou is credited with originating certain of its ideas. This book is one of the influences that converted Gandhi to pacifism. Walt Whitman, Edward Bellamy, and Emerson were among Tolstoy's favorite authors. Curiously, the archconservative, Pobyedonostsev, who guided Alexander III and Nicholas II along the path of Czarist-clerical reaction, admired Emerson intensely. It was perhaps the mysticism of the great transcendentalist that fascinated this Russian statesman who translated Emerson's *Essays* into Russian and always kept a volume of this work open upon his desk.

Lenin and Stalin had continued and considerably expanded the Czarist use of American technicians. They had made the slogan of matching and surpassing America almost an integral part of communist doctrine. On the intellectual side, Russia's interest in American books far outdid the vogue of Czarist days. According to Clarence Gohdes, between the years 1918-43 the Russians translated 217 American authors and distributed thirty-seven million copies of these books. Although the communists derided the "bourgeois realism" of the West in favor of "socialist realism," they translated innumerable American books of social protest for their direct propaganda value. Thus Jack London, an avowed socialist critic of contemporary America, was so popular that his books went through 567 editions and sold ten million copies. Apparently Mark Twain was considered sufficiently critical of his times to warrant his extraordinary popularity in Russia, for his works rated next to London's in popularity. Generally, however, the communists preferred to import the writings of leftist American writers like Upton Sinclair, Theodore Dreiser, Howard Fast, and John Steinbeck (until the latter offended communist sensibilities). Upton Sinclair's *The Jungle* could be used effectively to illustrate the alleged bourgeois lack of ethics. Howard Fast's novels frequently developed what the author considered to be the revolutionary tradition in America. Steinbeck's *Grapes of Wrath* or Farrell's *Studs Lonigan* could be interpreted by Marxists as evidence of the disintegration of bourgeois society. The fact that such interpretations were not always intended by the novelists did not disturb Soviet critics in this war of ideologies.

It is clear that America's cultural exports to the world consisted of far more than Yankee notions, gangster movies, Ely Culbertson's version of bridge, jazz discordancies, and cocktails. In architecture, Louis Sullivan, Frank L. Wright, and Albert Kahn had founded an international movement of functional modernism that affected almost every major country. Gershwin's symphonic jazz and Isadora Duncan's modern classical dance had a sustained effect abroad—Gershwin in France and England, Duncan in Russia. John Dewey had developed Froebel's principle of learning by doing into a democratic system of progressive education that had its disciples all over the globe. Alfred Thayer Mahan's idea of the role of sea power in history had fundamentally changed the tactical concepts of practically every nation that had a substantial navy and even affected the theories of land power. In Japan, under the occupational directives of MacArthur and Ridgway, the process of Americanization proceeded at breakneck speed—at least in externals. President Truman's Point Four promised, if fulfilled, to carry Americanization to the most primitive communities.

Nothing from the United States had been so contagious to Europeans as the liberal idealism expressed in firm accents of moral certainty. Woodrow Wilson's Golden Rule diplomacy aimed at imperialism had seemed quixotic to professional diplomats but he became for a time the symbol of justice to countless ordinary folk in Europe as well as in America. In his Mobile speech, Wilson had set a new standard for international relations, "It is a very perilous thing to determine the foreign policy of a nation in the terms of material interest." Even in New Deal times, when economic survival was uppermost, the United States continued the Anglo-American tradition of stating public issues in moral terms. At the Nuremberg trials of Nazi war criminals, Justice Robert H. Jackson insisted upon the American moral position that Wilson had asserted in 1919, namely, that guilt is personal and that wrongdoing must be punished. This was a far cry from the crude pragmatism and ethical relativism commonly attributed to the United States. Franklin D. Roosevelt's Four Freedoms had modernized the liberal Wilsonian formula of constitutional liberty and the self-determination of peoples by adding freedom from want and freedom from fear. This time, it was believed, the American people would lead the world in a disinterested effort to implement these rights.

Totalitarian propagandists thundered against American bourgeois decadence, but the youthful vitality of this country had never been greater and the nation was growing measurably in intellectual maturity. This coming of age did not mean an intolerant nationalism. The poisons of chauvinism had made slight inroads among a people whose ancestors had been born in every part of the world. There were those who would use the current fear of communist infiltration to destroy the heritage of civil liberty and moral idealism at home, but grounds for reasonable hope existed that the mid-century American would eventually recover from the Red scare as his parent had done after 1919. Fears of destruction by atomic warfare, bacteriological weapons, and other lethal instruments removed the old naïve optimism but they caused no appreciable faltering in national purpose. The extreme individualist faith in inevitable progress had gone but thoughtful Americans were ready to believe that the destiny of the individual was bound up with the salvation of all humanity. They could say with the English poet, John Donne, "No man is an Iland..."

Select Bibliography

· 1 – 3 ·

RECONSTRUCTION. THE NEW SOUTH.
SOUTHERN DEMAGOGUES AND LIBERALS

The most useful books that deal with the social and economic aspects of Reconstruction are E. Merton Coulter, *The South during Reconstruction, 1865-1877* (Louisiana State University, 1947); Francis B. Simkins and Robert H. Woody, *South Carolina during Reconstruction* (University of North Carolina, 1932); and W. E. Burghardt Du Bois, *Black Reconstruction* (Harcourt, Brace, 1935), which takes issue with the usual view that the Negro was a pawn of the Radicals. The first Klan is sympathetically but superficially presented in Stanley F. Horn, *Invisible Empire: The Story of the Ku Klux Klan, 1866-71* (Houghton Mifflin, 1939). Rupert B. Vance shows the social effects of physical cnvironment in *Human Geography of the South* (University of North Carolina, 1935), a very valuable study. The central biographic figures in these three chapters are dealt with in Manley W. Wellman, *Giant in Gray, a Biography of Wade Hampton* (Scribner, 1949), popularly written and sympathetic; Francis B. Simkins, *Pitchfork Ben Tillman* (Louisiana State University, 1944), scholarly; and C. Vann Woodward, *Tom Watson, Agrarian Rebel* (Macmillan, 1938), a thorough study.

For the history of the New South, C. Vann Woodward has covered most phases in the forthcoming *Origins of the New South, 1877-1913* (Louisiana State University), and R. B. Vance is scheduled to deal similarly with the next period in the same "A History of the South" series to be entitled, *The Present South, 1913-1946*. Two leaders of the New South are covered adequately in Raymond B. Nixon's *Henry W. Grady* (Knopf, 1943) and John K. Winkler's *Tobacco Tycoon: The Story of James Buchanan Duke* (Random House, 1942). Valuable for the movement of the cotton mills to the cotton fields is Broadus Mitchell's *The Rise of the Cotton Mills in the South* (Johns Hopkins, 1921).

Recent writers on the Negro show increasing awareness of his active role in history. Under the sponsorship of the Carnegie Corporation, Professor Gunnar Myrdal of the University of Stockholm prepared an objective historical and sociological study of the Negro in *An American Dilemma: The Negro Problem and Modern Democracy* (Harper, 1944), which contrasts the American creed of equality and the practice of inequality. John Hope Franklin has written a solid history of the Negro in *From Slavery to Freedom* (Knopf, 1947). Booker T. Washington has written simply and informatively in his autobiography, *Up from Slavery* (Doubleday, Page, 1906). His severest critic, W. E. B. Du Bois, assails the Washington program in *The Souls of Black Folk* (McClurg, Chicago, 1903). Special aspects of the race question are discussed in Charles S. Mangum, Jr., *The Legal Status of the Negro* (University of North Carolina, 1940), a synthesis mainly of court decisions; Paul Lewinson, *Race, Class, and Party: A History of Negro Suffrage and White Politics in the South* (Oxford University, 1932), very suggestive; and V. O. Key, *Southern Politics in State and Nation* (Knopf, 1949), unusually informative.

There are excellent essays on Southern social and cultural history in William T. Couch (ed), *Culture in the South* (University of North Carolina, 1934). Wilbur J. Cash has written brilliantly and critically in *The Mind of the South* (Knopf, 1941); see also Virginius Dabney, *Liberalism in the South* (University of North Carolina, 1932). For Southern education, there is much in Jessie P. Rice, *J. L. M. Curry* (King's Crown, 1949) and Dumas Malone, *Edwin A. Alderman* (Doubleday, 1940). In religious history, there are Hunter D. Farish, *The Circuit Rider Dismounts: A Social History of Southern Methodism, 1865-1900* (Dietz, Richmond, 1938) and George P. Jackson, *White Spirituals in the Southern Uplands* (J. J. Augustin, New York, 1943). Blake McKelvey shows the shortcomings of the Southern penal system in *American Prisons* (University of Chicago, 1936).

There is a good deal of literary history in Paul H. Buck's *The Road to Reunion, 1865-1900* (Little, Brown, 1937), a Pulitzer prize winner. Shields McIlwaine integrates social and literary history in *The Southern Poor White* (University of Oklahoma, 1939), outstanding. Other relevant works are: Aubrey H. Starke, *Sidney Lanier* (University of North Carolina, 1932); Charles R. Anderson, "*Charles Gayarré and Paul Hayne: The Last Literary Cavaliers,*" in David K. Jackson (ed.) *American Studies in Honor of William K. Boyd* (Duke University, 1940); and Ellen Glasgow, *A Certain Measure* (Harcourt, Brace, 1943), autobiographical and critical.

For Southern social, political, and economic theories see William Diamond, *The Economic Thought of Woodrow Wilson* (Johns Hopkins, 1943); Burton J. Hendrick, *The Life and Letters of Walter Hines Page* (2 vols., Doubleday, Page, 1922-25); Woodrow Wilson, *The State* (Heath, 1908) and his *Constitutional Government in the United States* (Columbia University, 1911); Alexander H. Stephens, *A Constitutional View of the Late War between the States* (National Publishing Co., 1868-70); Rudolph von Abele, *Alexander H. Stephens* (Knopf, 1946); and Harvey Wish, *George Fitzhugh, Propagandist of the Old South* (Louisiana State University, 1943).

· 4 ·

THE LAST FRONTIER AND FREDERICK JACKSON TURNER

The most convenient introduction to the Turner theories together with the chief criticisms is George R. Taylor (ed.), *The Turner Thesis* (Heath, 1949). Of the major contributions to the frontier thesis, the outstanding work has been Walter P. Webb's *The Great Plains* (Ginn, 1931). James C. Malin discusses Turner in relation to the "closed space" doctrines in "Space and History," *Agricultural History*, 18 (1944), 65-74, 107-126; Ray Billington uses the Turner approach in his comprehensive history, *Westward Expansion* (Macmillan, 1949); see also Le Roy R. Hafen and Carl C. Rister, *Western America* (Prentice-Hall, 1941). Everett Dick describes the social history of the frontier in *The Sodhouse Frontier, 1854-1890* (Appleton-Century, 1939) and *Vanguards of the Frontier* (Appleton-Century, 1941).

The story of the Nevada mining frontier is graphically told in George D. Lyman's *The Saga of the Comstock Lode* (Scribner, 1934) and in Richard G. Lillard's *Desert Challenge* (Knopf, 1942), which is rich in social history. For Utah see Nels Anderson, *Desert Saints: The Mormon Frontier* (University of Chicago, 1942). Other excellent regional histories with considerable social material include Bruce Nelson's fascinating story of the Missouri Valley in *Land of the Dacotahs* (University of Minnesota, 1946); R. R. Wilson, *Out of the West* (Wilson-Erickson, 1936); Roy Gettinger, *The Formation of the State of Oklahoma, 1803-1906* (University of Oklahoma, 1939); Carl C. Rister, *Southern Plainsmen* (University of Oklahoma, 1938), excellent for southwestern social history; Glenn C. Quiett, *They Built the West* (Appleton-Century, 1934); and Stuart R. Tompkins, *Alaska* (University of Oklahoma, 1945).

The conservation movement is interestingly told in Roy Robbins, *Our Landed Heritage* (Princeton University, 1942). Wayne Gard's *Frontier Justice* (University of Oklahoma, 1949), explains the violence and improvised justice of the Far West. Indispensable in its field is B. A. Botkin, *A Treasury of American Folklore* (Crown, 1944). The concepts of the West as reflected in literature are discussed in Henry Nash Smith, *Virgin Land: The American West as Symbol and Myth* (Harvard University, 1950).

The diffusion of the complex Central American Indian cultures through North America is traced by the anthropologist Paul Radin in *The Story of the American Indian* (Liveright, 1934). Of Clark Wissler's various books on the Indian, the best general survey is *Indians of the United States* (Doubleday, Doran, 1940). Loring B. Priest has written a detailed history of Indian reforms in *Uncle Sam's Step-Children: The Reformation of the United States Indian Policy, 1865-1887* (Rutgers University, 1942); see also Ruth Odell, *Helen Hunt Jackson* (Appleton-Century, 1939).

• 5 •

THE URBAN IMPACT ON RURAL LIFE

Of the various histories of American rural institutions, those especially valuable are Wayne C. Neely, *The Agricultural Fair* (Columbia University, 1935), which combines sociological and historical techniques; Boris Emmet and John E. Jeuck, *Catalogues and Counters: A History of Sears, Roebuck and Company* (University of Chicago, 1950), a many-sided interpretive history of the mail-order movement written by marketing specialists; and John S. Noffsinger, *Correspondence Schools, Lyceums, Chautauquas* (Macmillan, 1926), very informative. Charles H. Greathouse deals briefly with two rural institutions in "Development of Agricultural Libraries" and "Free Delivery of Rural Mails," both in *Yearbook of the Department of Agriculture: 1899* (Washington, D. C., 1900). James M. Williams presents an enlightening synthesis of rural social change in the East in *The Expansion of Rural Life* (Knopf, 1926).

For a general agricultural history with some incidental social history, see Fred A. Shannon, *The Farmer's Last Frontier, 1860-1897* (Farrar and Rinehart, 1945). James C. Malin offers a brilliant application of ecological concepts to agricultural history in *The Grassland of North America* (Privately published, J. C. Malin, Lawrence, Kansas, 1947); especially relevant here are chapters 12 to 21 inclusive. Pertinent biographies are Russell Lord, *The Wallaces of Iowa* (Houghton Mifflin, 1947); Rackham Holt, *George Washington Carver* (Doubleday, Doran, 1943); and Paul De Kruif's popular biographies of agricultural scientists, *Hunger Fighters* (Harcourt, Brace, 1928). The writer is especially indebted to Hamlin Garland's autobiographical *A Son of the Middle Border* (Macmillan, 1922). See the section on the Country Life Commission in Andrew D. Rodgers III, *Liberty Hyde Bailey* (Princeton University, 1949).

Rural literature may be studied in Frank L. Mott's *A History of American Magazines* (Harvard University, 1938), III; William P. Randel's *Edward Eggleston* (King's Crown, 1946); and the cited works of H. N. Smith, *Virgin Land* and B. A. Botkin, *A Treasury of American Folklore*.

· 6 ·

THE URBAN IMPACT ON THE HOME

The rise of the "emancipated woman" in American society is effectively told in Mary Earhart, *Francis Willard: From Prayers to Politics* (University of Chicago, 1944), which touches upon the temperance, suffrage, labor, and women's education movements; Arthur W. Calhoun, *A Social History of the American Family* (Arthur H. Clark, Cleveland, 1919), III; Elizabeth Cady Stanton, *Eighty Years and More* (European Publishing Company, New York, 1898); Mary R. Beard, *Woman as a Force in History* (Macmillan, 1946). Relevant chapters appear in Allen Nevins, *The Emergence of Modern America, 1865-1878* (Macmillan, 1927); Arthur M. Schlesinger, *The Rise of the City, 1878-1898* (Macmillan, 1933); and Harold U. Faulkner, *The Quest for Social Justice, 1898-1914* (Macmillan, 1931), all in the "History of American Life Series."

Specific urban problems are dealt with in Blake McKelvey, *American Prisons* (University of Chicago, 1936); Heywood Broun and Margaret Leech, *Anthony Comstock* (Boni, 1927), a critical view of Comstock's campaigns for strict morality; Lewis Mumford, *The Culture of Cities* (Harcourt, Brace, 1938), which stresses the unplanned nature of our urban environment; and John L. Gillen, *Criminology and Penology* (Appleton-Century, 1935), a useful textbook. The history of the settlement movement is autobiographically told in Jane Addams, *Twenty Years of Hull House* (Macmillan, 1942); Graham W. Taylor, *Pioneering on New Social Frontiers* (University of Chicago, 1930); and Lillian Wald, *The House on Henry Street* (Holt, 1915). Urban abuses are discussed by leading journalistic observers in Jacob Riis, *How the Other Half Lives* (Scribner, 1890), a picture of New York's tenements; William T. Stead, *If Christ Came to Chicago* (Laird and Lee, 1894), a severe arraignment of municipal corruption; and Lincoln Steffens, *The Autobiography of Lincoln Steffens* (Harcourt, Brace, 1931), an effort to present a pattern of civic corruption in the major cities.

Perhaps the most informative book on the history of American public health during this era is Mazyck P. Ravenel's collection of essays by authorities in *A Half Century of Public Health* (American Public Health Association, 1921). Howard D. Kramer has surveyed a basic aspect of this movement in "The Germ Theory and the Early Public Health Program in the United States," *Bulletin of the History of Medicine*, XXII (1948), 233-47. The *Encyclopedia of the Social Sciences* has many valuable articles concerning urban conditions: "Public Health," "Nursing," "Clinics and Dispensaries," "Child," "Food and Drug Regulation," "Temperance Movements," and "Juvenile Delinquency."

· 7 ·

URBANISM AND THE CHURCH

There are several excellent books on the social gospel movement. Charles H. Hopkins has explained the doctrinal and ideological strands in *The Rise of the Social Gospel in American Protestantism, 1865-1915* (Yale University, 1940). Aaron I. Abell deals thoughtfully with the institutions affected by the social gospel in *The Urban Impact upon American Protestantism, 1865-1900* (Harvard University, 1943); see also Henry F. May's careful analysis, *Protestant Churches and Industrial America* (Harper, 1949).

William W. Sweet's *The Story of Religion in America* (Harper, 1939) is weakest in the recent period. One phase of conservative Protestantism is covered in Stewart C. Cole, *The History of Fundamentalism* (R. R. Smith, 1931). The founder of the Christian Science Church is sympathetically presented in Lyman P. Powell's *Mary Baker Eddy* (Christian Science Publishing Society, Boston, 1950) and viewed critically in

Edwin F. Dakin's *Mrs. Eddy* (Scribner, 1929). Paxton Hibben is severely critical in his very informative and absorbing book, *Henry Ward Beecher* (Doran, 1927); in contrast, Gamaliel Bradford is almost reverent and only moderately enlightening in *Dwight L. Moody: A Worker in Souls* (Doubleday, Doran, 1928). Religion and Darwinism are dealt with historically in several essays in *Evolutionary Thought in America* (Yale University, 1950), edited by Stow Persons. Josiah Strong's *Our Country* (Baker, 1890) develops the missionary ideas and social philosophy of a Protestant leader. In the considerable literature of agnosticism, Robert G. Ingersoll has been prolific in his essays and books; best remembered is his *Why I Am An Agnostic* (Farrell, 1896). For American Catholicism, see the informative history by Theodore Maynard, *The Story of American Catholicism* (Macmillan, 1941) and the Reverend John A. Ryan's autobiographical *Social Doctrine in Action* (Harper, 1941), which shows the influence of the encyclicals on labor.

· 8 ·

THE CAPTAIN OF INDUSTRY, THE GILDED AGE, AND TAYLORIZATION

Veblen's idea of the captain of industry and finance capitalism can be studied in his book *The Theory of the Leisure Class* (Macmillan, 1899) and *The Theory of Business Enterprise* (Scribner, 1904). Joseph Dorfman has done the best biography, *Thorstein Veblen and His America* (Viking, 1934) and a detailed survey of economic thought relevant for this chapter in *The Economic Mind in American Civilization* (4 vols., Viking, 1946, 1949, 1951), of which the final volume is directly applicable. Thomas C. Cochran and William Miller offer a brilliant historical synthesis of entrepreneurial history in *The Age of Enterprise* (Macmillan, 1941). Especially revealing is William Miller's statistical analysis of American entrepreneurs, "American Historians and the Business Elite," *The Journal of Economic History,* IX (1949), 184-208; compare this study with Chester Destler's "Entrepreneurial Leadership among the Robber Barons," *Journal of Economic History,* VI (1946), 28-49. A classic on the inefficiency of the financial entrepreneur is Louis Brandeis' *Other People's Money* (Stokes, 1932); his best essays and interviews have been collected in *The Curse of Bigness* (Viking, 1934). The impact of the captain of industry on "society" and "culture" is entertainingly and analytically told in Dixon Wecter's *The Saga of American Society, 1607-1937* (Scribner, 1937) and in Ward McAllister's *Society As I Have Found It* (1890), a first-hand view by the famous arbiter of fashion.

Biographies of the captains of industry are mounting. Allan Nevins' *John D. Rockefeller* (2 vols., Scribner, 1940) is rather friendly in treatment. This interpretation is challenged by Chester McA. Destler, "Wealth against Commonwealth 1894 and 1944," *American Historical Review*, 50 (1944), 49-72, essentially a defense of Henry D. Lloyd's indictment of the Standard Oil Company. *The Autobiography of Andrew Carnegie* (Houghton Mifflin, 1920) has become a classic, but should be read together with the severely critical narrative of James H. Bridge, *The Inside History of the Carnegie Steel Company* (Aldine Book Co., 1903). An objective detailed study of Carnegie is badly needed. Louis F. Swift's *The Yankee of the Yards: Gustavus F. Swift* (A. W. Shaw, Chicago, 1927) is adulatory and only moderately informative. John Tebbel has written entertainingly and skilfully of a great dynasty in *The Marshall Fields* (Dutton, 1947). George Pullman's paternalistic labor philosophy is unfavorably interpreted in Almont Lindsey's *The Pullman Strike* (University of Chicago, 1942). Henrietta Larson's *Jay Cooke* (Harvard University, 1936) is a detailed scholarly monograph. Keith T. Sward has written a masterly criticism of Ford's reputation as an enlightened industrialist in a thoroughly documented work, *The Legend of Henry Ford* (Rinehart, 1948). A formerly tarnished reputation has been refurbished in Mark D. Hirsch, *William C. Whitney* (Dodd, Mead, 1948), which is based on considerable research. There are a number of excellent brief biographies of industrialists and financiers in the *Dictionary of American Biography:* John Wanamaker, William C. Whitney, Charles T. Yerkes, Philip D. Armour, Gustavus D. Armour, John D. Rockefeller, etc. The *Encyclopedia of the Social Sciences* has many first-rate articles on entrepreneurial development: "Private Fortunes," "Endowments and Foundations," "Frederick W. Taylor," and "Capitalism," the latter being Werner Sombart's summary of his own interesting, though highly controversial, theories on the subject.

· 9 ·

THE LABOR MOVEMENT (1865-1917)

Among the general American labor histories, the most analytical remains John R. Commons *et al.*, *History of Labour in the United States* (Macmillan, 1926), II, and Selig Perlman and Philip Taft, *History of Labor in the United States, 1896-1932* (Macmillan, 1935). A recent well-rounded and readable account is Foster R. Dulles' *Labor in America* (Crowell, 1949). Norman J. Ware has written the best postbellum study; *The Labor Movement in the United States, 1860-1895* (Appleton, 1929). There is a good deal of labor history based on the most recent sources in Harold U. Faulkner's *The Decline of Laissez-Faire, 1897-1917* (Rinehart, 1951).

For a biographic approach to labor and labor philosophy, see Terence V. Powderly, *The Path I Trod* (Columbia University, 1940), an autobiography of the conservative leader of the Knights of Labor; Louis I. Reed, *The Labor Philosophy of Samuel Gompers* (Columbia University, 1930); Samuel Gompers, *Labor and the Common Welfare* (Dutton, 1919) and *Seventy Years of Life and Labor* (2 vols., Dutton, 1925); Rowland H. Harvey, *Samuel Gompers* (Stanford University, 1935); Ray Ginger, *The Bending Cross, a Biography of Eugene V. Debs* (Rutgers University, 1949), very thorough and informative for the American Railway Union. There is considerable labor philosophy in Alpheus T. Mason's excellent *Brandeis: A Free Man's Life* (Viking, 1946).

On the major labor conflicts of this era there are Henry David, *A History of the Haymarket Affair* (Farrar and Rinehart, 1936); Almont Lindsey, *The Pullman Strike*, cited; and Samuel Yellen, *American Labor Struggles* (Harcourt, Brace, 1936). The prolabor policies of a great liberal are analyzed in Harvey Wish, "Altgeld and the Progressive Tradition," *American Historical Review*, 46 (1941), 813-31. For special labor topics covering this era, see Paul H. Douglas, *Real Wages in the United States, 1890-1926* (Houghton Mifflin, 1930); Willford I. King, *The Wealth and Income of the People of the United States* (Macmillan, 1915); and the articles "Workmen's Compensation," "Employer's Liability," "Freedom of Contract," and "Labor Injunction" in the *Encyclopedia of the Social Sciences*.

· 10 ·

THE PASSING OF THE OLD IMMIGRATION

Carl Wittke includes an interesting survey of the Old Immigration in *We Who Built America* (Western Reserve University, 1951) and deals with the German group in *The German-Americans and the World War* (Ohio State Archaeological and Historical Society, 1936), which emphasizes the role of Ohio's German language press. There is considerable light on the German-American press in Andrew J. Townsend, *The Germans of Chicago* (University of Chicago, 1927) and in Peter Olden and Harvey Wish, "The Influence of the *Illinois Staats-Zeitung* upon American Politics," *American German Review* (February, 1940), 30-39. Almost every phase of immigration history is covered in detail, though from a filiopietistic viewpoint in A. B. Faust, *The German Element in the United States* (2 vols., Houghton Mifflin, 1909). Two valuable sociological studies covering all groups are Maurice R. Davie, *World Immigration* (Macmillan, 1936) and Robert E. Park, *The Immigrant Press and Its Control* (Harper, 1922).

The best studies of the Scandinavians for this period are: Theodore C. Blegen, *Norwegian Immigration to America* (Norwegian-American Historical Association, Northfield, Minn., 1940); Adolph B. Benson and Naboth Hedin, *Americans from Sweden* (Lippincott, 1950); John Kolehmainen and George Hill, *Haven in the Woods* (State Historical Society of Wisconsin, Madison, 1951), dealing with the Finns in Wisconsin. Mary R. Coolidge combines scholarship and understanding in *Chinese Immigration* (Holt, 1909). For useful biographies of immigrant leaders mentioned in this chapter see the *Dictionary of American Biography*.

· 11 ·

THE NEW IMMIGRATION

A sociologist, Richard Schermerhorn, offers an intimate study of the New Immigration in *These Our People* (Heath, 1949), which is especially strong on the Italians, Czechs and Slovaks, Yugoslavs, Hungarians, and Jews. Another revealing sociological work is Robert E. Park and Herbert A. Miller, *Old World Traits Transplanted* (Harper, 1921). For other aspects see Merle Curti and Kendall Birr, "The Immigrant and the American Image in Europe, 1860-1914," *Mississippi Valley Historical Review*, XXXVII (1950), 203-30 and Edward G. Hartmann, *The Movement to Americanize the Immigrant* (Columbia University, 1948).

Among the books on the Italians, Phyllis H. Williams has written a fascinating narrative that is a model from both a sociological and historical viewpoint, *South Italian Folkways in Europe and America* (Yale University, 1938); still useful is Robert F. Foerster's *The Italian Emigration of Our Times* (Harvard University, 1919). A pithy, brief history of Jewish immigration is Oscar and Mary F. Handlin, "A Century of Jewish Immigration to the United States," *American Jewish Yearbook*, vol. 50 (1948-1949). Samuel Joseph has written a rather formal, economic survey in *Jewish Immigration to the United States from 1881 to 1910* (Columbia University, 1914); rather informative and interesting, but marred by a filiopietistic flavor is Anita L. Lebeson's *Pilgrim People* (Harper, 1950), dealing with recent Jewish immigration. Louis Wirth, the sociologist, offers real insight into the Chicago Jewish community in *The Ghetto* (University of Chicago, 1928). Mary Antin, a Jewish immigrant, has written a revealing autobiography, *The Promised Land* (Houghton Mifflin, 1912). The *Universal Jewish Encyclopedia* (10 vols., New York, edited by Isaac Landman) has exceptionally informative articles prepared by specialists on "Migrations of the Jews," "David Dubinsky," "Sidney Hillman," "International Ladies' Garment Workers' Unions," and "Amalgamated Clothing Workers of America." On the non-Jewish immigrants from Russia, Jerome Davis, the sociologist, has written sympathetically and acutely in *The Russian Immigrant* (Macmillan, 1922).

Not all immigrant groups have been the subject of extensive research, though all have had at least a volume or two written on them. Paul Fox's *The Poles in America* (Doran, 1922) shows strong Protestant partisanship in dealing with a Catholic group. Thomas Čapek reflects the point of view of the Czech freethinkers in *The Czechs in America* (Houghton Mifflin, 1920). Emil Lengyel's *Americans from Hungary* (Lippincott, 1948) is fascinating, though it lacks solidity. Both leading books on the Greeks are badly outdated: Henry P. Fairchild, *Greek Immigration to the United States* (Yale University, 1911) and Thomas Burgess, *Greeks in America* (Sherman, French and Company, Boston, 1913).

· 12 ·

INVENTION AND URBAN RECREATION

For the impact of invention on society see Roger Burlingame, *Engines of Democracy* (Scribner, 1940); G. S. Bryan, *Edison: The Man and His Work* (Knopf, 1926); and the relevant chapters of Nevins, Schlesinger, and Faulkner in the "History of American Life Series." The *Dictionary of American Biography* has useful articles on Alexander G. Bell, Edison, George Eastman, Nikola Tesla, Michael Pupin, and other inventors mentioned in this chapter.

One of the most brilliant special studies in the field of popular recreation is as yet available only through inter-library loan: Lewin A. Goff's "The Popular Priced Melodrama in America, 1890 to 1910," doctoral dissertation in English and Theatre Arts, Western Reserve University. A standard work on the theater is Arthur Hornblow's, *A History of the Theatre in America from Its Beginnings to the Present Time* (2 vols., Lippincott, 1919). The origins and development of American burlesque are developed from newspaper sources in Ettore Rella, *A History of Burlesque,* "San Francisco Theatre Research Series," San Francisco, 1940 (manuscript in possession of the Cleveland Public Library). Federal project studies have been utilized in Edmond M. Gagey, *The San Francisco Stage* (Columbia University, 1950). Harold E. Briggs and E. B. Briggs offer considerable new material in "The Early Theater on the Northern Plains," *Mississippi Valley Historical Review,* 37 (1950), 231-64. Contemporary criticisms of actors, dramatists, and plays are given in Montrose J. Moses and John M. Brown, *The American Theater as Seen by Its Critics, 1752-1932* (Norton, 1934). Among the better books dealing with other phases of stage and screen are Douglas Gilbert, *American Vaudeville* (Whittlesey House, 1940); Carl Wittke, *Tambo and Bones: a History of the American Minstrel Stage* (Duke University, 1930); Lewis Jacobs, *The Rise of the American Film* (Harcourt, Brace, 1939), which is analytical of social and economic forces in Hollywood as well as of the artistic factor. The best volume on American music is still John Tasker Howard, *Our American Music* (Crowell, 1939); popular music is the exclusive subject of Sigmund Spaeth's *A History of Popular Music in America* (Random House, 1948).

On the history of sports and games, Foster R. Dulles has written quite attractively and informatively in *America Learns To Play* (Appleton-

Century, 1940). Most of the books on sport are merely catalogues of events or exclusively descriptive. The *Encyclopedia Britannica* is surprisingly strong, even outstanding, in its articles on American sports such as baseball, football, and basketball. R. B. Weaver's *Amusements and Sports in American Life* (University of Chicago, 1939) is only a fair summary; much more informative is John A. Krout, *Annals of American Sport* (Yale University, 1929).

• 13 •

DARWINISM, PRAGMATISM, AND SCIENTIFIC DETERMINISM

The impact of Darwinism on American science is described analytically in Bert J. Loewenberg, "Darwinism Comes to America, 1858-1900," *Mississippi Valley Historical Review*, 28 (1941), 339-68, and "The Reaction of American Scientists to Darwinism," *American Historical Review*, 38 (1933), 687-701. The activities of Fiske in popularizing Darwin and Spencer can be followed in Ethel Fisk's *The Letters of John Fiske* (Macmillan, 1940). An important American Darwinist is the subject of Charles Schuchert and C. M. Le Vene, *O. C. Marsh, Pioneer in Paleontology* (Yale University, 1941). The influence of Charles Lyell and the new geology is part of the story in George P. Merrill, *The First Hundred Years of American Geology* (Yale University, 1924). There are a number of relevant biographies intended for the intelligent layman in Bernard Jaffe's *Men of Science in America* (Simon and Schuster, 1944).

The history of psychology in America has been told with considerable interpretation in Edwin G. Boring's *A History of Experimental Psychology* (Appleton-Century, 1950). Indispensable for the pioneer role of William James in psychology and philosophy is Ralph Barton Perry's monumental biography, *The Thought and Character of William James* (Little, Brown, 1935); see especially William James's own classic *Psychology* in the attractive edition of the World Publishing Company, Cleveland, 1948, and his *Pragmatism* (Longmans, Green, 1907). G. Stanley Hall discusses the early psychologists in his *Life and Confessions of a Psychologist* (Appleton-Century, 1923).

For the impact of Darwin on philosophy see the excellent essays by Robert Scoon and F. S. C. Northrop in Stow Persons' (ed.) *Evolutionary Thought in America* (Yale University, 1950). No less important is Paul A. Schilpp (ed.), *The Philosophy of John Dewey* (Vol. I of "The Library

of Living Philosophers," Northwestern University, 1939). The most
recent and authoritative work in its field is Herbert Schneider's *A
History of American Philosophy* (Columbia University, 1946). Very
useful are Philip Wiener's *Evolution and the Founders of Pragmatism*
(Harvard University, 1949) and Max Fisch (ed.), *Classic American
Philosophers* (Appleton-Century, 1951), dealing with Peirce, James,
Royce, Santayana, Dewey, and Whitehead. In the field of education,
Merle Curti has shown originality in analyzing the hitherto-neglected
underlying social philosophy of our educational leaders in *The Social
Ideas of American Educators* (Scribner, 1935). Hazen C. Carpenter has
related Emerson as well as Eliot to the origins of the elective system
in a significant article, "Emerson, Eliot, and the Elective System," *The
New England Quarterly*, XXIV (1951), 13-34.

· 14 ·

SOCIAL EVOLUTION AND THE SOCIAL STUDIES

The most thorough history of the Darwinian influence upon the social
studies is Richard Hofstadter's *Social Darwinism in American Thought,
1860-1915* (University of Pennsylvania, 1944). See also the enlightening essays of Edward S. Corwin on political thought and Joseph J.
Spengler on economic thought in Persons (ed.), *Evolutionary Thought
in America*, cited; Ralph Gabriel's analytical essays in *The Course of
American Democratic Thought* (Ronald Press, 1940), and Henry S.
Commager's thoughtful essays, *The American Mind* (Yale University,
1950).

On the post-Darwinian sociology, in addition to the above books, there
are William Graham Sumner's *Folkways* (Ginn, 1940), a classic; L. L.
and Jessie Bernard, *Origins of American Sociology* (Crowell, 1943);
Samuel Chugerman, *Lester F. Ward, the American Aristotle* (Duke University, 1939); and Bernhard J. Stern, *Lewis Henry Morgan, Social Evolutionist* (University of Chicago, 1931). The transmutation of proslavery
thought into an anti-evolutionary sociology is discussed in Harvey Wish.
"George Frederick Holmes and the Genesis of American Sociology,"
American Journal of Sociology, 46 (1941), 698-707.

There are excellent research articles on historians of this era in William
T. Hutchinson (ed.), *Marcus Jernegan Essays in American History* (University of Chicago, 1937) and in Howard Odum (ed), *American Masters*

of Social Science (Holt, 1927); see also Michael Kraus, *A History of American History* (Farrar and Rinehart, 1937). First-hand expositions of leading historical theories by their proponents are given in James Harvey Robinson, *The New History* (Macmillan, 1912); George R. Taylor (ed), *The Turner Thesis*, cited; and Henry Adams, *The Education of Henry Adams* (Houghton Mifflin, 1916). Valuable clues to many of Henry Adams' theories and vagaries can be found in his letters collected by Harold D. Cater (ed.), *Henry Adams and His Friends* (Houghton Mifflin, 1947). W. Stull Holt has edited many revealing letters in the correspondence of Herbert Baxter Adams in *Historical Scholarship in the United States* (Johns Hopkins, 1938). Edward Saveth treats of bias and racialist theories in *American Historians and European Immigrants, 1875-1925* (Columbia University, 1948). Among the newer biographies of historians that merit reading are Eric F. Goldman, *John Bach McMaster* (University of Pennsylvania, 1943) and John W. Caughey, *Hubert Howe Bancroft* (University of California, 1946).

For the economists and economic reformers there are Dorfman's *Thorstein Veblen and His America*, cited; Anna George de Mille, *Henry George* (University of North Carolina, 1950); Arthur E. Morgan, *Edward Bellamy* (Columbia University, 1944); and Sidney Fine's article, "Richard T. Ely, Forerunner of Progressivism. 1880-1901," *Mississippi Valley Historical Review*, 37 (1951), 599-624. For sociological jurisprudence see Roscoe Pound's article, "Jurisprudence," *Encyclopedia of the Social Sciences;* Max Lerner (ed.), *The Mind and Faith of Justice Holmes* (Little, Brown, 1945); and Alpheus Mason, *Brandeis,* cited. Daniel Aaron discusses Henry George, Edward Bellamy, Henry D. Lloyd, Thorstein Veblen, and others in *Men of Good Hope, a Story of American Progressives* (Oxford University, 1951).

· 15 ·

TOWARD LITERARY REALISM AND THE NEW JOURNALISM

Among the leading literary surveys for this era are: Arthur H. Quinn (ed.), *The Literature of the American People* (Appleton-Century, 1951), which includes literary history, drama, magazines, and some social theory as well as formal literature; Robert E. Spiller *et al., Literary History of the United States* (3 vols., Macmillan, 1948), vol. 3; William P. Trent *et al., The Cambridge History of American Literature* (3 vols., Macmillan, 1945 ed.), vol. 3; Vernon Parrington, *Main Currents in American*

Thought (3 vols., Harcourt, Brace, 1927, 1930), vol. 3; and, for the twentieth century particularly, Alfred Kazin, *On Native Grounds* (Reynal and Hitchcock, 1942) and Oscar Cargill, *Intellectual America* (Macmillan, 1941), which is unusual in its success in portraying the broad patterns of literary thought such as decadence, Freudianism, and the cult of the intelligentsia. Van Wyck Brooks has applied his panoramic social-literary method to this period in *New England: Indian Summer: 1865-1915* (Dutton, 1940). A detailed, somewhat conservative account of the novel's history is given in Arthur H. Quinn, *American Fiction* (Appleton-Century, 1936); many of the lesser figures are included in Alexander Cowie, *The Rise of the American Novel* (American Book Co., 1948).

The best books on the muckrakers are: Louis Filler, *Crusaders for American Liberalism* (Antioch Press, 1950); C. E. Regier, *The Era of the Muckrakers* (University of North Carolina, 1932); and Lincoln Steffens, *Autobiography*, cited. For other phases of literary history, see Frank L. Mott, *Golden Multitudes: The Story of Best Sellers in the United States* (Macmillan, 1947); Edmund Pearson, *Dime Novels* (Little, Brown, 1929); Henry Nash Smith, *Virgin Land*, cited; B. A. Botkin, *A Treasury of American Folklore*, cited; and James D. Hart, *The Popular Book: A History of America's Literary Taste* (Oxford University, 1950).

Among the leading anthologies that are relevant here are: Willard Thorp, Merle Curti, Carlos Baker (eds.), *American Issues* (2 vols., Lippincott, 1944), of which the first volume is *The Literary Record* and the second, *The Social Record;* Lyon N. Richardson, George H. Orians, and Herbert R. Brown (eds.), *The Heritage of American Literature* (2 vols., Ginn, 1951), both volumes of which are especially valuable for their analytical notes, extensive bibliography, and fresh selections; Harry R. Warfel, Ralph H. Gabriel, Stanley T. Williams, *The American Mind* (American Book Co., 1937); and Norman Foerster (ed.), *American Poetry and Prose* (Houghton Mifflin, 1934).

· 16 ·

TOWARD REALISM IN THE ARTS

Two art histories that integrate art and society are Oliver W. Larkin, *Art and Life in America* (Rinehart, 1949), highly detailed and well-illustrated, and Suzanne La Follette, *Art in America* (Harper, 1929). James T. Flexner's *A Short History of American Painting* (Houghton

Mifflin, 1950) is the most fascinating brief introduction to the subject. More detailed and conservative is the survey of Samuel Isham and Royal Cortissoz, *History of American Painting* (Macmillan, 1927). Among the better biographic studies of painters are Elizabeth McCausland, *George Inness* (American Artists, 1946); Lloyd Goodrich, *Winslow Homer* (Macmillan, 1944) and his *Thomas Eakins* (Whitney Museum, 1933). The author is especially indebted to the numerous excellent biographies of the *Dictionary of American Biography* such as those of Robert Henri, James A. M. Whistler, and John H. Twachtman.

On the history of architecture, Thomas E. Tallmadge has written a clear, comprehensive survey in *The Story of Architecture in America* (Norton, 1927). The best literature on functionalism includes Louis Sullivan, *Autobiography of an Idea* (American Institute of Architects, 1924); Hugh Morrison, *Louis Sullivan* (Norton, 1935); Frank Lloyd Wright, *Autobiography* (Longmans, Green, 1943); Commager, *The American Mind*, cited, chapter 19. A striking philosophic analysis of the relationship of Darwinism and functionalism has been written by Donald D. Egbert in "The Idea of Organic Expression and American Architecture," in Persons (ed.), *Evolutionary Thought in America*, cited. The Gothic rebellion of Ralph Adams Cram against modernism is told by himself in *The Gothic Quest* (Baker and Taylor, 1907) and *My Life in Architecture* (Little, Brown, 1936). Henry Russell Hitchcock, Jr., appraises the Richardson influence rather critically in *The Architecture of H. H. Richardson and His Times* (Museum of Modern Art, 1936). Lewis Mumford condemns the commercialized architecture of the Gilded Age in *The Brown Decades* (Harcourt, Brace, 1932) and points out the road to better living conditions and city planning in his later books, such as *The Culture of Cities* (Harcourt, Brace, 1944). Sculpture has not fared too well at the hands of art historians; the most convenient, though rather superficial, survey is Lorado Taft's *History of American Sculpture* (Macmillan, 1930). It would be better to read the sculpture sections in Oliver Larkin, *Art and Life in America*, cited.

· 17 ·

IMPERIALISM, PACIFISM, AND THE WAR TO END WAR

Albert K. Weinberg shows how the early American sense of a democratic mission and expansionism evolved into Manifest Destiny and imperialism in *Manifest Destiny* (Johns Hopkins, 1935). Julius Pratt's *Expansionists of 1898* (Johns Hopkins, 1936) is likewise an ideological study of imperialism, though limited to the period immediately preceding the Spanish-American War. Mahan's moralistic imperialism is keenly analyzed in Ralph Gabriel's *The Course of American Democratic Thought*, cited; much more detailed is William E. Livezey's *Mahan on Sea Power* (University of Oklahoma, 1947); Mahan is related to the "closed space" concept in James C. Malin, "Space and History," *Agricultural History*, 18 (1944), 65-74, 107-26. Claude G. Bowers portrays an extreme imperialist in *Beveridge and the Progressive Era* (Houghton Mifflin, 1932).

The foes of imperialism are treated in Fred Harrington, "Literary Aspects of Anti-Imperialism," *New England Quarterly*, X (1937), 211-30; Edwin Wagenknecht, *Mark Twain: the Man and His Work* (Yale University, 1935); Mark Twain, *Europe and Elsewhere* (Harper, 1932), which contains the famous "War Prayer"; Elmer Ellis, *Mr. Dooley's America* (Knopf, 1941). Merle Curti has a well-rounded study of the peace movement in *Peace or War: The American Struggle, 1636-1936* (Norton, 1936).

On the social-intellectual aspects of World War I, there is an excellent ideological study in Harley Notter, *The Origins of the Foreign Policy of Woodrow Wilson* (Johns Hopkins, 1937). Zechariah Chafee, Jr., discusses the Red scare and civil liberties in *Free Speech in the United States* (Harvard University, 1941), which has become a classic. The story of George Creel's Committee of Public Information is told fascinatingly in James R. Mock and Cedric Larson, *Words That Won the War* (Princeton University, 1939). The restricted role of scholarship in wartime is the subject of Merle Curti's article "The American Scholar in Three Wars," *Journal of the History of Ideas*, III, June, 1942. There is considerable social history from a newspaperman's viewpoint in Mark Sullivan's *Our Times: Over Here, 1914-1918*, V (Scribner, 1933). Foster R. Dulles has published a scholarly, readable history of the entire movement in *The American Red Cross* (Harper, 1950).

· 18 ·

POSTWAR REACTION, RACIALISM, AND IMMIGRANT RESTRICTION

On the Red scare of 1919 see Chafee, Jr., cited; Louis F. Post, *The Deportation Deliriums of Nineteen Twenty* (Kerr, Chicago, 1923), a vivid first-hand report; and G. L. Joughin and Edmund M. Morgan, *The Legacy of Sacco and Vanzetti* (Harcourt, Brace, 1948), which not only makes a thorough study of the case but notes its total impact upon American life and thought. Other aspects of intolerance are dealt with in Bessie Pierce, *Public Opinion and the Teaching of History in the United States* (Knopf, 1926); J. M. Mecklin, *The Ku Klux Klan* (Harcourt, Brace, 1924); and John Hope Franklin, *From Slavery to Freedom* (Knopf, 1947), which includes a section on the postwar Negro.

For postwar immigration history, see the bibliography for Chapter 11. The newer groups are discussed in detail in the following books: Manuel Gamio, *Mexican Immigration to the United States* (University of Chicago, 1930); Bradford Smith, *Americans from Japan* (Lippincott, 1948); Bruno Lasker, *Filipino Immigration* (University of Chicago, 1931); Leon E. Truesdell, *The Canadian-born in the United States* (Yale University, 1943); Oscar and Mary Handlin, *A Century of Jewish Immigration*, cited; Anita L. Lebeson, *Pilgrim People* (Jewish groups), cited; and T. J. Woofter, Jr., *Races and Ethnic Groups in American Life* (McGraw-Hill, 1933). A pro-immigration view is taken in William S. Bernard, *American Immigration Policy: A Reappraisal* (Harper, 1950).

· 19 ·

A BUSINESS CIVILIZATION

Among the best social histories or evaluations of the 1920's are Robert S. Lynd and Helen M. Lynd, *Middletown* (Harcourt, Brace, 1929), a unique sociological case study of Muncie, Indiana, which explains the psychology, social institutions, and habits of a Middle Western town; Charles Beard (ed.), *Whither Mankind* (Longmans, Green, 1928), a symposium of unusual value on the contemporary scene; Peter Odegard, *The American Public Mind* (Columbia University, 1930); Harold Stearns (ed.), *Civilization in the United States* (Harcourt, Brace, 1922), another symposium. Frederick L. Allen gives an impressionistic and nostalgic

view of the decade in *Only Yesterday* (Harper, 1931); also journalistic
is Mark Sullivan's *Our Times: The Twenties*, VI (Scribner, 1935). Pres-
ton W. Slosson covers the decade in the manner of the "History of
American Life Series" of which his book is a part in *The Great Crusade
and After, 1914-1928* (Macmillan, 1928). Harold J. Laski writes a severe
arraignment of our business civilization in his *The American Democracy*
(Viking Press, 1948). See also the sociological survey, Edmund S.
Brunner and J. H. Kolb, *Rural Social Trends* (McGraw-Hill, 1933).

For special aspects of the 1920's, there are: Foster R. Dulles, *Labor in
America* (Crowell, 1949); Sigmund Spaeth, *A History of Popular Music
in America* (Random House, 1948), which tends to be panoramic; Cecil
M. Smith, *Musical Comedy in America* (Robert M. MacGregor, New
York, 1950), exceptionally informative and explanatory; James P. Wood,
Magazines in the United States: Their Social and Economic Influence
(Ronald Press, 1949), invaluable for its portrayal of American reading
habits; Frank Luther Mott, *American Journalism* (Macmillan, 1941);
Walter Johnson (ed.), *Selected Letters of William Allen White* (Holt,
1947), which reveal the ideas of America's famous independent journalist.

· 20 ·

THE "LOST GENERATION" AND HENRY L. MENCKEN

Mencken's ideas may be followed from his own works, such as *Notes
on Democracy* (Knopf, 1926) and any group of essays in *Prejudices* (6
vols., Knopf, 1919-27). William Manchester has written a friendly biography in *Disturber of the Peace: The Life of H. L. Mencken* (Harper,
1951). There is a severe indictment of Mencken's alleged fascist tendencies, briefly stated, in Ludwig Marcuse, "Nietzsche in America," *The
South Atlantic Quarterly*, 50 (1951), 330-39. Mencken's severest critic,
Babbitt, elaborates his neo-humanistic ideas in *Democracy and Leadership* (Houghton Mifflin, 1925); see also Frederick Manchester and Odell
Shepard (eds.), *Irving Babbitt, Man and Teacher* (Putnam, 1941). The
unique New York atmosphere of the "Village" is analyzed sociologically
in Caroline Ware, *Greenwich Village, 1920-1930* (Houghton Mifflin,
1935).

For other aspects of the literary scene, see bibliography for Chapter 15.
Especially relevant here are: Malcolm Cowley (ed.), *After the Genteel
Tradition* (Norton, 1936); Joseph W. Beach, *American Fiction, 1920-*

1940 (Macmillan, 1941); Oscar Cargill, *Intellectual America*, cited; Alfred Kazin, *On Native Grounds*, cited; Henry S. Commager, *The American Mind*, cited, chapter 20. On the arts, see bibliography for Chapter 16 and R. L. Duffus, *The American Renaissance* (Knopf, 1928).

· 21 – 22 ·

THE IMPACT OF DEPRESSION AND WAR ON THE SOCIAL STRUCTURE AND CONSCIOUSNESS

The most useful social history for the 1930's is Dixon Wecter, *The Age of the Great Depression* (Macmillan, 1948). Walter Yust has edited a very informative topical survey of a decade in *Ten Eventful Years: 1936-1946* (Encyclopedia Britannica, Inc., Chicago, 1947). A critical view of the business pressures on American life is taken in Charles A. and Mary R. Beard, *America in Midpassage* (Macmillan, 1940), a history of the 1930's. A journalist's picture of the decade is the popular book of Frederick Allen, *Since Yesterday. The Nineteen-Thirties in America* (Harper, 1940). Perhaps the best symposium on the social-economic history of the decade is Harold Stearns (ed.), *America Now* (Scribner, 1938). Broadus Mitchell has written on the whole an excellent economic survey in *Depression Decade, 1929-1941* (Rinehart, 1947). A case history of the depression era is Robert S. Lynd and Helen M. Lynd, *Middletown in Transition* (Harcourt, Brace, 1937). A group of sociologists have summarized the era in a special issue, "Recent Social Trends," *American Journal of Sociology*, May, 1942. Harold Laski's critical analysis of contemporary American institutions, *The American Democracy*, cited, deserves study. John Gunther's *Inside U. S. A.* (Harper, 1947) gives a leading journalist's detailed picture of contemporary America in terms of regions and personalities.

Although the labor scene is discussed in most of the books listed above, there are very good special studies: R. R. Brooks, *When Labor Organizes* (Yale University, 1938); J. R. Walsh, C. I. O. *Industrial Unionism in Action* (Norton, 1937), a very detailed, interesting, and completely sympathetic account; Foster R. Dulles, *Labor in America*, cited; Horace R. Cayton and G. S. Mitchell, *Black Workers and the New Unions* (University of North Carolina, 1939).

For the social history of World War II, see Yust, cited; A. M. Lee and N. D. Humphrey, *Race Riot* (Dryden, 1943), dealing with the

Detroit riot of 1943; Bradford Smith, *Americans from Japan* (Lippin-cott, 1948), and Morton Grodzine, *Americans Betrayed* (University of Chicago, 1949), for the war relocation of Japanese-Americans; Robert A. Polson, "The Impact of the War on Rural Community Life; State and Local Viewpoint," *Rural Sociology,* June, 1943; Paul S. Taylor, "Effects of the War on the Social and Economic Status of Farm La-borers," *ibid.;* "The American Family in World War II," *The Annals of the American Academy of Political and Social Science* (entire issue), September, 1943; William F. Ogburn (ed.), *American Society in War-time* (University of Chicago, 1943).

· 23 ·

SOCIAL CONSCIOUSNESS DURING THE DEPRESSION AND
WAR YEARS

There are substantial sections on intellectual history in Beard's *America in Midpassage,* cited; and in Harold Stearns (ed.), *America Now,* cited. Especially useful for contemporary trends in philosophy, theology, and literature is Dixon Wecter *et al., Changing Patterns in American Civiliza-tion* (University of Pennsylvania, 1949). Valuable essays along similar lines appear in John W. Chase (ed.), *Years of the Modern: An American Appraisal* (Longmans, Green, 1949). F. S. C. Northrop has attempted to characterize philosophically American intellectual traits together with those for other areas in *The Meeting of East and West* (Macmillan, 1946).

For educational theory, see Robert Hutchins, *The Higher Learning in America* (Yale University, 1936) and a reply in Harry D. Gideonse, *The Higher Learning in a Democracy* (Farrar, 1937); I. L. Kandel, *The Impact of the War upon American Education* (University of North Caro-lina, 1949); *General Education in a Free Society* (Harvard, 1946), the significant Harvard Report on Education. On literature, see bibliography for Chapter 20 and S. J. Kunitz and Howard Haycraft, *Twentieth Cen-tury Authors* (H. W. Wilson, 1942); and for the arts, see bibliography for Chapter 16 and Hallie Flanagan, *Arena* (Duell, Sloan, and Pearce, 1940). The attitude of Americans on many social and economic issues can be studied from Hadley Cantril (ed.), *Public Opinion, 1935-1946* (Princeton University, 1951).

The new scientific trends are summarized for the layman in George W.

Gray, *The Advancing Front of Science* (McGraw-Hill, 1937); Bernard Jaffe, *Outposts of Science* (Simon and Schuster, 1935); David Dietz, *Atomic Energy in the Coming Era* (Dodd, Mead, 1945), which is unusually clear and includes an historical synopsis of the background of Hiroshima; and James Finney Baxter, *Scientists against Time* (Atlantic Monthly Press, 1948).

The present state of racial minorities has been discussed in numerous books and articles. Gunnar Myrdal's *An American Dilemma*, cited, has critically evaluated the background and status of the Negro. E. Franklin Frazier, the sociologist, has surveyed the subject with masterly skill in *The Negro in the United States* (Macmillan, 1949). Most minority groups are effectively treated in Richard Schermerhorn, *These, Our People*, cited; Arnold and Caroline Rose, *Divided America: Minority Group Relations in the United States* (Knopf, 1949); W. Lloyd Warner and Leo Srole, *The Social Systems of American Ethnic Groups* (Yale University, 1946), a sociological view; and Brewton Berry, *Race Relations* (Houghton Mifflin, 1951), which is exceptionally good from both sociological and historical viewpoints. President Truman's Committee on Civil Rights has issued the timely report, *To Secure These Rights* (Government Printing Office, Washington, D. C., 1947).

· 24 ·

THE COLD WAR: TWO WORLDS IN CULTURAL RIVALRY

On the Red scare and related questions, see the articles in the current yearbooks such as *Americana Annual, Britannica Book of the Year,* and the *New International Year Book;* and Francis Biddle, "The Tenney Committee," *The Nation,* August 4, 1951. The cultural impact of the United States on Europe has been traced in detail and with skill in Max N. Laserson, *The American Impact on Russia, Diplomatic and Ideological, 1784-1917* (Macmillan, 1950); Halvdan Koht, *The American Spirit in Europe* (University of Pennsylvania, 1949), a very favorable view of American influences abroad by a noted Scandinavian scholar; Richard H. Heindel, *The American Impact on Great Britain, 1898-1914* (University of Pennsylvania, 1940); Margaret Denny and William H. Gilman (eds.), *The American Writer and the European Tradition* (University of Minnesota, 1950), largely literary; "A Danger of Dependence?" *Time,* June 18, 1951, dealing with the Massey Report of the Canadian

Royal Commission on the Arts and Sciences regarding American cultural influences in Canada; Marcus Lee Hansen, *The Mingling of the Canadian and American Peoples* (Yale University, 1940); Harvey Wish, "Getting Along with the Romanovs," *South Atlantic Quarterly*, 48 (1949), 341-59, which contains a section on Russian-American cultural interaction; and William T. Stead, *The Americanization of the World* (H. Markley, New York, 1902). Robert Graves and Alan Hodge introduce a good many facts regarding American influences on England in their book, *The Long Week End: A Social History of Great Britain, 1918-1939* (Macmillan, 1941).

Index

605